Discovering Christ In Exodus

Volume 2

Discovering Christ

In Exodus

Volume 2

Donald S. Fortner

Go *publications*

Go Publications
Gibb Hill Farm, Ponsonby, Cumbria, CA20 1BX, ENGLAND.

© Go Publications 2020

ISBN 978-1-908475-20-6

This Book is Dedicated to

Pastor David Pledger

Table of Contents

The principal things contained in Exodus, are the accomplishment of God's promises made to Abraham concerning the increase of his seed; the rigorous treatment the Israelites suffered in Egypt; the Lord's emancipating them from bondage; and the ordinances of worship appointed in the wilderness. And as from several of the New Testament writers, we have authority to consider the deliverance from Egypt, as typical of a far more important deliverance of the church from the bondage of Sin and Satan; it should seem to follow, that nothing can more merit our attention than this sacred Book of God.

Robert Hawker

Foreword

Every book should have a foreword, even a volume 2. I am delighted therefore to be able to recommend this volume of Pastor Don Fortner's work on *Discovering Christ in Exodus*, while taking nothing away, I trust, from the principal contribution of Pastor Clay Curtis.

Volume 2 begins with an ending, as beginnings often do. This ending is the conclusion of over four centuries of Jacob's children living in Egypt. That story started well but ended badly. Now a new stage in Israel's history begins, a time of travel, miracles, battles, rebellion and judgment.

With the death angel's passing over Egypt a new day dawned for Israel, but slipping the chain of bondage and slavery would not be easy. The experience many hoped for came and passed quickly. The elation of liberty and deliverance gave way to the drudgery of need, and fearfulness in unbelief.

The history of Israel's deliverance from Egypt and subsequent wilderness wandering is a wonderful picture of a Christian's life-walk. We all encounter doubt, hardship, loss and tribulation. We all have our personal Wilderness of Sin. There are fine insights to be had in applying these picture-lessons to our own experience and many personal parallels can be made. But, as we shall see, a better blessing is to be discovered when we lift our eyes higher and see our wonderful Lord Jesus revealed in all these things. The Christ of God prefigured in the grand scheme and the smallest details.

By faith Old Testament believers glimpsed promises of grace and redemption in the types and symbols of law, sacrifice and tabernacle worship, and by the same faith of Christ New Testament believers discern in the person of their blessed Saviour He who is the substance and fulfilment of all these pictures of old.

Faith always looks to Christ. It did for those in Moses' day who had spiritual eyes to see, and it does for believers today. Some might wonder if we need to study the types and symbols since the fulfilment and reality has come. I believe we do for three reasons.

First, we learn from history how to understand our own experiences. Men's hearts have not changed, nor have our fleshly struggles diminished. We are as prone to complain and wander today despite the light of fulfilled revelation as men ever were under the shadows of the past. Therefore, we do well to remember the words, ways and dealings of God with His people in all ages.

Second, the word of God expressly declares, 'whatsoever things were written aforetime were written for our learning, that we through patience and comfort of the scriptures might have hope (Romans 15:4). There are lessons in these accounts to bring comfort and hope to weary travellers, and I am sure Pastor Fortner is an able guide to discovering them. They will reward careful attention.

Third, without question we shall learn more about our Lord Jesus Christ and His works and accomplishments by better understanding the analogies that point to Him. He is the sacrificial Lamb that was slain, the spiritual Rock from which the water of life gushed forth, the Bread of heaven come down to earth as did manna to nourish a hungry people. Moses wrote Exodus and Moses wrote of Christ. In the following pages you will be discovering Christ in Exodus.

I heartily recommend this volume to its readers. Blessings will be had in drinking at this fountain. The waters of Marah are bitter, but Jesus renders them sweet. We shall have sweet comfort and good hope as we see Christ in the book of Exodus.

Peter L. Meney
Sovereign Grace Church
Great Falls, Montana

Publisher's Preface

Pastor Don Fortner did not live to see the publication of this work though he knew it was imminent. The following letter was sent to him shortly before he passed into the presence of his Saviour. It has been edited slightly to remove some personal and family references but is largely intact.

Dear Don,

Thank you for being my friend and brother in Christ, and for all the help, support and encouragement you have provided to me over many years. It has been a privilege. I am grateful for your fellowship in the gospel of God and for your example as a preacher of the Lord Jesus Christ.

You supported New Focus magazine for many years with articles, advice and personal recommendations and your presence at our New Focus conferences was of great help in raising the profile of our venture and no doubt a principal draw for many people in the U.K. who came to hear you preach. I was honoured to share a platform with you whenever possible and grateful to witness the commitment to truth you provided in your Biblical expositions, clear gospel preaching, and wise counsel.

I also wish to say thank you for allowing me to help in the production of many of your books. I appreciate the faithfulness you have exhibited over these years in putting the fruit of your preaching and sermon preparation into written form. I know your books have been helpful already to many people and I feel sure, if the Lord tarry, your labours will prove to be valuable both to ordinary church members and gospel preachers and pastors for generations to come. Your constant desire to lift up the Lord Jesus, your own personal insights into scriptural truth and your endorsement of old, faithful writers will be treasured by the Lord's people everywhere.

All these have encouraged and assisted me, and having thanked the Lord for you it is only right I also convey my sincere gratitude to you personally. Presently, I am working on your Exodus manuscript 'Discovering Christ in Exodus'. You will be pleased to know I am almost finished. Thank you for your patience! It will be well over a thousand pages, and divide nicely into two volumes. When I have finished, and it is published, I shall at once turn my attention to 'Discovering Christ in Leviticus' and publish that, too, God willing. I intend, as we have discussed in the past, to take other works you have waiting to be produced and publish them in a similar format to these more recent works.

Over the past few decades we have seen the Lord open avenues for evangelism and ministry through travel and the expansion and enlargement of gospel preaching by cassette and video recording, CD and DVD, radio, television and now internet broadcasting. The growth of these media allowed you to reach many people with the gospel and I thank you, and your congregation in Danville, for your willingness to employ new technologies and trailblaze for some of the rest of us who have followed in your footsteps. The Lord enabled your ministry to go right around the world and I trust there will be much fruit evidenced in that great day to the glory of our Lord and Saviour.

Like the brethren in Ephesus, if we see your face no more this side of eternity we shall look forward to seeing you in glory. There we shall share with you an inheritance among all them which are sanctified. May the Lord Jesus comfort and keep you, and may He stand this night by your bed and speak your name.

Your brothers and sisters in the Lord send their greetings. Your preaching did our souls good, and we shall miss you.

Peter L. Meney

Chapter 61

'And It Came To Pass'

'And it came to pass, that at midnight the LORD smote all the firstborn in the land of Egypt, from the firstborn of Pharaoh that sat on his throne unto the firstborn of the captive that was in the dungeon; and all the firstborn of cattle ... And it came to pass the selfsame day, that the LORD did bring the children of Israel out of the land of Egypt by their armies.'
(Exodus 12:29-51)

Here are five words that are used hundreds of times in the Book of God, words that are used so often that we tend to ignore them; but they are tremendously instructive words. 'And it came to pass'. Everything that comes to pass is brought to pass by our God; and everything that our God has purposed shall come to pass. Everything predestined from eternity shall come to pass in time, because our God 'worketh all things after the counsel of his own will'. And everything that comes to pass in time was predestined in eternity 'according to the purpose of him who worketh all things after the counsel of his own will' (Ephesians 1:11). 'Shall there be evil in a city, and the LORD hath not done it?' (Amos 3:6). 'Who is he that saith, and it cometh to pass, when the Lord commandeth it not?' (Lamentations 3:37). 'I am the LORD, and there is none else. I form the light, and create darkness: I make peace, and create evil: I the LORD do all these things' (Isaiah 45:6, 7). And everything God has promised shall come to pass in time, because 'all the promises of God in Christ Jesus are yea, and in him Amen, unto the glory of God by us' (2 Corinthians 1:20).

Here, in Exodus 12, these words, 'and it came to pass', refer specifically to the destruction of Pharaoh and the land of Egypt, and the deliverance of Israel out of Egyptian bondage by the hand of God and according to the purpose of God.

All that came to pass that night in Egypt while actually real was also allegorical. It was a picture of the redemption, deliverance and salvation of God's elect in and by Christ Jesus. We read Israel's history without understanding, and with no profit to our souls, if we do not apply it spiritually to ourselves, as the Spirit of God intended (Romans 15:4; 1 Corinthians 10:11). In Exodus 12:29-51 the Holy Spirit gives us a tremendously instructive picture of our salvation in Christ, showing us six things involved in the deliverance of our souls from sin and Satan and the curse of the law.

Deliverance by a Great Slaughter

First, in verses 29 and 30, we see that the salvation of our souls is deliverance by a great slaughter. 'And it came to pass, that at midnight the LORD smote all the firstborn in the land of Egypt, from the firstborn of Pharaoh that sat on his throne unto the firstborn of the captive that was in the dungeon; and all the firstborn of cattle. And Pharaoh rose up in the night, he, and all his servants, and all the Egyptians; and there was a great cry in Egypt; for there was not a house where there was not one dead.'

That which came to pass that night in Egypt was exactly what the Lord God had purposed. 'And thou shalt say unto Pharaoh, Thus saith the LORD, Israel is my son, even my firstborn: And I say unto thee, Let my son go, that he may serve me: and if thou refuse to let him go, behold, I will slay thy son, even thy firstborn' (Exodus 4:22, 23). God's judgments are always just. Pharaoh had ordered the slaughter of God's firstborn (Exodus 1:22). In doing so, he ordered the slaughter of his own house. If you reap the wrath of God, you will but eat the fruit of your own ways. What a solemn warning! Hell is but the just retribution of God upon ungodly men and women.

But I see something more here than the certain judgment of God upon the wicked. These things are recorded to teach us God's method of grace, to show us how the Lord God saves his people from their sins.

There could be no deliverance from the wrath of God but by a great slaughter. And the slaughter was twofold. First, there was the slaughter of the paschal lamb. We could never have known the grace of God, mercy could never have come to our souls, we could not have been saved, except Christ our Passover be sacrificed for us. 'Without shedding of blood is no remission'! Second, in every house in Egypt one died that night, 'for there was not an house where there was not one dead' (v. 30).

In Pharaoh's house, and in the house of every Egyptian, there was one dead. The firstborn in every house, the one who represented the whole house, was killed that dark night when God sent destruction upon Egypt. That part of this history most everyone understands. Where were the children of Israel? Where did they live? Were not their houses in Egypt? Of course, they were. And the Word of God asserts plainly, 'There was not an house where there was not one dead'.

Does that mean that the firstborn in Israel were also slaughtered? Indeed, it does. In every Jewish home, also, there was a death. A lamb was sacrificed and the blood of that lamb protected God's chosen people from destruction. The lamb was slaughtered in the place and instead of the chosen object of deliverance. Typically and ceremonially, the Israelites died when the lamb died. 'Behold the Lamb of God, which taketh away the sin of the world' (John 1:29). When the Lord Jesus Christ died in our place, we died in him, and we died with him (John 10:11, 15; 1 Peter 3:18; 4:1, 2).

Deliverance with a Great Spoil

Second, in verses 31-36, we see that the salvation of God's elect is deliverance with a great spoil.

'And he called for Moses and Aaron by night, and said, Rise up, and get you forth from among my people, both ye and the children of Israel; and go, serve the LORD, as ye have said. Also take your flocks and your herds, as ye have said, and be gone; and bless me also. And the Egyptians were urgent upon the people, that they might send them out of the land in haste; for they said, We be all dead men. And the people took their dough before it was leavened, their kneadingtroughs being bound up in their clothes upon their shoulders. And the children of Israel did according to the word of Moses; and they borrowed of the Egyptians jewels of silver, and jewels of gold, and raiment: And the

LORD gave the people favour in the sight of the Egyptians, so that they lent unto them such things as they required. And they spoiled the Egyptians.'

Many speak of Israel's actions in borrowing the Egyptian's silver and gold as an evil thing, as something they should not have done. Do not be so foolish. This was done by God's express command (Exodus 3:21, 22; 11:2, 3). When the Egyptians 'lent' their silver and gold to the Jews, they 'lent' them in the same way Hannah 'lent' Samuel to the Lord. They had no thought of getting them back. They gladly gave the Israelites everything they asked, because God gave Israel 'favour' in the eyes of their enemies. He caused the Egyptians to gladly give them their riches, just to get rid of them. Why? He had promised 'ye shall spoil the Egyptians', 'and it came to pass'. So it is with you and me (Jeremiah 30:16; 50:10; Zephaniah 2:9; Zechariah 2:9; 14:1; Revelation 21:6; 21:24; Isaiah 53:10-12).

Deliverance on a Great Scale
Third, the salvation of God's elect is deliverance on a great scale. Read verses 37-39.

'And the children of Israel journeyed from Rameses to Succoth, about six hundred thousand on foot that were men, beside children. And a mixed multitude went up also with them; and flocks, and herds, even very much cattle. And they baked unleavened cakes of the dough which they brought forth out of Egypt, for it was not leavened; because they were thrust out of Egypt, and could not tarry, neither had they prepared for themselves any victual.'

This was not a small band of Jews who sneaked across the border out of Egypt. This was a great host, almost incalculable. Moses mentions just 600,000 men. These were men who were at least 20 years old. But the number does not include the women, the children or the aged. And it does not include the mixed multitude. Altogether there were, at the very least, two and a half million people who marched out of Egypt that night! 'And there was not one feeble person among their tribes' (Psalm 105:37). Israel marched out of Egypt triumphantly, ten thousand times ten thousand, and thousands of thousands, carrying with them everything they needed. What a picture! Need I say more? What a multitude! What a great multitude! What a rich multitude! What a mixed multitude! What a triumphant multitude!

'And they sung a new song, saying, Thou art worthy to take the book, and to open the seals thereof: for thou wast slain, and hast redeemed us to God by thy blood out of every kindred, and tongue, and people, and nation; And hast made us unto our God kings and priests: and we shall reign on the earth. And I beheld, and I heard the voice of many angels round about the throne and the beasts and the elders: and the number of them was ten thousand times ten thousand, and thousands of thousands; Saying with a loud voice, Worthy is the Lamb that was slain to receive power, and riches, and wisdom, and strength, and honour, and glory, and blessing. And every creature which is in heaven, and on the earth, and under the earth, and such as are in the sea, and all that are in them, heard I saying, Blessing, and honour, and glory, and power, be unto him that sitteth upon the throne, and unto the Lamb for ever and ever. And the four beasts said, Amen. And the four and twenty elders fell down and worshipped him that liveth for ever and ever' (Revelation 5:9-14).

'After this I beheld, and, lo, a great multitude, which no man could number, of all nations, and kindreds, and people, and tongues, stood before the throne, and before the Lamb, clothed with white robes, and palms in their hands; And cried with a loud voice, saying, Salvation to our God which sitteth upon the throne, and unto the Lamb. And all the angels stood round about the throne, and about the elders and the four beasts, and fell before the throne on their faces, and worshipped God, Saying, Amen: Blessing, and glory, and wisdom, and thanksgiving, and honour, and power, and might, be unto our God for ever and ever. Amen' (Revelation 7:9-12).

Deliverance by a Great Scheme
Fourth, the salvation of God's elect is deliverance accomplished by a great scheme. The scheme by which Israel sojourned in Egypt, multiplied in Egypt, gained wealth in Egypt, and came out of Egypt was a covenant of pure, free grace made with one man who represented the whole nation, a covenant based upon a great sacrifice. That is what we have before us in this chapter; and the whole thing speaks of God's covenant grace made with Christ for us, and its accomplishment in our deliverance (vv. 40-46; Genesis 15:1-21).

'Now the sojourning of the children of Israel, who dwelt in Egypt, was four hundred and thirty years. And it came to pass at the end of the

19

four hundred and thirty years, even the selfsame day it came to pass, that all the hosts of the LORD went out from the land of Egypt. It is a night to be much observed unto the LORD for bringing them out from the land of Egypt: this is that night of the LORD to be observed of all the children of Israel in their generations. And the LORD said unto Moses and Aaron, This is the ordinance of the passover: There shall no stranger eat thereof: But every man's servant that is bought for money, when thou hast circumcised him, then shall he eat thereof. A foreigner and an hired servant shall not eat thereof. In one house shall it be eaten; thou shalt not carry forth ought of the flesh abroad out of the house; neither shall ye break a bone thereof.'

It was not until the blood of the 'lamb' was shed that redemption was effected. As soon as the blood was shed, the very next morning, Israel marched forth a free people. 'All the hosts of the LORD (That includes the mixed multitude, not just the Jews.) went out from the land of Egypt' (v. 41). They were the Lord's purchased people, 'bought with a price', and that price was not 'corruptible things as silver and gold', 'but with the precious blood' of a lamb! All the redeemed, every sinner purchased by Christ at Calvary, must go out of bondage into liberty, out of darkness into light, out of death into life at God's appointed 'time of love' for his chosen.

Deliverance with a Great Seal
Fifth, our salvation in Christ is a deliverance with a great seal. The seal of Israel's deliverance was circumcision. 'All the congregation of Israel shall keep it. And when a stranger shall sojourn with thee, and will keep the passover to the LORD, let all his males be circumcised, and then let him come near and keep it; and he shall be as one that is born in the land: for no uncircumcised person shall eat thereof. One law shall be to him that is homeborn, and unto the stranger that sojourneth among you. Thus did all the children of Israel; as the LORD commanded Moses and Aaron, so did they' (Exodus 12:47-50).

Circumcision was an Old Testament sign by which the chosen nation was separated and distinguished from other people, a mark of identification in their bodies. It was an operation performed upon each new born boy in Israel by which all the promises and blessings of God's covenant were sealed to him for life. That legal ceremony of the Old Testament was typical of and pointed to the work of God the Holy Spirit in regeneration by which God seals to the hearts of chosen, redeemed sinners all the blessings of his covenant grace (Philippians 3:3; Colossians 2:11; Ephesians 1:13, 14).

Circumcision was a family mark of identification, a mark made in the flesh, a mark that was painfully made, a mark of divine favour, a mark of covenant blessedness, a mark of divine protection and care, and a permanent mark. That is an exact description of the work of God the Holy Ghost in us, called 'circumcision made without hands' (Colossians 2:11).

Deliverance by a Great Saviour

Sixth, verse 51 describes a deliverance performed by a great Saviour, 'the great God and our Saviour, Jesus Christ' (Titus 2:13). Salvation is the work of the Lord Jesus Christ, our great God; and his glory is great in the salvation he performs. 'And it came to pass the selfsame day, that the LORD did bring the children of Israel out of the land of Egypt by their armies.'

'Salvation is of the LORD.' Let the Lord alone be praised for it. Let us ever sing God's praise with rapture for the blessings of redemption, deliverance, and salvation in and by our great and glorious Saviour, the Lord Jesus Christ (Psalm 103:1-4; 107:1, 2; 108:1-6).

Whenever we contemplate God's goodness to Israel as it is recorded in this chapter, let us see our personal interest in all that is here recorded. If we do, we can never sufficiently adore the mercy, grace, and love of God. Oh, what deliverance that is which the Lord God accomplished for us! With what a high hand he has brought us out of bondage and into the glorious liberty of the sons of God! 'It is a night much to be observed unto the LORD of all the children of Israel in their generations forever. This month shall be to you the beginning of months, the first month of the year.' It is indeed a new month, a new year, new life, new privileges, and new joys. 'What hath God wrought.'

'O sing unto the LORD a new song: sing unto the LORD, all the earth. Sing unto the LORD, bless his name; show forth his salvation from day to day. Declare his glory among the heathen, his wonders among all people. For the LORD is great, and greatly to be praised: he is to be feared above all gods' (Psalm 96:1-4).

O blessed Son of God, our Passover, our Saviour, our Redeemer, our all, help us by the sweet influence of your Holy Spirit to keep the feast

21

of faith, 'not in the old leaven, neither with the leaven of malice and wickedness, but with the unleavened bread of sincerity and truth'. Oh, may the blood of the everlasting covenant be sprinkled upon our hearts, that it may be our security from the condemning sentence of the law, the guilt of sin, and from all the dreadful evils of iniquity. Enable us to feed upon your flesh and blood by faith. Make it to be meat indeed and drink indeed to our souls, to support and nourish us throughout the days of our pilgrimage. And grant that, like the believing Israelites, we may feed upon you, our Passover sacrificed for us, with our loins girded about with truth, and our feet shod with the preparation of the gospel of peace. Oh, give me grace, my Saviour, to feed upon you with my staff in my hand, ready to be gone and to depart in haste and be with you where you are forever!

Chapter 62

Harnessed By Grace

'And the LORD spake unto Moses, saying, Sanctify unto me all the firstborn, whatsoever openeth the womb among the children of Israel, both of man and of beast: it is mine … But God led the people about, through the way of the wilderness of the Red sea: and the children of Israel went up harnessed out of the land of Egypt … And the LORD went before them by day in a pillar of a cloud, to lead them the way; and by night in a pillar of fire, to give them light; to go by day and night: He took not away the pillar of the cloud by day, nor the pillar of fire by night, from before the people.'
(Exodus 13:1-22)

We should always read the historical books of Holy Scripture as they were intended, understanding they were written to teach us by types and pictures the wonders of redemption and grace in Christ. Without question, every portion of history in the Inspired Volume is an accurate and faithful transcript of what actually happened. They are true and infallible records of past events. Yet, they are not mere records of history. Each is also a prophetic picture, or metaphor, or illustration of God's mighty operations of grace toward, in, and upon his chosen.

The book of Exodus is no exception. This record of God bringing Israel out of Egypt by smiting the firstborn, leading them through the Red Sea, and guiding them through the wilderness into the land of Canaan, is written by the inspiration of God the Holy Spirit. It is a picture of our God's gracious, covenant mercy toward his people. God's elect are the people he separated from the Egyptians by covenant love and by the blood atonement of Christ. They are the people he separates from the Egyptians by the strong and mighty hand of his omnipotent, saving grace, bringing them out of the house of their bondage, and out of the land of their slavery. Read the record here given.

'Now the sojourning of the children of Israel, who dwelt in Egypt, was four hundred and thirty years. And it came to pass at the end of the four hundred and thirty years, even the selfsame day it came to pass, that all the hosts of the LORD went out from the land of Egypt. It is a night to be much observed unto the LORD for bringing them out from the land of Egypt: this is that night of the LORD to be observed of all the children of Israel in their generations' (Exodus 12:40-42).

All the children of Israel came out because of a covenant God made with their representative head long before any of them were ever born. The all came out of Egypt at once, by one sacrifice, in one night. They all came out gorgeously arrayed, decked with jewels of silver and gold, and fully supplied for their journey. They came out a great multitude, millions of them! All of Israel came out of Egypt, not one lacking. They all came out completely whole. 'There was not one feeble person in all their tribes' (Psalm 105:37). They all came out of Egypt by the mighty hand of God.

Let us look at the instructions God gave to Israel to mark this great deliverance throughout their generations. Israel came out of Egypt as a people harnessed by God for a long journey. I remind you, everything recorded in the Book of God about the Exodus was intended by our God to be a picture of the deliverance of our souls by Christ. God the Holy Spirit tells us so in 1 Corinthians 10:1-11. As you read these lines, if he has not already done so, I pray that the Lord God might harness you by his grace, bring you out of your bondage, and bring you into the glorious liberty of the children of God in Christ!

Sanctification Ordered
This chapter begins with a divine command, an order given by God to sanctify all the firstborn, both of man and beast.

'And the LORD spake unto Moses, saying, Sanctify unto me all the firstborn, whatsoever openeth the womb among the children of Israel, both of man and of beast: it is mine' (vv. 1, 2).

Remember, the instructions here are about keeping the passover in future generations. That Old Testament feast was given to the Jews in anticipation of Christ our Passover who is sacrificed for us. So, in these opening verses, the Lord God gives a command that points directly to our Lord Jesus Christ. The sanctification, setting apart, of the firstborn is intended to set our minds and hearts upon gospel mercy and grace in Christ Jesus, 'the Firstborn among many brethren', who was set apart by God the Father as our Redeemer and Saviour (John 17:19; Romans 8:29). Because Christ is the Firstborn and we are his, the church of God's elect is called 'the church of the firstborn' (Hebrews 12:23).

Unleavened Bread

Next, the Lord God gives specific instructions about the feast of unleavened bread. We read about the Jews keeping this feast many times in the Gospel narratives. The Old Testament Passover was the first day of a week-long celebration of deliverance called the Feast of Unleavened Bread. It commemorated the passing over of God's judgment and Israel's exodus out of Egypt, when they had no leavened bread, because they came out without making any provision for themselves. 'They were thrust out of Egypt, and could not tarry, neither had they prepared for themselves any victual' (Exodus 12:39).

'And Moses said unto the people, Remember this day, in which ye came out from Egypt, out of the house of bondage; for by strength of hand the LORD brought you out from this place: there shall no leavened bread be eaten' (v. 3).

God commanded Israel to 'Remember this day', because we are all terribly prone to forget the greatest of mercies, the greatest of blessings, and even the most wondrous experiences of his goodness. Yes, you and I are ever in danger of forgetting our spiritual deliverance from Egypt by the Lord Jesus Christ. Therefore, our Lord Jesus gave us two ordinances by which to remind us of it, that we might remember him.

By our baptism, being immersed, buried with Christ in the watery grave and rising up from the grave, believing sinners confess their faith in Christ. Baptism symbolically declares the fulfilling of righteousness by Christ's obedience unto death as our Substitute (Matthew 3:15) and our death and resurrection with him (Romans 6:4-11).

In our observance of the Lord's Supper, God's saints eat a piece of unleavened bread which portrays the body of Christ crushed to death under the weight of divine justice, when he was made sin for us; and we drink a cup of wine which portrays his blood shed for his elect for the remission of our sins. In doing this we are, as often as we eat the bread and drink the wine, graciously compelled to remember him who loved us and gave himself for us.

'This day came ye out in the month Abib. And it shall be when the LORD shall bring thee into the land of the Canaanites, and the Hittites, and the Amorites, and the Hivites, and the Jebusites, which he sware unto thy fathers to give thee, a land flowing with milk and honey, that thou shalt keep this service in this month' (vv. 4, 5).

The whole of Israel's deliverance was the work of God alone. It was the Lord God who brought them out of Egypt, and the Lord God who brought them into Canaan. So it is with us. Every step in our salvation is of the Lord (Ephesians 2:1-10).

'Seven days thou shalt eat unleavened bread, and in the seventh day shall be a feast to the LORD. Unleavened bread shall be eaten seven days; and there shall no leavened bread be seen with thee, neither shall there be leaven seen with thee in all thy quarters' (vv. 6, 7).

These seven days portray the whole, complete, perfect state of grace enjoyed by every sanctified soul. There is not the slightest portion of leaven (human filth) mixed with the work. Not only was Israel forbidden to mix leaven with their offering, none was allowed to remain in the house. There is no place for works in the house of grace!

'And thou shalt show thy son in that day, saying, This is done because of that which the LORD did unto me when I came forth out of Egypt' (v. 8).

When you and I come to the house of God to worship our Redeemer, in every aspect of our service to him, let us be wise and instruct our children in the matter, saying, like those fathers in Israel of old, 'We do this because of what the Lord God has done for us. We observe these ordinances of worship, we sing these hymns of praise, we offer our gifts, and we consecrate ourselves to our God, because of what the Lord God has done for us.'

'And it shall be for a sign unto thee upon thine hand, and for a memorial between thine eyes, that the Lord's law may be in thy mouth: for with a strong hand hath the LORD brought thee out of Egypt. Thou shalt therefore keep this ordinance in his season from year to year' (vv. 9, 10).

Redeem It or Kill It

In verses 11-16, the Lord's instructions about the firstborn are enlarged.

'And it shall be when the LORD shall bring thee into the land of the Canaanites, as he sware unto thee and to thy fathers, and shall give it thee, That thou shalt set apart unto the LORD all that openeth the matrix, and every firstling that cometh of a beast which thou hast; the males shall be the LORD'S. And every firstling of an ass thou shalt redeem with a lamb; and if thou wilt not redeem it, then thou shalt break his neck: and all the firstborn of man among thy children shalt thou redeem' (vv. 11-13).

Every unclean thing must either be redeemed or destroyed. With the birth of every firstborn, there was a choice to make. Redeem it or kill it. Devote it to God or send it to its death. This was a reminder that Pharaoh chose death for Egypt's firstborn; but the Lord God chose to redeem Israel.

'And it shall be when thy son asketh thee in time to come, saying, What is this? that thou shalt say unto him, By strength of hand the LORD brought us out from Egypt, from the house of bondage: And it came to pass, when Pharaoh would hardly let us go, that the LORD slew all the firstborn in the land of Egypt, both the firstborn of man, and the firstborn of beast: therefore I sacrifice to the LORD all that openeth the matrix, being males; but all the firstborn of my children I redeem. And it shall be for a token upon thine hand, and for frontlets between thine eyes: for by strength of hand the LORD brought us forth out of Egypt' (vv. 14-16).

Every jackass had to be redeemed by a lamb or have its neck broken. That jackass represents you and me, with apologies to the jackass! The ass is unclean. The ass is stubborn. And the ass is stupid and senseless. Like that jackass, the only thing that keeps our necks from being broken under the wrath of God is the fact we have been redeemed by the Lamb of God (Titus 2:13, 14).

God's Way

'And it came to pass, when Pharaoh had let the people go, that God led them not through the way of the land of the Philistines, although that was near; for God said, Lest peradventure the people repent when they see war, and they return to Egypt' (v. 17).

If you look at a map, you will see that the most direct route from Egypt to Canaan was from the northern part of Egypt to the southern part of Canaan. Such a route would take no more than a week, or at the most two. But that route would have led Israel directly in the path of war with the barbaric Philistines, a war they had not yet been prepared for.

The Lord God wisely and graciously compelled them to take another route, leading them in 'the right way'. God's way is always 'the right way' (Psalm 107:1-7). No other way would have taken them across the Red Sea. No other way would have destroyed Pharaoh and the armies of Egypt in the sea, in the process of delivering Israel. And a shorter route would not have proved the people.

Harnessed by Grace

Now, read verse 18. Israel was brought out of Egypt as a people harnessed.

'But God led the people about, through the way of the wilderness of the Red sea: and the children of Israel went up harnessed out of the land of Egypt.'

Robert Hawker was correct in suggesting that the harnessed state of Israel alluded to the church of God in this world, which is described as an army with banners coming up out of the wilderness (Song of Solomon 6:4; 8:5). The word 'harnessed' is used to speak of soldiers in ranks, five in a rank. The word here is a passive participle. It speaks of this great multitude being harnessed not by their own hands, but by the hand of God their Deliverer. They were harnessed 'five in a rank' and five is commonly used in Scripture to represent grace.

That is exactly what Christ has done for us. In the deliverance and salvation of our souls we are a people harnessed by grace, harnessed by our God and brought out of bondage, harnessed as a band of soldiers, but soldiers who stand still and see the salvation of the Lord, not soldiers who fight the battle. Yes, we have a battle to fight. We must fight the good fight of faith. We are at war with the world, the flesh, and the devil. But the victory was won for us by Christ our Redeemer, who brought us out of the house of bondage and death on that night long ago when he destroyed Satan and led captivity captive, as the Captain of our Salvation!

Joseph's Bones

'And Moses took the bones of Joseph with him: for he had straitly sworn the children of Israel, saying, God will surely visit you; and ye shall carry up my bones away hence with you' (v. 19).

By faith Joseph made the sons of Israel swear they would carry his bones up out of Egypt, promising them that God would preserve them, take care of them, and bring them up out of that land (Genesis 50:25, 26; Hebrews 11:22). Joseph died when he was 110 years old, was embalmed, and placed in a coffin in Egypt. The children of Israel passed that promise down generation after generation. For four hundred years, one generation said to the next, 'When the LORD God brings us up out of Egypt, we must take Joseph's bones out of this place and carry them to the land promised to our fathers Abraham, Isaac, and Jacob.'

Christ Our Guide

'And they took their journey from Succoth, and encamped in Etham, in the edge of the wilderness. And the LORD went before them by day in a pillar of a cloud, to lead them the way; and by night in a pillar of fire, to give them light; to go by day and night: He took not away the pillar of the cloud by day, nor the pillar of fire by night, from before the people' (vv. 20-22).

This was a standing miracle with Israel for forty years. The Holy Spirit, as we read in 1 Corinthians 10, tells us that this whole affair is to be understood by us with reference to our own experience of grace. Stephen said that Christ was in the church in the wilderness (Acts 7:37, 38). Without doubt, the pillar of cloud and of fire, this Shechinah, is representative of the Lord Jesus Christ, the great Angel of the Covenant. It is Christ our King and Saviour, the mighty Breaker, who goes before his people (Micah 2:13).

We have this same abiding miracle. Do we not? It is a voice behind us, or rather within us, saying, 'This is the way' (Isaiah 30:21; Psalm 78:14; 121:4-8; Isaiah 4:5; Matthew 28:20). May God give us grace ever to remember with joy his distinguishing mercies by which he manifests his great love to our souls! As we remember his great mercies upon us, let us never feast alone upon his bounties, hiding it from those around us, but let us proclaim the glad tidings to all who will hear us. May God the Holy Spirit ever give us wisdom and grace to distinctly remember his precept (v. 8) and teach our children, and our children's children, how the Lord has brought us out of the bondage of sin and death by his mighty arm and stretched out hand of grace.

Since our great God has been so gracious in bringing us out of Egypt, and in bringing us these many years through this wilderness, let us ever rejoice in confident hope and expectation. God who has wrought and is working his great mercy in us and for us will perform it until he brings us home to the good land he has promised us! Blessed Saviour, ever give us to see that however rough and thorny the way, it is 'the right way' to the city of habitation. Be our 'pillar of cloud' by day and our 'pillar of fire' by night, ever going before us in mercy to direct us in the way, surrounding us with the protection of your grace and your sweet presence. As you have borne us upon eagles' wings and brought us to yourself in grace, O gracious Saviour, bear us on your wings safely to yourself in glory.

Chapter 63

A Lamb For An Ass

'And it shall be when the LORD shall bring thee into the land of the Canaanites, as he sware unto thee and to thy fathers, and shall give it thee, That thou shalt set apart unto the LORD all that openeth the matrix, and every firstling that cometh of a beast which thou hast; the males shall be the LORD'S. And every firstling of an ass thou shalt redeem with a lamb; and if thou wilt not redeem it, then thou shalt break his neck: and all the firstborn of man among thy children shalt thou redeem.'
(Exodus 13:11-13)

Throughout the Mosaic dispensation, every day in the Jewish nation opened and closed with the sacrifice of a lamb. A lamb was offered upon God's altar at the door of the tabernacle every morning to begin the day; and another lamb was sacrificed every evening to conclude it. The Lord God said, 'I will meet you, to speak there unto thee' (Exodus 29:42). The lamb sacrificed was the place of meeting. God came to his people and his people came to him by a sacrificed lamb. There was no other way for the two to come together. If God came to man, it was by a lamb sacrificed. If man came to God, it was by a lamb sacrificed. That lamb sacrificed was given to the children of Israel for a token, a sign upon the hand that made the sacrifice, and in the eyes that beheld it. This is what the token promised, and what the Lord God intended by the sign. I will dwell among you and be your God, and this is how you 'shall be sanctified by my glory' (Exodus 29:38-46).

According to the typical revelation of the law given in Exodus 29, sanctification was by the sacrifice of a lamb; and in verse 43 we are told that it is by God's glory. Does the Lord God mean for us to understand that all our salvation and all his glory is in that Lamb to whom these typical lambs pointed, the Lamb of God, Christ our Passover, the Lamb of God sacrificed for us? Indeed, he does! All our salvation and all God's glory is in the Lamb of God slain for sinners.

In the second verse of chapter 13 the Lord God commands, 'Sanctify unto me all the firstborn, whatsoever openeth the womb among the children of Israel, both of man and of beast: it is mine'. But what about the unclean animals? The Lord God gave very specific command, forbidding that any unclean beast be offered to him (Leviticus 27:11). He makes two commandments that seem to contradict one another. If one was fulfilled, it would appear the other could not have been. He demanded that all the firstborn of man and beast be sanctified unto him. Yet, he also forbade offering anything unclean to him. How can such a law be fulfilled? How can all the firstborn be sanctified to the Lord, and no unclean thing be offered to him? The Lord God himself answers that question in Exodus 13:11-13. The ass was redeemed, made clean and accepted by God, by the sacrifice of a lamb.

There are four things in these verses I want you to see. Of course, everything here stated is to be understood typically. What was required by God in the law was typical of our Lord Jesus Christ and the salvation of our souls by his sacrifice of himself for us (Hebrews 10:9-14).

Unclean Unacceptable
First, the ass, being an unclean thing, could not be accepted by the holy Lord God. Even so, fallen man, being unclean, cannot be accepted by God. According to the law of God, no animal was considered clean except that which both divided the hoof and chewed the cud. By that standard of the ceremonial law, and certainly by the standard of the moral law, every man is unclean. But the Lord God sacrificed a Lamb, his own dear Son, the Lamb of God, for chosen sinners, and made the unclean altogether clean before him.

This is the great wonder of grace. Being redeemed by the precious blood of Christ, we are the sheep of God, the lambs of Christ's flock, made fit to sit far above principalities and powers in the heavenly places with Christ Jesus. Lost by sin through the fall, and utterly unclean,

God's super-abounding grace has made us perfectly clean, without spot and without blame, through the sin atoning blood of his own dear Son!

Like the unclean ass, fallen man is incapable of acceptance with God, 'we are all as an unclean thing, and all our righteousnesses are as filthy rags' (Isaiah 64:6). We are unclean, unclean at heart, unclean in nature, unclean in thought, and unclean in all our deeds That means it is impossible for any man to do anything acceptable to God. 'Who can bring a clean thing out of an unclean? Not one' (Job 14:4). We cannot obey God's law. We cannot do good. We cannot justify ourselves. We cannot make ourselves clean.

Consider the image given in Exodus 13. A man might shampoo an ass, and make it smell better; but still it would be unclean. He might separate the unclean thing from others like it, and put it in the field with his sheep; but an ass grazing with sheep is still an ass. It is still unclean. A man might even, by torturous devices, split the hooves of his ass and make it look like one of those clean animals that divided the hoof; but it was still unclean. There was one way only for the unclean ass to be made clean and acceptable with God, only one way it could be sanctified unto the Lord, a lamb had to die in its place.

So it is with fallen man. You and I cannot, ever, strive as we may, be made clean and accepted before the thrice holy God, any more than the ass could be acceptable at the altar of God, except by the sacrifice of Christ, the Lamb of God (Job 9:20, 30, 31; Psalm 143:2; Romans 3:20; Galatians 2:16, 21).

God's Claim

Second, the Lord God would not receive the ass. He refused to accept the ass because it was unclean. Yet, the Lord God would not relinquish his claim upon it. He said, 'It is mine' (v. 2). God claimed all the firstborn of man and beast, clean and unclean; a claim he refused to relinquish.

Nothing has changed. God still claims his rights as God. You and I are his. The sinner cannot be accepted by God, and cannot serve God. Still, God's claim is upon us. He still demands we be sanctified, holy and clean before him (Leviticus 20:7; 1 Peter 1:15, 16). Many tell us God does not require more of a man than he can perform, that man is not responsible for what he cannot do; but that simply is not true. As he commanded Abraham, so he commands you and me. 'I am the

Almighty God; walk before me, and be thou perfect' (Genesis 17:1). The gospel does not lower the standard. God's law demands redeem the ass or break its neck. And the same gospel that declares 'the gift of God is eternal life through Jesus Christ our Lord' declares 'the wages of sin is death'. Our inability to pay the debt does not remove the debt. Your inability to obey God's law does not relieve you of your responsibility to do so.

Can you imagine a man standing before a judge and saying, 'Your honour, I cannot help myself. I have such an irresistible tendency to steal that I simply cannot stop robbing people whenever I find the opportunity. Since I am a man without principle, the law has no claim upon me'?

Your inability to keep the law does not free you from the guilt and condemnation of God's broken law. The sinner's inability to trust Christ as his Saviour and Lord does not relieve him of his responsibility to do so. Man's inability is not his misfortune. It is his sin. It is written, 'He that believeth not shall be damned'. The Lord God says ...

'Turn you at my reproof: behold, I will pour out my spirit unto you, I will make known my words unto you. Because I have called, and ye refused; I have stretched out my hand, and no man regarded; But ye have set at nought all my counsel, and would none of my reproof: I also will laugh at your calamity; I will mock when your fear cometh; When your fear cometh as desolation, and your destruction cometh as a whirlwind; when distress and anguish cometh upon you. Then shall they call upon me, but I will not answer; they shall seek me early, but they shall not find me: For that they hated knowledge, and did not choose the fear of the LORD: They would none of my counsel: they despised all my reproof. Therefore shall they eat of the fruit of their own way, and be filled with their own devices. For the turning away of the simple shall slay them, and the prosperity of fools shall destroy them. But whoso hearkeneth unto me shall dwell safely, and shall be quiet from fear of evil' (Proverbs 1:23-33).

'He, that being often reproved hardeneth his neck, shall suddenly be destroyed, and that without remedy' (Proverbs 29:1).

The ass could not be accepted, but still the ass belonged to God. And fallen man cannot be received as is; sinful, guilty, and unclean. But God will not relinquish his claim. He says, 'Redeem the ass, sanctify it unto me, or break its neck'. The Lord Jesus declares, 'Every idle word that men shall speak, they shall give account thereof in the day of judgment' (Matthew 12:36). If you will not be sanctified unto him, he will condemn you. If you refuse to trust Christ, you shall be called to account in the day of judgment and cast into hell.

Redeemed by a Lamb

Third, the Lord God met the difficulty by providing a substitute for the unclean ass. Though the ass must be God's, it could not be, because it was unclean. The opening line of verse 13 reads, 'Every firstling of an ass thou shalt redeem with a lamb'. What a sweet, beautiful picture this is of the glorious gospel of Christ! The Lord God often compares man to an ass. It is written, 'God exacteth of thee less than thine iniquity deserveth ... For vain man would be wise, though man be born like a wild ass's colt' (Job 11:6, 12).

You and I are all born by nature 'like a wild ass's colt', foolish, senseless and stubborn, given to lust and debauchery, and wild. As the wild ass will not bear the yoke, so none will ever bow to the yoke of Christ, except the Son of God break him. Man by nature is like 'a wild ass used to the wilderness, that snuffeth up wind at her pleasure' (Jeremiah 2:24; Job 39:5).

In the movies you see old men and women riding donkeys, and you get the idea they are nice, gentle, sweet animals, the kind you would like to have for pets, if you just had the room. But that is never the case by nature. It is their nature to be mean. If you try to get one to ride, to carry a load, or to pull a cart, until he is broken and tamed, he will buck and kick and bite. If all else fails, he will just sit down.

That is a pretty good picture of man. Made by God and made for his glory, all men ought to gladly give thanks to him, submit to his rule, worship him, and give him his due. But just try to get one to worship God. Watch him kick! Tell the sweet, religious wild asses of this world the truth about man, about God, about Christ, and about redemption and grace. Watch them buck and bite!

Such wild asses we are by nature; unclean, unfit for God, unfit for service to God, unfit even to be sacrificed to God! Yet, the holy Lord God said, 'I will take the wild ass, the unclean thing, make it clean, use it for my service and show my glory in redeeming it with a Substitute, by the blood of the Lamb.' He said, they 'shall be sanctified by my glory'! He spared not his own Son, but delivered him up to die in our stead, as the Lamb of God, our Substitute (Romans 5:6-8; 2 Corinthians 4:4-6; 5:17-6:2). And that is his glory!

Substitution

Christ Jesus, the Lamb of God, was offered to God as a Substitute for ungodly, unclean, unacceptable man. Christ died, that we might never die. He was cursed, that we might not be cursed. He was rejected, that we might be accepted. He was despised, that we might be approved. He was forsaken, that we might never be forsaken. He was made sin for us, that we might be made the righteousness of God in him!

If we would understand the Word of God, we must begin and end with Substitution. The Book of God is all about Substitution. Charles Spurgeon put it like this, 'The heart of the gospel is redemption, and the essence of redemption is the substitutionary sacrifice of Christ.' That is the only hope of the sinner, and the joy of the true believer. The great transaction that took place at Calvary two thousand years ago, the great substitutionary work of Christ, the mighty transfer of sin from the sinner to the sinner's Surety, the punishment of the Surety in the sinner's place, the pouring out of the vials of divine wrath upon the head of our Substitute, the Lord Jesus Christ, which were due to us, is all our hope, all our joy, and all our salvation! This is the greatest transaction that ever took place upon the earth, the most marvellous sight men ever saw, and the most stupendous wonder heaven ever executed. Jesus Christ was 'made sin for us, that we might be made the righteousness of God in him'. Jesus Christ, the spotless Son of God, was made sin!

Christ Jesus came into the world to take our sins upon himself and to be punished for them. If Christ was punished for our sins, we cannot be punished for them. Justice will not allow it. Christ's being punished in our stead was the full discharge of our debt, the debt we owed to divine justice. If Christ died as a Substitute for me, if the Lamb of God was sacrificed to redeem this wild ass of a man, though I am nothing but an unclean ass in myself, I can no more be damned than Christ himself can be damned. Hell cannot have me! Either the ass or the lamb must be slain, but never both! If both were slain, where is the justice of God? Where is the honour of God? Where is his glory? What difference does the sacrifice make?

Perhaps you think, 'How may I know if Christ died for me?' Do you trust him? Will you trust him now? If you do, it is evidence that you have been redeemed by the Lamb of God. Christ took your place upon the cursed tree. You are without sin, altogether clean and righteous before God. God says so! You shall never die!

Let all who know what it is to be redeemed with the precious blood of God's dear Lamb tell it out everywhere to everybody. Tell the sick, tell the dying, tell the young, tell the old, tell sinners of every degree and in every place; salvation is not by what they do, nor by what they feel, but in what the Lamb of God has done! James Proctor wrote,

> Nothing, either great or small,
> Nothing, sinner, no;
> Jesus did it, did it all,
> Long, long ago.
>
> When He from His lofty throne
> Stooped to do and die,
> Everything was fully done:
> Hearken to His cry:
>
> 'It is finished!' Yes, indeed,
> Finished every jot:
> Sinner, this is all you need,
> Tell me, is it not?
>
> Weary, working, plodding one,
> Why toil you so?
> Cease your doing: all was done
> Long, long ago.
>
> Till to Jesus' work you cling
> By a simple faith,
> Doing is a deadly thing,
> Doing ends in death.
>
> Cast your deadly doing down,
> Down at Jesus' feet,
> Stand in Him, in Him alone,
> Gloriously complete!

Neck Broken

Bless God for the good news of those words, 'Every firstling of an ass thou shalt redeem with a lamb!' But there is a fourth thing I must tell you. The law declares, 'And if thou wilt not redeem it, then thou shalt break its neck'. There is no alternative. Every firstling of an ass must either be redeemed by a lamb, or it must be slain at God's altar. You must have Christ as your Substitute, or justice demands that you must be slain as the unclean ass you are. Calvary or hell! Christ or damnation! Forever clean or forever unclean! Turn or burn! Believe or be damned!

If now you believe on the Son of God, you have everlasting life; you have been redeemed by the sacrifice of God's Lamb. Oh, God enable you to believe on his Son! Come, bathe your soul in this Fountain, and be clean (Romans 8:1-4). If you will not believe on the Son of God, your neck shall be broken forever in hell, under the wrath of God.

Christ, the Clean, was made unclean, that he might make the unclean clean forever! Blessed Lamb of God! Blessed, blessed Saviour, adored be your matchless name forever! That is the gospel! God help you to believe it, for Christ's sake.

Chapter 64

Christ The Pillar Of Cloud And Fire

'And they took their journey from Succoth, and encamped in Etham, in the edge of the wilderness. And the LORD went before them by day in a pillar of a cloud, to lead them the way; and by night in a pillar of fire, to give them light; to go by day and night: He took not away the pillar of the cloud by day, nor the pillar of fire by night, from before the people.'
(Exodus 13:20-22)

When the Lord God brought Israel out of Egypt, 'He spread a cloud for a covering; and fire to give light in the night' (Psalm 105:39); and that pillar of cloud and fire was Christ the Saviour, the Lord Jehovah, who went before them. The Lord Jesus went before his people as their perpetual guide and protector by day and by night, until they were brought, at last, into Canaan, the land of their rest. And that which God did for his people of old he has promised to do for us throughout the days of our pilgrimage through this world (Isaiah 4:2-6).

One Pillar
The first thing to be observed about this pillar of cloud and fire is that it was one pillar, not two. It is needful for us ever to remember that our Lord Jesus Christ is one glorious Saviour. He is made many things to us, but he is One.

The pillar that followed Israel was something totally beyond the scope of human understanding, a miraculous thing that no man can explain or explain away. It was both a pillar of cloud and a pillar of fire. So, too, our Lord Jesus Christ is both God and man. Yet, he is one

Person, the God-man, our Mediator. This God-man Mediator, our Saviour, is 'the Man whose name is the BRANCH' (Zechariah 6:12); and the 'Man who is the Branch' is 'The LORD our Righteousness' (Jeremiah 23:6). He is made unto us 'wisdom, and righteousness, and sanctification, and redemption: That, according as it is written, He that glorieth, let him glory in the Lord' (1 Corinthians 1:30, 31).

Israel's Pillar
Second, I call your attention to the fact that this pillar of cloud and fire was Israel's pillar, Israel's guide, Israel's protection. It belonged to and was for Israel alone. It gave light to none but Israel. It gave protection to none but Israel. None but the people of God whom he brought out of the land of Egypt, none but the people of his choice and his covenant received any benefit from the pillar of his grace.

The pillar of fire was darkness to the Egyptians, though it was light to Israel. So, too, Christ is the salvation, joy, and comfort of his people, and a stumbling-stone and rock of offense to those who believe not. Christ is given as a Pillar to the Israel of God and only to the Israel of God. He is the Pillar 'over every dwelling place of Mount Zion, and above her assemblies'. Read Exodus 14:19, 20 and rejoice in God's distinguishing grace! 'And the angel of God, which went before the camp of Israel, removed and went behind them; and the pillar of the cloud went from before their face, and stood behind them: And it came between the camp of the Egyptians and the camp of Israel; and it was a cloud and darkness to them, but it gave light by night to these: so that the one came not near the other all the night.' There is nothing common or universal about the work of Jesus Christ. What he does, he does for his elect alone, and does it effectually. Universal love is useless love. Universal grace is useless grace. Universal redemption is no redemption at all.

Our Guide and Protector
Third, as the pillar going before them went before Israel to guide and protect them throughout their wilderness journey, so the Lord Jesus Christ is our Guide and Protector through this world, ever going before us. He guides us by his Word, by his Spirit, and by the hand of his grace. He has guided us all our days. He is guiding us now. He will guide us until he brings us, at last, into the land of immortality in heavenly glory.

'And on the day that the tabernacle was reared up the cloud covered the tabernacle, namely, the tent of the testimony: and at even there was upon the tabernacle as it were the appearance of fire, until the morning. So it was alway: the cloud covered it by day, and the appearance of fire by night. And when the cloud was taken up from the tabernacle, then after that the children of Israel journeyed: and in the place where the cloud abode, there the children of Israel pitched their tents. At the commandment of the LORD the children of Israel journeyed, and at the commandment of the LORD they pitched: as long as the cloud abode upon the tabernacle they rested in their tents. And when the cloud tarried long upon the tabernacle many days, then the children of Israel kept the charge of the LORD, and journeyed not. And so it was, when the cloud was a few days upon the tabernacle; according to the commandment of the LORD they abode in their tents, and according to the commandment of the LORD they journeyed. And so it was, when the cloud abode from even unto the morning, and that the cloud was taken up in the morning, then they journeyed: whether it was by day or by night that the cloud was taken up, they journeyed. Or whether it were two days, or a month, or a year, that the cloud tarried upon the tabernacle, remaining thereon, the children of Israel abode in their tents, and journeyed not: but when it was taken up, they journeyed. At the commandment of the LORD they rested in the tents, and at the commandment of the LORD they journeyed: they kept the charge of the LORD, at the commandment of the LORD by the hand of Moses' (Numbers 9:15-23).

The Lord Jesus Christ is our Guide, 'to give light to them that sit in darkness and in the shadow of death, to guide our feet into the way of peace' (Luke 1:79; Matthew 4:16; Isaiah 48:17).

'The LORD is my shepherd; I shall not want. He maketh me to lie down in green pastures: he leadeth me beside the still waters. He restoreth my soul: he leadeth me in the paths of righteousness for his name's sake. Yea, though I walk through the valley of the shadow of death, I will fear no evil: for thou art with me; thy rod and thy staff they comfort me. Thou preparest a table before me in the presence of mine enemies: thou anointest my head with oil; my cup runneth over. Surely goodness and mercy shall follow me all the days of my life: and I will dwell in the house of the LORD for ever' (Psalm 23).

Pillar of Cloud

By day, the pillar was a cloud over the camp of Israel, both to guide them through the wilderness and to cover and protect them from the scorching sun. By night it was a pillar of fire to give them light (Psalm 105:39). That is what Christ is to us. The Lord's our Rock of defence and our Cloud of covering. He is,

> Our shade by day defence by night,
> A Shelter in the time of storm!
> Secure whatever foes afright,
> A Shelter in the time of storm!

'He that dwelleth in the secret place of the most High shall abide under the shadow of the Almighty. I will say of the LORD, He is my refuge and my fortress: my God; in him will I trust. Surely he shall deliver thee from the snare of the fowler, and from the noisome pestilence. He shall cover thee with his feathers, and under his wings shalt thou trust: his truth shall be thy shield and buckler. Thou shalt not be afraid for the terror by night; nor for the arrow that flieth by day; Nor for the pestilence that walketh in darkness; nor for the destruction that wasteth at noonday. A thousand shall fall at thy side, and ten thousand at thy right hand; but it shall not come nigh thee. Only with thine eyes shalt thou behold and see the reward of the wicked. Because thou hast made the LORD, which is my refuge, even the most High, thy habitation; There shall no evil befall thee, neither shall any plague come nigh thy dwelling. For he shall give his angels charge over thee, to keep thee in all thy ways. They shall bear thee up in their hands, lest thou dash thy foot against a stone. Thou shalt tread upon the lion and adder: the young lion and the dragon shalt thou trample under feet' (Psalm 91:1-13).

How we ought to thank God for the Covering that is over us! God give us grace to trust him!

Pillar of Fire

The Lord Jesus is our Pillar of Cloud to cover us and guide us by day; and, blessed be his name forever, he is our Pillar of Fire to guide us by night! Fire suggests many things: light, heat, protection, and burning. Christ is a Pillar of Fire to our souls to guide us through the night of our mortality, lest we lose our way. The Lord Jesus is a Pillar of Fire to protect and guide our souls in the dark night of trouble and temptation, piercing through our spiritual darkness. He is a Pillar of Fire round about us to protect us from every evil (Psalm 34:7; 50:3; 97:3; 125:2; Zechariah 2:5). The Lord Jesus is a Pillar of Fire to our souls, not only to give us light, but also to give us heat and warmth in the bitter cold of night. By his Word and by his Spirit (which are both compared to fire), he keeps us from the natural coldness of our own sinful hearts, ever reviving us with the fire of his love, mercy, and grace.

Ever Present
Fourth, this pillar of cloud and fire was always with the children of Israel, from the moment they left Egypt, until they entered into and took possession of Canaan. The pillar never left them. It went before them, guided them, and protected them, until they no longer needed guidance and protection, until they no longer walked through the dark wilderness, until their enemies were all subdued (Nehemiah 9:19). So it is with our Saviour, our Pillar of Cloud and Fire. He has sworn, 'I will never leave thee nor forsake thee'. That is the sweet promise of God to every believer. 'I will never leave thee, nor forsake thee'. Read it as it is given repeatedly in his Word and rejoice (Hebrews 13:5, 6; Psalm 27:10; 73:25, 26; Isaiah 43:1-7). 'I will never leave thee, nor forsake thee'.

We have entirely too many fears for a people to whom the Lord Jesus Christ is an ever-abiding Pillar of Cloud and Fire, to whom the Lord has said, 'Fear thou not; for I am with thee; be not dismayed, for I am thy God; I will strengthen thee, yea, I will uphold thee with the right hand of my righteousness' (Isaiah 41:10). Why cannot we believe God? Has he not proved himself faithful to us? David heard God's promise and believed him. His faith in Christ quietened his fears. He said, 'Yea, though I walk through the valley of the shadow of death. I will fear no evil for thou art with me; thy rod and thy staff, they comfort me'. How I pray for the kind of grace exemplified by my friend, Pastor Rupert Rivenbark, as he stood by his daughter's casket many years ago, and said to the assembled congregation at her funeral service 'We are here to kiss the hand of God's providence'.

We have far too many doubts and fears concerning God's mercy, love, and grace to whom the Lord Jesus Christ is an ever-abiding Pillar of Cloud and Fire, for a people to whom the Lord has said, 'Him that cometh to me I will in no wise cast out' (John 6:37). 'I give unto them eternal life, and they shall never perish' (John 10:28). I know many of God's saints have trouble in this area. I acknowledge my own shameful, baseless, sinful doubts. But I will not excuse them! On what grounds dare we call into question the mercy, love, and grace of our God? We have absolutely no reason to entertain the slightest shade of doubt. Did he not promise never to cast out any who come to Christ? Will he not perform it? 'God is not a man that he should lie' (Numbers 23:19).

C. H. Spurgeon reasoned like this, 'The Scripture says, "He that believeth on the Son of God hath everlasting life", I believe the Son of God. I have life!' Why should we ever question that? Paul didn't! (2 Timothy 1:12; 4:6-8). 'If God be for us, who can be against us?' 'Who shall lay anything to the charge of God's elect?' 'Who is he that condemneth?' 'Who shall separate us from the love of God?'

I refuse to doubt God's love because of something I have thought, or said, or done. His love is free and unconditional. I refuse to question his grace because of my sin. While I acknowledge the abundance of my sin, I will rejoice in the superabundance of God's free grace in Christ. I am not going to be suspicious of his mercy because I do not deserve his mercy. Mercy is for the undeserving. We, to whom the Lord Jesus Christ is an ever-abiding Pillar of Cloud and Fire, spend entirely too much time grumbling and complaining about our trials and troubles. The Lord has said, 'In the world ye shall have tribulation, but be of good cheer; I have overcome the world' (John 16:33). We should not be surprised when troubles come. We ought to expect them. Every diamond that sparkles with beauty has been broken out of the earth, cut by sharp blows, and polished by rubbing. God has chosen us in the furnace of affliction (Isaiah 48:10). He will break, and cut, and polish his jewels. 'Beloved, think it not strange concerning the fiery trial which is to try you, as though some strange thing happened unto you' (1 Peter 4:12). Trouble is not strange to God's people. The absence of trouble is strange.

No matter the trial, the foe, or the heat we must endure, no matter the darkness through which we must pass, as the Lord God 'took not away the pillar of the cloud by day, nor the pillar of fire by night, from before the people' of old, the Lord Jesus Christ will never cease to be to our souls the Pillar of Cloud and Fire, until he has brought us into the land of our rest, in which we shall have neither enemy nor darkness!

Chapter 65

Burial Or Cremation?

'And Moses took the bones of Joseph with him: for he had straitly sworn the children of Israel, saying, God will surely visit you; and ye shall carry up my bones away hence with you.'
(Exodus 13:19)

Burial or cremation? Which should we practice? In some countries, cremation is far more common than burial. It has become more common in western countries where burial used to be the norm for people to cremate the bodies of the dead, rather than go to the time, trouble, and expense of burying them. I am frequently asked, 'Should believers be cremated?' Does the Bible give us an answer?

No, the Word of God does not give us a clear, definite answer. There are many things that are matters of indifference, things we may do or not do, as we think best for the glory of God. And we must always be content to allow our brethren to make their own determination about such things. 'Who art thou that judgest another man's servant? to his own master he standeth or falleth. Yea, he shall be holden up: for God is able to make him stand ... Let every man be fully persuaded in his own mind' (Romans 14:4, 5).

Still, I am often asked, 'Should a believer be cremated or buried?' While the Scriptures do not give any commandment in the matter, the burial of our bodies is more consistent with the faith of the gospel than cremation. Our Lord was buried. We confess our Saviour and our faith in him by a burial, in believer's baptism. There is an obvious connection between burial and our faith in Christ.

Moses's Faith

That which Moses did with Joseph's bones must have been very conspicuous to the nation of Israel as they made haste and left the land of Egypt. They left the land in haste, not as slaves secretly escaping from their captors in the night, but as slaves who had completely conquered, spoiled, and dispossessed their captors, in an open display of triumph and victory. As they left the land of captivity, we are told;

'Moses took the bones of Joseph with him: for he had straitly sworn the children of Israel, saying, God will surely visit you; and ye shall carry up my bones away hence with you'.

Why did he do that? In the eleventh chapter of the Book of Hebrews, God the Holy Spirit tells us it was an act of faith. Joseph made his brethren swear to carry his bones out of Egypt by faith. Moses carried his bones out of Egypt by faith. And Joshua buried his bones in Canaan by faith. Moses' action was an act of faith, faith in the resurrection of Christ our Redeemer, and of the resurrection of God's elect in, with, and by him. His faith, like our faith, was precisely the same faith that Job confessed (Job 19:25-27).

Jacob Embalmed

We read in the Book of Genesis that Abraham buried Sarah in the cave of Machpelah, in the land of Canaan; and when he died, Abraham's sons, Isaac and Ishmael, buried him in the same tomb (Genesis 23 and 25). And in Genesis 50, Joseph had his father, Jacob, embalmed, spent forty days mourning him, and obtained special permission from Pharaoh to carry his body up to Canaan. There he buried Jacob with Abraham and Isaac (Genesis 49:33-50:13).

'And when Jacob had made an end of commanding his sons, he gathered up his feet into the bed, and yielded up the ghost, and was gathered unto his people' (Genesis 49:33).

'And Joseph fell upon his father's face, and wept upon him, and kissed him. And Joseph commanded his servants the physicians to embalm his father: and the physicians embalmed Israel. And forty days were fulfilled for him; for so are fulfilled the days of those which are embalmed: and the Egyptians mourned for him threescore and ten days.

And when the days of his mourning were past, Joseph spake unto the house of Pharaoh, saying, If now I have found grace in your eyes, speak, I pray you, in the ears of Pharaoh, saying, My father made me swear, saying, Lo, I die: in my grave which I have digged for me in the land of Canaan, there shalt thou bury me. Now therefore let me go up, I pray thee, and bury my father, and I will come again. And Pharaoh said, Go up, and bury thy father, according as he made thee swear' (Genesis 50:1-6).

'And his sons did unto him according as he commanded them: For his sons carried him into the land of Canaan, and buried him in the cave of the field of Machpelah, which Abraham bought with the field for a possession of a buryingplace of Ephron the Hittite, before Mamre' (Genesis 50:12, 13).

No doubt many, as they watched this procession, must have thought, 'Why all this bother? Why all this expense? The man is dead. Don't they know his body is going to rot and decay and return to the dust? Doesn't Joseph know the body is just a shell, not the man?'

Joseph knew all that, and more. Joseph did what he did to honour his father, whom he dearly loved. Joseph embalmed his father because embalming was an indication that the one whose body was dead was really very much alive. The Scriptures do not tell us that but it was the reason the Egyptians embalmed their dead and built great pyramids for their kings. And our Lord Jesus tells us plainly that the death of the body is not, for God's elect, death at all, but the beginning of a better life (Psalm 116:15; John 11:25, 26; 2 Corinthians 5:1-5).

Joseph embalmed his father in hope of the resurrection (1 Corinthians 15:29; Acts 9:36, 37). When Paul speaks of the baptism of the dead in 1 Corinthians 15:29, the word baptism is used there as it is when the Scriptures speak of washing cups and pots and tables (Mark 7:4-8). The Apostle asserts that the reason for the practice of washing (embalming the dead) is the hope of the resurrection. Christ has redeemed our bodies as well as our souls. Surely, if the Lord Jesus Christ has redeemed the bodies of his elect, it is altogether proper for us to treat the bodies of the dead with the utmost respect and honour.

Joseph in a Coffin
That is what Joseph did for his father. He embalmed him and buried him in the land of Canaan, believing the Word and promise of God, that

he would live again in resurrection glory. In Genesis 50:22-26, God the Holy Spirit tells us that Joseph's last act as he was leaving this world was to secure his burial in the land of Canaan.

'And Joseph dwelt in Egypt, he, and his father's house: and Joseph lived an hundred and ten years. And Joseph saw Ephraim's children of the third generation: the children also of Machir the son of Manasseh were brought up upon Joseph's knees. And Joseph said unto his brethren, I die: and God will surely visit you, and bring you out of this land unto the land which he sware to Abraham, to Isaac, and to Jacob. And Joseph took an oath of the children of Israel, saying, God will surely visit you, and ye shall carry up my bones from hence. So Joseph died, being an hundred and ten years old: and they embalmed him, and he was put in a coffin in Egypt' (Genesis 50:22-26).

The Book of Genesis, the book of beginnings, closes with Joseph in a coffin. All God's dealings with Israel recorded in those 50 chapters, all the promises made to the patriarchs, and the glories of God's servant Joseph end with 'a coffin in Egypt'. For 300 years Israel was left with nothing but a mummy and a word of promise. The elaborately embalmed body of Joseph lay in a coffin, perhaps on public display somewhere in Goshen for 300 years! For three centuries, that silent 'coffin in Egypt' preached its mighty message. What did it say?

First, it was a silent reminder of mortality. The shrivelled, colourless lips that lay in that coffin, wrapped with linen, had left as their last utterance, 'I die, but God will surely visit you'. No man is necessary. No mere mortal is indispensable. God's Israel will survive the loss of the strongest and wisest. God lives, though a hundred Josephs die. Joseph died,

'And the children of Israel were fruitful, and increased abundantly, and multiplied, and waxed exceeding mighty; and the land was filled with them' (Exodus 1:7).

So, life springs side by side with death. There are cradles as well as graves. But the fact is, you and I must soon die (Ecclesiastes 7:2-4; Psalm 90:12).

Second, that 'coffin in Egypt' was a herald of hope. Joseph's bones, lying in 'a coffin in Egypt', perpetually declared, God will bring you out of this place. That is precisely what the Scriptures teach us about the burial of God's saints in the earth (1 Thessalonians 4:13-18; 1 Corinthians 15:51-58).

Third, that 'coffin in Egypt' was a preacher of patience. No doubt, hope deferred for 300 years had made many hearts sick and caused many fainting Israelites to ask in unbelief, 'Where is the promise of his coming?' But, for all those years, the silent coffin laid before the children of Israel proclaiming, 'Though the vision tarry, wait for it.' Surely, we need the same lesson.

'The Lord is not slack concerning his promise, as some men count slackness; but is longsuffering to us-ward, not willing that any should perish, but that all should come to repentance. But the day of the Lord will come as a thief in the night; in the which the heavens shall pass away with a great noise, and the elements shall melt with fervent heat, the earth also and the works that are therein shall be burned up. Seeing then that all these things shall be dissolved, what manner of persons ought ye to be in all holy conversation and godliness, Looking for and hasting unto the coming of the day of God, wherein the heavens being on fire shall be dissolved, and the elements shall melt with fervent heat? Nevertheless we, according to his promise, look for new heavens and a new earth, wherein dwelleth righteousness. Wherefore, beloved, seeing that ye look for such things, be diligent that ye may be found of him in peace, without spot, and blameless' (2 Peter 3:9-14).

Fourth, that 'coffin in Egypt' was a pledge of possession. It proclaimed, 'Canaan is yours and you shall possess it!' And, as we bury the bodies of God's saints in the earth, we bury them with the joyful knowledge that believing sinners are 'heirs of God and joint-heirs with Christ', possessors of eternal life (Romans 8:16-24).

Moses and Joseph's Bones
Let me show you the connection between Moses and Joseph's bones.

'Moses took the bones of Joseph with him: for he had straitly sworn the children of Israel, saying, God will surely visit you; and ye shall carry up my bones away hence with you' (v. 19).

Why does the Spirit of God tell us that Moses carried Joseph's bones out of Egypt? It is certain that Moses did not personally, physically carry that coffin containing Joseph's bones out of Egypt. Yet, our text declares that the carrying of Joseph's bones out of Egypt was specifically the work of Moses. Why? Moses represented the law of God. Joseph was typical of our Lord Jesus Christ, who was raised from the dead, because the law, death, had no more claim upon him. Joseph also represented God's elect who have been brought out of the bondage of sin and death because God's holy law has no claim upon us, since Christ has put away our sin (1 Peter 4:1, 2).

Joshua and Joseph's Bones

But Moses, the law, could never give Joseph and Israel the possession of the land of Canaan. That was a work that had to be done by another. Joshua 24 gives us one more sweet point of delight in the connection between Joshua and Joseph's bones.

Joseph's bones were buried in Canaan with Joshua's, after the Lord God fulfilled every promise he had made to Abraham and the nation of Israel concerning that land (Joshua 24:29-32). 'And it came to pass after these things, that Joshua the son of Nun, the servant of the LORD, died, being an hundred and ten years old. And they buried him in the border of his inheritance in Timnathserah, which is in mount Ephraim, on the north side of the hill of Gaash. And Israel served the LORD all the days of Joshua, and all the days of the elders that overlived Joshua, and which had known all the works of the LORD, that he had done for Israel. And the bones of Joseph, which the children of Israel brought up out of Egypt, buried they in Shechem, in a parcel of ground which Jacob bought of the sons of Hamor the father of Shechem for an hundred pieces of silver: and it became the inheritance of the children of Joseph' (Joshua 24:29-32).

So it shall be with you and me. As Joshua brought Joseph's bones into Canaan and laid him to rest with himself in the land of promise, so the Lord Jesus Christ, our great Joshua, shall give us rest in the land of God's promise. Our ever-gracious God, who cannot lie, has promised, 'They shall enter into my rest' (Romans 6:4-6; Hebrews 4:1-11). We bury our dead in the comfort and joy of knowing that their bodies rest in peace in the earth and their souls rest from their labour in heaven in anticipation, and in the confident hope of that day when body and soul shall be forever reunited in resurrection rest with Christ.

Chapter 66

Experiencing The Power Of God

'And the LORD spake unto Moses, saying, Speak unto the children of Israel, that they turn and encamp before Pihahiroth, between Migdol and the sea, over against Baalzephon: before it shall ye encamp by the sea ... And I, behold, I will harden the hearts of the Egyptians, and they shall follow them: and I will get me honour upon Pharaoh, and upon all his host, upon his chariots, and upon his horsemen ... Thus the LORD saved Israel that day out of the hand of the Egyptians; and Israel saw the Egyptians dead upon the sea shore. And Israel saw that great work which the LORD did upon the Egyptians: and the people feared the LORD, and believed the LORD, and his servant Moses.'
(Exodus 14:1-31)

Multitudes there are who are described by our Saviour as spiritually ignorant people, who always err, 'not knowing the Scriptures nor the power of God' (Matthew 22:29). They cannot understand the teachings of Holy Scripture, because they have never experienced them. They may be religious, outwardly very moral and righteous, and even orthodox in their doctrine, but God the Holy Ghost declares, 'They do alway err in their heart; and they have not known my ways' (Hebrews 3:10). Why? Because they are utterly ignorant of the power of God. They have never felt, they have never experienced the power of God.

They may sing, 'There is power, power, wonder working power, in the blood of the Lamb', but they have never felt the power of the blood in their souls. They may talk much about the power of God's irresistible, saving grace, but they have never experienced that power and grace for themselves.

Therefore they 'do always err in their heart'. To them redemption is only a doctrine. Regeneration is nothing but a principle. Righteousness is nothing but a legal standing. The new creation is a confusing puzzle. They have theories about these things, theories that must be adjusted, clarified, and changed year after year; but they know nothing by experience. They know nothing about 'the power of God' by which sinners are saved.

Exodus 14 gives us a picture of men and women experiencing the power of God. In this chapter, the Holy Spirit gives us the history of the children of Israel coming out of Egypt and crossing the Red Sea, experiencing the mighty power of God. What they experienced is held before us throughout the Scriptures as a type and illustration of every saved sinner's experience of grace. Here are seven things experienced by every sinner God saves by his marvellous grace.

Utter Helplessness

The first work of God the Holy Spirit upon the soul in the experience of grace is a painful, withering work. He brings the sinner to whom God is gracious to a state of utter helplessness, causing him or her to be entangled in hopelessness (vv. 1-9).

'And the LORD spake unto Moses, saying, Speak unto the children of Israel, that they turn and encamp before Pihahiroth, between Migdol and the sea, over against Baalzephon: before it shall ye encamp by the sea' (vv. 1, 2).

Israel was brought out of Egypt in a manner altogether contrary to that which any earthly wisdom would have chosen. The Lord God took them in a path that led them directly toward the Red Sea, where they were easily trapped by Pharaoh and the Egyptians. But God's way was 'the right way' (Psalm 107:7). He brought them forth through 'Pihahiroth', which means 'a hole', and marched them directly in front of 'Baalzephon', one of the gods of the Egyptians, the very god who was worshipped as the god who would prevent the escape of their servants!

What a delightful picture! God causes his elect to pass through the dark hole of despair, with Satan (Pharaoh) seeking their destruction, and brings them through that dark hole in mockery of 'the prince of darkness', who would hold us captive still.

Do not fail to observe it was by the hand of Moses that Israel was brought into this dark hole and ensnared. There must be a work of death wrought in us by the law. We cannot be raised to life by God's grace until we have been slain by his holy law (Romans 7:9). The Lord God brought Israel in the path he did, that he might make a display of his sovereignty in the destruction of Pharaoh (Romans 9:15-18).

'For Pharaoh will say of the children of Israel, They are entangled in the land, the wilderness hath shut them in. And I will harden Pharaoh's heart, that he shall follow after them; and I will be honoured upon Pharaoh, and upon all his host; that the Egyptians may know that I am the LORD. And they did so. And it was told the king of Egypt that the people fled: and the heart of Pharaoh and of his servants was turned against the people, and they said, Why have we done this, that we have let Israel go from serving us? And he made ready his chariot, and took his people with him: And he took six hundred chosen chariots, and all the chariots of Egypt, and captains over every one of them. And the LORD hardened the heart of Pharaoh king of Egypt, and he pursued after the children of Israel: and the children of Israel went out with an high hand' (vv. 3-8). All things, even Pharaoh and the Egyptians, even Satan and the reprobate shall glorify our God (Revelation 4:11; Proverbs 16:4). 'But the Egyptians pursued after them, all the horses and chariots of Pharaoh, and his horsemen, and his army, and overtook them encamping by the sea, beside Pihahiroth, before Baalzephon.'

Israel was shut up between the mountains behind and the raging sea before them, with death pursuing them. This is what God does with the sinner he pursues. He shuts the guilty sinner up between the mountains of offended justice and the swamps of inability. Satan roars, and the guilty conscience screams in agreement, 'God hath forsaken him: persecute and take him; for there is none to deliver him' (Psalm 71:11).

Shut up to Christ

What is the purpose of this? Why does God deal so with those who are the objects of his grace? Read verse 10, and you will see God's purpose is to shut us up to Christ.

'And when Pharaoh drew nigh, the children of Israel lifted up their eyes, and, behold, the Egyptians marched after them; and they were sore afraid: and the children of Israel cried out unto the LORD.'

Their situation, to all human appearance, was utterly hopeless. Before them was the Red Sea. Behind them Pharaoh and his armies were rushing to destroy them. They were surrounded by mountains. They were shut up to God, shut up to Christ, shut up to faith. That is what God does in Holy Spirit conviction. He shuts us up to Christ, sweetly forcing the chosen, redeemed sinner to call upon the Lord Jesus for mercy and grace to help in time of need (Galatians 3:23). Like the children of Judah before Ammon, sinners cry out for mercy only when they are shut up to faith. 'O our God, wilt thou not judge them? For we have no might against this great company that cometh against us; neither know we what to do: but our eyes are upon thee' (2 Chronicles 20:12). All earthly help was cut off. Israel could not make a move. They were shut up in confusion and dark despair.

'And when Pharaoh drew nigh, the children of Israel lifted up their eyes, and, behold, the Egyptians marched after them; and they were sore afraid: and the children of Israel cried out unto the LORD. And they said unto Moses, Because there were no graves in Egypt, hast thou taken us away to die in the wilderness? wherefore hast thou dealt thus with us, to carry us forth out of Egypt? Is not this the word that we did tell thee in Egypt, saying, Let us alone, that we may serve the Egyptians? For it had been better for us to serve the Egyptians, than that we should die in the wilderness' (vv. 10-12).

Salvation is near when the sinner is shut up to Christ. If the Lord God strips you of all hope and shuts you up to faith in Christ, I say to you as our Lord did to the rich young ruler, 'Thou art not far from the kingdom of God'.

Gospel Counsel

When the sinner is in such straits, helpless, suspended, as it were, over hell, he cries, 'What must I do?' So these people. They cried to Moses in confusion and despair, essentially saying, 'What are we to do?' Hear the good counsel Moses gives, it is gospel counsel, the only counsel God's prophets can give to the sinner God has shut in by his grace.

'And Moses said unto the people, Fear ye not, stand still, and see the salvation of the LORD, which he will show to you today: for the

Egyptians whom ye have seen today, ye shall see them again no more forever' (v. 13).

God does not arm Israel and tell them to go out and fight against Pharaoh. He did not strengthen their arms to bring salvation to them. He says, 'Stand still, and see the salvation of the LORD'. So it is with us! He says, our 'strength is to sit still' (Isaiah 30:7). He who is our mighty Jehovah knows how to deliver his own. We read in verse 14, 'The LORD shall fight for you, and ye shall hold your peace.'

Salvation is not something sinners obtain by effort (Romans 9:31-10:4). Salvation comes by revelation. 'Fear ye not, stand still, and see the salvation of the LORD, which he will show to you today.' And when you see God's salvation, you will see the Egyptians, your condemning sins, no more!

The Way Opened

Next, we see the way opened for God's chosen by God himself. As we read these next verses, understand their meaning. When the Lord God our Saviour saves sinners by the power of his grace, when he sets his captive prisoners free, giving them faith by his Spirit to come to him, he opens the way before them; but the way was opened long before it was opened to us. Christ our Passover opened the way by the blood of his cross, when he sacrificed himself for us. He opens the way before us in the sweet experience of grace by divine revelation, and brings us through the raging Red Sea of terror into the glorious liberty of the sons of God. This is how he does it (vv. 15-21).

First, he commands faith. He says 'Go forward' (v. 15). 'Believe on the Lord Jesus Christ, and thou shalt be saved!'

Second, he opens the way before us by the very rod of Moses, the rod of the law by which the Rock, Christ our God and Saviour, was smitten of God (vv. 16, 21, 22).

'But lift thou up thy rod, and stretch out thine hand over the sea, and divide it: and the children of Israel shall go on dry ground through the midst of the sea ... And Moses stretched out his hand over the sea; and the LORD caused the sea to go back by a strong east wind all that night, and made the sea dry land, and the waters were divided ... And the children of Israel went into the midst of the sea upon the dry ground: and the waters were a wall unto them on their right hand, and on their left.'

Third, he performs a work of sovereign, distinguishing grace to bring his elect through the sea (v. 19, 20).

'And the angel of God, which went before the camp of Israel, removed and went behind them; and the pillar of the cloud went from before their face, and stood behind them: And it came between the camp of the Egyptians and the camp of Israel; and it was a cloud and darkness to them, but it gave light by night to these: so that the one came not near the other all the night.'

Remember, this pillar of cloud and fire is our Lord Jesus Christ. He went before Israel to give them light and bring them through the sea; but he went behind them to confuse the Egyptians in darkness, lest they come near his chosen.

'Who maketh thee to differ from another? And what hast thou that thou didst not receive? Now if thou didst receive it, why dost thou glory, as if thou hadst not received it?' (1 Corinthians 4:7).

Fourth, the children of Israel were baptized unto Moses, 'And the children of Israel went into the midst of the sea upon the dry ground: and the waters were a wall unto them on their right hand, and on their left' (v. 22). The Spirit of God tells us, in 1 Corinthians 10:1, that this was a typical baptism, because the whole thing is a picture of faith. The children of Israel publicly consecrated themselves to Moses, committing themselves to Christ who led them through the sea. That is what believer's baptism is. It is our public avowal of consecration to Christ.

'Therefore we are buried with him by baptism into death: that like as Christ was raised up from the dead by the glory of the Father, even so we also should walk in newness of life. For if we have been planted together in the likeness of his death, we shall be also in the likeness of his resurrection: Knowing this, that our old man is crucified with him, that the body of sin might be destroyed, that henceforth we should not serve sin' (Romans 6:4-6).

Egyptians Destroyed

Remember, God said they would see the Egyptians no more; and the next thing we see is the destruction of Pharaoh and all the Egyptians in the sea (vv. 23-30). He troubled the Egyptians (v. 24). He took the wheels off of their chariots (v. 25). He fought against them (v. 25). He overthrew them in the midst of the sea (vv. 26, 27). 'There remained not so much as one of them' (v. 28). It is written of our God that he 'forgiveth all thine iniquities' (Psalm 103:3; Romans 8:1). He did all this by the same rod of Moses that opened the way before them (v. 26). And as they passed through the sea in faith, the children of Israel saw God's salvation (vv. 29, 30).

'But the children of Israel walked upon dry land in the midst of the sea; and the waters were a wall unto them on their right hand, and on their left. Thus the LORD saved Israel that day out of the hand of the Egyptians; and Israel saw the Egyptians dead upon the sea shore.'

Salvation Wrought

Thus, God wrought the salvation of Israel; and thus he still performs this great work of grace, by which he causes chosen sinners to experience the power of God, giving us faith in Christ (vv. 30, 31).

'Thus the LORD saved Israel that day out of the hand of the Egyptians; and Israel saw the Egyptians dead upon the sea shore. And Israel saw that great work which the LORD did upon the Egyptians: and the people feared the LORD, and believed the LORD, and his servant Moses.'

Israel saw the great work the Lord accomplished for them. When they saw it they worshipped the triune Jehovah. They feared him, calling upon his name. They experienced the power of God in salvation, and they believed on the Lord Jesus Christ who had delivered them.

Triumphant Song

Now, read the first verse of chapter 15. Here is the result of all this. The sinner saved by the omnipotent power of God's grace sings God's praise, triumphing over death, hell and the grave.

'Then sang Moses and the children of Israel this song unto the LORD, and spake, saying, I will sing unto the LORD, for he hath triumphed gloriously: the horse and his rider hath he thrown into the sea.'

Read the whole of Moses' song, and you will discover that in this song of praise to our great God and Saviour the saved people mention God's name (Thy, Thine, and Thou) twenty-four times. All praise goes to our God, because the work is all his (Psalm 115:1; 1 Corinthians 15:57; Revelation 19:1-6).

Discovering Christ In Exodus

Chapter 67

Trapped In Hopeless Despair

'And the LORD spake unto Moses, saying, Speak unto the children of Israel, that they turn and encamp before Pihahiroth, between Migdol and the sea, over against Baalzephon: before it shall ye encamp by the sea. For Pharaoh will say of the children of Israel, They are entangled in the land, the wilderness hath shut them in. And I will harden Pharaoh's heart, that he shall follow after them; and I will be honoured upon Pharaoh, and upon all his host; that the Egyptians may know that I am the LORD. And they did so. And it was told the king of Egypt that the people fled: and the heart of Pharaoh and of his servants was turned against the people, and they said, Why have we done this, that we have let Israel go from serving us? And he made ready his chariot, and took his people with him: And he took six hundred chosen chariots, and all the chariots of Egypt, and captains over every one of them. And the LORD hardened the heart of Pharaoh king of Egypt, and he pursued after the children of Israel: and the children of Israel went out with an high hand. But the Egyptians pursued after them, all the horses and chariots of Pharaoh, and his horsemen, and his army, and overtook them encamping by the sea, beside Pihahiroth, before Baalzephon. And when Pharaoh drew nigh, the children of Israel lifted up their eyes, and, behold, the Egyptians marched after them; and they were sore afraid: and the children of Israel cried out unto the LORD. And they said unto Moses, Because there were no graves in Egypt, hast thou taken us away

to die in the wilderness? Wherefore hast thou dealt thus with us, to carry us forth out of Egypt? Is not this the word that we did tell thee in Egypt, saying, Let us alone, that we may serve the Egyptians? For it had been better for us to serve the Egyptians, than that we should die in the wilderness. And Moses said unto the people, Fear ye not, stand still, and see the salvation of the LORD, which he will shew to you today: for the Egyptians whom ye have seen today, ye shall see them again no more forever. The LORD shall fight for you, and ye shall hold your peace. And the LORD said unto Moses, Wherefore criest thou unto me? speak unto the children of Israel, that they go forward.'
(Exodus 14:1-15)

Do you sometimes feel yourself trapped in hopeless despair at the end of a dead-end street with no place to go? If so, this portion of Holy Scripture is a message for you, a word of instruction from the God of Glory that is designed to give you clear direction in every dilemma you may face in this world. The instructions are clear. 'Stand still!'

A Furious Foe
God hardened Pharaoh's heart against the children of Israel; and he pursued them in fury, determined to take them captive again (Exodus 15:4-9). 'The Lord hardened the heart of Pharaoh king of Egypt, and he pursued after the children of Israel' (v. 8). With everything at his disposal, the enraged monarch of Egypt went after the children of Israel. 'But the Egyptians pursued after them, all the horses and chariots of Pharaoh, and his horsemen, and his army, and overtook them encamping by the sea, beside Pihahiroth, before Baalzephon' (Exodus 14:9).

That is a pretty good picture of our position in this world. You and I are pursued through this world by a furious foe, determined to destroy us.

In Revelation 12:12, the Apostle John tells us that Satan's fury against God's church, against Christ, his gospel and his people, the relentless venting of his enmity against the woman's Seed is the result of the fact that he is a defeated foe; and no foe is more furious that one who is defeated. He may have no power, he may have no arms, he may even be bound in chains, but his fury is unabated. Even so, we are told that Satan is in a rage, 'because he knoweth that he hath but a short time'. Though he is defeated, his rage has not diminished. He can do no harm to God's cause or his people. Therefore, there is cause for all heaven to rejoice. But, like a mad dog in a cage or a roaring lion on a chain, Satan's hatred of Christ is demonstrated in his growling and roaring against his church and people. Satan knows he has but a short time. Therefore he persecutes God's people with unimaginable fury; but his fury is the fury of impotence, because he is a defeated adversary (Revelation 12:13-16). That is the picture before us in Exodus 14.

The children of Israel have come out of Egypt. They have been completely delivered from their captors. Not a hoof was left behind in Egypt. All their cattle, all their children, and all their aged men and women had come out of the house of bondage. But the tyrant who had enslaved them was hardened against them and pursued them with greater wrath and fury than ever, determined to overtake them and make them his captives once more.

God the Holy Ghost tells us plainly that the experiences of Israel, from the time they came out of Egypt until they took possession of the land of Canaan, were typical of the experiences of God's elect in this world (1 Corinthians 10:1-11). As we make our way through this wilderness to our heavenly Canaan, Satan ever pursues us in fury. Therefore, we are urged to cast all our care upon our God, being assured that 'the God of all grace' will finish his work of grace (Philippians 1:6; 1 Peter 5:6-11).

Entangled in the Wilderness

Pharaoh said, concerning the children of Israel, 'They are entangled in the land, the wilderness hath shut them in' (v. 3). And when he overtook them, it is exactly how he found them, 'entangled in the land'. The Lord could easily have led them into Canaan in a far easier path, a path that would have avoided their entanglement; but he led them in the right way, the way by which he would most clearly display the glory of his grace. He led them to the edge of the Red Sea, surrounded by mountains they could not cross, with Pharaoh and all his forces roaring against them in fury. They were trapped in hopeless despair (vv. 10-12).

'And when Pharaoh drew nigh, the children of Israel lifted up their eyes, and, behold, the Egyptians marched after them; and they were sore afraid: and the children of Israel cried out unto the LORD. And they said unto Moses, Because there were no graves in Egypt, hast thou

61

taken us away to die in the wilderness? Wherefore hast thou dealt thus with us, to carry us forth out of Egypt? Is not this the word that we did tell thee in Egypt, saying, Let us alone, that we may serve the Egyptians? For it had been better for us to serve the Egyptians, than that we should die in the wilderness.'

God's primary purpose in all his works is the manifestation of his own glory; and that is pre-eminently the case in his great works of grace (Psalm 106:8; Isaiah 63:12-14). If God is to be glorified, man must be put out of the way. If he is to be glorified in the salvation of my soul, I have to be moved out of the way. If God is to be glorified in your salvation, you have to be put out of the way.

How does he move us out of the picture? He brings us to our wits' end, makes us conscious of our folly, our weakness, and our sin, that we may behold his glory when he performs our deliverance. Nothing so blinds us to God's glory as our high opinion of ourselves. Therefore, the Lord God leads us to Glory through the wilderness of this world, a place of much entanglement, where Satan pursues us and seeks to destroy us. Often the entanglements are of our own making; but even these could and would be avoided were that best for God's glory and best for our souls.

What entanglements we make for ourselves! How often we are trapped in hopeless despair, at the end of a dark dead-end road, with no place to turn, entangled with worldly care, with fleshly lusts, with ridicule, opposition and persecution, with religious curiosity, and with heavy trials.

Those who wade around little streams and shallow creeks, never learn much about God and his works. But they who 'go down to the sea in ships, and do business in great waters, these see the works of the LORD, and his wonders in the deep'. It is in waves of bereavement, poverty, temptation, and reproach that we learn the power of Jehovah. There we are made to know our own littleness. C. H. Spurgeon rightly observed, 'Self-esteem is that speck in the eye which most effectually mars human vision. The Great Surgeon of souls removes this from us chiefly by sanctified afflictions.'

At the mouth of the furnace, the Great Purifier sits as a Refiner to purify the sons of Levi; and when this work has been achieved and the divine purpose is accomplished, God's glory is manifested. Give thanks to God if he has led you down a rough road and through deep waters. It is in this way he gives you the experience of his great lovingkindness. Your troubles have enriched you with a wealth of knowledge you could never get in any other way. Your trials have been the cleft of the rock in which God has placed you, as he did his servant Moses, that you might behold his glory as he passed by. It is pain that creates a capacity for great pleasure, emptiness that creates a capacity for filling, and thirst that creates a capacity for refreshing!

The children of Israel were 'sore afraid' (v. 10). They thought they were about to die by the hand of Pharaoh (v. 11). In their desperation, they even thought it would have been better had they never come out of Egypt (v. 12). In the light of all they had already experienced, their fears and unbelief seem almost comical. The Lord God had graciously and miraculously preserved them in Egypt for four hundred years. They had seen all God's wonders in the Land of Ham. They had experienced the deliverance wrought by Jehovah on the night of the passover and the spoiling of Egypt. And, now, they were 'sore afraid'!

But, before we judge them too harshly, let us remember how often we are filled with the same fears and unbelief they expressed. We panic, just like they did; but there is no cause for alarm. Our God will never leave us, forsake us, or allow anything to harm us (1 Peter 1:3-9).

Direction for Every Dilemma

Read verses 13-15, and hear God's instruction to our souls. Here is divine direction for every dilemma.

'And Moses said unto the people, Fear ye not, stand still, and see the salvation of the LORD, which he will show to you today: for the Egyptians whom ye have seen today, ye shall see them again no more forever. The LORD shall fight for you, and ye shall hold your peace. And the LORD said unto Moses, Wherefore criest thou unto me? Speak unto the children of Israel, that they go forward.'

The direction the Lord commanded Moses to give us is fourfold. He tells us to do four specific things.

'Fear not!' How often our great God and Saviour speaks those words to us. How graciously he enforces them (Isaiah 41:10-14)

'Fear thou not; for I am with thee: be not dismayed; for I am thy God: I will strengthen thee; yea, I will help thee; yea, I will uphold thee with the right hand of my righteousness. Behold, all they that were incensed against thee shall be ashamed and confounded: they shall be as nothing; and they that strive with thee shall perish. Thou shalt seek them, and shalt not find them, even them that contended with thee: they that war against thee shall be as nothing, and as a thing of nought. For I the LORD thy God will hold thy right hand, saying unto thee, Fear not; I will help thee. Fear not, thou worm Jacob, and ye men of Israel; I will help thee, saith the LORD, and thy redeemer, the Holy One of Israel.'

All three persons in the triune Godhead have avowed themselves to help his wretched, weak, worthless worm, Jacob. 'I will help thee, saith the LORD', Jehovah. That is God our Father speaking. 'I will help thee, saith ... thy Redeemer'. That is God the Son, the second person of the Trinity, our Redeemer, speaking. 'I will help thee, saith ... The Holy One of Israel.' That is God the Holy Spirit speaking. 'If God be for us, who can be against us?' The Lord God of heaven and earth, the triune God; Father, Son, and Holy Spirit here makes eleven promises by which he would both remove our fears and encourage us to trust him.

(1) Are you alone? God says, 'Fear thou not; for I am with thee', not only within reach, but with you!

(2) Are you dismayed, by the power of your enemies or the greatness of your trial? The Lord says, 'Be not dismayed; for I am thy God', I am for you (Romans 8:28-39).

(3) Are you weak? Your God says, 'I will strengthen thee'.

(4) Are you destitute? God says, three times, 'I will help thee'.

(5) Are you about to fall, or already fallen? The Lord says, 'I will uphold thee with the right hand of my righteousness'.

(6) Are your enemies a terror to you? Your God says that he will confound them, bring them to nothing, and slay them every one (v. 12, 13). 'The Egyptians whom ye have seen today, ye shall see them again no more forever'!

(7) Are you fearful of failure? The Lord your God says, 'I will hold thy right hand' (v. 13). That means: I will walk hand in hand with you as your Father and your friend. I will guide you and lead you in your way (Proverbs 3:5, 6). I will hold you up when you are weak, wavering and trembling. I will pick you up when you fall. God will silence your fears as you walk with him, 'saying unto thee, Fear not; I will help thee'. He will say to you, to your heart, by his Spirit, 'Fear not', and make you hear his assuring promise, 'I will help thee'. 'The Lord shall fight for you, and ye shall hold your peace'!

(8) Are you now made to weep? 'Thou shalt rejoice in the LORD'. He will make you triumphant at last.

(9) Are you now abased? 'Thou shalt glory in the Holy One of Israel' (v. 16). Glory awaits you. You will yet glory in the Lord, in your interest in him, in your relation to him, in what he has done for you.

(10) Do the heavens appear to be as brass to you? God says, 'I the LORD will hear them' (v. 17).

(11) Does it sometimes seem that God has forsaken you? He has not. He says, 'I the God of Israel will not forsake them' (v. 17).

> How firm a foundation, ye saints of the Lord,
> Has laid for your faith in His excellent Word!
> What more can ye say, than to you He hath said,
> To you who for refuge to Jesus have fled?

Mark these promises and realize that though you are a worm, you have a mighty and a great God, and you have no reason to fear anything or anyone, ever!

'Stand still'! The people of God are in a great strait, even at their wits' end. Perish they must, to all human appearance. A wide ocean is before them. Inaccessible mountains surround them. An enraged Pharaoh pursues them. Death is before them. Yet, Moses says, 'Fear not'. Unbelief and carnal reason might suggest, 'What? Do not be afraid when inevitable destruction must be our doom? Why does Moses talk to us with such ignorance?' But, in the view of apparent destruction, Moses tells them of certain salvation and commands them to stand still and behold it. We do not hear one word from Moses to soothe their fears or comfort their minds, from any considerations of what they were in themselves, or what they had done to entitle them to the Lord's favour. No; but they were at this very moment indulging the murmurs of unbelief: 'Why hast thou brought us forth! Better to serve the Egyptians, than to perish here.'

In times of difficulty, in seasons of distress, when sin rages, conscience accuses, the law condemns, unbelief prevails, and we poor sinners are at our wits' end; seeing justice pursuing, all hope and help failing, and despair at the door, then the salvation of the Lord is our only hope. How blessed! How delightful! How this quells our fears, composes our souls, and comforts our hearts!

But, what is it to stand still and see the salvation of the Lord? Is it to cease from prayer and all other means of grace? No; in the midst of fears, in the sight of dangers, and in the dread of destruction, to stand still is to cease from all self-confidence and trust Christ.

'See the Salvation of the LORD'! This is an imperative command. Yet, it is a matter of certainty. You must behold 'the salvation of the LORD'. And as you stand still before him, you shall 'see the salvation of the LORD'! You will see the salvation he purposed in eternity. The salvation he purchased at Calvary. The salvation he performs in grace. The salvation he preserves in his own. The salvation he promises in resurrection glory.

'Assemble yourselves and come; draw near together, ye that are escaped of the nations: they have no knowledge that set up the wood of their graven image, and pray unto a god that cannot save. Tell ye, and bring them near; yea, let them take counsel together: who hath declared this from ancient time? who hath told it from that time? have not I the LORD? and there is no God else beside me; a just God and a Saviour; there is none beside me. Look unto me, and be ye saved, all the ends of the earth: for I am God, and there is none else' (Isaiah 45:20-22).

'Go forward'! That is our only path. 'Go forward'! That is the only path for fugitives pursued by justice, an army under orders from the Captain, a chosen people on the way to Canaan, a covenant people in great trouble, a people under divine commission to possess the land and slay the Canaanites, a people who soon must cross the Jordan and enter the land of rest.

Chapter 68

When God Is Not There

'And the angel of God, which went before the camp of Israel, removed and went behind them; and the pillar of the cloud went from before their face, and stood behind them: And it came between the camp of the Egyptians and the camp of Israel; and it was a cloud and darkness to them, but it gave light by night to these: so that the one came not near the other all the night.'
(Exodus 14:19, 20)

When the children of Israel came out of Egypt, as they approached the edge of the wilderness, the Lord God gave them a visible token of his presence, by which he would lead and protect them throughout their sojourn through the wilderness (13:20-22).

'And they took their journey from Succoth, and encamped in Etham, in the edge of the wilderness. And the LORD went before them by day in a pillar of a cloud, to lead them the way; and by night in a pillar of fire, to give them light; to go by day and night: He took not away the pillar of the cloud by day, nor the pillar of fire by night, from before the people'.

Christ's Presence
They saw in the sky above them a pillar of cloud. At night, it became a flame of fire. This was not something that looked like a cloud during the day, and a column of fire at night, something that appeared to be guiding and protecting them. This was a supernatural thing. God gave it; and it never departed from his chosen, so long as they walked through the wilderness. But, great as the symbol was, the reality was greater.

The pillar that protected and led them was not just a symbol of Christ's presence, that pillar was the Lord Jesus himself, their God and Saviour, who had before sworn, 'I will never leave thee, nor forsake thee.'

'He spake unto them in the cloudy pillar' (Psalm 99:7). Wherever the cloud went, Israel followed. It was their constant companion, their conductor, lest they go astray. The cloud was a huge umbrella, covering the whole of the great congregation, protecting them from the burning heat of the desert by day. At night, it was a clear, bright and shining light. The children of Israel could as easily march through the wilderness at night as they could by day. Well might they sing, as David did in Psalm 84:11, 'The LORD God is a sun and shield!' They experienced the fulfilment of the promise given many years later, 'The sun shall not smite thee by day, nor the moon by night' (Psalm 121:6).

This blessed symbol of God's presence must have been a very great joy and comfort. It must have been a glorious sight. Every man, woman, and child in Israel (millions of them) could see it floating above them as the constant, abiding banner of Jehovah's love, approval, and tender care. Moses declares, 'He took not away the pillar of the cloud by day, nor the pillar of fire by night, from before the people'. The Lord Jesus Christ, our God and Saviour is always with us. He has promised, 'I will never leave thee, nor forsake thee'. In the night of sorrow and in the day of joy, he is with us. But we do not always perceive his presence. We do not always enjoy it. He never leaves us, but we sometimes think he has. The sun always shines; but when the earth turns, or clouds gather in the sky, we cannot see the shining sun. Sometimes, he who is the glory of Israel removes the manifestation of his presence and stands, as it were, behind us; and we are troubled because of his absence. Then, when God is not here, or appears not to be, we cry, with Job, 'Oh that I knew where I might find him! that I might come even to his seat!'

But even when the Lord God seems to have forsaken us, he is with us, saving us, doing us good. 'And the angel of God, which went before the camp of Israel, removed and went behind them; and the pillar of the cloud went from before their face, and stood behind them: And it came between the camp of the Egyptians and the camp of Israel; and it was a cloud and darkness to them, but it gave light by night to these: so that the one came not near the other all the night' (Exodus 14:19, 20).

There are two passages in Isaiah's prophecy very similar to this (Isaiah 52:9-12; 58:8-14). 'Break forth into joy, sing together, ye waste places of Jerusalem: for the LORD hath comforted his people, he hath redeemed Jerusalem. The LORD hath made bare his holy arm in the eyes of all the nations; and all the ends of the earth shall see the salvation of our God. Depart ye, depart ye, go ye out from thence, touch no unclean thing; go ye out of the midst of her; be ye clean, that bear the vessels of the LORD. For ye shall not go out with haste, nor go by flight: for the LORD will go before you; and the God of Israel will be your rereward' (Isaiah 52:9-12).

The word, 'rereward', is 'rearward'. It means 'towards the rear' or 'rear guard'. The Lord God of Israel is sometimes out of sight, behind us; but he is still the Lord God of Israel who is fighting for us. Read Isaiah 58:8-14. 'Then shall thy light break forth as the morning, and thine health shall spring forth speedily: and thy righteousness shall go before thee; the glory of the LORD shall be thy rereward. Then shalt thou call, and the LORD shall answer; thou shalt cry, and he shall say, Here I am ... And the LORD shall guide thee continually, and satisfy thy soul in drought, and make fat thy bones: and thou shalt be like a watered garden, and like a spring of water, whose waters fail not ... If thou turn away thy foot from the sabbath,[1] from doing thy pleasure on my holy day; and call the sabbath a delight, the holy of the LORD, honourable; and shalt honour him, not doing thine own ways, nor finding thine own pleasure, nor speaking thine own words: Then shalt thou delight thyself in the LORD; and I will cause thee to ride upon the high places of the earth, and feed thee with the heritage of Jacob thy father: for the mouth of the LORD hath spoken it.'

The Lord's evident presence is our great joy; his absence our misery. If God smiles, none can make me miserable; but when he hides his smiling face, none can give me joy. Still, though we see neither the cloud by day nor the flame by night, God our Saviour is with us, fighting for us, and saving us. Read one more passage in Isaiah (54:7-17). 'For a small moment have I forsaken thee; but with great mercies will I gather thee. In a little wrath I hid my face from thee for a moment; but with everlasting kindness will I have mercy on thee, saith the LORD thy Redeemer. For this is as the waters of Noah unto me: for as I have

---

[1] Christ is our Sabbath. We rest in him by faith, and cease from our own works and ways, trusting Christ alone for all our salvation (Matthew 11:28-30; Hebrews 4:9, 10; 1 Corinthians 1:30).

sworn that the waters of Noah should no more go over the earth; so have I sworn that I would not be wroth with thee, nor rebuke thee. For the mountains shall depart, and the hills be removed; but my kindness shall not depart from thee, neither shall the covenant of my peace be removed, saith the LORD that hath mercy on thee. O thou afflicted, tossed with tempest, and not comforted, behold, I will lay thy stones with fair colours, and lay thy foundations with sapphires. And I will make thy windows of agates, and thy gates of carbuncles, and all thy borders of pleasant stones. And all thy children shall be taught of the LORD; and great shall be the peace of thy children. In righteousness shalt thou be established: thou shalt be far from oppression; for thou shalt not fear: and from terror; for it shall not come near thee. Behold, they shall surely gather together, but not by me: whosoever shall gather together against thee shall fall for thy sake. Behold, I have created the smith that bloweth the coals in the fire, and that bringeth forth an instrument for his work; and I have created the waster to destroy. No weapon that is formed against thee shall prosper; and every tongue that shall rise against thee in judgment thou shalt condemn. This is the heritage of the servants of the LORD, and their righteousness is of me, saith the LORD.'

Presence Removed
Sometimes the Lord Jesus mysteriously removes himself from before us. Moses tells us, 'The angel of God, which went before the camp of Israel, removed and went behind them' (v. 19). The symbol of God's presence was removed from before Israel, just as the fearful Israelites could feel the hot breath of Pharaoh's chariot horses breathing down upon them. From the day they entered the desert, they had seen the fiery, cloudy pillar before them. Now, suddenly, it was gone! As they obeyed God's command to 'go forward', as they neared the raging sea, they looked forward, but saw nothing!

So it is with us at times. Sometimes the Lord our God hides himself from us, takes away his manifest presence, and refuses to show himself. Sometimes, as we walk in the light of God's countenance, enjoying sweet fellowship with Christ our Redeemer, bathing in the consolation of the Spirit, suddenly, we look up and see nothing but darkness before us. Like the beloved spouse in Solomon's Song, we cry, 'I sought him, but I found him not'. Everything seemed bright and cheerful. We expected to go on from strength to strength, from victory to victory, until we came to the mount of God, to dwell forever in his rest. Then, darkness, sudden darkness, nothing but darkness! Then, nothing seems sure. Clouds return. Fears assail. We cry, 'Oh that I knew where I might find him!' John Newton expressed it like this, we start to look within, and cry with tears ...

'Tis a point I long to know,
Oft it causes anxious thought:
Do I love the Lord, or no?
Am I His, or am I not?

If I love, why am I thus;
Why this dull, this lifeless frame?
Hardly, sure, can they be worse,
Who have never heard His name.

Could my heart so hard remain,
Prayer a task and burden prove;
Every trifle give me pain,
If I knew a Saviour's love?

When I turn my eyes within,
All is dark and vain, and wild;
Filled with unbelief and sin,
Can I deem myself a child?

If I pray, or hear, or read,
Sin is mixed with all I do;
You that love the Lord indeed,
Tell me, is it thus with you?

God's promise seems to fall to the ground. Our circumstances seem to contradict it. Our hearts sink to the depths, crying, 'If the foundations be destroyed, what can the righteous do?' We begin to call into question the very Word of God, which once caused us to hope. We have said, 'This God is our God for ever and ever: he will be our guide even unto death!' But when he withdraws from before us, nothing seems sure. We begin to think, 'Is his mercy clean gone forever? Doth his promise fail for evermore?' In our souls, we cry, 'My God, my God, why hast thou forsaken me? Why art thou so far from helping me, and from the words of my roaring? O my God, I cry in the daytime, but thou hearest not!'

Do you know what I am talking about? The trouble may be caused by outward trials, personal faults, or inward corruption. That was David's case when he kept silence and refused to confess his sin. You try to read God's Word; but it is empty. You try to pray; but the heavens are brass. You assemble with God's saints to hear a word from heaven, but hear only the sound of a man's voice. There is no light, only thick darkness before you. What are we to do in such circumstances? The very worst thing to do is what we are most prone to do. Do not turn your eyes within. Look out of yourself to God on his throne. That is what he tells us to do (Isaiah 50:10).

'Who is among you that feareth the LORD, that obeyeth the voice of his servant, that walketh in darkness, and hath no light? Let him trust in the name of the LORD, and stay upon his God.'

Here, in Exodus 14, the children of Israel were in a time of dark necessity. Never did they more need the light of God's presence. But he removed himself and went behind them! Why? They must have thought, 'The Lord has forsaken us to punish us for our murmuring and unbelief'. Not so. The fact is our God often sends his messengers of love on a black horse of trouble. For the believer, darkness of soul is not the result of God's anger, but the fruit of his love. It does us good, teaches us patience, proves our faith, destroys self-confidence, makes us seek him, and softens our hearts toward others who walk in darkness.

When the cloudy and fiery pillar removed from before the children of Israel and went behind them, it was because it was most needed behind them. So it is with us. When the Lord removes his manifest presence, there is always a 'needs be' for it.

> God in Israel sows the seeds
> Of affliction, pain and toil:
> These spring up and choke the weeds
> That would else o'erspread the soil.

When the Lord Jesus hides himself for a moment, it is to make us value him the more (Song of Solomon 4:16-5:8).

With us Still

Though the pillar of cloud and fire was not seen, though it was removed from before them, it was with them still. The angel of the Lord removed, but he 'removed and went behind them'. He was just as much with them when he was at the rear, as when he went before them. Though it appeared that the Lord had utterly forsaken them, he was fighting for them. Their Sun was hidden from their eyes, but he was still their Shield behind. 'The glory of the Lord was their rereward.'

Troubled, downcast child of God, the Lord is with you still, and fighting for you, when you cannot see him. He is still your Salvation. He is still saving you. The Lord's presence is not to be determined by our awareness of it. When you are sighing and crying after him, those very sighs and cries are the fruit of his secret presence. Indeed, I suspect he is more really near when we think he has gone; when our hearts break for him, than when we are 'at ease in Zion' and speak confidently.

In verse 19, Moses tells us 'the pillar of the cloud went from before their face, and stood behind them'. It 'stood behind them'. I like that! It stood, firmly fixed behind them. The Angel of the Lord, shrouded in the cloud, stood with his drawn sword at the rear of Israel, saying to Pharaoh, 'Proceed no further. You shall not touch my chosen.' He lifted up his vast shield of darkness, and held it before the tyrant king. All that night horses and chariots and soldiers with swords ran around in circles. Then, 'they were as still as a stone till thy people passed over, O LORD, till thy people passed over whom thou hadst purchased' (15:16). God stood behind his people; and their enemy could not touch them.

So it is with us! There are times when we can see nothing before us to give us hope and joy; but the living God stands behind us to fight off the adversary. He cannot forsake his own. He says to us, 'Can a woman forget her sucking child, that she should not have compassion on the son of her womb? Yea, they may forget, yet will I not forget thee'.

Look at this again. If the children of Israel had simply looked back, they would have seen the Lord behind them just as clearly as they had seen him before them. If your soul is troubled and heavy because you cannot see the Lord before you, look back and see how the Lord has helped you hitherto. Look back. What do you see behind you? Loving-kindness and tender mercy, and nothing else. As I look back upon my own life, I cannot find anything but Christ. I cannot find anything but goodness and mercy. 'Truly God is good to Israel!' 'His mercy endureth forever!' Not one good thing has failed me. He has never left me, nor forsaken me. I have received blessings through my joys, and even greater blessings through my sorrows. The Lord's way has been all goodness, all the days of my life. I look back, and see the light of his presence shining like the sun. It is as a morning without clouds. I am overwhelmed with his boundless mercy, grace, and love! He has been mindful of us; he will bless us. He gave us mercies yesterday; and he is the same today and forever. Past mercies are the assurance of present mercy, and the promise of mercies to come. Electing love, redeeming blood, and saving grace assure us of God's mercy to preserve us and goodness to keep us. 'Surely, goodness and mercy shall follow me all the days of my life; and I will dwell in the house of the LORD forever!'

If the rainbow were always visible, it might not be so assuring a token of the covenant. So, the Lord wisely reveals it sparingly. But the covenant of which the bow speaks is as sure as it is everlasting. Spurgeon said, 'The Lord deals with us in all wisdom and prudence. His modes change, but the changes are all from the same motive, and with the same reason, all to make us sick of self and fond of him'.

Sweetly Revealed
In verse 20 we see the Lord's presence sweetly revealed when the time was right. 'And it came between the camp of the Egyptians and the camp of Israel; and it was a cloud and darkness to them, but it gave light by night to these: so that the one came not near the other all the night.'

Can you imagine Israel's joy when they saw that pillar of fire lighting the night before them? The children of Israel were commanded to 'go forward' to the Red Sea; and they must 'go forward' by faith, trusting nothing but the Word of God. Therefore, the pillar withdrew from before them and stood behind them.

Faith performs her greatest feats in the darkest places. These Israelites were to march right down into the heart of the Red Sea. It was a raging torrent. The Spirit of God says, by his servant Moses, 'The floods stood upright as an heap, and the depths were congealed in the heart of the sea'. Yet, 'the children of Israel walked upon dry land in the midst of the sea; and the waters were a wall unto them on their right hand, and on their left.' The fact that they walked through the sea, between two huge walls of water, tells me they walked before God in faith. I do not know, but it seems to me it would be far easier to get out of a little boat on a stormy sea and walk across the water, as Peter did, than to walk through two huge walls of water. Yet, these millions descended into the abyss believing God. Moses lifted up his rod and the waters rolled apart to open the way before them. They marched forward, not with fear and trembling, not with haste, or by flight (Isaiah 52:12), but in faith, believing God, with fiery and cloudy pillar behind them, not before them. That is faith. Faith is not saying I believe God. Faith is hazarding life itself upon God. They could not have acted in such great faith had the fiery and cloudy pillar gone before them.

We always want to be coddled and cuddled, like babies. We always want love-visits and delights. We want all the promises sealed to our hearts all the time. If we could, we would eat candy all the time, and be rolled into heaven in a stroller. But our heavenly Father will not have it so. He commands us to 'go forward' in faith; and he sees to it that we do. He commands us to grow in 'the grace and knowledge of our Lord Jesus Christ' and graciously sees that we do. He is always with us, holding our hands, upholding us by the right hand of his righteousness; but he does not always reveal his presence, or the firmness of his grip.

Our heavenly Father never spoils his children. He makes them grow. He makes us grow, or we never would. He takes away his manifest presence that we may follow him by faith. Job would never have become the man he was, had he not lost everything. Then, he cried out in faith, 'Though he slay me, yet will I trust in him.' We would never have known the name of Abraham, had he not been called out of Ur, called to forsake everything, even to sacrifice his son Isaac. Only by such great trials as God brought upon him did he come to know the Lord Jesus by his name, Jehovah-jireh.

Then, at the best, most suitable time, when patience has done her perfect work, through manifold trials, the Lord appears in his great glory and grace, and gives light by night to his own, just as he did to Israel, as they walked into the sea. Israel knew his presence, yet there was no token of his presence before them. Israel walked in the light, though all was darkness around them. Israel walked in the light, in a straight path, while the Egyptians were utterly confused by darkness.

They cast their care upon him who cared for them, and they knew their way. They knew God's way. They knew it with absolute certainty because there was no other way to go. In , the Holy Ghost tells us all these things happened to teach us something.

'There hath no temptation taken you but such as is common to man: but God is faithful, who will not suffer you to be tempted above that ye are able; but will with the temptation also make a way to escape, that ye may be able to bear it' (1 Corinthians 10:13).

God promised these people, 'Fear ye not, stand still, and see the salvation of the LORD, which he will shew to you today: for the Egyptians whom ye have seen today, ye shall see them again no more forever' (Exodus 14:13). And they never saw them again. Let me apply that to you and me. There are your sins; will you look back on them for a minute? Look steadily. They are as dreadful as the Egyptian horsemen and chariots. I have looked intently, and I cannot see a sin remaining. You may ask, 'What, have you lived so perfectly that you have never sinned?' You know better. I mourn countless offenses, but I cannot see one of them now, for my sin is gone. It has been drowned in the Red Sea of Christ's precious blood. 'The blood of Jesus Christ his Son cleanseth us from all sin.' It is written, 'The iniquity of Israel shall be sought for, and there shall be none; and the sins of Judah, and they shall not be found; for I will pardon them whom I reserve'. The Egyptians shall not come near us all the night of this life; and when the morning breaks, we shall see them dead upon the shore. Then shall we sing unto the Lord, 'for he hath triumphed gloriously', and our transgressions and sins he has cast into the depths of the sea. Then, the glory of the Lord that has been our rereward shall shine everlastingly before us!

> Far from a world of grief and sin,
> With God eternally shut in!

'Thus the LORD saved Israel that day out of the hand of the Egyptians; and Israel saw the Egyptians dead upon the sea shore. And Israel saw that great work which the LORD did upon the Egyptians: and the people feared the LORD, and believed the LORD, and his servant Moses' (Exodus 14:30, 31).

Chapter 69

'Thus, The Lord Saved Israel'

'Thus, the LORD saved Israel that day out of the hand of the Egyptians; and Israel saw the Egyptians dead upon the sea shore. And Israel saw that great work which the LORD did upon the Egyptians: and the people feared the LORD, and believed the LORD, and his servant Moses.' (Exodus 14:30, 31)

How does God save his people? The first fourteen chapters of Exodus were written to answer that question. I am certain of that because it is exactly how Moses was inspired of God to summarize all he wrote in those first chapters of the Book of Exodus. The summary Moses was inspired of God to give of these chapters is the text that heads this page.

Did you ever wonder where the children of Israel got the weapons of war with which they defeated their many enemies in the wilderness and the Canaanites? They had none in Egypt, and carried none out of Egypt. But on the seventh day after the passover night, when 'all the hosts of the LORD went out from the land of Egypt' (Exodus 12:41), Israel crossed the Red Sea by the mighty hand of God and 'saw the Egyptians dead upon the sea shore'. All their foes were drowned in the sea and their bodies washed up upon the shore. There, spread before them were all the armies of Egypt dead upon the shore, with all their weapons beside them. Moses and the Israelites gathered up the weapons of their defeated foes. Thus, the Lord God not only defeated the Egyptians for them, but also armed his chosen with the weapons by which the Egyptians hoped to destroy them. When I think of that, I am reminded of two most blessed declarations of Holy Scripture, Romans 8:35-39 and Isaiah 54:17.

'Who shall separate us from the love of Christ? Shall tribulation, or distress, or persecution, or famine, or nakedness, or peril, or sword? As it is written, For thy sake we are killed all the day long; we are accounted as sheep for the slaughter. Nay, in all these things we are more than conquerors through him that loved us. For I am persuaded, that neither death, nor life, nor angels, nor principalities, nor powers, nor things present, nor things to come, nor height, nor depth, nor any other creature, shall be able to separate us from the love of God, which is in Christ Jesus our Lord' (Romans 8:35-39).

'No weapon that is formed against thee shall prosper; and every tongue that shall rise against thee in judgment thou shalt condemn. This is the heritage of the servants of the LORD, and their righteousness is of me, saith the LORD' (Isaiah 54:17).

There is a reference to Exodus 14:30, 31 in Psalm 74. God's people are described by the psalmist as his congregation which he purchased, his inheritance which he redeemed and wherein he dwells (v. 2) and his turtledove (v. 19), the people of his covenant (v. 20). In verses 12-14, he describes God's salvation of Israel on the day they crossed the Red Sea. 'God is my King of old, working salvation in the midst of the earth. Thou didst divide the sea by thy strength: thou brakest the heads of the dragons in the waters. Thou brakest the heads of leviathan in pieces, and gavest him to be meat to the people inhabiting the wilderness' (Psalm 74:12-14).

This is Moses' inspired summary of the whole thing. 'Thus, the LORD saved Israel that day out of the hand of the Egyptians.' How did he save them? How does the Lord God save his people by his grace? Let us camp a little while by the waters of the Red Sea, and consider how it is, according to the Book of God, that God saves his elect. May God the Holy Spirit give us eyes to see Christ's glories here, as plainly as we see them on the shores of Galilee.

A Cradle of Miracles

Henry Law described Israel's beginning as an 'infancy in a cradle of miracles'. I cannot think of a better way to describe it. The nation of Israel came into being by the power of God giving Abraham a son in his old age. Remember, Abraham was 100 years old when Isaac was born, Sarah was 90. Isaac and his sons prospered and prevailed miraculously, against all odds, in the clear sunshine of God's intervening hand. The Lord watched over them and blessed them, not in obscurity, but in the open manifestations of his miraculous care. These things were a manifest display of what God's children should always expect. Our experience is but the echo of those constant, miraculous interventions of divine providence. 'God is my King of old, working salvation in the midst of the earth.'

At last, they came down into Egypt, just seventy souls in great need, brought there by the direct arrangement of Joseph, their brother, the man they betrayed and sold into bondage, the man they thought they had killed. But Joseph was on the throne in Egypt. Everything in Egypt had been placed in the hands of Joseph to save much people alive. Though they were oppressed in Egypt, persecuted and terribly abused by their taskmasters, 'the children of Israel were fruitful, and increased abundantly, and multiplied, and waxed exceeding mighty; and the land was filled with them' (Exodus 1:7).

Hedged In
After 400 years of affliction the children of Israel are brought out of Egypt by the mighty hand of God. How they must have danced as they marched out of that horrible place of slavery and misery on that passover night, carrying with them all the treasures of Egypt! 'It is a night to be much observed unto the LORD' (Exodus 12:42).

But their dancing did not last long. Soon the children of Israel were hedged in on every side. At first, they marched like soldiers in a dress parade returning from a great victory. Then, suddenly, Pharaoh and the Egyptians were on their back. They ran until they could run no further. Every door of escape was shut before them. Their joy turned to fear. Hope withered and despair set in. The fiery and cloudy pillar they followed led to the very jaws of destruction. In front of them broke the billows of the Red Sea. On either side stood a wall of rocks impossible to climb. Behind them were the enraged Egyptians. Within them were evil hearts of unbelief, quaking with fear. If they move forward, they marched into a watery grave. If they do not, they would be mowed down like dry grass by the Egyptians' swords. Everything was ready to devour them. A cruel, shameful death seemed certain and imminent.

Every child of God knows something about these things. Those who have never been in bondage have never been set free. Those who have never been in the pit, wherein is no water, have never been delivered from the pit. Those who have never been the Lord's prisoners have never become the Lord's freemen. Many dreary years I slaved at bricks, beneath the yoke of hell's foul prince. Then the Spirit of God called me to peace and freedom by the gospel. I thought my chains would break with ease. Canaan's sweet rest seemed near. But suddenly terrors gathered around my soul. The memory and guilt of sin spread like a vast ocean of blackness before me. 'Deep called unto deep at the noise of thy waterspouts: all thy waves and billows went over me' (Psalm 42:7). The Lord 'cast me into the deep, in the midst of the seas; and the floods compassed me about: all thy billows and thy waves passed over me' (Jonah 2:3). The law thundered loud in my soul, with the fierce sword of justice glittering before me. My corruptions, my iniquities, my transgressions, and my sins rose like mountains reaching to the skies around me.

All hope was gone, because all hope in self was gone. I was shut in and hedged about on every side. Five things suddenly dawned upon my soul, by which all my carnal hopes were slain, by which I was, at last, brought to faith in Christ. Sooner or later, you are going to have to deal with these five things.

I saw my sin. God the Holy Ghost convinced me of my sin (John 16:8); of the sinfulness of my sinful deeds, the sinfulness of my heart and nature, and the sinfulness of my righteousness. I saw that even my noblest deeds are filthy rags in God's sight.

I saw the infinite holiness of God's law. The law of God requires perfection. God cannot and will not accept anything less than absolute perfection (Leviticus 22:21; Matthew 5:20). Whatever I bring to God, if he accepts it, it must be perfect.

I saw that the only hope for sinners is a perfect substitute. I must have someone to obey the law of God and secure righteousness for me. I must have someone to make an infinite, justice-satisfying atonement for my sins. That Substitute I found in Jesus Christ the Son of God (Romans 3:24-26; 2 Corinthians 5:21).

I saw that faith in Christ is the only way a sinner can ever find acceptance with God. God's gracious salvation comes to sinners through faith in Christ (Ephesians 2:8). All who believe on the Son of

God have everlasting life (John 3:36). But I could not believe. I could not muster faith from within myself.

And I saw that faith in Christ is the gift of God. Faith in Christ is not within the realm of human ability. It is the gift of God (John 1:12, 13; Ephesians 2:8, 9). Faith is the operation of God, the work of grace in a man's soul (Colossians 2:12). It is not the result of man's imaginary 'free will'. Faith is given to sinners according to God's sovereign will (Romans 9:16). I was shut up to a sovereign God, shut up to the will of God. He could save me, or he could damn me. He could give me faith or leave me alone. It was entirely up to him.

By these five truths, I was slain; all hope in myself was gone. I was made to fall before Christ, suing for mercy, crying, 'God, be merciful to me, the sinner ... Lord, if you will, you can make me whole'.

Now, 'I through the law am dead to the law'. Because I have been crucified with Christ (Galatians 2:19-21), I am, absolutely dead to the law (Romans 7:4). There is no hope held out to any man in the law. The sinner's only hope of salvation is faith in Christ. You must trust the Son of God. By faith in Christ, we who believe fulfil the law of God (Romans 3:31). We must never allow anyone to bring us back under the yoke of the law (Galatians 5:1). The Son of God says, 'Look unto me, and be ye saved', and sweetly hems us in on every side, forcing us by omnipotent mercy to look upward to him, crying, 'Bring my soul out of prison, that I may praise thy name' (Psalm 142:7). And 'he brought me forth also into a large place; he delivered me, because he delighted in me' (Psalm 18:19). How I thank God for the grace that shut me up to Christ! 'Thus, the Lord saved Israel that day'!

God's Messenger
'Faith come by hearing, and hearing by the Word of God'. So, to create faith in his unbelieving people, the Lord God sent them a messenger, a prophet to lead them in the way. Look at Israel's messenger. Moses rides above this swell of trouble, in all the calmness of unshaken faith. Faith in Christ is a door to let in peace and a bolt to shut out fear. Moses saw the raging sea before them. He heard the rattle of the Egyptians' swords behind them. He saw the mountainous rocks surrounding them. But he was undaunted. He knew that all is well when Christ goes before! All is safe when God protects! All is sure when he gives his promise! And he had God's promise.

'And he said, Certainly I will be with thee; and this shall be a token unto thee, that I have sent thee: When thou hast brought forth the people out of Egypt, ye shall serve God upon this mountain' (Exodus 3:12).

Moses had been taught that the almighty Saviour, the incarnate God, would spring from the tribe of Judah. The tribe must be preserved that held the promised Seed. Therefore, he confidently looked for God's salvation, and commanded the children of Israel to believe God.

'And Moses said unto the people, Fear ye not, stand still, and see the salvation of the LORD, which he will show to you today: for the Egyptians whom ye have seen today, ye shall see them again no more forever. The LORD shall fight for you, and ye shall hold your peace' (Exodus 14:13, 14).

What shall we fear, when the gospel banner flies before us? Faith defies fear and foe. 'If God be for us, who can be against us? He that spared not his own Son, but delivered him up for us all, how shall he not with him also freely give us all things? Who shall lay anything to the charge of God's elect? It is God that justifieth. Who is he that condemneth? It is Christ that died, yea rather, that is risen again, who is even at the right hand of God, who also maketh intercession for us. Who shall separate us from the love of Christ?'

The waves are deep. Our foes are many and strong. There is no help in self. What shall we do? 'Stand still, and see the salvation of the LORD!' Here is a gospel warning. There is no hope in self, no help in your will, your works, or your worth! Here are gospel tidings. 'See the salvation of the LORD!' Christ has finished all. He paid the debt. He satisfied each claim of God's holiness, justice, and truth. Alone, he brought in everlasting righteousness. He trod the winepress alone. He conquered death, hell, and the grave. He put away sin by the sacrifice of himself. The work was gloriously accomplished by him alone. 'Stand still and see the salvation of the LORD!' 'The LORD will fight for you!' You need only to be still. Who can resist when he uplifts his arm? Omnipotence is your defence!

Neither the wrath of man, nor the malice of devils, nor the rage of hell can harm, when the Good Shepherd says, 'I give unto them eternal life, and they shall never perish'. Someone said, 'Stand, then, behind a fighting God, and you are high as heaven above all harm. Raise not the battle-cry, as if the charge was yours. Let all your breath be prayer and praise.'

Then the Lord spoke by his messenger again. He said, 'Speak unto the children of Israel, that they go forward' (Exodus 14:15). That is the watchword for God's Israel. Forward, onward, upward, heaven-ward! Dangers threaten. Go forward! Ease allures. Go onward! Worldly pleasures seduce. Look upward! Hell rages. Look heaven-ward! God speaks distinctly. 'Go forward!' He will not lead except in safety's path.

I hear carnal reason say, '"Go forward" contradicts "Stand still."' But, when grace gives light, faith has sight and sees all that God speaks as one harmonious whole. We take no step to expiate our sins, to pay our debts, to appease divine justice and wrath, or to procure redemption or righteousness. Yet, seeing the salvation of the Lord, the believing sinner goes forward in faith, growing in the grace and knowledge of Christ, ever looking to him (Philippians 3:7-15; Hebrews 12:1-3).

Heaven is reached, not by toil, but in toil. Blessings descend, not for deeds, but on deeds. Faith comes with empty hand. Christ fills it with salvation. The hand Christ fills with himself, and fills with his grace, then brings the sacrifices acceptable and well pleasing to God by Christ Jesus; sacrifices of praise, devotion, love, and obedience. 'Thus, the LORD saved Israel that day.' He sent a messenger. He commanded faith. He wrought faith in them. He led them forward.

Christ Himself

Now, let us look away from the Egyptians. Look away from the sea. Look away from Israel. And look away from the Lord's messenger. Look now at the Lord Jesus Christ himself, the Angel of the Lord, who performed the work of salvation for his people.

'And the angel of God, which went before the camp of Israel, removed and went behind them; and the pillar of the cloud went from before their face, and stood behind them: And it came between the camp of the Egyptians and the camp of Israel; and it was a cloud and darkness to them, but it gave light by night to these: so that the one came not near the other all the night' (Exodus 14:19, 20).

Thus, the Lord Jesus is a high wall of defence for us. He encompasses his blood-bought flock. They who would injure his redeemed must first defeat omnipotence. There is no passage for the destroyer's sword, but through him who is our Shield. But he who is to us a pillar of fire is to the world a pillar of darkness. He who is our confidence is confusion to the unbelieving. What floods of light flow from the crucified Christ to the believing heart! But to the unbelieving, the preaching of the cross is foolishness. The Foundation Stone upon which we are built is to the unbelieving a Stone of Stumbling and a Rock of Offence.

Next, the Angel of the Lord, our blessed Christ, opened the sea by the rod of Moses. 'And Moses stretched out his hand over the sea; and the LORD caused the sea to go back by a strong east wind all that night, and made the sea dry land, and the waters were divided. And the children of Israel went into the midst of the sea upon the dry ground: and the waters were a wall unto them on their right hand, and on their left' (Exodus 14:21, 22).

Moses lifted his rod with his hand and the sea parted before Israel. Do you remember when the Lord first appeared to Moses he made his hand leprous, and then made it clean? That is the hand he used to deliver his people. There is much to be learned from that; but I see something more here. Moses, as you know, represents the law of God; and here we see the Angel of the Lord accomplishing the salvation of his chosen, performing the wonders of his grace by his law. The very law of God that would have condemned us without Christ, now, because Christ has fulfilled all its demands, opens the way and demands the deliverance of our souls. Justice satisfied, demands that every blood-bought sinner must go free!

> Christ Jesus my discharge procured,
> The whole of wrath divine endured:
> The law's tremendous curse He bore;
> Justice can never ask for more.
>
> Payment God cannot twice demand,
> First at my bleeding Surety's hand,
> And then demand the price from me,
> For whom Christ died at Calvary.
>
> Be still, my soul, and find sweet rest
> The merits of my great High Priest,
> His righteousness and precious blood,
> Have satisfied the Holy God.

I'll trust Christ's efficacious blood,
And never fear the wrath of God,
Since Jesus Christ has died for me,
And lives for me to intercede.

The Result of God's Salvation

In verse 30, the Spirit of God says, 'Thus the LORD saved Israel that day out of the hand of the Egyptians'. Then, he tells us what the result of this great salvation was. The result is fivefold; and it is exactly the same today. These are the things that always accompany salvation.

1. 'Israel saw the Egyptians dead upon the sea shore.' Sin is slain by Christ crucified.

2. 'And Israel saw that great work which the LORD did upon the Egyptians.' Sin has been judged, condemned, and forever put away by the sacrifice of the Son of God.

3. 'And the people feared the LORD.' Sinners saved by the grace of God, call upon the name of God, worshipping him as God.

4. 'The people believed the LORD.' All who truly worship God as God, all who have been raised from death to life by the power of God's omnipotent grace, trust the Lord Jesus Christ alone for salvation (1 Corinthians 1:30).

5. Those who are saved by the Lord God give him, and him alone all the praise (Exodus 15:1, 2).

'Then sang Moses and the children of Israel this song unto the LORD, and spake, saying, I will sing unto the LORD, for he hath triumphed gloriously: the horse and his rider hath he thrown into the sea. The LORD is my strength and song, and he is become my salvation: he is my God, and I will prepare him an habitation; my father's God, and I will exalt him.'

The Holy Spirit erected this memorial on the shore of the Red Sea. 'Thus, the LORD saved Israel that day!' It tells of the glory of God and the glory of the gospel. It reveals to us the way God saves his people by his free grace in Christ. The Lord saved Israel: according to his purpose; to fulfil his covenant promise; because of his choice; by the blood of Christ our Passover Lamb; by effectual distinguishing grace; by the word of God declared by a man; fully, every foe conquered, never to rise again, and for his own glory, for the glory of his own great name.

85

Chapter 70

The Old Testament Doctrine Of Baptism

'And the angel of God, which went before the camp of Israel, removed and went behind them; and the pillar of the cloud went from before their face, and stood behind them: And it came between the camp of the Egyptians and the camp of Israel; and it was a cloud and darkness to them, but it gave light by night to these: so that the one came not near the other all the night. And Moses stretched out his hand over the sea; and the LORD caused the sea to go back by a strong east wind all that night, and made the sea dry land, and the waters were divided. And the children of Israel went into the midst of the sea upon the dry ground: and the waters were a wall unto them on their right hand, and on their left. And the Egyptians pursued, and went in after them to the midst of the sea, even all Pharaoh's horses, his chariots, and his horsemen. And it came to pass, that in the morning watch the LORD looked unto the host of the Egyptians through the pillar of fire and of the cloud, and troubled the host of the Egyptians, And took off their chariot wheels, that they drave them heavily: so that the Egyptians said, Let us flee from the face of Israel; for the LORD fighteth for them against the Egyptians. And the LORD said unto Moses, Stretch out thine hand over the sea, that the waters may come again upon the Egyptians, upon their chariots, and upon their horsemen. And Moses stretched forth his hand over the sea, and the sea returned to his strength when the morning appeared; and the Egyptians fled against it; and the LORD overthrew the

Egyptians in the midst of the sea. And the waters returned, and covered the chariots, and the horsemen, and all the host of Pharaoh that came into the sea after them; there remained not so much as one of them. But the children of Israel walked upon dry land in the midst of the sea; and the waters were a wall unto them on their right hand, and on their left. Thus the LORD saved Israel that day out of the hand of the Egyptians; and Israel saw the Egyptians dead upon the sea shore. And Israel saw that great work which the LORD did upon the Egyptians: and the people feared the LORD, and believed the LORD, and his servant Moses.' (Exodus 14:19-31)

Baptism is a New Testament ordinance; but it is taught here in the Old Testament by a very clear, visible picture. In fact, the gospel ordinance of believer's baptism is not taught anywhere in the Old Testament except here and in Genesis 6-8. There are no other references to or pictures of baptism in the Old Testament

Baptism not Circumcision
Contrary to the opinion of many, baptism is not taught or in any way symbolized in the Old Testament rite of circumcision. In fact, there is no evidence in the Word of God that there is any correlation at all between the Old Testament rite of circumcision and the New Testament ordinance of baptism. Circumcision in the flesh in the Old Testament was symbolic, not of baptism, but of the new birth, regeneration, the circumcision of the heart, and that circumcision made without hands by God the Holy Spirit. Circumcision in the Old Testament ceremonially sealed to the circumcised child all the blessings of God's covenant with Abraham, so by the new birth God the Holy Spirit, giving us faith in Christ, seals to the heaven-born soul all the blessings of God's covenant grace in Christ (Romans 2:28, 29; Ephesians 1:12-14; Philippians 3:3; Colossians 2:10-12).

Baptism is not taught in the Old Testament rite of circumcision. It is not a sacrament, a means of grace, or a ceremony by which grace is conferred to a person. Baptism is not, as we are often told, 'an outward sign of inward grace'. But baptism is taught in Exodus 14:19-31.

After reading his portion of Exodus 14, and reading what I have just stated, you might be scratching your head and saying to yourself, 'There is no mention of baptism here.' But there is; and we know there is, for

God the Holy Ghost tells us plainly in 1 Corinthians 10 that this passage is talking about baptism (1 Corinthians 10:1-13; Romans 15:4).

'Moreover, brethren, I would not that ye should be ignorant, how that all our fathers were under the cloud, and all passed through the sea; And were all baptized unto Moses in the cloud and in the sea; And did all eat the same spiritual meat; And did all drink the same spiritual drink: for they drank of that spiritual Rock that followed them: and that Rock was Christ' (1 Corinthians 10:1-4).

'Now all these things happened unto them for ensamples: and they are written for our admonition, upon whom the ends of the world are come' (1 Corinthians 10:11).

The things recorded in Exodus 14, the Spirit of God tells us, happened to the children of Israel as examples to us that we might learn from them. 'For whatsoever things were written aforetime were written for our learning, that we through patience and comfort of the scriptures might have hope' (Romans 15:4).

What was involved in Israel's baptism unto Moses? What does their baptism teach us about the New Testament gospel ordinance of baptism? Israel was 'baptized unto Moses' in a manner typical of our being 'baptized unto Christ' (Romans 6:3; Galatians 3:27). The word translated 'unto' in 1 Corinthians 10:2 is the very same word that is translated 'into', when the Spirit of God speaks of our baptism with reference to Christ in Romans 6:3 and Galatians 3:27

Unto, not Into

Obviously, the word is better translated 'unto'. The children of Israel were not baptized into Moses, but 'unto Moses', with reference to Moses; and we are not baptized into Christ, but unto Christ, with reference to Christ. Baptism does not put us in Christ. We are in Christ by grace and power, and the operation of God (1 Corinthians 1:30, 31). We are baptized unto Christ, with reference to him and his work for us (Romans 6:2-7).

Type and Antitype

Look at both the type and the antitype, the typical picture here at the Red Sea and its fulfilment in believer's baptism.

First, consider the physical picture. Those who teach sprinkling as a substitute for baptism tell us the outward sign is not important, but only the spiritual meaning. That sounds very pious; but if the sign is corrupt the meaning is corrupt. Baptism is truly a spiritual act; but it involves a physical act. Israel was 'baptized … in the cloud and in the sea'. They passed through the sea with Moses, under the cloudy pillar; and the sea became the grave of Israel's enemies.

Our baptism unto Christ also, of necessity, involves a physical act. Just as Israel was baptized in a watery grave, we are baptized in a watery grave, according to the commandment and example of our Saviour (Matthew 3:13-17; 28:19). Our baptism is always portrayed as a burial in a watery grave. We are baptized with Christ symbolically, buried in the watery grave with reference to Christ and our salvation by him.

Picture of Death

Second, baptism, then, is a picture of death. When Israel walked into the Red Sea, they walked into a grave; and God's children today, by their baptism, identify themselves with the Lord Jesus Christ in his death, burial, and resurrection. Baptism separated Israel from Egypt; and baptism symbolically separates believers from unbelievers, truth from error, and true religion from false religion. Israel's baptism in the Red Sea was an act of complete commitment to Moses; and our baptism is our publicly avowed commitment to Christ. Israel came out of their watery grave as a resurrected people; and we come out of the waters of baptism to walk with Christ as a resurrected people, in newness of life. Israel came up out of the Red Sea in hope of entering into and possessing the Land of Canaan; and the believer comes up out of the watery grave in hope of eternal life with Christ in heaven.

An Initiation

Third, Israel's baptism unto Moses was an initiation into an entirely new state of existence. Here is a mob of unruly people led out of Egypt by Moses. Until they came to the edge of the Red Sea, they were nothing but that, just a mob. They had no organization and no government. They were simply a mass of people who were following a leader out of bondage, out of slavery, into what they hoped would be freedom. All they had to unite them was the fact they were fleeing from something they did not like.

Then they went through the sea; and as they came out onto the other side, they were no longer an unruly mob. They were a unified nation under the leadership of one man. They belonged together. They were made a unit, a body under the direction of Moses. Moses was their leader; all that Moses stood for, they stood for. From then on, Moses was the recognized authority and the spokesman for God unto that people. Now, they are called 'the church in the wilderness' (Acts 7:38).

Their baptism united the whole nation to one man, even Moses, just as our baptism unites all believers to one Man, the God-man our Saviour, the Lord Jesus Christ. And as they were all united to Moses, they were all united to one another. So it is with God's church. We are united to one another as one body, because we are all united to Christ our Head.

Israel's baptism unto Moses was a baptism experienced by none except those who had just been delivered from what is called the 'house of bondage' (Exodus 13:3, 14). Similarly, baptism unto Christ is an ordinance reserved for believers, for those who have been delivered from the 'snare of the devil' (2 Timothy 2:26), for those who have experienced God's saving grace. In a word, baptism is reserved for believers only. It is the first act of obedience required by the Lord Jesus. It is our initiation into the church and kingdom of God (Matthew 28:19; Mark 16:16; Acts 2:38, 41; 22:16).

Israel's baptism unto Moses was immediately followed by their eating 'spiritual meat' and drinking 'spiritual drink' from Christ the Rock. So, too, the believer's baptism unto Christ is followed by his partaking of the Lord's Supper, in which we feast upon Christ's body and blood, symbolized by the bread and wine of the Lord's Supper (Matthew 26:26-28; 1 Corinthians 11:23-25).

Declared Allegiance
Fourth, Israel's baptism unto Moses was a declaration of their allegiance to Moses. Following Moses into the Red Sea, they became his disciples, obligating themselves to acknowledge him as the only mediator between themselves and God in that day (Deuteronomy 5:5; Galatians 3:19).

In the same way, by our baptism unto Christ, God's elect declare their allegiance to Christ. We declare ourselves to be his disciples, men and women voluntarily obligated to him, as the only Mediator between us and God (1 Timothy 2:5).

Passing through the Red Sea at his command, Israel defiantly renounced Pharaoh, and committed themselves to Moses, and voluntarily bound themselves to obey him. And our baptism, if it means anything, is a line drawn across our lives, proclaiming that we are now the pledged servants of the Son of God, our Lord and Saviour.

Thus Saved

Fifth, remember, this whole passage is talking about Israel's baptism unto Moses. And in Exodus 14:30 we read, 'Thus the LORD saved Israel.' Does that mean baptism is saving? Of course not! Look at two more passages: Matthew 3:13-17 and 1 Peter 3:21. Believer's baptism is God's ordained, symbolic picture of salvation by Christ.

'Then cometh Jesus from Galilee to Jordan unto John, to be baptized of him. But John forbad him, saying, I have need to be baptized of thee, and comest thou to me? And Jesus answering said unto him, Suffer it to be so now: for thus it becometh us to fulfil all righteousness. Then he suffered him. And Jesus, when he was baptized, went up straightway out of the water: and, lo, the heavens were opened unto him, and he saw the Spirit of God descending like a dove, and lighting upon him: And lo a voice from heaven, saying, This is my beloved Son, in whom I am well pleased' (Matthew 3:13-17).

Our Saviour's baptism by John the Baptist did nothing to fulfil righteousness. So what is the meaning of our Lord's word to John? Baptism portrays the bringing in of everlasting righteousness for sinners by the life, death, burial, and resurrection of Christ, the sinner's Substitute. By his obedience unto death, God's elect are made the righteousness of God (1 Corinthians 15:1-3; 2 Corinthians 5:17-21; Romans 4:25-5:11).

The Apostle Peter was inspired by God the Holy Ghost to tell us exactly the same thing, using the salvation of Noah and his family by the ark. Just as God saved Noah and his family by the ark, baptism pictures the salvation of God's elect in Christ by his suffering all the fury of God's holy wrath and justice as our Substitute

'For Christ also hath once suffered for sins, the just for the unjust, that he might bring us to God, being put to death in the flesh, but quickened by the Spirit: By which also he went and preached unto the spirits in prison; Which sometime were disobedient, when once the longsuffering of God waited in the days of Noah, while the ark was a preparing, wherein few, that is, eight souls were saved by water. The like figure whereunto even baptism doth also now save us (not the putting away of the filth of the flesh, but the answer of a good conscience toward God,) by the resurrection of Jesus Christ: Who is gone into heaven, and is on the right hand of God; angels and authorities and powers being made subject unto him' (1 Peter 3:18-22).

As Noah's ark was a picture of Christ and salvation by him, it was also a picture of baptism and our salvation by Christ. As the ark was God's ordinance, and not man's, so baptism is the ordinance of God, not the ordinance of man. As in the ark Noah and his family were immersed in the wrath of God, in baptism the believer is immersed in the watery grave, the symbol of judgment, death, and wrath, but never experiences that judgment, death and wrath. Baptism does not save by putting away sin, the filth of the flesh, but it is the figure (the picture) of salvation, and the answer of a good conscience toward God, by which we profess and portray our salvation in, by, and with the Lord Jesus Christ in and by whom all righteousness has been forever and perfectly fulfilled for sinners.

A Solemn Warning
Sixth, 1 Corinthians 10 gives us a very solemn warning. Many who were baptized unto Moses in the Red Sea perished in the wilderness, being overcome with temptations they faced in their pilgrimage.

'Moreover, brethren, I would not that ye should be ignorant, how that all our fathers were under the cloud, and all passed through the sea; And were all baptized unto Moses in the cloud and in the sea; And did all eat the same spiritual meat; And did all drink the same spiritual drink: for they drank of that spiritual Rock that followed them: and that Rock was Christ. But with many of them God was not well pleased: for they were overthrown in the wilderness. Now these things were our examples, to the intent we should not lust after evil things, as they also lusted. Neither be ye idolaters, as were some of them; as it is written, The people sat down to eat and drink, and rose up to play. Neither let us commit fornication, as some of them committed, and fell in one day three and twenty thousand. Neither let us tempt Christ, as some of them also tempted, and were destroyed of serpents. Neither murmur ye, as some of them also murmured, and were destroyed of the destroyer. Now all these things happened unto them for ensamples: and they are written for our admonition, upon whom the ends of the world are come. Wherefore let him that thinketh he standeth take heed lest he fall. There hath no temptation taken you but such as is common to man: but God is faithful, who will not suffer you to be tempted above that ye are able; but will with the temptation also make a way to escape, that ye may be able to bear it. Wherefore, my dearly beloved, flee from idolatry. I speak as to wise men; judge ye what I say. The cup of blessing which we bless, is it not the communion of the blood of Christ? The bread which we break, is it not the communion of the body of Christ? For we being many are one bread, and one body: for we are all partakers of that one bread' (1 Corinthians 10:1-17).

In all these things, the children of Israel are examples to us. Examples to warn us of danger, the dangers of this world, of covetousness which is idolatry, and the danger of unbelief. Examples to warn us against presumption. Examples to assure us of God's faithfulness. Examples to remind us that we are one in Christ. Let us deal with one another as the members of Christ.

That is the Old Testament doctrine of baptism, and the New Testament doctrine of baptism, too. May God the Holy Spirit give us grace, day by day, to walk with Christ according to the profession of our baptism in newness of life. 'Knowing this, that our old man is crucified with him, that the body of sin might be destroyed, that henceforth we should not serve sin' (Romans 6:6).

Chapter 71

Moses' Song

'Then sang Moses and the children of Israel this song unto the LORD,
and spake, saying, I will sing unto the LORD, for he hath triumphed
gloriously: the horse and his rider hath he thrown into the sea. The
LORD is my strength and song, and he is become my salvation: he is
my God, and I will prepare him an habitation; my father's God, and I
will exalt him. The LORD is a man of war: the LORD is his name.
Pharaoh's chariots and his host hath he cast into the sea: his chosen
captains also are drowned in the Red sea. The depths have covered
them: they sank into the bottom as a stone. Thy right hand, O LORD, is
become glorious in power: thy right hand, O LORD, hath dashed in
pieces the enemy. And in the greatness of thine excellency thou hast
overthrown them that rose up against thee: thou sentest forth thy wrath,
which consumed them as stubble. And with the blast of thy nostrils the
waters were gathered together, the floods stood upright as an heap, and
the depths were congealed in the heart of the sea. The enemy said, I will
pursue, I will overtake, I will divide the spoil; my lust shall be satisfied
upon them; I will draw my sword, my hand shall destroy them. Thou
didst blow with thy wind, the sea covered them: they sank as lead in the
mighty waters. Who is like unto thee, O LORD, among the gods? Who
is like thee, glorious in holiness, fearful in praises, doing wonders?
Thou stretchedst out thy right hand, the earth swallowed them. Thou in
thy mercy hast led forth the people which thou hast redeemed: thou hast
guided them in thy strength unto thy holy habitation. The people shall

hear, and be afraid: sorrow shall take hold on the inhabitants of Palestina. Then the dukes of Edom shall be amazed; the mighty men of Moab, trembling shall take hold upon them; all the inhabitants of Canaan shall melt away. Fear and dread shall fall upon them; by the greatness of thine arm they shall be as still as a stone; till thy people pass over, O LORD, till the people pass over, which thou hast purchased. Thou shalt bring them in, and plant them in the mountain of thine inheritance, in the place, O LORD, which thou hast made for thee to dwell in, in the Sanctuary, O Lord, which thy hands have established. The LORD shall reign forever and ever. For the horse of Pharaoh went in with his chariots and with his horsemen into the sea, and the LORD brought again the waters of the sea upon them; but the children of Israel went on dry land in the midst of the sea. And Miriam the prophetess, the sister of Aaron, took a timbrel in her hand; and all the women went out after her with timbrels and with dances. And Miriam answered them, Sing ye to the LORD, for he hath triumphed gloriously; the horse and his rider hath he thrown into the sea.'
(Exodus 15:1-21)

When reading the Word of God, it is always important to mark the first mention of a thing. The first mention of anything usually gives us a clear indication of how that particular thing is to be understood throughout the Scriptures. That rule, or principle of interpretation, is sometimes referred to as 'The Law of First Mention'.

We have before us the first song recorded upon the pages of Holy Scripture. There may have been others before this; but this is the first song of which we have record. The text which heads this page is the oldest poem in the world. It was written hundreds of years before Homer's Iliad. Its sublimity and grandeur is unsurpassed by any of the poetry that has followed it. Yet, this piece of poetry is rarely, if ever, mentioned, much less studied in any high school or university literature class.

Try to picture this huge choir, millions of people standing on the Canaan side of the Red Sea, as Moses lined out his hymn, singing the high praises of God for the redemption they had just experienced. When Moses had finished leading the children of Israel in his song, Miriam and the women of Zion took out their tambourines and danced as they repeated the chorus.

Parts of this sweet song of redemption are found throughout the Old Testament Scriptures. Both David and Isaiah use some of the exact words of this song in their praises of the triune God. This great song of praise to our God is so great, so significant that it is specifically named as one of the songs that will be sung by the redeemed in the New Jerusalem (Revelation 15:3, 4).

It is obvious, from the many allusions to this song in Holy Scripture, that it is full of spiritual instruction. It teaches us to give praise to God for the overthrow of all the powers of evil and the redemption and deliverance of his chosen. C. H. Spurgeon wrote:

'It is God's intent that from the day of Moses downward, even to the hour when flames of fire shall lick up the works of men, and the heavens themselves shall be dissolved with fervent heat, that this shall be the song of the chosen people everywhere, "Sing unto the LORD, for he hath triumphed gloriously".'

I cannot tell you how often I have repeated portions of this song in my worship of our God, as he has graciously delivered me from the hellish assaults of the prince of darkness against my soul. How often, when I thought I was about to be crushed, the Lord Jesus, our mighty Man of War, the Captain of our Salvation, arose and cast Pharaoh and his chariots into the depths of the sea, and I came away singing,

'I will sing unto the LORD, for he hath triumphed gloriously! The horse and his rider hath he thrown into the sea. The LORD is my strength and song, and he is become my salvation. He is my God, and I will prepare him an habitation ... Thy right hand, O LORD, is become glorious in power: thy right hand, O LORD, hath dashed in pieces the enemy ... Sing to the LORD, for he hath triumphed gloriously; the horse and his rider hath he thrown into the sea.'

May God the Holy Spirit, who dictated this song to Moses, write it afresh upon our hearts. Breathe on us, O Blessed Spirit, that we also may be filled with the praises of Jehovah!

The Time
To everything there is a season, and a time for every purpose under heaven. There is a time of the singing of birds; and there is a time for the singing of saints. 'Then sang Moses.' When did Moses and the children of Israel sing this great song? They sang this song of praise as soon as they had experienced God's salvation (Exodus 14:30-15:1).

'Thus the LORD saved Israel that day out of the hand of the Egyptians; and Israel saw the Egyptians dead upon the sea shore. And Israel saw that great work which the LORD did upon the Egyptians: and the people feared the LORD, and believed the LORD, and his servant Moses' (Exodus 14:30, 31).

'Then sang Moses and the children of Israel this song unto the LORD.' Only a redeemed people, conscious of their deliverance, can truly worship and praise Jehovah, the Deliverer. Those who are yet dead in trespasses and sins may practise a form of godliness and sing words; but the only people in this world who can and will worship God and sing his praise are those who have experienced his grace.

There was no singing while in Egypt. Only sighing, crying, groaning, and lamentation was heard in the land of bondage. There was no singing even at the celebration of the paschal supper on that dreadful night when the people ate the lamb in haste with their loins girded and their staves in their hands. There was no singing as they came out of Egypt. And even when they were crossing the Red Sea, there was no word of song. In all those events, the children of Israel had many emotions; fear and joy, excitement and dread, but not a word of song. They marched on steadily, but they were not ready to take out their tambourines, to sing and dance. Only when they had crossed the sea, and the waters of the sea rolled back upon and drowned their enemies, only when the depths completely covered Pharaoh and the Egyptian armies, only when they stood together on dry ground on the Canaan side of the Red Sea do we read, 'Then sang Moses and the children of Israel this song unto the LORD'. When their slavery was altogether a thing of the past, they sang Jehovah's praise.

Jehovah's Praise
The song of Moses, the song Israel sang when they had experienced God's deliverance, was a song of praise to Jehovah. Moses and the children of Israel sung their song 'unto the LORD'.

This song was not an exhibition of musical skill, but a pouring forth of gratitude, thanksgiving, and praise from the heart to God upon his throne. Jehovah had redeemed them with blood. Jehovah had brought them out of Egypt. Jehovah had brought them through the Red Sea. Jehovah had destroyed Pharaoh and the Egyptians in the Sea. Jehovah alone must have the praises of their song.

'Then sang Moses and the children of Israel this song unto the LORD.' Their song was entirely about Jehovah. They not only sang unto the Lord, but they sang about him. This song was all about the Lord. There is nothing in it about the people. The word 'LORD' is found twelve times in this song, in just 19 verses. The pronouns 'he', 'him', 'thy', 'thou', and 'thee' are found thirty-three times. How significant and how searching that fact is. How different this is from modern religious songs. Modern religious songs, like modern religion, are all about man, full of sentimentality and emotionalism. Instead of adoring, exalting, and praising the God of all grace, they focus our thoughts upon ourselves. They announce our love to God instead of his love for us. They recount our experiences, instead of God's mercies. They dwell more upon human attainments, than on Christ's atonement.

This first song, the Song of Moses, is different. 'I will exalt him' (v. 2) sums it all up. 'I will sing unto the LORD, for he hath triumphed gloriously: the horse and his rider hath He thrown into the sea' (v. 1). The theme of this song is the Lord God himself and that which he has done.

It is sweet and good to rejoice in God's mercies; but it is far sweeter and far better to rejoice in the God of mercies (Isaiah 61:10; Joel 2:23; Philippians 3:1, 3; 4:4-6).

Baptismal Song
The Holy Spirit tells us distinctly that the children of Israel were here 'baptized unto Moses in the cloud and in the sea'. So, this first song in Holy Scripture is a baptismal song, a song of clear consecration to God.

When Pharaoh and his hosts had been destroyed, Israel stood for the first time as a nation separated from Egypt. The Red Sea was the dividing line. Israel became a distinct people, a race redeemed from among men. They would never again feel the yoke of bondage. They would not return to Egypt. Pharaoh would hurt them no more. They were now a distinct people consecrated unto Jehovah. To them God would reveal himself. Among them he would dwell.

Their passage through the Red Sea was in type their death, their burial, and their resurrection to a new life. It was their national baptism unto God. Therefore, they sang this new song to the Lord. No song can exceed in sweetness that heavenly Canticle, 'I am my Beloved's, and my Beloved is mine'. There is no greater joy than to know that the Lord has chosen us unto himself to be his own, peculiar people. Conscious of redemption by blood and separation unto Jehovah, their God, 'Then, sang Moses and the children of Israel this song unto the Lord'. This is a song of personal praise, a congregational song, an experimental song, a joyous song of worship to God for his great salvation.

Come, young men and maidens, men, women and children, let us praise the Lord on the high-sounding cymbals and let us spend the rest of our days in crying, 'Sing ye unto the Lord, for he hath triumphed gloriously'.

The Content
Let us look briefly at the content of this blessed, instructive song.

'Then sang Moses and the children of Israel this song unto the LORD, and spake, saying, I will sing unto the LORD, for he hath triumphed gloriously: the horse and his rider hath he thrown into the sea' (v. 1).

Triumph implies warfare. Read the twelfth chapter of Revelation, and understand two things: first, there is an ongoing, relentless warfare between the seed of the woman and the serpent's seed, between Christ and the devil, between the church and the world, between the flesh and the Spirit; and second, Christ has fought and won the battle. He has triumphed gloriously.

'The LORD is my strength and song, and he is become my salvation: he is my God, and I will prepare him an habitation; my father's God, and I will exalt him' (v. 2).

In the first verse Moses adores the Lord God for his salvation. Here he adores him for those blessed covenant relations into which our great God condescends to bring himself. Do we know anything of this? Can you say he is my God (Isaiah 12:2; Zechariah 13:9)?

Christ is my Strength. He is the Strength of his spiritual Israel, the Author and Giver of strength to his own. He is the Strength of our lives, our hearts, and our graces. It is Christ who strengthens us to do his will, to exercise every grace, to withstand our inward corruptions, to resist our outward temptations, to bear afflictions, and to overcome every enemy. Therefore, he is our Song. He alone is my Salvation; and he became my salvation in the sweet experience of his deliverance. He is my father's God, the God of Abraham, Isaac, and Jacob, the God of the covenant.

'The LORD is a man of war: the LORD is his name' (v. 3).

This character given to our blessed God and Saviour is a striking one (Psalm 24:8; Isaiah 27:4; 45:9; Revelation 19:11). John Trapp wrote,

'He alone is a whole army of men, van and rear both (Isaiah 52:12). He sends the sword (Ezekiel 14:17), musters the men (Isaiah 13:4), orders the ammunition (Jeremiah 50:25) and gives the victory. Whence, he is here styled by the Chaldee, The Lord and Victor of wars.'

'Pharaoh's chariots and his host hath he cast into the sea: his chosen captains also are drowned in the Red sea' (v. 4).

Read the entire song spiritually for the profit of your soul. Pharaoh is but a type of Satan, the great enemy of our souls. His chosen captains typify all evil, the terrors of the law, and particularly all our countless sins. Our Lord Jesus Christ, the Angel of the Lord, Jehovah, our Immanuel, our great Man of War, destroyed them all in his fury when he redeemed us with his blood (Exodus 14:17, 24-28; Colossians 2:13-15; Revelation 12:9-11). Our defeated foe, the Devil, is in a rage, 'because he knoweth that he hath but a short time' (Revelation 12:12). Read on,

'Pharaoh's chariots and his host hath he cast into the sea: his chosen captains also are drowned in the Red sea. The depths have covered them: they sank into the bottom as a stone. Thy right hand, O LORD, is become glorious in power: thy right hand, O LORD, hath dashed in pieces the enemy. And in the greatness of thine excellency thou hast overthrown them that rose up against thee: thou sentest forth thy wrath, which consumed them as stubble. And with the blast of thy nostrils the waters were gathered together, the floods stood upright as an heap, and the depths were congealed in the heart of the sea. The enemy said, I will pursue, I will overtake, I will divide the spoil; my lust shall be satisfied upon them; I will draw my sword, my hand shall destroy them. Thou didst blow with thy wind, the sea covered them: they sank as lead in the mighty waters' (vv. 4-10).

What a blessed, joyful picture this is of sin pardoned through Immanuel's blood (Micah 7:18, 19).

'Who is like unto thee, O LORD, among the gods? Who is like thee, glorious in holiness, fearful in praises, doing wonders?' (v. 11).

Unlike the many gods of Egypt, unlike the many gods of this world, he who is God indeed, the Lord Jehovah, is 'glorious in holiness' (Isaiah 6:3; Revelation 4:8). It was in this character that the Lord Jesus addressed his Father, calling him 'Holy Father', in his prayer (John 17:11). By the expression, 'fearful in praises', Moses declares that even in ascribing praise to him, God's people bow before him with humility, fearful of saying or doing something unbecoming the worship and praise of God. He who is our great God is God 'doing wonders'. All his works are like himself Wonderful. His work of creation is wonderful. All his works of providence are wonderful. We read in Revelation 12:16 'And the earth helped the woman, and the earth opened her mouth, and swallowed up the flood which the dragon cast out of his mouth'. How wonderful is our God's work of redemption (Romans 3:24-26; 2 Corinthians 5:18-21; Galatians 3:13, 14). And all his works of grace in the new creation are wonderful (2 Corinthians 5:17).

'Thou stretchedst out thy right hand, the earth swallowed them' (v. 12).

When the Lord God stretched out his right hand, drew forth his angry, glittering sword of justice, and slaughtered his darling Son as our Substitute, and buried him in the earth, the earth swallowed our sins. Three days later, the earth cast out her dead, and our Saviour arose without sin, 'justified in the Spirit'.

'Thou in thy mercy hast led forth the people which thou hast redeemed: thou hast guided them in thy strength unto thy holy habitation' (v. 13).

How sweet it is to behold God's distinguishing grace set forth with such clarity (Exodus 8:22; Matthew 13:49; Isaiah 65:13; 1 Corinthians 4:7). All his people obtained mercy. All who obtained mercy were redeemed. All who were redeemed were brought out of Egypt. All who were brought out were brought out by God's omnipotence. And all for whom mercy was designed, to whom redemption was granted, and for whom deliverance was accomplished were brought by that same omnipotence into God's 'Holy Habitation!' Notice that Moses sings of this as something already done, though Israel would wander about in the wilderness for forty years. So it is with us.

'The works were finished from the foundation of the world' (Hebrews 4:3; Romans 8:29, 30; Ephesians 1:3-6).

'The people shall hear, and be afraid: sorrow shall take hold on the inhabitants of Palestina. Then the dukes of Edom shall be amazed; the mighty men of Moab, trembling shall take hold upon them; all the inhabitants of Canaan shall melt away. Fear and dread shall fall upon them; by the greatness of thine arm they shall be as still as a stone; till thy people pass over, O LORD, till the people pass over, which thou hast purchased' (vv. 14-16).

This was fulfilled to Israel and it shall be fulfilled to us (Deuteronomy 2:4; Numbers 22:3; Joshua 2:9, 10). When the time comes for you and me to pass over the sea into eternal bliss with Christ, our great Saviour shall silence every foe. Satan may seek to raise Moses up to condemn us, but Christ will stand by his Joshua, and Moses shall have nothing to say (Zechariah 3:1-10).

'Thou shalt bring them in, and plant them in the mountain of thine inheritance, in the place, O LORD, which thou hast made for thee to dwell in, in the Sanctuary, O Lord, which thy hands have established' (v. 17).

If the Lord God has brought you out of Egypt, depend upon it, he will bring you into the heavenly Canaan (John 10:27, 28).

'The LORD shall reign forever and ever' (v. 18).

What a great reason for joy amidst all the disappointments of life (Psalm 97:1; Revelation 11:15). Blessed be his name, the Lord Jesus Christ, our Saviour, our God, our King, reigns. Else we would be without hope!

'For the horse of Pharaoh went in with his chariots and with his horsemen into the sea, and the LORD brought again the waters of the sea upon them; but the children of Israel went on dry land in the midst of the sea. And Miriam the prophetess, the sister of Aaron, took a timbrel in her hand; and all the women went out after her with timbrels and with dances' (vv. 19, 20).

Miriam, an Old Testament name, is the same as Mary in the New. The name means 'bitter'. But now the bitter is made sweet, and joins in the song. As in fasting all mourn (Joel 2:16), so in praising all should partake. It was a common thing in the church of old to celebrate the praises of the Lord our God (Judges 5:1; 1 Samuel 18:6). Let us follow their example and celebrate incessantly the high praises of our God, for he has triumphed gloriously! Sing, O my soul, sing unto the Lord!

John Trapp wrote, 'A good soul is altogether unsatisfiable in sanctifying God's name, and setting forth his goodness. Should I do nothing else all the days of my life, said that martyr, yea, as long as the days of heaven shall last, but kneel on my knees and repeat David's Psalms; yet should I fall infinitely short of what I owe to God.'

'And Miriam answered them, Sing ye to the LORD, for he hath triumphed gloriously; the horse and his rider hath he thrown into the sea' (v. 21).

Awake, my heart! Awake, my soul! Sing unto the Lord forever! Did the Lord bring his people out of Egyptian bondage; and did Israel sing his mercies at the Red Sea? And shall not I, whom he has brought out of nature's darkness, and out of the bondage of sin and Satan, shout aloud his praise and sing of the salvation of the Lord?

'The LORD hath appeared of old unto me, saying, Yea, I have loved thee with an everlasting love: therefore with lovingkindness have I drawn thee. Again I will build thee, and thou shalt be built, O virgin of Israel: thou shalt again be adorned with thy tabrets, and shalt go forth in the dances of them that make merry' (Jeremiah 31:3, 4).

Oh, blessed and only Potentate, King of kings, and Lord of lords, infinite and eternal Jehovah; Father, Son, and Holy Ghost, you have brought me out of the iron furnace, out of the horrible pit, the mire, and the clay! You have set my feet upon the rock Christ Jesus and established my goings! You have put a new song in my mouth, even praise unto my God forever! Many shall see it, and fear, and shall trust in the Lord!

'Not unto us, O LORD, not unto us, but unto thy name give glory, for thy mercy, and for thy truth's sake' (Psalm 115:1).

Chapter 72

The Solitariness Of God

'Who is like unto thee, O LORD, among the gods? who is like thee, glorious in holiness, fearful in praises, doing wonders?'
(Exodus 15:11)

Everyone knows that God is great in wisdom, wondrous in power, and abundant in mercy. But in these degenerate days of religious perversion, most people know nothing of God's being, his nature, and his attributes. There are very few who understand that God is infinite, majestic, great beyond imagination, and glorious. I hope that this study will be blessed of God to inspire you to trust, adore, and reverently worship him. There is no one and nothing in all the universe like our God. He is infinitely higher and greater than all his creation. It is the solitary excellence of God that inspires reverence for him, faith in him, and obedience to him. Yet, at the outset, it must be acknowledged that our God is incomprehensibly great.

Isaac Watts teaches in the following verses that no mortal can fully know or fathom our eternal God.

> Can creatures to perfection find,
> The eternal, uncreated mind?
> Or can the largest stretch of thought,
> Measure and search his nature out?

'Tis high as heaven, 'tis deep as hell;
And what can mortals know or tell?
His glory spreads beyond the sky,
And all the shining worlds on high.

Here are seven facts about God which show his solitariness, seven things which distinguish him from and set him apart from all his creatures, infinitely.

There is One God
The Word of God universally and with the utmost clarity states there is only one God (Deuteronomy 6:4; 1 Corinthians 8:6; 1 Timothy 2:5; Ephesians 4:4-6). God alone is solitary in his being. There are many angels, many men, and many of all other creatures; but God is One. He 'only hath immortality, dwelling in the light which no man can approach unto; whom no man hath seen nor can see; to whom be honour and power everlasting. Amen' (1 Timothy 6:16). Because there is one God, our allegiance is due to him alone. Our affections are to be directed to him alone. And all who know, trust, and worship him are one body.

God is Eternal
Angels are not eternal. Men are not eternal. And matter is not eternal. But God is eternal. In Genesis 1:1 we read, 'In the beginning God'. In the beginning, there was nothing and no one but God. There was a 'time' before time began, when God dwelt alone in the ineffable glory of his own great being. There was no heaven in which to set his throne and manifest his glory. There was no earth to be his footstool and engage his care. There were no angels to sing his praise. There was no universe to be upheld by the word of his power. There were no men created in his image and after his likeness. There were no hours, days, months, years, or ages. From everlasting, in old eternity, God was alone in his glory. He is the great 'I AM', 'the eternal God', who says, 'I live forever'. The psalmist says of him, 'Thy throne is established of old; thou art from everlasting' (Psalm 93:2). He is the first and the last, 'the high and lofty One that inhabiteth eternity' (Isaiah 57:15). This great God, who alone is eternal, is and must be the Creator of all things, the Possessor of all things, the Ruler of all things, and the Disposer of all things.

106

God is Spirit

Our Lord Jesus Christ declares, 'God is a Spirit: and they that worship him must worship him in Spirit and in truth' (John 4:24). That does not mean God is one spirit among many, but that he is Spirit, without the limitations of a body. The Bible often ascribes to God terms such as 'the hand of the Lord', 'the mouth of the Lord', 'the eyes of the Lord', 'the arm of the Lord', and 'the ear of the Lord'. But these terms are mere accommodations of language to help our puny brains understand the works of God. They are anthropomorphic terms, human terms, to describe the works of the Lord. They do not, in any way, represent the nature and being of God.

As you read the Bible you cannot fail to notice that never once were men given any kind of physical, visible, tangible representation of God's being. Even under the types and shadows of the Old Testament age of ceremonial worship, nothing was given as a representation of God's being. All the types and shadows of the law represented his work of redemption through Christ. But nothing represented God himself. Why? Because God is Spirit. He is the infinite, incomprehensible, invisible, immutable, omnipresent Spirit.

Because God is Spirit, he expressly forbids every form of idolatry (Exodus 20:3-6). The first and second commandments forbid the acceptance of any other god or any intrusion of anyone or anything in our hearts in the place of God, as the object of our affections or the ruler of our lives. These two commands also forbid the worship of God using any image, the representation of God by anything visible, and the use of religious images, symbols or pictures, such as pictures of Christ, crosses, crucifixes, religious relics, angelic forms, etc.. Do not look upon this as an extreme position. Those who make use of such religious symbols and emblems, who would be shocked to be charged with practising idolatry, only need to read 2 Kings 18:1-7 to see how serious this breach of God's law is.

All true worship and service rendered to God must be spiritual, heart worship. It is not sufficient to come before God on bended knee, with prostrate body, or with words of praise. We must worship God in and by his Holy Spirit, and with our spiritual nature; our souls, our hearts, our minds, and our wills. True worship is heart worship (John 4:23, 24; Philippians 3:3). We must worship God alone. We must worship him spiritually. We must worship God sincerely. And we must worship him in truth, in accordance with revealed truth. The doctrine of Scripture and the outward duties of public and private worship must never be neglected or altered (1 Chronicles 15:13); but the essence of worship must be found in the heart. Otherwise the outward acts of worship are an abomination to the Lord God (Isaiah 1:10-15).

God is a Trinity

We worship one God in the trinity, or tri-unity, of his sacred persons. We do not have three Gods. We worship one God, who subsists in three distinct persons; the Father, the Son, and the Holy Ghost. And these three persons are equal in all things. This is precisely what is stated in 1 John 5:7. 'For there are three that bear record in heaven, the Father, the Word, and the Holy Ghost: and these three are one.'

From the very beginning, God revealed that there are three persons in the Godhead. God the Father created all things through his Son, the Word (Genesis 1:1; John 1:1-3). God the Spirit moved upon the face of the waters (Genesis 1:2). God said, 'Let us make man in our image and in our likeness' (Genesis 1:26). And God promised to send his Son, the Seed of the woman, to redeem fallen man (Genesis 3:15).

In the New Testament, the doctrine of the Trinity is, as we have seen, expressly declared in 1 John 5:7; and it is frequently represented to us. When our Lord was baptized, the Father spoke from heaven, the Son was immersed in the Jordan river, and the Holy Spirit descended upon him from heaven (Matthew 3:16, 17). God's servants are commanded to administer the ordinance of baptism in the name of the Trinity. 'Go ye therefore, and teach all nations, baptizing them in the name of the Father, and of the Son, and of the Holy Ghost' (Matthew 28:19). The apostolic benediction (2 Corinthians 13:14) pronounces the blessings of grace upon God's saints in the name of the triune God. Our Lord Jesus Christ himself plainly declares the trinity of persons in the Godhead (John 14:16). And all three persons in the Trinity are involved in the work of salvation. The salvation of God's elect was planned by God the Father, purchased by God the Son, and applied by God the Spirit (Ephesians 1:3-14). The Word of God reveals one God in three persons. The Father is God (Romans 1:7). The Son is God (Hebrews 1:8). The Holy Spirit is God (Acts 5:3, 4). 'And these three are One'.[2]

---

[2] Though the Son is voluntarily subject to the Father (John 10:16-18), and the

God is Independent and Self-sufficient

God is solitary in his being, in his eternality, in his spirituality, and in his trinity. And God is solitary in his independence and self-sufficiency. God alone needs nothing. God does not need you, me, or anyone else. God needs nothing but himself. In old eternity, when God dwelt alone in the glory of his triune persons, he was self-contained and self-sufficient, in need of nothing. He needed nothing to make him happy, glorious, and complete. And he is still independent, self-sufficient, in need of nothing. The creation of the world added nothing to God. He is immutable. He changes not (Malachi 3:6; James 1:17). His essential glory could never be increased or diminished.

God was under no constraint, obligation, or necessity to create the world. God who 'worketh all things after the counsel of his own will' (Ephesians 1:11), freely chose to create the world simply because it was his sovereign pleasure to do so. He created the world, not to get glory to himself, but to display and manifest his glory in it. God gains nothing from his creatures. Even the praises of redeemed sinners add nothing to the glory of his being. Read Nehemiah 9:5. 'Stand up and bless the Lord, your God, forever and ever; and blessed be thy glorious name, which is exalted above all blessing and praise.' Even the salvation of God's elect adds nothing to his solitary, self-sufficient, and independent glory. He predestinated his elect to eternal salvation to the praise of the glory of his grace, 'according to the good pleasure of his will' (Ephesians 1:5). He chose to save us to show forth his glory in us (Ephesians 2:7), but not that he might increase his glory (Psalm 16:2, 3). We add nothing to him.

I have often heard it said, 'Because God is love, there was a great vacuum in God's heart. He needed someone to love. Therefore, he created man.' That was not the case at all. 'God is love.' But there was from eternity a perfect self-sufficiency even in his love. The Father, Son, and Holy Ghost dwelt together in perfect love from everlasting. We gain everything from God; but God gains nothing from his creatures (Romans 11:34-36). And, if God gains nothing from man, then it is impossible for man to bring God into any obligation to him (Read Job

---

Spirit is voluntarily subject to the Son and the Father (John 14:16) in the covenant of redemption and grace, for the salvation of God's elect, there is no subordination of Persons in the Godhead.

35:7, 8). Every mercy, every blessing, every benefit we receive from the Almighty is a matter of his own free favour.

By the same token, God loses nothing by the wickedness of his creatures (Job 35:6). As man can add nothing to God's glory, so man can never diminish God's glory. God made all things to show forth his glory, and all things shall serve their end (Revelation 4:11). The glory of his wisdom and power shall be seen in all creation and providence. The glory of his love and justice is seen in redemption. The glory of his mercy and grace is seen in the salvation of his elect. The glory of his truth and righteousness is seen in the eternal ruin of his enemies.

The God of the Bible is so great that he is self-sufficient in the glory of his own holy being. There was no vacuum in God's heart that had to be filled by man. Had it pleased him to do so, he might have dwelt alone in his solitary glory forever without making his glory known to any. All that we experience of his grace and goodness we experience because of his sovereign good pleasure alone (Psalm 115:3; 135:6).

God is totally independent of his creatures and self-sufficient without us (Isaiah 40:15-23; 1 Timothy 6:15, 16). This is the God of the Bible. He is still, in this reprobate religious age, 'the unknown God' (Acts 17:23). Because he is unknown in this religious world, we seek to make him known. This is a God to be reverenced, worshipped, and adored. A. W. Pink wrote, 'He is solitary in his majesty, unique in his excellency, peerless in his perfections. He sustains all, but is himself independent of all. He gives to all, and is enriched by none.'

God is Unknowable
This great, solitary God can only be known by revelation. I have offered no arguments to prove the existence of God. That is not because arguments cannot be produced. God's being is a self-evident truth of creation and providence, so that all men and women are without excuse before him (Romans 1:20). But no man will ever come to know the living God by the light of nature (Job 11:7, 8; 26:14). A savage might find a watch in the sand and conclude there was a watchmaker; but he would never be able to know the watchmaker by looking at the watch. Even so, a man may know that God is by the light of nature; but he can never come to know God by the light of nature. God cannot be known by man, except as God is pleased to reveal himself to us (John 3:3; 1 Corinthians 2:14). And God has been pleased to reveal himself to men.

God has revealed himself to men in the person and work of the Lord Jesus Christ, his dear Son (John 1:18; Hebrews 1:1-3). God has revealed himself to men in the inspired volume of Holy Scripture (2 Timothy 3:15-17). God reveals himself to sinners through the preaching of the gospel (Romans 1:16, 17). Yet, no sinner will ever see and know the living God until he reveals himself in the sinner's heart by the irresistible grace and power of the Holy Spirit (2 Corinthians 4:6). Everything depends upon God! Even when we have been made to see and know the glory of God in the face of Jesus Christ, our spiritual knowledge, at best, is a fragmentary knowledge. We ever need to grow in the grace and knowledge of the Lord Jesus Christ. Knowing him, let us each seek grace that we 'might walk worthy of the Lord unto all pleasing, being fruitful in every good work, and increasing in the knowledge of God' (Colossians 1:10).

God Forgives Sin

God alone forgives sin freely, without any reparations being made by the one forgiven. Sinners are 'justified freely by his grace through the redemption that is in Christ Jesus' (Micah 7:18-20). No god dreamed up and made by fallen, depraved man forgives freely. But he who is God forgives freely. He does not demand and will not accept any reparations made by man, but only the reparation and restitution made by himself for men in the sacrifice of his dear Son, the Lord Jesus Christ. He who is God will accept no payment or satisfaction for sin, except the payment and satisfaction he has made for sin in the sacrifice of his dear Son, the Lord Jesus Christ.

Oh, how we ought to thank God for so arranging the affairs of the universe that he might make himself known to sinners in redemption by Christ (Romans 6:17, 18; 2 Corinthians 4:6).

'Who is like unto thee, O LORD, among the gods? Who is like thee, glorious in holiness, fearful in praises, doing wonders?'

111

Discovering Christ In Exodus

Chapter 73

The Waters Of Marah

'So Moses brought Israel from the Red sea, and they went out into the wilderness of Shur; and they went three days in the wilderness, and found no water. And when they came to Marah, they could not drink of the waters of Marah, for they were bitter: therefore the name of it was called Marah. And the people murmured against Moses, saying, What shall we drink? And he cried unto the LORD; and the LORD shewed him a tree, which when he had cast into the waters, the waters were made sweet: there he made for them a statute and an ordinance, and there he proved them, And said, If thou wilt diligently hearken to the voice of the LORD thy God, and wilt do that which is right in his sight, and wilt give ear to his commandments, and keep all his statutes, I will put none of these diseases upon thee, which I have brought upon the Egyptians: for I am the LORD that healeth thee. And they came to Elim, where were twelve wells of water, and threescore and ten palm trees: and they encamped there by the waters.'
(Exodus 15:22-27)

We read in the Book of Proverbs, 'The full soul loatheth an honeycomb; but to the hungry soul every bitter thing is sweet' (27:7). Are you hungry or full? If you are hungry, here is a bitter thing upon which I trust the Spirit of God will feed you. If he will do so, you shall find this bitter thing sweet and satisfying, and you shall be filled. Let us go to the waters of Marah; sitting down by the stream of bitter waters, ask God the Holy Spirit to be our Teacher, and ask him to write upon our hearts the lessons that bitter place is intended to teach us.

After God had so graciously delivered the children of Israel across the Red Sea, miraculously opening a path for them in the sea and then drowning Pharaoh and the armies of Egypt in the depths of the sea, he brought Israel into the wilderness of Shur, where for three days they wandered without water. Their cattle were perishing. Their children's tongues were swollen. Their lips were parched. They had roamed for three days in the barren wilderness without water.

Then, at last, they came to the plentiful fountains of Marah. When they saw the waters of Marah, how their hearts must have rejoiced in hope and expectation. As they approached Marah, they could almost taste the water. They could almost feel the cool, refreshing water in their mouths. But when they got there, the waters were so bitter they could not drink them! What frustration they must have felt!

Immediately, they turned on Moses, to murmur and complain. Actually, they turned on the Lord who had brought them to this place. Though the Lord had led them by the fiery and cloudy pillar, though he was with them, though he had miraculously and graciously delivered them from the bondage of Egypt and promised to do them good, they could not see him. All they could see, all they could think about were the bitter waters before them and the thirst within them. Because they saw nothing good in God's providence, they despised it. Do you know anyone like that? I blush to tell you I do. It is he who writes these lines. When these chosen, redeemed people should have remembered God's goodness, they thought only of their troubles. When they should have looked to their merciful Deliverer, they looked only upon Marah's bitter waters. When they should have prayed, they murmured. When they should have believed, they grumbled. 'But God, being full of compassion, forgave their iniquity, and destroyed them not ... For he remembered that they were but flesh' (Psalm 78:38, 39).

They had just before sung the song of salvation on the borders of the Red Sea. They had that great sight fresh in their minds. They had been redeemed. All their enemies were swallowed up in the sea. They were now on the march toward the Promised Land. Three days they have travelled into the wilderness, and found no water. When they came to Marah, though water was there in abundance, it was bitter and they could not drink it. They murmured against Moses; and Moses cried unto the Lord. When he did, the Lord showed him a tree, which when cast into the waters made them sweet.

114

Personal Application
Let every ransomed soul personally apply these things to himself. The Lord my God has brought me out of spiritual Egypt. He has led me by a new and living way, through the red sea of Christ's blood. He has put a new song in my heart, the Song of Moses and the Lamb. He has made himself my Strength, my Salvation, and my Redemption.

He brought Israel through the wilderness of Shur, so he is bringing you and me through the wilderness. We ought to expect experiences such as one is likely to find in a wilderness. This is not the Land of Promise. This is the wilderness. We ought never call into question the wisdom and goodness of our God for leading us through the wilderness. We should never doubt our Father's mercy, love, and grace because he sends us some bitter thing by which he has purposed to sweeten our souls and to sweeten himself to our souls!

O Lord God, as often as you bring me to the waters of Marah, show me the tree you showed Moses that day, Jesus Christ my crucified Saviour, cast him into my soul's experience, and make every bitter thing sweet!

God's Direction
Remember, it was God who brought Israel to Marah. He brought them here to teach them and to make himself known to them. And he did it to teach us and make himself known to us. 'All these things happened unto them for ensamples: and they are written for our admonition' (1 Corinthians 10:11). In his wise and adorable providence, The Lord Jesus, the God of Israel, brought the children of Israel to the bitter waters of Marah, so that he might make himself known to them as 'The LORD that Healeth Thee'.

Three Observations
Reading this portion of Holy Scripture and this experience in Israel's history, three things are obvious.

1. God does not deal with all people alike. This is evident from the picture before us. To the Egyptians, God's presence brought nothing but darkness and destruction. To the children of Israel, the presence of the Lord was their light and their salvation. Jehovah brought plagues to Egypt. He brought healing to Israel. God overthrew the armies of Egypt in the Red Sea. But he brought Israel through the sea upon dry ground.

Why did God treat the two nations with such distinct difference? The Jews certainly were not better people than the Egyptians. On the whole, the Israelites were just as wicked and corrupt as the Egyptians. So, the difference was not in themselves. The difference between Israel and Egypt was the difference of God's distinguishing grace. The Lord God made himself the God of Israel, by his own sovereign choice and covenant mercy. Thanks be unto God, he made a difference between Israel and Egypt, because he chose to make a difference. And he has done the same for us (1 Corinthians 4:7). Let us ever adore the grace of God, the sovereign grace of God that brings salvation to his elect people. Thanks be unto God, he has not dealt with us after our sins, nor rewarded us according to our iniquities! We gladly acknowledge, 'By the grace of God I am what I am'.

2. God does not deal with his own elect as we might expect. God seldom does things the way we expect him to. He does not deal with us according to our wishes, but according to his own infinite wisdom. He does not act according to our pleasure, but according to his own purpose. His ways are not our ways. And his thoughts are not our thoughts. Who would ever have imagined that God, who had given Egypt for the ransom of these Israelites, would then lead them into the wilderness of Shur? Who would have thought that God, who divided the Red Sea, would send his chosen ones three days into the desert without water? They looked for a Promised Land of milk and honey, but found Marah! We might have expected that Almighty God would cause water to gush out of the ground as soon as his people began to thirst, as he later caused it to gush out of the Rock; but it did not. God was determined, in love and mercy, to prove his children. So, they must be tried. He was determined to make himself known as 'The LORD that Healeth Thee'. But in order for him to be known as the Lord that heals, his beloved people had to be brought down to the place that they needed healing. Do you see the parallel? We are not in a dress parade. We are pilgrims in this world, marching through a bleak and barren wilderness to our land of promised rest. And ours is a stern march over rough ground, which flesh and blood would never choose. All along the way, God is proving us, teaching us, and preparing us for our promised rest.

The Egyptians had plenty of water. They had so much water they were drowned in it. But God's chosen ones did not even have enough water to quench their thirst. If they would drink, they had to seek water from the hand of their God. That is just the way it is in this world. The wicked seem to possess an abundance of the goods and comforts of this world, while God's elect must seek their daily bread by faith and prayer. Do not envy the prosperity of the wicked. The waters of a full cup are wrung out to them because God intends by these things to drown them in his wrath (Psalm 73:1-20; 92:7).

The Lord was teaching Israel to trust him. He was teaching them to long for and earnestly seek after the Land of Promise. And that is what he is doing for us. With every trial, he is saying, 'This is not your place of resting. Seek those things which are above, where Christ sitteth on the right hand of God. Set your affection on things above not on things on the earth. For ye are dead, and your life is hid with Christ in God' (Colossians 3:1-3). The only way to the City Beautiful is through the Slough of Despond and up the Hill Difficulty. This is the way to Canaan. This is the way you must go. We must through much tribulation enter into the kingdom of God. This is God's way, not ours. And God's way is best. The sooner we learn it the better.

3. There is a need for every trial and a necessity for every heartache that our heavenly Father sends. God has a reason for doing things the way he does them. And his reason is always gracious, loving, wise, and good. He will never cause his child a needless tear. By this grievous trial, the Lord caused Israel to see something of the corruption, unbelief, and vile ingratitude that was in their hearts.

If there had been no wilderness within, they would not have had to go through the wilderness of Shur. If there had not been a drought in their souls, they would not have had to endure the drought of the desert. If there had been no bitterness in their hearts, they would not have had to experience the bitter waters of Marah. God intends by our trials to show us our corruption, to teach us to trust him, and to correct his erring children. Child of God, there is a needs be for the things you suffer (Hebrews 12:5-12). I repeat, our Father's hand will never cause his child a needless tear.

Not only did God intend to show his people what was in them, he brought them to Marah because he was determined to show them what is in him. God brought Israel down to Marah so he might reveal himself to them under this name 'The LORD that Healeth Thee'. This is God's purpose in all the experiences of his people upon the earth. It is that we may know more and more of him. The Lord leads his people into the

117

wilderness of affliction, pain, and sorrow and causes us to thirst and cry after him, so that he might make us know his wisdom, power, goodness, and love to us in Christ Jesus. C. H. Spurgeon observed, 'Our lives are the canvas upon which the Lord paints his own character'. Whatever your trial, when it is over, if you belong to God, you will say as David, 'It is good for me that I have been afflicted' (Psalm 119:71). There is a need for your trials, else you would not have them. There is a necessity for every affliction, else you would not be required to endure it.

Healer of Trouble
First, the Lord Jesus is the healer of all our troubles. Who among God's saints has not learned by bitter experience that, though our days on earth be few, they are full of trouble? Perhaps you are going through a trial of great trouble right now. Perhaps God has brought you into trouble so that he might teach you to know him as 'The LORD that Healeth Thee'. I know whereof I speak by personal experience. 'This poor man cried, and the LORD heard him, and saved him out of all his troubles' (Psalm 34:6; 3:1-8; 2 Samuel 22:1-7, 17-20, 31).

When the children of Israel came to Marah, they found themselves in great trouble. The waters were bitter. They were dying of thirst. They had nothing to drink. They seemed to be mocked. There was plenty of water, but not an ounce to drink. Then, God intervened! He delivered them from their trouble by healing Marah's bitter waters. The Lord makes our waters of bitter trouble to be sweet in many ways.

Sometimes he simply changes our circumstances. How often have you been so greatly oppressed that you thought you could not endure another day of abuse? But, just when it looked as though you would be overcome, the Lord God removed the oppressor, or took you out of his reach. Many times I have been in a strait, not knowing what to do, or how to order my steps. I have come to the point where some decision must be made, but I knew not what to do. Then, the Lord stepped in and completely altered the whole affair. He opened the way before me. He took me by the hand and said, 'This is the way, walk in it'.

Sometimes the Lord turns our sorrow to joy and makes bitter waters sweet by injecting something unexpected that changes everything. He showed Moses a tree and directed him to cast it into the waters. 'When he cast it into the waters, the waters were made sweet'. The waters Israel could not endure became sweet to them because of the tree.

That tree, of course, refers to the person and work of our Lord Jesus Christ (Psalm 1:3; Song of Solomon 2:3; Revelation 22:2). No doubt this tree had always been at Marah. But God had to show it to Moses. And our Lord Jesus is always present with us in our troubles. He is the One who brings them. They come to us because of his gracious work as our Mediator. But until he reveals himself we cannot see him. But once we see his hand, the hand of our Redeemer, in our bitter waters, those waters become sweet (1 Thessalonians 5:16-18; Genesis 50:20).

Frequently, the Lord Jesus makes our waters of bitter trouble to be sweet simply by giving us satisfaction with his will. Nothing removes trouble from our hearts like submission to the will of God in the trouble he brings. Acquiescence in the will of God brings peace to the troubled heart quicker and more effectually than anything else (John 12:28). How often we cry out with Jacob, 'All these things are against me'. But, then, the Lord takes us down to the land of plenty and shows us our beloved Joseph upon his throne; and we are ashamed that we ever questioned his goodness.

All we have experienced should teach us that our God is able to make the most bitter things sweet. Past grace is his pledge of future grace. The name of God our Saviour is 'The LORD that Healeth Thee'. In the midst of all our troubles, let us ever worship him and trust him (John 14:1-3).

Healer of Sickness
Second, our ever-gracious God and Saviour is the healer of all our sicknesses. Certainly, sickness and disease are included in this promise of healing. They are specifically named. We are not among the foolish and ignorant charismatics, who pretend to have the apostolic gifts of healing. No man today possesses those gifts of the apostolic age. But let no one misunderstand this promise of God, or diminish its fulness. The name of God our Saviour is 'The LORD that Healeth Thee'.

This portion of Holy Scripture certainly assures us that all sickness and disease is the result of sin. Read verse 26 again. It is plainly stated that if we had no sin we would have no disease. If we were perfectly righteous, obedient, and sinless, we would never get sick. Though our bodies are redeemed by Christ, they are not yet changed. The change for our bodies will come later. The resurrection will do for our bodies what regeneration has done for our souls. But until these bodies are raised incorruptible, so long as we live in this world, we will have to suffer sickness and disease in one form or another. This body is yet under the sentence of death because of sin. It is left under the sentence of death, by divine purpose, to remind us of the effects of sin and its consequences.

If Christ had not redeemed us from sin, we would have to suffer eternal death in hell. And he has wisely left bodily sickness in us, sickness that will eventually bring bodily death, to remind us constantly what he has done for us in redemption, to make us both grateful and humble. All men get sick and die, young and old, because all are sinners. But those who are redeemed by the blood of Christ and saved by his grace have nothing to fear of either sickness or death.

Still, the Lord our God, 'The LORD that Healeth Thee', does heal his people from bodily sickness and disease. Our Lord Jesus is so much concerned about his tried and afflicted saints that he makes our bed in times of sickness (Psalm 41:3). He 'took our infirmities, and bare our sicknesses' (Matthew 8:17). He tells us plainly how to seek his healing power (James 5:14, 15).

Often the Lord heals us of sickness and disease by graciously preventing them (Psalm 91:4-16). We do not often think of it, but God's prevention of disease ought to be as much a matter of praise as his curing us of it. But, with us, what should inspire constant gratitude creates indifference. The healing hand of God is more conspicuously seen when we have been sick and graciously restored to health. Let us never attribute praise to the medicine we have taken, the doctors who have treated us, or to some ingenuity of our own. It is God alone who wounds and God alone who heals. Let God alone be praised.

Israel's experience at the waters of Marah also shows us plainly that our God uses ordained means for the healing of his sick people. The Lord God could have simply spoken the word and made the waters of Marah sweet. But he chose to use a specific means. Had Moses not cast in the tree, the waters would not have been healed. The use of means does not hinder faith. It proves faith. Believing God, Moses took a worthless tree and cast it into the waters. And the waters were healed. This is the first reference of healing mentioned in the Bible, and it was accomplished by the use of means. The healing was done by God. That tree had no healing virtue. But God used the tree to accomplish the healing.

In a similar way, the Lord healed the waters of Jericho when Elisha cast salt into them (2 Kings 2:19-22). God told Isaiah to lay a lump of figs upon Hezekiah's boils to heal him (2 Kings 20:7). Paul told Timothy to use a little wine for his stomach disorders (1 Timothy 5:23). And James told the sick to use both prayer and the anointing of oil for the healing of the sick (James 5:14, 15).

In every healing we experience, we have a pledge of the resurrection of the body. 'The LORD that Healeth Thee', who brings us up from the gates of death, will, at the time appointed, bring us up from the very pit of corruption. He who restores health to our bodies will restore life to our bodies in the resurrection.

Healer of Souls

This great God of ours, who heals the bitter waters of earthly trouble and bodily disease, is also the Healer of our souls!

He says, 'I am the LORD that healeth thee'. These bitter waters of Marah are an emblem of the bitter curses of the law, for that bitter thing sin, which makes for the bitter work of repentance. The law demands bitter plagues upon every sinner, even a bitter death in hell. It cannot give us peace. But Christ, the Tree of Life, was immersed under the curse of the law, and made a curse for us. He endured in our place the bitter wrath of God and suffered the bitter curses of the law to the full satisfaction of divine justice. Now, the law of God, once so bitter to our souls, is sweet, pleasant, lovely and comforting, because it is fully satisfied by Christ, our Substitute.

How is it God heals the sin sick soul? How does he remove the plague of our hearts? Look at Marah again, and you will see the answer.

First, the Lord made the people know how bitter the water was. There was no healing for the water until they had tasted its bitterness. But once they knew how bitter it was by nature, the Lord miraculously made it sweet to them. That is what happens in conversion. The Lord first makes sin bitter to us. He makes us see how corrupt and wretched we are by nature. He squeezes the cry from our hearts, 'O wretched man that I am'. Then, he heals us by his grace. This is God's way with men. First, he wounds, then he heals. First, he strips, then he clothes. First, he humbles, then he exalts. First, he kills, then he makes alive.

Second, before the waters were healed, prayer was made to God. The prayer of Moses did not heal the waters. But until he called upon the name of the Lord, the waters were not healed. And you will not be healed of your sin and your heart's plague until you call upon God for mercy through Christ Jesus (Romans 10:9-13).

Still, something else was needed. So, third, the waters were healed when the tree was cast into them. You know what the tree represents? It speaks of two things. The tree is a picture of Christ himself (Revelation 22:2), and a picture of the cross upon which our Saviour put away our sins and brought in everlasting righteousness for us (1 Peter 2:24). We can only be saved, healed of our soul's plague, when the work of Christ is imputed to us and his grace and righteousness are imparted to us. We are saved when Christ himself comes into our hearts by the power of his Spirit and makes all things new.

Fourth, once the tree was cast into the waters, they were completely healed. The waters of Marah, once so vile and bitter, were made to be the sweetest waters on the earth, once the tree was cast in. And God's elect, so vile and bitter in themselves, are made perfect and holy once they have Christ, and have his work put in them. When God heals a soul, it is healed forever, and healed completely, so there is not even a trace of sin or its bitterness.

This is the name of God our Saviour, 'The LORD that Healeth Thee'. He heals all our troubles. He heals all our sicknesses. And he heals our souls. If you have not yet trusted him, trust him now. He can and will heal you by the power of his grace!

Healer All-sufficient
'And they came to Elim, where were twelve wells of water, and threescore and ten palm trees: and they encamped there by the waters' (v. 27).

Israel found twelve wells of water and seventy palm trees at Elim, a well for every tribe and a tree for every elder. This tells us that there are 'times of refreshing' to follow the waters of Marah (Acts 3:19). And it tells us that the grace of our Lord Jesus Christ is grace sufficient for our souls, grace sufficient for all the Israel of God. May the Lord God, 'The LORD that Healeth Thee', make that grace yours, for Christ's sake.

Chapter 74

'Between Elim And Sinai'

'And they took their journey from Elim, and all the congregation of the children of Israel came unto the wilderness of Sin, which is between Elim and Sinai, on the fifteenth day of the second month after their departing out of the land of Egypt. And the whole congregation of the children of Israel murmured against Moses and Aaron in the wilderness: And the children of Israel said unto them, Would to God we had died by the hand of the LORD in the land of Egypt, when we sat by the flesh pots, and when we did eat bread to the full; for ye have brought us forth into this wilderness, to kill this whole assembly with hunger ... And Moses said unto Aaron, Take a pot, and put an omer full of manna therein, and lay it up before the LORD, to be kept for your generations. As the LORD commanded Moses, so Aaron laid it up before the Testimony, to be kept. And the children of Israel did eat manna forty years, until they came to a land inhabited; they did eat manna, until they came unto the borders of the land of Canaan. Now an omer is the tenth part of an ephah.'
(Exodus 16:1-36)

In this chapter God the Holy Ghost shows us two gifts of grace given to the church of God in the wilderness of Sin. Elim was a place of palm trees and wells of water (Exodus 15:27). There the children of Israel enjoyed great refreshing from the presence of the Lord. It was a place of bounteous blessing, signifying the all-sufficient grace of God in Christ for his elect. In Elim there were twelve wells of water, a well for each of the twelve tribes of Israel. There were seventy palm trees, symbols of victory in Elim, one for each of Israel's seventy elders. Elim represents God's all-sufficient, unfailing and distinguishing grace in Christ, it also represents the bounty and fulness of our inheritance in the world to come as the Israel of God, with Christ our Saviour.

Sinai was the place where God gave his law by the hand of Moses. Elim portrays grace. There is nothing at Sinai but darkness, thunder, lightning and curses. In Exodus 16 we find the children of Israel between Elim and Sinai, between the place of blessedness and the place of everlasting cursedness, in a place called 'The Wilderness of Sin'.[3]

---

[3] Robert Hawker's Poor Man's Portions (July 22 – Evening) My soul! Thou art still in a wilderness state, not yet arrived home to thy Father's house; and thou art frequently exercised with wilderness dispensations. Perhaps, under the Spirit's teaching, an evening's meditation on the wilderness of sin, where Israel sojourned, will be profitable to thee. Let faith lead thee thither, and see what subjects are there opened before thee.

Was there ever an instance like Israel, which was brought out with a high hand, and stretched out arm, from the tyranny of Egypt? Did the sea open a path for them to march through; and that memorable spot, which to them became the way of salvation, became to their enemies that pursued them, the pit of destruction? Did the Lord go before them in a pillar of cloud by day and cover them from danger by the pillar of fire by night? After such miracles, yea, in the moment of receiving the same continuance of divine favour, while on their way to Canaan, what was there in the people's passing through the wilderness of sin, that should have discomposed their minds, or made them call in question God's faithfulness and his love? Thou knowest, my soul, what the Scripture hath recorded of the events of the wilderness to Israel. Though their history furnisheth a continued series of the Lord's mercies over them, yet, on their part, little else can be found but rebellion, unthankfulness, and sin.

Pause, and let the apostle's question have its full weight upon thee. 'What then? (saith he) are we better than they? No, in no wise; for we have before proved, both Jews and Gentiles, that they are all under sin.' Was there ever an instance of grace like this, my soul, so great, so distinguishing, so abounding, when the Lord found thee in the Egypt of thy fallen nature, and when he brought thee out with a sovereign hand? Did Jesus open to thee a new and living way through his blood? And dost thou not know, that his cross, which is thy glory, and thy salvation, will be the condemnation of all the enemies who despise it? Is thy Lord leading thee, going before thee, and following thee, in grace, and goodness, and mercy, all the days of thy life, like the pillar of cloud, and the pillar of fire, to Israel, and bringing thee by a 'right way, to a city of

The word used for Sin here means 'thorn'. It is where you and I live in this world. 'The Wilderness of Thorns!' This world is a place of pain and discomfort, a place of thorns, because of sin. Every pleasant, appealing berry that grows in this 'wilderness of sin', is surrounded with thorns. To enjoy the berry you will feel the prick of the thorn.

---

habitation?' Are these among the daily manifestations of thy Lord? And shall thy passage (for thou knowest that it is but a passage) through the wilderness of sin make thee for a moment lose sight of Jesus?

True, thou art exercised; and thine exercises appear to thee so peculiarly distressing, as if no one of God's people before had ever been so circumstanced. But in them thou shouldest mark the wisdom, as well as the love of him that appoints them. Didst thou trace Jesus in all, thou wouldest find a sanctified blessing in all; and the issue of thy heaviest trials would then bring in an exact proportion of the sweetest comforts.

It is because they are peculiar, that they are suited to thee. There are numberless things which occur in the exercises of thy brethren, which to thee would be no exercises at all. They feel them, and know their pressure, and the love of Jesus in sending them, and the tenderness of Jesus in helping them under them, and bringing them out of them. All these things thou seest and knowest in others, and findest cause both to admire and to adore the divine faithfulness in the dispensations. But in the study and improvement of the exercises in thine own heart, which, of all others, is the most important, here thou failest. And yet thou art convinced, in a cool hour, when grace is alive, that if a synod of angels were to arrange the circumstances of thy state, they could not order them with the wisdom and love that they are now ordered with. Go then, my soul, go by faith, frequently to the wilderness of sin. Look at Israel's history, and look up for wisdom to gather suitable instruction. Behold Jesus in every dispensation. Whatever tends to lead thee to him must be blessed. It is impossible that any trial, be it what it may, can be otherwise than blessed, which opens to the view Jesus therein, and endears and makes Jesus precious thereby.

And, my soul, while I wish thee frequently to go by solemn meditation to the wilderness of sin, let each renewed visit remind thee that thou art getting through it. Like children at school, every day brings on the festival which will take us home to our Father's house. A few steps more, a few exercises more, and Jesus will send his chariot for us. Yea, he will come himself to fetch us; and we shall take an everlasting farewell both of the wilderness of sin and this world of sorrow together.

'Haste, haste, my beloved, and be thou like to a roe, or to a young hart, upon the mountains of spices.'

Our Depravity

The first thing that strikes me as I read this chapter in Israel's history is that we are a depraved, sinful people, in constant need of grace and forgiveness (Exodus 16:2, 3). Remember, it has only been a month since they came out of Egypt. In just one month they experienced deliverance by the Lord God through the blood of the paschal lamb, spoiled the Egyptians, walked through the Red Sea, saw Pharaoh and his armies slain upon the shores of the sea, and sang with Moses and Miriam the praises of Jehovah.

'And the whole congregation of the children of Israel murmured against Moses and Aaron in the wilderness: And the children of Israel said unto them, Would to God we had died by the hand of the LORD in the land of Egypt, when we sat by the flesh pots, and when we did eat bread to the full; for ye have brought us forth into this wilderness, to kill this whole assembly with hunger' (Exodus 16:2, 3).

How like these murmuring Israelites we are! We ought to look at our trials and the trials of our brethren and think of God's providence, the benefit of the chastening rod and the sweetness of the Father's tender care, never causing his child a needless tear. O Spirit of God, graciously teach us not to murmur against our God, but to 'rejoice in the Lord', and in everything to give thanks, knowing that whatever we experience is 'the will of God in Christ Jesus concerning' our souls.

Heavenly Manna

Yet, as they murmured, God bestowed mercy! As they grumbled, he was gracious! They deserved wrath, he gave grace. The food provided for the chosen tribes had never been seen before by human eye, nor touched by human hand. 'They knew not what it was.' Manna stands before us as a type and emblem of our Lord Jesus Christ, the Bread of Life, salvation's feast (John 6:31-35, 41-43, 48-58).

'Our fathers did eat manna in the desert; as it is written, He gave them bread from heaven to eat. Then Jesus said unto them, Verily, verily, I say unto you, Moses gave you not that bread from heaven; but my Father giveth you the true bread from heaven. For the bread of God is he which cometh down from heaven, and giveth life unto the world. Then said they unto him, Lord, evermore give us this bread. And Jesus said unto them, I am the bread of life: he that cometh to me shall never hunger; and he that believeth on me shall never thirst' (John 6:31-35).

'The Jews then murmured at him, because he said, I am the bread which came down from heaven. And they said, Is not this Jesus, the son of Joseph, whose father and mother we know? how is it then that he saith, I came down from heaven? Jesus therefore answered and said unto them, Murmur not among yourselves' (John 6:41-43).

'I am that bread of life. Your fathers did eat manna in the wilderness, and are dead. This is the bread which cometh down from heaven, that a man may eat thereof, and not die. I am the living bread which came down from heaven: if any man eat of this bread, he shall live forever: and the bread that I will give is my flesh, which I will give for the life of the world. The Jews therefore strove among themselves, saying, How can this man give us his flesh to eat? Then Jesus said unto them, Verily, verily, I say unto you, Except ye eat the flesh of the Son of man, and drink his blood, ye have no life in you. Whoso eateth my flesh, and drinketh my blood, hath eternal life; and I will raise him up at the last day. For my flesh is meat indeed, and my blood is drink indeed. He that eateth my flesh, and drinketh my blood, dwelleth in me, and I in him. As the living Father hath sent me, and I live by the Father: so, he that eateth me, even he shall live by me. This is that bread which came down from heaven: not as your fathers did eat manna, and are dead: he that eateth of this bread shall live forever' (John 6:48-58).

Gracious God

What a gracious God our God is! Let us learn this from the manna that fell in the wilderness. The children of Israel were hungry. Oppressed with great hunger, the journeying multitude murmured from their fretting hearts against the Lord. Their muttering reached the ears of the Most High. But he did not react to their murmurings as we might expect. The Lord Jehovah does not send forth swift bolts of lightning to destroy the ungrateful, murmuring mob! No!

The Lord our God is full of pity. He delights in mercy. He who is our God is love. He opens heaven, and pours down mighty supplies of bread. The supply is a miracle, a miraculous display of our blessed Saviour, teaching us today and feeding us today, as clearly as it did those millions of old. Upon thankless sinners, the Lord God pours out tender mercies!

But God's goodness in bestowing food pales into insignificance in the bright and shining light of Christ's redemption and gift of eternal life in him! If we would see grace in its zenith, we must look to Mount Calvary. In Adam's loins we stood before the holy Lord God; lost, ruined, and undone as one leprous mass of misery and sin, shameless, tearless, and prayerless. Then mercy took up the cause of the fallen, and promised that a Saviour would descend from heaven, the Seed of a woman, the incarnate God!

The manna fell upon the earth in darkness. It was in the night when this soft shower fell upon the earth. 'When the dew fell upon the camp in the night, the manna fell upon it'. So it was when Christ came. Spiritual blindness was the world's thick shroud when the Sun of Righteousness arose with healing in his wings. And so, it is when his grace first touches the sinner's heart. Our great Saviour finds the heart of man all darkness, a black mass of midnight gloom.

When morning came, the dew became manna and was obvious to the sight of all. Henry Law observed, 'Thus for a while Jesus lies hidden in the Word and ordinances, and gospel-rites, which fall in thick and sparkling abundance around our homes. It is not until the Sun of Righteousness arises, that the real treasure is discerned.'

The manna was small, and round, and white and sweet. Each of these things tells much about our Saviour. It was small. It was like a little seed on the ground. Pride might look upon it and sneer. Can this insignificant thing be from heaven? So it was with our blessed Christ. He appeared in utter humility. No signs of royalty or divinity were upon him. No place was found for him. He came in the lowliness of our nature. He appeared as the lowliest of men. His highest station upon earth was in the deep valley of humiliation (2 Corinthians 8:9; Philippians 2:5-8). Meekness was his majesty. Abasement was his glory. He put on our flesh, to clothe us in his bright glory. He sank to nothingness, to exalt us above all greatness. He lived and died in shame, contempt, and pain, that we might reign in all the honour of his glory.

The manna was round. Its circle was without beginning and without end. Behold our eternal Saviour! Who can tell his beginning? Who can calculate the length of his days? Look through the ages of eternity past. In all he lives unchanged, unchangeable. Look through the ages of eternity to come. He still lives unchanged, unchangeable. What an ocean of delight this is, as wide as the breadth and length of our Saviour's love! He declares himself to be he who 'was, and is, and is to come' (Revelation 4:8). In all the vast expanse of his eternality, our great High Priest has had us in his hand and in his heart. That will never change. We are forever one with him!

The manna was white. It covered the muck and mire of the filthy earth, stained by the feet and waste of man and beast. The manna's spotless hue proved its descent to be from above. Again, we see our blessed Lord Jesus. Every look of his eye, every word of his mouth, and every step of his feet are as dazzling and bright as the holiness of heaven. He was the Righteousness of God embodied in the flesh of man. He walked through this earth as perfect as God is perfect, the perfect God-man. He ever shined as the Light of the world, untainted as a beam from the mid-day sun. It could not be otherwise. Redemption required it. He who would redeem us from sin must be without sin. Would you be blameless, without sin before God? Eat this Manna. Trust the Lord Jesus Christ.

The manna was sweet, too. It was nourishing; and the nourishment brought pleasure to the taste. 'The taste of it was like wafers made with honey' (v. 31). Our Lord Jesus Christ is all sweetness to the feasting soul. Taste and see it is so! What can be sweeter than the redemption that is ours in Christ? In and by him all our sins are fully and forever pardoned, all guilt fully and forever cancelled, all debt fully and forever paid, all pledges of glory faithfully and forever pledged!

How delightful and sweet it is to our souls to gaze with open eye on a reconciled Father's smile, to enjoy the comfort, instruction, strength, and guidance of the indwelling Spirit of God, to know that the angels of God are ministering spirits sent forth to minister to our souls, to realize all things work together for our good and that all things present and to come are our sure heritage, because we are Christ's and Christ is ours! Christ is this sweet manna. Feast upon him and live forever.

Gathered by All
Each day the manna fell; but it had to be gathered by every man in Israel. Every day the multitude was busy in the field. The manna fell thick, in great abundance, and was gathered by the hands of hungry Israelites. O my soul, let it be my daily work to gather the Bread of Heaven! Christ must be received by faith (John 1:12). Each one must receive Christ for himself, and we must feed upon our Saviour daily.

For each one there was exact sufficiency. Each one had enough. Those who gathered much had nothing left over; and those who gathered little had plenty. Great as our souls' needs are, Christ is sufficient, his grace is sufficient. Though our sins abound beyond measure, where sin abounds his grace still much more abounds. Live, child of God, every day, bathe in the Saviour's blood, trust the Saviour's righteousness, and seek the Saviour's grace. You will find his grace sufficient. Then, with Jacob, you can say, 'I have enough' (Genesis 33:11). You will have enough but none to spare. Each one must gather according to his own eating for himself. 'According to your faith be it unto you' (Matthew 9:29). Gather the children's Bread and live forever. Even if you gather only the crumbs, you will find this Bread sufficient for all your soul's needs. But the manna was daily food, only good for the day it was gathered. It could not be hoarded or stored for the future. So, Christ is our daily bread.

Though the manna did not come by human effort, it did not encourage or cause sloth or indifference. So, it is with Christ and his salvation. He is altogether free. He saves sinners freely by his grace, without them exercising any effort or doing anything. Yet, saved sinners serve him and one another with fervent love and zeal. The manna sustained the bodies of the children of Israel for a little while; but it could not keep anyone from dying. Though they gathered manna and ate in the wilderness, they died there, too. But Christ is the Bread of Life. He is manna that gives eternal life to all who eat. He promises, 'I am the living bread, which came down from heaven, if any man eat of this bread, he shall live forever; and the bread that I will give is my flesh, which I will give for the life of the world.'

Standing Miracle
The manna was a standing miracle in the wilderness for forty years. It was found every day, six days a week, for forty years, throughout the wilderness march. That, too, is a picture of our dear Saviour. He is a standing miracle of grace, an enduring supply for all life's weary way.

The manna began to fall from heaven from the time the Israelites arrived in the wilderness of Sin, which was the sixteenth day of the second month after their departure from Egypt, until they came to Canaan. Yet, it never fell on the sabbath. The miracle is even more astounding when we remember there was enough manna every morning to satisfy the daily hunger of millions of people for all those forty years. Remember, too, that every Friday there was twice as much manna on the ground. The manna was so delicate and perishable that, if kept for just one day, it bred worms and stank. Yet, to teach Israel to reverence the sabbath, that which was kept for the sabbath did not spoil. The omer laid up before the Lord in the ark of the covenant was preserved for hundreds of years.

Unrelenting Mercy

The manna was to Israel a gift of enduring mercy. Though they rebelled and often sinned against the Lord, there was never a day the manna was not provided.

'And the children of Israel did eat manna forty years, until they came to a land inhabited; they did eat manna, until they came unto the borders of the land of Canaan' (Exodus 16:35).

What a fit portrayal this is of our blessed Saviour, the Lord Jesus Christ, and God's unrelenting mercy to our poor souls in and by him! Though we rebel against him, mercy is not suspended. Though we murmur, his grace still abounds. Though we sin and forget him, he will not forget us, and will not forget to be gracious. Though we fail in our duty, our Saviour does not fail in his love. Morning after morning, mercy still comes. Day after day, grace is sure. Not a day, or an hour is omitted. Our blessed Saviour is all this and more. 'For it shall come to pass, that before my people call, (he declares) I will answer; and while they are speaking, I will hear' (Isaiah 65:24).

Here is another sweet thought. As Israel had no other sustenance until they came into the Land of Canaan, so God's elect have no other sustenance in this world than Christ, and desire no other, until they come into their Canaan above. In Christ, there is a boundless fulness of grace and life, and of glory, too. Help me, my Lord, to feed on you and on your great salvation by faith. O Spirit of God, let my meditation of him be sweet! 'I will sing unto the LORD as long as I live: I will sing praise to my God while I have my being. My meditation of him shall be sweet: I will be glad in the LORD' (Psalm 104:33, 34).

When time's crumbs are no more needed, eternity's full feast begins. Sweet is the present taste of grace; but what will be the heavenly feast?

An Instructive Memorial

In verses 33 and 34 a specific command was given to Aaron to gather an omer of manna to be kept as a memorial to Israel of God's great provision for his people. 'Moses said unto Aaron, Take a pot, and put an omer full of manna therein, and lay it up before the LORD, to be kept for your generations. As the LORD commanded Moses, so Aaron laid it up before the Testimony, to be kept.'

An omer of manna was placed in a golden pot inside the ark of the covenant, under the mercy seat. That ark of the covenant was itself located in the Holy of Holies, where the high priest sprinkled the atonement blood once a year. The manna under the blood was a lasting declaration to Israel that they obtained deliverance, were sustained by bread in the wilderness, and came into the land of rest by the blood of the paschal lamb.

The whole thing is a picture of Christ and our salvation by him. Christ is the Paschal Lamb slain for us, by whom God's elect are delivered from death, hell, and sin, and redeemed from the curse of the law, by whom we have salvation. Christ is our Salvation, the Bread upon which we feed day by day in this world. Christ will bring us into our heavenly Canaan. He is our acceptance in the holy place. And our blessed Lord Jesus has given us a reminder of these things in the bread and wine of the Lord's Supper.

Blessed Sabbath Rest

Bread is a great blessing. Indeed, bread is a necessity. Without it, we could not live. It is a great gift of grace that is ours in Christ. Let us never cease to give thanks to our God for Christ our daily Bread. But there is another necessity of life, one that is equally necessary and equally blessed. That is rest.

'And it came to pass, that on the sixth day they gathered twice as much bread, two omers for one man: and all the rulers of the congregation came and told Moses. And he said unto them, This is that which the LORD hath said, Tomorrow is the rest of the holy sabbath unto the LORD: bake that which ye will bake to day, and seethe that ye will seethe; and that which remaineth over lay up for you to be kept until the morning. And they laid it up till the morning, as Moses bade: and it did not stink, neither was there any worm therein. And Moses said, Eat that today; for today is a sabbath unto the LORD: today ye shall not find it in the field. Six days ye shall gather it; but on the seventh day, which is the sabbath, in it there shall be none. And it came to pass, that there went out some of the people on the seventh day for to gather, and they found none. And the LORD said unto Moses, How long refuse ye to keep my commandments and my laws? See, for that the LORD hath given you the sabbath, therefore he giveth you on the sixth day the bread of two days; abide ye every man in his place, let no man go out of his place on the seventh day. So, the people rested on the seventh day' (Exodus 16:22-30).

Here we have the first mention of the sabbath. Notice how the sabbath is described in verse 23. It is called 'the rest of the holy sabbath unto the LORD'. Like the manna and like the water gushing out of the rock, this blessed sabbath rest is a picture of our Lord Jesus Christ and the boundless grace of God given to us in him.

> The sabbath day, that day of rest,
> Was sanctified and blest,
> To point us to our Saviour Christ,
> In whom alone is rest.
>
> That legal sabbath ended when
> Christ died and rose again.
> Yet, there's a sabbath that remains,
> A rest that's found in Him.
>
> 'Come unto Me', the Saviour said,
> 'And I will give you rest'.
> O weary sinners, cease from works,
> Trust Christ and find sweet rest.
>
> Ah, sweet refreshment for my soul,
> The rest of faith is rest!
> Ceasing from works, I trust God's Son,
> Christ is my Sabbath Rest!

This ordinance of sabbath observance was established by God in the wilderness at the same time that manna was given from heaven. The manna portrayed God's provision of life in Christ, the Bread of Life. The sabbath portrayed God's provision of rest in Christ. It is specifically called, 'the rest of the holy sabbath unto the LORD'. 'So, the people rested on the seventh day.'

The children of Israel were commanded not to do any work on the sabbath. They were not even allowed to pick up manna on the seventh day of the week. In Exodus 20:8-11 God's law strictly prohibited any man from doing any work on Saturday, and prohibited him from having anyone under his authority do any work for him. Those who would impose upon us the carnal ordinance of sabbath keeping, who would bring us back under the yoke of bondage to the law, compelling us to keep the sabbath day, compel us to do what they themselves cannot do. I know many teach sabbath-keeping as a 'rule of life'. They would impose upon God's saints strict rules and regulations for sabbath day observance. But all their teaching and preaching in that regard is sheer hypocrisy. Not one of them observes the sabbath day. Their teaching regarding the sabbath is just 'a fair show in the flesh' (Galatians 6:12, 13), and no more. Their pretended reverence for the law of God, when examined closely reveals a total disregard for God's law. They sift through the commandments, pick out what they like, and ignore the rest. Let me show you what I mean. Here are four things required in God's law for the observance of the sabbath day. If the sabbath day is observed it must be observed in such a way as to include all four of these things.

The sabbath day must be observed on Saturday, the seventh day of the week (Exodus 20:10). Sunday is not the sabbath day. It never has been. Sunday is once called 'the Lord's Day', but only once, and then with no instructions of any kind about the matter. It was the day of Christ's resurrection. But nowhere in the Bible are we commanded, or even permitted, to observe the sabbath on Sunday.

No work can be done on the sabbath. None! (Exodus 20:10). Works of necessity and works of mercy were permitted on the sabbath; but no one was allowed to do any work of any kind for himself, or to benefit himself. If you want to keep the sabbath day, in accordance with God's holy law, then you must not, under penalty of death, light a fire for cooking (Exodus 35:3), gather wood for burning (Numbers 15:32-36), carry any burden (Jeremiah 17:21, 22), travel (Exodus 16:29), or do any business (Amos 8:5). Anything which might be construed as a matter of personal profit or pleasure was expressly forbidden on the sabbath day (Isaiah 56:2; 58:13; Ezekiel 20:12, 21). The essence of sabbath worship was absolute, unreserved, unconditional, all-encompassing self-denial. It was an utter renunciation of self and an utter dedication of one's self to the Lord God.

In addition, any genuine observance of the sabbath day necessitates a return to the ceremonial law of the Old Testament. The sabbath day cannot be observed without the offering of a double sin offering, a double meal offering, and a double drink-offering; and those offerings must be made in the temple at Jerusalem (Numbers 28:9, 10).

There is one more point, which cannot be ignored. Those who insist upon keeping the sabbath must also demand the execution of all sabbath breakers (Exodus 31:15). The same law that required the observance of the sabbath also required the death of those who broke the sabbath. If a man wants to keep the sabbath, he must also be willing to stone to death anyone who breaks the sabbath, even his own son or daughter.

Do you know anyone who observes the sabbath day this way? I do not. Not even the most orthodox Jew, the most strict Adventist, or the most heretical Russellite in the world observes such a sabbath. And those who pretend to observe a Sunday sabbath do not even come close to the requirements of God's Word regarding sabbath observance.

It is obvious no one observes the sabbath day in a literal sense, and no one has for more than 2,000 years. Jews do not observe it. Catholics do not observe it. Protestants do not observe it. Reformed people do not observe it. Those who pretend to observe it only make a mockery of the sabbath by their hypocrisy. Their sabbath keeping is nothing but a fleshly show!

Christ is our Sabbath. True sabbath rest is faith in Christ. 'Come unto me, all ye that labour and are heavy laden, and I will give you rest. Take my yoke upon you, and learn of me; for I am meek and lowly in heart: and ye shall find rest unto your souls. For my yoke is easy, and my burden is light' (Matthew 11:28-30).

Here the Son of God, the Lord of glory, the God-man Mediator, our all-glorious Christ, bids weary, heavy laden sinners to come to him and find rest for their souls. 'Come unto me, all ye that labour and are heavy laden, and I will give you rest.' There is no salvation to be had, but by coming to Christ. There can never be any true, peaceful, satisfying rest for our souls, except we come to Christ, trusting him alone as our Lord and Saviour, his blood for our atonement, his obedience our only righteousness. Only he can give weary sinners rest.

Here is the Master's word to us all, both to the unbeliever and the believer. 'Take my yoke upon you, and learn of me; for I am meek and lowly in heart: and you shall find rest unto your souls.' In all circumstances of life, we find rest unto our souls only as we voluntarily submit to the rule and dominion of the Son of God as our Lord and King. The only way to find rest is to willingly slip our necks under his yoke. When we do, and only when we do, we will find his yoke really is easy and his burden really is light. I bid you now, whatever your circumstances, take the Master's yoke upon you, and find rest unto your soul. Take upon you the yoke of his grace, bowing to him as your Lord (Luke 14:25-33). Take upon you the yoke of his doctrine, his gospel, bowing to him as your Prophet (Jeremiah 6:16). Take upon you his yoke of providence, trusting him as your God and Saviour (Psalm 31:1, 5, 7, 15). Only in this way do we find rest for our souls.

'Come unto me, all ye that labour and are heavy laden, and I will give you rest. Take my yoke upon you, and learn of me; for I am meek and lowly in heart: and ye shall find rest unto your souls. For my yoke is easy, and my burden is light.' The call of the gospel is a call to rest, the blessed rest of faith in Christ. It is this rest that the Old Testament sabbath day pointed to and typified. All things relating to sabbath law in the Old Testament pointed to the necessity and blessedness of the rest of faith which believers enjoy in Christ.

Let every hungry soul, 'Come and dine'. Feast upon the Manna, the Bread of Life, Christ Jesus, and live forever. Let every weary, heavy-laden sinner 'Come and rest'. Quit your works and come to Christ; and he will give you rest.

Chapter 75

Christ The Smitten Rock

'And all the congregation of the children of Israel journeyed from the wilderness of Sin, after their journeys, according to the commandment of the LORD, and pitched in Rephidim: and there was no water for the people to drink. Wherefore the people did chide with Moses, and said, Give us water that we may drink. And Moses said unto them, Why chide ye with me? Wherefore do ye tempt the LORD? And the people thirsted there for water; and the people murmured against Moses, and said, Wherefore is this that thou hast brought us up out of Egypt, to kill us and our children and our cattle with thirst? And Moses cried unto the LORD, saying, What shall I do unto this people? They be almost ready to stone me. And the LORD said unto Moses, Go on before the people, and take with thee of the elders of Israel; and thy rod, wherewith thou smotest the river, take in thine hand, and go. Behold, I will stand before thee there upon the rock in Horeb; and thou shalt smite the rock, and there shall come water out of it, that the people may drink. And Moses did so in the sight of the elders of Israel. And he called the name of the place Massah, and Meribah, because of the chiding of the children of Israel, and because they tempted the LORD, saying, Is the LORD among us, or not?'
(Exodus 17:1-7)

How bitter that trial was that Israel experienced at Marah! Marah's bitter waters mocked their parched lips. But sweet relief was near. The Lord showed Moses a tree, which he cast into the waters. As soon as he cast that tree into Marah's bitter waters, the bitter was made sweet, and vexation was turned into joy. Painful as that trial was, it was but the prelude to more painful and more bitter trials to follow.

Now we find the congregation of the Lord in Rephidim, in the depths of the desert. There are no streams of water, no wells, just dry, barren desert. They thirst and search for water; but their search is in vain. There is nothing before them but dry sand. As with Israel in the wilderness, so it is for God's elect in this world. Troubles die only to live again.

This is the experience of Zion's pilgrims. Darkness flees as the sun rises; but soon it returns. Afflictions clear away, but soon reappear, often with greater heaviness. Joseph escapes the pit, then the dungeon binds him fast. David, safe from Adullam's cave, must seek refuge in Engedi's wilds. Troops of lusts we hoped had been conquered by grace, with mustered force assail us again when least expect. Weeds of evil, long ago plucked up, rear their noxious heads over and over again. Satan lays Abraham low in Egypt, and shoots an arrow from the same shaft in Gerar. Be certain, the ebbing tide will roll in again tomorrow.

We must never dream of undisturbed rest in this world. Until we drop this flesh forever, we live in a ceaseless cycle of temptation and sorrow. But we must not despise the trials of providence by which our heavenly Father teaches his children to trust him and the Saviour weans us from this world. The chastening rod in our Father's hand has a teaching voice. 'The LORD'S voice crieth unto the city, and the man of wisdom shall see thy name: hear ye the rod, and who hath appointed it' (Micah 6:9). Spirit of God, give me grace to hear the rod.

By these trials the hidden vileness of our hearts and the vast riches of our Saviour's grace are both made known to us. Is that not obvious here in Exodus 17? The murmurings of the chosen people betray the bias of the human heart to what is evil. Yet, against the black backdrop of Israel's sin, the light of God's goodness shines brightly and we see the golden glories of the Lord. The people chide and tempt their God. Moses seeks the open refuge of a mercy seat. How precious is this spot! A gracious answer allays all fears, and soon supplies all need.

'And the LORD said unto Moses, Go on before the people, and take with thee of the elders of Israel; and thy rod, wherewith thou smotest the river, take in thine hand, and go. Behold, I will stand before thee there upon the rock in Horeb; and thou shalt smite the rock, and there shall come water out of it, that the people may drink. And Moses did so in the sight of the elders of Israel' (vv. 5, 6).

Moses did just as he was told; and as the leaders looked on, water gushed out. Let us draw near in reverence. The ground upon which we stand is holy ground. That Rock is Christ. That gash is his wounded side. Those streams are his abundant grace.

The Spirit of God declares plainly in 1 Corinthians 10:11, 'Now all these things happened unto them for ensamples (types): and they are written for our admonition, upon whom the ends of the world are come'. Be sure you get this. It is impossible to understand the covenants, the promises, the worship, or the events of the Old Testament until you see their spiritual significance and spiritual fulfilment in Christ.

The children of Israel enjoyed many great blessings from God, typical of the blessings we receive in Christ. Having been delivered from the bondage of Egypt by the blood of the paschal lamb, which was a type of our redemption by Christ, the whole nation of Israel began a pilgrimage to the promised place of rest. Their journey through the wilderness to Canaan was a picture of the believer's life in this world. This world is a wilderness. We are strangers and pilgrims passing through this land, pressing onward toward heaven, the promised place of rest. Here we live by faith. We are fed, clothed, refreshed, and protected in our pilgrimage by the hand of God. Read 1 Corinthians 10:1-4. There the Apostle Paul, writing by divine inspiration, shows us some of the blessings the typical people enjoyed in their pilgrimage.

'Moreover, brethren, I would not that ye should be ignorant, how that all our fathers were under the cloud, and all passed through the sea; And were all baptized unto Moses in the cloud and in the sea; And did all eat the same spiritual meat; And did all drink the same spiritual drink: for they drank of that spiritual Rock that followed them: and that Rock was Christ' (1 Corinthians 10:1-4).

At the beginning of the journey, they were all baptized (vv. 1, 2). They were all fed with bread from heaven (v. 3). The manna that fell from heaven was a picture of Christ the Bread of Life (John 6:31-58). They were all refreshed with the same spiritual drink (v. 4). God gave them water from the Rock which Moses had smitten, just at the time they were about to die of thirst. That water was to them the water of life, which represents the Holy Spirit, the Water of Life, that we who believe receive from Christ.

'In the last day, that great day of the feast, Jesus stood and cried, saying, If any man thirst, let him come unto me, and drink. He that believeth on me, as the scripture hath said, out of his belly shall flow rivers of living water. (But this spake he of the Spirit, which they that believe on him should receive: for the Holy Ghost was not yet given; because that Jesus was not yet glorified)' (John 7:37-39).

Then Paul plainly tells us, 'that Rock was Christ'. That Rock which was smitten by Moses, from which the life-giving water gushed out to save the children of Israel, was a typical picture, representation, and symbol of the Lord Jesus Christ, our Saviour, the smitten Lamb of God from whom, in whom, with whom, and by whom we have eternal life. The Lord Jesus Christ is the Rock of Salvation, smitten by God, out of whom the Living Water of Life flows to perishing sinners.

The Rock

First, I want you to see that the Rock itself is a clear type of the Lord Jesus Christ. 'The Rock' is a title frequently given to the Lord Jesus, by which he identifies himself, and by which his people honour and worship him. In his song of praise to God, Moses lamented that Israel 'forsook God who made him and lightly esteemed the Rock of his salvation' (Deuteronomy 32:15). David also sang praises to the Rock, saying, 'The LORD is my rock, and my fortress, and my deliverer: The God of my rock; in him will I trust: he is my shield, and the horn of my salvation, my high tower, and my refuge, my saviour; thou savest me from violence' (2 Samuel 22:2, 3). The Psalmist admonishes us to sing to God our Rock. 'O come, let us sing unto the LORD: let us make a joyful noise to the rock of our salvation' (Psalm 95:1). And the prophet Isaiah spoke of the coming of Christ in these words: 'A man shall be as an hiding place from the wind, and a covert from the tempest; as a river of water in a dry place, as the shadow of a great Rock in a weary land' (Isaiah 32:2). Then, while he was upon the earth, our Lord Jesus Christ spoke of himself and said, 'Upon this rock I will build my church; and the gates of hell shall not prevail against it' (Matthew 16:18). The rock is a type of Christ, our God and Saviour. It symbolizes him beautifully.

The rock is a symbol of strength and stability. Bildad said to Job, 'Shall the rock be removed out of his place?' (Job 18:4). This is a source of great joy and peace to the believing heart: The Rock upon which we are built cannot be shaken. A flood of trials may come, and winds of temptation may beat violently against us, but the house built on the rock will stand (Matthew 7:25). Christ is our mighty Rock, strong and stable.

The rock is a mass of might. The billows beat against it in vain. The raging storm never disturbs its rest. It is fixed. There it stands. All the changing ages find it still unchanged. That Rock is Christ our God and Saviour. Another characteristic of the rock is durability. The rocks will outlast the storms of time. Waters will not wash them away. Mighty winds will not remove them from their foundations. Many a ship has been broken to pieces upon a rock, but the rock stands unchanged. Christ is our Rock, the unchanged, unchangeable, immutable, durable One (Malachi 3:6; Matthew 21:42-44, Hebrews 13:8). Either you will be built upon him or you will be destroyed by him.

Strong and durable is our Rock, Christ Jesus. Mark his decrees. Eternal love arranged salvation's scheme. The hand of sovereign grace drew the wise record of his wondrous kingdom. This chart of history was drawn, framed, and fixed forever by his omnipotent hand, in his omniscient mind, by his all-wise decree. To blind reason, chance may appear to rule, and man's wild will may appear to hold the helm. But all things serve the counsels of his will. The falling sparrow and the tottering throne, the fading leaf and the declining empire, obey his fixed resolve. His purpose cannot be moved. He is a Rock.

The rock is also a symbol of elevation and exaltation. The mighty rock towers high above man. It is a landmark and symbol throughout the country where it is situated. Christ is our high, elevated, exalted Rock. His throne is in the heavens, where he is seated at the right hand of the Majesty on High. 'The name of the LORD is a high tower; the righteous runneth into it and is safe' (Proverbs 18:10). Flee to this Rock, fall on him, hide in him, and you will find safety from the wrath of God, the assaults of men, the temptations of Satan, and the trials of life.

Remember, child of God, God is our Rock, and the high God our Redeemer (Psalm 61:1-4; 62:1, 2; 78:35). The Rock is near. It is your one support, your only refuge. Be wise, and lay your every sin on him. The weight, indeed, would weigh down worlds. But he can bear all. He can bear all away. Be wise, and cast your every care on him. Cares come rapidly and threaten to overwhelm. But let them waft you to the mercy seat, where Christ waits to be gracious. In faith and prayer, roll them all on him. They cannot over-burden him. He is the Rock.

Rock Smitten

Second, I want you to see the typical significance of Moses being commanded of God to smite the Rock. In Exodus 17 the Holy Spirit gives us this vivid, typical picture of the death of our Lord Jesus Christ.

The children of Israel had journeyed from the wilderness of Sin and pitched their tents in Rephidim. Again, they murmured against God, because there was no water in that place. They refused to believe God in spite of all he had done. They, like us, were prone to unbelief, ever doubting God, ever walking by sight and not by faith. Let us be warned.

The Lord God told Moses to take his rod and smite the Rock, and from it the fountain of waters would be given. It is important to notice the connection between Exodus 16 and 17. In chapter 16 God sent manna from heaven. In chapter 17 God told Moses to smite the rock. The manna was a type of our Lord's incarnation. The smitten rock was a picture of his crucifixion. The Lord Jesus had to descend from heaven to earth, as the manna did, or he could not become the Bread of Life for his people. Then he had to be smitten in death by the rod of divine justice, or he could never have poured out the Water of Life upon us.

The Rock was smitten because of sin and for the sake of sinners. Israel murmured against God and were ready to stone his servant. They refused to believe God's Word, power, goodness, and faithfulness, saying, 'Is the LORD among us, or not?' (v. 7). The rock was smitten for a rebellious, unbelieving people, a people who deserved no grace or favour from God. The parallel is clear, the Lord Jesus Christ was crucified because of sin, to put away sin (Hebrews 9:26; Romans 8:1-4). Had there been no sin, or had it been possible for sin to be put away by some other means, our Lord would not have been crucified. The Son of God was crucified for a rebellious, sinful people (Romans 5:6-10).

Christ came to save sinners. Christ died in the place of sinners. Christ shows mercy to sinners. If you want the Water of Life, come as a guilty, helpless sinner, and fall upon the smitten Saviour.

The Rock was smitten by the rod of Moses. Moses' rod was the symbol of God's law, God's justice, and God's judgment. This is the rod which became a serpent, the sign of God's curse. This rod turned the Nile River into blood. It delivered Israel across the Red Sea and drowned the armies of Pharaoh in the depths. The Lord Jesus Christ was smitten by the rod of God's strict justice (Romans 3:24-26).

The water could not be given until the Rock was smitten. And God could not and would not save sinners, pouring upon us the Water of Life, until the sinner's Substitute was smitten in justice. Moses must smite the Rock in full fury. Christ must be smitten by the law and justice of God in the full fury of an angry God. The sinner's Surety must satisfy

God's violated law, if the sinner is to go free. Thus, when Christ was made sin for us, justice demanded his death. And now that Christ has been slain for sinners, it is a righteous and just thing for God to forgive sinners and open to us the Fountain of Life (Zechariah 13:1; 1 John 1:9).

The Rock was smitten by the will, decree, and purpose of God. God told Moses when to smite the Rock, where to smite the Rock, how to smite the Rock, and what the result of smiting the Rock would be. So, the Lord Jesus Christ was crucified and slain for sinners according to the will, purpose, and decree of God (Acts 2:23; Isaiah 53:10-12).

God set the time of his Son's death (Romans 5:6). God ordained the means of his Son's death (Galatians 3:13). God determined the place of his Son's death. God himself brought to pass the death of his beloved Son. Christ voluntarily gave his life. God the Father slew his Son. God determined and secured the results of his Son's death as the sinner's Substitute. Nothing was left to chance.

Here is something even more astounding. God himself was represented in the Rock. The Lord said to Moses, 'I will stand before thee upon the rock in Horeb; and thou shall smite the rock' (v. 6). In smiting the Rock, Moses was smiting God himself. Never let it be forgotten that the Lord Jesus Christ, our Substitute, is himself God (Acts 20:28; 1 John 3:16). In order to redeem our souls, God was forsaken by God! God was wounded by God! God was slain by God!

> Well might the sun in darkness hide
> And shut his glories in,
> When God the mighty Maker died
> For man, the creature's sin.

The rock was smitten for the benefit of a particular people. The rock was smitten specifically for the people of Israel, 'that the people may drink' (v. 6). There was no water from this rock for the Amalekites, the Amorites, or the Moabites. The rock was smitten for the Israelites. The water flowed for the Israelites. The Israelites were saved by the water.

Even so, the Lord Jesus Christ was wounded for our transgressions. He was bruised for our iniquities. The chastisement of our peace was upon him. And with his stripes we are healed. God says, 'For the transgression of my people was he stricken'. And all of God's elect receive the benefits of his death. Christ died particularly and only for his own elect. Christ effectually accomplished redemption for his elect, all his elect, and none but his elect.

Behold the clefts of the smitten Rock. They are made for sinners, made to hide offenders from pursuing justice. Flee to them. Enter in. Hide yourself, your soul, your sins, in those deep wounds. Secreted there, you are safe, safe from all foes, safe for all ages. No curse can touch you. No wrath can find you. Satan cannot reach you. Guilt cannot ruin you. The pierced side is a God-wrought and a God-strong refuge.

Water from the Rock

Third, from the smitten Rock water flowed out to Israel. The water is a picture of the Holy Spirit, the gift of the crucified Christ. Just as the water poured out of the rock, the Holy Spirit was poured out upon chosen sinners as the Spirit of Life from the crucified, risen, exalted Christ (John 7:37, 38; Galatians 3:13, 14).

The water flowed out of the rock in fulfilment of God's covenant. 'He opened the Rock, and the waters gushed out: they ran in the dry places like a river. For he remembered his holy promise, and Abraham his servant' (Psalm 105:41, 42). So it is that the Holy Spirit comes to God's elect giving us eternal life in Christ, 'which God, that cannot lie, promised before the world began' (Titus 1:2). This is the fulfilment of God's covenant. 'I will put my Spirit within you' (Ezekiel 36:27).

All the children of Israel drank the water that gushed from the Rock (1 Corinthians 10:4). Even so, all of God's elect receive the gift of the Holy Spirit. In the new birth, all God's elect receive the Spirit of God, the Water of Life (Galatians 4:6). 'If any man have not the Spirit of Christ, he is none of his' (Romans 8:9).

This water gushed out of the Rock upon the children of Israel, just when they were ready to die of thirst. When they could find no other water to quench their thirst, God gave his people water to drink. That is the way our Lord works. Christ refreshes the souls of poor sinners who come to him just when they are ready to perish, when they can find no help, comfort, or refreshing anywhere else. When a man is brought to the place that he sees that without Christ he must perish, when his soul begins to thirst for him, the water of Life will gush out from the wounded Christ to his poor soul.

That water which gushed out of the Rock could not be dried up. Benjamin Keach said, 'The water out of the rock followed the children of Israel, through the wilderness, over all hills and valleys, unto Canaan. All the dryness of that dry and barren desert could not dry it up. So, the waters of life streaming from Christ, that sacred Rock, follow the true Israel of God, quite through the wilderness of this world, until they come to the heavenly Canaan. Yea, all the persecutions and temptations in the world cannot dry it up.'

Smitten Again

Fourth, we must not leave this picture of Christ our smitten Rock, without briefly remembering the second striking of the rock. It is recorded in Numbers 20:7-13.

'And the LORD spake unto Moses, saying, Take the rod, and gather thou the assembly together, thou, and Aaron thy brother, and speak ye unto the rock before their eyes; and it shall give forth his water, and thou shalt bring forth to them water out of the rock: so, thou shalt give the congregation and their beasts drink. And Moses took the rod from before the LORD, as he commanded him. And Moses and Aaron gathered the congregation together before the rock, and he said unto them, Hear now, ye rebels; must we fetch you water out of this rock? And Moses lifted up his hand, and with his rod he smote the rock twice: and the water came out abundantly, and the congregation drank, and their beasts also. And the LORD spake unto Moses and Aaron, Because ye believed me not, to sanctify me in the eyes of the children of Israel, therefore ye shall not bring this congregation into the land which I have given them. This is the water of Meribah, because the children of Israel strove with the LORD, and he was sanctified in them.'

This incident took place 40 years later. Everything here is a contrast to what happened in Exodus 17. In Exodus 17 the rock pictured Christ on the cross. Here the Rock pictures Christ exalted. The word used for 'rock' in Numbers 20:8 means 'an elevated rock'. In Exodus 17 Moses was told to strike the Rock. Here God tells him to speak to the Rock. In Exodus 17 Moses was told to use his own rod, the rod of judgment. Here God told him to take Aaron's rod, the rod of blessing (Numbers 17:10). It seems obvious that the Holy Spirit tells us of this second striking of the rock to teach us three lessons.

Our Lord's one sacrifice for sin is sufficient and effectual. The rock must not be smitten the second time, but only spoken to. It is written, 'Christ, being raised from the dead, dieth no more; death hath no more dominion over him. For in that he died, he died unto sin once; but in that he liveth, he liveth unto God' (Romans 6:9, 10). 'Now once in the end of the world hath he appeared to put away sin by the sacrifice of himself ... Christ was once offered to bear the sins of many' (Hebrews 9:26, 28). Christ made one sacrifice for sin. Our Lord's one sacrifice for sin is all God requires and all God will accept for sin's atonement. To offer God any other sacrifice, either in the place of Christ or in addition to Christ, is to make the blood of Christ of no effect.

God will slay anyone who brings any other sacrifice, just as he killed Moses for striking the Rock the second time. Christ's one sacrifice is sufficient. All the streams of salvation flow to us as guilty sinners through the merits of accomplished redemption.

Sinners smitten by the rod of God, the great host of God's elect, having been crucified with Christ at Calvary, shall never be punished again for sin. The rod of Moses, the rod of judgment was worn out on the back of Christ. Now, the great High Priest in heaven holds out the rod of Aaron, the rod of blessing. The only thing required to receive the Water of Life from the Smitten Rock is faith in Christ. And the word of faith, by which sinners speak to the Rock and obtain the Water of Life is, 'God be merciful to me, the sinner'.

In giving the Water from the Rock, God acted in marvellous grace. Where sin abounded, grace did much more abound. And it was grace acting in righteousness. Not until the Rock was smitten did the waters flow out to perishing men. Not until Christ, the Son of God was smitten of God could the grace of God flow out to sinners such as we are.

What is the response of your heart to this amazing, abundant grace of God? I am sure every believing heart must swell with gratitude for Christ, the Smitten Rock, and say, 'Thanks be unto God for his unspeakable gift'. Come, come thirsty soul. Come, drink of the water of life freely. Drink often. Drink abundantly. And thirst no more.

Chapter 76

A War To Which God Has Sworn Himself

'Then came Amalek, and fought with Israel in Rephidim. And Moses said unto Joshua, Choose us out men, and go out, fight with Amalek: tomorrow I will stand on the top of the hill with the rod of God in mine hand. So, Joshua did as Moses had said to him, and fought with Amalek: and Moses, Aaron, and Hur went up to the top of the hill. And it came to pass, when Moses held up his hand, that Israel prevailed: and when he let down his hand, Amalek prevailed. But Moses' hands were heavy; and they took a stone, and put it under him, and he sat thereon; and Aaron and Hur stayed up his hands, the one on the one side, and the other on the other side; and his hands were steady until the going down of the sun. And Joshua discomfited Amalek and his people with the edge of the sword. And the LORD said unto Moses, Write this for a memorial in a book, and rehearse it in the ears of Joshua: for I will utterly put out the remembrance of Amalek from under heaven. And Moses built an altar, and called the name of it Jehovah-nissi: For he said, Because the LORD hath sworn that the LORD will have war with Amalek from generation to generation.'
(Exodus 17:8-16)

The Book of Exodus gives us a wonderful and wide variety of spiritual instruction. Always read the Book of God with great care, asking God the Holy Spirit to open it to you. Even the smallest detail of the most obscure section has profound significance. Moses typified Christ our

Saviour. Pharaoh represented Satan. Egypt was typical of the world. Israel groaning in bondage pictures the sinner in his native misery. Israel delivered from its cruel task-masters speaks of redemption by power and blood. The people's journey through the wilderness points to our life of faith in this world, with its many trials and temptations.

In Exodus 17:8-16 we see Israel assaulted by and prevailing over Amalek. The assault of Amalek upon God's Israel, and the triumph of Israel over Amalek by the prevailing intercession of Moses, with Aaron and Hur holding up his hands, is intended to teach us that as long as we are in this world we will be engaged in a war, a war from generation to generation, but a war we are sure to win. It is the war that takes place continually in the heart of every heaven-born soul, the war of our two natures; the raging, relentless conflict between flesh and spirit.

In the first seven verses of this chapter we saw the rock smitten by the rod of Moses. A stream of water flowed out of that smitten rock to the chosen people; and they all drank the water that flowed from the rock. Moses smiting the rock typified the smiting of our blessed Saviour, the Lord Jesus Christ, by the hand of divine justice. The water that flowed from the rock typified God the Holy Ghost who comes to redeemed sinners in saving grace, because they have been redeemed by that great act of divine justice, the sacrifice of our Lord Jesus Christ in our room and stead (Galatians 3:13, 14).

But after the Holy Spirit comes in saving grace, after he takes up his abode within us, after a new and holy nature of his creating has been implanted, a strange conflict is experienced, something altogether unknown before. 'The flesh lusteth against the spirit, and the spirit against the flesh; and these are contrary the one to the other' (Galatians 5:17). That is the picture we have before us in Exodus 17:8-16.

A Divine Nature Created
The teaching of Scripture in this regard is of great practical importance. Ignorance of what the Word of God teaches concerning the two natures of the believer has caused untold distress in many souls. Many have thought and been taught, that when a sinner is born again God changes the heart and sin is vanquished forever. But 'a change of heart' is nowhere spoken of in Scripture. God never changes anything about fallen man. The old nature, called 'the old man', and 'the flesh', is neither destroyed, nor set aside, nor altered in any way.

In the new birth something altogether new is created in us. God the Holy Spirit imparts new life and creates that which is righteous, holy and divine in us by God's omnipotent grace. The Christian is a person who has been 'born again'. The new birth is receiving a new nature: 'that which is born of the Spirit, is Spirit' (John 3:6). Being born of God, we have been made 'partakers of the divine nature' (2 Peter 1:4).

In the new birth a spiritual, divine nature, is created in and communicated to us. This new nature is created by God the Holy Spirit. He plants the 'seed' of the Word of God in us (1 Peter 1:23) and forms Christ in us by grace (2 Corinthians 5:17; Colossians 1:27; 1 John 3:9). In justification righteousness is imputed and we are declared righteous. In sanctification righteousness is imparted and we are made righteous. 'Christ in you, the hope of glory' is that 'holiness without which no man shall see the Lord' (Colossians 1:27; Hebrews 12:14).

But when the new nature is communicated by God to the one born again, while Christ is formed in us, and though the holiness without which no man shall see the Lord is created in us, the old sinful nature remains, and remains unchanged until we leave this world.

In every heaven-born soul there are two natures: one sinful, the other sinless; one born of the flesh, the other born of God; one carnal and beastly, one spiritual and holy. These two natures differ from each other in origin, in character, in disposition, and in deed. They have nothing in common. They are completely opposed to each other.

The two natures in the believer are illustrated in the life of Abraham. He had two sons: Ishmael and Isaac. Ishmael represents that which is 'born of the flesh'. Isaac typifies that which is 'born of the Spirit'. Ishmael was born according to the common order of nature. Isaac was not. Isaac was born as the result of a miracle. God supernaturally quickened both Abraham and Sarah, when they were both too old to have children. Ishmael, born first, was of 'the bond-woman'. Isaac was born of the 'free-woman' (Galatians 4:22). But after Isaac was born a bitter conflict erupted and Ishmael assaulted Isaac (Genesis 21:9). That is what God the Holy Spirit tells us about Abraham's two sons and their mothers in Galatians 4:22-29. Their conflict was representative of the same warfare today. 'But as then he that was born after the flesh persecuted him that was born after the Spirit even so it is now.'

These two natures in us, the flesh and the spirit, are also illustrated in the life of Isaac's son Jacob. Jacob had two names: one he received from his earthly parents, and one he received from God. The Lord God called him 'Israel' (Genesis 32:28). From that point on, his life was a series of paradoxes. He exhibited a dual personality, two distinct natures. One minute we see him trusting God with implicit confidence, the next he gives way to an evil heart of unbelief. Throughout the Scriptures, the Holy Spirit refers to the patriarch in one place as 'Jacob', and in the next place as 'Israel'.

When God tells us of something evil he did, he calls him 'Jacob'. When he refers to his faith or obedience he calls him 'Israel'. When Joseph's brothers returned to their father from Egypt and told him his favourite son was yet alive and was now governor over all the land of Egypt, we are told, 'And Jacob's heart fainted for he believed them not' (Genesis 45:26). But, 'They told him all the words of Joseph, which he had said unto them; and when he saw the wagons which Joseph had sent to carry him, the spirit of Jacob their father revived: And Israel said, It is enough; Joseph my son is yet alive' (Genesis 45:48). Then we read, 'When Jacob had made an end of commanding his sons, he gathered up his feet into the bed, and yielded up the spirit ... and the physicians embalmed Israel' (Genesis 49:33; 50:2). 'Jacob' died. 'Israel' was embalmed. At death only the new nature will be preserved!

The Warfare
Throughout every believer's life on this earth there is a conflict between the flesh and the spirit, a raging warfare within. Just as Ishmael 'persecuted' Isaac, 'the flesh lusteth against the spirit, and the spirit against the flesh; and these are contrary the one to the other; so that ye cannot do the things that ye would' (Galatians 5:17). Sometimes we act like Jacob, sometimes we act like Israel. Usually, we act like both.

This is exactly what Paul tells us he experienced. 'I know that in me (that is, in my flesh,) dwelleth no good thing ... The evil which I would not, that I do ... When I would do good, evil is present with me' (Romans 7:18-21). Why? Why am I in this condition? Why is sin so prominent in my nature? Why is evil always present with me? Why this constant warfare in my soul? These are questions I am asked frequently by concerned souls who honestly acknowledge their sin. And these are questions I frequently ask myself.

The Word of God alone supplies us with the answer to them. 'That which is born of the flesh is flesh; and that which is born of the Spirit is spirit' (John 3:6). It is as simple and yet as profound as that. All true believers are people with two natures: 'flesh' and 'spirit'. Those two natures constantly war with one another. The spirit will never surrender to the flesh and the flesh will never bow to the spirit. We do not live after the flesh, or walk in the flesh. We live after the Spirit and walk in the Spirit. And those who walk in the Spirit do not fulfil the lusts of the flesh. Yet, we never escape those lusts. We will never be free from 'the body of this death' until we have dropped this body in death.

Painful as this condition is, it is best for us that we may be reminded of three things while we live in this world. First, the only thing distinguishing us from others is the grace of God (1 Corinthians 4:7). Second, our only ground of acceptance with God is the blood and righteousness of Christ (1 Corinthians 1:30). Third, we should never become content with our existence in this world (2 Corinthians 5:1-9).

Amalek ... The Flesh

'Then came Amalek, and fought with Israel in Rephidim' (17:8). The possession of water and wells was a cause of trouble among the ancients (Genesis 21:25; 26:19, 20; Exodus 2:17; Numbers 20:19; Judges 5:11). The camp of Israel had a river of water gushing out of a rock; and the Amalekites were determined to take it. So, they attacked Israel.

The name 'Amalek', we are told, implies 'warlike'. Our Amalek, our flesh, ever lusts against our souls, making war (1 Peter 2:11). Amalek was the grandson of Esau (Genesis 36:12), 'who for one morsel of meat sold his birthright, and when he would have inherited the blessing was rejected'. That is our flesh. Amalek was Israel's first enemy, just as the flesh is ours; but Amalek was conquered by Joshua. And just as Christ has prevailed over sin, Satan, death, and hell, so our flesh shall perish forever.

'And he took up his parable, and said, Balaam the son of Beor hath said, and the man whose eyes are open hath said: He hath said, which heard the words of God, and knew the knowledge of the most High, which saw the vision of the Almighty, falling into a trance, but having his eyes open: I shall see him, but not now: I shall behold him, but not nigh: there shall come a Star out of Jacob, and a Sceptre shall rise out of Israel, and shall smite the corners of Moab, and destroy all the children of Sheth. And Edom shall be a possession, Seir also shall be a possession for his enemies; and Israel shall do valiantly. Out of Jacob

151

shall come he that shall have dominion, and shall destroy him that remaineth of the city. And when he looked on Amalek, he took up his parable, and said, Amalek was the first of the nations; but his latter end shall be that he perish forever' (Numbers 24:15-20).

The Time

Be sure to take note of the time when this warfare began. It was after the rock was smitten and the water flowed out of it, 'Then came Amalek and fought with Israel'. The Holy Spirit calls our attention to this for a reason. It was when Moses smote the rock and the waters were given that Amalek made war on Israel. Then, for the first time, Israel was called upon to do some fighting (cf. Exodus 13:17). They had done no fighting in the house of bondage. They were not allowed to fight the Egyptians at the Red Sea. But now having been given the water out of the Rock which typified the Holy Spirit, their warfare began. 'It was that', A. W. Pink observed, 'which typified the Holy Spirit that caused the Amalekites to attack Israel! Wonderfully accurate is the type.'

Only when the chosen, redeemed sinner is born of God, made partaker of the divine nature (2 Peter 1:4), does the inward conflict begin. Before that, he is dead in trespasses and sins, and insensible to the claims of God's holiness. Until the Holy Spirit begins to shed his light on our wicked hearts we do not realize the depths and power of the evil within us. When the new born soul is made to know the plague of his own heart, he is astounded by the discovery of the evil remaining in him, evil he never knew was there before. The religious professor knows nothing of this conflict between the two natures. Mere religionists know nothing of inward corruption and heart depravity. The unregenerate are entirely under the dominion of the flesh, serving its lusts and doing its will. The 'flesh' does not make war with its subjects. It rules over them. But as soon as Christ comes the conflict begins.

Notice this, too, it was not Israel who attacked Amalek, but Amalek who attacked Israel. The new nature in the believer delights to feed upon the Word, to commune with God, and be engaged with spiritual things. But the flesh will not let him live in peace. The Devil delights to rob the believer of joy, and works upon the flesh to accomplish his fiendish designs. 'The flesh lusteth against the spirit.' Yet, the spirit will not yield. It is written, 'and the spirit against the flesh; and these are contrary the one to the other' (Galatians 5:17).

Joshua Defeats Amalek

Next, we are told Israel prevailed. But it was Joshua who discomfited Amalek. It was Joshua who whipped the enemy.

'And Moses said unto Joshua, Choose us out men, and go out, fight with Amalek: tomorrow I will stand on the top of the hill with the rod of God in mine hand. So, Joshua did as Moses had said to him, and fought with Amalek: and Moses, Aaron, and Hur went up to the top of the hill. And it came to pass, when Moses held up his hand, that Israel prevailed: and when he let down his hand, Amalek prevailed. But Moses' hands were heavy; and they took a stone, and put it under him, and he sat thereon; and Aaron and Hur stayed up his hands, the one on the one side, and the other on the other side; and his hands were steady until the going down of the sun. And Joshua discomfited Amalek and his people with the edge of the sword' (vv. 9-13).

There is a great variety of opinion about the typical significance of the four men named in these verses and the things they did. But there is no reason to limit the typical teaching. Certainly, we see here a picture of the believer prevailing over his enemy, Satan, and indwelling sin, by prayer. Israel prevailed over Amalek by the uplifted hand of Moses. 'And it came to pass, when Moses held up his hand, that Israel prevailed; and when he let down his hand Amalek prevailed' (v. 11).

The uplifted hand suggests prayer, supplication before the throne of God. 'Hear the voice of my supplications, when I cry unto thee, when I lift up my hands toward thy holy oracle' (Psalm 28:2). 'I will therefore that men pray everywhere, lifting up holy hands, without wrath and doubting' (1 Timothy 2:8). Then 'Moses' hands grew heavy.' How soon we grow weary in prayer! 'Men ought always to pray and not to faint' (Luke 18:1), our Saviour tells us. But how miserably we fail! How quickly our hearts get 'heavy'. But, blessed be God, Moses was not left to himself! Aaron and Hur were with him and 'stayed up his hands, the one on one side and the other on the other side'. Moses represents the demands of God's law; satisfaction, justice, truth, and holiness. His drooping hands represent the law's inability to save (Romans 8:3, 4). Aaron represented Israel's priesthood, God's Sacrifice, our Lord Jesus Christ. Hur means 'light'. He is the emblem of divine holiness, and so points to the Holy Spirit of God. How do we prevail over sin and Satan? We prevail by blood and by the grace of God given to us and working in us; supported on both sides, both the earthly and the heavenly. The

Lord Jesus Christ, the Angel of God's Presence, the Messenger of the Covenant, stands 'at the altar having a golden censer; and there was given unto him much incense, that he should offer it with the prayers of all saints upon the golden altar which was before the throne' (Revelation 8:3). And we prevail by the Spirit of God who works in us to will and do of his good pleasure. 'Likewise, the Spirit also helpeth our infirmities. For we know not what we should pray for as we ought; but the Spirit Himself maketh intercession for us with groanings which cannot be uttered' (Romans 8:26). The Lord Jesus, by his grace, and the Holy Spirit, by his reviving influences, like Aaron and Hur, uphold and sustain our drooping souls in this world.

Let us pray, ever pray for ourselves and for one another. 'The effectual, fervent prayer of a righteous man availeth much.' But this fact is clear: if you and I prevail over sin and Satan, it will not be because of our prayers. We will prevail by Christ alone, our great Prophet, Priest, and King. Put Moses the prophet, Aaron the priest, and Hur the prince (Miriam's husband) together, and you have the picture.

Here (vv. 9-13) is the first mention of Joshua. He is called 'Jesus' in Acts 7:45 and Hebrews 4:8. I know that the Greek for Joshua is Jesus; and I know why that is the case. Joshua represents our blessed Saviour, the Lord Jesus Christ. Here he is set before us as a Man of War, the Captain of the Lord's hosts, a mighty Conqueror, Israel's great Saviour.

Moses was weak but Joshua was strong. Moses' hands sagged, but Joshua's were victorious. Christ, our great Joshua, fights all our battles for us, and makes us more than conquerors by his grace (Isaiah 40:28-31; Hebrews 7:24, 25; Romans 8:37-39; Revelation 12:11).

Defeated Not Destroyed

It is important to note that Amalek was defeated by Joshua, but not destroyed. We are told 'Joshua discomfited Amalek'. The fact is, there is no destroying or eradicating the evil nature within us. Though discomforted and put to flight by grace, it is very much alive and still at war. Let us ever be mindful of these things and give praise to our great Saviour for his grace.

'Remember what Amalek did unto thee by the way, when ye were come forth out of Egypt; How he met thee by the way, and smote the hindmost of thee, even all that were feeble behind thee, when thou wast faint and weary; and he feared not God' (Deuteronomy 25:17, 18).

Jehovah-nissi

We are sure this whole account is written in the Book of God to point us to Christ our Saviour and to illustrate our great salvation in and by him, because the Lord commanded Moses to write a memorial, build an altar, erect a banner over it and name the place Jehovah-nissi. By this he assured Moses, Joshua, and Israel, 'I will utterly put out the remembrance of Amalek from under heaven'.

'And the LORD said unto Moses, Write this for a memorial in a book, and rehearse it in the ears of Joshua: for I will utterly put out the remembrance of Amalek from under heaven. And Moses built an altar, and called the name of it Jehovah-nissi' (vv. 14, 15).

'Jehovah-nissi' means 'the Lord our Banner'. Christ is our Banner. The banner is the symbol of victory. The banner is the rallying point.

'And in that day there shall be a root of Jesse, which shall stand for an ensign of the people; to it shall the Gentiles seek: and his rest shall be glorious' (Isaiah 11:10).

'We will rejoice in thy salvation, and in the name of our God we will set up our banners: the LORD fulfil all thy petitions. Now know I that the LORD saveth his anointed; he will hear him from his holy heaven with the saving strength of his right hand. Some trust in chariots, and some in horses: but we will remember the name of the LORD our God' (Psalm 20:5-7).

Still, there is more. This is a war to which the triune God has sworn himself. 'For he said, Because the LORD hath sworn that the LORD will have war with Amalek from generation to generation' (v. 16).

'So shall they fear the name of the LORD from the west, and his glory from the rising of the sun. When the enemy shall come in like a flood, the Spirit of the LORD shall lift up a standard against him. And the Redeemer shall come to Zion, and unto them that turn from transgression in Jacob, saith the LORD. As for me, this is my covenant with them, saith the LORD; My spirit that is upon thee, and my words which I have put in thy mouth, shall not depart out of thy mouth, nor out of the mouth of thy seed, nor out of the mouth of thy seed's seed, saith the LORD, from henceforth and forever' (Isaiah 59:19-21).

The Lord God has laid his hand upon his own throne and swears by himself that he will utterly root out and destroy Amalek; and he will. Soon, he will make a new heavens and a new earth; and there will be 'no more sin'. The very slime of the serpent will be eradicated from

155

God's creation and from us! In resurrection glory, this corruptible shall put on incorruption and this mortal shall put on immortality forever!

How blessed to know that when our God makes all things new, our blessed Saviour shall 'change our vile body, that it may be fashioned like unto his glorious body according to the working whereby he is able even to subdue all things unto himself' (Philippians 3:21).

Chapter 77

Moses' Great Mistake

'So, Moses hearkened to the voice of his father in law, and did all that he had said.'
(Exodus 18:1-27)

Thus far in the Book of Exodus we have seen the Lord God performing both judgment and mercy, judgment upon Egypt and mercy upon Israel. In the exercise of his mighty grace, the Lord visited and redeemed his people; bringing them forth out of the land of Egypt, delivering them, first from the hand of Pharaoh then from the hand of Amalek. We have seen, in the manna falling from heaven, a type of Christ the Bread of Life coming down from heaven to give us life. In the rock that followed Israel through the wilderness, we saw a type of Christ smitten for his people. In the stream gushing out of the smitten rock, the Lord God gave us a typical picture of God the Holy Spirit, 'the blessing of Abraham', given to us by our crucified Redeemer (Galatians 3:13, 14).

In Exodus 18, Moses and the children of Israel are encamped at Rephidim, at 'the mount of God'. There are clear lessons set before us in this chapter we need to understand and lay to heart. May God the Holy Spirit be our Teacher.

Moses' Faithfulness
Let it be clearly understood that Moses was a man of remarkable faith and faithfulness. Exodus 18 begins with Jethro, Moses' father-in-law, bringing his wife, Zipporah, and his two sons, Gershom and Eliezer, back to him.

'When Jethro, the priest of Midian, Moses' father in law, heard of all that God had done for Moses, and for Israel his people, and that the LORD had brought Israel out of Egypt; Then Jethro, Moses' father in law, took Zipporah, Moses' wife, after he had sent her back, And her two sons; of which the name of the one was Gershom; for he said, I have been an alien in a strange land: And the name of the other was Eliezer; for the God of my father, said he, was mine help, and delivered me from the sword of Pharaoh: And Jethro, Moses' father in law, came with his sons and his wife unto Moses into the wilderness, where he encamped at the mount of God: And he said unto Moses, I thy father-in-law Jethro am come unto thee, and thy wife, and her two sons with her' (vv. 1-6).

It had been a long, long time, at least a year, since Moses had seen Zipporah and their two sons, and their parting had not been exactly pleasant. You will remember God met Moses in an inn back in chapter four and almost killed him because he had not circumcised one of his sons. When Moses submitted to the will of God, Zipporah was required to perform the ordinance; but she did not like it. And she and Moses had words.

'And it came to pass by the way in the inn, that the LORD met him, and sought to kill him. Then Zipporah took a sharp stone, and cut off the foreskin of her son, and cast it at his feet, and said, Surely a bloody husband art thou to me. So, he let him go: then she said, A bloody husband thou art, because of the circumcision' (Exodus 4:24-26).

Moses learned that obedience is a matter of immense importance. He also learned that any child of God who marries someone who will not worship God with him marries trouble. When Moses was finally compelled by God to obey him, as all believers are, Zipporah took the boys and went home to her father. Actually, Moses 'sent her back' (v. 2), because she would have been a hindrance to him in the work of God. Moses went on to Egypt to do what God had called him to do. Now, a full year later, after Jethro heard what God had done with Moses, he brought Zipporah and the boys back to him.

Typical Picture
There is a typical picture here of Christ and his church. Zipporah being reconciled to Moses may be taken to represent the reconciliation of God's elect to Christ. Zipporah was a black woman, a Midianite, an

Ethiopian (Numbers 12:1), a sinful woman, from a cursed race. She came to Moses with two sons: Gershom (A Stranger) and Eliezer (God is my Help, God is my Salvation). She and Moses were reconciled 'at the mount of God', the place of divine justice. Furthermore, Moses was a husband of blood to Zipporah. They were reconciled by covenant blood, by the fulfilment of a covenant in a work of circumcision.

A Faithful Account

On the day Jethro, Zipporah, and his sons came to meet him, Moses faithfully reported to his family all that the Lord had done.

'And Moses went out to meet his father in law, and did obeisance, and kissed him; and they asked each other of their welfare; and they came into the tent. And Moses told his father-in-law all that the LORD had done unto Pharaoh and to the Egyptians for Israel's sake, and all the travail that had come upon them by the way, and how the LORD delivered them' (vv. 7, 8).

Moses told Jethro about passover and God's sacrifice for his people, Israel's deliverance across the Red Sea by the hand of God, the pillar of cloud and fire, and the Lord's conquest over Pharaoh and Egypt (chapters 12-14). No doubt, he rehearsed with him the song of redemption when Israel triumphed over the Egyptians (chapter 15). He surely told his father-in-law about the sweetened waters of Marah and Jehovah's revelation of himself as 'The Lord that healeth thee', and the manna that fell from heaven, Christ the Bread of Life (chapter 16). He told of the water of God flowing from the smitten rock, revealing Christ crucified, and the stream of water gushing from the smitten rock, typifying the gift of God the Holy Ghost to his people through Christ's blood atonement (chapter 17). And Jethro, I am confident, heard Moses' witness about the marvellous display of God's goodness, grace, and power in his deliverance of Israel from Amalek, revealing himself as 'Jehovah-nissi', 'the LORD our Banner' (Exodus 17:8-16).

When Jethro heard Moses' report of God's wondrous works he was ecstatic.

'And Jethro rejoiced for all the goodness which the LORD had done to Israel, whom he had delivered out of the hand of the Egyptians. And Jethro said, Blessed be the LORD, who hath delivered you out of the hand of the Egyptians, and out of the hand of Pharaoh, who hath delivered the people from under the hand of the Egyptians. Now I know that the LORD is greater than all gods: for in the thing wherein they dealt proudly he was above them. And Jethro, Moses' father-in-law, took a burnt offering and sacrifices for God: and Aaron came, and all the elders of Israel, to eat bread with Moses' father-in-law before God' (vv. 9-12).

Jethro's heart was unchanged; but he was so excited by what he saw and heard that he rejoiced in God's goodness. He extolled the Lord God, not as the only Lord God, but as the greatest of all gods. He even made sacrifices to Jehovah according to the law. But his heart was still unchanged. Jethro was still an idolater.

Here is another remarkable thing about Moses. The arrival of his family did not deter him from the worship and service of his God.

'And it came to pass on the morrow, that Moses sat to judge the people: and the people stood by Moses from the morning unto the evening' (v. 13).

Moses had not seen his family in more than a year. But the day after they got there, he went out to do what God had called him to do, what God had given him the singular responsibility to do. His family arrived in the evening. The next morning Moses went into the congregation of the Lord. As John Gill said, 'Though his father-in-law was come to visit him, yet, he did not neglect the care of his people, and the business that lay upon his hands for their good.'

We would be wise to follow Moses' example in this matter. If you want to do your family good, do not allow your family to keep you from the worship and service of God. And do nothing that would keep your family from the worship and service of God.

Honoured of God

This man Moses, a man of great faith and faithfulness, was highly honoured of God. Moses honoured God, and God honoured Moses.

'Wherefore the LORD God of Israel saith, I said indeed that thy house, and the house of thy father, should walk before me forever: but now the LORD saith, Be it far from me; for them that honour me I will honour, and they that despise me shall be lightly esteemed' (1 Samuel 2:30).

The Lord God of Israel had made his servant Moses the judge and pastor, the leader and the teacher of a congregation of more than four million people.[4] The work the Lord God had imposed upon Moses was a great work (Ephesians 3:8), a demanding work, and a work involving great honour. But it was a work for which God equipped him and constantly supplied him. 'Our sufficiency is of God!'

'And Moses said unto his father in law, Because the people come unto me to inquire of God: When they have a matter, they come unto me; and I judge between one and another, and I do make them know the statutes of God, and his laws' (vv. 15, 16).

Yet, when Jethro saw what Moses was doing, he said, 'The thing that thou doest is not good. Thou wilt surely wear away, both thou, and this people that is with thee: for this thing is too heavy for thee; thou art not able to perform it thyself alone … Hearken now unto my voice, I will give thee counsel … Appoint judges to help you … God will be with you.' Obviously, God was already with him; but Jethro went on with his counsel. 'So, shall it be easier for thyself.' Easy Street is always a Wrong Way Boulevard! But Jethro just knew he was wiser than God. So, he continued with his counsel. 'They shall bear the burden with thee … Thou shalt be able to endure' (vv. 17-23).

A Horrible Mistake
Moses made a horrible mistake. He followed the counsel of carnal reason. 'So, Moses hearkened to the voice of his father in law, and did all that he had said' (v. 24). Jethro's counsel probably arose from loving concern for Moses' health. It was, in a fleshly sense, wise and prudent. But Moses did wrong in obeying Jethro's counsel. He made a mistake from which there was no recovery. That becomes obvious, as we proceed through the record given by God the Holy Ghost in a moment.

Remember, Jethro was an unbeliever, a heathen priest. He had no spiritual discernment. The servant of God must never allow himself to be guided by natural principles (Galatians 1:16). What is best for me? What is best for my family? What would family and friends have me to do? Consider those things, and you will never do what the Lord God directs you to do. Had Abraham considered those issues, he would never have gone with Isaac to the mount of sacrifice, and would never have known the Lord Jesus in his character as Jehovah-jireh.

---

[4] There were 600,000 footmen, not counting women, children, and aged people in the congregation.

That man who is engaged in the service of God must never heed the counsel of carnal wisdom. We take our orders only from our Master. 'Whatsoever he saith unto you, do it' (John 2:5). If we would obey our God, and serve him in any area of life, our actions must be determined only by the Word of God, the will of God, and the glory of God.

A Great Burden

What was once Moses' highest honour and greatest privilege became a great burden to him once he began to consider himself. How sad!

A son or a daughter in a young family is nothing but a delight to a loving mother. The cries of the child do not annoy her. The dirty diapers are not repulsive to her. The aching breasts do not make her resentful. But let that mother begin to think of herself and all that the child is costing her, and that new born child may be in grave danger at its mother's own hands. So it was with Moses.

When he began to consider himself rather than the will of God, the glory of God, and the people of God, he began to look upon his service as a great burden and greatly resented it.

'And Moses said unto the LORD, Wherefore hast thou afflicted thy servant? And wherefore have I not found favour in thy sight, that thou layest the burden of all this people upon me? Have I conceived all this people? Have I begotten them, that thou shouldest say unto me, Carry them in thy bosom, as a nursing father beareth the sucking child, unto the land which thou swarest unto their fathers? Whence should I have flesh to give unto all this people? For they weep unto me, saying, Give us flesh, that we may eat. I am not able to bear all this people alone, because it is too heavy for me. And if thou deal thus with me, kill me, I pray thee, out of hand, if I have found favour in thy sight; and let me not see my wretchedness' (Numbers 11:11-15).

Moses was willing to relinquish the work and the post of high honour to which God had called him. True, his responsibility was immense. But faith would have said, 'God's grace is sufficient'. Instead Moses' heart failed him. 'I am not able to bear all this people alone, because it is too heavy for me' (Numbers 11:14).

God never called him to bear the burden of his people alone and God had never left him alone. Moses was only the instrument. God was carrying the load. And God was doing the work. Any place where God puts me is a place of honour. Any work God puts in my hands is honourable work. The same is true of you. That is a lesson we need to learn early, learn well, and learn daily.

'For ye see your calling, brethren, how that not many wise men after the flesh, not many mighty, not many noble, are called: But God hath chosen the foolish things of the world to confound the wise; and God hath chosen the weak things of the world to confound the things which are mighty; And base things of the world, and things which are despised, hath God chosen, yea, and things which are not, to bring to nought things that are: That no flesh should glory in his presence' (1 Corinthians 1:26-29).

Moses' relinquishing of his burden had the appearance of humility; but it was only an appearance of humility. Many fail here. With his lips, he was saying, 'I am not sufficient'. But he was really saying, 'God, you are not sufficient!' We must never thrust ourselves into any work, presuming and pretending we have been called and sent of God, when that is not the case. But to shrink from any work or responsibility God has put upon us is both cowardice and unbelief. 'Is anything too hard for the Lord?' No work is too great. C. H. Mackintosh rightly observed, 'With him the weight of a mountain is nothing; without him, the weight of a feather is overwhelming.' 'I can do all things through Christ which strengtheneth me' (Philippians 4:13). No burden is too heavy for God.

It is never an act of humility or faith to depart from any divinely appointed post, or any divinely appointed work for any reason. Difficulties are nothing to God. The Red Sea stands forever as a monument to that fact. Needs are nothing to God. When Israel needed it, God caused the Egyptians to give them both their silver and their gold, gladly! When they were hungry, the Lord God rained manna from heaven to feed them. When they were thirsty, he caused water to gush out of the rock for them to drink! Proud men are nothing to God. He raised up Pharaoh to prove that to the world, and to us, his people! And our inabilities are nothing to God (1 Corinthians 1:26-29). 'When I am weak, then am I strong.'

Our God can draw a straight line with a crooked stick. He can conquer a nation by an old man. And he can speak to the hearts of sinners by a stuttering, stammering tongue. God can speak as easily by a jackass as by a man. The power by which we do his work is not ours, but his!

163

The Burden Removed

When Moses complained about the burden God so graciously had given him, the Lord quickly took it away.

'And the LORD said unto Moses, Gather unto me seventy men of the elders of Israel, whom thou knowest to be the elders of the people, and officers over them; and bring them unto the tabernacle of the congregation, that they may stand there with thee. And I will come down and talk with thee there: and I will take of the spirit which is upon thee, and will put it upon them; and they shall bear the burden of the people with thee, that thou bear it not thyself alone' (Numbers 11:16, 17).

God will never force us to serve him. If I do not want to speak for him, he can raise up stones to do so. If I do not want to wash and kiss the Master's feet, somebody will. If I do not want to break my alabaster box of ointment and anoint him, somebody will. If I do not want to be bothered by serving Christ, he will not force me to do so. He does not need me. And he does not need you.

If the honour and privilege God has given us in his service becomes a burden to us and we want to lay it down, he will let us. We can step down from the place of dignity if we want to, and sink into the place where base unbelief is sure to put us. Thus, God took the burden away! Read Numbers 11:16, 17 again.

'And the LORD said unto Moses, Gather unto me seventy men of the elders of Israel, whom thou knowest to be the elders of the people, and officers over them; and bring them unto the tabernacle of the congregation, that they may stand there with thee. And I will come down and talk with thee there: and I will take of the spirit which is upon thee, and will put it upon them; and they shall bear the burden of the people with thee, that thou bear it not thyself alone.'

If the Lord God has condescended to give you the privilege of preaching the gospel, he has given you a great, great privilege, a high, high honour. If the Lord God has given any local church the gospel of his grace, has made that church a light house for the gospel of his glory, he has given that congregation a great, great privilege, a high, high honour.

'Unto me, who am less than the least of all saints, is this grace given, that I should preach among the Gentiles the unsearchable riches of Christ' (Ephesians 3:8).

'We have this treasure in earthen vessels, that the excellency of the power may be of God, and not of us' (2 Corinthians 4:7).

Oh, what a blessing! Yet, the blessing is a burden. It is 'The burden of the word of the LORD'. It is and always will be a burden involving opposition, heartbreak, gut-wrenching pain and agony, disappointment, sorrow, sacrifice, and labour. And it will, relentlessly, involve the heavy, heavy burden of being misunderstood by those we dearly love and for whom we labour. If the burden gets to the point where it becomes greater to us than the blessing, we can lay it down. But, when you are tempted to lay it down, remember what happened when the Lord God granted Moses' desire and took away the burden. The Lord God took the spirit with which he had invested Moses, and the power which had resided in Moses, and divided it among seventy men. Nothing was gained. No more work was done than before. But Moses lost his place of dignity and honour as the leader and judge of the people. What Moses alone had done before was now done by seventy men. God's purpose was not hindered; but his servant was greatly injured, because he gave up the blessing of the burden.

Moses Withered

When the Lord relieved Moses of his burden, he also relieved him of his honour, the blessing of the burden, and Moses withered.

'And Moses said, The people, among whom I am, are six hundred thousand footmen; and thou hast said, I will give them flesh, that they may eat a whole month. Shall the flocks and the herds be slain for them, to suffice them? Or shall all the fish of the sea be gathered together for them, to suffice them? And the LORD said unto Moses, Is the LORD'S hand waxed short? Thou shalt see now whether my word shall come to pass unto thee or not' (Numbers 11:21-23).

The man of great faith, who brought Israel across the Red Sea, when he relinquished his burden, when he sought to retire from the field of service, became a man of great unbelief. Those who do nothing for God expect nothing from God. Those who attempt great things for God expect great things from God.

Trouble Followed

After wreaking havoc by his 'wise counsel', Jethro went back to Midian and went back to his gods; and Moses was left to live with the mess he had made. 'And Moses let his father-in-law depart; and he went his way into his own land' (v. 27).

'And Moses said unto Hobab, the son of Raguel the Midianite, Moses' father-in-law, We are journeying unto the place of which the LORD said, I will give it you: come thou with us, and we will do thee good: for the LORD hath spoken good concerning Israel. And he said unto him, I will not go; but I will depart to mine own land, and to my kindred' (Numbers 10:29, 30).

What trouble followed! The trouble with Korah (Numbers 16) began right here (Numbers 10:31). Once Moses hearkened to Jethro's counsel, he grovelled before him. 'Come with us Jethro, we need you. You shall be God's eyes to us! God and his people need you.' Jethro said, 'Well, if God needs me, I don't need God.'

Jethro, whose other name was Hobab, preferred his gods to Jehovah. He preferred the comforts of Median to the troubles of the wilderness. He chose the people of Midian over the people of God. He preferred the pleasures of life in Midian to the blessings of life with God. This is the man whose counsel Moses followed.

Would to God that every faithful man and woman, every faithful gospel preacher, pastor, and missionary, and every faithful local church might learn the blessing of the burden of serving Christ and his cause in this wilderness! The blessings we have do involve a burden. If ever we choose to relinquish the burden of the work, we will also choose to relinquish the blessing.

The greatest privilege and the highest honour any man or woman can ever enjoy in this world is the privilege and honour of being allowed to do something for God. Be sure you understand what I am saying. The Lord God does not need us for anything. He does not need us to give him anything. He owns the cattle on a thousand hills, and all the gold in the deep mines of the earth belongs to him. There is no lack on God's part that his creatures supply. There is no vacuum in his being that must be filled by us. We add nothing to the happiness, glory, and majesty of the Almighty! He is independent and self-sufficient. He does not need us. The solitariness of God is the majesty of God. God does not need man. He created us without our assistance (Genesis 1:26, 27). He redeemed us without our aid (Galatians 3:13). Righteousness is his work alone. Atonement is his work alone. He saved us without our co-operation (Ephesians 2:1-9). We are his creation. He chose us. We did not choose him. He called us. We did not call him. He came to us. We did not come to him. He found us. We did not find him. He gave us life. We did not give ourselves life. 'Salvation is of the LORD.'

Do you understand what I am saying? God does not need man. He does not need us for anything. Yet, in great, condescending mercy, love, and grace, this great and mighty Lord God does use men to accomplish his work in this world. The holy Lord God permits some men and women, fallen depraved men and women, to do some things for him. Imagine that! What a privilege! When God allows a man or a woman to do something for him, he places that person in the position of highest privilege, honour, and favour. If God honours you by giving you a work to do for Christ, rejoice in it. Do not murmur and complain. God just might take away the blessing that is such a burden to you.

O may he give us hearts to serve him cheerfully, resolutely, and faithfully for the glory of Christ and the interests of his kingdom. Do what you can for Christ, for his honour and his glory; honour him, and watch him honour you.

Read, again, about one woman who did what she could for the Lord Jesus, and about the high honour bestowed upon her for doing what she could.

'And being in Bethany in the house of Simon the leper, as he sat at meat, there came a woman having an alabaster box of ointment of spikenard very precious; and she brake the box, and poured it on his head. And there were some that had indignation within themselves, and said, Why was this waste of the ointment made? For it might have been sold for more than three hundred pence, and have been given to the poor. And they murmured against her. And Jesus said, Let her alone; why trouble ye her? She hath wrought a good work on me. For ye have the poor with you always, and whensoever ye will ye may do them good: but me ye have not always. She hath done what she could: she is come aforehand to anoint my body to the burying. Verily I say unto you, Wheresoever this gospel shall be preached throughout the whole world, this also that she hath done shall be spoken of for a memorial of her' (Mark 14:3-9).

This poor woman wrought a good work on Christ. It seemed like nothing, even a waste to all others. But she did what she could; and our Master called it 'a good work'. It was a good work because it was a work done for Christ alone. It was a good work because it was a work of faith. It was a good work because it involved great, personal sacrifice. It was a good work because it was the work at hand and the work she could do. And, because she did this good work, the Lord Jesus made it a perpetual honour to her.

Spirit of God, give me grace to do some good work for God my Saviour while I live in this world. Let me count the burden of the work a blessing, and never the blessing a burden. O my Heavenly Father, as you promised in blessing Abraham to make him a blessing, make me a blessing to your people, make me a blessing to many in this the day you have given me, for the glory of your dear Son. Amen.

Chapter 78

Grace At Sinai

'In the third month, when the children of Israel were gone forth out of the land of Egypt, the same day came they into the wilderness of Sinai … An altar of earth thou shalt make unto me, and shalt sacrifice thereon thy burnt offerings, and thy peace offerings, thy sheep, and thine oxen: in all places where I record my name I will come unto thee, and I will bless thee. And if thou wilt make me an altar of stone, thou shalt not build it of hewn stone: for if thou lift up thy tool upon it, thou hast polluted it. Neither shalt thou go up by steps unto mine altar, that thy nakedness be not discovered thereon.'
(Exodus 19:1-20:26)

When you think about the law of God and the giving of the law at Sinai are you a little uneasy? When you think about the Ten Commandments, do you feel a little uncomfortable? Or, are you one of the very few people in this world who understands why the law was given at Sinai and what the law teaches?

Exodus chapters 19 and 20 should always be read together. Their message is one message. The law given at Sinai was 'our schoolmaster to bring us unto Christ' (Galatians 3:24). The purpose of God in giving the law was to show us our need of a Saviour and to point us to his dear Son as our Saviour.

God's Promise
When the children of Israel left Rephidim, the place of murmuring, they came to the Mount of God at Sinai. While Israel was camped before the

Mount of God, Moses went up to meet God. And the very first word the Lord God gave to his people at Sinai was a promise of pure, free grace (Exodus 19:1-6). The Lord gave Moses a specific message for his people. Notice in verse 3 how he referred to his people as both Jacob and Israel. He wanted them to remember what they are by nature and what he made them by grace. 'Thus shalt thou say to the house of Jacob, and tell the children of Israel.'

'In the third month, when the children of Israel were gone forth out of the land of Egypt, the same day came they into the wilderness of Sinai. For they were departed from Rephidim, and were come to the desert of Sinai, and had pitched in the wilderness; and there Israel camped before the mount. And Moses went up unto God, and the LORD called unto him out of the mountain, saying, Thus shalt thou say to the house of Jacob, and tell the children of Israel; Ye have seen what I did unto the Egyptians, and how I bare you on eagles' wings, and brought you unto myself. Now therefore, if ye will obey my voice indeed, and keep my covenant, then ye shall be a peculiar treasure unto me above all people: for all the earth is mine: And ye shall be unto me a kingdom of priests, and an holy nation. These are the words which thou shalt speak unto the children of Israel' (19:1-6).

First, the Lord reminded the children of Israel of what he had done for them already, reminding them specifically of the grace and power of God they had already experienced. 'Ye have seen what I did unto the Egyptians, and how I bare you on eagles' wings, and brought you unto myself' (v. 4). Then he promised that he would make these chosen people, the people he had redeemed to himself, his own peculiar treasure above all people, a kingdom of priests, and a holy nation.

Yes, there were conditions to the promise (v. 5). The Lord said he would do these things for Israel, 'if' they would obey his voice and keep his covenant. But, remember, that which God requires of his people he always gives to his people. So, the 'ifs' of God are not to be read by us as conditions we must meet but as promises of God, assuring us he will meet the conditions he requires. I will show you evidence of that fact.

Presumed Goodness
God made his promises of grace to his people and sent Moses to declare them to the people at the foot of the mountain. Then, as soon as Moses proclaimed God's promise, the elders of Israel gave a unified answer

that exposed the great evil plaguing the hearts of all men by nature. That is pride. How horribly proud we all are! How horribly God hates pride! Yet, there is in us all a presumption of inward goodness that makes all men think they can, by one means or another, to some degree or another, merit God's favour. That is what we have before us in verses 7 and 8.

'And Moses came and called for the elders of the people, and laid before their faces all these words which the LORD commanded him. And all the people answered together, and said, All that the LORD hath spoken we will do. And Moses returned the words of the people unto the LORD' (19:7, 8).

What an outburst of self-righteousness and ignorance! Until the greatness and holiness of God is seen, and the exceeding sinfulness of sin felt, man is ever ready to make empty promises to God, presuming he is really good and not evil, that he is really able to do what God requires and not utterly impotent. The rich young ruler was just like these Israelites at Sinai (Mark 10:17-22).

A Mediator Provided

Now, in verse 9, the Lord God provides a mediator for his poor, sinful, ignorant people. 'And the LORD said unto Moses, Lo, I come unto thee in a thick cloud, that the people may hear when I speak with thee, and believe thee forever. And Moses told the words of the people unto the LORD' (19:9).

Throughout these two chapters, Moses is clearly typical of our Lord Jesus Christ as our great Mediator. The law, Paul tells us in Galatians 3:19, 'was ordained by angels in the hand of a mediator'. No less than ten times, the Spirit of God tells us, Moses went up to the Mount to speak to God for the people, and came down again to speak to the people for God. Oh, how we ought to give thanks to God continually for that one Mediator between God and men, the man Christ Jesus!

God's Requirement

'And the LORD said unto Moses, Go unto the people, and sanctify them today and tomorrow, and let them wash their clothes, And be ready against the third day: for the third day the LORD will come down in the sight of all the people upon mount Sinai' (19:10, 11).

The word 'sanctify', means 'set apart'. Yet, the act by which the people had to be sanctified tells us they must be set apart, prepared and made ready to meet the holy Lord God by being made pure, holy, and clean before God. This purity was symbolized by a ceremonial washing.

If you and I would be ready to meet God, we must be readied both by blood atonement, through the precious blood shed by Christ our Substitute, and by the sanctifying work of God the Holy Ghost in the washing of regeneration (Titus 3:5, 6).

'But after that the kindness and love of God our Saviour toward man appeared, Not by works of righteousness which we have done, but according to his mercy he saved us, by the washing of regeneration, and renewing of the Holy Ghost; Which he shed on us abundantly through Jesus Christ our Saviour; That being justified by his grace, we should be made heirs according to the hope of eternal life' (Titus 3:4-7).

A Strict Prohibition
There is something particularly instructive about the third day in Scripture. The Lord told Moses to make the people ready 'against the third day', because he would come to them the third day (vv. 11, 15, 16). On the third day God raised the earth from chaos and caused it to bud with life (Genesis 1:9-13). On the third day Abraham offered Isaac on Mount Moriah (Genesis 22:4) and learned of God's provision 'Jehovah-jireh' (Genesis 22:14). On the third the flesh of the sacrifice was burned before the Lord (Leviticus 7:17). And our Lord Jesus Christ was raised on the third day. Throughout Scripture, the third day was the day of deliverance and victory, the day of resurrection and life. And, here in verses 12-15, the Lord God said, I will come down to my people on the third day; but they cannot come up to me.

'And thou shalt set bounds unto the people round about, saying, Take heed to yourselves, that ye go not up into the mount, or touch the border of it: whosoever toucheth the mount shall be surely put to death: There shall not an hand touch it, but he shall surely be stoned, or shot through; whether it be beast or man, it shall not live: when the trumpet soundeth long, they shall come up to the mount. And Moses went down from the mount unto the people, and sanctified the people; and they washed their clothes. And he said unto the people, Be ready against the third day: come not at your wives' (19:12-15).

No one was allowed to even touch the Mount of God with his hand, let alone climb it. If they dared do so, they were to be stoned or shot on the spot. Remember, the whole congregation had boasted that they could do whatever God required to give them acceptance with him. Here, the Lord God says, if you even try to satisfy me with your polluted hands, I will destroy you. The touch of your polluted hand upon God's ark will result in eternal ruin for you, just as Uzza's touching the ark of God killed him. If we attempt to add anything to Christ, our Ark, for acceptance with God, we shall be forever damned. The gaze of your curious, speculative eye (19:21) upon God's salvation; the wonders and mysteries of God, will be the everlasting ruin of your soul, just as those 50,000 men of Bethshemesh were slaughtered by God's wrath for daring to lift the lid and look into the ark (1 Samuel 6:19, 20).

The obvious message of God to Israel in verses 12-15 is, 'You cannot come to me, but I will come to you. But on the third day I will come to you and sanctify you.' And he did just that. We could never come to God. He will not accept us until he has come to us himself, sanctified us, and made us holy. And in the third day of time, 'in due time', the holy Lord God came to his people in the person of his dear Son. By his obedience and death, by his work of justice and grace, the Lord Jesus Christ sanctified us, made us the righteousness of God, and made us holy. In Christ, the Lord our Righteousness, our Sanctification and Redemption, we are free to draw near to God by faith in 'that holiness without which no man shall see the Lord'.

Unapproachable Holiness
In verses 16-25 the Lord God gives a magnificent display of his unapproachable holiness.

'And it came to pass on the third day in the morning, that there were thunders and lightnings, and a thick cloud upon the mount, and the voice of the trumpet exceeding loud; so that all the people that was in the camp trembled. And Moses brought forth the people out of the camp to meet with God; and they stood at the nether part of the mount. And mount Sinai was altogether on a smoke, because the LORD descended upon it in fire: and the smoke thereof ascended as the smoke of a furnace, and the whole mount quaked greatly. And when the voice of the trumpet sounded long, and waxed louder and louder, Moses spake, and God answered him by a voice. And the LORD came down upon mount Sinai, on the top of the mount: and the LORD called Moses up to the top of the mount; and Moses went up. And the LORD said unto Moses, Go down, charge the people, lest they break through unto the

LORD to gaze, and many of them perish. And let the priests also, which come near to the LORD, sanctify themselves, lest the LORD break forth upon them. And Moses said unto the LORD, The people cannot come up to mount Sinai: for thou chargedst us, saying, Set bounds about the mount, and sanctify it. And the LORD said unto him, Away, get thee down, and thou shalt come up, thou, and Aaron with thee: but let not the priests and the people break through to come up unto the LORD, lest he break forth upon them. So, Moses went down unto the people, and spake unto them'.

When the Lord God came down upon Sinai, his coming was announced by a sevenfold, or perfect, expression of his terrible majesty and unapproachable holiness: thunder, lightning, cloud, fire, smoke, quaking, and a trumpet. There was nothing to encourage hope, attract the guilty, or pacify the accusing conscience. Such is the character of the great Judge of all the earth, who must do right. He is all terror! There is no mention made of blood-atonement. So, there is no hope for man this way. 'Our God is a consuming fire' (Hebrews 12:29). Well might we cry, like those men of Bethshemesh who remained, 'Who is able to stand before this holy LORD God?'

Sin Exposed
In chapter 20, with the giving of the Ten Commandments, the Lord God exposed the sin and guilt of this people who had boasted, 'All that the LORD hath spoken, we will do' (19:8).

'And God spake all these words, saying, I am the LORD thy God, which have brought thee out of the land of Egypt, out of the house of bondage. Thou shalt have no other gods before me. Thou shalt not make unto thee any graven image, or any likeness of anything that is in heaven above, or that is in the earth beneath, or that is in the water under the earth: Thou shalt not bow down thyself to them, nor serve them: for I the LORD thy God am a jealous God, visiting the iniquity of the fathers upon the children unto the third and fourth generation of them that hate me; And showing mercy unto thousands of them that love me, and keep my commandments. Thou shalt not take the name of the LORD thy God in vain; for the LORD will not hold him guiltless that taketh his name in vain. Remember the sabbath day, to keep it holy. Six days shalt thou labour, and do all thy work: But the seventh day is the sabbath of the LORD thy God: in it thou shalt not do any work, thou, nor thy son, nor thy daughter, thy manservant, nor thy maidservant, nor thy cattle, nor thy stranger that is within thy gates: For in six days the LORD made heaven and earth, the sea, and all that in them is, and rested the seventh day: wherefore the LORD blessed the sabbath day, and hallowed it. Honour thy father and thy mother: that thy days may be long upon the land which the LORD thy God giveth thee. Thou shalt not kill. Thou shalt not commit adultery. Thou shalt not steal. Thou shalt not bear false witness against thy neighbour. Thou shalt not covet thy neighbour's house, thou shalt not covet thy neighbour's wife, nor his manservant, nor his maidservant, nor his ox, nor his ass, nor any thing that is thy neighbour's' (20:1-17).

The law's purpose is to identify sin, condemn sin, and condemn the sinner. The people were appalled, not by what God required, that was all holy and good, but by their own sinfulness that they now knew prevented them from doing what God required. When they saw that God demands perfection, they withdrew from the mount as quickly as they could (v. 18).

'And all the people saw the thunderings, and the lightnings, and the noise of the trumpet, and the mountain smoking: and when the people saw it, they removed, and stood afar off.'

A Mediator Desired
The purpose of God in giving his holy law at Sinai was to show his people their need of a Mediator, to shut us up to Christ and faith in him. It is exactly what happened with these Israelites at Mount Sinai (20:19-21; Job 9:30-33). The terrors of Sinai reveal the need for Calvary!

'And they said unto Moses, Speak thou with us, and we will hear: but let not God speak with us, lest we die. And Moses said unto the people, Fear not: for God is come to prove you, and that his fear may be before your faces, that ye sin not. And the people stood afar off, and Moses drew near unto the thick darkness where God was' (20:19-21).

This was all the nearness to God they could accomplish when their imaginary goodness was exposed for the evil it was. Sin exposed, guilt felt, causes needy souls to desire a mediator. We cannot come to God without Christ!

'If I wash myself with snow water, and make my hands never so clean; Yet shalt thou plunge me in the ditch, and mine own clothes shall abhor me. For he is not a man, as I am, that I should answer him, and we should come together in judgment. Neither is there any daysman betwixt us, that might lay his hand upon us both' (Job 9:30-33).

The Way Revealed

As we read Exodus 20:22-26, remember we are still at Mount Sinai. We are still learning 'what the law saith'. In these last verses of Exodus 20 the Lord God shows us the Way by which sinners may and must come to him, not by works but by blood, the precious blood of Christ.

'And the LORD said unto Moses, Thus thou shalt say unto the children of Israel, Ye have seen that I have talked with you from heaven. Ye shall not make with me gods of silver, neither shall ye make unto you gods of gold. An altar of earth thou shalt make unto me, and shalt sacrifice thereon thy burnt offerings, and thy peace offerings, thy sheep, and thine oxen: in all places where I record my name I will come unto thee, and I will bless thee. And if thou wilt make me an altar of stone, thou shalt not build it of hewn stone: for if thou lift up thy tool upon it, thou hast polluted it. Neither shalt thou go up by steps unto mine altar, that thy nakedness be not discovered thereon.'

The burnt offering is Christ. The peace-offering is Christ. The sheep and the oxen portray Christ, our sin atoning Sacrifice. The altar upon which we come to God is Christ. He is our Altar who is the Altar of God's making, 'an altar of earth'. And 'an altar of stone', but not hewn stone. Our hands contribute nothing. Our hands have no part in the work of salvation. And we do not come to God upon stairs, step by step, but by faith in Christ alone. Anything we contribute, anything we add to Christ's work, all our imaginary righteousness only exposes our nakedness, our sin, and pollutes the altar by which we would draw near to and find acceptance with the holy Lord God.

God's Gift

In the Book of God, God's 'ifs' are not conditions we must meet, but promises God will keep. God's 'if' in Exodus 19:5 is to be read, not as a condition that must be met by us, but as God's promise to us that he would meet the condition, supplying for Jacob and Israel, the whole house of his elect, everything connected with the promise. So, read the promise again (Exodus 19:5, 6).

'Now therefore, if ye will obey my voice indeed, and keep my covenant, then ye shall be a peculiar treasure unto me above all people:

for all the earth is mine: And ye shall be unto me a kingdom of priests, and an holy nation. These are the words which thou shalt speak unto the children of Israel.'

In Christ, by his obedience unto death as our Substitute and covenant Surety, every sinner who comes to God upon this Altar, by this Sacrifice, by faith in Christ, has perfectly obeyed his voice and kept his covenant. And now, because of our perfection in Christ, the things promised in Exodus 19:5, 6 are ours.

There is therefore now no condemnation to them which are in Christ Jesus, who walk not after the flesh, but after the Spirit. For the law of the Spirit of life in Christ Jesus hath made me free from the law of sin and death. For what the law could not do, in that it was weak through the flesh, God sending his own Son in the likeness of sinful flesh, and for sin, condemned sin in the flesh: That the righteousness of the law might be fulfilled in us, who walk not after the flesh, but after the Spirit (Romans 8:1-4).

'Ye also, as lively stones, are built up a spiritual house, an holy priesthood, to offer up spiritual sacrifices, acceptable to God by Jesus Christ. Wherefore also it is contained in the scripture, Behold, I lay in Sion a chief corner stone, elect, precious: and he that believeth on him shall not be confounded. Unto you therefore which believe he is precious: but unto them which be disobedient, the stone which the builders disallowed, the same is made the head of the corner, And a stone of stumbling, and a rock of offence, even to them which stumble at the word, being disobedient: whereunto also they were appointed. But ye are a chosen generation, a royal priesthood, an holy nation, a peculiar people; that ye should show forth the praises of him who hath called you out of darkness into his marvellous light: Which in time past were not a people, but are now the people of God: which had not obtained mercy, but now have obtained mercy' (1 Peter 2:5-10).

John Berridge, the English preacher and hymnwriter, described the contrast between law and gospel thus,

> The law demands a weighty debt,
> And not a single mite will bate;
> But gospel sings of Jesus' blood,
> And says it made the payment good.

177

The law provokes men oft to ill,
And churlish hearts makes harder still;
But gospel acts a kinder part,
And melts a most obdurate heart.

'Run, run, and work,' the law commands
Yet, finds me neither feet nor hands;
But sweeter news the gospel brings;
It bids me fly, and lends me wings.

[Such needful wings, O Lord, impart,
To brace my feet and brace my heart;
Good wings of faith and wings of love
Will make a cripple sprightly move.]

With these a lumpish soul may fly,
And soar aloft, and reach the sky;
Nor faint nor falter in the race,
But cheerly work, and sing of grace.

Chapter 79

'On Eagles' Wings'

'Ye have seen what I did unto the Egyptians, and how I bare you on eagles' wings, and brought you unto myself.'
(Exodus 19:4)

When a soldier is severely wounded in battle it is of little benefit to him to be told there are doctors at the hospital who can bind up his wounds and give him medicine that will ease him of all the pains that wrack his body. What that wounded warrior needs is someone to carry him to the hospital, and a doctor to administer the care he needs and give him the medicine that will help. So it is with us. All the promises of God and all the doctrine of the gospel are of no benefit to our souls, until the Lord God, by his own gracious hand, applies them to us. We are thirsty, but too faint to crawl to the waterhole. We must be carried to the water. We are too weak even to drink. Someone must put the water to our lips and tenderly put it in our mouths.

That is what the Lord our God does for us by his Spirit. God the Holy Ghost, the blessed Spirit of Truth, takes of the things of Christ and applies them to us. Do not imagine that our blessed Saviour has placed his promises, his blessings, and his mercies on heavenly shelves that we may climb up to heaven and get them for ourselves. That is not the case at all. He comes to us and sheds his mercy, love, and grace abroad in our hearts by his Spirit. Yes, he bids us come boldly to the Throne of Grace, that we might obtain mercy and find grace to help in time of need. But, blessed be his name, he does much more than that!

He who is our God and Saviour, the Lord Jesus Christ, comes to our poor souls and pours in the oil and wine of grace, by which he renews us day by day. Oh, bless his name forever! Child of God, if you are labouring under deep distresses, your God does not give you promises and then leave you to yourself, to draw them up from the Word like buckets of water from a well. Oh, no! The promises he has written in the Word, he will write anew on your heart. He will manifest his love to you, and by his blessed Spirit dispel your cares and troubles. It is God's prerogative and God's work to wipe every tear from the eyes of his chosen. The good Samaritan not only gives you the sweet wine of the promise, he also holds the golden chalice to your lips and pours the life-blood into your soul. The poor, sick, way-worn pilgrim is not merely strengthened to walk, but he is borne 'on eagles' wings', until he has reached the Mount of God above!

Glorious gospel! God our Saviour provides help for the helpless and brings grace to us before we seek it. So, he gets as much glory in the giving as in the gift. That is what the Lord God declares in Exodus 19:4. It is precisely what is portrayed for us in Israel's deliverance out of Egyptian bondage. 'Ye have seen what I did unto the Egyptians, and how I bare you on eagles' wings, and brought you unto myself'. What a blessed, blessed word this is from God our Saviour to us!

Christ's Redemption

What a picture this is of our God's tender mercy toward us in Christ! First, here is a picture of our blessed Saviour's wondrous work of redemption. The eagle is declared in the Levitical law to be an unclean bird (Leviticus 11:13-16). Yet, our Lord delights to use the unclean eagle as a representation of himself as our Saviour. He says, in Exodus 19:4, 'I bare you on eagles' wings, and brought you unto myself.' Certainly, this speaks of his protection of us. But it also seems to me to allude to the fact he took our uncleanness, our sins, upon himself, making our sins his own, making himself unclean before the holy Lord God. He bears his redeemed on eagles' wings, makes us the very righteousness of God in him, that he might bring us to God.

What unspeakable mercy this is! He, who in such infinite love and grace became both sin and a curse for us (2 Corinthians 5:21; Galatians 3:13), compares himself to the unclean eagle, when made sin for us, that we might be made the righteousness of God in him.

God's Providence

This word from God to us is used to describe the wondrous mystery of providence in Revelation 12:1-17. God's church, his elect, constantly persecuted by Satan, is there described as a 'woman given two wings of a great eagle, that she might fly into the wilderness, into her place, where she is nourished.'

Our Pilgrimage

In Deuteronomy 32, Moses was inspired of God to use this same emblem of Israel being carried 'on eagles' wings' as a description of our pilgrimage through this world. As the children of Israel were pilgrims in the wilderness, so God's saints are pilgrims in this world, carried through their pilgrimage 'on eagles' wings'. Moses is here giving his last word of instruction to the children of Israel. As he does, he begins his instruction with a song of praise to the Lord God, who had led Israel through the wilderness, caring for, providing for, and protecting them for forty-years. According to God's wise and good purpose, causing them to walk 'in a straight way', the children of Israel made an 11-day trip in 40 years! Moses' purpose here is threefold.

He wants to exalt and extol the Lord God who redeemed and brought his people out of the land of bondage. He begins his instructive song by calling the people of God to 'ascribe greatness unto our God' (Deuteronomy 32:1-3).

You will remember the Lord God proclaimed his name to Moses back in Exodus 34:6, 7, when he hid him in the cleft of the rock and showed him his glory. When Moses talks about publishing the name of the Lord, he is talking about our Lord Jesus Christ, Jehovah the Son. Remember, his name is what he is, his character and his attributes. He is saying, 'I will proclaim the glorious attributes of God my Saviour, in whom I trust'. There are many names by which the Lord God reveals himself to us in Holy Scripture.[5]

As he tells us to publish the name of the Lord, Moses calls for us to do so by ascribing greatness to our God. 'Ascribe ye greatness unto our God.' Truly, he who is our God is great. He alone is great! Then, in Deuteronomy 32:4, he tells us four specific aspects of the greatness of God our Saviour. First, 'He is the Rock.' The Rock of Salvation, the

---

[5] See p. 218

Rock of Refuge. Second, 'His work is perfect.' His work is all one; and it is perfect. Third, 'All his ways are judgment.' All his ways are both righteous and wise. Fourth, 'A God of truth and without iniquity, just and right is he.' He who is God our Saviour is the God of Truth, the God who is Truth, and the God who performs Truth.

Moses' primary purpose was to extol and honour the Lord Jesus, our great God and Saviour. His next object, here in Deuteronomy 32, was to remind us of God's great goodness to us, to inscribe upon our hearts and minds the memory of his gracious works for us, with us, and in us, inspiring us with gratitude, love, and devotion to our God.

God's faithful servant begins by reminding us we are corrupt, sinful people, altogether undeserving of the least of his favours (vv. 5, 6). He tells us to 'remember the days of old' (vv. 7, 8). Remember, everything God does in this world is according to his everlasting, immutable, electing love and purpose of grace toward his people (v. 8). Remember, children of God, you are the Lord's chosen portion and the lot of his inheritance (v. 9). Remember where you were and what you were when he called you by his grace (v. 10; Isaiah 51:1).

Those words give us a biographical sketch of every saved sinner's life. He found us. We did not find him. He found us in a desert land, in a waste and howling wilderness. He has led us about all the days of our lives. He has instructed us. He has kept us as the apple of his eye. His providence has been good, only good. It is described in vv. 13, 14.

'He made him ride on the high places of the earth, that he might eat the increase of the fields; and he made him to suck honey out of the rock, and oil out of the flinty rock; Butter of kine, and milk of sheep, with fat of lambs, and rams of the breed of Bashan, and goats, with the fat of kidneys of wheat; and thou didst drink the pure blood of the grape.'

Moses' third object, in this chapter was to inspire our faith in Christ, our God and Saviour. He does this by using this very graphic, tender illustration of our God's gracious oversight of his people (vv. 11, 12).

'As an eagle stirreth up her nest, fluttereth over her young, spreadeth abroad her wings, taketh them, beareth them on her wings: So the LORD alone did lead him, and there was no strange god with him.'

This is a tremendous, instructive picture of the great mercy and grace of our blessed Saviour in his dealings with us.

'As the Eagle'

Like other creatures of our God, the eagle not only appears to show great affection for her young, but manifests tremendous superiority over other winged creatures in taking care of her brood. She provides for them and protects them, as other birds of the air do. But, in training them, she constantly shelters them from danger, far more than other birds do their young. The Lord our God seems to have created her with such excellence, that she might be illustrative of his affection for, tender care of, and protection of, his children.

John Gill wrote, 'Of all animals the eagle is most affectionate to its young, and most studiously careful of them. When it sees anyone coming to them, it will not suffer them to go away unpunished, but will beat them with its wings and tear them with its nails.'

Stirs Up

'She stirreth up her nest'. Though they might be naturally inclined to do so, the eagle will not allow her young to be lethargic. She stirs her nest, calling them to life and excitement. As she stirs her nest, she 'fluttereth over them', over her young. The eagle does not go into her nest suddenly. She first makes a noise and awakens her chicks with her wings, striking them against a tree or its branches. Being awakened, they receive her gladly, without fear.

On Her Wings

She 'spreadeth abroad her wings, taketh them, beareth them on her wings'. In this way, she both teaches them to fly and protects them. Other birds carry their young in their talons. Held in their claws, the young might be easily snatched away and killed by some bird of prey. If someone from the ground should shoot at the bird, her young might be killed and the bird herself unharmed. But the eagle carries her young on her wings, so that no arrow from beneath can touch the young, until it has first pierced the heart of the old bird.

I am aware some people refer to this text as 'proof' the Bible contains errors, asserting, 'Eagles do not carry their young on their wings or on their backs, but in their claws, as other birds'. Even if that were true, it would not prove an error in Holy Scripture, Moses is simply giving us a metaphor, by divine inspiration, picturing our Saviour's care of his people.

God's Grace

This picture also gives us a vivid view of our God's wondrous operations of grace in salvation. 'So, the LORD alone did lead them.' With those words, Moses portrayed the grace and power of our God in our experience of his great salvation.

He who was made sin for us is our omnipotent Saviour. His wings, like the eagle's, are broad and strong enough to carry his own. Our great God, 'the God of all grace', by the irresistible power of his Holy Spirit, stirs up his nest. He will not allow his children, chosen, redeemed sinners, to remain as they are born into this world. He would not allow us to sleep forever in the unawakened state of sin and death. He has brought us out of our unregenerate state of spiritual death.

We were at ease and had no desire to be awakened and stirred out of our death slumber. But the Lord our God, because of his great love for us, awakened us, stirred us up, and brought us out, by sending a gospel preacher in the power of his Spirit to arouse us. He sent his law into our consciences, working in us a sense of guilt, wrath, and death. By his Spirit, revealing Christ in us, he convinced us of our sin, of Christ's righteousness, and of judgment finished. Exerting the omnipotent power of his grace, he plucked us as brands out of the burning. Taking us up on his omnipotent wings of mercy, he taught us to fly with heart aspirations after him, setting our hearts upon Christ and things above.

This mighty work of grace he performs by the preaching of the gospel (Romans 10:17; Hebrews 4:12; James 1:18; 1 Peter 1:23-25). The gospel preacher is sent of God like 'a flying eagle' (Revelation 4:7), with the word of grace to his chosen.

God our Saviour has led us and fed us all the days of our lives. He has, as it were, hovered over us, though we knew it not, from our mothers' wombs. Even now, he causes us to 'mount up with wings as eagles', to soar aloft in the exercise of faith, hope, and love, entering within the veil, into the holiest of all by the blood of Christ, living in the constant and comfortable expectation of 'the mercy of our Lord Jesus Christ unto eternal life'. He lifts us up from our low estate and raises us in sweet communion with himself, bearing us on his heart, in his hands, and on his arms, supporting us in all our temptations and afflictions, and carrying us through all our troubles and difficulties, safe to eternal glory and happiness.

Reviving Grace

Yet, we are ever inclined to lethargic indifference. Are we not? Do you not often find yourself so? I know I do. But, blessed be his name, 'As an eagle stirreth up her nest, fluttereth over her young, spreadeth abroad her wings, taketh them, beareth them on her wings: So the LORD' stirs and awakens our souls, spreads abroad his mighty wings of grace, bears us upon them, and so, God our Saviour revives our languishing hearts with grace.

How often I sleep, though my heart wakes. How often when my Saviour comes, I refuse him. Yet, he puts his hand into my heart, dropping the sweet-smelling myrrh of his grace into my wretched heart, and graciously causes me to awake, arise, and seek him, until at last I find him. Then, he brings me into his banqueting house and spreads his banner of love over me, and causes me to know more fully, with every experience of his love, that many waters cannot quench his love, neither can the floods of my sin drown it!

'Bless the LORD, O my soul: and all that is within me, bless his holy name. Bless the LORD, O my soul, and forget not all his benefits: Who forgiveth all thine iniquities; who healeth all thy diseases; Who redeemeth thy life from destruction; who crowneth thee with lovingkindness and tender mercies; Who satisfieth thy mouth with good things; so that thy youth is renewed like the eagle's' (Psalm 103:1-5).

'He giveth power to the faint; and to them that have no might he increaseth strength. Even the youths shall faint and be weary, and the young men shall utterly fall: But they that wait upon the LORD shall renew their strength; they shall mount up with wings as eagles; they shall run, and not be weary; and they shall walk, and not faint' (Isaiah 40:29-31).

> Compassed with trouble, in distress,
> What fears possess my mind!
> Saviour, I long to see Your face,
> For grace and peace divine!
>
> With broken heart, and waiting long,
> Beneath this crushing load,
> I own my sin, confess my wrong,
> And stretch my hands to God.

My wretched heart, my God, I mourn;
And for my sin I weep!
With every lust obscene I burn,
And sink into the deep!

As Satan raises Moses up,
And roars against my soul,
Lord Jesus, my poor cause take up,
And make Your servant whole!

Arise, O Lord! Shine forth in grace!
Your precious blood apply!
Embrace my soul, dear Prince of Peace,
Blest Rock higher than I!

Speak, Saviour, let me hear Your voice,
Show me, again, Your face!
Oh! Hear my inmost groans and cries.
Revive my soul with grace!

God's Election

The eagle also portrays God's sweet and blessed election of some to salvation in Christ. I have read that the eagle will usually lay three eggs, but normally only hatches and rears one, devoting everything to its chosen. So, the Lord our God has chosen One, even our Lord Jesus Christ, as his Elect; and, blessed be his name, he has chosen us in him and as one with him. Though all the rest of Adam's fallen race are left to themselves, as the unhatched eggs in the eagle's nest, our great God devotes himself entirely to his chosen.

Let every ransomed sinner rejoice and give thanks for this sweet, comforting word of grace from our God. 'As an eagle stirreth up her nest, fluttereth over her young, spreadeth abroad her wings, taketh them, beareth them on her wings; so, the LORD alone did lead him'. Christ, our God and Saviour, has borne and still bears us upon eagle's wings. He stirred us up and brought us to himself. He will not allow any of his little ones to perish. It is written, 'he that toucheth you toucheth the apple of his eye'. While on his omnipotent wings of mercy, nothing can touch us, until it first touches him. Nothing can harm us, until it first harms him. Nothing can destroy us, until it first destroys him! How safe, how secure we are on his wings!

Christ Alone
Then, in verse 12 we read, 'The LORD alone did lead him'. It was the Lord alone who performed all this work for his people of old. It is the Lord alone who has performed all this great work for us. 'Salvation is of the LORD.' He alone separated us from the sons of Adam in eternal election, by special redemption, and in effectual calling. He alone chose us as his portion. He alone found us by his grace. He alone has led us about. He alone has instructed us by his Spirit. He alone has kept us as the apple of his eye. He alone spreads abroad his omnipotent wings, takes us up, and carries us on his wings to the Mountain of God in eternal glory. He alone shall have our praise forever (1 Corinthians 4:7).

Go back to Exodus 19:4-6. I want you to see this and rejoice. In the Book of God, God's 'ifs' are not conditions we must meet, but promises God will keep. God's 'if' in Exodus 19:5 is to be read, not as a condition that must be met by us, but as God's promise to us that he would meet the condition, supplying for Jacob and Israel, the whole house of his elect, everything connected with the promise. Read the promise again (Exodus 19:5, 6). First, as we have it in the King James Version.

'Ye have seen what I did unto the Egyptians, and how I bare you on eagles' wings, and brought you unto myself. Now therefore, if ye will obey my voice indeed, and keep my covenant, then ye shall be a peculiar treasure unto me above all people: for all the earth is mine: And ye shall be unto me a kingdom of priests, and an holy nation. These are the words which thou shalt speak unto the children of Israel' (Exodus 19:4-6).

Now, those verses as they appear in Young's Literal Translation.

'You have seen what I did to bondage; and I bore you on wings of eagles and brought you to Me. And now if listening you will listen to My voice, and will keep My covenant, you shall become a special treasure to Me above all the nations, for all the earth is Mine. And you shall become a kingdom of priests for Me, a holy nation. These are the words which you shall speak unto the children of Israel' (Exodus 19:4-6).

As he promised, so he has performed the work.

'Ye also, as lively stones, are built up a spiritual house, an holy priesthood, to offer up spiritual sacrifices, acceptable to God by Jesus Christ. Wherefore also it is contained in the scripture, Behold, I lay in Sion a chief corner stone, elect, precious: and he that believeth on him shall not be confounded. Unto you therefore which believe he is precious: but unto them which be disobedient, the stone which the builders disallowed, the same is made the head of the corner, And a stone of stumbling, and a rock of offence, even to them which stumble at the word, being disobedient: whereunto also they were appointed. But ye are a chosen generation, a royal priesthood, an holy nation, a peculiar people; that ye should show forth the praises of him who hath called you out of darkness into his marvellous light: Which in time past were not a people, but are now the people of God: which had not obtained mercy, but now have obtained mercy' (1 Peter 2:5-10).

After commenting on this portion of Scripture, Robert Hawker made the following supplication to our God. Blessed are those whose hearts echo his prayer.

'Oh Lord, give me grace rightly to enjoy and use such marvellous blessings. And since, to the wisdom and strength of the eagle, thou hast now added the tenderness and solicitude of the hen, do thou, Lord, gather me under thy wings, and nourish me with thy love and favour, that I may be thine forever, and live here by faith, as hereafter I hope to live with thee in glory.'

Chapter 80

The Ten Commandments

'And God spake all these words, saying, I am the LORD thy God, which have brought thee out of the land of Egypt, out of the house of bondage. Thou shalt have no other gods before me ... Ye shall not make with me gods of silver, neither shall ye make unto you gods of gold. An altar of earth thou shalt make unto me, and shalt sacrifice thereon thy burnt offerings, and thy peace offerings, thy sheep, and thine oxen: in all places where I record my name I will come unto thee, and I will bless thee. And if thou wilt make me an altar of stone, thou shalt not build it of hewn stone: for if thou lift up thy tool upon it, thou hast polluted it. Neither shalt thou go up by steps unto mine altar, that thy nakedness be not discovered thereon.'
(Exodus 20:1-26)

When we read the twentieth chapter of Exodus, we are standing at the foot of Mount Sinai. Moses declares, 'The LORD came from Sinai, and rose up from Seir unto them; he shined forth from mount Paran, and he came with ten thousands of saints: from his right hand went a fiery law for them' (Deuteronomy 33:2). But Sinai is all darkness, until Zion's Sun of Righteousness rises upon it. Then, the darkness flees before the rising Sun. The angry roars are hushed by the sound of grace. The terrors of darkness are dispersed by the Light of Life. The quaking is settled by the Prince of Peace, as we are made to see that Sinai opens the way to Zion and its blissful slopes of mercy, love, and grace.

How vast and infinitely important God's righteous law is! It was delivered with such awful solemnity on Mount Sinai that all the children of Israel were filled with fear, as they stood before the quaking mountain. That fact alone should fill our hearts with constantly increasing joy, praise, and thanksgiving for the unspeakable gift of God, our Lord Jesus Christ, our precious, blessed, holy, law-fulfilling, law-satisfying Surety! He answered all the demands of Sinai's law for us; and, answering those demands, he is declared to be 'the end of the law for righteousness to everyone that believeth' (Romans 10:4).

With every renewed view of our blessed Saviour, who has, with his own blood, redeemed us from the curse of the law, let us renew our praises to the God of all grace. With every renewed conviction of sin, as we remember our iniquities, transgressions and sins, let us lift our hearts with renewed gratitude and adoration to our ever gracious, triune Jehovah.

Blessed Spirit of God, by the sweet influences of your grace in our hearts, teach us to cherish the redemption that is ours in Christ Jesus, and to cherish our Redeemer. In great love for our souls, he stood forth as our Surety in old eternity. He undertook our cause. By his doing and dying as our Substitute, the Son of God obtained eternal redemption for us. By his blood and righteousness, we now draw nigh to God and are 'accepted in the Beloved'. Blessed be God, the boundary which kept Israel from approaching God and kept God from approaching Israel, is removed. We are come to Jesus, the Mediator of the new covenant, and to his precious blood of sprinkling. Drawing nigh to God, in this new and living way, we arrive at the fountain-head of mercies, the throne of God and the Lamb, the throne of grace, and obtain the mercy and grace we need.

God Identifies Himself

Before giving his law, the Lord God identifies himself, and identifies himself by the salvation he has performed (vv. 1, 2).

'And God spake all these words, saying, I am the LORD thy God, which have brought thee out of the land of Egypt, out of the house of bondage.'

Who was it that brought Israel to the foot of Mount Sinai? Who has the right to lay such claims upon us as are given in these Ten Commandments? It is God, the Supreme One, Elohim your Creator. It is the Lord thy God, our covenant God, God in covenant with us. It is the Lord Jehovah, the self-existent, eternal God of all redemption, salvation, and grace. It is the triune God, our omnipotent Saviour, 'which have brought thee out of the land of Egypt, out of the house of bondage'.

It is the God of everlasting grace who speaks from Sinai. His mercy looked upon Israel's enslavement in Egypt and protected them. He burst their bonds and crushed their foes. He fed them morning after morning with bread from heaven. He sent streams gushing from the smitten rock to quench their thirst. Now he brings them to Sinai. Sinai will be a platform upon which God will show his Christ to chosen sinners.

The children of Israel heard a voice speaking to them from heaven. Who was it that spoke? The voice was that of their Redeemer and ours, Christ Jesus. The Holy Spirit tells us that the Angel, the Messenger, of the eternal covenant, communed with Moses on the mount. If it is Christ who speaks, the message will be full of tender love and rich mercy. He says, as he introduces himself, 'Ye have seen what I did unto the Egyptians, and how I bare you on eagles' wings, and brought you unto myself' (Exodus 19:4).

Surely, he did not bear them on eagle's wings out of Egypt, just to crush them with woe upon Sinai! No! The sound of thunder upon the mount and the flashes of lightning shooting from heaven announce fresh rain from heaven, new revelations of grace. Special preparation must be made. The sin soiled people must be purified, before they draw near to God.

That is what everything spoken at Sinai declares. We must be purged of all sin, purified from all iniquity and cleansed of all guilt before we can come to God, or God can come to us. So, when the Lord God speaks from Sinai's fiery mount, with his very first word, before he gives his ten commandments, he identifies himself as God our Saviour. 'I am the LORD thy God, which have brought thee out of the land of Egypt, out of the house of bondage.' Redemption is our Saviour's claim upon our hearts and lives (1 Corinthians 6:19, 20; Psalm 116:16, 17).

Understand this first and foremost, the hand that holds the glittering sword of law and justice and shakes it over a terrified world of guilty sinners, declaring, 'the soul that sinneth it shall die', is the hand of our crucified Christ. The reason for the giving of the law was to make sinners, like you and me, know our need of him.

The Commandments

In verses 1 and 2, the Lord God identifies himself. Second, in verses 3-17, he gives us the Ten Commandments. These Ten Commandments were written upon two tables of stone by the finger of God. On the first table, we have the first four commandments, revealing our duty to God. On the second table, the Lord God wrote out six commandments revealing our duty to one another, man's duty to man. Let us look briefly at these Ten Commandments.

The First Commandment

'Thou shalt have no other gods before me' (v. 3). Here the Lord God demands that we reverence him alone as God, that we serve him with a perfect heart and a willing mind (1 Chronicles 28:9). Martin Luther wrote, 'In this first commandment the keeping of all the other nine is commanded.' We must worship the triune God alone as God. And worship him in faith, hope, and love. This commandment is a prohibition of idolatry, of will worship, of mixing the worship of God and the worship of idols. But our Lord Jesus gives us the best commentary upon his words in Matthew 22:37, 38, where he tells us plainly what this great commandment of the law is.

'Jesus said unto him, Thou shalt love the Lord thy God with all thy heart, and with all thy soul, and with all thy mind. This is the first and great commandment.'

The Second Commandment

'Thou shalt not make unto thee any graven image, or any likeness of anything that is in heaven above, or that is in the earth beneath, or that is in the water under the earth: Thou shalt not bow down thyself to them, nor serve them: for I the LORD thy God am a jealous God, visiting the iniquity of the fathers upon the children unto the third and fourth generation of them that hate me; And showing mercy unto thousands of them that love me, and keep my commandments.'

This second commandment is a strict prohibition of idolatrous, religious images, icons, relics, etc.. Not only are we to acknowledge none as God, except God, we are never to have or make use of religious symbols in the worship of God; no images of angels, crosses, pictures of Christ, etc. (Isaiah 40:18; Deuteronomy 4:15).

192

Included in this is the requirement that we love and obey our God, worshipping him with the heart, in spirit and in truth.

The Third Commandment

'Thou shalt not take the name of the LORD thy God in vain; for the LORD will not hold him guiltless that taketh his name in vain' (v. 7). In this day of religious blasphemy, when men and women are taught that God is nothing and can do nothing without them, the profaning of God's name is as common as breathing. Sadly, it is all too common among those who truly reverence and worship him. But by careless speech, arising from a failure to make the reverence of God a matter of thoughtful, deliberate choice, true believers often take God's name in vain, joking about God and heavenly things and using God's name, or substitutes for it, as by-words.

'Holy and reverend is his name' (Psalm 111:9). Let us reverence and sanctify his name in thought, and word, and deed. Any use of God's name without the intention of exalting and honouring his name is taking the name of the Lord our God in vain. Let us take care never to do so.

The Fourth Commandment

'Remember the sabbath day, to keep it holy. Six days shalt thou labour, and do all thy work: But the seventh day is the sabbath of the LORD thy God: in it thou shalt not do any work, thou, nor thy son, nor thy daughter, thy manservant, nor thy maidservant, nor thy cattle, nor thy stranger that is within thy gates: For in six days the LORD made heaven and earth, the sea, and all that in them is, and rested the seventh day: wherefore the LORD blessed the sabbath day, and hallowed it'.

This fourth commandment (vv. 8-11), like the first three, has to do with our duty toward God. It stands here as the last commandment relating to our relationship with and reverence for God. Yet, our Lord Jesus declares, 'The sabbath was made for man' (Mark 2:27). Standing as it does between the two tables of the law, at the end of the first and the beginning of the second, it might be best to understand it as the hinge upon which both our duty to God and our duty to man hang. I will come back to that shortly. For now, let me simply and dogmatically declare that there is nothing written in the Bible and nothing required of man that is more important than this fourth commandment. Perhaps that is the reason Satan has raised so much confusion about it.

193

The Fifth Commandment

'Honour thy father and thy mother: that thy days may be long upon the land which the LORD thy God giveth thee' (v. 12). The fifth is called by the Apostle Paul 'the first commandment with promise' (Ephesians 6:2). God promises length of days to those who honour their parents, to those who honour authority, which is no more and no less than honouring God.

The Sixth Commandment

'Thou shalt not kill' (v. 13). Again, I refer to the words of our Lord Jesus in Matthew's Gospel as the best commentary there is upon the sixth commandment.

'Ye have heard that it was said by them of old time, Thou shalt not kill; and whosoever shall kill shall be in danger of the judgment: But I say unto you, That whosoever is angry with his brother without a cause shall be in danger of the judgment: and whosoever shall say to his brother, Raca ('Raca' means worthless one), shall be in danger of the council: but whosoever shall say, Thou fool, shall be in danger of hell fire' (Matthew 5:21, 22). God himself makes inquisition for blood (Psalm 9:12; Genesis 4:8-12, 23, 24). For one man to take another man's life, or disdain another as a worthless thing, is for man to assume the place of God to himself.

The Seventh Commandment

'Thou shalt not commit adultery' (v. 14). This seventh commandment refers not merely to the sexual infidelity of married people, but to all sexual evil, having its roots in the sensual lusts of our hearts.

'Ye have heard that it was said by them of old time, Thou shalt not commit adultery: But I say unto you, That whosoever looketh on a woman to lust after her hath committed adultery with her already in his heart' (Matthew 5:27, 28).

John Trapp, commenting on this seventh commandment, made this tremendously perceptive observation: 'Adultery only is named; because bestiality, sodomy, and other uncleannesses, though more heinous, yet they do not directly fight against the purity of posterity and human society, which the law mainly respects.'

The Eighth Commandment

'Thou shalt not steal' (v. 15). Stealing is taking, by any method, that which is not your own. It is fraud and cheating, as well as open theft. Any disrespect of private property as private property is stealing (Ephesians 4:28; 1 Thessalonians 4:6).

The Ninth Commandment

'Thou shalt not bear false witness against thy neighbour' (v. 16). Do not bear false witness, and do not hear it (Deuteronomy 19:16-20). Gossip and slander would die very quickly if there were no ears anxious to hear and tongues anxious to bear them. If you love the lie, you are as guilty as if you had made it (Revelation 22:15).

The Tenth Commandment

'Thou shalt not covet thy neighbour's house, thou shalt not covet thy neighbour's wife, nor his manservant, nor his maidservant, nor his ox, nor his ass, nor anything that is thy neighbour's' (v. 17). This tenth commandment points to the root of evil in the desire of the heart. It shows us that by thinking as well as by doing evil, we break the law of God. When Paul saw that this, like all the commandments of the law, was something altogether inward and spiritual, sin revived and the law slew him (Romans 7:9), shutting him up to Christ.

With these ten words of law, with these Ten Commandments, the Lord God said, 'Walk before me and be thou perfect ... Be ye holy for I am holy ... Love me perfectly, with all your heart, and love your neighbour as yourself.' God demands perfection. He will not and cannot accept anything except perfection. He demands perfect righteousness, perfect purity, and perfect holiness (Galatians 3:10-12, 24; Psalm 1, 15, 24).

'For as many as are of the works of the law are under the curse: for it is written, Cursed is every one that continueth not in all things which are written in the book of the law to do them. But that no man is justified by the law in the sight of God, it is evident: for, The just shall live by faith. And the law is not of faith: but, The man that doeth them shall live in them' (Galatians 3:10-12).

'Wherefore the law was our schoolmaster to bring us unto Christ, that we might be justified by faith' (Galatians 3:24).

A Mediator Wanted

Third, in verses 18 and 19, we are told that as soon as they heard what the Lord God required of them, the children of Israel wanted a mediator, someone to stand before God in their stead. 'And all the people saw the thunderings, and the lightnings, and the noise of the trumpet, and the mountain smoking: and when the people saw it, they removed, and stood afar off. And they said unto Moses, Speak thou with us, and we will hear: but let not God speak with us, lest we die.'

Blessed be God, there is one Man, only one, who has fulfilled these commandments of God; and that Man is our Lord Jesus Christ, the God who spoke at Sinai. Read about him in Psalm 1; 15; and 24. As you do, remember our Lord Jesus Christ is our Representative man, by whom we are reconciled to God (Romans 5:19).

When he fulfilled the law's righteousness by his obedience in life and in death, our blessed Mediator and Surety, the Lord Jesus, fulfilled all the law's righteousness and all the law's justice, satisfying all the claims of the holy Lord God for his elect. Behold him, now in heaven's glory, speaking to God for you, and rejoice (1 John 2:1, 2; Hebrews 7:22-25; 10:12-14).

What a sweet, blessed picture Moses is here in Exodus 20 of our Lord Jesus Christ, of whom God declares, 'I will cause him to draw near, and he shall approach unto me: for who is this that engaged his heart to approach unto me? saith the LORD' (Jeremiah 30:21).

'And Moses said unto the people, Fear not: for God is come to prove you, and that his fear may be before your faces, that ye sin not. And the people stood afar off, and Moses drew near unto the thick darkness where God was' (Exodus 20:20, 21).

One Way

Fourth, even as he gives the law at Sinai, the Lord God declares that there is only one way sinners can come to him, and that is by an Altar of his making, our crucified Redeemer (vv. 22-26).

'And the LORD said unto Moses, Thus thou shalt say unto the children of Israel, Ye have seen that I have talked with you from heaven. Ye shall not make with me gods of silver, neither shall ye make unto you gods of gold. An altar of earth thou shalt make unto me, and shalt sacrifice thereon thy burnt offerings, and thy peace offerings, thy sheep, and thine oxen: in all places where I record my name I will come unto thee, and I will bless thee. And if thou wilt make me an altar of stone, thou shalt not build it of hewn stone: for if thou lift up thy tool upon it, thou hast polluted it. Neither shalt thou go up by steps unto mine altar, that thy nakedness be not discovered thereon.'

Robert Hawker wrote, 'Is not this altar of earth intended to show, that as the earth is the Lord's, and the fulness thereof, and nothing of creature property is to be mixed with it, so salvation is all the Lord's; nothing of human merit or work composing any part of it? ... And doth not the prohibition of lifting up a tool upon the altar, imply that nothing can be offered of ours upon that Altar, (which is Christ himself) that sanctifieth the gift, without polluting it?'

Our blessed Redeemer claims the salvation of our souls as his work, and his alone. Anyone who dares to mix any effort of his own with that of Christ, does so upon penalty of everlasting death in hell.

'And I looked, and there was none to help; and I wondered that there was none to uphold: therefore mine own arm brought salvation unto me; and my fury, it upheld me' (Isaiah 63:5).

Rest Your Way
If God requires perfection and no man can give it, except Christ, and the Lord God forbids us to even try to perform it, how can anyone be saved? I promised I would come back to the fourth commandment (vv. 6-10). The whole reason the law of the sabbath was given was to show us that the only way to heaven is to rest your way there. To keep the sabbath, you had to quit working, trusting God to provide everything needed, and living entirely upon God's provision. Christ is the Sabbath. We keep the sabbath and fulfil the whole law by trusting him, only by trusting him. By faith in Christ, and only by faith in Christ, we keep God's commandment and establish God's law (1 John 3:23; Romans 3:31).

Christ is our Sabbath (Hebrews 4:9-11). We rest in him. And his rest is glorious (Isaiah 11:10). Finding rest in Christ, we 'call the Sabbath a delight' (Isaiah 58:13, 14). To all who attempt to keep the law by their works and pretend to observe the sabbath day carnally, the law and the sabbath it requires, are irksome duties that only cause pain.

Satan in his great craftiness and subtlety, has turned the law of the sabbath, the law of rest, into a work. Do not fall for his lie. Come to Christ and rest your way to heaven (Matthew 11:28-30).

God give us grace ever to reverence his holy law, and never lose sight of the fact that, rather than that one jot or tittle of the law should fail, he gave his own dear Son to be our great, glorious, all-sufficient Surety, to be made sin for us, that we might be made the righteousness of God in him.

With every remembrance of God's holy law, with every remembrance of his precepts, with every thought of his commands, let me acknowledge my sin, confess my guilt, and cling to my Saviour. Spirit of God, make every word of the law a love token from our God to endear our Redeemer to our hearts. Let me never be found going about to establish my own righteousness, but be found in Christ, who of God is made unto me righteousness, trusting him who is 'the end of the law for righteousness to everyone that believeth' (Romans 10:4).

Chapter 81

Christ The Servant

'Now these are the judgments which thou shalt set before them. If thou buy an Hebrew servant, six years he shall serve: and in the seventh he shall go out free for nothing. If he came in by himself, he shall go out by himself: if he were married, then his wife shall go out with him. If his master have given him a wife, and she have born him sons or daughters; the wife and her children shall be her master's, and he shall go out by himself. And if the servant shall plainly say, I love my master, my wife, and my children; I will not go out free: Then his master shall bring him unto the judges; he shall also bring him to the door, or unto the door post; and his master shall bore his ear through with an aul; and he shall serve him forever.'
(Exodus 21:1-6)

In Exodus 21 the Lord God begins to give his judgments, or civil statutes to Israel, by which he typified and portrayed redemption, grace, and salvation by Christ.[6] Here we have the first of the civil statutes given to Israel. It appears to be a basis for all that follows it.

---

[6] Ever remember, the law of God, these civil statutes, ceremonial rites, and all the commandments were Messianic. They were given to Israel alone and applied to Israel alone. The law of the Old Testament has absolutely nothing to do with Gentiles. It was never given to Gentiles. The law was Messianic. It pointed to Christ, who is the fulfilment and the end of the law.

Exodus 21:1-6 gives us the law of God concerning the bond-servant. This, the very first civil statute given to Israel, was a blessed picture of redemption and grace by our Lord Jesus Christ.

This law describes a man who would voluntarily make himself a bond-servant to his master for life. The servant spoken of in this passage of Scripture, by type and picture, is the Lord Jesus Christ our Saviour. The Lord Jesus Christ, the Son of God, became the Servant of God that he might redeem and save sinners chosen of God from the foundation of the world (Matthew 1:21). He 'came not to be ministered unto, but to minister and to give his life a ransom for many' (Mark 10:45). How blessed it is to see and know Christ in this relationship! The eye of faith sees Christ the Servant and rejoices in all his work. Let me show you five things about this law of the bond-servant, by which our Lord Jesus Christ was typified.

Voluntary Servant
First, the Lord Jesus Christ chose to become Jehovah's Servant. We understand and rejoice to know this Servant is himself God. He is one with the Father in being, glory, and greatness; in all things equal with the Father. In his eternal Deity, as God the Son, our Saviour is altogether equal with the Father. But he became a man, our Surety, our Mediator, that he might subject himself to and obey his Father's will as a man for the salvation of God's elect, 'to the praise of the glory of his grace' (Ephesians 1:6; 2 Corinthians 8:9; Philippians 2:6-8).

Let it be clearly understood: the Son of God is and must be God, the second Person of the blessed Trinity. We are Trinitarians. We believe, according to the Scriptures, that there is one God, subsisting in three eternal Persons, in all things equal to one another (1 John 5:7). The Son of God is not, and cannot possibly be, inferior to the Father in his divine nature. If Jesus Christ is God manifest in the flesh, as the Scriptures declare, there cannot be any measure of inequality between the Father and the Son. Augustus Toplady, wrote, 'The uncreated and eternally begotten Son of the Father Almighty is and must be as truly a divine being as the Father who begat him.'

When we read in the Scriptures of Christ being the Servant of God, subjecting himself to the will of God, and obeying the commandment of God, we are assured that his servitude is and must be by his own free and voluntary consent. He is, indeed, the Servant of God; but his service was no forced work. 'He gave himself for us, that he might redeem us from all iniquity, and purify unto himself a peculiar people, zealous of good works' (Titus 2:14). 'Christ loved the church, and gave himself for it' (Ephesians 5:25). Our Lord himself declares, 'As the Father knoweth me, even so know I the Father: and I lay down my life for the sheep' (John 10:15).

There was a perfect understanding between the Father and the Son from eternity. Let there be no misunderstanding in our own minds. Christ became the Servant of Jehovah by his own will (John 10:16-18; Isaiah 50:5-7; 42:1-4).

Christ's Service
Second, the Lord Jesus served. From the moment of his birth, until his final breath in this world, the Lord Jesus served. He was ever Jehovah's righteous and faithful Servant. He said, to his disciples, 'I am among you as he that serveth' (Luke 22:27).

'Wherefore when he cometh into the world, he saith, Sacrifice and offering thou wouldest not, but a body hast thou prepared me: In burnt offerings and sacrifices for sin thou hast had no pleasure. Then said I, Lo, I come (in the volume of the book it is written of me,) to do thy will, O God. Above when he said, Sacrifice and offering and burnt offerings and offering for sin thou wouldest not, neither hadst pleasure therein; which are offered by the law; Then said he, Lo, I come to do thy will, O God. He taketh away the first, that he may establish the second. By the which will we are sanctified through the offering of the body of Jesus Christ once for all. And every priest standeth daily ministering and offering oftentimes the same sacrifices, which can never take away sins: But this man, after he had offered one sacrifice for sins for ever, sat down on the right hand of God; From henceforth expecting till his enemies be made his footstool. For by one offering he hath perfected for ever them that are sanctified' (Hebrews 10:5-14).

Six Years
According to Exodus 21:2, a servant could only serve for six years, no more, except he become a voluntary bond-servant forever. Six years was the measure of a man's obedience. That is not accidental. Six is the number of man, the number of incompletion, frustration, and failure. The Lord Jesus Christ came to accomplish, as Jehovah's Servant, what

201

no man had ever done before. He came here to make up for man, to make reconciliation for man, to make atonement for iniquity, to make an end of sin, to make restitution for transgressions, and to bring in everlasting righteousness (Daniel 9:24; Romans 8:1-4). If you will take time to read this section at one sitting (Exodus 21-23), you will see that all these civil laws given to Israel are laws requiring equity, justice, and righteousness. Wherever a breach was found, wherever an offense was committed, restitution was required. Honour must be served and respect restored for reproach inflicted; an eye for an eye, a tooth for a tooth, an ox for an ox, and a life for a life.

So, too, Christ became Jehovah's Servant to make restitution for us; and, blessed be his name, he did what he came here to do (Daniel 9:24; Romans 8:1-4). This Servant of God fulfilled the law perfectly, bringing in everlasting righteousness. The Lord Jesus Christ put away the sins of his people by the sacrifice of himself. He finished the transgression and made an end of sins.

The Servant's Option
Third, the servant, according to the law, had an option. Had he chosen to do so, he could have gone out free. Our blessed Saviour could have gone out free. It was the servant's choice whether he remained a servant or went out free.

So it was with our Saviour, even after he had come into the world. Living here as a Man, the Lord Jesus had perfectly honoured and pleased his Father (Matthew 17:5). Even in Gethsemane, the Lord Jesus told Peter he was under no constraint, except the constraint of his own voluntary will, to die in our place at Calvary (Matthew 26:52-54). But, had he gone out free, he would go out by himself.

Freedom Refused
So, fourth, I want you to see that our Lord would not go out by himself. 'If the servant shall plainly say, I love my master, my wife, and my children; I will not go out free' (Exodus 21:5). Oh, how I thank God that our all-glorious Christ, Jehovah's Righteous Servant, said, 'I will not go out free'. Rather, 'he stedfastly set his face to go to Jerusalem' (Luke 9:51; John 12:27-32; Isaiah 50:7).

Try to picture in your mind the great covenant of grace. The Lord Jesus, back before the world was made, stood before God the Father, and said, 'I love my Master'. Why did the Lord Jesus Christ come into this world? The answer is found in these words. Christ came here because of his great love for his Father, to glorify God the Father. The first Adam, who was made for the glory of God, failed miserably. The last Adam succeeded gloriously. He restored that which he took not away. He was altogether competent for the work he came here to do, because this man is God, because this God-man was altogether without sin. 'In him is no sin' (1 John 3:5). 'He knew no sin' (2 Corinthians 5:21). 'He did no sin' (1 Peter 2:22). When tempted of the devil, Satan found nothing in him by which to seduce him.

He had no work, no ambition, no will, except to do his Father's will. When he was a boy, he corrected his mother on this subject, saying, 'Wist ye not that I must be about my Father's business' (Luke 2:49). There was never a boy who loved, honoured, and sought to please his mother like this boy; but there was someone he loved more, sought to honour more, sought to please more, someone more important than his mother. He loved his Father too much to be detracted from his work by the sorrows of his mother. When he was a man, he said, 'I do always those things that please him' (John 8:29). When his labour was ended, when his work was done, when the faithful Servant gave an account of the work he had done, he said, 'I have glorified thee on the earth: I have finished the work which thou gavest me to do' (John 17:4). In glorifying the Father our covenant Surety ensured that elect sinners are eternally justified and saved with an everlasting salvation. The love of God for us and the love of Christ for his Father is the source and cause of it all.

Next, the Servant says, 'I love my wife'. You who are loved of Christ cannot fail to see your Beloved here. Here we see something of the marvellous love of Christ for his bride, the church. What David said concerning Jonathan, we say from the heart concerning our Redeemer. 'Thy love to me was wonderful' (2 Samuel 1:26). Oh, that we might know the unknowable! Oh, 'that Christ may dwell in your hearts by faith; that ye, being rooted and grounded in love, may be able to comprehend with all saints what is the breadth, and length, and depth, and height; and to know the love of Christ, which passeth knowledge, that ye might be filled with all the fulness of God' (Ephesians 3:17-19).

Where can we find illustrations of Christ's great love for his elect bride? Jacob's love for Rachel was rewarded with deceit (Genesis 29:18-20); but it did not dampen his love. Our Saviour's love for us caused him shame and suffering beyond human understanding; but the more he endured the more his love was made manifest. His love for us is stronger than death and as firm as the very life of the eternal God!

Adam's love for Eve gives us another illustration of our Saviour's love for us. Nowhere do we see the love of Christ, the last Adam, for his bride more fully illustrated than in the love of the first Adam for his wife Eve (Genesis 2:23; Ephesians 5:25-27). The Holy Spirit tells us plainly that Adam was not deceived by the devil (1 Timothy 2:14). He knew exactly what he was doing. He sinned with his eyes wide open. He saw Eve in the depths of her sin, guilt and shame. Yet, he loved her. Because of his love for her, before he would be separated from her, he chose to be damned with her. He cleaved to his wife, for they were one. He plunged himself into ruin. He freely, deliberately plunged himself under the wrath of God. He made himself sin for Eve's sake, because he loved Eve. In this Adam stands as a type of Christ, who loved us and gave himself for us (2 Corinthians 5:21; Galatians 3:13, 14).

Next, the Servant says, 'I love my children'. Even back then, in the covenant of grace, before the world began, the predestined children of God were given a family relation with the Son of God. Is he the Son of God? So are we, by divine adoption and special predestination, from eternity. Thomas Bradbury wrote,

'Through the perfection of his righteousness, the preciousness of his blood, the power of his resurrection, and the prevalency of his intercession, he brings forth the progeny of grace (his seed – a seed to serve him) from the womb of the eternal purpose, to serve, praise, and adore the eternal Three-in-One to all generations.'

In us Christ sees the fruit and satisfaction of his soul's travail. In him is all our salvation (1 Corinthians 1:30). In him we were chosen to salvation. In him we have been redeemed from all sin. In him we are begotten again unto a lively hope by his resurrection. In him we have been quickened into spiritual life by his Spirit. In him we have been born again never to die. In him we are saved. He carries us in the bosom of his everlasting love. He washed us from every stain of sin in his own precious blood. He has justified us with his spotless righteousness. He shall at last present us faultless to the Father in perfect holiness (Hebrews 2:13).

Why did Christ become the Servant of God? Because he loved his Father, he loved his wife, and he loved his children.

Servant Forever

We read in Exodus 21:6, 'He shall serve him forever'. So, the fifth thing we see is our Lord Jesus Christ serving forever. How delightful and blessed it is to our hearts to see the willingness of Christ to bow, to humble himself, to become obedient to the Father's will, to suffer and die for us. How he loved us! He said, 'I will not go out free!' He had his ear bored. He solemnly and publicly, before the Father, before the Spirit, before the heavenly angels, declared himself to be Jehovah's Servant forever, and never had a second thought about it.

A human body was prepared for the Son of God; and he came into this world as Jehovah's Servant in that body, saying to his Father, 'A body hast thou prepared me'. What a glorious sight for the comfort of every believing heart! The Son of God wears and forever dwells in a human body! He has a real human heart to feel the sorrows and sufferings of his loved ones in this world, real human eyes to watch over his people, to weep with those who weep, to weep for those who cannot weep for themselves. He has real human ears ever attentive to the cries of his beloved, real human hands to minister to the necessities of his family, real human feet frequently weary in errands of mercy for his beloved. Our dear Saviour has real human lips ever filled with grace, ever flowing with words of love and life for his chosen, a real human soul which was troubled and sorrowful, even unto death, that his sinful, sorrowing people might be sinless and joyful to all eternity. Blessed be God forever, yonder in heaven's highest glory there is a man, a real man, Jesus, the Christ, Jehovah's Servant, my Saviour!

Consider what our Lord has done and is doing as Jehovah's Servant. He brought in everlasting righteousness by his obedience to God as our Representative. He put away sin by the sacrifice of himself. He lives in heaven to make intercession for transgressors, according to the will of God. He sends his Spirit to regenerate and save his redeemed ones in the time of love. He keeps and preserves his believing people secure unto eternal glory. He rules the world for the good of his redeemed ones. He is coming again to gather his elect up to glory and present them before the throne of the triune Jehovah in all the perfection and beauty of his own perfection and beauty; holy, unblameable, unreprovable, without spot, or wrinkle, or any such thing, 'to the praise of the glory of his grace', 'that God may be all in all' (Ephesians 5:25-27; Jude 24, 25; 1 Corinthians 15:24-28).

All praise to Christ, the Servant! 'Unto him that loved us, and washed us from our sins in his own blood, and hath made us kings and priests unto God and his Father; to him be glory and dominion for ever and ever. Amen' (Revelation 1:5, 6). Whatever our need may be, it is supplied from the unfailing stores of our heavenly Bridegroom. The time of our destitution and helplessness gave him opportunity to exercise his love and care. When we were lost and loathsome, he came to us in love. When we were naked, he clothed us with the garments of salvation (Isaiah 61:10). When hungry, he feeds us. When fainting, he restores us. When helpless, he upholds us. Do we long for glory? He will bring us in!

The time of our Saviour's service is 'forever'. Hear what he, himself, says about it. 'Blessed are those servants, whom the lord when he cometh shall find watching: verily I say unto you, that he shall gird himself, and make them to sit down to meat, and will come forth and serve them' (Luke 12:37). Time will not terminate his service of love. In the ages to come God will show the exceeding riches of his grace toward us through Christ Jesus. When time shall be no more, the Lamb in the midst of the throne will feed us, lead us to fountains of living water, and bless us with eternal joy in his presence 'forever'.

Forever adore, love, and trust the Lord Jesus Christ, who stooped so low to lift us so high. If Christ our Saviour is the Servant of God, let us imitate him as we endeavour to serve our God and one another. 'Let this mind be in you, which was also in Christ Jesus' (Philippians 2:5; John 13:13-15).

Chapter 82

Restitution Required

'...restore five oxen for an ox and four sheep for a sheep ... Make full restitution ... If a thief be found, let him pay double ... For I am gracious ... The innocent and the righteous slay thou not; for I will not justify the wicked ... '
(Exodus 21:7-23:8)

In this portion of Holy Scripture we are given a lengthy series of laws, statutes, and judgments by which the Lord God sets before us his wisdom and justice, as well as his mercy, love, and grace. Here, the guilty are required, by divine justice, either to make restitution or to suffer punishment. Reading the law, we cannot avoid noting that the law and justice of God considers only guilt or innocence. It forbids any mercy on the basis of the offender's circumstances and condition.

'Thou shalt not follow a multitude to do evil; neither shalt thou speak in a cause to decline after many to wrest judgment: Neither shalt thou countenance a poor man in his cause ... Thou shalt not wrest the judgment of thy poor in his cause' (Exodus 23:2, 3, 6).

As far as the law is concerned, no sympathy is to be given and no injustice tolerated merely because of poverty. As the Scriptures put it, 'The soul that sinneth, it shall die' (Ezekiel 18:4, 20). Justice is blind and cannot be bribed. By that same justice, the guiltless and innocent are protected. 'Keep thee far from a false matter; and the innocent and righteous slay thou not: for I will not justify the wicked' (Exodus 23:7).

How often the Lord God forbids the slaying, or even the punishment of 'the innocent and righteous' (Proverbs 17:15; 24:24; Isaiah 5:22, 23).

By these divinely given precepts we see that the death of our Lord Jesus Christ was a penal sacrifice. He died at the hand of justice as the sinner's substitute, because he deserved the fury of God's holy justice and wrath. 'He who knew no sin was made sin for us that we might be made the righteousness of God in him' (2 Corinthians 5:21). 'Thanks be unto God for his unspeakable gift!' The God of Glory found a way, in his infinite wisdom, to be both just and the Justifier of chosen sinners in the person of his Son, our Saviour, the Lord Jesus Christ (Job 33:24; Isaiah 45:21; Romans 3:25, 26). The holy Lord God will not and cannot justify the wicked, except by making the wicked perfectly righteous in Christ.

Exodus 21 enumerates specific laws of restitution. God required restitution be made to a betrothed maid servant who was dealt with deceitfully. If her master put her away, he was required to redeem her and provide for her (vv. 7-11). The law of God required eye for eye, tooth for tooth, ox for ox, sheep for sheep, and life for life.

Atonement

Twelve times God says, 'restore', or 'make it good', or 'pay double', or 'make restitution'. Those are four different English translations for the same Hebrew word. The word has such wide meaning that our translators give four translations of it in just one chapter. It means 'restore', 'make good', 'pay double', 'make restitution', 'make safe', 'make complete', 'make amends', 'recompense', 'make perfect', 'make an end', 'finish full', and 'make peaceable by performing restitution'. Obviously, the passage is talking about reconciliation and atonement.

Then some crimes are listed, so base, vile and offensive to God that no restitution could be made for them.

'Thou shalt not suffer a witch to live. Whosoever lieth with a beast shall surely be put to death. He that sacrificeth unto any god, save unto the LORD only, he shall be utterly destroyed' (Exodus 22:18-20).

The fact these laws were made gives us a hint at the depravity of the human heart. Witchcraft, bestiality and idolatry were common things in Egypt and in Canaan. C. H. Mackintosh rightly observed,

'There are crimes here forbidden which would seem to place man, as regards his habits and tendencies, below the level of a 'dog'; yet do those very statutes prove, beyond all question, that the most refined and cultivated member of the human family carries about in his bosom the seeds of the very darkest and most horrifying abominations.'

208

Next, in verses 21-27, the Lord God demands by law that his people not be oppressive or severe, but merciful, and gives the reason in verse 27. 'For I am gracious!' In Exodus 22:28 we are told we are never to speak evil of our civil magistrates, whom he calls 'gods' over us. We are to honour those who are in authority as God's servants for good.

Shall be Holy

In verses 29 and 30 God reminds us again that the first fruits and the firstborn are his and they must not be withheld from him. Then, in verse 31, he gives us the reason for the giving of all these laws. 'And ye shall be holy men unto me.' That is to say, 'You shall be separated from all other people. You shall be sanctified unto me.'

How are we to be made holy? How can sinners be separated from sinners and sanctified unto the holy Lord God. The answer is in what we have read. We shall be made holy by a complete restitution made for all our offenses. I remind you, this long list of laws, laws of restitution, is introduced by the law of the bond slave (Exodus 21:1-6). The Lord God has made us holy by the obedience of Christ, his voluntary bond slave, Jehovah's Righteous Servant. Our Lord Jesus Christ, because of his love for his Father and his love to us his captive wife and children, cheerfully bowed to be Jehovah's Servant, to have his ear opened, and would not go out free, until he had accomplished all the work he was called to do and had satisfied all demands as our Surety in the everlasting covenant of grace. Robert Hawker wrote,

'Oh! Thou precious God of my salvation, thou who, though rich, yet for my sake didst become poor; and though in the form of God, and with whom it was no robbery to be equal with God, yet didst make thyself of no reputation, and didst take upon thee the form of a servant; mercifully grant, that the same mind may be in me which was so strikingly displayed by thyself. May it be the language of my soul, "I love my Lord, I love my Master, I love his service, in it I would dwell: I will not go out free, but I will abide in it forever".'

'Thou shalt not delay to offer the first of thy ripe fruits, and of thy liquors: the firstborn of thy sons shalt thou give unto me. Likewise shalt thou do with thine oxen, and with thy sheep: seven days it shall be with his dam; on the eighth day thou shalt give it me' (Exodus 22:29, 30).

Read Exodus 23:7. The Lord God declares that in order for any sinner to be justified before him, he must be made holy, righteous, and just. 'Keep thee far from a false matter; and the innocent and righteous slay thou not: for I will not justify the wicked.' Only by the sacrifice of Christ can the wicked be made innocent, righteous, and just before God.

Christ the Key

It is sad but true that most who read the Bible and most who preach and teach from it, see nothing in the Old Testament but historic facts, legal precepts, carnal ceremonies, and moral ethics. To the vast majority of the religious people I meet, the Old Testament is a sealed Book, without meaning or message. They simply cannot unlock it, because they do not have the key. They are like those whom Isaiah describes in Isaiah 6. Seeing they see not. Hearing they hear not. Understanding, they understand not the things written in the Old Testament Scripture.

The Key to the Old Testament is Christ. What a great blessing it is to have the Key! Yet, there is no room for boasting here. If we see, hear, and understand the Scriptures, it is because God has graciously caused the light of his glory and grace to shine in our hearts by his Spirit and we have been taught of God. It is the Lord who opens our understanding that we might understand the Scriptures (Luke 24:45). 'Blessed are your eyes, for they see: and your ears, for they hear' (Matthew 13:16).

Blessed is that enlightened soul who, by the grace of God, is able to see Christ in the Old Testament as well as in the New. Blessed are those eyes that behold the Lord Jesus Christ in all the promises, precepts, and prophecies of the Old Testament, as well as in the proclamations of the New. Blessed are those hearts that see the beauty and glory of Christ in the ordinances, types, and shadows of the law, as well as in the shining light of the gospel. Nowhere is man's spiritual blindness more evident than in the things written by religious men about the Mosaic law.

The law of God requiring restitution for any wrong done by one person to another was not intended merely to teach the moral precept of restitution. Rather, these things were written to teach by precept and by picture that the Lord Jesus Christ would, by his great work of redemption, turn the tables and make a full restitution of all things to the everlasting praise and glory of the triune God. They all testify of that which is written of him in Psalm 69:4. 'Then I restored that which I took not away.' Soon, very soon, our Lord Jesus Christ shall appear in his glory and there shall be a manifest restitution of all things to God by him (Acts 3:18-21; Ephesians 2:4-7). God hasten the day!

210

Benefit by the Injury

The law of God demanded that anyone wronged by another should not only have the wrong repaired, but also be made to benefit and gain by the injury done. It is God primarily who has been wronged in all his rights by sin. Yet, man too has been wronged. But the Lord God has, in wisdom, fixed it so both he and his people will gain by the injury done. The fall of Satan and the entrance of sin into the world by the fall of our father Adam has been, is being, and shall yet be made to redound to the everlasting riches of God's elect and the glory of his great name.

Yes, the God of Glory works all things together for the good of his people and the everlasting glory of his own great name. Satan will gain nothing by the havoc he has wrought in God's world. He will achieve absolutely nothing! This is the glory of the cross. 'Where sin abounded, grace did much more abound!' These laws of restitution declare, 'Where sin abounds, grace shall much more abound'. I have chosen my words deliberately. Yes, both God and man have gained more by the forgiveness of sin through the blood of Christ than was lost by the sin and fall of our father Adam.

The Lord God has arranged all things, even the sin and fall of our father Adam, for the everlasting good and happiness of his people. We shall lose nothing, but only gain by what happened in the garden. We are gainers, not by sin, but by redemption! Indeed, the sin and fall of Adam was itself, by divine purpose, a picture of redemption by Christ (Romans 5:12-20). Martin Luther rightly exclaimed, with regard to Adam's sin in the Garden, 'O blessed fall!' Had there been no fall, no sin, no condemnation, we could never have known the wonders of redemption, we could never have known the glories of grace. Grace not only cuts up sin by the roots and ultimately destroys it, grace makes chosen, redeemed sinners everlasting beneficiaries of Satan's work.

Still, there is more. The holy Lord God has gained more by redemption than ever he lost (if I can be permitted to use such language) by the fall. The Lord God reaps a richer harvest of glory in the fields of grace than he could ever have reaped in the garden of innocence (Ephesians 1:3-14; 2:7). The sons of God raise a more lofty song of praise around the empty tomb of the crucified Christ than we could ever have raised in the Garden of Eden. The injury done by sin has not only been perfectly atoned for and remedied by the blood of Christ, but God has gained by the cross the praise of the glory of his grace. As it is

211

written, 'Surely the wrath of man shall praise thee: the remainder of wrath shalt thou restrain' (Psalm 76:10).

God's Glory Seen

This is a stupendous truth. The eternal, triune, holy Lord God has gotten himself great gain by the work accomplished by our all-glorious Christ at Calvary! Who could ever have conceived such a thing? When we see man and the creation over which he was lord laid in a heap of ruins at the feet of Satan, how could we ever imagine that from those ruins the great God of Glory would gather a crown for his holy head which could not be gotten in any other way? Yet, it was ever the immutable purpose of the all-wise God to glorify himself and reveal his glory to all creation by the accomplishments of his darling Son at Calvary (Isaiah 40:1-5).

The glory of the Lord is the Lord Jesus Christ, the incarnate God-man, our Mediator, our Surety, our Substitute, our Saviour. Christ is the embodiment of 'the glory of the Lord' but he is more. The Lord Jesus Christ is essentially and emphatically 'the glory of the Lord', for in him dwells all the fulness of the Godhead bodily (Colossians 2:9, 10). When Isaiah said, 'the glory of the Lord shall be revealed', he spoke prophetically of the incarnation of Christ. He was saying, God the Son shall come in human flesh possessing all the glory of the glorious God; and in him God shall be seen of all men, for this man is God. God's glory was revealed in his Son when he was sent here on the mission of mercy to redeem and save his people. Yet, the meaning of Isaiah's words is fuller still.

The glory of the Lord is displayed in the attributes of his being. His glory is what sets him apart from all his creatures and identifies him as God over all, blessed forever. Isaiah declared that the glory of God, the glory of all his attributes, would be revealed in Christ at Calvary.

David said, 'The heavens declare the glory of God' and they do, but only in part. Great as the glory of God revealed in the heavens is, believing sinners see in the cross a display so wonderful that the glory of his wisdom and power in creation pales by comparison. The glory of the cross, the glory of the Lord revealed in the crucified Christ, the glory of the Lord revealed in the salvation of poor, fallen, helpless, doomed, damned sinners, that is the glory of the Lord! Sin has blinded us to the glory of God; but grace reveals it far more fully than it could ever have been known otherwise. The glory of God is revealed in the gospel; but it is hidden from them that are lost (2 Corinthians 4:4-6). Look to Christ, the crucified, risen, exalted, saving Christ, and behold the glory of God. In him and by him restitution has been made, and both God and man have gained more in him than ever was lost by the sin and fall of Adam, for in him the glory of the Lord is revealed.

Wisdom and Knowledge

I see in the cross of Christ the glory of God's wisdom and knowledge revealed more fully than it could have been in any other way (Romans 11:33-36). Adam saw the wisdom of God in creation more clearly than any man has seen it since the fall. But Adam did not and could not see the glory of God's wisdom in redemption until he experienced it.

I know, cavilling will-worshippers cry, 'If that is true, if God has ordained all things, then let us sin that grace may abound.' Let none be so foolish. Though it is the wisdom of God that ordained sin, it is the justice of God to punish it. Believing hearts do not challenge God's wisdom (Jude 4). We adore it!

Here is the glory of God's wisdom. It is written, 'By mercy and truth iniquity is purged' (Proverbs 16:6). But iniquity could never be purged and truth maintained, unless some way known only to infinite wisdom is found to do it. Unless some infinitely wise arrangement could be made to satisfy the rigid requirements of truth, while exercising absolute mercy. Righteousness and peace could never have kissed each other had not God in infinite wisdom found a way to make it happen. The glory of God's wisdom is revealed in that way. It is called substitution. Salvation by a Substitute of infinite worth makes it possible and certain that iniquity shall be purged by mercy and by truth. Behold the cross of Christ and sing the praises of Jehovah!

'Surely his salvation is nigh them that fear him; that glory may dwell in our land. Mercy and truth are met together; righteousness and peace have kissed each other. Truth shall spring out of the earth; and righteousness shall look down from heaven' (Psalm 85:9-11).

Mercy, Grace, and Love

I see in the cross of our Lord Jesus Christ the glory of God's mercy, grace, and love revealed. I do not suggest that the love of God is not revealed in other ways, in other acts of his goodness, or in other places. It is. I am certain that Adam, before the fall, knew God's love in benevolence, goodness, and sweet communion. He knew the love of God as his Creator, his Maker, and his Companion. But Adam did not know and could not know the glory of God's love. Indeed, it would not have been possible for anyone to know the glory of God's love had there been no fall. The glory of God's love is revealed in the cross of our Lord Jesus Christ. We read of God's everlasting, electing love and rejoice. We give thanks to our God for his eternal, adopting love (Jeremiah 31:3; 1 John 3:1). But the glory of the love of God is revealed at Calvary (John 3:16; Romans 5:6-8; 1 John 3:16; 4:9, 10).

Love is known by its deeds; but love is also known by comparison. Those who imagine they are wiser than God tell us God loves all men. Others among them would have us believe that the love of God would have been more greatly revealed had there been no entrance of sin into the world. But it was the wisdom of God that ordained the entrance of sin into the world. That wisdom is displayed here. By ordaining the sin and fall of our father Adam and the ruin of all the human race in him, the Lord God shows the glory of his love in saving some.

If the Lord God had kept all from sinning, or if he had saved all, how could we know the intensity, devotion, and freeness of his love for us? Love is displayed by these two things: self-sacrifice and comparison. I know the love of God because he loved me and gave himself for me; and I know the love of God, the glory of his love, because he loved me and not multitudes far better than me. If God loved all, where is the glory of his love? But once a sinner is made to see that the Lord God has loved him, and loved him immutably from all eternity, passing by many who were more noble, more useful, more appealing than him, then the chosen, redeemed, called sinner sees the surpassing glory of the love of God in the face of Jesus Christ, and is conquered by his love.

We see the glory of God's love in the fact that God's love is discriminating love. Solomon tells us man cannot know love or hatred by anything except God's distinguishing mercy (Ecclesiastes 8:17-9:1) We know the glory of God's love because he said, to the praise of his glory, 'Jacob have I loved, but Esau have I hated!' Therefore, 'we love him, because he first loved us'.

Truth, Justice, and Holiness
As I behold the Son of God hanging upon the cursed tree, made sin for me, bearing all the terror of God's holy wrath for me, forsaken of God,

and slain for me, I see the glory of God's absolute truth; his infinite, inflexible justice, and infinite, immaculate holiness.

In Christ crucified, the glory of God's justice is revealed as it could not be revealed in any other way. Adam knew the threat of justice before he fell. Sinners in hell know the severity of God's justice. We see tokens of justice every day. Justice demands punishment, a just and righteous punishment for every offence. Justice demands a victim. No pleadings, no tears, no repentance, no works of restitution can turn away the sword of justice. Mercy may implore leniency, and love beg for pardon, but justice is unaffected and unbending. Justice 'will by no means clear the guilty'. But God, in infinite wisdom and love, found a way to both punish the sinner and forgive him.

Behold the glory of God's justice in the face of his darling Son when he was made sin for us. Believing sinners are justified freely by the grace of God through the redemption that is in Christ Jesus ...

'Whom God hath set forth to be a propitiation through faith in his blood, to declare his righteousness for the remission of sins that are past, through the forbearance of God; To declare, I say, at this time his righteousness: that he might be just, and the justifier of him which believeth in Jesus' (Romans 3:25, 26).

When God Almighty looks on the shed blood of his darling Son, he says, 'Enough'. Here is the glory of God's justice revealed! Oh, how holy, how just, how true the God of glory must be! When the holy Lord God found sin on his own beloved Son, he spared not his own darling Son. When God the Son bore the wrath of God in his own body, in his soul, and in his heart on the cursed tree, he satisfied the justice of God. God, the holy Lord God, will indeed punish sin, for he must. Justice demands it.

God is Gracious

I see in the cross of Christ the glory of the Lord's absolute sovereignty and great goodness revealed, and revealed in such full splendour, as it could never have been known otherwise. In the cross, by which the law is finished, we hear the God of glory speak clearly what he said in the dark shadows of the law. 'I am gracious.'

When Moses asked the Lord to show him his glory, he said 'I will make all my goodness to pass before thee; and I will be gracious to whom I will be gracious'. Here is the glory of God's sovereign

215

goodness, the glory of his grace. God is gracious. God will be gracious to whom he will be gracious. Our great God is so sovereign in his graciousness that he makes even the wrath of man to praise him and work for the good of his chosen. He is so sovereign in his graciousness that he makes Satan, who dared imagine he could thwart the purpose of the Almighty and led a rebellion in heaven and leads the rebellion of men and demons on earth and in hell, to be his servant to accomplish his purpose of grace toward his elect.

His glory is great in salvation, indescribably greater than ever it could have been had Adam not fallen, had sin never entered into the world, had the Lord Jesus Christ not died at Calvary, had he not saved his people from their sins. This is what the laws of restitution tell us. Behold the cross of our Lord Jesus Christ and understand, when you hear the Son of God cry, 'It is finished', that restitution has been made and the glory of God is revealed.

Be sure you do not miss the intent of this revelation of God. If the glory of God is most fully and perfectly revealed in the salvation of sinners, how that fact ought to inspire poor, needy sinners with hope. Surely, if God is glorified in saving sinners, he would be glorified in saving me! I will, upon that ground, like David of old, sue for mercy! 'For thy name's sake, O Lord, pardon mine iniquity; for it is great' (Psalm 25:11).

Chapter 83

'I Am Gracious'

'Thou shalt neither vex a stranger, nor oppress him: for ye were strangers in the land of Egypt. Ye shall not afflict any widow, or fatherless child. If thou afflict them in any wise, and they cry at all unto me, I will surely hear their cry; And my wrath shall wax hot, and I will kill you with the sword; and your wives shall be widows, and your children fatherless. If thou lend money to any of my people that is poor by thee, thou shalt not be to him as an usurer, neither shalt thou lay upon him usury. If thou at all take thy neighbour's raiment to pledge, thou shalt deliver it unto him by that the sun goeth down: For that is his covering only, it is his raiment for his skin: wherein shall he sleep? And it shall come to pass, when he crieth unto me, that I will hear; for I am gracious.'
(Exodus 22:21-27)

Here is the reason God gives for giving all the commandments of the law, both the commandments of restitution in verses 1-20 and the commandments of mercy to the stranger, the widow, the fatherless, and our neighbours that we have before us in verses 21-27: 'For I am gracious.' He commands us to be gracious because he is gracious.

God's Character
'I am gracious.' That is the character of our God. 'I am gracious.' That is the reason he does what he does. 'I am gracious.' 'Thou art a God ready to pardon, gracious and merciful, slow to anger, and of great

kindness ... Thou art a gracious and merciful God' (Nehemiah 9:17, 31). The fact that God is gracious is set before us as a matter of constant praise in the psalms (Psalm 86:15; 103:8; 111:4; 112:4; 116:5; 145:8).

The gracious character of our God inspires hope in needy sinners, confident faith in believing sinners, and loving gratitude in saved sinners (Isaiah 30:18, 19; 33:2). 'Turn unto the LORD your God: for he is gracious and merciful, slow to anger, and of great kindness' (Joel 2:13). The Lord our God, the triune Jehovah; Father, Son and Holy Spirit, declares himself gracious; and he proves himself gracious in all his works.

The source and fountain of grace is God the Father (Ephesians 1:3), who purposed in himself the everlasting salvation of an elect multitude before the world began. On behalf of that elect multitude he made a covenant of grace with his Son, ordered in all things and sure before ever the worlds were made.

The mediatorial channel of grace is God the Son (John 1:17). The grace of God is revealed and given to men only by the mediation of the Lord Jesus Christ. 'The law was given by Moses, but grace and truth came by Jesus Christ'. That does not mean that God did not save his elect by grace before the incarnation of Christ. He did. Salvation has always been by grace (Genesis 6:8). And that grace has always been found and given in Christ (Romans 3:24-26). But grace and truth were fully revealed in the substitutionary sacrifice of Christ. Christ alone always has been, is now, and shall forever be the solitary channel of grace (Romans 5:15, 17, 21; 1 Timothy 2:5). Grace does not come through the church. Grace cannot be conferred by some pretentious, earthly priest. And grace is not given through the ordinances of baptism and the Lord's Supper. Grace comes to sinners through Christ alone.

The great bestower of grace is God the Holy Spirit, who is called 'the Spirit of grace' by the prophet Zechariah (12:10). He is the One who applies the gospel to the hearts of sinners with saving power. He quickens God's elect while they are yet spiritually dead. He conquers the rebel's will, melts the hard heart, opens the blind eye, and cleanses the soul. He gives ears to hear, eyes to see, and a heart to believe on the Lord Jesus Christ.

The gospel of God is the message of grace. It is called 'the gospel of the grace of God' (Acts 20:24). To the self-righteous religionist, it is a stumbling block. To the learned, philosophical worldling, it is foolishness. Why? Because there is nothing in the gospel to gratify the pride of man. The gospel of God declares that man can never be saved, but by the grace of God. It declares that apart from Christ, the unspeakable gift of God's grace, there is no salvation and the state of every human being is desperate, hopeless, and irretrievable. The gospel addresses men and women as depraved, guilty, condemned, perishing sinners. It puts us all upon one level. The gospel declares that the purest moralist is in the same condition as the vilest profligate, the zealous religionist to be no better off than the most profane infidel. Without Christ, without grace, all are lost.

The gospel addresses every descendant of Adam as a fallen, polluted, hell-bent, hell-deserving sinner, utterly incapable of changing his ruined condition. The grace of God is our only hope. All men, by nature, stand before God's holy law as justly condemned felons, awaiting the execution of his wrath upon them (John 3:18, 36; Romans 3:19). Our only hope is grace! George S. Bishop put it like this,

'Grace is a provision for men who are so fallen that they cannot lift the axe of justice, so corrupt that they cannot change their own nature, so averse to God that they cannot turn to him, so blind that they cannot see him, so deaf that they cannot hear him, and so dead that he must himself open their graves and lift them into resurrection.'

Our only hope of salvation and eternal life is the grace of God freely bestowed on sinners through Jesus Christ, the sinner's Substitute.

Character of Grace
All the religious world talks about salvation by grace. But few understand the character of God's grace as it is revealed in the Word of God. As soon as grace is defined in biblical terms, man's opposition to it comes to surface. Let us look at the character of God's grace as it is revealed in Holy Scripture. When the Lord God declares, 'I am gracious' he is declaring his great, glorious attribute of grace.

Grace is an attribute of God which, like his love, is exercised only toward his elect. Nowhere in the Bible do we read of universal grace, or common grace, or of grace bestowed upon mankind in general. The mercy of God is 'over all his works' (Psalm 145:9); but the grace of God is upon his elect alone. The mercy of God is life upon this earth. The grace of God is eternal life. Mercy is anything short of eternal wrath. The grace of God is eternal salvation. Grace is the solitary source

219

from which the goodwill, love, and salvation of God flow to his chosen people. Abraham Booth described grace as 'the eternal and absolute free favour of God, manifested in the vouchsafement (infallible promise) of spiritual and eternal blessings to the guilty and unworthy'. Arthur W. Pink said, 'Divine grace is the sovereign and saving favour of God exercised in bestowing blessings upon those who have no merit in them and for which no compensation is demanded.'

Grace is completely unmerited and unsought. Grace cannot be bought, earned, or won by anything in us or done by us. If it could, it would cease to be grace. Grace is bestowed upon sinners without attraction, without condition or qualification. When it comes, it comes as a matter of pure charity; unasked and undesired. In Bible terms grace is directly opposed to works, worthiness, and merit in the creature.

'Now to him that worketh is the reward not reckoned of grace, but of debt. But to him that worketh not, but believeth on him that justifieth the ungodly, his faith is counted for righteousness' (Romans 4:4, 5).

'And if by grace, then is it no more of works: otherwise grace is no more grace. But if it be of works, then is it no more grace: otherwise work is no more work' (Romans 11:6).

'For by grace are ye saved through faith; and that not of yourselves: it is the gift of God: Not of works, lest any man should boast' (Ephesians 2:8, 9).

God 'hath saved us, and called us with an holy calling, not according to our works, but according to his own purpose and grace, which was given us in Christ Jesus before the world began, but is now made manifest by the appearing of our Saviour Jesus Christ, who hath abolished death, and hath brought life and immortality to light through the gospel' (2 Timothy 1:9, 10).

Grace and works will not mix. Any attempt by man to mix the grace of God with the works of man or the will of man is both blasphemy and a total denial of grace. Search the Scriptures, and you will find that there are four things which always characterize the grace of God. Whenever men speak contrary to these four things they deny the grace of God.

The grace of God is eternal (Romans 8:28-30; 2 Timothy 1:9). Grace does not originate in time and cannot be controlled or directed by anything in time. Grace is eternal.

The grace of God is free. Paul declares we are justified freely by his grace, through the redemption that is in Christ Jesus (Romans 3:24).

When God declares in his Word that his grace is free, he is telling us that his grace is without cause, without qualification, without condition, and without change.

The grace of God is sovereign (Romans 5:20, 21). Grace reigns, everywhere, over all things. If grace reigns, then it reigns from a throne. The One who sits upon the throne is sovereign. The throne of the sovereign God is called 'the throne of grace' (Hebrews 4:16). When the Bible declares that grace is sovereign, it is stating that God is gracious to whom he will be gracious (Romans 9:11-18). Salvation and eternal life is the gift of God (Romans 6:23). If it is a gift, it cannot be claimed as a right. If it is a gift, it cannot be earned. If it is a gift, the giver is free to bestow it upon whom he will. Nothing so riles man and stirs his hatred of God as the declaration that grace is free, sovereign, immutable, and eternal. This is the offence of the gospel. Grace is abasing to man's proud heart, putting all upon one level. Grace gives no recognition to the righteousness of man. Grace makes fallen man utterly dependent upon the goodness of God for salvation. And grace is the sovereign prerogative of the sovereign Lord.

The grace of God is discriminating and distinguishing (1 Corinthians 4:7). Grace discriminates, segregates and differentiates between men. Grace chooses some and passes by others. God has his favourites, whom he has from eternity singled out from the rest of Adam's race, to whom he will be gracious. Indeed, the word 'grace' means 'favour'. 'Gracious' means 'favourable'. Grace separated Abel from Cain, and separated Abraham from the rest of his family. Grace separated Isaac from Ishmael, and distinguished between Jacob and Esau. Grace separated David from his brothers. The only difference between the children of God and the children of the devil is grace. Every child of God knows it and gladly acknowledges, 'By the grace of God I am what I am' (1 Corinthians 15:10).

Works of Grace

We know that God is gracious as we experience and know his great works of grace. Let me remind you of those works of God's grace as they are set forth in the Word of God.

I will not spend much time here. But I want you to understand that everything involved in the salvation of sinners is the work of God's grace. There is nothing required for our salvation that is in any way dependent upon, determined by, or conditioned upon man in the least, not the worth of man, not the works of man, and not the will of man. We are saved by grace alone (Ephesians 1:3-2:10).

God's election is the election of grace (Romans 11:5, 6). God's covenant is the covenant of grace (Psalm 89:2, 3). Our adoption into the family of God was by grace (Ephesians 1:5, 6). The redemption of our souls by Christ was a marvellous work of God's grace (Hebrews 2:9). We are justified by grace (Romans 3:24). We are forgiven by grace (Ephesians 1:7). Our regeneration and calling are by the grace and power of God the Holy Spirit (Galatians 1:15, 16). Our sanctification is by the grace of God (1 Corinthians 1:30). Our preservation in grace is by grace (John 10:28-30). And our resurrection shall be the work of God's grace (John 5:25-28).

From the gates of hell to the gate of heavenly glory, we owe our salvation to grace alone. When our great, almighty God and Saviour has finished the work, he shall 'bring forth the headstone thereof with shoutings, crying, Grace, grace unto it!' (Zechariah 4:7).

Trophies of Grace
The glory of God's gracious character shines forth most splendidly when we behold the trophies of his grace and observe the unworthiness of those sinners he has saved by his marvellous grace (1 Corinthians 1:26-31). Here are four trophies of grace which will serve to illustrate the grace of our God, who declares, 'I am gracious'.

Manasseh, the King of Judah (2 Chronicles 33:1-13 was a barbaric monster. He sacrificed his own children on the burning altars of his chosen idols. He filled Jerusalem with innocent blood. His sacrilegious indecencies perverted the whole nation. He led Judah into corruptions unmentionable, even among the heathen. Yet, the grace of God touched his heart, renewed his soul, forgave his sin, and made him an heir of heavenly glory.

Saul of Tarsus (Acts 9) was a blood thirsty persecutor of God's church, hell-bent upon the destruction of God's lambs, and determined to annihilate Christianity. His thirst for violence and murder was insatiable. His rancorous heart was filled with violence. Never did a man live who, in the opinion of human judgment, was more certainly deserving of eternal damnation. Yet, this godless wretch is today seated with Christ upon his throne, a trophy of the grace of God.

The Corinthians (1 Corinthians 6:9-11) were the most sensual, profligate people of the ancient Roman world. They were vile in the vilest age in the annals of human history. Yet, through the infinitely tender mercies of our ever-gracious God, a great multitude of them today are robed in white and crowned with glory.

And not least, the man who writes these lines. I am Gomer. I am Onesimus. I am the wild Gadarene. I am the prodigal son. I am the sinner saved by grace. Grace chose me. Grace redeemed me. Grace preserved me. Grace called me. Grace keeps me. Grace will bring me home. Soon I shall be seated around the throne of God and of the Lamb, robed in white garments of purity, without spot, without sin, and without blame!

> Amazing grace! How sweet the sound
> That saved a wretch like me!
> I once was lost, but now am found;
> Was blind, but now I see.
>
> 'Twas grace that taught my heart to fear,
> And grace my fears relieved;
> How precious did that grace appear
> The hour I first believed.
>
> Through many dangers, toils and snares,
> I have already come;
> 'Tis grace hath brought me safe thus far,
> And grace will lead me home.
>
> The Lord has promised good to me,
> His Word my hope secures;
> He will my Shield and Portion be,
> As long as life endures.
>
> Yea, when this flesh and heart shall fail,
> And mortal life shall cease,
> I shall possess, within the veil,
> A life of joy and peace.

> The earth shall soon dissolve like snow,
> The sun forbear to shine;
> But God, who called me here below,
> Will be forever mine.

John Newton

Hear this word from the triune God and rejoice. 'I am gracious!'

Chapter 84

The Stranger's Heart

'Also thou shalt not oppress a stranger: for ye know the heart of a stranger, seeing ye were strangers in the land of Egypt. And six years thou shalt sow thy land, and shalt gather in the fruits thereof: But the seventh year thou shalt let it rest and lie still; that the poor of thy people may eat: and what they leave the beasts of the field shall eat. In like manner thou shalt deal with thy vineyard, and with thy olive yard. Six days thou shalt do thy work, and on the seventh day thou shalt rest: that thine ox and thine ass may rest, and the son of thy handmaid, and the stranger, may be refreshed. And in all things that I have said unto you be circumspect: and make no mention of the name of other gods, neither let it be heard out of thy mouth.'
(Exodus 23:9-13)

When the Lord God gave his law at Sinai and commanded the children of Israel to honour him in all things, he gave two reasons: first, he said, 'For I am gracious', and second, 'For ye were strangers in the land of Egypt'. These two things we must never forget. He who is our God is gracious; and we were strangers in Egypt, when he sought us out and saved us by his grace.

Do not ever forget who you were, what you were, and where you were when God saved you by his grace. The Lord God frequently commands us to remember we were bondmen in the land of Egypt, urging us to look unto the rock whence we were hewn by the hammer of omnipotent mercy and to the hole of the pit whence we have been dug by his almighty grace (Isaiah 51:1). There are some things we must never forget. We must never forget the price of our redemption (Galatians 3:13, 14; 1 Peter 1:18-20). We must never forget what God has done for us (1 John 3:1). We must never forget what we are by nature and what God has saved us from, by his almighty grace (1 Corinthians 1:26-31; 6:9-11).

Here, in Exodus 23:9-13, the Lord God himself calls us to remember we were 'strangers in the land of Egypt' when he came to us, sought us out, and saved us. The Lord our God commands us neither to vex nor oppress a stranger. He commanded us not to 'vex' (22:21), suppress, mistreat, or act violently toward a stranger in our midst. The Lord commands us not to 'oppress' a stranger here. The word 'oppress' is weightier than the word 'vex'. It means 'afflict, crush, force down, hold down, or thrust yourself upon'. Look at the reasons he gives in this portion of Holy Scripture for this command, by which he teaches us to treat graciously those people we are naturally apt to treat with cruelty. Mark them. There are three of them: 'For ye know the heart of a stranger' (v. 9). 'Seeing ye were strangers in the land of Egypt' (v. 9). 'And the stranger may be refreshed' (v. 12).

The Stranger's Heart

If we are truly his, the Lord God declares of you and me, 'Ye know the heart of a stranger'. Do we? Do you and I know the stranger's heart? Do we know what it is like to grope about in darkness, as a stranger in Egypt? If so, we above all people ought to pity the stranger.

Oh, yes, I know the heart of a stranger in a strange land; and you do too. You who have tasted that the Lord is gracious know 'the heart of a stranger' and we know it well. It will be profitable to our souls to look back and again call to our remembrance what we are by nature. Lord God, help me never to forget! Child of God, ever 'consider thyself'. Believer, seek grace from God the Holy Ghost that you may ever live in relentless awareness of the plague of your own heart (1 Kings 8:38).

Never was mercy more seasonable, more abundant, more unexpected, unlooked for, and unmerited, than when bestowed upon me, when the Lord Jesus passed by me, spread his skirt over me, and said to me, 'Live!' And, here, he says to me, 'Ye know the heart of a stranger'.

Oh, for grace to rightly apprehend, and always apprehend, that state out of which the Lord God has brought me by his grace! I was living as a stranger to the commonwealth of Israel, 'without hope, and without God in the world', when Christ Jesus reached down for me.

'Ye know the heart of a stranger'. What is the heart of a stranger? The stranger's heart is a heart of utter enmity against God (Romans 8:7), a heart without the slightest knowledge of the triune God, a heart utterly ignorant, blind, senseless, unconscious of sin, and unconscious of danger, a heart of sin; base, vile and corrupt (Isaiah 51:1). We were hewn from the rock of human depravity by the hammer of omnipotent grace. We did not break ourselves from the rock. God broke us from it. We did not fall from the rock. We did not evolve from the rock. We were hewn from it, with the violence of God's omnipotent hand. We were dug from the pit of human corruption and degradation by the hand of God's irresistible mercy (Genesis 6:5; Jeremiah 17:9; Mark 7:21-23).

Your heart and mine are by nature as black as the heart of Judas. Whatever sin there is, has been, or ever will be in this world, is in your heart and mine by nature. The germ of all evil is in us all. It does not matter who your parents are, for that which is born of the flesh is flesh. Corruption brings forth corruption. It can never give birth to purity. The history of our race, when honestly read, is a history of corruption and depravity. War, persecution, ambition, greed, rape, murder, and debauchery of every kind has been the history of humanity.

Things have not changed in our day of education, and reason. Every day, the news is the same. Self-serving politicians and preachers are exposed for their hypocrisy. Captains of industry practise to deceive. Athletes cheat, artists indulge, artificers defraud. Adultery, fornication, and rape are widespread. Rioting, murder, and abortion run rampant. Homosexuality, paedophilia, and even cannibalism are practiced by educated, civilized, enlightened reprobates, religious and irreligious!

Yes, I know the heart of a stranger, for I know the present corruption of my depraved heart! How I thank God for his forgiveness of my sin and for the righteousness that is mine in Christ. I thank God for the new nature of grace he has established in me, causing me to love him and love righteousness. But there is a real warfare in my soul between the old man and the new, between the flesh and the spirit, between that in me which is of the devil and that in me which is born of God (Romans 7:14-25; Galatians 5:17; 1 John 3:1-10).

227

A Stranger's Condition

Yes, we know the heart of a stranger. That alone ought to make us merciful to strangers. But the Lord gives another reason why we should be merciful to strangers. He says, 'Thou shalt not oppress a stranger: for ye know the heart of a stranger, seeing ye were strangers in the land of Egypt'. We should never oppress, abuse, hold down, afflict, or thrust ourselves on a poor sinner, 'a stranger', because we were once strangers in Egypt, this land of darkness and oppression (Ephesians 2:11-13).

We were strangers to the blessed Lord Jesus. We knew him not. We loved him not. We desired him not. His love, his grace, his pity, his mercy were concepts that never entered our hearts. Neither his person nor his salvation, nor the merits of his blood, nor his righteousness, were precious in our eyes. There was nothing in us but contempt for the ever-blessed Son of God who loved us and gave himself for us. 'Dead in trespasses and sins', we were strangers to grace and strangers to God, strangers to Christ and strangers to the Holy Spirit. We were, every second, exposed to the tremendous horrors of 'the second death', where we would have been strangers to God and to Christ to all eternity!

What deep impressions this ought to make upon our hearts! You and I ought to be broken, humble, and contrite people. Pride ought not exist in us. God hates it; and we ought to. Nothing in us is more dreadful than pride. Pride of race, pride of place, even pride of grace runs wild in our hearts. 'Who maketh thee to differ from another? and what hast thou that thou didst not receive? now if thou didst receive it, why dost thou glory, as if thou hadst not received it?' (1 Corinthians 4:7).

Humbling and shameful as these facts are, they ought to encourage us with regard to our own salvation. Only saved sinners truly know and confess such things about themselves. How hopeful we ought to be with regard to those who are yet without Christ. If God saved me, he can save you. How kind and gracious we ought to be toward one another for Christ's sake (Ephesians 4:32-5:1). How committed, devoted, and consecrated we ought to be to God our Saviour (Romans 12:1, 2).

I once read about a young pastor who had dinner with a very wealthy man in his congregation. The man lived with his family on a large piece of property, in a huge, spacious, beautiful and magnificently furnished house. The young preacher had never been inside such a place. Needless to say, he was both surprised and impressed by everything he saw, and asked permission to walk through the house. When he did, he was very surprised to find, adjacent to the beautifully finished basement, one particular room. When he opened the door, he found a room with a dirt floor, a little rough, crude furniture; a small table and a couple of odd chairs, and bare, unpainted walls. As he sat with his host, he could not keep from asking why the man had such a room in such a house. The man replied, 'Pastor, that is my remembrance room. The Lord has blessed me in countless ways. I am a wealthy man. My business enterprises have been successful. But I hope never to forget where I came from. I keep that remembrance room and go there often.'

The Lord our God graciously reminds us, throughout Holy Scripture, who we are and what we are by nature, and where we were when he sought us out, found us, and saved us by his almighty free grace. He would have us never forget.

A Stranger's Refreshment
Yes, 'we know the heart of a stranger;' and we were 'strangers in the land of Egypt'. But there is a third thing that is precious beyond words. Read it again and understand that the Lord God specifically tells us he gave the law of the sabbath that 'the stranger may be refreshed'.

'Also thou shalt not oppress a stranger: for ye know the heart of a stranger, seeing ye were strangers in the land of Egypt. And six years thou shalt sow thy land, and shalt gather in the fruits thereof: But the seventh year thou shalt let it rest and lie still; that the poor of thy people may eat: and what they leave the beasts of the field shall eat. In like manner thou shalt deal with thy vineyard, and with thy olive yard. Six days thou shalt do thy work, and on the seventh day thou shalt rest: that thine ox and thine ass may rest, and the son of thy handmaid, and the stranger, may be refreshed. And in all things that I have said unto you be circumspect: and make no mention of the name of other gods, neither let it be heard out of thy mouth' (Exodus 23:9-13).

The word 'refreshed' in verse 12 means 'to breathe passively, to be renewed by a breath of air, to be breathed upon, or to be made to breathe passively'. It is used in Ezekiel 37.

'So I prophesied as I was commanded: and as I prophesied, there was a noise, and behold a shaking, and the bones came together, bone to his bone. And when I beheld, lo, the sinews and the flesh came up upon them, and the skin covered them above: but there was no breath in them. Then said he unto me, Prophesy unto the wind, prophesy, son of man, and say to the wind, Thus saith the Lord GOD; Come from the four winds, O breath, and breathe upon these slain, that they may live. So I prophesied as he commanded me, and the breath came into them, and they lived, and stood up upon their feet, an exceeding great army' (Ezekiel 37:7-10).

The Lord Jesus fulfilled all the law in the room and stead of chosen sinners and died on the cross as the Surety for strangers, that they might be breathed upon and refreshed by the Spirit of grace in regeneration. Christ was made a stranger when he was made sin for us, that we might live before God and rest forever in him (Psalm 69:8; Proverbs 6:1-5; 27:13, 14). Bless God for his grace! In Christ, at the throne of grace, there is grace and mercy for strangers, 'yea, for the rebellious also!'

'If there be in the land famine, if there be pestilence, blasting, mildew, locust, or if there be caterpillar; if their enemy besiege them in the land of their cities; whatsoever plague, whatsoever sickness there be; What prayer and supplication soever be made by any man, or by all thy people Israel, which shall know every man the plague of his own heart, and spread forth his hands toward this house: Then hear thou in heaven thy dwelling place, and forgive, and do, and give to every man according to his ways, whose heart thou knowest; (for thou, even thou only, knowest the hearts of all the children of men;) That they may fear thee all the days that they live in the land which thou gavest unto our fathers. Moreover concerning a stranger, that is not of thy people Israel, but cometh out of a far country for thy name's sake; ... Hear thou in heaven thy dwelling place, and do according to all that the stranger calleth to thee for: that all people of the earth may know thy name, to fear thee, as do thy people Israel; and that they may know that this house, which I have builded, is called by thy name. If thy people go out to battle against their enemy, whithersoever thou shalt send them, and shall pray unto the LORD toward the city which thou hast chosen, and toward the house that I have built for thy name: Then, hear thou in heaven their prayer and their supplication, and maintain their cause' (1 Kings 8:37-45).

Let us be humbled in the dust before our God and ascribe all our mercies to his distinguishing grace. Everlastingly cry, my ransomed soul, 'Not unto us, O LORD, not unto us, but unto thy name give glory, for thy mercy, and for thy truth's sake!' Let us ever return praise to give God all glory and honour (Luke 17:17, 18).

Chapter 85

Let None Come Empty

'And six years thou shalt sow thy land, and shalt gather in the fruits thereof: But the seventh year thou shalt let it rest and lie still; that the poor of thy people may eat: and what they leave the beasts of the field shall eat. In like manner thou shalt deal with thy vineyard, and with thy olive yard. Six days thou shalt do thy work, and on the seventh day thou shalt rest: that thine ox and thine ass may rest, and the son of thy handmaid, and the stranger, may be refreshed. And in all things that I have said unto you be circumspect: and make no mention of the name of other gods, neither let it be heard out of thy mouth. Three times thou shalt keep a feast unto me in the year. Thou shalt keep the feast of unleavened bread: (thou shalt eat unleavened bread seven days, as I commanded thee, in the time appointed of the month Abib; for in it thou camest out from Egypt: and none shall appear before me empty:) And the feast of harvest, the firstfruits of thy labours, which thou hast sown in the field: and the feast of ingathering, which is in the end of the year, when thou hast gathered in thy labours out of the field. Three times in the year all thy males shall appear before the Lord GOD. Thou shalt not offer the blood of my sacrifice with leavened bread; neither shall the fat of my sacrifice remain until the morning. The first of the firstfruits of thy land thou shalt bring into the house of the LORD thy God. Thou shalt not seethe a kid in his mother's milk.'
(Exodus 23:10-19)

We often urge sinners to come to Christ as 'empty handed beggars'. But the law of God specifically requires that none appear before the holy Lord God empty. 'They shall not appear before the Lord empty.' That is the language of the law. If we come to God, we must bring something with us. What does God require us to bring to him? We will be wise to read the Book of God, to diligently search the Scriptures, and find out what it is that he requires us to bring to him. In this portion of Holy Scripture, the Lord God tells us we cannot and must not come to him empty. If we come to God, we must bring him that which he requires.

Sabbath Refreshment

There are multitudes who talk about keeping a sabbath day in the most severe and morbid terms imaginable; but here (vv. 10-12) sabbath observance is spoken of as a time of rest and refreshment, and as a special provision for the poor. Sabbath keeping was central and essential to the worship of God in the typical days of ceremonial, Old Testament law. God could no more be worshipped without sabbath observance than he could be worshipped without blood. Sabbath keeping was as essential to the worship of God as the blood of a lamb on the day of atonement. Therefore, before giving the children of Israel instructions about the three annual feasts for which every man in Israel was required to gather at God's altar, Moses was inspired by God the Holy Ghost to expand and elaborate upon the fourth commandment. 'Remember the sabbath day to keep it holy' (Exodus 20:8).

In verses 10 and 11 we see that God required Israel to observe a yearly sabbath as well as the weekly sabbath. Every seventh year he required the children of Israel to let the land rest. They were not allowed to plant their crops, or prune their vineyards, or gather the fruits the orchards and fields brought forth on their own (Leviticus 25:3-7). In verse 12 the Lord commanded the observance of a weekly sabbath every Saturday. These sabbath laws served to remind Israel and to teach us that we have our bread by the hand of God, not by the labour of our own hands. We are to live in dependence upon our God, not depending upon the arm of the flesh. Let us ever remember that 'the earth is the LORD'S'. We are temporary tenants on the land. It belongs to God. We own nothing.

But notice the reasons God gives for these commandments in verse 11 and 12: 'that the poor of thy people may eat', 'thou shalt rest', 'the stranger may be refreshed'. The sabbath was to be kept every week and every year, as a constant reminder to Israel of that sweet rest which Adam lost in the Garden, and of the blessed rest that could and would be recovered only in and by Christ. The sabbath was entirely intended and only intended to typify salvation in Christ, the blessed rest of life, and faith, and reconciliation to God in him.

'No work' was to be done on the sabbath, because salvation is a matter of grace, a work of grace alone, enjoyed by faith in Christ, without our works of any kind. No other festival in the Old Testament had such a strict injunction put on it except the day of atonement.

Do you see the significance of that? The rest of faith is the same as the rest of perfect atonement, and the rest of complete reconciliation to God. This is what was typified in the beginning, when the Lord God rested from all his works on the seventh day.

Is it so with your soul? Do you have such rest in Christ with God, as if you had never sinned? Do you have no more conscience of sin? This is the rest Christ has won for all who trust him. Come to the Lord Jesus Christ and rest! Cease from all work and labour. Rest and be refreshed in him (Matthew 11:28-30; Hebrews 4:3, 7).

Here is 'a feast of fat things, a feast of wines on the lees, of fat things full of marrow, of wines on the lees well refined' (Isaiah 25:6). This rest of faith and this sabbath feast is good, oh, how good! But the rest of heaven will be glorious (Hebrews 4:9). 'There remaineth therefore a rest to the people of God.'

In verse 13, we are admonished to strictly and circumspectly observe these things. 'And in all things that I have said unto you be circumspect: and make no mention of the name of other gods, neither let it be heard out of thy mouth.' I take this to mean that God counts the mixture of our works with the work of his Son for our salvation to be nothing but blasphemy and base idolatry. Let us not take the name of the heathen's god, 'Free Will', to our lips, except to condemn it.

Three Feasts of Faith
In verses 14-17 the Lord God commanded the children of Israel to observe three annual feasts in which he required all the men of Israel to come to his altar and worship for a week: the feast of unleavened bread, the feast of harvest, and the feast of ingathering. These three annual feasts of worship were great feasts of faith. Keeping them was an

outward display of faith and a ceremonial picture of the salvation that is ours by faith in Christ.

'Three times thou shalt keep a feast unto me in the year. Thou shalt keep the feast of unleavened bread: (thou shalt eat unleavened bread seven days, as I commanded thee, in the time appointed of the month Abib; for in it thou camest out from Egypt: and none shall appear before me empty:) And the feast of harvest, the firstfruits of thy labours, which thou hast sown in the field: and the feast of ingathering, which is in the end of the year, when thou hast gathered in thy labours out of the field. Three times in the year all thy males shall appear before the Lord GOD' (Exodus 23:14-17).

Women and children were allowed to come and did; but every man was required to come to each of these feasts, because the man is the head of the house and the representative of the family.

The Feast of Unleavened Bread

The feast of unleavened bread, though distinct from the passover, is commonly looked upon as a continuation of the passover feast. On the passover night the children of Israel ate the Lamb with their coats on their backs, their shoes on their feet, and their staffs in their hands, ready to go out of Egypt. The passover sacrifice was the cause of deliverance. The feast of unleavened bread represents the effects of redemption. The sacrifice of Christ our Passover is the effectual cause of pardon. The sweet fellowship of faith, pictured in the feast of unleavened bread, is the effect, the sure and certain result of Christ's death as our Substitute.

This feast was a constant reminder of God's great work of grace in bringing Israel out of Egypt by his mighty power and stretched out arm, because of the blood that was shed for them (Exodus 12-14). But it was more than that. The passover and this feast of unleavened bread that followed it were, together, a picture and constant reminder of God's promise to send a Redeemer, even Christ our Passover, who is sacrificed for us (1 Corinthians 5:7).

Three things were prominent in the first passover: a lamb, blood, and deliverance. It was pre-eminently 'the LORD'S passover'. It was called 'the LORD'S passover' because the whole of the work was wholly his. He ordained it. He provided the lamb. He accepted the lamb. He passed over the people. He brought them out of Egypt and across the Red Sea. And he alone was praised for it (Exodus 15).

The feast of unleavened bread pictures faith in Christ (John 6:53-56). Do not miss the connection of the feast of unleavened bread with the feast of passover. The feast of unleavened bread began the next day after the passover was ended. So, too, the gift of life and faith in Christ follows the accomplishments of Christ at Calvary. All who were redeemed by blood shall be made to live and feed upon Christ at God's appointed time (Galatians 3:13, 14). As one great family, the children of Israel kept the first day of this feast as a 'holy convocation'. No servile work was done. It was a blessed time of rest, picturing the perpetual sabbath rest of faith in Christ. The people were all joined together, united in one holy body of redeemed souls remembering what God had done for them. They were bought with the same blood. They were saved by the same power. They were going to the same homeland. They ate the same bread (Ephesians 3:18, 19; 4:1-7).

As often as we eat the bread and drink the wine at the Lord's Table, like Israel of old, in the feast of unleavened bread, we show forth the Lord's death until he comes again, in remembrance of him: in remembrance of redemption finished (Blood Atonement), and in hope of redemption future (Resurrection Glory).

What does God require us to bring to him? Remember, what God requires, he gives; and the only thing he will ever accept is that which he himself has given. His name is Jehovah-jireh. He will provide. He will provide himself, and he will be seen in the provision he makes. God required the observance of this feast of unleavened bread with this assurance in the last line of verse 15, 'And none shall appear before me empty'. That which the children of Israel brought to the Lord God was that which he had given them to bring: the passover lamb and the firstfruit sheaves. That is exactly what the Lord tells us in Deuteronomy 16:16, 17. 'Every man shall give as he is able, according to the blessing of the LORD thy God which he hath given thee.' Christ is what we must bring: his blood and his righteousness. Grace is what we receive by the Sacrifice we bring; free, bounteous, infinite grace (Romans 5:20, 21; 1 Peter 1:18-20; Psalm 115:1).

The Feast of Harvest
The feast of harvest is Pentecost the same as the feast of weeks (Leviticus 23:15-22; Deuteronomy 16:16, 17). It was held fifty days i.e. seven weeks and a day, a sabbath day, after the feast of firstfruits. It is

commonly called 'Pentecost' because it was held on the fiftieth day. This is the harvest, or ingathering feast. This great harvest feast speaks of the ingathering of God's elect by Christ.

The risen Christ gave us a delightful picture and foretaste of the ingathering of his elect in Acts 2:1-4. When the Day of Pentecost was fully come, he poured out his Spirit upon all flesh and three thousand souls were gathered into the fold of his grace at one time. Just as the harvest followed the firstfruits, the salvation of God's elect follows the resurrection of Christ. Indeed, all the redeemed shall be gathered unto God by the risen Christ (Isaiah 43:5-7; John 10:15-18; Romans 11:26).

In Leviticus 23, Moses gives a much larger, more complete declaration of God's law regarding these feasts. In the twenty-second verse of that chapter we read, 'And when ye reap the harvest of your land, thou shalt not make clean riddance of the corners of thy field when thou reapest, neither shalt thou gather any gleaning of thy harvest: thou shalt leave them unto the poor, and to the stranger: I am the LORD your God'. Even in requiring Israel never to gather all their harvest, the Lord teaches us about his grace. Boaz left some handfuls of purpose for Ruth, so the Lord God always provides for his own. In the Old Testament there was a remnant according to the election of grace among the Gentiles. The Lord said, 'You take care that you provide for them'. In this Gospel Age, there is still a remnant according to the election of grace. The Lord says, 'You take care that you provide for them'.

In other words, the Lord would have us ever mindful of the needs of others, specifically of the fact that he has a people to whom he will be gracious; and he gives us the privilege of serving their souls' needs by the preaching of the gospel.

The Feast of Ingathering
'The feast of ingathering, which is in the end of the year, when thou hast gathered in thy labours out of the field' (v. 16), is the feast of tabernacles. This was a time when Israel was reminded that they dwelt in booths in the wilderness and God dwelt with them in the cloudy and fiery pillar. But it spoke of more than that. It spoke of that time when God came here and tabernacled in human flesh that he might at last bring God and man together in eternal glory and perfect fellowship, with sin and every evil consequence of it expiated, put away, purged, gone, and forgotten forever (Psalm 72:16-19; Revelation 21:1-7).

The Eighth Day

The eighth day was considered the great day of the feast of tabernacles (John 7:37). On the eighth day, the harvest was completed. Everything was gathered. What a time of celebration it was! The joy of harvest and the shouting and dancing associated with the treading of the winepresses must have been something to behold. This Gospel Age is the eighth day of the feast, the last day there is. Hear the Son of God, as he speaks on this, the eighth day, the great day of the feast.

'In the last day, that great day of the feast, Jesus stood and cried, saying, If any man thirst, let him come unto me, and drink. He that believeth on me, as the scripture hath said, out of his belly shall flow rivers of living water' (John 7:37, 38).

He who is God our Saviour promises to forever quench the thirst of our souls, the thirst he has created in us by his grace.

'And he that sat upon the throne said, Behold, I make all things new. And he said unto me, Write: for these words are true and faithful. And he said unto me, It is done. I am Alpha and Omega, the beginning and the end. I will give unto him that is athirst of the fountain of the water of life freely. He that overcometh shall inherit all things; and I will be his God, and he shall be my son' (Revelation 21:5-7).

Strict Prohibitions

In Exodus 23:18, 19, the Lord God makes some very strict prohibitions. If we would worship God we must worship him by faith alone, trusting Christ alone as our Saviour. No leaven of our works, no leaven of our righteousness can be mixed and mingled with the sacrifice of our dear Saviour's blood and righteousness. 'Thou shalt not offer the blood of my sacrifice with leavened bread; neither shall the fat of my sacrifice remain until the morning' (v. 18). God the Holy Ghost gives these same prohibitions in the New Testament (1 Corinthians 5:7; Galatians 5:1-4).

'Purge out therefore the old leaven, that ye may be a new lump, as ye are unleavened. For even Christ our passover is sacrificed for us' (1 Corinthians 5:7).

'Stand fast therefore in the liberty wherewith Christ hath made us free, and be not entangled again with the yoke of bondage. Behold, I Paul say unto you, that if ye be circumcised, Christ shall profit you nothing. For I testify again to every man that is circumcised, that he is a debtor to do the whole law. Christ is become of no effect unto you, whosoever of you are justified by the law; ye are fallen from grace' (Galatians 5:1-4).

In verse 19 there is another strict prohibition that teaches the same thing. 'The first of the firstfruits of thy land thou shalt bring into the house of the LORD thy God. Thou shalt not seethe a kid in his mother's milk.' We worship God by bringing to him that which he has given us, Christ the Firstborn, the Firstfruit, with no mixture of the idolatrous religious superstition of will-worship. That is exactly what is meant by the command, 'Thou shalt not seethe a kid in his mother's milk.'

This remarkable prohibition is found three times in the Scriptures (Exodus 23:19; 34:26; Deuteronomy 14:21). By this prohibition, the Lord God, our heavenly Father, tenderly guards us from the idolatrous inventions of men in the practices of barbaric human religion. The heathen around Israel were all idolaters. They practised the most obscene and ridiculous religious customs imaginable. It was common for them in their harvest feasts to seethe (boil) a kid in its mother's milk and then sprinkle their fields, vineyards and orchards with the liquid for 'good luck' from their gods! True worship is altogether spiritual worship, the worship of God by faith in Christ, nothing else (Philippians 3:1-3). We dare not come before the holy Lord God empty. Yet, we dare not bring him any idolatrous mixture of our own making, of our own will and works. We come to God with the Sacrifice he has provided: Christ our Passover! Christ the Firstborn! Christ the Firstfruit! We have no other confidence. 'Christ is All.'

'Now where remission of these is, there is no more offering for sin. Having therefore, brethren, boldness to enter into the holiest by the blood of Jesus, By a new and living way, which he hath consecrated for us, through the veil, that is to say, his flesh; And having an high priest over the house of God; Let us draw near with a true heart in full assurance of faith, having our hearts sprinkled from an evil conscience, and our bodies washed with pure water' (Hebrews 10:18-22).

Chapter 86

The Angel Sent Before: Christ Our Protector

'Behold, I send an Angel before thee, to keep thee in the way, and to bring thee into the place which I have prepared. Beware of him, and obey his voice, provoke him not; for he will not pardon your transgressions: for my name is in him. But if thou shalt indeed obey his voice, and do all that I speak; then I will be an enemy unto thine enemies, and an adversary unto thine adversaries. For mine Angel shall go before thee, and bring thee in unto the Amorites, and the Hittites, and the Perizzites, and the Canaanites, the Hivites, and the Jebusites: and I will cut them off. Thou shalt not bow down to their gods, nor serve them, nor do after their works: but thou shalt utterly overthrow them, and quite break down their images. And ye shall serve the LORD your God, and he shall bless thy bread, and thy water; and I will take sickness away from the midst of thee. There shall nothing cast their young, nor be barren, in thy land: the number of thy days I will fulfil. I will send my fear before thee, and will destroy all the people to whom thou shalt come, and I will make all thine enemies turn their backs unto thee. And I will send hornets before thee, which shall drive out the Hivite, the Canaanite, and the Hittite, from before thee. I will not drive them out from before thee in one year; lest the land become desolate, and the beast of the field multiply against thee. By little and little I will drive them out from before thee, until thou be increased, and inherit the land. And I will set thy bounds from the Red sea even unto the sea of the Philistines, and from the desert unto the river: for I will deliver the inhabitants of the land into your hand; and thou shalt drive them out before thee. Thou shalt make no covenant with them, nor with their gods. They shall not dwell in thy land, lest they make thee sin against me: for if thou serve their gods, it will surely be a snare unto thee.' (Exodus 23:20-33)

Have you ever looked at the rugged mountain ranges those early pioneers had to cross to reach the west of America, and thought, 'What inspired them? What rare, rugged men and women they must have been!' With no promise of anything but rugged mountains, wild beasts, and permanent isolation from family, friends, and the rest of the world, they headed west. To me that is amazing.

But just suppose things had been different. Suppose before leaving, those who followed the trail west had been assured, upon good authority, that there was a land beyond those rugged mountains of unimaginable peace and prosperity, indescribable life and health, a land they could have simply by planting their feet upon the ground. Then, it was promised, upon that same good authority, that every enemy they might meet in the way would flee from them and every obstacle would be removed from their path. And then, one more promise, they were promised that God himself would send an Angel before them to lead the way, keep them in the way, and bring them into the land. With such assurances and promises I would have signed up in a heartbeat. As God's ambassador to your soul, I call you to join me for such a journey to a land of unimaginable peace and prosperity, indescribable life and health, a land of immortality and glory.

After giving his law to the children of Israel at Mount Sinai, the chosen nation was about to proceed in their journey toward the land of Canaan. The Lord God had given them plain directions for the regulation of their lives. Now, at the end of Exodus 23, as he is about to thrust them into the wilderness where he will try them and prove them for forty years, he graciously encourages them. He promised his people the care of his infinite love and assured them he would send an Angel before them to keep them in the way and to bring them into the land he had prepared for them.

As we read this portion of Holy Scripture, let us remember that these things were written 'for our learning, that we through patience and comfort of the Scriptures might have hope' (Romans 15:4). This is more than a historic record. This is the Word of God to you and me. The promises contained here are not merely ancient promises to an ancient people. They are the present promises of our ever-present God to his 'holy nation', to his church, called by his Spirit 'the Israel of God' (Galatians 6:16). And, just as the Lord God fulfilled all his promises to that physical nation (Joshua 23:3, 9-12, 14), so he will fulfil every promise of his grace to us.

The Angel
'Behold, I send an Angel before thee, to keep thee in the way, and to bring thee into the place which I have prepared' (Exodus 23:20).

The Land of Canaan was specifically created and prepared by God for the children of Israel. It is used in Scripture to represent two things. First, the Land of Canaan represents Heaven. That is obvious, because it is the Land of Promise; therefore it is used in Scripture to represent our final place of rest with Christ. But Canaan also represents the believer's present life in Christ. That, too, is obvious, because there were in the Land of Canaan many enemies and much trouble.

Thus, Canaan represents our whole experience of grace, culminating in Heaven's everlasting glory. Here the Lord God promises to send an Angel before us; and this Angel has two specific assignments, two tasks and two responsibilities. First, it is his responsibility to keep us in the way. Second, it is his responsibility to bring us into the place the Lord God has prepared for us.

Who is this Angel? This is not one of the created angels sent forth to minister to those who shall be the heirs of salvation (Hebrews 1:14). This Angel is our dear Saviour, the Lord Jesus Christ, the Angel of God's presence, that One who spoke to Moses out of the bush, the Angel who was with the Israelites at Sinai and in the wilderness, who saved them, redeemed them, bore them, and carried them all the days of old, the One against whom they rebelled, and the One they tempted for forty years in the wilderness.

To say that Christ is 'an Angel' does not in any way contradict the fact of his eternal Deity. The word 'angel' simply means 'messenger'. And our Lord Jesus Christ is both Jehovah and Jehovah's Messenger. In his eternal Deity, our Saviour is God himself, over all and blessed forever. In his mediatorial capacity, as our Surety and Substitute, he is 'the Angel of the LORD'. When the Scriptures speak of our Saviour as 'the Angel of the LORD', appearing in the form of a man before he actually assumed our nature in the incarnation, they are telling us that God's own Son, the Surety and Mediator of the covenant, the man Christ Jesus, is the Revelation of God. Jesus Christ, our Mediator, is, always was, and ever shall be the only one in whom and by whom God makes himself known to men. Christ is God's Message; and Christ is God's Messenger.

Two things in this passage make it unmistakably clear this Angel is our Saviour. I am certain he is because in verse 21 we are told this Angel has the authority and ability to forgive sin; and the Lord God declares, at the end of verse 21, 'my name is in him'.

Christ our Lord is that Angel of whom the prophets spoke describing him as our Saviour and Protector (Isaiah 63:9; Psalm 34:7). He is the Angel of the Lord standing among the myrtle trees, defending his people, interceding for us. He is Michael the Archangel, who resisted Satan when he accused Joshua, and the Angel who stands as God to defend his feeble ones in the earth (Zechariah 1:11, 12; 3:1-7; 12:8).

This is what the Lord God declares to us about Christ as the Angel of the Lord sent before us. 'Behold, I send an Angel before thee, to keep thee in the way, and to bring thee into the place which I have prepared.'

First, he declares 'I send an Angel before thee'. Christ our Angel, Messenger and Heavenly Proctor, is sent before us. He was sent before us as our Surety in old eternity. He was sent before us to judgment as our Substitute, dying under the wrath of God to put away our sins. The Lord Jesus was sent before us as our Forerunner into heaven. He has walked this path before us and leads the way to Heaven. Blessed be God, just as 'he must needs go through Samaria' to save the Samaritan woman at the appointed time of love, our Lord Jesus is sent before his chosen, as our Saviour, to save the people of his choice at the appointed time of mercy. Our Lord Jesus was sent before us into Heaven to be our great Benefactor, our mighty Joseph.

Second, the Lord God here promises that our Saviour, the Lord Jesus, his Angel, will keep us in the way. He is the Way. He put us in the Way. He leads us in the Way. And he keeps us in the Way.

Third, it is the work and responsibility of Jehovah's Angel, Christ our Protector, to bring us at last into heaven. 'Behold, I send an Angel before thee, to keep thee in the way, and to bring thee into the place which I have prepared.' Is that not what he tells us in John 10?

'I am the good shepherd, and know my sheep, and am known of mine. As the Father knoweth me, even so know I the Father: and I lay down my life for the sheep. And other sheep I have, which are not of this fold: them also I must bring, and they shall hear my voice; and there shall be one fold, and one shepherd. Therefore doth my Father love me, because I lay down my life, that I might take it again. No man taketh it from me, but I lay it down of myself. I have power to lay it down, and I have power to take it again. This commandment have I received of my Father' (John 10:14-18).

The Obedience Required

All God's promises of grace are free and unconditional. But, in verses 21 and 22, a condition is set before us. Everything is conditioned upon obedience, obedience to the Angel who is God.

'Beware of him, and obey his voice, provoke him not; for he will not pardon your transgressions: for my name is in him. But if thou shalt indeed obey his voice, and do all that I speak; then I will be an enemy unto thine enemies, and an adversary unto thine adversaries' (Exodus 23:21, 22).

Does this mean that God's grace is conditional? Does God require obedience from us as a condition of mercy? Does God's promise depend upon our obedience? Certainly not! You may be thinking, 'But, these verses seem to read that way.' Let us see. Did the children of Israel obey the Lord? Did they obey his commands? By no means! He declares, again and again, that 'they provoked him to anger' with their high places, their counsel, and their iniquities (Psalm 78; 106). Did their disobedience keep the Lord from fulfilling every word of his promise? By no means! (Psalm 106:8; Joshua 23:3, 9-12, 14)

What obedience does God require of us? It is not the obedience of our hands, but 'the obedience of faith' (Romans 16:26), by which we establish the law (Romans 3:31).

The Lord God declares that Christ, his Angel, 'will not pardon your transgressions, for my name is in him' (v. 21). And in a strict, legal sense that is exactly the case. Our blessed Saviour never just 'pardons' sin. He put our sins away! He removed them altogether, so thoroughly so that they are not and never can be the slightest barrier to God's fulfilment of his promised mercy!

Salvation Sure

'For mine Angel shall go before thee, and bring thee in unto the Amorites, and the Hittites, and the Perizzites, and the Canaanites, the Hivites, and the Jebusites: and I will cut them off' (Exodus 23:23).

In verses 23-26 the Lord God again demands that we keep ourselves from idols and from idolatry, promising his unfailing grace to all who worship him.

'Thou shalt not bow down to their gods, nor serve them, nor do after their works: but thou shalt utterly overthrow them, and quite break down their images. And ye shall serve the LORD your God, and he shall bless thy bread, and thy water; and I will take sickness away from the midst of thee. There shall nothing cast their young, nor be barren, in thy land: the number of thy days I will fulfil' (Exodus 23:24-26).

To our enemies, Christ is an enemy. To our adversaries, he is an adversary. He blesses our bread and water, making them nourishing and refreshing to us. He frees his own from sickness and disease, from all the consequences of sin. In the kingdom of grace there are no barren, fruitless souls (Galatians 5:22, 23). Every heaven born soul shall have his days fulfilled (Psalm 91:1-16).

Our Enemies

'I will send my fear before thee, and will destroy all the people to whom thou shalt come, and I will make all thine enemies turn their backs unto thee' (Exodus 23:27).

Our enemies are not the people of this world. We spend our lives preaching the gospel to the people of this world, seeking their everlasting salvation. But if men set themselves in opposition to God's church, they shall fail. If men and women resolve to hurt or injure God's people, they shall find themselves fleeing, though no one is pursuing them (Proverbs 28:1).

'And I will send hornets before thee, which shall drive out the Hivite, the Canaanite, and the Hittite, from before thee' (Exodus 23:28).

Only God could drive out armies and destroy nations with hornets!

But, really, our greatest enemies, those with whom we must constantly do battle, those with whom we are continually at war, are like the Amorites and Hittites, the Perizzites and Hivites and Jebusites; enemies within. They are the Canaanites dwelling in our hearts, the lusts of our flesh. Yet, for wise and holy purposes known only to him, in his great mercy, the Lord our God, the God of all grace, promises that these foes shall not be quickly destroyed.

'I will not drive them out from before thee in one year; lest the land become desolate, and the beast of the field multiply against thee. By little and little I will drive them out from before thee, until thou be increased, and inherit the land' (Exodus 23:29, 30).

It is best we live with our old, fallen, depraved nature, until we inherit the land of our inheritance. It is best for us to live in this world, struggling with the lusts of our flesh, that we might ever remember that salvation is God's work of grace. It is best for us to live in this body of flesh, that we might ever be reminded the only difference between us and others is the distinguishing grace of our God. It is best for us to live in this state of relentless warfare, that we might prove day by day that his grace is sufficient!

The Lord God has set the bounds of our habitation from the river to the ends of the earth, for these are the bounds of our Saviour's dominion (vv. 31-33; Psalm 72:8; Zechariah 9:10).

'And I will set thy bounds from the Red sea even unto the sea of the Philistines, and from the desert unto the river: for I will deliver the inhabitants of the land into your hand; and thou shalt drive them out before thee. Thou shalt make no covenant with them, nor with their gods. They shall not dwell in thy land, lest they make thee sin against me: for if thou serve their gods, it will surely be a snare unto thee' (Exodus 23:31-33).

Does the Lord Jesus go before us? That thought should revive our hearts continually. Let everything in me remember him! Let me never lose sight of him going before me and having gone before me! The Angel of the Lord! The Angel of the Covenant! The Angel of God's Presence! Rejoice, my heart, Jehovah's name, his character and being, are in him who is my Saviour, my Redeemer, and my Protector!

Oh, blessed Angel of Grace, Son of God, send your Spirit in a constantly renewing work of grace to subdue and drive out the corruptions of my heart before you. Make me the conquest of your mercy, and do the same for my fellow-pilgrims in this hostile land! Safely carry us through the whole of this wilderness journey. Bring us soon into that heavenly Canaan prepared for us from eternity, that home you have gone before to prepare for us, where we shall see you face to face, and sorrow and sighing shall flee away forever!

Chapter 87

'Behold The Blood'

'And he said unto Moses, Come up unto the LORD, thou, and Aaron, Nadab, and Abihu, and seventy of the elders of Israel; and worship ye afar off. And Moses alone shall come near the LORD: but they shall not come nigh; neither shall the people go up with him. And Moses came and told the people all the words of the LORD, and all the judgments: and all the people answered with one voice, and said, All the words which the LORD hath said will we do. And Moses wrote all the words of the LORD, and rose up early in the morning, and builded an altar under the hill, and twelve pillars, according to the twelve tribes of Israel. And he sent young men of the children of Israel, which offered burnt offerings, and sacrificed peace offerings of oxen unto the LORD. And Moses took half of the blood, and put it in basons; and half of the blood he sprinkled on the altar. And he took the book of the covenant, and read in the audience of the people: and they said, All that the LORD hath said will we do, and be obedient. And Moses took the blood, and sprinkled it on the people, and said, Behold the blood of the covenant, which the LORD hath made with you concerning all these words. Then went up Moses, and Aaron, Nadab, and Abihu, and seventy of the elders of Israel: And they saw the God of Israel: and there was under his feet as it were a paved work of a sapphire stone, and as it were the body of heaven in his clearness. And upon the nobles of the children of Israel he laid not his hand: also they saw God, and did eat and drink. And the LORD said unto Moses, Come up to me into the mount, and be there:

and I will give thee tables of stone, and a law, and commandments which I have written; that thou mayest teach them. And Moses rose up, and his minister Joshua: and Moses went up into the mount of God. And he said unto the elders, Tarry ye here for us, until we come again unto you: and, behold, Aaron and Hur are with you: if any man have any matters to do, let him come unto them. And Moses went up into the mount, and a cloud covered the mount. And the glory of the LORD abode upon mount Sinai, and the cloud covered it six days: and the seventh day he called unto Moses out of the midst of the cloud. And the sight of the glory of the LORD was like devouring fire on the top of the mount in the eyes of the children of Israel. And Moses went into the midst of the cloud, and gat him up into the mount: and Moses was in the mount forty days and forty nights.'
(Exodus 24:1-18)

Exodus 24 opens with an expression of the law's strictness and severity; a divine prohibition is given and a wall of separation between God and man is erected.

'And he said unto Moses, Come up unto the LORD, thou, and Aaron, Nadab, and Abihu, and seventy of the elders of Israel; and worship ye afar off. And Moses alone shall come near the LORD: but they shall not come nigh; neither shall the people go up with him' (Exodus 24:1, 2).

The Lord God commanded the seventy elders and the children of Israel to worship 'afar off'. He said, 'they shall not come nigh'. Throughout the legal dispensation, under the types and shadows of the law, the people were never allowed to draw nigh. Those two precious words, 'draw nigh', could never be heard from the top of Sinai's fiery mount. The law says, 'Stay away. Keep back. If so much as the hand of a beast touch the mount, it shall be slain!' Those sweet words, 'draw nigh', could only be uttered at heaven's side of the empty tomb of our risen Redeemer. But, blessed be God, there is now a Door open in Heaven; and over the Door the Lord God has written these words in the precious blood of Christ, 'Draw nigh'. The blood of the cross has opened the way for sinners to draw nigh unto God!

Yet, at the same time, this twenty-fourth chapter of Exodus introduces us to a scene without parallel in all the history of the Old Testament. Before the chapter closes, we see Moses and Aaron, Nadab and Abihu, and seventy of the elders of Israel in the very presence of the holy Lord God, and not only are we told that 'He laid not his hand on them', but they were thoroughly at ease in his presence, for they did 'eat and drink' before him (v. 11).

Moses, A Type of Christ
Why was an exception made for Moses? Jehovah called Moses up into the mount, and only he was allowed to draw nigh. Aaron, Nadab, Abihu, the elders, and the children of Israel were forbidden to come near. In verse 13, we see that Moses brought Joshua with him into the mount. These two were allowed access to God in the mount. Why? Were they better than the others? No. Were they more holy? No. Were they more righteous? No. Were they personally entitled to this great and high privilege? Again, the answer is no. But Moses and Joshua were both types of our Lord Jesus Christ as divinely appointed mediators between God and his people.

Moses represents justice satisfied. And justice satisfied demands release. Joshua means 'Jesus' or 'Jehovah saves'. How often the Lord God would have destroyed Israel in the wilderness had not Moses stood between God and his people (Exodus 32:10, 11, 32; Deuteronomy 9:19, 25; 10:10; Psalm 106:23).

'They forgat God their saviour, which had done great things in Egypt; Wondrous works in the land of Ham, and terrible things by the Red sea. Therefore he said that he would destroy them, had not Moses his chosen stood before him in the breach, to turn away his wrath, lest he should destroy them' (Psalm 106:21-23).

Moses represented the law and justice of God. And Moses represented the Lord Jesus Christ, our Saviour, by whom the law and justice of God are fully satisfied. Moses and Joshua together represented the perfect mediation of Christ, his acceptance with God as our Mediator, and our acceptance with God in him.

An Altar and Sacrifices
'And Moses came and told the people all the words of the LORD, and all the judgments; and all the people answered with one voice, and said, All the words which the LORD hath said will we do' (v. 3). The 'words of the LORD' refer to the Ten Commandments recorded in Exodus 20. 'The judgments' refer to those statutes found in chapters 21 to 23. The

children of Israel presumptuously and ignorantly, with one unanimous voice, said, 'All the words which the LORD hath said will we do'. Then Moses built an altar.

'And Moses wrote all the words of the LORD, and rose up early in the morning, and builded an altar under the hill, and twelve pillars, according to the twelve tribes of Israel. And he sent young men of the children of Israel, which offered burnt offerings, and sacrificed peace offerings of oxen unto the LORD' (vv. 4, 5). Without question, the altar was built according to the instructions given in Exodus 20:24-26. It was an altar made of God's material, without steps, portraying Christ our Altar (Hebrews 13:10).

Near this altar, Moses set twelve pillars to represent the twelve tribes of Israel. The young men sent to offer sacrifices unto the Lord were probably the firstborn of the children of Israel, from whom the Levites would later be taken. The burnt offerings and peace offerings they sacrificed upon the altar unto the Lord were sacrifices of thanksgiving. They gave thanks to God for the law he had given, revealing God's holiness, and for the law's fulfilment by a mediator, by a representative man. They gave thanks for all that was typified and prophesied by these things: God's acceptance of his people by the Mediator-man, through the Altar and Sacrifice of his own making and providing, Christ Jesus.

Behold the Blood

Everything we have from God is by blood; the precious, sin atoning blood of Christ. Every approach of God to man is by the blood. And every approach of man to God must be by the blood. The Word of God puts special sanctions upon blood, the blood of beasts as well as the blood of men, because 'the life of the flesh is in the blood' and 'ye who sometimes were far off are made nigh by the blood of Christ'.

'And Moses took half of the blood, and put it in basins; and half of the blood he sprinkled on the altar. And he took the book of the covenant, and read in the audience of the people: and they said, All that the LORD hath said will we do, and be obedient. And Moses took the blood, and sprinkled it on the people, and said, Behold the blood of the covenant, which the LORD hath made with you concerning all these words' (Exodus 24:6-8).

'Behold the blood of the covenant.' Those words, uttered by Moses as he sprinkled the people with the crimson life-stream, forcibly remind us of John's, 'Behold the Lamb of God, which taketh away the sin of the world' (John 1:29). A covenant is an agreement between two parties. In the Scriptures, it is a testament, a divine disposition, a pledge of grace, a bond of perpetual blessedness. The covenant was beautifully expressed in Exodus 12, 'The blood shall be to you for a token'. That was the experience and assurance of the covenant in man, 'When I see the blood'. That was the safety and security of Israel. It was covenant blood that Israel was called to behold. Such is the blood of his cross. We have been 'reconciled to God through the death of his Son'. When he instituted the Supper, our Saviour said, 'This cup is the new testament (covenant) in my blood, which is shed for you' (Luke 22:20).

Be sure to observe when this blood was shed. As with the death of Christ, so with the sacrifice here. It was after God was honoured by his servant Moses. 'Come up unto the LORD ... and worship' (v. 1). Before the cross was reached, Christ had this testimony, that he pleased God (Matthew 3:17). Moses came near the Lord, while the others worshipped 'afar off'. The Lord Jesus was transfigured upon the mount, just as Moses was here called up to God before the people, as if to indicate God's acceptance of his obedience as our Representative.

The blood was shed after the Word of the Lord had been revealed. 'Moses told the people all the words of the LORD' (v. 3). Christ did not die until he had finished the work and declared the words the Father gave him. 'I have given unto them the words which thou gavest me' (John 17:8). The way was made plain before the sun went down. The blood was shed after an altar had been built. Christ our Altar was made by the incarnation, when a body was prepared for him by the Holy Ghost, by which redemption could be accomplished (Hebrews 10:1-7).

What does the blood signify? Blood shed declares that sin has come in, that the law has been broken, that God's holiness has been violated. But, blessed be his name, the blood of innocent victims suggests substitution and the removal of sin by a divinely accepted substitute. That Substitute is our Lord Jesus Christ. He suffered for us, the just for the unjust, that he might bring us to God (2 Corinthians 5:21; Galatians 3:13; 1 Peter 2:24). Blood shed and accepted by God declares salvation accomplished, redemption obtained and sin put away. Isaac was saved when the ram took his place on the altar (Genesis 22:13). God's elect were saved by the blood of Christ when the Lamb who is God took our place (Revelation 13:8).

Behold the blood again, and see where this blood was sprinkled. It was sprinkled on the altar. 'Moses took half of the blood and sprinkle it on the altar' (v. 6). The altar represents the claims of God's holiness and justice. Before the people could be blessed, his justice must be satisfied. Before the sinner can be saved, Christ must offer himself without spot unto God. The halving of the blood between the altar and the people indicates the double character of the sacrifice of Christ. He both fulfils the law and makes peace. By doing the Father's will, he obtained redemption for us. In him every attribute of God is satisfied, and every need of man fully met. He both brings in everlasting righteousness and gives us peace. 'Oh, that men would praise the LORD for his goodness' (Psalm 107:8).

Then, 'Moses took the blood and sprinkled it on the people, and said, Behold the blood of the covenant which the LORD hath made with you'. The blood on the people speaks of the work of God the Holy Ghost applying to our hearts the redemption Christ accomplished. It speaks of life bestowed. The blood sprinkled brings us into contact with life, the life that was offered to God for us. 'The life is in the blood.' All the value of the sacrifice is now ours. 'We have redemption through his blood, even the forgiveness of sins' (Ephesians 1.7). Blood sprinkled speaks of reconciliation. It was the blood of the covenant (Hebrews 9:14). We are 'made nigh by the blood' (Ephesians 2:13). Blood sprinkled brings faith. Israel had presumptuously asserted their ability to obey God's law. Now, as far as it is pictured before us here, they speak not of their ability, but of faith in Christ. After the blood was sprinkled on them, Moses read the book of the covenant, of God's promise, in the audience of the people, declaring Christ's work finished, and they said, 'All that the LORD hath said will we do, and be obedient' (v. 7). With that expressed faith in the Substitute, the blood was sprinkled upon them (v. 8). The blood unites redeemed sinners to God.

'Then went up Moses, and Aaron, Nadab, and Abihu, and seventy of the elders of Israel: And they saw the God of Israel: and there was under his feet as it were a paved work of a sapphire stone, and as it were the body of heaven in his clearness. And upon the nobles of the children of Israel he laid not his hand: also they saw God, and did eat and drink' (Exodus 24:9-11).

Here is a blood-sprinkled nation, 'an holy nation', by virtue of God's own covenant and God's own sacrifice, in communion with the holy

Lord God. They are eating and drinking with pleasure, in the fulness of their welcome and acceptance in the beloved Sacrifice! There we are, living in the blessedness, peace, and joy of God's immediate presence, rejoicing in God's sovereignty, in his grace, and in his salvation, rejoicing in God our Saviour (Revelation 7:14, 15).

Redemption Portrayed
'And the LORD said unto Moses, Come up to me into the mount, and be there: and I will give thee tables of stone, and a law, and commandments which I have written; that thou mayest teach them. And Moses rose up, and his minister Joshua: and Moses went up into the mount of God. And he said unto the elders, Tarry ye here for us, until we come again unto you: and, behold, Aaron and Hur are with you: if any man have any matters to do, let him come unto them. And Moses went up into the mount, and a cloud covered the mount. And the glory of the LORD abode upon mount Sinai, and the cloud covered it six days: and the seventh day he called unto Moses out of the midst of the cloud. And the sight of the glory of the LORD was like devouring fire on the top of the mount in the eyes of the children of Israel. And Moses went into the midst of the cloud, and gat him up into the mount: and Moses was in the mount forty days and forty nights (Exodus 24:12-18).

In the remainder of this chapter Moses is separated from Aaron, Nadab and Abihu, and the seventy elders of Israel, resuming his mediatorial position, to receive from God the two tables of stone which he had written. For this purpose, he is called up to meet the Lord in the Mount, where he remained forty days and nights alone with God. During this time the glory of the Lord was displayed before the eyes of Israel for seven days, a glory 'like devouring fire' and then the Lord gave him a pattern of redemption, by which he was commanded to make the ark of the covenant, the mercy seat, the golden candlestick, the table of Shewbread, and the tabernacle, all portraying Christ our Redeemer and our salvation by him. Behold the blood, and believe God! Behold the blood, and rejoice in Lord!

Chapter 88

The Golden Candlestick

'And thou shalt make a candlestick of pure gold: of beaten work shall the candlestick be made: his shaft, and his branches, his bowls, his knops, and his flowers, shall be of the same. And six branches shall come out of the sides of it; three branches of the candlestick out of the one side, and three branches of the candlestick out of the other side: Three bowls made like unto almonds, with a knop and a flower in one branch; and three bowls made like almonds in the other branch, with a knop and a flower: so in the six branches that come out of the candlestick. And in the candlestick shall be four bowls made like unto almonds, with their knops and their flowers. And there shall be a knop under two branches of the same, and a knop under two branches of the same, and a knop under two branches of the same, according to the six branches that proceed out of the candlestick. Their knops and their branches shall be of the same: all it shall be one beaten work of pure gold. And thou shalt make the seven lamps thereof: and they shall light the lamps thereof, that they may give light over against it. And the tongs thereof, and the snuffdishes thereof, shall be of pure gold. Of a talent of pure gold shall he make it, with all these vessels. And look that thou make them after their pattern, which was shewed thee in the mount.' (Exodus 25:31-40)

The tabernacle and its furnishings, the priesthood, the sacrifices, the ceremonies, the sabbaths, the holy days, and the events of the Old

Testament were all types and pictures of heavenly things by divine design. They were all intended to portray Christ and God's salvation in him. This is stated by divine inspiration, with regard to the tabernacle and its furnishings and sacrifices, in Hebrews 9:1-12. In Hebrews 9:23 we are told these carnal things were 'patterns of things in the heavens'. And in Hebrews 10:1 we read they were 'a shadow of good things to come'. That is exactly what we read about these things in Exodus 25:40. 'And look that thou make them after their pattern, which was showed thee in the mount.'

Try to get a picture of the tabernacle in your mind's eye. As you approach it, the very first thing that strikes your eye is the brazen altar, the place of sacrifice. Between that brazen altar and the door of the tabernacle stands the laver of brass, the place of cleansing. Then, if you pull back the curtain, you enter the outer court of the tabernacle 'which is called the sanctuary'. In the sanctuary, the holy place, there were three pieces of furniture. On your right is the golden table of shewbread, with twelve loaves of bread and incense on it. In the back, just before you get to the veil separating the sanctuary from the 'Holiest of all', is the golden altar of incense. On the left side is the golden candlestick, a candelabra with seven candles burning constantly.

Then, if you could go with Aaron behind the veil on the day of atonement into the inner sanctuary, 'which is called the Holiest of all', you would see just one piece of furniture, the centre of Israel's worship, the ark of the covenant, overlaid with pure gold. Inside the ark is a golden pot of manna, Aaron's rod that budded, and the tables of God's law. Over the ark, completely covering it, is the mercy seat, the place of atonement, symbolizing the very throne of God, the throne of grace. At each end of the mercy seat are cherubs facing one another, looking constantly upon the mercy seat. This is where God declared he would meet with and commune with men (Exodus 25:22).

The spiritual significance of these things should be obvious to all who read the Scriptures. Those things involved in the tabernacle worship were given in vision to Isaiah (Isaiah 6:1-8), Ezekiel (Ezekiel 1-10), Daniel (Daniel 7:9-14), Zechariah (Zechariah 3:1-4:14), and to the Apostle John (Revelation 1:10-20; 4:1-5:14). Exodus 25:31-40 describes just one of the three pieces of furniture in the outer court of the sanctuary the golden candlestick. In Leviticus 24, we have a few additional instructions about the candlestick and its seven lamps.

'And the LORD spake unto Moses, saying, Command the children of Israel, that they bring unto thee pure oil olive beaten for the light, to cause the lamps to burn continually. Without the veil of the testimony, in the tabernacle of the congregation, shall Aaron order it from the evening unto the morning before the LORD continually: it shall be a statute for ever in your generations. He shall order the lamps upon the pure candlestick before the LORD continually' (Leviticus 24:1-4).

We do not have to guess what this candlestick represents. The Holy Spirit specifically tells us that this candlestick represents the church of God in this world (Revelation 1:20). More particularly, it represents the Lord Jesus Christ the Light of the world in glory (John 8:12; 9:5) and his mystical body the church, which is the light of the world on earth (Matthew 5:14).

The Oil

God required the children of Israel to bring pure olive oil from the olives of their own olive trees, to the priests to be burned in the candlestick (Leviticus 1, 2). It had to be 'pure', the very best, undiluted and clear. It must be oil 'beaten' from the olive, prepared with the greatest of care. I see four very important lessons here.

The oil represents God the Holy Spirit and the grace he gives. True worship always involves personal cost, be it time, effort or money. There is no such thing as worshipping God without sacrifice (2 Samuel 25:24). In all things, we are to bring our best to our God. And our great and gracious God would have us worship him in the full assurance of acceptance with him by Christ.

By requiring the children of Israel to bring the oil to be burned in the candlestick by the priests, the Lord gave assurance of acceptance. Accepting their oil, he said, 'I have accepted you'. By this seemingly insignificant gesture, he was saying to his people, 'This candlestick and the light it gives burns for you. Though you are not in the holy place personally, you are there representatively in your priest; and all that goes on in that holy place, all the transactions of the sanctuary are for you. You have an interest in them.' Believer, read Hebrews 10:16-22 and rejoice in your assured acceptance with God in Christ.

'This is the covenant that I will make with them after those days, saith the Lord, I will put my laws into their hearts, and in their minds will I write them; And their sins and iniquities will I remember no more.

Now where remission of these is, there is no more offering for sin. Having therefore, brethren, boldness to enter into the holiest by the blood of Jesus, By a new and living way, which he hath consecrated for us, through the veil, that is to say, his flesh; And having an high priest over the house of God; Let us draw near with a true heart in full assurance of faith, having our hearts sprinkled from an evil conscience, and our bodies washed with pure water.'

The Lamps

These seven lamps and the candlestick holding them are highly significant. God commanded 'Make it a candlestick of pure gold' (Exodus 25:31, 37; Leviticus 24:4). This candlestick made of pure gold had seven lamps at the ends of seven branches, upheld by one shaft. As such, it was typical of God's church in the world, upheld by Christ, the shaft of gold, being constantly supplied with light, life and grace by the Holy Spirit. Put this together with John's vision in Revelation, and we see how Christ upholds and sustains his church in all its branches. The number seven suggests the fulness and completion of the church. Each true gospel church being represented in the seven branches of the candlestick. The Holy Spirit indwells his church, each individual believer and each local assembly. Every true gospel church is 'an habitation of God through the Spirit'. And our Lord Jesus Christ, who dwells in his church by the Spirit, upholds it and walks in the midst of the seven golden candlesticks, protecting both his church and the angels of the churches.

These lamps were to be kept burning continually (Leviticus 24:4). That does not mean that they were never allowed to go out. They were. The priests did not keep them burning when they were moving from place to place in the wilderness, but only when they were encamped in a specific place for a time. The lamps were trimmed, filled with oil and lit every morning. They burned until nightfall. In the evening they were trimmed, filled with oil and lit again, and burned until the next morning. You may recall that the Lord first called Samuel after he and Eli had gone to bed, 'before the lamp of God went out in the temple' (1 Samuel 3:3). The lamps were kept burning continually to tell us that the grace of God and the supply of it to our souls is constant, both in the day when the sun shines brightly and in the night when our vision is dim. Our experience does not, in any way, affect or alter God's goodness!

Yet, the lamps were permitted to go out to teach us our unceasing need of the light and grace of God's Spirit, and to keep us ever mindful that all light and grace bestowed upon us comes to us through the sanctuary work or intercession of our great High Priest, the Lord Jesus Christ. Our great Aaron orders the light and the candlestick before the Lord continually, from evening until morning (Leviticus 24:3, 4). The lamps were kept burning all through the day to teach that something more than the light of nature is needed to lead us out of this wilderness to the throne of God. And the candlestick was kept burning throughout the night, until the dawning of the new day, to teach us that the church of God in this world of darkness gives light and shall continue to give light, be it dim or bright, until the Daystar, Christ Jesus, comes in saving grace to call his elect in regeneration and conversion (2 Peter 1:19; 2 Corinthians 4:4-6), and until he comes in the glory of his second advent to gather us to himself in resurrection glory (Revelation 2:28; 22:16).

Let no one be deceived by those self-serving religious teachers who assert that God has ceased to minister through the local church. That will not happen, so long as time shall stand. So long as the Son of God walks in the midst of the seven golden candlesticks the light of the gospel will shine from them!

The Light in the Lamps

Let us take a careful look at this pure, golden candlestick, as it is stood in the tabernacle. This candlestick stands not in the most holy place, which symbolises heaven, but in the sanctuary, which refers to heavenly things enjoyed on earth. Our Lord Jesus Christ, our High Priest after the order of Melchizedek, uses this candlestick to speak of himself and his churches in this world (Revelation 1:20).

The seven lamps of fire burning before the throne of God signifies the sevenfold Spirit of our God (Revelation 4:5). The shaft, we have seen speaks of Christ. The seven lamps, we are told in Revelation 1:20, represent the church. But, in Revelation 4, we are told they represent the seven Spirits, or sevenfold Spirit, of our God. There is no contradiction here, but a delightful, instructive picture. Christ is the Candlestick. He upholds the lamps, his church and each member of it. Without him, we would all fall and come to utter ruin in a heartbeat (John 10:28-30; Jude 24, 25). The light we have, the oil of grace we enjoy, is ours because we are in him and one with him.

The Lord Jesus gives light, life and grace in this world by his Spirit; but he does so through the instrumentality of his church, using such things as we are, to carry the light of his grace and glory into the corners of this dark, dark world. As the Apostle Paul stated, 'We have this treasure in earthen vessels, that the excellency of the power may be of God, and not of us' (2 Corinthians 4:7).

The olive oil feeding the flame is God the Holy Spirit. He is the unction, the anointing in and upon us, giving light, knowledge and understanding (1 John 2:20-27). He is given to us by Christ, by the merit, mediation and power of our Saviour (Revelation 3:1). As all the light shining from the lamp comes from the oil. All grace is the gift and operation of God the Holy Spirit. Christ pours out his Spirit upon us by the merit of his sacrifice (Galatians 3:13, 14) continually, as the priest poured oil into the lamp in the tabernacle. He gives us his oil in the day and in the night.

The care of the lamps is all his. As our great High Priest, the Lord Jesus upholds the lamps, his churches and his people in this world. He feeds them with oil. He lights them and keeps them burning. He trims them. He carries away the ashes. The priest setting the lamps in order daily portrays our great Saviour's unceasing work of grace causing his people to receive and give forth light. You and I are the representatives of Christ himself, who shined as light in the midst of darkness (Philippians 2:15; Matthew 5:16). May he cause us to be like John the Baptist, burning and shining lights all the days of our lives, shining clearly and constantly, always shining on Christ.

The candlestick shined only upon the golden table of shewbread and the golden altar. It shined to give light only upon those two things. The bread on the table speaks of Christ, the Bread of Life, who gave his life for us. The golden altar of incense speaks of Christ exalted and accepted and full, complete salvation in him. Let us shine the light of the gospel forth, pointing the eyes of needy souls to him who alone is life!

May God give us grace to constantly hold before men the light of the gospel and the adorable name of Christ. We must never cover the light with religious ceremony, carnal reason, or religious traditions and customs. Let it be ours ever to hold forth that Word of life, not to set up new lights, or to defend old ones, but to faithfully proclaim the gospel of God's boundless free grace in Christ. Let the light of our lamp be the light of the pure candlestick, the message of pure, free grace in Christ.

There is a blessed unity about this candlestick and its lamps. The candlestick is one (Ephesians 4:1-7). And the light of each lamp is exactly the same. As the oil was pure, without mixture, the gospel is all grace. There is not a sputter of works or free will in it.

God's Interpretation
In Zechariah 4 God the Holy Spirit gives us his own interpretation of this typical picture. In Zechariah 3 we are given a picture of a sinner saved by the grace of God. Such men are men who shall never cease to be 'men wondered at'. Then, in the opening verses of chapter 4, we learn that if we would see the light of the gospel, the light of this candlestick, we must be awakened by the Spirit of God (Zechariah 4:1, 2). The Lord God tells us the meaning of the candlestick's light is salvation by grace alone in Christ alone (Zechariah 4:4-9).

'And the angel that talked with me came again, and waked me, as a man that is wakened out of his sleep, And said unto me, What seest thou? And I said, I have looked, and behold a candlestick all of gold, with a bowl upon the top of it, and his seven lamps thereon, and seven pipes to the seven lamps, which are upon the top thereof: And two olive trees by it, one upon the right side of the bowl, and the other upon the left side thereof. So I answered and spake to the angel that talked with me, saying, What are these, my lord? Then the angel that talked with me answered and said unto me, Knowest thou not what these be? And I said, No, my lord. Then he answered and spake unto me, saying, This is the word of the LORD unto Zerubbabel, saying, Not by might, nor by power, but by my spirit, saith the LORD of hosts. Who art thou, O great mountain? before Zerubbabel thou shalt become a plain: and he shall bring forth the headstone thereof with shoutings, crying, Grace, grace unto it. Moreover the word of the LORD came unto me, saying, The hands of Zerubbabel have laid the foundation of this house; his hands shall also finish it; and thou shalt know that the LORD of hosts hath sent me unto you' (Zechariah 4:1-9).

Chapter 89

Where Does God Live?

'And the LORD spake unto Moses, saying, Speak unto the children of Israel, that they bring me an offering: of every man that giveth it willingly with his heart ye shall take my offering. And this is the offering which ye shall take of them; gold, and silver, and brass, and blue, and purple, and scarlet, and fine linen, and goats' hair, and rams' skins dyed red, and badgers' skins, and shittim wood, oil for the light, spices for anointing oil, and for sweet incense, Onyx stones, and stones to be set in the ephod, and in the breastplate. And let them make me a sanctuary; that I may dwell among them. According to all that I shew thee, after the pattern of the tabernacle, and the pattern of all the instruments thereof, even so shall ye make it.'
(Exodus 25:1-9)

Do you remember how perplexed you were by your children's first questions about God? At first, they seemed silly and childish; but when you took time to think about them they were simple and profound. I remember one of my daughter's first questions about God. One day, after playing by herself for a good while, Faith walked into my office and asked, 'Daddy, where does God live?' We find the answer in Exodus 25:1-9.

The Lord God commanded Moses to gather materials from the children of Israel. The materials were gifts involving tremendous sacrifice and thoughtfulness, but gifts given with willing hearts, and gifts only from the children of Israel. Using these gifts, Moses was required to make a sanctuary, an earthly dwelling place for the Lord our God; and he was required to make it exactly according to the pattern the Lord showed him in the mount.

Tabernacle's Importance

There is more written in the Scriptures about the tabernacle than there is about any other single subject, except, of course, the Lord Jesus Christ himself. The subject begins in Exodus 25 and ends in chapter 40. In Exodus 25-31 the Lord God gave Moses the heavenly design and picture by which the tabernacle's structure and furniture must be made and its priesthood patterned. Then in chapters 32-34 we have an interval. In those chapters we are given very important words of instruction. In chapters 35-40 the tabernacle is constructed.

God tells the whole story of creation in just two chapters; but when he tells us about the tabernacle; its courts, its furniture, and its rituals, he does so with deliberate and elaborate detail involving thirteen chapters. Almost the whole second half of the book of Exodus is devoted to describing the tabernacle.

Why has the Lord given us so much detail about the tabernacle? Because the tabernacle, with all its furniture and priesthood, all its sacrifices and ceremonies, was designed by God himself to be a picture and type of our Lord Jesus Christ and his salvation. I have no idea how much Moses knew about the things God showed him in the mount, or how much light the Lord gave him, but I am sure he saw much and knew much, much more than most imagine about the person and work of the incarnate God, our Lord Jesus Christ, and the redemption he would accomplish by the sacrifice of himself upon the cursed tree.

Again and again in the New Testament the Holy Spirit makes reference to the tabernacle, its furniture and the priesthood. In fact, it is impossible to understand the book of Hebrews without reference to the books of Exodus and Leviticus. The visions of Isaiah, Ezekiel, and Zechariah involved visions of the tabernacle. John's visions recorded in the book of Revelation also involved visions of the tabernacle. The tabernacle is central in the Revelation of God. It is central in the unfolding of God's purpose of redemption and grace in and by the Lord Jesus Christ.

Three Meanings
The tabernacle has at least three typical meanings. First, it is a type, a visible illustration, of that heavenly place in which God has his dwelling. Second, the tabernacle is typical of Jesus Christ, who is the meeting-place between God and man. Third, the tabernacle is a typical picture of Christ dwelling in his elect, the church, a picture of our union and communion with the Son of God.

First, the tabernacle is a type of heaven, a visible illustration of that heavenly place in which God has his dwelling (Hebrews 9:21-24). The tabernacle was made to be a sanctuary, a holy dwelling place for Jehovah (Exodus 25:8). It was symbolic of God's dwelling. It was an earthly picture of the heavenly reality. Where does God live? He lives in Heaven. That is the first answer.

Heaven is God's sanctuary, the place of his residence and the manifestation of his glorious presence. Solomon, confessed, and confessed correctly, 'Behold, and the heaven of heavens cannot contain thee' (2 Chronicles 6:18). Jeremiah said, 'A glorious high throne from the beginning is the place of our sanctuary' (17:12). The visions of Ezekiel and John set before us the heavens opened, a throne, and the appearance of a man above upon the throne. That man is the God-man, our Saviour in whom the glory of the triune God is revealed. He who sits yonder, upon the throne of heaven, who sits upon the mercy seat is our Divine Surety, 'He that sweareth to his own hurt and changeth not' (Psalm 15:4). His dwelling place is on high (Psalm 113:5; Isaiah 33:5).

John said, 'And after that I looked, and, behold, the temple of the tabernacle of the testimony in heaven was opened' (Revelation 15:5). Heaven is his tabernacle, the holy hill upon which he resides, the place of his dwelling (Psalm 24:3). 'Exalt the LORD our God, and worship at his holy hill; for the LORD our God is holy' (Psalm 99:9).

Second, the tabernacle is a type of the Lord Jesus himself (John 1:14). 'The Word was made flesh and dwelt (tabernacled) among us' (John 1:14). The tabernacle had particular reference to our Saviour's incarnation and his dwelling among men here on earth during the days of his humiliation. Just as the tabernacle was Jehovah's dwelling-place in the midst of Israel so are we told that, 'God was in Christ reconciling the world unto himself' (2 Corinthians 5:19). We read in Colossians 2:9, 10, 'For in him dwelleth all the fulness of the Godhead bodily. And ye are complete in him, which is the head of all principality and power'.

265

The tabernacle was not something that originated in the mind of Israel, or even of Moses. It was designed by God. So, too, the manhood of our blessed Saviour and the redemption of our souls by the sacrifice of Christ was God's work alone. The human body which enshrines his eternal Deity, is a body specifically prepared by God for the accomplishment of the great work (Hebrews 10:5). Where does God live? He lives in Christ. That is the second answer to our question.

Third, the tabernacle was a picture of Christ dwelling in us. Where does God live? He lives in his people. In the new birth, by a wondrous, mysterious work of grace, God himself takes up permanent residence in his people (John 14:16-18, 23; Colossians 1:27; 1 John 3:23, 24; 4:12; 1 Corinthians 3:16, 17; 6:19, 20). Daniel W. Whittle wrote,

> Once far from God and dead in sin,
> No light my heart could see;
> But in God's Word the light I found,
> Now Christ liveth in me.
>
> As rays of light from yonder sun,
> The flowers of earth set free,
> So life and light and love came forth,
> From Christ living in me.
>
> As lives the flower within the seed,
> As in the cone the tree,
> So, praise the God of truth and grace,
> His Spirit dwelleth in me.
>
> Christ liveth in me,
> Christ liveth in me,
> Oh! what a salvation this,
> That Christ liveth in me.
>
> With longing all my heart is filled,
> That like Him I may be,
> As on the wondrous thought I dwell
> That Christ liveth in me!

Redemption Portrayed
The tabernacle was God's dwelling place. As such, it portrayed and typified heaven, the incarnate Christ and God dwelling in us in grace, giving life eternal in, by, and with the Lord Jesus Christ. But the tabernacle also portrayed the whole work of redemption by which the triune God delivers his elect from sin and death by Christ. Israel's high priest typified Christ our High Priest. The sacrifices of the tabernacle portrayed Christ our Sacrifice and Passover. The brazen altar pictured Christ our Altar. The golden laver represented Christ a fountain opened for sinners. The golden candlestick was a symbol of Christ the Light of the World. The table of shewbread showed forth Christ the Bread of Life. The altar of incense represented Christ our Acceptance. The ark and its mercy seat typified Christ our Propitiation. In the tabernacle, upon the mercy seat, the Lord God met his people and communed with them. The ark of the covenant was the throne where God manifested his holiness and his grace. It was called 'the mercy seat'. It is all covered with blood. Upon it sits the Lamb of God our Saviour (Hebrews 4:16).

In all the offerings and sacrifices God was manifested as just and merciful, just in punishing sin and merciful in forgiving the sinner. There God and the sinner met. So throughout the tabernacle there was the manifestation of God, not to terrify, but to bring his covenant people into communion with himself. In the tabernacle our fellowship with God was symbolized in the priestly mediations, blood sacrifices, and countless offerings that were made. But in Christ all the types are perfectly and eternally fulfilled. 'Behold, the tabernacle of God is with men, and he will dwell with them, and they shall be his people, and God himself shall be with them, and be their God' (Revelation 21:3)

Christ the Antitype
Of all that the tabernacle typified, Christ is the antitype, the fulfilment. The key to the tabernacle is Christ. In the volume of the Book of God, Christ is the subject. It is all written of him. A. W. Pink wrote, 'As a whole and in each of its parts the tabernacle foreshadowed the person and work of the Lord Jesus. Each detail in it typified some aspect of his ministry or some excellency in his person.'

'The Word was made flesh, and dwelt among us, (and we beheld his glory, the glory as of the only begotten of the Father,) full of grace and truth' (John 1:14).

The reference here is to the incarnation of our Lord Jesus Christ, the first advent of God's dear Son to this earth. The language John uses takes us back to the book of Exodus.

The tabernacle was a temporary dwelling place. It was just a tent, a convenience. The children of Israel used it for less than thirty-five years. Our Lord Jesus tabernacled among us in humiliation for less than thirty-five years, in a body of flesh that was destroyed by wicked men but raised up a glorious body in three days by the Saviour himself.

The tabernacle was a common, ordinary thing, humble, and unattractive in outward appearance. There was nothing about it to attract the flesh or please the carnal eye. Nothing but plain boards and skins. So it was with the incarnate Christ. His Divine majesty was hidden beneath a veil of flesh. He had no form or comeliness, no beauty that would cause anyone to desire him. But the tabernacle was God's dwelling place. There, in the midst of Israel's camp, the God of Glory took up his abode. Between the cherubim, upon the mercy seat he made his throne. In the holy of holies he manifested his presence in Shekinah glory. And the triune God dwells in the Word that was made flesh and tabernacled among men (Colossians 2:9, 10), showing forth his glory in him who is our Saviour. We behold the glory of the triune God in our all-glorious Saviour, the Lord Jesus Christ (2 Corinthians 4:6).

The tabernacle was the place where God met with man. If an Israelite desired to draw near unto Jehovah, he had to come to the tabernacle, the place of sacrifice, the place of atonement. God said, 'And thou shalt put the mercy seat above upon the ark, and in the ark thou shalt put the testimony that I shall give thee. And there I will meet with thee, and I will commune with thee' (Exodus 25:21, 22). How perfect the picture! Christ is the meeting-place between God and man. 'Jesus saith unto him, I am the way, the truth, and the life: no man cometh unto the Father, but by me' (John 14:6). There is but one mediator between God and men, the man Christ Jesus (1 Timothy 2:5). He spans the gulf between the holy Lord God and fallen humanity.

The tabernacle was the place where the law was preserved. The first two tables of stone, on which Jehovah had inscribed the Ten Commandments, were broken (Exodus 32:19). The second set was placed in the ark, beneath the mercy seat, in the tabernacle for safe keeping (Deuteronomy 10:2-5). It was there, only there, within the holy of holies, that the law was preserved unbroken, magnified, and made honourable. Again, how clearly and beautifully this speaks of Christ who magnified the law and made it honourable as our Substitute.

The tabernacle was the place where sacrifice was made. In its outer court stood the brazen altar, to which the animals were brought, and on which they were slain. There it was the blood was shed and atonement was made for sin. So it was with the Lord Jesus. He fulfilled in his own person the typical significance of the brazen altar and of everything else in the tabernacle. The body in which he tabernacled on earth was nailed to the cursed tree. The cross was the altar upon which God's Lamb was slain, where his precious blood was shed, where complete atonement for sin was made.

The tabernacle was the place where the priestly family was fed. In Leviticus 6:16-26 the Lord instructed the priests to eat of the sacrifices 'in the court of the tabernacle of the congregation'. Christ is the Food of God's priestly family, that royal priesthood of believers to whom Christ is precious (1 Peter 2:5-9).

The tabernacle was the place of worship. Believing Israelites brought their offerings to the tabernacle. They turned to the tabernacle when they desired to worship the Lord. At its door they heard his voice. Within its courts the priests performed their sacred service. And so it is today. By Christ we offer our sacrifices of praise and thanksgiving to God (Hebrews 13:15). In him alone, and by him alone, we worship the Father. Through him alone we have access to the throne of grace. The tabernacle had just one door. The outer court, with its solid walls of white curtains, was broken open by one gate only, telling us there is but one way into the presence of the holy God. Christ is the Door, the only door by which sinners have access to God (John 10:9).

The materials used in the tabernacle tell us Christ is Lord over all the earth and all creation shall be made to honour him. The Lord God arranged for materials from every part of creation to be used in the construction and service of the tabernacle. The mineral kingdom supplied the metals and the precious stones. The vegetation of the earth gave the wood, linen, oil and spices. Animals furnished the skins and goat hair for curtains, and of course, the sacrifices upon the altar. In Christ and by Christ there is a day appointed when all creation shall be made to show forth the praises of our God (Acts 3:21; Ephesians 1:11; Colossians 1:19, 20).

Purposed and Performed

If you will read Exodus 25 through 40 at one sitting, you will see clearly that the Holy Spirit has given us two full accounts of the construction of the tabernacle. First, we have the blueprints for the tabernacle given to Moses in the mount (Exodus 25-31). God showed Moses the pattern and said, 'Make the tabernacle exactly according to this pattern.' Then, in Exodus 32-34, there is an interruption, a parenthesis, in which we see a terrible fall involving great corruption and judgment. After the fall, the tabernacle is constructed exactly according to the plan revealed in the mount.

Surely, none can fail to see the beauty and clarity of the parallel. God purposed the salvation of his elect in and by Christ before the world was made. Indeed, our salvation was accomplished in eternity (Romans 8:28-30; Ephesians 1:3-6). Then came the sin and fall of our father Adam. Then the Lord God began to perform in the earth his great purpose of grace, as it is revealed in Romans 8:28-30.

Someone wrote, 'Christ had been already provided, but man must feel the need of the Divine salvation by the actual experience of sin. It is touching beyond degree to know that all the time that man was rebelling against God, God's remedy was waiting in that mount of grace.' When the fulness of time was come, God sent forth his Son. Where sin abounded, grace did much more abound.

The Spirit's Work

The tabernacle was, at last, constructed by the agency of God the Holy Spirit. 'And Moses said unto the children of Israel, See, the LORD hath called by name Bezaleel the son of Uri, the son of Hur, of the tribe of Judah; And he hath filled him with the Spirit of God, in wisdom, in understanding, and in knowledge, and in all manner of workmanship' (Exodus 35:30, 31).

Christ came to tabernacle among us by the power and agency of God the Holy Spirit in the incarnation (Luke 1:34, 35). And he comes to dwell in chosen, redeemed sinners by that same divine agency, by the power and grace of God the Holy Ghost.

This is the message of the tabernacle: 'Salvation is of the LORD' in its planning, in its purchase, in its performance, in its preservation, and in its praise!

Chapter 90

The Ark Of The Covenant

'And they shall make an ark of shittim wood: two cubits and a half shall be the length thereof, and a cubit and a half the breadth thereof, and a cubit and a half the height thereof. And thou shalt overlay it with pure gold, within and without shalt thou overlay it, and shalt make upon it a crown of gold round about. And thou shalt cast four rings of gold for it, and put them in the four corners thereof; and two rings shall be in the one side of it, and two rings in the other side of it. And thou shalt make staves of shittim wood, and overlay them with gold. And thou shalt put the staves into the rings by the sides of the ark, that the ark may be borne with them. The staves shall be in the rings of the ark: they shall not be taken from it. And thou shalt put into the ark the testimony which I shall give thee. And thou shalt make a mercy seat of pure gold: two cubits and a half shall be the length thereof, and a cubit and a half the breadth thereof. And thou shalt make two cherubims of gold, of beaten work shalt thou make them, in the two ends of the mercy seat. And make one cherub on the one end, and the other cherub on the other end: even of the mercy seat shall ye make the cherubims on the two ends thereof. And the cherubims shall stretch forth their wings on high, covering the mercy seat with their wings, and their faces shall look one to another; toward the mercy seat shall the faces of the cherubims be. And thou shalt put the mercy seat above upon the ark; and in the ark thou shalt put the testimony that I shall give thee. And there I will meet with thee, and I will commune with thee from above the mercy seat, from between the two cherubims which are upon the ark of the testimony, of all things which I will give thee in commandment unto the children of Israel.'
(Exodus 25:10-22)

After commanding Moses to take offerings from his people, the Lord God told his servant to use those gifts of the people to make a sanctuary for him, that he might dwell among his chosen people. Then he proceeded to tell him exactly how he was to make the tabernacle and everything to be put in it. In verses 10-22, God told Moses to make an ark of shittim wood, overlay it with gold, and place a mercy seat of pure gold upon it.

What heart can conceive or tongue describe the blessedness of this word from our God? What a wonderful, heavenly revelation this is! At all times, under all circumstances, and in all places the God of all grace has provided and established a mercy seat, a throne of grace; and he bids sinners meet him there! There is a place where God and sinners can meet, a place where God can meet me and I can meet God, freely and without hindrance of any kind!

No place is at a distance so far from the mercy seat that we cannot meet God there immediately. No circumstance is so dark that the penetrating eye of God who sits upon this throne of grace cannot see through it. No covering is so thick that it can obscure me from his sight. No circumstance is so gloomy and dark, so heavy and black that my God cannot behold me. 'Can any hide himself in secret places that I shall not see him? saith the LORD. Do not I fill heaven and earth? saith the LORD' (Jeremiah 23:24). 'If I say, Surely the darkness shall cover me; even the night shall be light about me. Yea, the darkness hideth not from thee; but the night shineth as the day; the darkness and the light are both alike to thee' (Psalm 139:11, 12).

By night upon our bed, by day in our various occupations, in the crowded streets, or alone in the open field, surrounded by the ungodly, or in the company of God's saints, we may, if God the Holy Spirit enables us, lift our hearts to heaven and meet our God upon his throne of grace, upon the mercy seat. With a sigh or a groan, with a heartfelt word, a groan of confession, or a deep desire that cannot be put into words, we may instantaneously meet God, the God of all grace, our heavenly Father. He bids us do so (Hebrews 4:16), and promises, 'There will I meet with you'. We meet him with sin. He meets us with forgiveness. We meet him with guilt. He meets us with pardon. We meet him with need. He meets us with grace. We meet him with misery. He meets us with mercy. We meet him with heaviness. He meets us with strength. We meet him with darkness. He meets us with light. We meet him with confusion. He meets us with direction. We meet him with sorrow. He meets us with solace.

How? How can this be? How can God and sinners meet together? If God the Holy Spirit will graciously teach us the meaning of this ark and its mercy seat, if he will show us the typical significance of this piece of furniture made to be put in the tabernacle, in the holy of holies, this centre piece of Old Testament ceremonial worship, we will see how it is that God and sinners can, and do, meet together on the mercy seat.

In the ninth chapter the Book of Hebrews, God the Holy Spirit uses the tabernacle and the furniture in it as typical things to show us the excellence, pre-eminence, and glory of the Lord Jesus Christ as our divine Redeemer and Saviour.

'Then verily the first covenant had also ordinances of divine service, and a worldly sanctuary. For there was a tabernacle made; the first, wherein was the candlestick, and the table, and the shewbread; which is called the sanctuary. And after the second veil, the tabernacle which is called the Holiest of all; Which had the golden censer, and the ark of the covenant overlaid round about with gold, wherein was the golden pot that had manna, and Aaron's rod that budded, and the tables of the covenant; And over it the cherubims of glory shadowing the mercyseat; of which we cannot now speak particularly' (Hebrews 9:1-5).

These are the things we read about in Exodus 25, the golden pot that had manna, Aaron's rod that budded, the tables of the covenant, the cherubims of glory, and the mercy seat. In its day, under the ceremonial, typical religious service of the Old Testament, the ark of the covenant was one of the 'ordinances of divine service' which beautifully typified and pictured the Lord Jesus Christ and our redemption by him. John saw this clearly. 'The temple of God was opened in heaven, and there was seen in his temple the ark of his testament' (Revelation 11:19).

Each time we read about these Old Testament pictures of our Redeemer, let us beg grace from God the Holy Ghost to seek him of whom the ark speaks, the Lord Jesus Christ, and grace to find him. All the 'ordinances of divine service', all the rites and ceremonies, and the 'worldly sanctuary' itself, the tabernacle, were types of Christ. You will not understand the Old Testament Scriptures until you see that everything in them represented, pointed to, and pictured Christ, our Substitute (Luke 24:27; 44, 45). The tabernacle portrayed Christ, our God-man Mediator, glorious within and humble without. The brazen

273

altar spoke of our Redeemer's sufferings and death. The laver represented Christ our Fountain, opened for cleansing. The candlestick typified Christ the Light of the World. The table of shewbread foreshadowed Christ the Bread of Life. The altar of incense prefigured Christ as our Advocate and Intercessor. The veil was Christ the Door. The ark of the covenant was typical of Christ our Reconciliation.

In this portion of Holy Scripture (Exodus 25:10-22) God the Holy Ghost takes us into 'the Holiest of all', by the 'golden censer' of our Saviour's merits. Here we see our Lord Jesus Christ beautifully typified in the ark of the covenant. It was made of shittim wood, a cedar-like wood, overlaid inside and outside with pure gold, representing both the incorruptible humanity and glorious deity of our Saviour. The ark was the symbol of God's holiness, power and glory. It was carried about from place to place upon the shoulders of the priests by staves, fitted into rings attached to the ark. Even so, Christ is carried throughout the world upon the shoulders of chosen men by the preaching of the gospel.

There are many good studies of the tabernacle and its furnishings, showing the correspondences to be drawn from the materials by which those things were made and our Lord Jesus. But I want us to look beyond those factual comparisons, good as they are, to the message those things are intended to declare. With that in mind, let us by faith do what no mortal ever was allowed to do with their physical eye. Let us look inside the ark. What can be found in the Ark Christ Jesus?

God's Preachers

If you could go behind the veil with the high priest on the Day of Atonement, into the holy of holies, the very first thing you would see would be 'the cherubims of glory shadowing the mercyseat'. Those cherubs represent God's preachers (Exodus 25:18-20; Psalm 80:1; Isaiah 6:1-7).

'And thou shalt make two cherubims of gold, of beaten work shalt thou make them, in the two ends of the mercy seat. And make one cherub on the one end, and the other cherub on the other end: even of the mercy seat shall ye make the cherubims on the two ends thereof. And the cherubims shall stretch forth their wings on high, covering the mercy seat with their wings, and their faces shall look one to another; toward the mercy seat shall the faces of the cherubims be' (Exodus 25:18-20).

We know these cherubs represent gospel preachers because they are the same as those living creatures John saw when he was called up to heaven to behold the throne of God (Revelation 4:6-11). It is not possible for a sinner to find, know, or come to God apart from the instrumentality of a gospel preacher (Romans 10:14-17; James 1:18; 1 Peter 1:23-25; 1 Corinthians 1:23; Hebrews 4:12).

God's preachers are not priests. We detest idolatrous priestcraft, be it Roman, Anglican, Mormon, or Baptist. But God's preachers are his angels, his messengers of mercy and grace to his people in this world, angels of the churches they serve (Revelation 3, 4). And they ought to be treated as such (Isaiah 52:7). Their eyes are always toward Christ the Mercyseat. They all see eye to eye (Isaiah 52:8). Their message is the message of sins forgiven by blood atonement, and Jesus Christ crucified (1 Corinthians 2:2; Galatians 6:14). The glory of God is revealed by the message they proclaim!

God's Propitiation

But upon entering the holy of holies in the tabernacle, you would not look long at the cherubim. Their eyes, their faces, their wings direct your attention away from themselves to the mercy seat. That mercy seat represents Christ, God's propitiation (Exodus 25:17, 21, 22; 1 John 4:9, 10; Romans 3:24-26).

'And thou shalt make a mercy seat of pure gold: two cubits and a half shall be the length thereof, and a cubit and a half the breadth thereof' (Exodus 25:17).

'And thou shalt put the mercy seat above upon the ark; and in the ark thou shalt put the testimony that I shall give thee. And there I will meet with thee, and I will commune with thee from above the mercy seat, from between the two cherubims which are upon the ark of the testimony, of all things which I will give thee in commandment unto the children of Israel' (Exodus 25:21, 22).

'In this was manifested the love of God toward us, because that God sent his only begotten Son into the world, that we might live through him. Herein is love, not that we loved God, but that he loved us, and sent his Son to be the propitiation for our sins' (1 John 4:9, 10).

'Being justified freely by his grace through the redemption that is in Christ Jesus: Whom God hath set forth to be a propitiation through faith in his blood, to declare his righteousness for the remission of sins that are past, through the forbearance of God; To declare, I say, at this time his righteousness: that he might be just, and the justifier of him which believeth in Jesus' (Romans 3:24-26).

The mercy seat was the place where the blood of the paschal lamb was sprinkled, the place of propitiation, the place of reconciliation. That is Christ! He alone is the Propitiation, the satisfaction of justice for his people. Christ our Passover being sacrificed for us (1 Corinthians 5:7) is not propitiation, reconciliation, atonement, and satisfaction merely provided and offered. Christ our Passover being sacrificed for us is propitiation, reconciliation, atonement, and satisfaction accomplished and accepted! Christ our Mercyseat is the place of substitution, sacrifice, and satisfaction. The Son of God, by his blood, has obtained eternal redemption for every sinner for whom he died upon the cursed tree (Hebrews 9:12; Galatians 3:13). His propitiation for sin is effectual redemption accomplished. This is what we commonly call 'Limited Atonement' because it is atonement made for God's elect, atonement by which chosen sinners are effectually redeemed.

God's Presence
Standing in the holiest of all with Christ, our Aaron, our great High Priest, suddenly, we realize we are standing before the mercy seat, the symbol of God's presence. With blood upon the mercy seat, covering the broken tables of the law (Exodus 25:16), we see the glory of God in the pardon of sin by the sacrifice of Christ. That is the revelation of the glory of God in the face of our Lord Jesus Christ (Leviticus 9:23, 24; Psalm 85:9-11; Isaiah 6:1-6).

'And Moses and Aaron went into the tabernacle of the congregation, and came out, and blessed the people: and the glory of the LORD appeared unto all the people. And there came a fire out from before the LORD, and consumed upon the altar the burnt offering and the fat: which when all the people saw, they shouted, and fell on their faces' (Leviticus 9:23, 24).

'Surely his salvation is nigh them that fear him; that glory may dwell in our land. Mercy and truth are met together; righteousness and peace have kissed each other. Truth shall spring out of the earth; and righteousness shall look down from heaven' (Psalm 85:9-11).

'In the year that king Uzziah died I saw also the Lord sitting upon a throne, high and lifted up, and his train filled the temple. Above it stood the seraphims: each one had six wings; with twain he covered his face, and with twain he covered his feet, and with twain he did fly. And one cried unto another, and said, Holy, holy, holy, is the LORD of hosts: the whole earth is full of his glory. And the posts of the door moved at the voice of him that cried, and the house was filled with smoke. Then said I, Woe is me! for I am undone; because I am a man of unclean lips, and I dwell in the midst of a people of unclean lips: for mine eyes have seen the King, the LORD of hosts. Then flew one of the seraphims unto me, having a live coal in his hand, which he had taken with the tongs from off the altar' (Isaiah 6:1-6).

God not only meets us upon the Mercyseat, Christ Jesus. Here, and here alone God meets with and abides with us. No matter where you are, if you are in Christ, the name of the place is Jehovah-Shammah, the Lord is There. Your life is hid with Christ in God (Isaiah 43:1-5).

God's Purpose
Now, we do by faith what no mortal ever could do actually, we lift up the mercy seat and look inside the ark. Remember, I am talking of the Lord Jesus Christ. What do you see? You see the two tables of the law of God, which we have broken. The broken law, all our sin, is under the mercy seat, under the blood. This broken law under the blood, represents God's purpose.

The Law was written upon tables of stone, signifying both the hardness of our hearts and the inflexibility of God's law. The law represents our curse and condemnation by reason of sin. This law was always kept in the ark, under the mercy seat (Exodus. 25:16, 21), representing perfect redemption by Christ. 'And thou shalt put into the ark the testimony which I shall give thee' (v. 16). 'And thou shalt put the mercy seat above upon the ark; and in the ark thou shalt put the testimony that I shall give thee' (v. 21).

And that perfect redemption of his elect is the purpose of God (Romans 8:28-31). The law of God, being perfectly satisfied by Christ, cries for and demands the everlasting salvation of God's elect just as fully, just as strongly, just as effectually as the grace of God. In Christ, being justly redeemed by his blood, God's elect, every sinner who trusts the Lord Jesus Christ is free from the law (Romans 6:14, 15; 7:4; 10:4; Galatians 3:13).

God's Power

Look again, there is something else inside the ark. There is Aaron's rod that budded. That rod exemplifies God's power. Aaron's rod that budded is the gospel of Christ, the Man whom God has chosen.

'And the LORD said unto Moses, Bring Aaron's rod again before the testimony, to be kept for a token against the rebels; and thou shalt quite take away their murmurings from me, that they die not' (Numbers 17:10).

Christ our Rock was smitten by Moses' rod, the law. The Water of Life flows freely out to sinners by Aaron's rod, the gospel. The gospel of Christ is the mighty power of God, before which all must fall (Romans 1:16, 17).

God's Provision

We see one more thing inside the ark, the golden pot which had manna. That golden pot of manna is a picture of Christ, God's provision for his elect in, by, and with Christ.

'And Moses said unto Aaron, Take a pot, and put an omer full of manna therein, and lay it up before the LORD, to be kept for your generations. As the LORD commanded Moses, so Aaron laid it up before the Testimony, to be kept' (Exodus 16:33, 34).

It was a golden pot. It was a big pot, holding an omer of manna. And it had manna, the bread of heaven for God's children throughout their appointed wilderness journey. What a sweet and blessed picture that is of our Saviour! All God's provision for sinners is in Christ Jesus. His name is Jehovah-jireh, the Lord will provide (Ephesians 1:3-6). All God's provisions of grace are in Christ. All God's provisions of providence come through Christ and direct us to Christ. And all the provisions of heaven are ours in Christ. Come, needy soul, to the Ark Christ Jesus! The way is open. All who come to God by Christ are forever saved! All you need, all God requires, all that heaven can bestow is in the Ark, Christ Jesus.

'Hear my cry, O God; attend unto my prayer. From the end of the earth will I cry unto thee, when my heart is overwhelmed: lead me to the rock that is higher than I. For thou hast been a shelter for me, and a strong tower from the enemy. I will abide in thy tabernacle for ever: I will trust in the covert of thy wings. Selah' (Psalm 61:1-4).

Chapter 91

The Table Of Shewbread

'Thou shalt also make a table of shittim wood: two cubits shall be the length thereof, and a cubit the breadth thereof, and a cubit and a half the height thereof. And thou shalt overlay it with pure gold, and make thereto a crown of gold round about. And thou shalt make unto it a border of an hand breadth round about, and thou shalt make a golden crown to the border thereof round about. And thou shalt make for it four rings of gold, and put the rings in the four corners that are on the four feet thereof. Over against the border shall the rings be for places of the staves to bear the table. And thou shalt make the staves of shittim wood, and overlay them with gold, that the table may be borne with them. And thou shalt make the dishes thereof, and spoons thereof, and covers thereof, and bowls thereof, to cover withal: of pure gold shalt thou make them. And thou shalt set upon the table shewbread before me always.' (Exodus 25:23-30)

Here are seven things I want fixed in your mind, but more importantly, I pray that God the Holy Ghost will stamp them upon your heart.

(1) All who believe on the Lord Jesus Christ are numbered among the elect of God: chosen, redeemed, and called. (2) All God's elect are in Christ by sovereign, eternal election, by the regenerating work of God the Holy Spirit, and by God's blessed gift of faith in Christ. (3) All God's elect are accepted in Christ, with Christ, for Christ's sake, as Christ himself is accepted. (4) All God's elect are supplied and provided for by Christ. (5) All God's elect are safe and secure in Christ. (6) All God's elect are a part of that royal priesthood, described by Peter, who

serve God in the sanctuary. (7) All God's elect are one in Christ. The Church of God is one body, the body of Christ, with many members.

The portion of Holy Scripture that heads this chapter contains the instructions the Lord God commanded Moses to give to Aaron and the children of Israel regarding the table of shewbread in the tabernacle.

Three Pieces of Furniture
You will remember there were three pieces of furniture in the first section of the tabernacle, in the outer sanctuary. As the priest walked into that holy place, before the veil that separated the holy place from the holy of holies and the ark of the covenant, he would see these three things. Standing in the back, right in front of the veil, he would see the golden altar of incense. On his left, he would see the golden candlestick. On his right, he would see the golden table of shewbread, with its twelve loaves of bread in two rows, with golden dishes, golden bowls, and golden spoons, and frankincense upon each row of bread.

This piece of furniture is described in detail here in Exodus 25:23-30. Here we are given the physical description of the table of shewbread. This same description is given again in Exodus 37:10-16. In Leviticus 24:5-9, the Holy Spirit gives the instructions Aaron was given concerning the table and its bread.

'And thou shalt take fine flour, and bake twelve cakes thereof: two tenth deals shall be in one cake. And thou shalt set them in two rows, six on a row, upon the pure table before the LORD. And thou shalt put pure frankincense upon each row, that it may be on the bread for a memorial, even an offering made by fire unto the LORD. Every sabbath he shall set it in order before the LORD continually, being taken from the children of Israel by an everlasting covenant. And it shall be Aaron's and his sons'; and they shall eat it in the holy place: for it is most holy unto him of the offerings of the LORD made by fire by a perpetual statute.'

This golden table of shewbread and the bread upon it give us much typical instruction concerning our Lord Jesus Christ and God's bounteous provisions of grace for his people in him.

The Table
First, I want you to see that the golden table of shewbread is itself typical of our great Saviour. The name given to this table, 'the table of

shewbread' (Numbers 4:7), might better be translated, 'the table of the bread of presence'. It speaks of Christ ever present with God and ever present with us. There never was a time when the Lord Jesus Christ was not present with God for us. 'I was set up from everlasting, from the beginning, or ever the earth was ... Then I was by him, as one brought up with him: and I was daily his delight, rejoicing always before him; Rejoicing in the habitable part of his earth; and my delights were with the sons of men' (Proverbs 8:23, 30, 31). And the materials of the table clearly speak of our Redeemer. It was made of shittim wood, overlaid with pure gold. These were the same materials used to make the ark of the covenant.

The shittim wood, a wood like our cedar that did not decay or rot, portrays our Saviour's humanity, which never saw corruption. In order to redeem and save us, the Son of God took on himself our nature. He became one of us. Yes, Jesus Christ, our God, is a real man. He has taken our human nature into union with himself, indivisibly and permanently. He who would redeem man must himself be a man. But this man was born of a virgin and had no sin. He had no sin, did not sin, and knew no sin. Yet, he was made sin for us, that we might be made the righteousness of God in him (2 Corinthians 5:21).

Sin is that which has corrupted God's universe, corrupts our race, and shall at last corrupt our bodies in the grave; but it did not corrupt Christ's body. Though he was made sin for us, when he had put away our sins by the sacrifice of himself, he arose from the grave before his body could see corruption. Now, yonder in heaven, seated upon the throne of God, is God in our nature, the God-man, the Lord Jesus Christ. It is written, 'He that hath suffered in the flesh hath ceased from sin'. The shittim wood being overlaid with pure gold speaks of our Saviour's perfect and eternal divinity. That man who is our Saviour is God, perfectly and fully God, shining forth from eternity and for evermore, in the golden brilliance of his divinity. Though he was a perfect man, though he had died as our Substitute, his sacrifice could never have availed for our eternal salvation, except he be himself God incarnate.

> Well might the sun in darkness hide
> And shut his glories in,
> When God the mighty Maker died,
> For man, the creature's sin!

The table, wearing a crown of pure gold, speaks of Christ's exaltation and glory as our great King. God the Father has made him both Lord and Christ. He has placed upon the head of the God-man, our Mediator, the crown of universal monarchy. He has given him power and dominion over all flesh, that he might give eternal life to all his redeemed ones. Yes, the God-man, our Saviour, holds the reins of the universe in his hands. He rules the entire universe, absolutely, for the salvation and everlasting good of his people to the glory of God.

The Table's Place

Second, be sure you do not fail to see the place where the table of shewbread stood. The table of shewbread, the bread of presence, stood in the holy place in the tabernacle, before the presence of the Lord. The bread was symbolically set before God himself. It stood there before the Lord God continually, as bread fit for God, offered to God, honoured by God, and accepted by God. It stood there symbolically as the Bread of God. Our Redeemer, speaking of himself, said, 'the bread of God is he which cometh down from heaven, and giveth life unto the world' (John 6:33).

The Lord Jesus Christ, the Bread of Life for our souls, is the very Bread of God. He is the Food of Heaven. That is to say, our all-glorious Christ, his person and work, is he upon whom God feasts and delights, and the One in whom alone the infinite, holy, triune Jehovah finds satisfaction.

The Loaves

Third, we are told that twelve cakes or loaves of bread were to be set upon the golden table. 'And thou shalt set upon the table shewbread before me alway' (v. 30).

'And thou shalt take fine flour, and bake twelve cakes thereof: two tenth deals shall be in one cake. And thou shalt set them in two rows, six on a row, upon the pure table before the LORD' (Leviticus 24:5, 6).

Twelve is the number of God's Israel, his elect, the 144,000 sealed ones in the earth (Revelation 7:4; 14:1-3). Without question, these twelve loaves of bread typify our Lord Jesus Christ, the Bread of Life, as we have seen. But that the bread is specifically required to be in twelve loaves shows that the loaves represent Christ in connection with his people, represented in the twelve tribes of Israel, the twelve names inscribed upon Aaron's breastplate, the twelve stones of the altar erected by Joshua when Israel crossed over Jordan, the twelve stones of Elijah's altar on Mount Carmel before the prophets of Baal, the twelve apostles, the twelve foundations of the New Jerusalem, and the twelve gates of the heavenly city.

The twelve loaves in the Holy Place, upon the table before God, tells us symbolically that Christ the High Priest of God, our great High Priest, has an abundant supply for all whose names are inscribed upon his breastplate. Therefore, none shall perish.

Hear our Saviour, hear him, needy soul, and rejoice. In our Father's house there is 'bread enough and to spare' (Luke 15:17). The supply is abundant, super-abundant. Did you notice in Leviticus 24:5 that each loaf had 'two tenth deals' of fine flour; two omers? That was double any man's daily provision of manna in the wilderness. In each loaf of bread, sitting on the table in the holy place, there was symbolically twice as much bread for every person in Israel as he needed. 'Where sin abounded, grace did much more abound.' My Saviour's supply is infinite, boundlessly infinite! And his supply is mine. His supply, my brother, my sister, is yours! It is a bountiful supply. All grace is ours in him (Ephesians 1:3). All glory is ours in Christ Jesus (John 17:22). All things are yours in Christ (1 Corinthians 3:21).

> Feasting on the Bread of God's providing,
> Jesus crucified, my soul is satisfied.
> Feasting on the Bread of God's providing,
> O wonderful and bountiful supply!

Bread for Sinners
Are you hungry? Are you a poor, needy, starving sinner? Is your soul made hungry by grace? Do you hunger and thirst for righteousness before God? Come and eat. In Christ, there is bread enough for you! There is such an infinite sufficiency and abundance of life, mercy, love, and grace in Christ that, though untold multitudes live by eating this Bread, the Bread is undiminished. There is still just as much as in the beginning. 'Come, now, let us reason together'. You may not know your name is in the Book of Life. You may not know your name is on the breastplate of our great, sin atoning High Priest. But this you should

know, because our text and the whole Word of God declares it, there is plenty of Bread on God's table, plenty of Bread for your needy soul in Christ, and you are welcome to it. Come and eat; and you will discover that the table was set specifically for you! If you perish, the fault will be all your own, and no one else's.

Perhaps you think, 'But no one's hand was allowed to touch that bread except the priest's.' Satan has a fiendish way of turning the truth of God into a lie and of making what should be most encouraging horribly discouraging. It is true, no hand could touch that bread but the priest's. But that ought to tell you that the Bread of Life is for sinners who need a Priest! The priest alone must manage the table and keep bread on it all the time. The Bread is in the holy place, so sinners may get it as they come to God by faith in Christ.

Priests' Bread
There is much typical instruction in the fact that only God's priests were allowed to eat the shewbread, and to eat it only in the holy place. Certainly, this was God's provision for his servants. Those who preach the gospel are to live by the gospel (1 Corinthians 9:14). What is represented here is intended to show us that the salvation of God's elect by the will of God is Christ's bread, the bread that satisfies his very soul. Still, the shewbread is for us. It speaks of Christ who is our Bread.

We are told none but God's priests could eat this bread. If I come to Christ the Bread of Life and eat him, I am, I must be, one of those made to be in him 'a chosen generation and a royal priesthood' before God! The proof is in the pudding, we are told. Well, in this case, the proof is in the Bread, in eating the Bread of God. That is exactly what our Saviour tells us in John 6:54-58.

'Whoso eateth my flesh, and drinketh my blood, hath eternal life; and I will raise him up at the last day. For my flesh is meat indeed, and my blood is drink indeed. He that eateth my flesh, and drinketh my blood, dwelleth in me, and I in him. As the living Father hath sent me, and I live by the Father: so he that eateth me, even he shall live by me. This is that bread which came down from heaven: not as your fathers did eat manna, and are dead: he that eateth of this bread shall live forever'.

Come my soul, come my brother, come my sister, come needy sinner. There is Bread abundant on the table. There are twelve loaves.

Each loaf has twice as much as you can take in. The Bread sits on a table with four corners, pointing to sinners everywhere. The Bread is there all the time, and the table is the King's table. Here, Mephibosheth eats, with his crippled legs covered, as one of the King's sons. Eat, O my soul, eat and be satisfied!

Two Rows
Next, we are told that the bread was to be set on the table in two rows (Leviticus 24:6). Try to picture the scene. There is a priest, Aaron or one of his sons, standing before this table with twelve loaves of bread before him. There is Christ, standing in the holy place, ever busy, never idle, his hands constantly and bountifully providing Bread for his people: the bread of his immutable grace, the bread of his adorable and wise providence, the bread of his sweet consolation, the bread of his blessed presence, and the bread of his tender care.

Taken from Israel
The bread was to be taken from the children of Israel (Leviticus 24:8), because the Lord God would have all his people know it was for them. So, too, the Lord Jesus Christ, the Bread of Life, is Bread taken from among men, that we might know that all he is he is for us, and all he does he does on our behalf.

'Then thou spakest in vision to thy holy one, and saidst, I have laid help upon one that is mighty; I have exalted one chosen out of the people' (Psalm 89:19). 'For every high priest taken from among men is ordained for men in things pertaining to God, that he may offer both gifts and sacrifices for sins: Who can have compassion on the ignorant, and on them that are out of the way; for that he himself also is compassed with infirmity' (Hebrews 5:1, 2).

The Frankincense
Fourth, it was required of God that each row of bread have some frankincense upon it for a memorial of burnt offering to the Lord. 'And thou shalt put pure frankincense upon each row, that it may be on the bread for a memorial, even an offering made by fire unto the LORD' (Leviticus 24:7).

The bread was to be eaten; but the frankincense was to be burned. The frankincense speaks of our acceptance with God, and of the

285

acceptance of our worship, praise, and sacrifices, the acceptance of our very prayers by Christ. All God's spiritual Israel, typified by the twelve loaves, are made through Christ a sweet savour to him. Our prayers and sacrifices, worship and service, our very lives come up before God for a memorial of a sweet, acceptable savour to him (Acts 10:4; 1 Peter 2:5; Ecclesiastes 9:7).

Renewed Weekly

Fifth, the Lord required Aaron to set fresh bread on the golden table every sabbath (Leviticus 24:8). There is more here than this, I am sure, but this is distinctly a word of instruction to God's servants. The bread was to be prepared before it was brought to the tabernacle. Yet, it was to be freshly prepared. Then, every Saturday the priest was required to set fresh bread on the table in the house of God.

Gospel preachers must come to the house of God with fresh Bread and set that upon the table before the Lord, feeding his children with the Bread of God. God's servants dare not bring stale bread to his people and dare not bring any other food to feed them. Displays of oratory eloquence, great learning, and vain philosophy, theological speculation, denominational dogma, and religious ceremony, history, moralism, and civic duties are all a breach of this perpetual statute. The only bread with which God's servants are to feed his children is Jesus Christ and him crucified, the Bread of Life.

The Sabbath

Sixth, as the bread was brought out before the people and placed in the holy place on the golden table on the sabbath day. Christ is our Sabbath, and the rest wherewith the Lord causes 'the weary to rest, and their refreshing'. 'Return unto thy rest, O my soul; for the LORD hath dealt bountifully with thee' (Psalm 116:7). 'This is the rest wherewith ye may cause the weary to rest; and this is the refreshing' (Isaiah 28:12).

Our Lord Jesus Christ, the Bread of God, is brought out and set before men in this blessed gospel sabbath by the preaching of the gospel. And he shall be brought out on the morning of that great eternal sabbath awaiting us and set gloriously before his people forever. He is set before us continually upon the table of God, the table of God's preparing, the table of God's presence, the table of God's showing. Christ is the Bread of the gospel table. He is the Bread of the table prepared for me in the presence of my enemies. Our dear Saviour is the Bread of our souls as we feast at the Lord's table, remembering him. And our all-glorious Christ shall be the Bread of our souls forever on the table at the marriage supper of the Lamb.

Blessed Fellowship

Seventh, the two rows of bread, six loaves to a row, sitting upon that golden table, suggests the blessed fellowship, unity, and oneness of God's church. God's Israel in this gospel age is just one tribe.

'The cup of blessing which we bless, is it not the communion of the blood of Christ? The bread which we break, is it not the communion of the body of Christ? For we being many are one bread, and one body: for we are all partakers of that one bread' (1 Corinthians 10:16, 17). We are one in Christ. This is our strength, our peace, our joy, our hope.

These loaves sat on the table, one beside the other, each closely connected with the other. We read the words 'one another' in Colossians 3 again and again. 'Lie not one to another; forbearing one another, and forgiving one another', 'in all wisdom teaching and admonishing one another'. That is the way believers are to live. We live not for ourselves, but to love and serve one another (Ephesians 4:1-5:2).

God's Israel, God's church is ever one before him. These twelve loaves, covered with pure frankincense, arranged in divine order on the table of pure gold, standing in the holy place before the Lord, standing in the light of the golden candlestick, display the indissoluble unity of God's Israel. Even after the revolt of the ten tribes there were twelve loaves on the table (2 Chronicles 13:11), because, 'the purpose of God according to election' stands unaltered (Romans 9:11; 2 Timothy 2:19). The church of God is one body, the body of Christ, already seated with him in glory. Not one member shall be severed from that body. All Israel shall be saved!

This is the everlasting memorial of God's honour and glory. Like the twelve stones taken out of Jordan and laid together as a memorial to God, and those twelve stones erected as an altar by Elijah before the altars of Baal, these twelve loaves in the tabernacle declare to the glory of God our Saviour, whose name is called Jesus, 'He shall save his people from their sins'.

287

Chapter 92

Covers To Wrap Yourself In

'Moreover thou shalt make the tabernacle with ten curtains of fine twined linen, and blue, and purple, and scarlet: with cherubims of cunning work shalt thou make them. The length of one curtain shall be eight and twenty cubits, and the breadth of one curtain four cubits: and every one of the curtains shall have one measure. The five curtains shall be coupled together one to another; and other five curtains shall be coupled one to another. And thou shalt make loops of blue upon the edge of the one curtain from the selvedge in the coupling; and likewise shalt thou make in the uttermost edge of another curtain, in the coupling of the second. Fifty loops shalt thou make in the one curtain, and fifty loops shalt thou make in the edge of the curtain that is in the coupling of the second; that the loops may take hold one of another. And thou shalt make fifty taches of gold, and couple the curtains together with the taches: and it shall be one tabernacle. And thou shalt make curtains of goats' hair to be a covering upon the tabernacle: eleven curtains shalt thou make. The length of one curtain shall be thirty cubits, and the breadth of one curtain four cubits: and the eleven curtains shall be all of one measure. And thou shalt couple five curtains by themselves, and six curtains by themselves, and shalt double the sixth curtain in the forefront of the tabernacle. And thou shalt make fifty loops on the edge of the one curtain that is outmost in the coupling, and fifty loops in the edge of the curtain which coupleth the second. And thou shalt make fifty taches of brass, and put the taches into the loops, and couple the tent together, that it may be one. And the remnant that remaineth of the curtains of the tent, the half curtain that remaineth, shall hang over the backside of the tabernacle. And a cubit on the one side, and a cubit on the other side of that which remaineth in the length of the curtains of the tent, it shall hang over the sides of the tabernacle on this side and on that side, to cover it. And thou shalt make a covering for the tent of rams' skins dyed red, and a covering above of badgers' skins.' (Exodus 26:1-14)

As soon as Adam sinned in the Garden of Eden, he sought a refuge from God. He made some fig leaves and tried to hide from God among the trees of the garden. Men have been making refuges ever since. Every sinner has a refuge, something by which he tries to hide himself from an angry God. When the Lord God comes in saving mercy, when God comes to save a sinner by his grace, the very first thing he does is a work of demolition. He tears down every false refuge in which the sinner seeks to hide. That is what we told in Isaiah 28:14-20.

In Exodus 26, God the Holy Spirit shows us an instructive, clear picture of the refuge we must have for our souls, Christ Jesus, and the covers in which we must wrap ourselves. Here, in verses 1-14, the Lord God tells Moses to make four thick coverings for the tabernacle. These coverings, called 'curtains' in our Authorized Version, are great, instructive pictures of our Lord Jesus Christ and his great salvation.

First Covering
The first covering is actually ten coverings of fine twined linen, bound together as one, with cherubs of cunning work interwoven in it. Remember, the tabernacle in the wilderness was typical of Christ himself, the Word made flesh, who dwelt among us, full of grace and truth (John 1:14), of the church of God in this world (1 Corinthians 3:9), and of every believer (Ephesians 2:19-22).

'Moreover thou shalt make the tabernacle with ten curtains of fine twined linen, and blue, and purple, and scarlet: with cherubims of cunning work shalt thou make them. The length of one curtain shall be eight and twenty cubits, and the breadth of one curtain four cubits: and every one of the curtains shall have one measure. The five curtains shall be coupled together one to another; and other five curtains shall be coupled one to another' (vv. 1-3).

The curtains were coupled together with loops because God's people are one, joined by the love of Christ, in one body (Ephesians 2:21, 22; 4:16). Our Lord says of his church, 'My dove, my undefiled is but one. The daughters saw her, and blessed her' (Song of Solomon 6:9).

'And thou shalt make loops of blue upon the edge of the one curtain from the selvedge in the coupling; and likewise shalt thou make in the uttermost edge of another curtain, in the coupling of the second' (v. 4).

The coupling of these two great curtains together, to make one tabernacle, seems to suggest that God's elect both in heaven and earth are but one body, one church, one people (Ephesians 1:10; 3:15).

'Fifty loops shalt thou make in the one curtain, and fifty loops shalt thou make in the edge of the curtain that is in the coupling of the second; that the loops may take hold one of another. And thou shalt make fifty taches of gold, and couple the curtains together with the taches: and it shall be one tabernacle' (vv. 5, 6).

These fifty 'taches', or buckles, of gold might have reference to 'the unity of the Spirit in the bond of peace' (Ephesians 4:3-5).

Second Covering
The second covering was a covering made by combining eleven coverings made of goats' hair.

'And thou shalt make curtains of goats' hair to be a covering upon the tabernacle: eleven curtains shalt thou make. The length of one curtain shall be thirty cubits, and the breadth of one curtain four cubits: and the eleven curtains shall be all of one measure. And thou shalt couple five curtains by themselves, and six curtains by themselves, and shalt double the sixth curtain in the forefront of the tabernacle. And thou shalt make fifty loops on the edge of the one curtain that is outmost in the coupling, and fifty loops in the edge of the curtain which coupleth the second. And thou shalt make fifty taches of brass, and put the taches into the loops, and couple the tent together, that it may be one. And the remnant that remaineth of the curtains of the tent, the half curtain that remaineth, shall hang over the backside of the tabernacle. And a cubit on the one side, and a cubit on the other side of that which remaineth in the length of the curtains of the tent, it shall hang over the sides of the tabernacle on this side and on that side, to cover it' (vv. 7-13).

John Trapp observed, "The tabernacle was goats' hair without and gold within. God hid his Son under the carpenter's son. 'The king's daughter is all glorious within' (Psalm 45:13). And all her sons are princes in all lands (Psalm 45:16). Howbeit, they must be content to pass to heaven as Christ their Head did, as concealed men. 'Therefore the world knoweth us not, because it knew not him' (John 1:10). 'Our life is hid with Christ' (Colossians 3:4) as the life of flowers in winter is hid in the root."

Third and Fourth

The third and fourth coverings are given in the very brief statement of verse 14. 'And thou shalt make a covering for the tent of rams' skins dyed red, and a covering above of badgers' skins.' There were four 'curtains' or coverings for the tabernacle. Each one was different from the other. Like the four Gospels, each represented different aspects of the character and work of our blessed Saviour, whose name is Wonderful. Just as we have four independent records describing the Saviour in the four Gospels, so we have before us in these coverings, four pictures of our great God and Saviour, the Lord Jesus Christ. Each Gospel narrative, like each curtain, is complete in itself; but all four are needed to give us a full revelation of the God-man, our Mediator. In the 'badger's skins' covering, as in Matthew's Gospel, we see Christ our King; but his royalty is disguised in humility. In the covering of 'rams' skins' dyed red our Lord Jesus is portrayed as Jehovah's suffering Servant, as he is presented in the Gospel of Mark. In the third covering of 'goats' hair' the Lord Jesus is set before us as the sacrifice God requires, as the Son of Man, pure and holy, obedient and pleasing to God, as he is portrayed in the Gospel of Luke. And in the innermost covering of 'fine twined linen' our Saviour is portrayed, as he is in the Gospel of John, as God the Son, who is one with his people.

The Covering of Fine Twined Linen

The gorgeous covering of fine twined linen, the covering of blue, scarlet and purple, with its cherubim interwoven in it, was actually ten coverings made into one. Because this is the innermost covering, seen from within the tabernacle, and because it is made of ten curtains looped together, it seems obvious to me that it refers to the law of God given in the ten commandments at Sinai. This covering was laid over the golden boards and formed the interior roof of the house, or, the 'covering of the tabernacle' as seen from the inside. Christ, who is the end of the law (Romans 9:30-10:11), is here exhibited in all the perfection of his glorious character as Jehovah-tsidkenu, the Lord our Righteousness (Jeremiah 23:6). This covering represents Christ our Saviour and all the fulness of his redemptive grace and glory.

Notice the colours used in making this covering. It was blue. This points our eyes to the heavens. How calm and impressive is the deep blue of heaven. Clouds may obscure it, but nothing can pollute it. It is high above all. No human eye can pierce it. It is illimitable, unchangeable, and eternal. How like the divine nature of the Son of Man, how like him who was with the Father before the world was. In Christ the uncreated glory, the deep blue of the unfathomable majesty of the triune God is made visible to the eyes of understanding created in us in the new birth.

The covering was also scarlet. This colour compels us to look downward and think of the red earth from which man at first was made. You will remember that the name of our father Adam means 'red earth'. As the blue tells of our Saviour's divinity, the scarlet proclaims his glorious humanity. The one points to him as the Son of God, the other as the Son of Man. The hunger, weariness, and tears of our blessed Lord tell how truly human he was.

And this first covering was purple. Purple suggests royalty; but there is more than the implication of royalty here. Purple is a new colour that is formed by mixing blue and the scarlet together. The union of these two colours forms a third and distinct one. How beautiful! Christ is divine, Christ is human, and Christ is both in one distinct Person. He is the God-man, the Man-God, our Saviour, all God and all man in one Person, Jesus Christ the Godman! In the purple, then, we behold our Lord Jesus in his mediatorial glory, the only Mediator between God and men, the Man Christ Jesus.

Cherubim

This covering of fine twined linen had figures of cherubs meticulously interwoven in it. What do these cherubs represent? Why are they interwoven into the covering that is seen from within the tabernacle?

Perhaps there is a suggestion here that our Lord Jesus is Lord also over the holy angels, as he certainly is. It may be that these cherubs represent gospel preachers, who are the angels of the churches, as the seraphs overshadowing the mercy seat represent God's messengers.

I think there is something very precious that is represented by these cherubs worked into, interwoven in, the fine twined linen covering of blue, scarlet, and purple. These cherubs represent God's elect, Christ's redeemed ones, the children of God who are so completely united to Christ that we are one with him, so truly one with him that we have been made part of him, 'bone of his bone and flesh of his flesh'. We are described by the Spirit of God as 'his body, the fulness of him that filleth all in all'. The Church was interwoven with Christ, 'the Lamb slain from before the foundation of the world' (Revelation 13:8), by the will and decree of God, in the eternal purpose of grace which he purposed in himself. Wonderful thought! Oh, the unsearchable riches of his grace! We were 'chosen in him before the foundation of the world' (Ephesians 1:4).

When I went to my concordance and tried to find out what the name 'cherubims' means, I ran into trouble. Cherubims are simply defined as 'angelic creatures'. What does the word itself mean? I want to know what the name 'cherub' means. In Ezra 2:59, the word is used as the name of a city, a place. It is the same word; but as it is used to describe a thing, or used as a name, the word 'cherub' means 'blessing'.

These 'cherubims' interwoven in the covering of fine twined linen of blue, scarlet, and purple are blessings. Christ is 'the Blessed God' and 'the Blessed and only Potentate;' and we are in-Christ, woven into him! We are one with him!

The Covering of Goats' Hair
The covering of goats' hair was made of goats' hair spun by women whose hearts stirred them up in wisdom (Exodus 35:26). It was made from the white, downy wool at the roots of goats' hair, the goats' hair from which cashmere wool is woven. This goats' hair covering was laid over and rested on the first one of fine twined linen. Nothing wears more comfortably than cashmere; and nothing wears so comfortably on our souls as the gospel of Christ!

Here, in the goats' hair covering, we see the spotless righteousness and holiness of God's elect in Christ. Without this perfect righteousness and spotless holiness that is ours in Christ, we could never enter into God's holy hill in heaven (Hebrews 12:14; Psalm 24:3, 4). But, blessed be his name forever, all who wash their robes and make them white in the blood of the Lamb shall live with him (Revelation 7:14, 15).

Only righteousness can be accepted with the righteous Lord God. Only holiness can dwell in communion with the holy Lord God. Our Lord Jesus Christ is made of God unto us righteousness in free justification. He is the righteousness of God imputed to us, giving us a righteous standing before God. And Christ is made of God unto us righteousness in sanctification, too. He is our holiness, without which no man shall see the Lord. He is the righteousness of God imparted to us in the new birth (1 Corinthians 1:30, 31).

The Covering of Rams' Skins

Neither fine linen nor goats' hair imply suffering, but skins cannot be gotten without sacrifice. 'Rams' skins dyed red' suggest both death and transformation. The Lord Jesus is before us here as the 'Man of Sorrows', with dyed garments, as the Lamb of God who takes away the sin of the world.

Let us put the shoes off our feet as we enter Gethsemane and see there the skin of the Sacrifice being dyed red with the blood of agony. Try to get a picture of our Lord Jesus when he rose up in Gethsemane and went forth to meet the soldiers. He went forth to meet those representatives of the law, with his garments dyed red in his own blood. Surrendering himself to his tormenters, he commanded his captors to let his people go their way, completely free!

In this covering we have Christ our Redemption. In the 'goats' hair', Christ our Righteousness. In the 'fine linen', Christ our Salvation. But these 'rams' skins dyed red' speak to us as believers, as sinners united to Christ by grace. We are indebted to the cleansing power of Christ's atoning blood for our fitness to dwell in his holy presence.

The white curtain was under the red one. Purity before God cannot be had, but by the blood of Christ. Under the blood we are pure! We must be crucified with Christ if we are to live unto God. As the white covering was kept clean by the crimson covering, so may we be kept clean by a constant, ever-cleansing blood (1 John 1:7-9).

The Covering of Badgers' Skins

The covering of 'badgers' skins' was designed to protect the tabernacle from the elements. It was not designed for beauty, but for protection. Here, again, we see our Lord. This covering pictures Christ in his humiliation (Isaiah 52:13-53:3).

Like our Saviour, the badger skin covering had to bear the heat of the day. It was exposed to the storm and the tempest. Think of our loving, gracious Lord Jesus. How he was misunderstood while being made a curse for us. Thank God, he bore it all. He answered not a word. Satan came, but found nothing in him. To the world there was no beauty in him; but to God the Father he is all-glorious, that One in whom he is well pleased, with whom his delights have always been. And to all who know him in the experience of his saving mercy, he is precious.

Those who only saw the badger skins saw nothing of the hidden glory within. Though Christ is still, to the world, 'a root out of a dry ground', to the child of God, to the believing sinner, who has access within the veil, he is altogether lovely.

Oh, that our hearts may be like the heart of the tabernacle, the habitation of God, or like the King's daughter, 'all glorious within'. Although our faces may have the uncomely badger's skin appearance, yet in heart may we have the beauty of the Lord our God upon us.

Our Experience

These four coverings also show us a picture of the believer's experience in relation to Christ. In our natural state of spiritual ignorance and blindness, we could only see the blessed Redeemer as the 'badgers' skins' covering speaks of him, having no beauty, no attractiveness, because we had no sense of our guilt or need. In the 'rams' skins dyed red' we have been cleansed and changed by the power of his atoning blood. In the 'goats' hair' covering we experience what it is to be made the righteousness of God in Christ. In the innermost curtain of 'fine twined linen' we walk in the light, as he is in the light, beholding his glory and filled with all the fulness of God.

Is this our experience? Do you know what it is to live within the holy of holies, in sweet, unbroken fellowship with the Holy One? This is our privilege in Christ Jesus.

Chapter 93

Buckles, Boards, Bases, And Bars

'And thou shalt make fifty taches (buckles) of gold, and couple the curtains together with the taches (buckles): and it shall be one tabernacle ... And thou shalt make boards for the tabernacle of shittim wood standing up ... And thou shalt make bars of shittim wood; five for the boards of the one side of the tabernacle, And five bars for the boards of the other side of the tabernacle, and five bars for the boards of the side of the tabernacle, for the two sides westward. And the middle bar in the midst of the boards shall reach from end to end. And thou shalt overlay the boards with gold, and make their rings of gold for places for the bars: and thou shalt overlay the bars with gold. And thou shalt rear up the tabernacle according to the fashion thereof which was showed thee in the mount.'
(Exodus 26:6-30)

The Lord God told Moses to make 50 taches (buckles) of gold and 50 buckles of brass, and 48 boards. Each board was to have two sockets of silver, that is two foundations or bases of silver under it. And he was commanded to make 15 bars of shittim wood overlaid with gold.

What was represented by these buckles, boards, bases, and bars? As we seek to understand the typical meaning of the tabernacle and its furnishings, we should do so by following the direction of God the Holy Spirit. In the book of Hebrews, he gives us four distinct statements about the tabernacle and the ceremonies of carnal worship connected with it. He tells us these things were: 'the shadow of heavenly things'

(Hebrews 8:5), 'the patterns of things in the heavens' (Hebrews 9:23), 'the figures of the true' (Hebrews 9:24), and 'a shadow of good things to come' (Hebrews 10:1). In other words, the things we read about here in the book of Exodus were designed to be shadows, patterns, types, and figures of those heavenly, spiritual things now revealed in the gospel of Christ. Specifically, the Holy Spirit tells us that the tabernacle in the wilderness was typical of Christ himself, the Word made flesh, who dwelt among us, full of grace and truth (John 1:14), of the church of God in this world (1 Corinthians 3:9), of every believer (Ephesians 2:19-22), and of the whole of God's salvation wrought out for and given to chosen sinners in Christ (Hebrews 9:1-15).

May God the Holy Ghost give us grace as we come to the tabernacle, as Simeon came to the temple looking for the Consolation of Israel, looking for Christ. Seeing our Saviour and God's great salvation in him in such carnal things as buckles, and boards, and bases, and bars, may he cause our hearts, like those disciples on the road to Emmaus, to burn within us, as he talks with us by the way.

God's Command
In Exodus 25:8, God gave his command to build the tabernacle, 'And let them make me a sanctuary; that I may dwell among them'. What a remarkable command that is! The Lord God commands sinful men to make a tabernacle for him, that he might dwell among them! Does God desire the company and companionship of such things as we are? He does indeed; but he will not come to us and we cannot come to him except in a way that honours him in all his holy character. The tabernacle was designed to show, by constant, daily sacrifice and service, how God and man are united in the person and work of Christ.

Those who constructed the tabernacle were a chosen, covenant people. They were people who had been redeemed by the blood of a lamb. They were a people delivered from death in the Red Sea and sanctified to God by the work of his Wind, the constant representation of God the Holy Spirit in Scripture (John 3:8; 1 Corinthians 3:16).

The Pattern
God took Moses up into the mount and showed him the pattern according to which he must make the tabernacle. He showed Moses the accomplishment of redemption by the sacrifice of the incarnate Son of

God. 'See, saith he, that thou make all things according to the pattern shewed to thee in the mount' (Hebrews 8:5; Exodus 25:9, 40).

Because these carnal things had spiritual meaning, they were to be made to a heavenly pattern. The tabernacle, as salvation, was according to the purpose of God. 'Thus saith the LORD' was the rule of everything. No man's opinion was sought; and no man's opinion was given. Everything was done to show forth the greatness and glory of our Saviour, the Lord Jesus Christ. It was done for the glory of God alone and designed to display God's marvellous scheme of redemption and grace by the substitutionary sacrifice of his darling Son at Calvary.

The Materials
Remember, God required the children of Israel to bring the materials by which the tabernacle was to be made (Exodus 25:1-8). He would only accept that which was offered willingly; though the offering was received by divine command. How can a sacrifice be a willing sacrifice, if it is commanded? Actually, the only way we will ever offer ourselves or make any offering of sacrifice of any kind to God is if he commands it. It is written, 'Thy people shall be willing in the day of thy power'.

Where did these pilgrims, dwelling in a desert, get all the rich and rare materials necessary for such a costly enterprise? Where on earth did they get all the silver and gold and precious stones that God received from their hands to make the tabernacle? The Lord God himself put into their hands that which he now received from their hands (Exodus 12:36). So it is with us (1 Chronicles 29:14). In Exodus 36:6, we are told that these redeemed sinners, fresh out of Egypt, gave with such willing hearts, so liberally, that Moses had to tell them to stop giving.

The Workman
In Exodus 31, Moses shows us the workmen God used to do the job.

'And the LORD spake unto Moses, saying, See, I have called by name Bezaleel the son of Uri, the son of Hur, of the tribe of Judah: And I have filled him with the spirit of God, in wisdom, and in understanding, and in knowledge, and in all manner of workmanship, to devise cunning works, to work in gold, and in silver, and in brass, and in cutting of stones, to set them, and in carving of timber, to work in all manner of workmanship. And I, behold, I have given with him Aholiab, the son of Ahisamach, of the tribe of Dan: and in the hearts of all that are wise hearted I have put wisdom, that they may make all that I have commanded thee' (Exodus 31:1-6).

Bezaleel led a whole crew of skilled artisans. Bezaleel means 'In the shadow of God'. Bezaleel, like God the Holy Spirit, gave to 'every man his work', and imparted to each workman the wisdom needed to perform his work. Bezaleel stands before us as one typical of God the Holy Spirit, foreshadowing his great work in the building of God's spiritual temple, the church, which is 'an habitation of God through the Spirit'. The Lord used many to make his sanctuary; but Bezaleel alone was skilled 'in all manner of workmanship;' and he alone devised curious works (Exodus 35:30-32).

The Buckles

Let us look briefly at the buckles, boards, bases, and bars spoken of in Exodus 26. We will begin with the fifty buckles of gold and the fifty buckles of brass (vv. 6 and 11).

'And thou shalt make fifty taches of gold, and couple the curtains together with the taches: and it shall be one tabernacle' (Exodus 26:6). 'And thou shalt make fifty taches of brass, and put the taches into the loops, and couple the tent together, that it may be one' (Exodus 26:11).

The number 50 is itself an indication these taches (buckles) which held the loops of the curtains together represent God the Holy Spirit, fifty being the number for Pentecost. Added to the symbolic number 50, both gold and brass are used in Scripture as emblems of divinity. We are twice told the purpose for these buckles was to hold all together, to 'couple the tent together, that it may be one'. That is the work of God the Holy Spirit. He makes of many one in Christ (Ephesians 4:1-7).

The Bases

Before looking at the boards, think about the bases upon which the boards were set. Each board was set in two sockets of silver, which formed the foundation for the tabernacle. These sockets of silver were made to serve as the two tenons, or hands, that held the boards upright and held them all together.

'And thou shalt make boards for the tabernacle of shittim wood standing up. Ten cubits shall be the length of a board, and a cubit and a half shall be the breadth of one board. Two tenons shall there be in one board, set in order one against another: thus shalt thou make for all the boards of the tabernacle. And thou shalt make the boards for the tabernacle, twenty boards on the south side southward. And thou shalt make forty sockets of silver under the twenty boards; two sockets under one board for his two tenons, and two sockets under another board for his two tenons. And for the second side of the tabernacle on the north side there shall be twenty boards' (Exodus 26:15-20).

Knowing this house is typical of heavenly and eternal things, we may be sure something very special is to be seen here. These bases formed the one foundation upon which the whole tabernacle was erected and upon which it sat. In Exodus 30 we are told that every man had to give half a shekel as atonement for his soul. In Exodus 38 we find the 'atonement money', the price of souls, was to be made into sockets, in which the boards of the tabernacle were to rest.

What does all that mean? The Foundation, upon which the whole tabernacle and all the services of the tabernacle sat was Atonement. Here Peter was inspired to make reference to this very thing, when speaking of our redemption by the Lord Jesus Christ's precious blood.

'Forasmuch as ye know that ye were not redeemed with corruptible things, as silver and gold, from your vain conversation received by tradition from your fathers; But with the precious blood of Christ, as of a lamb without blemish and without spot: Who verily was foreordained before the foundation of the world, but was manifest in these last times for you' (1 Peter 1:18-20).

The tabernacle had no standing apart from the atonement; and the church of Christ, God's House, has no foundation but the sin atoning, precious blood of our Lord Jesus Christ. To deny the redeeming power and efficacy of Christ's blood is to deny the only foundation laid by God upon which it is possible to build true worship and acceptable service. 'Other foundation can no man lay' (1 Corinthians 3:11).

The Boards

The bases, the foundation, represent the atoning work of Christ. The boards resting on and fixed therein typify the redeemed of the Lord. The boards represent us, the Israel of God always portrayed in the number 12 or multiples of 12. Each board was fifteen feet long, twenty-seven inches broad with two tenons (hands) holding the silver socket.

The boards say more than you may imagine, they represent every believer's experience of grace, by which we are built on Christ. Boards have to be cut down. Saul had this experience on his way to Damascus, and every chosen, redeemed sinner must be brought down in the dust of repentance before the throne of God. The boards could not be used until they were completely dried up. The sap of pride and self-righteousness must be dried up in us. David knew about this when he cried, 'Thy hand was heavy upon me. My moisture is turned into the drought of summer' (Psalm 32:4). The boards also had to be cleansed and covered, clad and completely encased in pure gold. Beauty was put on them that is altogether foreign to boards. So it is with God's elect. 'The righteousness of God which is by faith of Jesus Christ unto all and upon all them that believe' (Romans 3:22).

The boards were fitly framed together, joined by skilled hands, representing God given faith in Christ, holding the foundation and holding us to the foundation. When planted in their bases, forming one foundation, they were joined one to another. True spiritual union can only come through our being joined together in Christ. Each board resting on the silver sockets of atonement stood as one with the other.

The Bars

Then, the Lord God commanded Moses to make fifteen strong bars of shittim wood overlaid with gold. These bars encircled the golden boards like the arms of omnipotent mercy and grace, keeping them on the foundation, keeping them upright, keeping them together, and pointed heavenward. Marvellous grace!

As each board had three rings, through which the bars ran, each believer has three golden rings through which we are united by almighty grace to God our Saviour and to one another: faith, hope, and love. 'The grace of the Lord Jesus Christ, the love of God, and the communion of the Holy Ghost' (2 Corinthians 13:14). 'These three, and the greatest of these is love' (1 Corinthians 13:13).

The tabernacle is often referred to as 'the tabernacle of witness' (Numbers 17:7, 8; 18:2; 2 Chronicles 24:6; Acts 7:44). Like the church of God, it was a witness in the wilderness to the mercy and holiness, and justice and grace, and faithfulness and truth of God. That is precisely what we are, as trophies of his grace. We are God's tabernacle of witness in this world. Witnessing everywhere of God's greatness and grace, his glory and goodness, and his free salvation in his dear Son, our Saviour, the Lord Jesus Christ.

Chapter 94

Where's The Middle Bar?

'And thou shalt make bars of shittim wood; five for the boards of the one side of the tabernacle, and five bars for the boards of the other side of the tabernacle, and five bars for the boards of the side of the tabernacle, for the two sides westward. And the middle bar in the midst of the boards shall reach from end to end. And thou shalt overlay the boards with gold, and make their rings of gold for places for the bars: and thou shalt overlay the bars with gold. And thou shalt rear up the tabernacle according to the fashion thereof which was showed thee in the mount.'
(Exodus 26:26-30)

The tabernacle of the Congregation, which is described in such great detail in Exodus 25-40, is without question the fullest, most instructive type and picture of Christ that was given in the Old Testament Scriptures. It typified and portrayed our blessed Saviour himself; and it typified and portrayed our salvation in him

It began with a plan. God showed Moses the pattern that had to be rigidly followed (Exodus 25:9, 40; Romans 8:28-31). Everything in the tabernacle focused on a sacrifice; the altar of sacrifice, the laver of cleansing, and the veil of separation (Revelation 13:8). The central thing in the tabernacle was the mercy seat, the place of atonement (Exodus 25:22; Romans 3:24-26; 1 John 2:1, 2). The Shekinah above the mercy seat spoke of divine acceptance by the blood of the sacrifice

(Ephesians 1:6). The bread on the table spoke of Christ the Bread of Life. The light of the golden candlestick spoke of Christ the Light of the World. The curtains over the tabernacle represented the covering of our souls with Christ's garments of salvation. The loops and buckles (taches) spoke of our union in Christ by God the Holy Spirit, who joins us together as one tabernacle. The forty-eight boards of the tabernacle declared that all God's elect shall be joined to Christ. The bases, the sockets of silver in which each board was set, signified the atonement, being made from the atonement money, and comprised the singular foundation of the whole structure. The bars of shittim wood overlaid with pure gold spoke of our security in the omnipotent arms of our Redeemer. We read about these bars that wrapped the boards and held them together in Exodus 26:26-30 and in Exodus 36:31-34.

How we ought to rejoice and give thanks to our God for the security of our souls in his arms of mercy. It is a security that involves every attribute of the triune God; his immutability and his faithfulness, his mercy and his grace, his justice and truth, his righteousness and his holiness.

Moses speaks of five bars on each of the three enclosed sides of the tabernacle, fifteen in all. But if you will look at any picture or model of the tabernacle, you will never be able to find more than twelve. Count them, and count them again. There are only four bars on each side of the tabernacle. I have a model of the tabernacle sitting before me, as I write. I can see four and feel four; two upper and two lower bars on each side; but I cannot see, or feel, or find the fifth one. So, I've got a question that just has to be answered. Where is the middle bar? Read verse 28 again. 'And the middle bar in the midst of the boards shall reach from end to end.'

We are told where this middle bar was placed in Exodus 36.

'And he made bars of shittim wood; five for the boards of the one side of the tabernacle, and five bars for the boards of the other side of the tabernacle, and five bars for the boards of the tabernacle for the sides westward. And he made the middle bar to shoot through the boards from the one end to the other. And he overlaid the boards with gold, and made their rings of gold to be places for the bars, and overlaid the bars with gold' (Exodus 36:31-34).

The middle bar was seen by no one. It ran inside the boards. It was shot 'through the boards from the one end to the other'. Everything else in the tabernacle could be seen by the eye of man, be it from the outside or the inside; but this middle bar no mortal eye could see. Everyone knew it was there; but no one could see it, except the Lord God himself.

What do you suppose that middle bar represented? Read Colossians chapter one. As you read the chapter, you will immediately see what the middle bar of the tabernacle represented. God our Father, 'hath made us meet to be partakers of the inheritance of the saints in light: Who hath delivered us from the power of darkness, and hath translated us into the kingdom of his dear Son: In whom we have redemption through his blood, even the forgiveness of sins: Who is the image of the invisible God, the firstborn of every creature: For by him were all things created, that are in heaven, and that are in earth, visible and invisible, whether they be thrones, or dominions, or principalities, or powers: all things were created by him, and for him: And he is before all things, and by him all things consist. And he is the head of the body, the church: who is the beginning, the firstborn from the dead; that in all things he might have the preeminence. For it pleased the Father that in him should all fulness dwell; And, having made peace through the blood of his cross, by him to reconcile all things unto himself; by him, I say, whether they be things in earth, or things in heaven. And you, that were sometime alienated and enemies in your mind by wicked works, yet now hath he reconciled in the body of his flesh through death, to present you holy and unblameable and unreproveable in his sight: If ye continue in the faith grounded and settled, and be not moved away from the hope of the gospel, which ye have heard, and which was preached to every creature which is under heaven; whereof I Paul am made a minister; Who now rejoice in my sufferings for you, and fill up that which is behind of the afflictions of Christ in my flesh for his body's sake, which is the church: Whereof I am made a minister, according to the dispensation of God which is given to me for you, to fulfil the word of God; Even the mystery which hath been hid from ages and from generations, but now is made manifest to his saints: To whom God would make known what is the riches of the glory of this mystery among the Gentiles; which is Christ in you, the hope of glory: Whom we preach, warning every man, and teaching every man in all wisdom; that we may present every man perfect in Christ Jesus: Whereunto I also labour, striving according to his working, which worketh in me mightily' (Colossians 1:12-29).

The middle bar represented Christ in you, the hope of glory. Everything else in the tabernacle represented the works of Christ for us. The middle bar represented the work of Christ in us. Without the middle bar the tabernacle would not have been complete. And there is no salvation for any sinner, no hope of glory, until Christ is in you. Christ in you is the hope of glory (Colossians 1:27). The essence of God's salvation is Christ himself. The sweetness of it is Christ in you. The anticipation of it, the hope of it, is glory.

The gospel of God's free and sovereign grace in Christ is a mystery hidden from the unregenerate man, hidden from every unbeliever, but revealed by his Spirit to his saints, 'To whom God would make known what is the riches of the glory of this mystery among the Gentiles; which is Christ in you, the hope of glory.'

The Riches of Glory
First, all the riches promised, proclaimed, and presented to sinners in the gospel are in Christ. The riches of the gospel are spiritual riches. They are called, 'the riches of the glory of this mystery', because the glory of the gospel is, in great measure, to be seen in the riches of grace it holds in store for sinners who trust Christ.

What are these riches? They are the rich truths of grace, compared to gold, silver, and precious stones, by which God builds his holy temple (1 Corinthians 3:11-16). They are the rich truths of the gospel: sovereign election, substitutionary redemption, irresistible grace and the infallible preservation of God's saints in grace.

The riches Paul speaks of are the rich treasures of grace laid up for sinners in Christ. In Christ there are immense and infinite treasures of grace laid up in store for God's elect (John 1:16; Ephesians 1:3; Colossians 2:9, 10). All the promises of God relating to this life and to the life to come are in Christ yea and amen, sure and infallible. In Christ we have free justification (Romans 3:24-26), absolute pardon (Ephesians 1:7), complete reconciliation (2 Corinthians 5:17), eternal adoption (1 John 3:1, 2), and eternal life (Romans 3:23).

The Glory of the Gospel
Second, Christ is also the glory of the gospel. Read Colossians 1:27 again. 'To whom God would make known what is the riches of the glory of this mystery among the Gentiles; which is Christ.'

It is written, 'His glory shall be great in thy salvation' (Psalm 21:5). The gospel is the revelation of the glory of God; and the glory of God is Christ. We see the glory of God in the face of Christ. That is to say, by faith in Christ every believer sees that which was revealed to Moses in Exodus 34, God's glorious, sovereign goodness and inflexible justice in the exercise of his saving grace in Christ (Isaiah 45:20-22). God's glory is known and revealed only in Christ, the incarnate God, the sinner's Substitute (John 1:18; 17:3; 2 Corinthians 4:6).

The Hope of Glory
Third, the believer's hope of glory is Christ. 'Christ in you, the hope of glory.' We live in hope of immortality and eternal life in heavenly glory, 'looking for the mercy of our Lord Jesus Christ unto eternal life'. The basis, foundation, and ground of our hope is 'Christ in you, the hope of glory'. The cause of our hope is the grace of God in Christ. The basis of our hope is the finished work of Christ. Our hope itself is 'Christ in you, the hope of glory'.

'Christ in you' is what the middle bar represented, and 'the hope of glory' is the subject of Colossians 1. The glory the saints will have with Christ will be the enjoyment of him forever in heaven. This hope of glory in which we live is brought to light by the gospel (2 Timothy 1:9, 10). Christ is our hope of glory. Christ crucified is the basis of our hope. But Christ crucified is not our hope. Christ in you is the hope of glory. It is Christ in us that gives us hope, the confident expectation of glory. Christ in you, formed in you, living in you, reigning in you, is the hope, the confident, pleasurable expectation of eternal glory.

Religion that is all experience and feeling is worthless, useless religion. But religion that has neither experience nor feeling is just as worthless and useless. Hope, like faith and love, is an internal thing, something felt, experienced, and known in the soul. You can talk about faith all you want to, and define it with unmistakable precision, but until you experience it, you will never know what it is. You can read books about love, and even write books about love, but you will never know what it is until you experience it. And once you experience it, you will laugh at the definitions men attach to it. The same is true of hope. Hope is not a theory, a doctrine, or just something to talk about. Hope is something born in you, something felt in the heart and known only by experience. 'Christ in you, the hope of glory.'

'Glory itself is in his hands', said John Gill, 'the gift of it is with him and through him. He has made way by his sufferings and death for the enjoyment of it, and is now preparing it for us by his presence and intercession. His grace makes us worthy of it. His righteousness gives us title to it. And his Spirit is the earnest of it.'

Three Facts Revealed
The hope of glory which we have in Christ is built upon Christ himself alone. It is a hope founded upon his blood, righteousness, intercession and grace. Here are three facts revealed in the Scriptures which assure us our hope of glory is a good, well grounded, and sure hope. I hope to go to heaven when I die. I have hope of eternal life with Christ. I confidently expect the mercy of our Lord Jesus Christ unto eternal life. I am looking for and expecting immortality and eternal life in glory with Christ. But is that reasonable; or is it just a pipe dream? Let us see.

God's Promise
God has promised eternal life and glory to his elect. It is written, 'The Lord will give grace and glory' (Psalm 84:11). God promises to believing sinners not only spiritual life that now is, but also eternal life which is to come (1 Timothy 4:8). This promise of eternal life, life with Christ forever in glory, is the principle, all-encompassing promise of the gospel. It is the centre of all the promises of God. Indeed, all other blessings of grace terminate in this. 'This is the promise that he promised us, even eternal life' (1 John 2:25).

It is a promise made by God, who cannot lie, before the world began (Titus 1:2). This is a promise to be depended upon. It is sure and certain. When this life is over, God's saints will enter into eternal life in glory. 'Blessed is the man that endureth temptation: for when he is tried', when he has been proved by the trials and afflictions of life in this world, 'he shall receive the crown of life, which the Lord hath promised to them that love him' (James 1:12). And the crown of life is the 'crown of glory that fadeth not away' (1 Peter 5:4).

Christ's Preparation
The glory of eternal life in heaven is a glory God has prepared for his elect. It is a glory unseen, unheard of, and inconceivable to the minds of men and women in this world. But it is a glory prepared by God for

them that love him and revealed to us by his Spirit (1 Corinthians 2:9, 10). This preparation of eternal happiness was made for us before the world began. Heaven is a kingdom prepared for God's elect from the foundation of the world (Matthew 25:34). It was prepared in the counsels and purposes of God, which cannot be defeated, frustrated, or made void by any means. This kingdom of glory was prepared for us by our blessed Saviour's sin atoning death as our Substitute (John 14:1-3). And this kingdom of glory will, most assuredly, be given to those men and women for whom it was prepared by God (Matthew 20:23).

It will not be given to any but those for whom it was prepared. It cannot be purchased, earned, won or in any way merited by the works of men. It will be given freely to those for whom God has prepared it.

Grace Experienced
God's elect in this world are men and women he has prepared unto glory (Romans 9:23). Not only has God promised and prepared a kingdom of glory for his elect, but his elect are 'vessels of mercy which he had afore prepared unto glory'. Every work of God's grace is a preparatory work by which he prepares his people to enter into and enjoy everlasting glory.

God prepared us unto glory in sovereign predestination, having ordained us unto eternal life. He has prepared us for glory by blood atonement. And he prepares us for glory by the experience of his grace, making us partakers of the divine nature, putting Christ in us by the mighty operations of his Spirit. At God's appointed 'time of love' (Ezekiel 16:8), those who were ordained unto eternal life are given grace to believe on the Lord Jesus Christ and effectually caused to come to him in faith by the Spirit of grace (Acts 13:48; Psalm 65:4).

Those God has ordained to eternal life and caused to believe on Christ shall most assuredly enjoy that life in eternity to which they were ordained from eternity. The means of bringing God's elect into eternal life in glory as well as eternal life itself has been infallibly fixed by God's decree (2 Thessalonians 2:13, 14).

'God hath from the beginning chosen you to salvation', not from the beginning of your repentance, faith, and conversion, but from the beginning of all things, from the beginning of time, from eternity. All who now believe, and all who ever shall believe were chosen by God to salvation before the world began. The means by which God

309

determined to save us is plainly revealed. 'Through sanctification of the Spirit' that is regeneration, 'And belief of the truth' that is faith in Christ, 'Whereunto he called you by our gospel' that is, the preaching of the gospel of Christ.

That salvation and eternal life to which we have been elected, predestinated and called is eternal glory – 'To the obtaining of the glory of our Lord Jesus Christ'. We shall obtain that very same glory which Christ has entered into and now possesses for us. He has it in his hands to give to God's elect (John 17:2). He declares it is ours (John 17:5, 22). We have been predestinated to it (Romans 8:29). He has prepared it for us and us for it. And we shall have it (Romans 8:28-31).

Here is a marvellous, golden chain of grace which cannot be broken. It begins in predestination and ends in glorification. 'Whom he did predestinate, them he also called: and whom he called them he also justified: and whom he justified, them he also glorified.'

We read in Exodus 26:30, 'And thou shalt rear up the tabernacle according to the fashion thereof which was shewed thee in the mount.' The whole tabernacle was set up by just one man, Moses, who also typified the Lord Jesus Christ. The whole work of salvation was finished and reared up by one man, Christ Jesus the Lord, according to the pattern of God's eternal decree, to the praise of the glory of his grace! He is the middle board shot 'through the boards from the one end to the other', who holds everything together.

Chapter 95

The Veil Of Separation

'And thou shalt make a vail of blue, and purple, and scarlet, and fine twined linen of cunning work: with cherubims shall it be made: And thou shalt hang it upon four pillars of shittim wood overlaid with gold: their hooks shall be of gold, upon the four sockets of silver. And thou shalt hang up the vail under the taches, that thou mayest bring in thither within the vail the ark of the testimony: and the vail shall divide unto you between the holy place and the most holy. And thou shalt put the mercy seat upon the ark of the testimony in the most holy place. And thou shalt set the table without the vail, and the candlestick over against the table on the side of the tabernacle toward the south: and thou shalt put the table on the north side. And thou shalt make an hanging for the door of the tent, of blue, and purple, and scarlet, and fine twined linen, wrought with needlework. And thou shalt make for the hanging five pillars of shittim wood, and overlay them with gold, and their hooks shall be of gold: and thou shalt cast five sockets of brass for them.' (Exodus 26:31-37)

In the tabernacle, and later in the temple, the Lord God commanded that a veil of separation be hung between the holy place of daily service and the holy of holies. It formed a wall of separation between God and men. None but the high priest could enter in within the veil; and he could do so only once a year, only on the day of atonement, and even then only with the blood of God's appointed sacrifice, the paschal lamb. We do not have to speculate about the spiritual significance of this veil. The Scriptures tell us plainly it speaks of our Lord Jesus Christ.

'Then verily the first covenant had also ordinances of divine service, and a worldly sanctuary. For there was a tabernacle made; the first, wherein was the candlestick, and the table, and the shewbread; which is called the sanctuary. And after the second veil, the tabernacle which is called the Holiest of all; which had the golden censer, and the ark of the covenant overlaid round about with gold, wherein was the golden pot that had manna, and Aaron's rod that budded, and the tables of the covenant; and over it the cherubims of glory shadowing the mercyseat; of which we cannot now speak particularly. Now when these things were thus ordained, the priests went always into the first tabernacle, accomplishing the service of God. But into the second went the high priest alone once every year, not without blood, which he offered for himself, and for the errors of the people: The Holy Ghost this signifying, that the way into the holiest of all was not yet made manifest, while as the first tabernacle was yet standing: which was a figure for the time then present, in which were offered both gifts and sacrifices, that could not make him that did the service perfect, as pertaining to the conscience; which stood only in meats and drinks, and divers washings, and carnal ordinances, imposed on them until the time of reformation. But Christ being come an high priest of good things to come, by a greater and more perfect tabernacle, not made with hands, that is to say, not of this building; Neither by the blood of goats and calves, but by his own blood he entered in once into the holy place, having obtained eternal redemption for us' (Hebrews 9:1-12).

The veil of separation points to our Saviour who has, with his blood, entered 'heaven itself, there to appear in the presence of God for us'.

That Which Conceals

First, it should be noted that a veil is a covering. It covers, hides, or conceals. Something hidden behind it cannot be seen. As the veil on Moses' face screened the glory beaming forth from that man who had been in the mount with God, so to this day there is a veil on the hearts of men that keeps them from seeing the glory of God in the face of Christ. How blessed of God we are when the veil is taken away and Christ is revealed! (See 2 Corinthians 3:8-18; 4:6; Hebrews 10:19-21).

The veil of the tabernacle hid, or came between, the people and the glory of the divine presence, which rested on the mercy seat in the holy of holies. That veil typified the body of the Lord Jesus Christ. He took upon him 'the likeness of sinful flesh' (Romans 8:3). His flesh, like a veil, concealed the glory of his divine character. On the Mount of Transfiguration, when he was transfigured before Peter, James, and John, the glory that dwelt within burst forth, as Moses and Elijah spoke to him about the death he must accomplish at Jerusalem. That glory, the divine majesty, was always there, but the body of flesh veiled it.

Indeed, there is a sense in which our own bodies are veils that hide from us the face of our glorified Lord. The death of this body will be but the rending of the veil, the opening of the way for our access into his immediate, glorious presence. 'To be absent from the body, and to be present with the Lord' (2 Corinthians 5:8). How sweet the thought! There is only a veil between my soul and my Saviour, a veil that will soon be taken away!

The Materials
Second, the materials with which the veil of separation was made are highly symbolic. If you look back at the first verse of this chapter, you will see this veil of separation was made of the same materials, and in the same way as the curtains of the tabernacle.

It was made of 'fine linen', which represented the purity of Christ's nature as the God-man, the holiness of his life as our Mediator, and the righteousness of God which he brought in by his obedience unto death as our Representative and Surety. The veil was made of 'twined linen', representing our Redeemer's strength as our God-man Mediator. 'Fine twined', that is the texture of his being. God and man are finely twined in one in the person of our Lord Jesus. This veil was made 'of cunning work'. Our Saviour's incarnation and birth was by the 'cunning work' of God the Holy Spirit (Luke 1:35; 1 Timothy 3:16).

And it was made of 'of blue, purple, and scarlet'. These same colours appeared in the 'hanging for the door' (v. 36). The colours are the same, because both the veil of separation and the door of access speak of Christ. It is Christ, the one and only God-man, our one and only Mediator, who brings us to God. The blue speaks of him who came from heaven. The scarlet speaks of him who is man, born of woman. The purple is formed by combining scarlet and blue, by combining God and man. Purple is the colour of royalty, representing Christ our Royal Priest and King. Let us sing with Mary, 'My soul doth magnify the Lord, and my spirit hath rejoiced in God my Saviour' (Luke 1:46).

313

These colours, blue, and purple, and scarlet, may have reference to the graces of the Spirit, with which our Redeemer's humanity was adorned: his flaming zeal for his Father's glory and the good of his people, his bloody wounds, sufferings and death, the preciousness of his blood, the dignity of his person, and his glorious exaltation; purple and scarlet being the colours worn by kings.

This veil of separation was made 'with cherubims' embroidered in it. Something wonderful and magnificent is in this. The cherubims were made as one piece of beaten work of gold with the mercy seat (Exodus 25:17-20). They were embroidered into the curtain over the tabernacle. And they were embroidered in this veil of separation. Why? Because Christ and his people are one.

Its Position
Third, the position of the veil is highly significant and instructive. In verse 32 we read, 'And thou shalt hang it upon four pillars of shittim wood overlaid with gold: their hooks shall be of gold, upon the four sockets of silver'. The veil was so large, so thick and heavy that it took four pillars to hold it. John Gill suggested these pillars represent the divinity of our Saviour, which upheld and sustained his humanity in all his undertakings and accomplishments as our Substitute, giving merit, virtue and efficacy to all. The shittim wood overlaid with gold spoke of the eternality of our Redeemer and his accomplishments for us which are eternal. The veil was hung upon hooks of gold and set upon sockets of silver, linking God and man through the atonement.

This thick, heavy veil of separation was hung directly in front of the mercy seat. It separated the holy of holies from the holy place. Symbolically, it separated God from man. This, too, is simply magnificent. The veil of separation, the very thing that separated God from man, represented him by whom God and man are reconciled. There was no access to God but through this veil. And it is through Christ Jesus alone that poor, fallen sinners have access to God. Our Saviour declares, 'I am the Way' (John 14:6).

Aaron, Israel's high priest, could enter in behind the veil only once a year, and then only with the blood of the paschal lamb. What a solemn time that must have been for God's priest! As he pushed the heavy veil aside, he knew he was pushing his way into the presence of God, before whom no man can stand without the blood he symbolically carried in his hand. As he pushed the veil of separation aside, the priest was saying symbolically, 'The incarnate God must be removed, taken away by death, before man can come to God. Christ must be removed. The holy One must be put to death before man can, through his sin atoning blood, enter into fellowship with God.'

The Rending of the Veil

Fourth, look, now, at the rending of the veil. The fullest and most delightful explanation of the veil of separation was given in the moment of our Lord's death on the cross. When the Lord Jesus bowed his sacred head and gave up the ghost, immediately, we are told, 'the veil of the temple was rent in twain, from the top to the bottom' (Matthew 27:51). By the invisible hand of the invisible God, the veil was ripped from the top to the bottom.

The meaning of this is obvious. From the highest heaven to the lowest earth, Christ Jesus has opened a new and living way by his blood. Not only has he entered himself within the veil, but he has entered in as the Forerunner of his redeemed; and we shall, most assuredly, follow him, that where he is there we shall be also.

As the Lord Jesus has, by his death, opened a new and living way for his people, so he has broken down all the veils of separation between himself and his redeemed. The Jew and the Gentile were now brought into one fold. The veil of mysteries hidden from men in ages past, of ordinances and shadows of the law, has been taken away in his holy mountain the church.

'And in this mountain shall the LORD of hosts make unto all people a feast of fat things, a feast of wines on the lees, of fat things full of marrow, of wines on the lees well refined. And he will destroy in this mountain the face of the covering cast over all people, and the veil that is spread over all nations. He will swallow up death in victory; and the Lord GOD will wipe away tears from off all faces; and the rebuke of his people shall he take away from off all the earth: for the LORD hath spoken it. And it shall be said in that day, Lo, this is our God; we have waited for him, and he will save us: this is the LORD; we have waited for him, we will be glad and rejoice in his salvation' (Isaiah 25:6-9).

The veil was divinely rent. It was rent from the top. Rent from above, rent by God. Had it been the work of man it would have been torn from the bottom. Though it is true that 'with wicked hands' men crucified and slew the Lord of glory, yet, our Saviour died by the will of God, by the hand of God, and for the glory of God. It was God who made our sins to meet on him and made him sin for us (2 Corinthians 5:21). The veil was rent from the top; the hands of God were stretched forth, they took hold of it and opened it up, indicating that the death of his beloved Son has met every claim of righteousness and justice, setting before us open access to the mercy seat.

The veil was rent in the midst. Not down the side. It was no side entrance Christ made for us by his sin atoning blood! The ark, with its mercy seat and Shekinah glory, stood in the centre of the Holy of holies and close to the veil. The veil, being rent in the midst, was rent right in front of the mercy seat. The veil was rent in twain. It did not fall to pieces and was not torn to shreds. The rent was clean and straight. Perhaps this exact division into two parts symbolized the separation of Christ's soul from his body in death. Perhaps it symbolized the throwing open of the great door between earth and heaven, as John saw in his vision, indicating the complete reconciliation of the fellowship between God and his people by the blood of Christ (2 Corinthians 5:17-21; Revelation 4:1, 2).

The veil was completely rent. Not a thread was left in the way. Grace began it and grace completed it. 'It is finished!' Christ has, indeed, perfected that which concerns us. Every difficulty in God's way of saving men is now removed and removed by God himself. Sin has been put away. Justice has been satisfied. Righteousness is brought in. The law has been fulfilled, completely and forever fulfilled, for us by our Substitute.

The veil was rent from the top to the bottom. It was not rent from side to side, nor from the bottom to the top, which might have suggested it was simply worn out from usage. It was rent from the top to the bottom, showing that the power which rent it was from above, not from beneath; that the rending was not of man but of God. It was man that crucified the Lord of glory, but, 'it pleased the Lord to bruise him; He hath put him to grief'. Beginning with the roof and ending with the floor, the rending was complete; for God in heaven had done it. From the roof to floor there remained not one fragment of the old veil. So from heaven to earth, from the throne of God, down to the dwelling of man, there exists not one remnant nor particle of a barrier between sinners and God.

He who openeth and no man shutteth, has with his own hand, in his boundless mercy, love, and grace, thrown open to the chief of sinners the throne of grace, and bids us come in and draw near (Hebrews 4:16).

The rent veil declares that Christ is the end of the law. He finished and fulfilled it. He satisfied and completed it. Now, we have free and open access to the throne of God. The rending of the veil was done, as if the temple itself mourned for and testified abhorrence at the crucifixion of Christ. The temple rent, as it were, its garments at the death of its Lord. The veil was rent to show that the Lord, who had taken up his residence in the most holy place between the cherubim, over the mercy seat, in thick darkness, had now moved out and left the house desolate. The rending of the veil signified the rending of Christ's flesh, the breaking of his body for us, which was typified by the veil (Hebrews 10:20).

The veil was rent to signify the clear, full, revelation of God and his saving grace proclaimed in the gospel, proclaiming the way into the holiest of all, into heaven itself, where Christ is who entered by his own blood as our Forerunner (Hebrews 10:9-22).

The veil was rent in the presence of the Jewish priests. They were in the holy place, outside the veil, of course, officiating, lighting the lamps, or placing incense on the golden altar, or arranging the shewbread on the golden table. When they saw the solemn rending of the veil, they must have been shocked and terrified. I can picture them covering their eyes lest they should see the hidden glories of that holy chamber they were forbidden to enter. Perhaps Isaiah's words rang in their ears, 'Woe is me, for I am undone; I am a man of unclean lips, and I dwell among a people of unclean lips; for mine eyes have seen the King, the Lord of Hosts' (Isaiah 6:5).

But the veil was rent before their eyes to disclose the true mercy seat, Christ Jesus, our Saviour, and the glory of God. It is no longer profanity to handle the holy things of the sanctuary, or to gaze upon the golden floor and walls all stained with sacrificial blood, or to go up to the mercy seat and sit down beneath the very shadow of the glory of God. Indeed, the safest and the most blessed place for our needy souls is the Mercy-Seat, Christ Jesus. Come into the holy place and handle him (1 John 1:1-3; 2:1, 2).

The veil was rent at the time of the evening sacrifice. About three o'clock, when the sun began to set, the lamb was slain and laid upon the brazen altar. Just at the moment when its blood was shed, and the smoke arose from the fire that was consuming it, the veil was rent in twain. There was an unseen link between the altar and the veil, between the sacrifice and the rending, between the blood-shedding and the removal of the barrier. It was blood that had done the work. It was blood that had rent the veil and thrown open the mercy seat: the blood of 'the Lamb, without blemish, and without spot'.

The veil was rent precisely at the moment when the Son of God died on the cross. His death did it. His death opened God's heaven for our souls. His death opened for us the way of life and brought us into life. It was from the cross that the power emanated which rent the veil. From that place of weakness, and shame, and agony, came forth the omnipotent command, 'Lift up your heads, O ye gates, and be ye lifted up, ye everlasting doors'. The 'it is finished' upon Golgotha was the appointed signal; and the instantaneous response was the rending of the veil. The pierced hands of our accepted Sacrifice rent the veil separating God and man. It was the cross of Christ that rent the veil and opened the new and living way into the holiest of all.

When the veil was rent, the cherubim which were embroidered on it were rent with it. Those cherubim symbolized the Church of God's elect. Being embroidered into the veil, we see a picture of our identification with Christ in his death. We were nailed with him to the cross. We were crucified with him. With him we died, and were buried, and rose again. In that rent veil we have the symbol of the apostle's doctrine, concerning our union and oneness with Christ in life and death. 'I am crucified with Christ.' 'Ye are dead, and your life is hid with Christ in God.'

The rent veil declares that all the law is fulfilled, satisfied, and ended. 'Christ is the end of the law for righteousness to everyone that believeth.' 'There is therefore, now, no condemnation to them that are in Christ Jesus.'

The broken body and shed blood of our Lord opened the sinner's way into the holiest. These were the tokens of grace and of righteousness. The rending of the veil was not merely an act of God's power. It was not merely an act of his grace. Righteousness did it. Righteousness rolled away the stone. Righteousness burst the gates of brass and cut in sunder the bars of iron. The barrier of separation has been righteously removed. We have a righteous as well as a gracious entrance into the holy place. God gives sinners a righteous as well as a gracious welcome at his throne.

That which the blood of bulls and goats could never do, Christ has done with his own precious blood. Thank God forever, his is better blood! It knocks but once, and the gate flies open. It but once touches the sword of fire, and it is quenched. Not a moment is lost. The fulness of the time has come. God has unbarred the door. He has thrown open his mercy seat to poor, needy sinners, and rushes to receive his banished ones.

The veil has been rent in twain from the top to the bottom by the cross of our Lord Jesus Christ. The way is open. The blood is sprinkled. The mercy seat is accessible. The voice of our Great High Priest, seated on that mercy seat, bids us enter in, and enter in boldly, without fear. 'Having, therefore, boldness to enter into the holiest by the blood of Jesus, by a new and living way which He hath consecrated for us, through the veil, that is to say, his flesh, and having an high priest over the house of God, let us draw near with a true heart, in the full assurance of faith' (Hebrews 10:19-22).

Let us therefore enter in and find the mercy and grace we need in him. Entering in is our only security and our only joy. The only way we can enter in by Christ the Way is in the confident boldness of 'the full assurance of faith', trusting him alone as our all-sufficient, gloriously effectual Saviour. Not to come with such boldness is unbelief. Not to come in the full assurance of faith is presumption. To draw near with an 'evil conscience' is to declare our belief that the blood of the Lamb is not of itself enough to give the sinner a good conscience and fearless access to the throne of grace.

May I then draw near, just as I am, by the virtue and the efficacy of the sprinkled blood? Yes, I may. Yes, you may! How else could we come? May I be bold at once? Indeed, you may. If ever you see the blood upon the mercy seat, that will give you the boldness and full assurance of faith by which you may enter it. Do you see it? Has God the Holy Spirit given you eyes to see? Then come boldly. Come boldly now. Come in the full assurance of faith, not supposing it possible that God who has provided such a mercy seat can do anything but welcome you. Christ, our mercy seat is the place of pardon.

The rent veil is liberty of access. The sprinkled blood is boldness for needy sinners. The rent veil has a voice. The blood is the voice. It speaks pardon, peace, salvation, and eternal life to sinners. 'Today, if ye will hear his voice, harden not your heart'. Make haste and enter in!

Open Door

Verses 36 and 37 speak of the door of the tabernacle. The outer door, by which God's priests entered into the holy place.

'And thou shalt make an hanging for the door of the tent, of blue, and purple, and scarlet, and fine twined linen, wrought with needlework. And thou shalt make for the hanging five pillars of shittim wood, and overlay them with gold, and their hooks shall be of gold: and thou shalt cast five sockets of brass for them' (Exodus 26:36, 37).

Because Christ has entered into heaven, having obtained eternal redemption for us, chosen, redeemed sinners are made priests unto God (1 Peter 2:5-9; Revelation 1:6; 5:10). Entering in by Christ the Door, sinners like you and me are accepted in the holy place completely sanctified and 'meet for the Master's use' (2 Timothy 2:21), living in continual fellowship with the triune Jehovah!

Lord Jesus, come now in the hearts of your redeemed, and take away the veil of unbelief. Open to the comfort of our souls sweet, soul-ravishing views of your grace and glory. Just imagine, my brother, my sister, what a glorious object will that day, that wonderful day, open to our souls, when Christ Jesus removes the last veil in the resurrection, when our dear Lord appears in all his beauty to take his redeemed home to himself. Then, when we awake in his likeness, we shall be fully and eternally satisfied with his presence forever within the veil!

Chapter 96

Christ Our Altar

'And thou shalt make an altar of shittim wood, five cubits long, and five cubits broad; the altar shall be foursquare: and the height thereof shall be three cubits. And thou shalt make the horns of it upon the four corners thereof: his horns shall be of the same: and thou shalt overlay it with brass. And thou shalt make his pans to receive his ashes, and his shovels, and his basins, and his fleshhooks, and his firepans: all the vessels thereof thou shalt make of brass. And thou shalt make for it a grate of network of brass; and upon the net shalt thou make four brazen rings in the four corners thereof. And thou shalt put it under the compass of the altar beneath, that the net may be even to the midst of the altar. And thou shalt make staves for the altar, staves of shittim wood, and overlay them with brass. And the staves shall be put into the rings, and the staves shall be upon the two sides of the altar, to bear it. Hollow with boards shalt thou make it: as it was showed thee in the mount, so shall they make it.'
(Exodus 27:1-8)

As the chosen sinner came to worship God in the days of Moses, he would approach the tabernacle in the wilderness. It was not much to look at from the outside. It was a tent, covered with badgers' skins, surrounded by an enclosed court. There was only one way of access into the tabernacle, one gate or door, really just a curtain. But that was the only way the worshipper could come to God. He must come through that one entrance.

As he pulled back the curtain and passed through the door, the first thing he saw was a huge bronze altar 7½ feet wide, 7½ feet long, and 4½ feet high. It had four large horns, one on each corner. This great brazen altar was the first thing to meet the eye, as the sinner came to worship God. It is described here in Exodus 27:1-8, and again in Exodus 29:36, 37.

'And thou shalt offer every day a bullock for a sin offering for atonement: and thou shalt cleanse the altar, when thou hast made an atonement for it, and thou shalt anoint it, to sanctify it. Seven days thou shalt make an atonement for the altar, and sanctify it; and it shall be an altar most holy: whatsoever toucheth the altar shall be holy'.

This brazen altar was the place where the blood was shed, and the victim consumed in the fire. It was the place that gave meaning to everything else connected with the tabernacle. Without this brazen altar nothing was accomplished. This brazen altar typified Christ our Altar (Hebrews 13:10).

As the brazen altar was the very first thing the ancient worshipper saw as he approached the thrice holy God upon his throne, so Christ crucified is the first thing the sinner sees as he comes to God. The very first thing the Spirit of God teaches the heaven-born soul is accomplished redemption by the sacrifice and blood-atonement of the Lord Jesus Christ.

The brazen altar first arrested the eyes of any who drew near to God. Every eye must first behold the altar. Every step must first approach this hallowed structure. There is no coming to God any other way. So it is that all heaven-taught souls are made to acknowledge Christ Jesus as the Altar of the Church. 'We have an altar, whereof they have no right to eat which serve the tabernacle' (Hebrews 13:10).

Christ (his obedience, his blood, his sacrifice, his atonement) is first and foremost in the knowledge and worship of God. Let him be first and foremost in the affection of our hearts. Let him be first and foremost in all our doctrine, in all our preaching, in all our hymns of worship, in all our prayers, in all our praise!

That which is represented in the brazen altar is the sacrifice of Christ by which sinners are brought to God. This is the heart of the gospel; and this is the heart of all gospel preaching. The Lamb of God, our Lord Jesus Christ, died in our place as our Sacrifice. As the bloody offerings were brought to the altar, each was consumed by the fire on the altar.

But Christ is the Sacrifice that consumed the fire of God's holy wrath and justice. All the beauty of religion is vain without the blood of this altar.

Altar of Sacrifice
This brazen altar is called the altar of burnt offering in Exodus 40:29. It was the place of sacrifice. It stood in the court between the gate of the court and the tabernacle itself. The burnt offering, remember, was a sweet savour offering to the Lord (Leviticus 1:9).

'And the LORD called unto Moses, and spake unto him out of the tabernacle of the congregation, saying, Speak unto the children of Israel, and say unto them, If any man of you bring an offering unto the LORD, ye shall bring your offering of the cattle, even of the herd, and of the flock. If his offering be a burnt sacrifice of the herd, let him offer a male without blemish: he shall offer it of his own voluntary will at the door of the tabernacle of the congregation before the LORD. And he shall put his hand upon the head of the burnt offering; and it shall be accepted for him to make atonement for him. And he shall kill the bullock before the LORD: and the priests, Aaron's sons, shall bring the blood, and sprinkle the blood round about upon the altar that is by the door of the tabernacle of the congregation. And he shall flay the burnt offering, and cut it into his pieces. And the sons of Aaron the priest shall put fire upon the altar, and lay the wood in order upon the fire: And the priests, Aaron's sons, shall lay the parts, the head, and the fat, in order upon the wood that is on the fire which is upon the altar: But his inwards and his legs shall he wash in water: and the priest shall burn all on the altar, to be a burnt sacrifice, an offering made by fire, of a sweet savour unto the LORD' (Leviticus 1:1-9).

In fulfilling this picture, our Lord Jesus died upon the cursed tree as our sin offering; and his death is declared to be a 'sweet smelling savour' offering to God (Ephesians 5:2).

The brazen altar was made by the hands of men; but it was made according to the pattern and purpose of God. So, by the hands of men, our Lord was led outside Jerusalem and nailed to the cursed tree; but he died there according to the eternal decree and unalterable purpose of the triune God (Acts 2:23). Christ submitted to men that he might offer himself a burnt offering and sacrifice to God and a sin offering for chosen sinners (Hebrews 9:12, 26-28).

'Neither by the blood of goats and calves, but by his own blood he entered in once into the holy place, having obtained eternal redemption for us ... Now once in the end of the world hath he appeared to put away sin by the sacrifice of himself. And as it is appointed unto men once to die, but after this the judgment: So Christ was once offered to bear the sins of many; and unto them that look for him shall he appear the second time without sin unto salvation.'

That is redemption. The Lord Jesus Christ put away sin by the sacrifice of himself. The brazen altar was not a type, or emblem, or picture of the cross. The cross is not our altar. We glory in the gospel doctrine of the cross, Christ crucified, but not in the physical cross, or shape of the cross. The cross is not our altar. Christ is our Altar. The brazen alter typified our Saviour, but not the cross on which he died.

The altar was the place of sacrifice. Every animal sacrificed to God was laid out on this huge altar. How large it looked, with a little turtle-dove laying on it. Yet, how small it must have looked with a year old calf laying on it. But on what altar can the Christ of God place himself? What altar can sustain the weight of this sacrifice? The promised God-man came to die. What arms might be able to bear him up?

All things below are worse than worthless for such glorious use. If a structure could be raised, in which each stone were brighter than a million suns, it would be black beside him. Creation has nothing that can hold him. When Jehovah's own fellow came to die, none could possibly sustain him but himself. We cannot imagine the burdens that pressed him down. The least transgression of God's righteous law is a load beyond all thought. Its weight sinks the sinner deeper and deeper through unending ages in the unfathomable gulfs of hell!

But our Lord Jesus Christ bore all the weight of the countless sins of multitudes, when he was made sin for us. What could support him when the avenging fire of infinite justice fell, and he cried, 'My God, my God, Why hast thou forsaken me?' No angel could uphold the weight of such a sacrifice. The help of multiplied worlds would crumble into dust. Earth could supply no prop or pillar to sustain him. Where is the altar to hold this sacrifice? Christ himself is the Altar! Christ alone could uphold himself, with all the load and weight of our sin and our guilt, with all the load and weight of God's furious anger. Christ's only altar is himself. Hear him, as he speaks of his work and his sacrifice in Isaiah 63.

'I have trodden the winepress alone; and of the people there was none with me: for I will tread them in mine anger, and trample them in my fury; and their blood shall be sprinkled upon my garments, and I will stain all my raiment. For the day of vengeance is in mine heart, and the year of my redeemed is come. And I looked, and there was none to help; and I wondered that there was none to uphold: therefore mine own arm brought salvation unto me; and my fury, it upheld me.'
(Isaiah 63:3-5)

Pause now, my ransomed soul. Behold God's Altar and God's Offering. Christ stood as the sacrificing, fire-applying Priest. Christ came as the fire burned Lamb. Christ bore all as the fire-sustaining Altar. Christ died as the fire-consuming Sacrifice!

Yes, blessed be his name, our Lord Jesus Christ is the sacrifice that consumed the fire on the altar. This sacrifice satisfied forever the wrath, and fury, and justice of the holy Lord God. All was sufficient, for all was divine. There was enough in all, for God was in all. The wrath broke forth. The fury was poured out. Vengeance demanded her due. The law exacted its curse. But this one great burnt offering was fully adequate and satisfactory. Every divine attribute was magnified. Every sin of the whole family of God was expiated. Christ bore the whole, because he is the Altar of God's making, who is himself God. He is the Priest who made the sacrifice, the Sacrifice offered, and the Altar that sustained the Sacrifice. There is no sweeter thought on earth, there is no louder song in heaven, than praise to the Priest who offered, to the Lamb who suffered, to the Altar who sustained the whole.

The Components of the Altar

Look at the specified components of this great brazen altar and behold the magnificence of Christ our Altar. The shittim wood speaks of our Lord's humanity. The brass represents his deity. The frame was made of choice wood, combined, overlaid with, and encased in brass. The wood alone could not suffice. The flames would have consumed it. An altar of unmingled brass would be too heavy to carry through the wilderness. The union of wood and brass made an altar fit for its destined purpose (John 1:14). The altar was square, solid and strong, able to bear every weight put upon it. It stands the massive symbol of solidity. It cannot be overthrown. Faith sees this and rejoices. Christ our Altar is our stronghold. He is our Rock and our Salvation.

The altar had four horns. The horns represented power. Christ our Altar and our Sacrifice is omnipotent, prevailing, and effectual. Adonijah and Joab fled to the altar and took hold of its horns, hoping to escape the fury of King Solomon; but they were slain holding the horns of that physical altar. If you flee to a physical altar, take refuge in a physical altar, and take hold of the horns of any physical altar, you will not escape the fury of God's wrath. But any sinner who takes hold of the horns of this Altar shall live forever. Christ's sacrifice alone is sufficient and efficacious for satisfaction, forgiveness, justification, and for victory of death, and hell, and sin, and Satan. Like the unicorn of scripture that pushes with power that none can resist, so our Lord Jesus Christ's sacrifice is an omnipotent, efficacious sacrifice. 'Canst thou bind the unicorn?' These four horns, one on each corner, show that Christ's one great sacrifice for sin reaches to the four corners of the earth.

Every Sacrifice
Every sacrifice was offered to God upon this one altar. No Israelite could get ceremonial absolution for his sins, or a blessing from the priest, except he come to this altar with a sacrifice. He claimed the victim laid on the altar as his substitute, laying his hands upon its head, and was accepted. He was pronounced ceremonially clean. Everything and everyone brought to the altar was sanctified and accepted by the altar. The altar's main design was to receive burnt offerings. Early in the morning, throughout the day, and at evening's close the flames were bright, the spire of smoke ascended. So it is today.

'And thou shalt offer every day a bullock for a sin offering for atonement: and thou shalt cleanse the altar, when thou hast made an atonement for it, and thou shalt anoint it, to sanctify it. Seven days thou shalt make an atonement for the altar, and sanctify it; and it shall be an altar most holy: whatsoever toucheth the altar shall be holy' (Exodus 29:36, 37).

What wondrous, blessed words are those! 'Whatsoever toucheth the altar shall be holy!' Me, my prayers, my praise, my service, my gifts, my insignificant cup of cold water, my very life, all I am is accepted of God by Christ my Altar (Ecclesiastes 9:7-10).

'We have an altar, whereof they have no right to eat which serve the tabernacle. For the bodies of those beasts, whose blood is brought into the sanctuary by the high priest for sin, are burned without the camp. Wherefore Jesus also, that he might sanctify the people with his own blood, suffered without the gate. Let us go forth therefore unto him without the camp, bearing his reproach. For here have we no continuing city, but we seek one to come. By him therefore let us offer the sacrifice of praise to God continually, that is, the fruit of our lips giving thanks to his name' (Hebrews 13:10-15).

'To whom coming, as unto a living stone, disallowed indeed of men, but chosen of God, and precious, Ye also, as lively stones, are built up a spiritual house, an holy priesthood, to offer up spiritual sacrifices, acceptable to God by Jesus Christ' (1 Peter 2:4, 5).

'Go thy way, eat thy bread with joy, and drink thy wine with a merry heart; for God now accepteth thy works. Let thy garments be always white; and let thy head lack no ointment. Live joyfully with the wife whom thou lovest all the days of the life of thy vanity, which he hath given thee under the sun, all the days of thy vanity: for that is thy portion in this life, and in thy labour which thou takest under the sun. Whatsoever thy hand findeth to do, do it with thy might; for there is no work, nor device, nor knowledge, nor wisdom, in the grave, whither thou goest' (Ecclesiastes 9:7-10).

One Altar

There is but one Altar by which sinners can come to God; that is the Altar of God's own making, the Lord Jesus Christ (Exodus 20:24-26).

'An altar of earth thou shalt make unto me, and shalt sacrifice thereon thy burnt offerings, and thy peace offerings, thy sheep, and thine oxen: in all places where I record my name I will come unto thee, and I will bless thee. And if thou wilt make me an altar of stone, thou shalt not build it of hewn stone: for if thou lift up thy tool upon it, thou hast polluted it. Neither shalt thou go up by steps unto mine altar, that thy nakedness be not discovered thereon.'

Yet, in every age Satan erects many counterfeit altars. He decks them with gaudy disguises. He slopes them with a flowery path into his bewitching snare. He smooths with skilful hand the slippery ascent. He sets forth the altar of man's imagined worth. He causes a man to dream that dung, dug from his own bowels and shaped by his own foul hands, and beautified by the tools of his own heart's sewer, is an altar by which he can come to God. He raises the altar of man's mighty will. He erects the gradually ascending altar of man's imaginary holiness. He always puts man upon an altar that exposes his nakedness. Christ is the only Altar of God's making; and coming to God by this Altar, our nakedness is always completely covered.

Christ must be all, or nothing! He must do all the work, have all the merit, and possess all the glory. Every other altar stands on ruined ground and will carry you to hell. We must come to Christ the Altar, if we would come to God. But this is an Altar to which no man will come until the Sacrifice on the Altar has been brought to him (Isaiah 6:1-7). Isaiah experienced this. He saw the awful distance between his soul and God, and he cried, 'Woe is me'. His neighbour's sins troubled him more than his own in chapter five. He pronounced six woes upon others; but when he saw the holiness of the Holy One, his seventh woe was for himself. He passed judgment on himself and took his place in the dust. Then he saw the altar and its provision.

'In the year that king Uzziah died I saw also the Lord sitting upon a throne, high and lifted up, and his train filled the temple. Above it stood the seraphims: each one had six wings; with twain he covered his face, and with twain he covered his feet, and with twain he did fly. And one cried unto another, and said, Holy, holy, holy, is the LORD of hosts: the whole earth is full of his glory. And the posts of the door moved at the voice of him that cried, and the house was filled with smoke. Then said I, Woe is me! for I am undone; because I am a man of unclean lips, and I dwell in the midst of a people of unclean lips: for mine eyes have seen the King, the LORD of hosts. Then flew one of the seraphims unto me, having a live coal in his hand, which he had taken with the tongs from off the altar: And he laid it upon my mouth, and said, Lo, this hath touched thy lips; and thine iniquity is taken away, and thy sin purged'. (Isaiah 6:1-7)

Oh, may God bring you to himself by Christ our Altar, our Sacrifice, our Priest, our All in all! Amen.

Chapter 97

The Tabernacle Fence: Christ Our Mediator

'And thou shalt make the court of the tabernacle: for the south side southward there shall be hangings for the court of fine twined linen of an hundred cubits long for one side: And the twenty pillars thereof and their twenty sockets shall be of brass; the hooks of the pillars and their fillets shall be of silver. And likewise for the north side in length there shall be hangings of an hundred cubits long, and his twenty pillars and their twenty sockets of brass; the hooks of the pillars and their fillets of silver. And for the breadth of the court on the west side shall be hangings of fifty cubits: their pillars ten, and their sockets ten. And the breadth of the court on the east side eastward shall be fifty cubits. The hangings of one side of the gate shall be fifteen cubits: their pillars three, and their sockets three. And on the other side shall be hangings fifteen cubits: their pillars three, and their sockets three. And for the gate of the court shall be an hanging of twenty cubits, of blue, and purple, and scarlet, and fine twined linen, wrought with needlework: and their pillars shall be four, and their sockets four. All the pillars round about the court shall be filleted with silver; their hooks shall be of silver, and their sockets of brass. The length of the court shall be an hundred cubits, and the breadth fifty everywhere, and the height five cubits of fine twined linen, and their sockets of brass. All the vessels of the tabernacle in all the service thereof, and all the pins thereof, and all the pins of the court, shall be of brass. And thou shalt command the children of Israel, that they bring thee pure oil olive beaten for the light, to cause the lamp to burn always. In the tabernacle of the congregation without the vail, which is before the testimony, Aaron and his sons shall order it from evening to morning before the LORD: it shall be a statute forever unto their generations on the behalf of the children of Israel.' (Exodus 27:9-21)

In the first part of this chapter we see Christ our Altar portrayed in the brazen altar. Here we see Christ our Mediator portrayed in the linen fence surrounding the tabernacle.

'And thou shalt make the court of the tabernacle: for the south side southward there shall be hangings for the court of fine twined linen of an hundred cubits long for one side' (Exodus 27:9).

The tabernacle court was about 175-180 feet long and 75-80 feet wide. What a small enclosure for those who were worshippers of the one and only true and living God! It seems to have been, even in its size, a declaration that God's people in this world are few among many, 'a remnant according to the election of grace'. Yet, few as they are, even now, in this Gospel Age the measure of the true tabernacle, the Church of God is beyond the calculation of man (Malachi 1:11; Matthew 18:20). The 'hangings for the court of fine twined linen' (Exodus 27:10-21) formed the fence around the tabernacle.

Oil and Priests

The 'pure oil olive beaten for the light' is typical of God the Holy Spirit in all his gifts, graces, and operations bestowed upon the church. None but he can enlighten the darkened minds of poor, lost, and ruined sinners. He alone gives us the light of the knowledge of the glory of God in the face of Jesus Christ.

'Then answered I, and said unto him, What are these two olive trees upon the right side of the candlestick and upon the left side thereof? And I answered again, and said unto him, What be these two olive branches which through the two golden pipes empty the golden oil out of themselves?' (Zechariah 4:11, 12).

It is by God the Holy Spirit that God's servants are called and gifted for their work. By this 'pure oil olive' their lips, as golden pipes pouring out the oil, preserve the knowledge and worship of God from one generation to another. The 'oil olive beaten' signifies the labour of God's servants in the Word, as they prepare their messages and their hearts to shine forth the light of the gospel.

The work of God's priests, as declared in verse 21, shows us the work of God's servants in his house. The pastor, the gospel preacher, is to rule the house of God as a husband is to rule his house (1 Timothy 3:5), ordering the worship of God by the revealed will of God given in Holy Scripture. If we would worship God, we must worship him 'in spirit and in truth' (Philippians 3:3) 'after the due order' (1 Chronicles 15:13).

The Fence
The whole structure was enclosed by a fence made of white linen which hung from sixty pillars, twenty on each side and ten on each end. Revelation 3:12 shows us that these pillars represented the church of God's elect, 'the Israel of God', 'the pillar and ground of the truth' (1 Timothy 3:15). Remember, the number twelve and multiples of twelve, of which sixty is, are used in Scripture to represent God's Israel.

'Him that overcometh will I make a pillar in the temple of my God, and he shall go no more out: and I will write upon him the name of my God, and the name of the city of my God, which is new Jerusalem, which cometh down out of heaven from my God: and I will write upon him my new name' (Revelation 3:12).

The four pillars of the eastern end, facing the rising sun, formed the gate of entrance into the tabernacle. The tabernacle was God's designated dwelling place. The camp was the dwelling place of the people. This linen fence stood between God and man. I remind you again that the tabernacle, in all its parts and in all its furnishings, in all its sacrifices and ceremonies, set forth our Lord Jesus Christ in his being, work, and glory as our God and Saviour.

Our Mediator
Linen, being made from the fibres of the flax plant, is an earthly thing. It is used in the Scriptures to represent the righteousness of God's saints (Revelation 19:8). Our righteousness is our Lord Jesus Christ (1 Corinthians 1:30). This linen fence, standing between God and man, speaks of our Saviour's perfect humanity, symbolizing Christ our Mediator, specifically symbolizing his accomplishments as our Mediator.

A mediator is one who takes an official, legal, and accepted position between two parties that are at odds. He is a Daysman, a go-between,

331

who offers something that will satisfy both parties. By satisfying each, he is able to reconcile them and make them friends. That is what the Lord Jesus Christ is to us; our perfect, God-man Mediator (1 Timothy 2:5; Hebrews 8:6, 12:24).

Brass Bottoms

The tops of the pillars were silver. The bottoms, or bases, were brass (Exodus 27:10). The brass, from which the bottoms of these pillars was formed represents the righteousness of Christ our Mediator.

Brass is a composition that will stand the test of fire; and fire is set forth in Scripture as a symbol of the judgment of God (Isaiah 29:6, 30:30, 66:15). What can stand the test of the fire of divine judgment? Righteousness, perfect righteousness, and nothing else (Nahum 1:5, 6; Isaiah 59:16; 63:1-5).

Man's righteousness is obnoxious to God. It is an offence. Our imaginary, pretended righteousness is the most foul, filthy, obnoxious thing in the universe to the Holy Lord God. Our righteousnesses are filthy rags before him (Isaiah 64:6). Offer the holy God your righteousness, and you will be eternally ruined, consumed by his fury, destroyed in his wrath, and damned forever in hell.

How, then, can I be saved? I must have righteousness, perfect righteousness, a righteousness worthy of, accepted by and well pleasing to the holy Lord God, a righteousness that has endured the fire. You and I can never stand in God's presence with anything short of perfect righteousness. It must be righteousness of infinite merit; but it must be the righteousness of a man. That is what the linen fence represents, righteousness accomplished and brought in by the doing and dying of the Son of God, our God-man Mediator!

When God the Holy Spirit comes to a sinner in the saving operations of his grace, giving the chosen, redeemed sinner faith in Christ, he convinces that sinner of righteousness. He convinces the redeemed sinner that righteousness has been finished, accomplished, and brought in by the obedience of Christ, righteousness with which God himself is well pleased (John 16:7-11).

Silver Tops

But God requires more than righteousness. Sin must be punished. Justice must be satisfied. God demands atonement (satisfaction), the satisfaction of his holy justice. That is what is represented by the silver tops on those sixty pillars, set in sockets of brass in the linen fence encompassing the tabernacle.

As no man can bring in righteousness, so no mere man can satisfy the justice of God, even for himself, let alone another. But the Son of God, who came to earth in a 'linen' body, the God-man Mediator, Christ Jesus, did. As the sockets of brass typified the righteousness of Christ that has stood the furious fire of God's holy wrath and judgment for us, the tops of silver typified the silver of our Saviour's precious blood, his atonement, by which justice has been satisfied and sin has been put away. Silver was frequently used in the ceremonies of the law in connection with atonement (Exodus 30:12-16; Leviticus 5:15, 16).

Christ's obedience as our God-man Mediator is our righteousness before God, our only righteousness. His obedience is the righteousness imputed to us, reckoned to be ours, in justification (Romans 5:19; 2 Corinthians 5:21). And his righteous nature is the righteousness imparted to us, formed in us, in sanctification and regeneration, making us 'partakers of the divine nature' (2 Peter 1:4), giving us that 'holiness without which no man shall see the Lord' (Hebrews 12:14). It is this righteousness in which we shall be raised and into which we shall be transformed, in glorification at the last day, and the righteousness for which we shall be rewarded in the day of judgment. Christ alone is our righteousness. He is our righteousness and all who are born of God are made the righteousness of God in him (Jeremiah 23:6; 33:16). His precious blood, the atonement he obtained by his blood, the blood by which our sins were put away at Calvary, is our only atonement for sin (2 Corinthians 5:17-21; Galatians 3:13, 14).

The sixty pillars portray God's elect, all saved sinners. The sockets of brass pictured Christ our righteousness. The tops of silver typify Christ our atonement, our redemption. The linen fence was representative of the Man Christ Jesus, our Mediator, by whom, in whom, and with whom we have righteousness and atonement, by whom, in whom, and with whom we stand accepted before the Holy Lord God. By the pure silver of his blood and the pure gold of his Deity, by the white linen of his perfect righteousness in our humanity, he is our God-man Mediator and Saviour!

The Son of God was obedient unto death for us. He met our sentence and expiated our guilt when he was made sin for us. And, as he was made sin for us, that he might be damned in our stead, we are made the righteousness of God in him, that we might live in him. The believer is joined to Christ as one spirit (1 Corinthians 6:17). We are members of his body, bone of his bone, and flesh of his flesh (Ephesians 5:30). I cannot explain that, but I can believe it and rejoice in it. I am one with Christ and Christ is one with me! That is the message of God the Holy Spirit in the tabernacle's linen fence, with its pillars and their silver tops and brass sockets. Christ is our God-man Mediator, by whom God is reconciled to us and we are reconciled to God.

Chapter 98

God's Priest And God's Priests

'And take thou unto thee Aaron thy brother, and his sons with him, from among the children of Israel, that he may minister unto me in the priest's office, even Aaron, Nadab and Abihu, Eleazar and Ithamar, Aaron's sons. And thou shalt make holy garments for Aaron thy brother for glory and for beauty. And thou shalt speak unto all that are wise hearted, whom I have filled with the spirit of wisdom, that they may make Aaron's garments to consecrate him, that he may minister unto me in the priest's office. And these are the garments which they shall make; a breastplate, and an ephod, and a robe, and a broidered coat, a mitre, and a girdle: and they shall make holy garments for Aaron thy brother, and his sons, that he may minister unto me in the priest's office … And Aaron shall bear the names of the children of Israel in the breastplate of judgment upon his heart, when he goeth in unto the holy place, for a memorial before the LORD continually … And thou shalt put in the breastplate of judgment the Urim and the Thummim; and they shall be upon Aaron's heart, when he goeth in before the LORD: and Aaron shall bear the judgment of the children of Israel upon his heart before the LORD continually … And thou shalt make a plate of pure gold, and grave upon it, like the engravings of a signet, HOLINESS TO THE LORD. And thou shalt put it on a blue lace, that it may be upon the mitre; upon the forefront of the mitre it shall be. And it shall be upon Aaron's forehead, that Aaron may bear the iniquity of the holy things, which the children of Israel shall hallow in all their holy gifts; and it

shall be always upon his forehead, that they may be accepted before the LORD ... And thou shalt embroider the coat of fine linen, and thou shalt make the mitre of fine linen, and thou shalt make the girdle of needlework ... And for Aaron's sons thou shalt make coats, and thou shalt make for them girdles, and bonnets shalt thou make for them, for glory and for beauty. And thou shalt put them upon Aaron thy brother, and his sons with him; and shalt anoint them, and consecrate them, and sanctify them, that they may minister unto me in the priest's office. And thou shalt make them linen breeches to cover their nakedness; from the loins even unto the thighs they shall reach: And they shall be upon Aaron, and upon his sons, when they come in unto the tabernacle of the congregation, or when they come near unto the altar to minister in the holy place; that they bear not iniquity, and die: it shall be a statute for ever unto him and his seed after him.'
(Exodus 28:1-43)

The Lord Jesus Christ is our one and only sin atoning High Priest, our only Advocate and Heavenly Intercessor before God. We call no man a priest but the God-man our Saviour. We pray to none, worship none, and revere none but that man who is God, the Lord Jesus Christ. Yet, every saved sinner is, in and with Christ, a priest. God's elect are called by God the Holy Spirit 'an holy nation' and 'a royal priesthood' (1 Peter 2:9). Christ makes all his redeemed to be priests unto God (Revelation 1:6; 5:10; 20:6). Priests are the members of the priestly family, those who live upon the sacrifice of God, ever doing business in the holy place, serving God in the sanctuary.

In Exodus 28, Aaron represents Christ, our great, sin atoning High Priest; and Aaron's sons represent believing sinners, you and me, whom Christ has made priests unto God forever. The Lord Jesus is called both the Apostle and the High Priest of our profession in Hebrews 3:1. An apostle is one who comes out from God with a message to men. A priest is one who goes in to God on behalf of men. The Lord Jesus Christ is both our Apostle from God and our High Priest before God. He came from God, and he went back to God. The great work of the priest was to minister unto the Lord (28:3). 'I delight to do thy will, O my God', is the language of our great High Priest; and that is our souls' great delight, if we are among those walking in the white robes of God's holy priesthood (Revelation 1:6).

I urge the reader, before he proceeds, to read the twenty-eighth chapter of Exodus, the eighth chapter of Leviticus, and the seventh chapter of the book of Hebrews. Read all three chapters consecutively, asking God the Holy Ghost to give you understanding as you read.

God's Priest

Aaron, God's priest, was typical of the Lord Jesus Christ, our great High Priest. The priest had to be ceremonially perfect. No man that had a blemish of any kind could offer the offering of the Lord (Leviticus 21:23). And our High Priest, the Lord Jesus, was 'holy, harmless, undefiled, and separate from sinners' (Hebrews 7:26). Man could find no fault in him, and God was infinitely pleased with him. But there is much more to the type before us than ceremonial perfection. Everything we are told about Aaron in Exodus 28 and Leviticus 8 is typical of Christ.

The first thing mentioned in this chapter is God's calling and appointment of Aaron to be Israel's high priest. 'No man taketh this honour unto himself, but he that is called of God, as was Aaron' (Hebrews 5:4). 'Every high priest is ordained' of God (Hebrews 8:3). Even so, the Lord Jesus Christ, our High Priest, was chosen and appointed of God. He is the only divinely ordained High Priest, the only 'mediator between God and man' (1 Timothy 2:5).

Not only was Aaron called, in Leviticus 8:6 we are told he and his sons were washed with water. They must be clean who bear the vessels of the Lord. Aaron is a brilliant type of Christ; but our Lord Jesus needed no such washing. Obviously, this washing was required to show us that though we are one with our Saviour, God's elect must be washed with the washing of regeneration by the Word as well as redeemed with the blood of atonement.

Third, God commanded Moses to clothe his priest with such magnificent garments as are described in this chapter for specific reasons. For his own glory and beauty (vv. 2, 40). To consecrate him as one worthy to minister before the Lord in the holy place (v. 3). That he might bear the names of the children of Israel before the Lord continually (v. 12). That he might, with Light (Urim) and Perfection (Thummim) bear the judgment of the children of Israel upon his heart continually (v. 30). That he might bear the iniquity of the holy things, and yet be accepted and die not (v. 38).

The coat, the robe, and the ephod were put upon him. And our great High Priest was robed in garments of glory and beauty. These holy robes were typical both of his character and of his righteousness, the garments of salvation he puts upon us.

Fourth, the priest was crowned. The mitre, or holy crown, was put on his head. The priestly dress was not complete without the crown (Zechariah 3:1-5). The priest must be one fit to wear a crown. The Mediator between God and man must be one able to wear and worthy of the glorious crown. The crown of holiness is his by right.

Fifth, Aaron was anointed. 'Moses poured the anointing oil upon Aaron's head' (Leviticus 8:12). The anointing Spirit was poured out on the head of God's Beloved as he stood by the Jordan. The Spirit, like a dove, crowned him with glory and honour. He is the Lord's Anointed.

Sixth, Aaron was sprinkled with the blood, consecrated to the work, and had his hands filled for the Lord (Leviticus 8:24-27). He was claimed by God as his priest; and God filled his hands with the work he must perform.

'And he brought Aaron's sons, and Moses put of the blood upon the tip of their right ear, and upon the thumbs of their right hands, and upon the great toes of their right feet: and Moses sprinkled the blood upon the altar round about. And he took the fat, and the rump, and all the fat that was upon the inwards, and the caul above the liver, and the two kidneys, and their fat, and the right shoulder: And out of the basket of unleavened bread, that was before the LORD, he took one unleavened cake, and a cake of oiled bread, and one wafer, and put them on the fat, and upon the right shoulder: And he put all upon Aaron's hands, and upon his sons' hands, and waved them for a wave offering before the LORD' (Leviticus 8:24-27).

The voice from Heaven said, 'This is my beloved Son', as the Father claimed the Saviour. The Spirit was given unto him without measure; and his hands were filled. His holy hands were indeed filled for God and for man (Matthew 1:21).

Aaron, the priest, fed on the bread of consecration (Leviticus 8:31; 21:22). The holy bread was his. What none other could touch was his by right of his character as priest. The Lord Jesus once said to his disciples, 'I have meat to eat that ye know not of'.

'And Moses said unto Aaron and to his sons, Boil the flesh at the door of the tabernacle of the congregation: and there eat it with the bread that is in the basket of consecrations, as I commanded, saying, Aaron and his sons shall eat it' (Leviticus 8:31).

'He shall eat the bread of his God, both of the most holy, and of the holy' (Leviticus 21:22).

No man that had a blemish could come nigh to offer the offering of the Lord (Leviticus 21:23). The Lord Jesus Christ, our High Priest, was 'holy, harmless, undefiled, and separate from sinners' (Hebrews 7:26). No blemish could be found in him.

God's Priests

As Aaron was typical of Christ, God's Priest, Aaron's sons represented God's priests, who belong to that 'royal priesthood' of saved sinners, all who come to God by faith in Christ. May God the Holy Spirit now take the things which are Christ's and reveal them to us, showing us they are ours by virtue of our union with him. Both here in Exodus 28 and in Leviticus 8, I see some matters of tremendous importance and blessedness, though they are commonly missed by those whom I have read in my studies.

First, the names of the priest and the priests are constantly set before us in very close association. Twenty-eight times we read these words together 'Aaron and his sons'. They were chosen together. They were called, ordained, and accepted together. They were clothed with the holy garments together.

Oh, the depths! We were chosen in Christ 'before the foundation of the world'. Called, clothed, and accepted with him as one with him from eternity!

Aaron's sons were all priests by birth; so are we. We are priests because we are sons. We are the sons of God, blood relatives to the Great High Priest, bone of his bone, flesh of his flesh.

Second, Aaron and his sons had the same calling. Their hands were filled with the same work. 'As my Father hath sent me', says our Lord Jesus, 'even so send I you' (John 20:21). He has made us priests unto God. Let all who are born of God and called, abide in our high and holy calling.

Third, Aaron and his sons had the same white linen garments. Aaron had robes of glory and beauty that belonged to him alone. They were distinctly his as God's only high priest. Yet, all his sons wore the pure linen garments he wore. Undoubtedly, there are glories that belong to the Lord Jesus as the divine and eternal One which we can never possess; but, like him, we are clothed with fine linen, clean and white.

With His spotless garments on
Holy as the Holy One!

Fourth, they had the same anointing. They were accepted by the same blood and anointed with the same oil. Christ entered into the holy place by his own blood, and so did we in and with him. The same Spirit that came upon him is our anointing, the unction of the Holy One (1 John 2:27). How unerring the type. The oil was first poured upon Aaron's head before it was given unto his sons. The Spirit was given unto Christ without measure that he might give the Spirit to his redeemed. 'The promise is unto you, and to your children' (Acts 2:39; Galatians 3:13, 14).

Fifth, both Aaron and his sons had their hands filled with the same offering. We have nothing else to offer God on our behalf than that which Christ, our Aaron, offered. We wave before the Lord that which our blessed Lord Jesus waves: obedience; his perfect righteousness, and satisfaction; our complete atonement.

Sixth, both Aaron and his sons ate the same food. They fed on the same holy bread. The Lord Jesus lived by faith, so must we. His soul rested on and was strengthened by the promises of his Father. This also is our high privilege. We live as he lived, walking with God by faith. He 'leaving us an example, that we should follow his steps' (1 Peter 2:21). But I think there is more here. As our Lord's sacrifice satisfies him as our just God and Saviour, so it satisfies our souls!

Seventh, Aaron and his sons were priests by the same authority. They had their rightful place in the holy place by the sacrifice they brought, because they were ordained of God to bring the sacrifice.

Priestly Garments
The garments set before us in this chapter, made specifically for God's priest and his priests, reveal much about both our great Saviour and the poor souls saved by his accomplishments as our Great High Priest.

The coat was made of 'fine white linen', and worn next to the body. 'Fine linen is the righteousness of the saints' (Revelation 19:8). The white linen is given to cover nakedness, our sin and shame.

340

The robe was worn over the white linen coat and was 'all of blue'. It was 'curiously wrought', and 'without seam'. As the 'white linen' speaks of the perfect man, so 'all of blue' speaks of the Lord from Heaven. 'Curiously wrought' in his incarnation, and, with regard to his eternal existence, 'without seam'. This robe of blue was worn by the high priest alone. It represents something belonging to Christ which cannot be put upon his people: his eternal Godhead.

Attached to the skirt of this robe were 'golden bells' and 'pomegranates'. The bells speak of a harmonious, joyful sound. 'Fear not ... I bring you good tidings of great joy ... for unto you is born ... a Saviour, which is Christ the Lord' (Luke 2:10, 11). The bells and pomegranates, with their joyful sound ringing in the court, seem to speak of the joy with which our blessed Saviour performed and performs his work as our Great High Priest!

The ephod of the priestly attire was worn above the 'robe of blue'. It was made of the same materials as the veil, 'blue, purple, and scarlet'. We have the same order here as in the curtains. The white coat represents the character and the righteousness of Christ.

There was also a girdle connected with the ephod, made of the same materials. The girdle speaks of service. Thus, we learn that even while the priest was clothed with these 'robes for glory and beauty', he was still in the attitude of serving. Our great High Priest, now seated upon his throne and robed with glory and beauty, still wears the golden girdle of service, ever serving his elect (Revelation 1:13).

The breastplate was nine inches square, and formed with 'cunning work of gold, blue, purple, and scarlet' (Exodus 28:28). It was not to be 'loosed from the ephod'. It is therefore typical of something which belongs to Christ as our Mediator. Twelve stones were sewn in it in four rows, one for each tribe in Israel, bearing their names. Thus, the high priest carried the people of God on his bosom, written on his heart. This is a precious thought for everyone redeemed by the blood of Christ. We are ever remembered by him, ever before him. Our place with him is on his heart, held up before God, and ever accepted in him. The priest could not take off the breastplate without stripping himself of his garment of glory.

The Urim and Thummim were mysterious stones connected with the breastplate, they mean 'Lights and Perfections' and were used when seeking to know the mind and will of the Lord (Numbers 27:21; 1

Samuel 28:6). We are not told how, but in some way God's mind was revealed through them. Perhaps they either brightened or grew dim according to God's 'Yes' or 'No'. Is not our Lord Jesus the Light and Perfection by which sinners are led and brought into the kingdom of light? Perhaps the Urim and Thummim have reference to the work of God the Holy Spirit, the great gift that has come to his people by our Lord's entrance into heaven (Hebrews 9:12; Galatians 3:13, 14). As the Urim and Thummim, through the high priest, revealed the will of God, the Holy Spirit, coming to us through Christ our High Priest, leads us into all truth.

The mitre was the head piece, or 'holy crown' of the priest. It was made of fine white linen and had a plate of pure gold in the forefront, with these solemn words clearly engraved upon it, 'HOLINESS TO THE LORD' (Exodus 28:36). While the truth taught here is a deeply humbling one, it is full of comfort. This holy crown was put upon Aaron that he might bear the 'iniquity of the holy things'. There is in our most holy things much to mar and disfigure them; but our Representative and High Priest is crowned with holiness, and we are in him, one with him. Our service to our God is as fully accepted as his!

It is added 'It shall be always upon his forehead, that they may be accepted before the LORD' (Exodus 28:38).

'Who is he that condemneth? It is Christ that died, yea rather, that is risen again, who is even at the right hand of God, who also maketh intercession for us' (Romans 8:34).

Who or what can separate us from him who has bound us to his shoulder and his heart with the cords of love and power? I am nothing; he is everything. Of myself I can only say, 'Unclean!' But he is 'Holiness to the LORD'. 'Ye are complete in him', perfect, entire, lacking nothing!

Chapter 99

The Urim And The Thummim

'And Aaron shall bear the names of the children of Israel in the breastplate of judgment upon his heart, when he goeth in unto the holy place, for a memorial before the LORD continually. And thou shalt put in the breastplate of judgment the Urim and the Thummim; and they shall be upon Aaron's heart, when he goeth in before the LORD: and Aaron shall bear the judgment of the children of Israel upon his heart before the LORD continually.'
(Exodus 28:29, 30)

The Urim and the Thummim are mentioned five times in the Scriptures (Exodus 28:30; Leviticus 8:8; Deuteronomy 33:8; Ezra 2:63; and Nehemiah 7:65). Yet, these two pieces in the breastplate of God's high priest were very significant and typically instructive. The first time they are mentioned is here in Exodus 28.

Typical Priesthood
Aaron was an eminent type and picture of our Great High Priest, the Lord Jesus Christ, as God the Holy Ghost tells us in Hebrews 7.

'But this man, because he continueth ever, hath an unchangeable priesthood. Wherefore he is able also to save them to the uttermost that come unto God by him, seeing he ever liveth to make intercession for them. For such an high priest became us, who is holy, harmless, undefiled, separate from sinners, and made higher than the heavens; Who needeth not daily, as those high priests, to offer up sacrifice, first for his own sins, and then for the people's: for this he did once, when he offered up himself. For the law maketh men high priests which have infirmity; but the word of the oath, which was since the law, maketh the Son, who is consecrated for evermore' (Hebrews 7:24-28).

As Aaron was a priest chosen and appointed by God himself, the Lord Jesus is the Priest of God's choice and God's appointment. As Aaron alone made atonement ceremonially for the sins of Israel on the day of God's appointment, the Lord Jesus by the sacrifice of himself made real atonement for God's true Israel on the day appointed by God from eternity. As Aaron ministered in the holy place, representing God's chosen nation, the Lord Jesus ministers in heaven itself, representing God's elect. As Aaron's priesthood was ceremonially effectual for all Israel, securing the blessing of God upon the people of Israel, Christ's priesthood is in reality effectual for all God's true Israel.

Moses put the special, holy garments of the High Priest upon Aaron by God's command, those holy garments made specifically as the Lord God had prescribed: the coat, girdle, robe, ephod, breastplate and mitre. Those holy garments were put on Aaron to symbolize what our Lord has done for us. Christ did not wear ceremonial garments of a priest. Our High Priest made garments of salvation and put them on us.

Moses, symbolizing the law of God, put the golden plate, the holy crown, on Aaron's head. There never was a priest in Israel who was also a king, yet the priestly garments were not complete without this holy crown on the head of the high priest (Zechariah 3:1-5). Why? Aaron represented the Lord Jesus, who is a Priest upon a throne, a Royal Priest. Christ is the Priest who wears the crown as Zion's King.

There are many things about Aaron and his priestly garments that are highly symbolical and instructive. But, perhaps, that which is given the least consideration by commentators is the Urim and the Thummim. These two aspects of Aaron's priestly attire are often ignored, but they are highly instructive. I want to show you what I can of their meaning.

Their Meaning
'Urim' means 'lights' and 'Thummim' means 'perfections', both words are always plural. There is no way for us to know what the Urim and Thummim were. The Scriptures never tell us what they were, only what their use and purpose were; and history gives nothing but tradition and speculation. Intriguing as it might be to look at the possibilities of what they were, I will leave that alone. This much we know from the Word

of God. The Urim and Thummim were placed along with the names of the twelve tribes of Israel in the breastplate worn by Aaron. Specifically, they were worn upon the heart of God's high priest. And it was by these, through the intercessory work of the high priest, that God gave direction to the children of Israel and settled all important matters of judgment and justice, as Moses tells us in verse 30.

'And thou shalt put in the breastplate of judgment the Urim and the Thummim; and they shall be upon Aaron's heart, when he goeth in before the LORD: and Aaron shall bear the judgment (the verdict and the discernment) of the children of Israel upon his heart before the LORD continually.'

Joshua was required to follow the direction of God's priest, who sought God's counsel by the Urim before the Lord (Numbers 27:21). The Urim and Thummim were lost during the time of the Babylonian captivity and never recovered. This is apparent from the instructions given by Nehemiah in the rebuilding of the temple at Jerusalem.

'And the Tirshatha (Governor - Nehemiah) said unto them, that they should not eat of the most holy things, till there stood up a priest with Urim and with Thummim' (Ezra 2:63).

Jehovah's Holy One

With those words, the Holy Spirit showed the deficiency and imperfection of the Levitical priesthood and the great need of another priest, not after the order of Aaron, but after the order of Melchizedek, a great High Priest over the house of God, with whom would be the true Urim and Thummim. That is the priest of whom Moses spoke in the prophecy of Deuteronomy 33:8.

'And of Levi he said, Let thy Thummim and thy Urim be with thy holy one, whom thou didst prove at Massah, and with whom thou didst strive at the waters of Meribah' (Deuteronomy 33:8).

The Lord Jesus Christ, our Saviour and Redeemer, is Jehovah's 'Holy One'. He is the holy God and the holy man. In fact, the words of Deuteronomy 33:8, 'thy holy one', might better be translated 'the man, thy holy one'. Christ alone fits that character. He is 'the man, God's holy One' in his conception and birth, in his nature, and in all the acts and deeds he performed. Thus, he is a suitable High Priest for his people, 'holy, harmless, undefiled, separate from sinners, and made higher than the heavens'.

Not only is Christ the 'Holy One' spoken of here, he is also that One whom Israel 'didst prove at Massah and with whom Israel didst strive at Meribah' in the wilderness (Exodus 17:1-7). 'For he is our God; and we are the people of his pasture, and the sheep of his hand. Today if ye will hear his voice, harden not your heart, as in the provocation, and as in the day of temptation in the wilderness: When your fathers tempted me, proved me, and saw my work' (Psalm 95:7-9).

The true Urim (Lights) and Thummim (Perfections) belong to and are found in the Lord Jesus Christ, our Saviour. Deuteronomy 33:8 might be properly paraphrased, as John Gill suggested, 'And of the tribe of Levi, he said, Let thy Thummim and thy Urim (or thy Perfections and thy Lights, O God) be with thy Holy One, Christ Jesus, whom thou, O Levi, with the rest of the tribes of Israel, didst tempt at Massah, and strive with at the waters of Meribah.'

Christ The Urim
Our Lord Jesus Christ is the true Urim and Thummim, the true lights and perfections of his people. All light and perfection are found in Christ and only in Christ. Apart from Christ there is no light of any kind; and apart from him there is no perfection. 'For it pleased the Father that in him should all fulness dwell' (Colossians 1:19). 'In whom are hid all the treasures of wisdom and knowledge' (Colossians 2:3).

Christ is the Urim. Christ is the Light in whom all light is found and from whom all light comes. Light on the earth is but the reflected light of the sun, so the light that is in us is but the reflection of Christ, who is the Sun of our souls and the Light of the world. 'That was the true Light, which lighteth every man that cometh into the world' (John 1:9).

All natural light in men comes from Christ. The light of nature in fallen man is nothing compared to what it was before the fall. Yet, there is a sense in which all men are enlightened by Christ. This natural light is not sufficient to save; but it does render all men without excuse before God. By this natural light, given by Christ, all men and women know God is, know he is holy, mighty, and to be worshipped. This light even causes the natural man, to some degree, to know the difference between good and evil, and the necessity of an atonement for sin to satisfy his offended Creator. This light of Christ, sometimes called 'the light of nature', also teaches natural, unregenerate men and women how to behave, at least in measure (Romans 1:20; 2:14, 15).

When John says that Christ is that true Light, 'which lighteth every man that cometh into the world', he is not talking about the light of grace that comes to regenerate men in the new creation. Christ does not give every man the light of grace. There are many who never even receive the light of the gospel, much less the light of grace. Besides, in the context, John is not talking about the new creation of grace, but about the physical creation and the things of nature (John 1:3, 4). As all men have their natural life and being from Christ, their divine Creator, the Creator of all things, so all men have all natural light from him.

The light of grace is found in and comes from Christ as well. When I speak of the light of grace, I mean that spiritual light which comes to poor sinners born in darkness, raised and living in darkness, walking in darkness, and loving darkness. Light causes them to be made 'light in the Lord'. The light of grace causes sinners to see what they could not see before; their lost condition, the depravity of their hearts, the guilt of sin, the necessity of a Redeemer, the fulness and glory of Christ as their Redeemer, and the finishing of redemption and salvation by him.

Sinners enlightened by Christ, enlightened with the enlightenment of grace, testify with the man in John 9:25 'One thing I know, that, whereas I was blind, now I see'. God's saints are called 'children of light', because we have been called by the almighty, irresistible power and grace of God the Holy Spirit out of darkness into light, out of the darkness of depravity, death, and sin, into the marvellous light of life, grace, and righteousness in Christ. If anyone receives this light, it is by the gift and grace of Christ our God (Ephesians 5:14). If any are called to light, it is by Christ. If any walk in the light, they walk in Christ. He is given of God the Father, 'a Light to lighten the Gentiles'.

Christ gives us the light of the perfections and attributes of God. It is true, as we have already seen, that some of God's perfections are shown forth in creation to all men. But the light of the knowledge of the glory of God is manifest and made known only in the face of Jesus Christ our crucified, risen, and exalted Saviour (2 Corinthians 4:6). He is the brightness of the Father's glory, the express image of his Person. Salvation is more than a religious creed, experience, or feeling. Salvation is knowledge of the living God as he is revealed and made known in Jesus Christ (John 7:3).

Unbelievers know God as Creator. Believers are people who know God in Christ. We see the wisdom of God in the scheme of salvation by

Christ. We see the riches of his mercy, love, and grace in the mission of Christ as our Surety. We see the justice and grace, holiness and truth, faithfulness and severity of the Almighty in the sufferings and death of Christ as our Substitute. Indeed, in Christ crucified we see the perfect harmony of all the attributes of God, fully displayed, entirely satisfied, and in complete agreement (Psalm 85:10; Proverbs 16:6).

His Own Light

We see the sun in its own light, it being impossible for us to see it in any other light than its own. So we see Christ, the Sun of Righteousness, in his own light, and it is impossible for us to see him in any other (John 1:14). In his own light we see him as the brightness of the Father's glory and the express image of his Person. In his own light we see him as the only Mediator between God and men. In his own light we see him as the only and all-sufficient Saviour for guilty sinners. In his own light we see the glory and efficacy of his sin atoning blood, whereby he has perfected forever them that are sanctified. In his own light we see the perfection of his justifying righteousness. In his own light we see the treasures of grace and glory laid up in him for believing sinners.

The light of the knowledge of the gospel and the glorious truths of the gospel are from Christ, who is the Light and the Truth. Christ, by his Spirit, opens our understanding and causes us to learn the Scriptures. It is Christ who gives regenerate men and women to understand the mysteries of the kingdom. He sends his Spirit to his elect as the Spirit of Truth, to lead us into all truth. Otherwise, the Bible would be to us, as it is to all the world, a sealed Book, full of riddles, contradictions, and outdated morals. David understood this and prayed for light from Christ to understand the Word of God. We would be wise to follow his example. 'Open thou mine eyes, that I may behold wondrous things out of thy law' (Psalm 119:18).

The Light of Glory

As the light of nature and of grace is from Christ, the true Urim, so too is the light of glory. Heaven is a world, a state, a condition of blessed, glorious, eternal, satisfying light. The inheritance of God's saints is called the inheritance of light (Colossians 1:12). All the light of heaven's glory is Christ, God's Urim (Revelation 21:23). Soon, we will safely arrive in our glorious, heavenly, eternal home with Christ. Once we have reached Canaan's fair and happy land, we shall walk in perfect light forever! All the lingering darkness of infidelity, doubt, and fear that vexes us here will be completely dispelled in the twinkling of an eye. Our very souls will be radiant with the beams of light from Christ which shall forever strike our hearts with wonder, joy, and praise.

'The sun shall be no more thy light by day; neither for brightness shall the moon give light unto thee: but the LORD shall be unto thee an everlasting light, and thy God thy glory. Thy sun shall no more go down; neither shall thy moon withdraw itself: for the LORD shall be thine everlasting light, and the days of thy mourning shall be ended' (Isaiah 60:19, 20).

Christ the Thummim

Do you see what I have been talking about? The Urim is Lights; and Christ is the Light. He is the true Urim. The lights of nature, grace, and glory all come from him. Now, I want you to see that our Lord Jesus Christ is the true Thummim, too. All perfections are found in him, fully, completely, and everlastingly. Whenever we think about perfections, let us only think of Christ. He comprehends them all and possesses them all. All the perfections of the triune God are in him. 'For in him dwelleth all the fulness of the Godhead bodily' (Colossians 2:9).

Is eternity a divine perfection? Christ is the eternal God (Revelation 1:8). Is omnipotence a divine perfection? Christ declares himself to be 'the Almighty' his name is 'the mighty God'. Is omniscience a divine perfection? It is in Christ. He knows the thoughts of the heart (John 21:17). Is omnipresence a divine perfection? Christ is the everywhere present God (Matthew 18:20). Is immutability a divine attribute? Christ is the same yesterday, today, and forever (Hebrews 13:8). All the perfection of the gifts of the Spirit are in Christ and flow to us from Christ (Psalm 68:17-20).

All the perfection of grace is in Christ and comes to chosen, redeemed sinners through Christ and for Christ's sake. Our all-glorious Christ is full of grace. All justifying grace is in him and comes from him. All sanctifying grace, all preserving grace, all glorifying grace is in him and comes from him. Christ is our wisdom, righteousness, sanctification, and redemption. He is that holiness we must have, without which no man shall see the Lord. Indeed, in this matter of grace and salvation, 'Christ is all'.

All the perfection of the blessings and promises of God to sinners in the covenant of grace are in Christ. Christ is our Joseph. He owns and holds the keys to all the storehouse of God's grace. 'For all the promises of God in him are yea, and in him Amen, unto the glory of God by us' (2 Corinthians 1:20).

'Blessed be the God and Father of our Lord Jesus Christ, who hath blessed us with all spiritual blessings in heavenly places in Christ: According as he hath chosen us in him before the foundation of the world, that we should be holy and without blame before him in love: Having predestinated us unto the adoption of children by Jesus Christ to himself, according to the good pleasure of his will, To the praise of the glory of his grace, wherein he hath made us accepted in the beloved' (Ephesians 1:3-6).

We cannot come into any circumstance or condition but what there is a blessing and promise of God in Christ to meet our need, if only we had faith to see it and lay hold of it.

All the perfection of life is Christ himself. With him is the fountain of life. All the streams of life, particularly spiritual, eternal, everlasting life, flow to God's elect through him, through his mediation, merit, and power. Perhaps you ask, 'How is it that all life came to be in Christ the Mediator?' The answer is found in Psalm 21:4. As our Mediator and Surety, he asked his Father for it for all his seed, upon the grounds of his obedience and death; and the Father granted him his request. 'As thou hast given him power over all flesh, that he should give eternal life to as many as thou hast given him' (John 17:2). It was for this purpose that the Son of God came into the world, to remove all obstacles out of the way, that the streams of life might flow freely to his people forever.

All the perfection of strength is in Christ We are poor, weak, helpless creatures of flesh. Without him, we can do nothing. But Christ is the man of God's right hand, whom he has made strong for himself and for us. Though we can, of ourselves do nothing, we can do all things through Christ who strengthens us. The Lord is my Strength and my Salvation!

All the perfection of wisdom is in Christ. Christ is Wisdom (Proverbs 8). Without him, there is nothing but folly. And he is made of God unto us Wisdom to teach us, to guide us, and to protect us.

All the perfection of joy is found in our all-glorious Saviour. There is always a reason to rejoice in him: in his Person, in his righteousness, in his blood, in his intercession, his promises, and in his providence. All who worship God in the Spirit rejoice in Christ Jesus (Philippians 3:3).

All the perfection of comfort and consolation is in Christ as well. He is our Comfort and our Consolation. Any comfort and consolation found anywhere else is a deceit and a delusion (John 14:1-3).

Christ is the true Urim. All true light is in him and comes from him. And our great God and Saviour is the true Thummim. All perfections are in him and come from him.

Carried on His Heart

Look at Exodus 28:9-30 again. As Aaron, the typical high priest, carried the Urim and Thummim upon his heart, so Christ, God's true High Priest, carries his people upon his heart in all his priestly functions. He carries our judgment, our verdict and our discernment! Remember, the Urim and Thummim were carried upon the high priest's breastplate where the names of the twelve tribes of the children of Israel were engraved in precious stones. They were carried upon his heart before the Lord. This teaches us three glorious, soul-cheering gospel truths. God's elect are ever upon the heart of Christ, our great High Priest.

1. As the names of the children of Israel were upon Aaron's breastplate, so our names are engraved, not only upon the palms of his hands, but also upon our great Saviour's heart. He has set us as a seal upon his heart. We were upon his heart from eternity as the objects of his everlasting love. We were upon his heart when he came into the world to save us. We were upon his heart when he died at Calvary. We were upon his heart when he took his seat in heaven. We are upon his heart now and forever.

2. All Christ has done and shall do as our great High Priest, with the Urim and the Thummim, he does as our Representative, Mediator, and Substitute. When Aaron made atonement by sacrifice, he did so for the congregation of the Lord. So, Christ is sacrificed for us. He obtained eternal redemption with his own blood and entered and took possession of heaven as our Forerunner. He appears in the presence of God for us. He makes intercession for us. That is the very language of Holy Scripture. Thank God for particular grace and distinguishing love!

3. Christ, the true Urim and the true Thummim, is that One by whom we are guided and instructed. By the Urim and the Thummim God gave direction to his servants, and thus to his people.

'And he shall stand before Eleazar the priest, who shall ask counsel for him after the judgment of Urim before the LORD: at his word shall they go out, and at his word they shall come in, both he, and all the children of Israel with him, even all the congregation' (Numbers 27:21).

None but the high priest could ask counsel of God in the sanctuary. And Christ alone can speak to God for us. We cannot come to God without a Mediator, without a Priest, or without a Sacrifice. God's direction and blessing was sought upon the ground of Urim (Light) and Thummim (Perfection), upon the ground of God's omniscient judgment and absolute perfection being fully satisfied with Christ. Intercession was made and counsel sought for Israel alone, just as our Lord Jesus makes intercession for God's elect Israel alone. The Urim and the Thummim, all the lights and all the perfections of the triune God were engaged for a specific people. So, too, all that Christ does he does for a specific people, his redeemed, the people of his love!

And as that person for whom counsel was asked was to stand before the high priest, so we must each take our place before Christ, our great High Priest. We cannot come to God any other way, but by faith in his name. If the true Urim and Thummim, all true lights and perfections, are found in Christ, let us go to him for them. In our darkness, let us go to him for light. In our sinfulness, let us go to him for perfection.

If we are, as the elect of God, engraved upon the very heart of the Son of God, how dear we must be to him. Upon his heart we are loved. Upon his heart we are safe. Upon his heart we ought to be free of fear.

If Christ is our Urim and Thummim, our Light and our Perfection before God, we ought to confidently trust him to manage all our affairs. Trust him for our spiritual, eternal affairs; temporal, earthly affairs; domestic, family affairs. All our affairs!

'How delightful it is to see Jesus thus represented', wrote Robert Hawker, 'as bearing the persons of his redeemed, in his own light and perfection, when he goes in before the presence of God for us! Sweet and precious is the thought to the believer.'

This is no trivial matter. It is of such great importance that Moses, when dying, expressly prayed, 'Let thy Thummim and thy Urim be with thy Holy One'. O precious, glorious, gracious Lord Jesus, be the Urim and the Thummim, lights and perfections to our souls in grace here and in glory hereafter forever! Amen.

Chapter 100

'The Iniquity Of The Holy Things'

'And thou shalt make a plate of pure gold, and grave upon it, like the engravings of a signet, HOLINESS TO THE LORD. And thou shalt put it on a blue lace, that it may be upon the mitre; upon the forefront of the mitre it shall be. And it shall be upon Aaron's forehead, that Aaron may bear the iniquity of the holy things, which the children of Israel shall hallow in all their holy gifts; and it shall be always upon his forehead, that they may be accepted before the LORD.'
(Exodus 28:36-38)

How we lament the sin with which we serve our God! Our hearts mourn that evil is mixed with all we do. Our souls are heavy with the burden of felt iniquity when we read, or pray, or sing, or try to worship! We are compelled to lament, with John Newton, 'Sin is mixed with all I do!'

Here, in Exodus 28:36-38, the Spirit of God shows us a portion of Aaron's priestly garments that represents every covenant worshipper's condition before the Lord God. As the worshipper stood before the holy God represented by God's appointed priest and mediator, this part of Aaron's dress displayed both the personal iniquity and perfect holiness of the worshipper for whom Aaron stood. Here comes an ancient Israelite to worship the Lord God at the tabernacle. His heart is full of gratitude and praise. He understands the meaning of what was done for him on that great and glorious high day in Israel, the Day of Atonement. He appreciates and rejoices in the slain passover lamb and the scapegoat which foreshadowed Christ the Redeemer, in whom he trusted. He appreciates and rejoices in the Aaronic blessing ceremonially bestowed upon him through that sacrifice, symbolizing all blessings of grace and salvation bestowed upon chosen sinners, through the blood of Christ.

The worshipper comes with a gift of praise, a thank offering he wants to give to the Lord God his Saviour, for his glory, for his praise, just because he wants to. Ceremonially, he pictures a redeemed sinner, forgiven, accepted in the Beloved; justified and sanctified. Still, he cannot come to God except by God's high priest wearing this royal, mitre, with this plate of pure gold upon his forehead 'Holiness to the LORD'. The priest of God places the gift of the forgiven sinner upon the altar of God, bearing for the redeemed sinner 'the iniquity of the holy things … that he may be accepted before the LORD'.

As Aaron was set apart and distinguished from the common priests by his glorious garments, how glorious, how beautiful is the Lord Jesus in the eyes of God! How glorious and beautiful in our eyes! Spurgeon once said, 'The unveiled sight of him will be our heaven. Our present view of him is our salvation, comfort, strength, and sanctification.'

Why was Israel's high priest so majestically, so royally adorned? The Holy Spirit tells us, 'Such an high priest became us' (Hebrews 7:26). It was becoming for us to have the Lord Jesus, this gloriously arrayed High Priest. God himself declares, it is becoming that we should have a High Priest decked out in 'gold, and blue, and purple, and scarlet, and fine linen'. He has covered us with the robe of righteousness and made us comely with his comeliness which he has put upon us.

> Jesus, in Thee our eyes behold
> A thousand glories more,
> Than the rich gems, and polished gold,
> The sons of Aaron wore.

As Israel of old had need of one to bear the iniquity of their holy things, so you and I, as we come to our God with our gifts and sacrifices and thanksgiving, as we bring to him the praise of our lips and the services of our lives, must have One who is able to bear the iniquity of our holy things. We need one who is 'able to save them to the uttermost that come unto God by him, seeing he ever liveth to make intercession for them'. Blessed be his name, Christ Jesus our Lord is such an High Priest over the house of God! By the merit and efficacy of his perpetual intercession, by the merit and efficacy of his blood and righteousness, our Lord Jesus Christ makes us, our worship and service, our praise and sacrifices of thanksgiving 'accepted before the Lord'.

Jesus Christ the everlasting Representative by whom alone I come to God, by whom alone I offer myself and my sacrifices to the holy Lord God, is the One who wears upon his head the mitre of God's priest, and on his forehead the pure plate of golden 'Holiness to the Lord!'

Iniquity

The iniquity of our holy things is something we must recognize and confess (1 John 1:8-10). This is a subject we all prefer not to think about, let alone discuss. Oh, none of us minds a little self-deprecation. We take great pride in out-doing one another in that. But none of us wants to think about, 'The iniquity of the holy things which the children of Israel shall hallow in all their gifts'.

All we do for God and for others is deformed and tainted by our polluted hearts and dirty hands, both by human infirmity and sin. Even a casual scrutiny of our most saintly deeds discovers the leprosy of iniquity popping out in this body of flesh. Our apparent loveliness is horribly unlovely! Our greatest sanctity is evil! We have need to pray over our prayers, to weep over our tears, to repent of our repentance, and to confess the sin of our confessions!

When our most fervent prayer has been prayed, our most self-denying act performed, our most liberal offering given, our most powerful sermon preached, and our sweetest anthem poured forth, all must be bathed in the blood of Christ that 'cleanseth us from all sin'.

Holy Still

Yet, 'holy things' are still 'holy things' in God's sight, though they are holy things accompanied with our iniquity! Our prayers, our praises, our service to our God, these are holy things, though much iniquity accompanies them. They are holy because they are God's ordinances, things he has ordained for his own glory. He tells us to serve him. He calls for us to come to him in prayer. He has said, 'Whoso offereth praise glorifieth me'. And when we do what God tells us to do, the act is holy, because it is done in obedience to him, as the ordinance of God.

Such deeds are holy because they are designed to show forth God's glory. Those sacrifices the Israelites brought were meant to set forth Christ and his glorious work. That made them holy. They were 'hallowed' by the children to the Lord. So, our sacrifices, whatever they may be, are meant to be tokens of our gratitude, love, dedication, and homage to God our Saviour. Their design makes them 'hallowed', sanctified, holy things. Our heavenly Father teaches us much precious truth by every institution of the tabernacle, and the temple, and the gospel church; and that makes obedience to his ordinances holy.

These things called 'holy things' in the passage before us, were deeds that were holy in the intent of the worshipper. When he brought his turtle doves, or lamb, or bullock, he intended real reverence, true allegiance, and sincere gratitude to God. His intent was holy. Our God is so gracious that he calls our love, and faith, and labour, and patience, 'holy things', because he sees we truly desire to honour him by these things. He knows what is holy and what is not holy; and though there be a defilement about our 'holy things', yet holy things they are. I know they are 'holy things' because God himself calls them 'holy things'.

Iniquity Upon Them

They are 'holy things', yet there is iniquity upon our 'holy things'. You need no proof that there is much that must be called 'iniquity' in regard to our 'holy things'. Honest examination of our own hearts and lives will silence every objection. Our wandering thoughts in worship, our deadness in prayer, our meaningless Bible reading, our love of self, our love of the world, our lack of love for Christ, our lack of love for one another, the hypocrisy that defiles us, the littleness of our faith, our pride, the severity of our judgment regarding others, the contempt we display for others. If these are our 'holy things', how evil our other things must be! There is a terrible, indescribably horrible iniquity about our 'holy things'. A personal iniquity that makes all our righteousnesses filthy rags!

Holiness

Yet, in the same sentence in which the Lord God speaks of 'the iniquity' that is ours, iniquity by which we pollute everything, he also speaks of 'holiness', 'Holiness to the LORD!' How useful and striking the type!

'And thou shalt make a plate of pure gold, and grave upon it, like the engravings of a signet, HOLINESS TO THE LORD. And thou shalt put it on a blue lace, that it may be upon the mitre; upon the forefront of the mitre it shall be. And it shall be upon Aaron's forehead, that

Aaron may bear the iniquity of the holy things, which the children of Israel shall hallow in all their holy gifts; and it shall be always upon his forehead, that they may be accepted before the LORD.'

Thus, has Christ, our true Aaron, made a full atonement for the 'iniquity of our holy things' and the mitre is always upon his head, making both us and our offerings accepted before the triune Jehovah. This sweet gospel revelation is declared plainly in the Book of God.

'My little children, these things write I unto you, that ye sin not. And if any man sin, we have an advocate with the Father, Jesus Christ the righteous: And he is the propitiation for our sins' (1 John 2:1, 2).

In Jeremiah 2:3 the Lord God declares that Israel was 'holiness unto the LORD'. 'Moreover the word of the LORD came to me, saying, Go and cry in the ears of Jerusalem, saying, Thus saith the LORD; I remember thee, the kindness of thy youth, the love of thine espousals, when thou wentest after me in the wilderness, in a land that was not sown. Israel was holiness unto the LORD, and the firstfruits of his increase: all that devour him shall offend; evil shall come upon them, saith the LORD' (Jeremiah 2:1-3).

The word 'holiness' means 'sanctified' or 'consecrated'. That is what the Lord God declares us to be in and by Christ. 'Holiness to the LORD'! Being 'Holiness to the Lord', we have free access to him always (Jude 1; 1 Corinthians 6:9-11; Hebrews 10:10-14). Christ is our Holiness (Hebrews 12:14). He who is our Wisdom, Righteousness and Redemption, is our Sanctification, too (1 Corinthians 1:30). He perpetually makes us accepted before the Lord (2 Corinthians 5:7-21).

In Zechariah 14:20 the prophet of God declares that in this gospel day, even the horses shall have bells on their bridles that proclaim, 'Holiness to the Lord'. Horses are animals used for work, to pull a plough or a carriage. Zechariah is telling us that in Christ all our works, all our gifts, our labours for the glory of God are accepted of God, just as we are, just as Christ is, as 'Holiness to the LORD'. Is that not what the Spirit of God declares in 1 Peter 2:5? 'Ye also, as lively stones, are built up a spiritual house, an holy priesthood, to offer up spiritual sacrifices, acceptable to God by Jesus Christ.'

But there is more. In Zechariah 14:21 we are told that every pot in Jerusalem, that is, every utensil used by God's people in this world, every part of your life and mine, the totality of our lives, are, like the pots and bowls at God's altar in the temple 'Holiness to the LORD'.

'In that day shall there be upon the bells of the horses, HOLINESS UNTO THE LORD; and the pots in the LORD'S house shall be like the bowls before the altar. Yea, every pot in Jerusalem and in Judah shall be holiness unto the LORD of hosts: and all they that sacrifice shall come and take of them, and seethe therein: and in that day there shall be no more the Canaanite in the house of the LORD of hosts' (Zechariah 14:20, 21).

Imagine, that my brother! Imagine that, my sister! In Christ you are 'Holiness to the LORD'. Your gifts are 'Holiness to the LORD'. Your entire life is 'Holiness to the LORD'. I could not imagine such a thing, let alone say or write it, were it not plainly written in the Book of God by the Spirit of God.

'I beseech you therefore, brethren, by the mercies of God, that ye present your bodies a living sacrifice, holy, acceptable unto God, which is your reasonable service. And be not conformed to this world: but be ye transformed by the renewing of your mind, that ye may prove what is that good, and acceptable, and perfect, will of God' (Romans 12:1, 2). 'Go thy way, eat thy bread with joy, and drink thy wine with a merry heart; for God now accepteth thy works. Let thy garments be always white; and let thy head lack no ointment' (Ecclesiastes 9:7, 8) 'And thou shalt make a plate of pure gold, and grave upon it, like the engravings of a signet, HOLINESS TO THE LORD. And thou shalt put it on a blue lace, that it may be upon the mitre; upon the forefront of the mitre it shall be. And it shall be upon Aaron's forehead, that Aaron may bear the iniquity of the holy things, which the children of Israel shall hallow in all their holy gifts; and it shall be always upon his forehead, that they may be accepted before the LORD' (Exodus 28:36-38).

You and I are a people God calls holy, a people whose gifts he calls holy, a people whose lives he calls holy, because Christ bears the iniquity of our holy things always before the Lord. He bears the blood of our atonement always before the Lord, wearing the golden insignia of perfect holiness on his forehead as our High Priest, our Mediator, and our Surety!

Chapter 101

Are You A Consecrated Christian?

'And this is the thing that thou shalt do unto them to hallow them, to minister unto me in the priest's office: Take one young bullock, and two rams without blemish, And unleavened bread, and cakes unleavened tempered with oil, and wafers unleavened anointed with oil: of wheaten flour shalt thou make them ... Then shalt thou take the anointing oil, and pour it upon his head, and anoint him. And thou shalt bring his sons, and put coats upon them. And thou shalt gird them with girdles, Aaron and his sons, and put the bonnets on them: and the priest's office shall be theirs for a perpetual statute: and thou shalt consecrate Aaron and his sons ... And I will dwell among the children of Israel, and will be their God. And they shall know that I am the LORD their God, that brought them forth out of the land of Egypt, that I may dwell among them: I am the LORD their God.'
(Exodus 29:1-46)

A while back I read a few of those biographical blurbs men send out to advertise themselves. One advertised himself as a man whose 'heart beats for a church patterned after God's Word'. Another described himself as a man who 'has a passion to see believers live holy lives'. And a third said he is a man who 'possesses a genuine desire to lead his church in the purity of the gospel from both the pulpit and in his life'.

Those are very noble, laudable goals. But, when I read or hear about such goals, I want to know, 'What is a church patterned after the Word of God? Would that be a church like the church at Corinth, or the church at Galatia, or the church at Jerusalem, or the church at Colossae?' I want to know, 'By what means can I persuade believers to live holy lives? Is it possible for a person to be a believer and not be holy? Is holiness something we do, or something God gives? Are believers created in righteousness and true holiness? If we are, can we, by some means or other, lose it? If we lose it, can we get it back?' I want to know, 'How am I to lead people to live in the purity of the gospel, both from the pulpit and in my life? What is the purity of the gospel? Is it a revealed purity, or a purity I perform? Is it doctrinal purity, or a duty purity? Is it purity I proclaim, or a purity I promote and push on others?'

Being ignorant as I am about such lofty goals, I have searched the Scriptures for answers. And I have found the answers to my questions in Exodus 29. Are you a consecrated Christian? Carefully read the 46 verses of this chapter, asking God the Holy Ghost to give you the answer and you will find it. I am sure a hallowed and consecrated Christian is one whose life exemplifies the purity of the gospel and one who is holy. I am certain that a hallowed church, a consecrated church is a church reflecting the pattern of instruction given in God's Word.

In this chapter the Lord God told Moses how to consecrate Aaron and his sons as God's priests in his house. If I am consecrated to God, I must be consecrated to him just as Aaron and his sons were. If you are consecrated to God, you must be consecrated to him just as Aaron and his sons were. If we are consecrated Christians, we must be consecrated as they were. The first time the word 'consecrate' is found in the Bible is in this same context (Exodus 28:3); and the first time the word 'consecration' is used is here in Exodus 29. If there is any merit in the so-called 'law of first mention' then we may learn that to consecrate something is to hallow it, sanctify it, and make it holy. To set it as a gem in a piece of jewellery or in a crown.

All Are Priests
During the days of Moses and under the Mosaic law, only one family was allowed to serve God in the priestly office; but in this gospel day all God's saints are 'a chosen generation, a royal priesthood' (1 Peter 2:9). In the church of God no one group is set apart to the priesthood above the rest of their brethren. In this gospel day God's covenant promise is fulfilled in us. 'Ye shall be a kingdom of priests unto me.' God the Spirit tells us all to present our bodies a living sacrifice, holy acceptable unto God, which is our reasonable service.

It is the grand purpose of God in all the works of his grace, both for us and in us, to fit us for the office of the spiritual priesthood; and it will be the crown of our perfection when with all our brethren, we shall sing unto the Lord Jesus the new song, saying, 'Unto him that loved us, and washed us from our sins in his own blood, and hath made us kings and priests unto God and his Father; to him be glory and dominion for ever and ever'. According to 1 Peter 2, this honour belongs to every believer. It belongs even to new born babes in grace. If, even as you read these lines, you are born of God, you are born into God's priestly family. Every saved sinner forms a part of a holy priesthood, to offer up spiritual sacrifices, acceptable to God by Christ Jesus.

There is no such thing as 'clergy' and 'laity' in the church of God. We are all, in Christ, priests unto God. The Roman Church has its priests. The Episcopal Church has its priests. The Mormon Church has its priests. In each of these societies of wickedness; blind, ignorant, deluded men are kept in bondage and taught they cannot approach God except through the medium of a priest, who is himself only a sinful man. I tell you, on the authority of God's Holy Word, no man will ever draw near to God in faith, until he approaches God, not by the medium of some earthly priest, but through Jesus Christ, our only true Priest.

All who come to God by faith in the Lord Jesus Christ are themselves priests unto God. Every true believer in Christ Jesus is a priest, one who has perpetual access to God by faith through the merits of Christ, one who lives upon holy things at God's Altar continually.

We need no earthly priests, for we are priests ourselves. A person may not be able to read or write, but if he is truly converted, he is a priest unto God. You may not stand behind a pulpit, or lead the people of God in public prayer, but if you believe on Christ, you are a priest unto God. Our ladies are commanded of God to be silent in the public assembly of God's saints. Yet they too belong to this holy priesthood. All the children of God are priests. As in the Old Testament there was one sin atoning high priest, though all the sons of Aaron were priests in the service of God, even so, the Lord Jesus Christ alone is our great, sin atoning High Priest, and all the sons of God are priests in him.

A Chosen Family
The first thing I want you to see about the consecration, the holiness, the hallowedness set before us in Scripture is that it begins with God's

election. The Lord said to Moses, 'Take Aaron and his sons' (Leviticus 8:2; Exodus 28:1; 29:1-4). The priesthood was not something men decided upon, voted upon, or chose for themselves. Only those chosen, elected, and ordained by God were allowed to serve as priests (Hebrews 5:1-5; 1 Peter 2:5-9).

If you are a part of God's 'holy priesthood', it is because God from eternity chose you, elected you, and ordained you to be his own. Salvation does not begin with man's will, but with God's will. Salvation is not caused by man's will. It is caused by God's will. Men and women are not saved because they will to be saved. We are saved because God from eternity willed to save us. All who are born of God readily confess they are debtors to sovereign grace alone.

Aaron's family was a chosen family. He and his sons were specifically chosen by God to be his priests. 'No man taketh this honour upon himself, but he that was called thereunto as was Aaron.' Being chosen of God, Aaron and his sons were at God's command brought nigh unto the door of the tabernacle. None ever come to God except those who are brought to him. The King's spouse sings, 'He brought me into the banqueting house'. The Lord Jesus said, 'No man can come unto me except the Father which hath sent me draw him'. We are made nigh by the blood of Jesus and brought nigh by the irresistible drawings of God the Holy Ghost. Are you a chosen priest of God, brought to him by omnipotent mercy? Then, you will be interested in the ceremonies prescribed in the chapter before us. These ceremonies teach us how the Lord God makes chosen sinners priests in his holy nation.

Washed with Water

Verse 4 says, 'Aaron and his sons thou shalt bring unto the door of the tabernacle of the congregation, and shalt wash them with water'. The pure and holy God cannot be served by men of unclean hands and impure hearts. He would not embrace the unclean under the law; and he will not tolerate the unclean in this gospel day. He demands, 'Be ye clean that bear the vessels of the LORD', and, 'Be ye holy; for I am holy'. Those are unbending precepts. God will not accept that which is unclean. It was well said by the psalmist, 'I will wash mine hands in innocency, so will I compass thine altar, O LORD' (Psalm 26:6).

Moses (the Law) had to wash the priests. We must be washed in redemption (Zechariah 13:1) and we must be washed in regeneration

(Titus 3:3-7). Thus, both by the blood atonement of our Lord Jesus Christ and by the sanctifying operations of God the Holy Spirit, we are cleansed from all filthiness of the flesh and of the spirit, and made vessels fit for the Master's use (1 Corinthians 6:9-11).

Are you thus cleansed from all sin? Do you know, by the sweet experience of his grace, the blessedness of that man unto whom God will not impute sin? If so, 'being made free from sin, ye became the servants of righteousness'. God has made you a priest in his house.

Wondrously Clothed

After they were washed by Moses, the priests were wondrously clothed by him. 'And thou shalt take the garments, and put upon Aaron the coat, and the robe of the ephod, and the ephod, and the breastplate, and gird him with the curious girdle of the ephod: And thou shalt put the mitre upon his head, and put the holy crown upon the mitre. Then shalt thou take the anointing oil, and pour it upon his head, and anoint him. And thou shalt bring his sons, and put coats upon them. And thou shalt gird them with girdles, Aaron and his sons, and put the bonnets on them: and the priest's office shall be theirs for a perpetual statute: and thou shalt consecrate Aaron and his sons' (Exodus 29:5-9).

They must not wear one garment that belonged to them beforehand. Even their underwear was provided! Within and without their clothing was new, appropriate, divinely provided, and put upon them. They wore what was given, nothing more, nothing less. No man can serve God in filthy rags of his own righteousness. We must have both the fine linen of Christ's righteousness imparted and imputed for glory and beauty.

Every priest had a coat put upon him. These priestly coats were like the coat worn by our Lord Jesus, all of one piece, woven from top to bottom, hanging from the shoulder and draping the body. That coat represents the righteousness of Christ imputed to us from eternity and given to us at the moment of conversion (Leviticus 8:13).

Until God puts this robe upon you, you cannot serve him. But as soon as you come to Christ, he will put this robe upon you.

Every priest was also girded with a girdle. We are told that our Lord Jesus Christ, as our great High Priest, is 'girt about the paps with a golden girdle' (Revelation 1:13). That is the girdle of his faithfulness, truth, and love. And Christ Jesus gives each of his own a girdle of faithfulness, truth, and love.

Girdles were used as huge belts to hold up the long, flowing garments men used to wear and to lend strength and support to the body. Men engaged in labour, travel, or battle, strapped on a girdle to brace themselves and hold their robes up. Every priest of Christ is given a girdle of faithfulness to carry him through his appointed labours.

And each priest was given a bonnet, or a turban. These turbans distinguished the priests from other men. They were given for glory and beauty. This, too, applies to us. The Lord has made his people glorious, honourable, and beautiful in his own eyes. We are not merely accepted, but beloved. We are not merely washed, but admirable. We are not merely free from condemnation, but full of imparted beauty, being made new creatures in Christ and partakers of the divine nature (Ezekiel 16:8-14; 2 Corinthians 5:7; 2 Peter 1:4).

The Lord Jesus says to every saved sinner, 'Thou art all fair, my love; there is no spot in thee ... Thou hast ravished my heart' (Song of Solomon 4:7, 9). Our Saviour so admires the purity and perfection of each saved sinner, that his own heart is captured.

These garments were all provided for Aaron and his sons at no cost. They contributed nothing to the expense of buying them, or the labour of weaving them, or in the skill of making them. So it is with us. The garments of our salvation are ours freely, put upon us by God himself. And the priestly garments formed a complete suit, a complete outfit for priestly service. It is true, as Spurgeon wrote, 'They had no shoes upon their feet, but they would have been superfluous, for the place whereon they stood was holy ground. They were sandaled with reverence.'

All the dress provided was absolutely necessary to be worn. No priest was to offer sacrifice without the appointed garments, for we read, 'They shall be upon Aaron, and upon his sons, when they come in unto the tabernacle of the congregation, or when they come near unto the altar to minister in the holy place; that they bear not iniquity, and die' (Exodus 28:43).

Divinely Anointed

The priests of God were and are divinely anointed. 'Then shalt thou take the anointing oil, and pour it upon his head, and anoint him' (v. 7). Aaron was anointed with the holy oil poured upon his head. Then all the sons of Aaron were anointed (Leviticus 8:30). Even so, the Lord Jesus Christ was anointed with the Holy Spirit without measure; and all who are in Christ by faith are also anointed as priests unto God. All of God's elect have the anointing of the Holy Spirit symbolized by the holy oil (1 John 2:20, 27). I know men talk about this anointing of the Holy Spirit, as though it were some mystical, second work of grace, which some believers have, and others have not. But that is not the case. This anointing flows to all believers freely from and through the Lord Jesus Christ. According to John, the thing that distinguishes the believer from the unbeliever is this anointing of the Spirit (1 John 2:19, 20).

I do not suggest there are no demonstrations of divine power, special fillings of the Spirit, or manifestations of the Spirit's presence, by which we are enabled to carry out the work he would have us to do. Without the power of the Holy Spirit, our praying, preaching, worship, singing, witnessing, writing, all our labour for Christ is vain. We must have the Holy Spirit. I do not minimize his power or his work. Without him, we are nothing and we can do nothing for Christ. But understand, all of God's children are complete in Christ. The Holy Spirit is the 'Heirloom' our Saviour passed along to his children (Galatians 3:13, 14).

This anointing of the Spirit is our sanctification in the experience of grace. As Aaron and his sons were sanctified symbolically by the anointing oil poured out upon them, we are truly sanctified, made holy, by the Spirit of God's anointing in regeneration. In election we were set apart for holy purposes, separated unto God and sanctified (Jude 1). In redemption we were declared to be holy; sanctified by the blood of Christ (Hebrews 10:10). In regeneration we are made holy; sanctified by the grace of God imparting to us and creating in us a holy nature (2 Thessalonians 2:13), giving us that 'holiness without which no man shall see the Lord' (Hebrews 12:14).

A Sin Offering

Aaron and his sons, came to God and were accepted by God as his priests by one common sin offering (vv. 11-14). You know who our sin offering is! It is our blessed Christ! 'Now then we are ambassadors for Christ, as though God did beseech you by us: we pray you in Christ's stead, be ye reconciled to God. For he hath made him to be sin for us, who knew no sin; that we might be made the righteousness of God in him' (2 Corinthians 5:20, 21). See also 1 Peter 1:18-20; 2:24; 3:18.

The bullock of the sin offering being brought to the altar, Aaron and his sons were to lay their hands upon it. Read the tenth verse. They 'shall put their hands upon the head of the bullock'. The Hebrew word means more than lightly placing the hand; it gives the idea of pressing hard upon the bullock's head. They came each one and leaned upon the victim, each laying the burden of his guilt and sin upon God's appointed substitute. That is a picture of faith in Christ.

The bullock was killed by Moses (v. 11) a token that just as the poor beast was slain, so they deserved to die for their sins. The blood was caught in bowls and taken to the altar. There it was poured out, at the bottom of the altar, round about. There must have been a pool of blood all around the altar. What did it signify? Our only access to God is by blood! These men were washed and robed and anointed; and yet they could not come to the altar until the blood was poured out at the altar.

This done, the choice and more vital parts of the bullock were taken and burned upon the altar (v. 13). That was done to show that even when our Lord Jesus is viewed as our sin offering, he is still a sweet savour unto God. Though the Lord God hid his face from his Son when he made him sin for us, yet it is this very Saviour, this Substitute, this sin offering that is well -pleasing to God! Therefore, the inner pieces of the bullock were burned on the altar where nothing could be presented but that which was a sweet savour to God. Blessed, blessed Lamb of God!

But because the bullock was a sin offering, and therefore obnoxious to God, its flesh, and its skin, and all that remained were carried outside the camp and burned with a quick, consuming fire, as a thing worthy to be destroyed. Because sin was upon it, it must be burned up (v. 14).

The Burnt Offering

These priests were consecrated to God by blood, specifically by the blood of the burnt offering (vv. 15-18).

'Thou shalt also take one ram; and Aaron and his sons shall put their hands upon the head of the ram. And thou shalt slay the ram, and thou shalt take his blood, and sprinkle it round about upon the altar. And thou shalt cut the ram in pieces, and wash the inwards of him, and his legs, and put them unto his pieces, and unto his head. And thou shalt burn the whole ram upon the altar: it is a burnt offering unto the LORD: it is a sweet savour, an offering made by fire unto the LORD.'

This burnt offering differed widely from the sin offering. The sin offering indicated Christ as bearing our sin. The burnt offering portrays Christ as presenting an acceptable offering unto the Lord. God required of us perfect obedience; he demanded from us a pure and holy life. That is what we see in the burnt offering. We are consecrated to God by Christ's obedience unto death as our Surety.

Ram of Consecration
In verses 19-22, we read about the consecration of the priests to God by the blood of the 'ram of consecration' (v. 22).

'And thou shalt take the other ram; and Aaron and his sons shall put their hands upon the head of the ram. Then shalt thou kill the ram, and take of his blood, and put it upon the tip of the right ear of Aaron, and upon the tip of the right ear of his sons, and upon the thumb of their right hand, and upon the great toe of their right foot, and sprinkle the blood upon the altar round about. And thou shalt take of the blood that is upon the altar, and of the anointing oil, and sprinkle it upon Aaron, and upon his garments, and upon his sons, and upon the garments of his sons with him: and he shall be hallowed, and his garments, and his sons, and his sons' garments with him. Also thou shalt take of the ram the fat and the rump, and the fat that covereth the inwards, and the caul above the liver, and the two kidneys, and the fat that is upon them, and the right shoulder; for it is a ram of consecration' (Exodus 29:19-22).

The blood of Christ applied to our hearts by the Holy Spirit, causes us to be consecrated to the Lord. This consecration is not perfect, but it is entire. The whole man is consecrated to Christ. God's priests are not partially consecrated to Christ. They are entirely consecrated to him.

The believer's ear is consecrated to God by the blood of Christ. The consecrated ear hears the voice of God. The believer hears what unregenerate men cannot hear. He hears the voice of God in his Word, in the preaching of the gospel, and in providence. He listens not for an audible voice from heaven, but for the still, small voice within, saying, 'This is the way, walk ye in it'.

The believer's hand is consecrated to God by the blood of Christ. The hand refers to work and labour, and to all the activities of life. The believer is a person who works for God. All that he does is done with an eye to his God. Whether he eats or drinks, works in the factory or labours in the ministry, all he does, he does for the glory of God. His garments are praise. His meals are feasts unto the Lord. His work is service to God. All his days are sabbath days. The blood is upon his hand, so all he does is consecrated to God.

And the believer's foot is consecrated to God by the blood of Christ. As the ear refers to hearing and the hand to working, the foot refers to your manner of life as you travel through this world. The consecrated foot follows his Master. The believer's life is governed not by riches, pleasures, or comforts, but by Christ. He seeks not wealth, or even economic stability. He seeks Christ.

'Tell me, O thou whom my soul loveth, where thou feedest, where thou makest thy flock to rest at noon: for why should I be as one that turneth aside by the flocks of thy companions?' (Song of Solomon 1:7).

Consecrated feet carry people to the house of God, never away from it. Consecrated feet carry us in the way of obedience, never in the way of rebellion. Consecrated feet pursue the cause of Christ, not the interests of self. The whole man was thus consecrated to God by blood.

Remember, the priests were all barefoot before God, like Moses before the bush. They were always on holy ground, always in the presence of God. That which makes the ground upon which we walk through this world holy ground is the blood of consecration upon our right toe.

Then these consecrated priests, in their holy garments, had their hands filled with wave offerings and heave offerings of praise to God (vv. 23-29). In verse 30 we see that every priest, being consecrated to God, wore these garments of consecration for seven days. By these priests continually feeding upon the sacrifices they offered to God in the tabernacle, God promised to make himself known to Israel.

'This shall be a continual burnt offering throughout your generations at the door of the tabernacle of the congregation before the LORD: where I will meet you, to speak there unto thee. And there I will meet with the children of Israel, and the tabernacle shall be sanctified by my glory. And I will sanctify the tabernacle of the congregation, and the altar: I will sanctify also both Aaron and his sons, to minister to me in the priest's office. And I will dwell among the children of Israel, and will be their God. And they shall know that I am the LORD their God, that brought them forth out of the land of Egypt, that I may dwell among them: I am the LORD their God' (Exodus 29:42-46).

Are you a consecrated Christian? If you trust Christ you are, and as a priest unto God, you are accepted of God always (Ecclesiastes 9:7-10). Rejoice!

Chapter 102

The Other Altar

'And thou shalt make an altar to burn incense upon: of shittim wood shalt thou make it ... And Aaron shall make an atonement upon the horns of it once in a year with the blood of the sin offering of atonements: once in the year shall he make atonement upon it throughout your generations: it is most holy unto the LORD ... And as for the perfume which thou shalt make, ye shall not make to yourselves according to the composition thereof: it shall be unto thee holy for the LORD. Whosoever shall make like unto that, to smell thereto, shall even be cut off from his people.'
(Exodus 30:1-38)

In the twenty-seventh chapter of Exodus, we saw Christ our Altar magnificently represented in the great brazen altar that stood at the forefront of the tabernacle in the wilderness and at the forefront of all the ceremonial worship of the typical, Mosaic Age. How we thank God for our Altar, the one and only Altar, by which sinners can come to God, Christ Jesus! 'We have an altar, whereof they have no right to eat which serve the tabernacle' (Hebrews 13:10). The brazen altar of sacrifice typified our blessed Lord Jesus, the sin atoning Sacrifice, by whose blood we draw near to God.

But one altar alone was not sufficient to portray the work by which sinners are brought to God and find acceptance with him in Christ Jesus. The Lord God ordered another altar be made to represent our Redeemer, the Lord Jesus Christ, and our access to God by him. We read about the other altar in this chapter. This chapter speaks of five things in the tabernacle; the altar of incense (vv. 1-10), atonement money (vv. 11-16), a laver of brass (vv. 17-21), the anointing oil (vv. 22-33), and the incense (vv. 34-38).

The tabernacle in the wilderness, along with the priesthood, all the sacrifices, all the ceremonies and all the furnishings of the tabernacle, were designed to typify our Lord Jesus, our salvation by him and in him, and our worship of God in him. When the worshipping Israelite came to worship God, he could do so only in the way God prescribed. So it is with sinners today. If we worship God, we must worship him in the way he requires.

In the days of the tabernacle the sinner had to be typically redeemed. He must first be accepted by a sin atoning sacrifice offered upon, and consumed by, the fire of the brazen altar. The sacrifice had to be killed and offered by God's priest in the way God appointed. Then, the sinner, for whom atonement was made, had to be typically regenerated. He must wash in the laver of brass before the tabernacle. And the redeemed, regenerate sinner must be typically represented in the court of the tabernacle by God's priest. As God's priest went about the business of the holy place, we see the blood-bought, regenerate soul walking in the light of the golden candlestick – Christ our Light; feeding upon the bread of God upon the table of Shewbread – Christ our Bread spread upon the gospel table; perpetually accepted by the perpetual merit of Christ's shed blood – Christ our Passover sacrificed for us; who is our great High Priest and Advocate represented in the golden altar of incense before the tabernacle veil.

Its Purpose

'And thou shalt make an altar to burn incense upon' (v. 1). The altar of incense is not to be confused with the altar of burnt offering. No sacrifice was ever offered upon this altar. Nothing but incense was to be put upon its ever burning coals. The sacrifice was made outside, at the door of entrance. The incense of this blood-sprinkled altar speaks of the efficacious merit of Christ's sin atoning blood ascending up unto God, by which we have unceasing access to and acceptance with God on his throne (Hebrews 10:17-22).

Christ is our constant, all prevailing advocate on high (1 John 2:1, 2). It is through his precious name we make our requests known unto God. 'If ye ask anything in my name, I will do it' (John 14:14). 'His name is as ointment poured forth' (Song of Solomon 1:3). By him we and our works and our prayers and our praise are accepted of God (1 Peter 2:5).

Its Materials

This altar was made of incorruptible shittim wood (v. 1) overlaid with gold (v. 3) and had a crown of gold. There was a horn on each corner and a golden crown on top. It had four golden rings under the crown for the two staves by which it was to be carried. It occupied a position in the holy place directly in front of the veil. Burning coals were placed upon it and sweet incense was put upon the coals morning and evening. Fragrant white smoke ascended from it continually.

Like the great brazen altar outside, this altar of incense was also made of two different materials: not wood and brass as before, but wood and gold. Here, again, we see both the divinity and the humanity of Christ typified. In the brazen altar the wood was strengthened by the brass. In the altar of incense the wood, Christ's human nature, is glorified by the gold.

Gold was united with wood and Christ is the corresponding wonder. He who is equal to God in the Godhead's greatness is one with man in humanity's low state. He who rightfully sits upon Jehovah's throne willingly wears the rags of humanity. Such is the Saviour we have. Such is the Saviour we need! More cannot be needed. Less would be nothing.

He who was crucified in weakness has been raised in glory. He who was the 'man of sorrows' is now the Man in glory. He took upon himself the likeness of sinful flesh. Now that likeness, that body, our nature, our flesh, has been glorified in him. What an encouragement to prayer and faith and worship! Ever remember that the Lord of glory is still truly human! 'Consider him' (Hebrews 12:3). The altar of incense was much smaller than the one Ezekiel saw in his vision of the gospel day (Ezekiel 41:22), all things in the carnal worship of the legal dispensation were but 'a shadow of good things to come' (Hebrews 10:1). Now all worship is spiritual. 'God is a Spirit: and they that worship him must worship him in spirit and in truth' (John 4:24).

'For from the rising of the sun even unto the going down of the same my name shall be great among the Gentiles; and in every place incense shall be offered unto my name, and a pure offering: for my name shall be great among the heathen, saith the LORD of hosts' (Malachi 1:11).

Its Position

'And thou shalt put it before the veil that is by the ark of the testimony, before the mercy seat that is over the testimony, where I will meet with thee' (v. 6). The altar of incense stood within the door, in the centre of the holy place, in a straight line with the brazen altar, the laver of brass, and the ark of the covenant and the mercy seat. Those vessels which stood in line with the great altar and the mercy seat indicate the provision made for us to come to God by the blood of Christ, the new and living way. The mercy seat represented the throne of God. The altar of incense stood before it. This is exactly the position of it as John saw it spiritually in Revelation 8:3, 4. The whole thing points to Christ, our great High Priest, the Angel of the Lord, who is before the throne making intercession for us.

'And another angel came and stood at the altar, having a golden censer; and there was given unto him much incense, that he should offer it with the prayers of all saints upon the golden altar which was before the throne. And the smoke of the incense, which came with the prayers of the saints, ascended up before God out of the angel's hand' (Revelation 8:3, 4).

Our Lord Jesus, our great High Priest, not only prays for us, he takes our prayers and presents them with the incense of his infinite merit before the Father's throne. He takes our prayers and presents them before God in the fragrance of his high priestly character and on the basis of his perfect sacrifice.

'Seeing then that we have a great high priest, that is passed into the heavens, Jesus the Son of God, let us hold fast our profession. For we have not an high priest which cannot be touched with the feeling of our infirmities; but was in all points tempted like as we are, yet without sin. Let us therefore come boldly unto the throne of grace, that we may obtain mercy, and find grace to help in time of need' (Hebrews 4:14-16).

Its Height

This Golden Altar of Incense was 'two cubits' high (v. 2). That little bit of information tells us it was half a cubit higher than the other vessels in the tabernacle. Why?

He who humbled himself unto death has now been 'highly exalted'. God raised him from the dead and set him 'far above all' (Ephesians

1:20, 21). He is now Head over all to his church. In the estimate of God, the merit of his Son's death is far above all. Christ's precious blood exceeds everything! Praise his name! You and I may not be able to appreciate the full value of the Saviour's death, but God can, and God does! He saves his people according to his own high estimate of the worth of Christ's atoning work. He can and will bless us according to his own high estimate of the worth of Christ's atoning work.

Its Staves
The staves or poles (vv. 4, 5) by which the altar of incense was carried were not to be removed. They were always present with the altar. The altar was ever ready for the march, ready to move with the children of Israel. The intercessions of Christ are ours in every circumstance or place, and that continually. 'Lo, I am with you alway' (Matthew 28:20).

Always ready! What a privilege! Always near! What a blessing! Try to get hold of this, my brother, my sister. When we offer our prayers to our God, when we come into his house to worship him, when we go out to labour for him, as we seek to live for him, mingled with the sweet incense of the Saviour's precious name, we are standing between the two staves of his faithfulness and power! As the staves were the means by which the altar was carried, we are reminded that the gospel sound must go into all the earth. Place has no power to shut out Christ. By the staves of God's faithfulness and God's power, let us go forth with the good news of his grace!

Its Horns
At each corner of the altar was a golden horn (v. 2). Horns are symbols of power and fulness. Here they speak of the power of Christ's advocacy and intercession. They were four in number, because Christ has his elect in the four corners of the earth. 'Wherefore he is able also to save them to the uttermost that come unto God by him, seeing he ever liveth to make intercession for them' (Hebrews 7:25).

The power of Christ's intercession does not lie in his persuasiveness, but in his presence before God as the glorified Son of Man. That God has taken one Man into heaven, that he has exalted him to his own right hand in human form, gives us hope he might bring other men to glory, saved by the right hand of his great mercy. The wounds of Christ never fail in the eye of our gracious God. He is always 'the Lamb as it had been slain' (Revelation 5:6). He always has power to save and to keep us by His grace. He has the 'power to open the book' (Revelation 5:5).

The altar was square. Such also was the shape of the atoning brazen altar. Our salvation is exceeding strong. Christ cannot fail. His atoning work is firmly based on the might of God's own omnipotence forever!

Its Crown

On the top of the Altar of Incense there was a golden crown (v. 3). The crown is a royal emblem. Let Christ Jesus take it, then. It is his right. 'The government shall be upon his shoulder' (Isaiah 9:6). God the Father cries, 'Yet have I set my king upon my holy hill of Zion' (Psalm 2:6). Once, derision mocked him with its crown of thorns. But now in heaven he wears redemption's everlasting diadem. 'But', as Henry Law observed, 'though he rules thus high, his darling throne is the poor sinner's heart! His brightest crown is jewelled with saved souls.'

Around the top of the altar was a ridge, or crown, to keep the coals from falling off the altar. The coals of fire were protected by a crown of gold. Christ's priestly power is preserved and assured by his kingly might. He is now 'crowned with glory and honour' (Hebrews 2:9).

How comforting it must have been to the Israelite who was responsible to carry the altar over the rough desert that God had made provision against the falling of the coals of fire. Their feet might stumble; but the burning coals were still preserved by the crown of gold. Glorious truth this! What assurance! Our Priest is the King of the universe! Though Peter stumbled and fell, the coals of Christ's intercession failed not. He said to Peter, and he says to every believing sinner, 'I have prayed for thee' (Luke 22:32). We may fail; but the incense of his merit still ascends. When we read the seventeenth chapter of John, we should always remember this golden altar of incense in its magnificent portrayal of Christ our Intercessor.

The Incense

'And Aaron shall burn thereon sweet incense every morning: when he dresseth the lamps, he shall burn incense upon it. And when Aaron lighteth the lamps at even, he shall burn incense upon it, a perpetual incense before the LORD throughout your generations. Ye shall offer no strange incense thereon, nor burnt sacrifice, nor meat offering; neither shall ye pour drink offering thereon' (Exodus 30:7-9).

'And the LORD said unto Moses, Take unto thee sweet spices, stacte, and onycha, and galbanum; these sweet spices with pure frankincense: of each shall there be a like weight: And thou shalt make it a perfume, a confection after the art of the apothecary, tempered together, pure and holy: And thou shalt beat some of it very small, and put of it before the testimony in the tabernacle of the congregation, where I will meet with thee: it shall be unto you most holy' (Exodus 30:34-36).

Here is something very important. The fire on which the incense was placed was taken from the brazen altar where the sin offering was consumed (Leviticus 16:12, 13). No other fire could be used. Aaron, the high priest, did not make a fire of his own choosing. His sons, Nadab and Abihu, did burn incense on a fire of their own kindling. This is called 'strange fire' (Leviticus 10:1, 2). What did they do that was so abominable? Nadab and Abihu departed from the plain Word of Jehovah, and by their actions signified that worship may be offered to God on another foundation than acceptance through a crucified Christ. For that the Lord killed them and will kill anyone who dares to approach him in any way except through the bloody sacrifice of the divine substitute Christ Jesus (Hebrews 9:22).

The value of this altar lay in the incense. As we might expect, that which typifies the merit of God's sin atoning Son will have something peculiar and mysterious about it. It was made by the mingling of three spices, each part of equal weight (Exodus 30:34-38). What these spices, stacte, onycha and galbanum were, no one can tell. But I know exactly what they represent. They represent the sweet spice of Christ's merit and efficacy as our Redeemer, namely, the merit of his righteousness, that is, his obedience; the efficacy of his blood, that is, his atonement; and the prevalence of his advocacy, or his intercession.

Incense is a symbol of prayer (Psalm 141:2). As Aaron offered the incense, he was a figure of our Lord Jesus Christ in Heaven offering up prayer on behalf of those who are his (Hebrews 9:24). Aaron offered up this incense exclusively for the children of Israel, and our Lord Jesus prays only for those who are his (John 17:9). Those for whom that sacrifice died on the brazen altar were included in the prayers of the golden altar. The intercessory work of our Lord does not exceed or fall short of his sacrificial work. The fire fed on the sacrifice, so the fire of God's wrath fed upon, and was satisfied by, Christ our Substitute.

Our Lord as our great High Priest not only prays for us but takes our prayers and presents them like incense before the Father's throne. How he does this is illustrated in Revelation 8:3. He takes our persons and our prayers and our performances and presents them before God in the fragrance of his high priestly character and on the basis of his perfect sacrifice, giving us perpetual acceptance in all things with God (Ecclesiastes 9:7; 1 Peter 2:5).

This is the meaning of the type before us in Exodus 30. The intercession of our Lord Jesus Christ is based upon the cross and finds its efficacy in the cross; in the sacrifice of himself as the sin offering. The horns of the altar of incense were stained once a year with the blood of atonement from the brazen altar (Exodus 30:10). And the priesthood of Christ and his work of intercession on our behalf rests wholly in the blood of the cross. Had he not died and met the claims of divine justice against us, he could not make effectual intercession for us.

Inseparable Altars

These two altars are inseparable. The sacrifice was made on the brazen altar; but the atonement is complete on the golden altar. What do we see between the two altars? Resurrection! Our Lord died on the cross, the altar of sacrifice; and after his resurrection he took the blood of the cross to the throne of God in Heaven, having obtained eternal redemption for us! Had he not risen, his death would have been of no avail and our faith would be vain (1 Corinthians 15:17). Our High Priest rose from the dead, took his blood within the veil, consummated the atonement there, and made reconciliation. It was the blood that gave value to the incense; and it is the blood of Christ that makes both our persons and our prayers acceptable to God!

We dare not come to God, or seek to worship God, or bring any strange fire of free will or good works or law obedience to the thrice holy Lord God, lest, like Nadab and Abihu, he slay us in his wrath!

'And as for the perfume which thou shalt make, ye shall not make to yourselves according to the composition thereof: it shall be unto thee holy for the LORD. Whosoever shall make like unto that, to smell thereto, shall even be cut off from his people' (Exodus 30:37, 38).

Chapter 103

A Certain Number, Price And Result

'And the LORD spake unto Moses, saying, When thou takest the sum of the children of Israel after their number, then shall they give every man a ransom for his soul unto the LORD, when thou numberest them; that there be no plague among them, when thou numberest them. This they shall give, every one that passeth among them that are numbered, half a shekel after the shekel of the sanctuary: (a shekel is twenty gerahs:) an half shekel shall be the offering of the LORD. Every one that passeth among them that are numbered, from twenty years old and above, shall give an offering unto the LORD. The rich shall not give more, and the poor shall not give less than half a shekel, when they give an offering unto the LORD, to make an atonement for your souls. And thou shalt take the atonement money of the children of Israel, and shalt appoint it for the service of the tabernacle of the congregation; that it may be a memorial unto the children of Israel before the LORD, to make an atonement for your souls.'
(Exodus 30:11-16)

This is God's law regarding the numbering of the children of Israel and the atonement money they paid, so that no plague come upon them. Here we have a very instructive and blessed type and picture of our redemption, the ransom of our souls, by the precious blood of the Lord Jesus Christ.

We believe, rejoice in, and preach, without apology, the great and glorious gospel doctrine of particular and effectual redemption accomplished by the precious, sin atoning blood of the Lord Jesus

Christ, the doctrine sometimes called limited atonement. I defy anyone to find any place in the Book of God that even hints at the possibility that Christ shed his blood for those who perish in hell, as well as those who are saved by it. Where does the Word of God proclaim an atonement that does not atone, a redemption that does not redeem, a deliverance that does not deliver, a ransom that does not set free, or a Saviour who does not save? Nowhere!

The fact is, everywhere in the Book of God, in every place, every chapter, every verse, every prophecy, every picture, and every type which speaks of, or in any way explains, the great and glorious redemptive work of Christ, it is always set before us as the redemption of a specific people. It is a redemption that is effectually accomplished, a redemption by which those specific people are actually redeemed.

In our portion of Scripture we are told that the ransom money for atonement was paid for a certain number of people. 'The sum of the children of Israel.' A certain price was paid. The price for their ransom was 'half a shekel after the shekel of the sanctuary'. A certain result followed. Those who were redeemed according to the requirement of the law had 'no plague among them'.

Here are five blessed facts of divine revelation. All five are here so obviously set before us that only those who will not see do not see them.

A Chosen People

First, none was redeemed but God's chosen, the children of Israel, and all the children of Israel were redeemed. All the children of Israel were numbered with the adult males of the nation. They made up the specific number for whom this atonement money was paid, 603,550 men.

'And the silver of them that were numbered of the congregation was an hundred talents, and a thousand seven hundred and threescore and fifteen shekels, after the shekel of the sanctuary: A bekah for every man, that is, half a shekel, after the shekel of the sanctuary, for every one that went to be numbered, from twenty years old and upward, for six hundred thousand and three thousand and five hundred and fifty men' (Exodus 38:25, 26).

The children of Israel were a chosen people, representing God's elect in this world, who are called, 'The Israel of God' (Galatians 6:16). How we ought to rejoice in God's electing love! The Lord God himself describes it beautifully in Deuteronomy 7:1-9. God chose us in Christ.

He chose us before the world was made. He chose us in everlasting love. And having chosen us in Christ, the Lord God blessed us with all spiritual blessings in Christ from eternity (Ephesians 1:3-6; 2 Timothy 1:9, 10; Psalm 65:4). Election is the source and cause of all blessedness!

The atonement money was paid for 'the sum (total number) of the children of Israel' and Christ Jesus, our Redeemer, made atonement for and redeemed his elect, only his elect, and all his elect, 'the sum (total number) of the children of Israel'. It is written, 'for the transgression of my people was he stricken' and 'the good shepherd giveth his life for the sheep'.

Divine Measure

Second, the ransom price was determined by divine measure. Those who were redeemed were redeemed with 'half a shekel after the shekel of the sanctuary' (v. 13). The measurement of the silver by which atonement was made was not man's measure, but God's, 'the shekel of the sanctuary'. In other words, God's demand was measured out by God himself, exacted by God, and paid to God. Here is the measurement of the sanctuary: 'the precious blood of Christ'. The redemption price was a price that met the demand of the law, that met God's demand. Not only did the Lord God require they must each bring half a shekel, no more and no less, but it must be 'the shekel of the sanctuary', not the shekel of commerce, which might be debased in quality or diminished by wear and tear. The coin must be according to the shekel standard laid up in the holy place and determined by God himself. To make sure of its measure, we are told 'a shekel is twenty gerahs' (v. 13).

We bring to God the redemption that God himself has appointed, the blood of Christ, nothing more and nothing less. The ransom price is perfection; perfect righteousness and perfect atonement, perfect obedience unto death, and from it there must be no varying. The price satisfies the divine demand and satisfies it to the full.

And the price appointed effectually redeemed all for whom the price was paid. Multitudes think of the sacrifice of Christ upon the cursed tree in a blasphemous way, trampling under foot the blood of the Son of God, for they imagine that our Saviour made a sort of general atonement by which redemption was made possible for all men, but accomplished for none. Such an absurdity leaves it to the sinner to redeem himself by his works or by the power of his will!

The Scriptures teach that the particular and effectual redemption of Christ was for God's own chosen. Nothing else honours God. Nothing else gives hope to sinners. Nothing else can be true. All those for whom the atonement money of Christ's precious blood was paid are freed from the possibility of plague. That is what the numbering of the children of Israel teaches us (Proverbs 12:21; Psalm 91:10).

We only read of the children of Israel being numbered, totalled, twice in Old Testament Scripture. They were numbered once, as men commonly try to number them today, without atonement. Then, the plague of God broke out against them and killed 70,000 men (2 Samuel 24:15). But we read in the Book of Numbers about another numbering of Israel (Numbers 1:1, 2; 26:2-4), a numbering by atonement.

'And the LORD spake unto Moses in the wilderness of Sinai, in the tabernacle of the congregation, on the first day of the second month, in the second year after they were come out of the land of Egypt, saying, Take ye the sum of all the congregation of the children of Israel, after their families, by the house of their fathers, with the number of their names, every male by their polls' (Numbers 1:1, 2).

'Take the sum of all the congregation of the children of Israel, from twenty years old and upward, throughout their fathers' house, all that are able to go to war in Israel. And Moses and Eleazar the priest spake with them in the plains of Moab by Jordan near Jericho, saying, Take the sum of the people, from twenty years old and upward; as the LORD commanded Moses and the children of Israel, which went forth out of the land of Egypt' (Numbers 26:2-4).

We read of one more numbering, the numbering of the Israel of God, a numbering by atonement, a numbering that shall soon be performed, in Revelation 7; and there we see them that are numbered saved from every plague! 'And I heard the number of them which were sealed: and there were sealed an hundred and forty and four thousand of all the tribes of the children of Israel' (Revelation 7:4).

'After this I beheld, and, lo, a great multitude, which no man could number, of all nations, and kindreds, and people, and tongues, stood before the throne, and before the Lamb, clothed with white robes, and palms in their hands; And cried with a loud voice, saying, Salvation to our God which sitteth upon the throne, and unto the Lamb. And all the angels stood round about the throne, and about the elders and the four beasts, and fell before the throne on their faces, and worshipped God,

Saying, Amen: Blessing, and glory, and wisdom, and thanksgiving, and honour, and power, and might, be unto our God for ever and ever. Amen. And one of the elders answered, saying unto me, What are these which are arrayed in white robes? And whence came they? And I said unto him, Sir, thou knowest. And he said to me, These are they which came out of great tribulation, and have washed their robes, and made them white in the blood of the Lamb' (Revelation 7:9-14).

Faith in the Atonement
Third, in Romans 3:25 the Apostle Paul speaks about 'faith in his blood', faith in the blood of Christ, faith in his sin atoning sacrifice as our Substitute. All the chosen brought the atonement money in their hands. Even so, all God's elect must and shall come to God through faith in the blood of Christ, and the redemption accomplished by the Lord Jesus Christ. We come to God on his terms, trusting Christ as our Redeemer, accepting personally the price required. Christ's blood is a price of infinite worth. Yet, the atonement money paid was a price even the poorest of men could obtain, even if by begging alms. So it is with Christ. He is the free gift of God to and for sinners, the very poorest of sinners! His atonement may be had by any who are willing to have it. The atonement money must be personally brought by each worshipper.

How can I speak to you as I should about this? Spirit of God, help me to speak plainly and truthfully. You must trust the Lord Jesus Christ and trust him alone. Come to God by faith in his blood, and you cannot be turned away. Come any other way and you cannot be accepted (Hebrews 10:14-22). 'For by one offering he hath perfected for ever them that are sanctified. Whereof the Holy Ghost also is a witness to us: for after that he had said before, This is the covenant that I will make with them after those days, saith the Lord, I will put my laws into their hearts, and in their minds will I write them; And their sins and iniquities will I remember no more. Now where remission of these is, there is no more offering for sin. Having therefore, brethren, boldness to enter into the holiest by the blood of Jesus, by a new and living way, which he hath consecrated for us, through the veil, that is to say, his flesh; And having an high priest over the house of God; Let us draw near with a true heart in full assurance of faith, having our hearts sprinkled from an evil conscience, and our bodies washed with pure water' (Hebrews 10:14-22).

All Equal
Fourth, observe, 'the rich shall not give more, and the poor shall not give less than half a shekel, when they give an offering unto the LORD, to make an atonement for your souls' (v. 15). All Israel was equally redeemed; and all the Israel of God are equally redeemed. The Lord Jesus purchased all his people with an equal price, the price of his own precious blood. All are equally valued by God. All are equally loved by Christ. All are equally redeemed to the same inheritance. All are equally secure, bought with the same price. All are equally accepted, 'accepted in the beloved'. And all are equally respected, for 'his righteousness is unto all, and upon all, that believe; for there is no difference'.

Silver Sockets
Fifth, everything in the worship of God, everything involved in this thing called faith and salvation has its basis and foundation in the sin atoning sacrifice of our Lord Jesus Christ. Back in Exodus 26 all the boards of the tabernacle were fixed, each board in two 'sockets of silver'. Those sockets, connected to each other, formed the foundation of the tabernacle. If you look at Exodus 38, you will see where Moses got the silver to make the foundation that held everything together.

'And the silver of them that were numbered of the congregation was an hundred talents, and a thousand seven hundred and threescore and fifteen shekels, after the shekel of the sanctuary: A bekah for every man, that is, half a shekel, after the shekel of the sanctuary, for every one that went to be numbered, from twenty years old and upward, for six hundred thousand and three thousand and five hundred and fifty men. And of the hundred talents of silver were cast the sockets of the sanctuary, and the sockets of the veil; an hundred sockets of the hundred talents, a talent for a socket' (Exodus 38:25-27).

'The foundation of the worship of Israel', wrote C. H. Spurgeon, 'was redemption. The dwelling place of the Lord their God was founded on atonement. All the boards of incorruptible wood and precious gold stood upon the redemption price, and the curtains of fine linen, and the veil of matchless workmanship, and the whole structure rested on nothing else but the solid mass of silver which had been paid as the redemption money of the people.'

Blood atonement and redemption by Christ is everything in the house of God, in the worship of God, and to the people of God!

Chapter 104

Do You Want To Be Clean?

'And the LORD spake unto Moses, saying, Thou shalt also make a laver of brass, and his foot also of brass, to wash withal: and thou shalt put it between the tabernacle of the congregation and the altar, and thou shalt put water therein. For Aaron and his sons shall wash their hands and their feet thereat: When they go into the tabernacle of the congregation, they shall wash with water, that they die not; or when they come near to the altar to minister, to burn offering made by fire unto the LORD: So they shall wash their hands and their feet, that they die not: and it shall be a statute for ever to them, even to him and to his seed throughout their generations.'
(Exodus 30:17-21)

Man, by nature, is one vile mass of sin, polluted and filthy from the crown of his head to the soles of his feet. Throughout the Book of God, the God of Glory declares, 'Thou art vile'. Our thoughts, our affections, even our bodies are declared to be vile. If ever the Lord God is pleased to make you know yourself, you will, like Jeremiah, confess with shame before him, 'I am become vile' (Lamentations 1:11). If the Lord is pleased to have mercy upon you, he will cause you to become aware of your vileness before him, just as he did Job (Job 40:1-5).

Has the Lord God shown you your state before him? In Exodus 30:17-21 God shows us how the vilest of sinners can be made clean. He directed Moses to make a 'laver of brass', a bronze wash tub, in which every priest was required to wash before he entered the tabernacle of the congregation, or approached the altar to make a burnt offering.

Altar and Laver

The altar and the laver were both essential; but the altar preceded the laver. The laver stood between the altar and the door of the tabernacle, and right in line with the mercy seat and the altar of incense, signifying that no one can ever approach God, except by washing in this 'laver of brass'. In the brazen altar we see Christ dying for our sins. In the laver of brass we see the work of God the Holy Ghost causing sinners to wash and be made clean in the Fountain opened for sin and uncleanness (Titus 3:4-7; Zechariah 12:10-13:1). The laver comes after the altar. First, the cross, then Pentecost. First, justified by Christ's blood, then sanctified by God's Spirit in regeneration. The laver was filled with water. Water is used in Scripture to symbolize both the Word and the Spirit of God. The laver of brass in the tabernacle typified the awakening and cleansing work of God the Holy Ghost, as he makes the Word of God effectual to the hearts of chosen, redeemed sinners in the saving operations of his grace. This, of course, can come only as the result of and only through the blood of our Lord Jesus Christ shed for us in the accomplishment of redemption (Galatians 3:13, 14).

Women's Mirrors

The laver was made from the mirrors Israel's women brought out of Egypt. It was made of bronze, a strong metal, beaten out of those mirrors. It shadowed forth our Lord Jesus, the One of whom God the Holy Spirit always speaks, to whom the Spirit always points. Christ is our Strength. He came to save his people from their sins, to perform the mightiest work ever performed by God himself.

We read in Exodus 38:8 that the materials for this laver of brass were brought to Moses by the women the Lord brought out of Egypt. The Jewish women had mirrors made of beaten brass that they brought out of Egypt, mirrors the Egyptian women had given them. These mirrors they brought to Moses; and Moses used them to make this wash tub for the house of God. I think three things are significant in this fact.

First, and foremost, as this laver portraying our Saviour was made from that contributed by women, so our Lord Jesus Christ is the woman's Seed, 'made of a woman, made under the law', to redeem you and me from the curse of the law. Second, what once was used only for vanity was brought to the Lord God and accepted by him in his service, in his house, for the worship of his name. Third, as the mirror shows a person's face, so the only way we ever see ourselves as we really are is when we come to Christ, the Laver of our souls, and wash in him.

When, like these women, we stand at the door of the tabernacle and see ourselves in the light of the presence of a holy and sin hating God, like Job, we abhor ourselves and repent in sackcloth and ashes. As we behold Christ crucified, we see ourselves as we really are, 'abominable and filthy', 'unclean' and 'vile'. Yet, looking upon the Saviour in faith, bathing our souls in this Fountain opened for sin and uncleanness, we begin to see ourselves as we really are in him: justified, sanctified, fair, without spot, made beautiful through his beauty!

For Cleansing
The laver was made for the cleansing of God's priests. That was its purpose. It was a big wash tub, standing between the brazen altar of sacrifice and the door of the tabernacle. In Exodus 30:20 a strict command was issued that no priest should touch the altar or pass the door until his hands and feet had been washed in the laver. No defilement may approach the Lord God. But, and this is sweeter than honey, he who demands such purity provides the purifying stream. The Lord who says you must be cleansed, brings near his cleansing Laver, Christ Jesus, and says, 'Wash and be clean'.

Eternal love devised the plan. Eternal wisdom drew the pattern. Eternal grace provides the basin. But by whom can it be filled? The Lord Jesus Christ himself pours in the stream. He brings the rich supply. It is blood, blood from his own veins, blood from his very heart! Nothing in heaven or earth could help, but this. He bled to fill the washbasin. He died to open wide the cleansing Fountain. Plunge into this Fountain, and our sins are gone forever! No uncleanness can now be found!

God looks with an all-searching eye; but sin has fled as far as the east is from the west. It has vanished in the efficacy of Christ's perfect atonement. The blood, the all-powerful blood has washed it away. The Christ-bathed soul is pure and clean and bright and spotless and as fit for heaven, as Christ himself. It is so. It must be so. Hear the Spirit's witness. 'The blood of Jesus Christ his Son cleanses us from all sin' (1 John 1:7). Lift up your eyes! Behold the bright arrayed throng. What is their title to the heavenly home? It is the precious blood of Christ! So, too, is yours and mine.

But sins forgiven in the sight of God are not soon forgotten in the court of conscience. Satan finds entrance here. With savage voice and clamorous demand, he drags our old transgressions and our present iniquities before the bar of conscience. If he cannot cast us into hell, he will do his best to keep us half afraid of hell until we enter heaven's glory. What wild storms of fear he raises in weak, uninformed minds! He reads out long scrolls of iniquity, transgression, and sin, things we know full well we have done. He argues that souls so black as ours are only fuel for the endless flames of hell. But, when he would raise up Moses against us, our mighty Advocate rises in reply. By his Word and by his Spirit, Christ brings us again and again to the Laver to wash!

The only refuge for our sin polluted souls is the Laver of God, Christ Jesus! Would you have a conscience at ease and quiet, unruffled and calm before God? Would you have peace in your soul and quietness in your heart? Then wash in the Laver! Here blood-washed souls rejoice and confidently sing, 'God is appeased! Justice is satisfied! My sins are gone!' While the polished brass of the laver revealed the uncleanness, the water in the laver would cleanse it away. This is the work of God the Spirit, convincing the redeemed, blood-bought soul at once of sin, and of righteousness, and of judgment (John 16:7-11). The water in the laver was only for those who were redeemed at the altar. And the work of God the Holy Ghost in sanctification comes only to the redeemed of the Lord, and to all the redeemed.

The Spirit's Work

The laver of brass speaks of the work of God the Holy Spirit. We are not told what the dimensions of the laver were. When Moses received instruction to make 'the laver and its foot', no mention at all is made of size or shape. At first sight one might wonder, 'Is it an oversight?' God makes no mistakes. Every omission is as emphatic as a pronouncement. It is surely significant that the vessel which represents the work of the Holy Spirit was not limited to any particular form or size. 'The wind (Spirit) bloweth where it listeth; thou hearest the sound thereof, but canst not tell whence it cometh and whither it goeth' (John 3:8).

Why was the laver not made of wood and brass like the altar? The answer seems clear. Christ had two natures: God and man. The Holy Spirit is one Person. Let us adore the wisdom of God. Those who study and understand the types have no difficulty concerning the inspiration of the Scriptures. The other vessels of the tabernacle had staves or shafts by which they were to be carried. The laver had none. Not only is the work of God the Spirit represented in this laver, but also his Divine Person. We are saved by the redeeming work of the Lord Jesus Christ for us and by the regenerating or sanctifying work of God the Holy Spirit in us. Both are essential (Ezekiel 36:25, 26).

The work of the Spirit is as necessary to make us fit for heaven as the work of the Saviour. We must be redeemed; and we must be regenerated. We must be justified; and we must be sanctified. We must have a righteous record; and we must have a righteous nature. We must have righteousness imputed to us; and we must have righteousness imparted to us (2 Corinthians 5:17-21; 2 Peter 1:4). Are you a new creature in Christ? 'Except a man be born again, he cannot see the kingdom of God'. There is no heaven, but for people made holy by redemption and regeneration. Our title to heaven must be found in Christ; our fitness for heaven must be from him. Blood bought all pardon, confers all peace, and earned and bestows all sanctifying grace.

The Altar and the Laver

Pay close attention to the connection between the altar of sacrifice and the laver of cleansing. Like all the other vessels, there was a blood connection between the altar of burnt offering and the laver of cleansing. The laver was sprinkled with the blood of atonement. The laver could not be reached and used by any except those for whom blood had been shed.

The Spirit did not come till after the work of atonement was finished. The sprinkling of the laver with the blood symbolised the consecrating and imparting of divine authority for its work. When Christ entered into Heaven by his own blood, he sent the Holy Spirit. The work of the Holy Ghost in regeneration is the fruit of the sin atoning death of our Lord Jesus Christ. There is a vital connection between Calvary and Pentecost.

The laver was to be filled with water. Where did the water come from? The Smitten Rock! 'That Rock was Christ' (1 Corinthians 10:4). The laver could be filled, and men could be cleansed, because the rock was smitten. At the altar we see the blood of atonement. At the laver we see the water of cleansing. Both are needed and both come to us through our Blessed Redeemer, the Lord Jesus Christ. You remember that when they had pierced his side, 'forthwith came there out blood and water' (John 19:34), the blood first, then the water. The water, or ministry of the Spirit, always comes by way of the altar (Ezekiel 47:1-12). 'He shall take the things of Christ, and show them unto you' (John 16:13, 15). You believe in the forgiveness of sin; believe also in the indwelling Spirit. The water of the Spirit, the Water of Life, comes to us in the Laver, Christ Jesus. The two cannot be separated. The indwelling of the Spirit is 'Christ in you the hope of glory'.

They must be clean who would 'stand before God'. There was but one means of cleansing. There was but one laver; no other was needed. This was God's provision. They might wash themselves elsewhere, but it would not make them 'clean before the Lord'. Hear Job's testimony. 'If I wash myself and make my hands never so clean; yet shalt thou plunge me in the ditch' (Job 9:30, 31). Snow-waters of earth and self-will never avail, only the 'Fountain opened for sin and uncleanness' is effectual. The washing of regeneration is as much a matter of necessity as the blood of redemption. 'Ye must be born again'.

I travel abroad preaching the gospel of Christ at least twice every year. I have crossed the borders of the U.S.A. north, south, east, and west many times. Whenever I leave this country and cross into another, three things are required. I must have a passport and birth certificate to prove my citizenship. I must have a visa from the country receiving me. I must have a clean record, no criminal, record. Soon, I will leave this land of sorrow and sin. I hope to enter the glory of heaven. I hope to be accepted as a citizen of New Jerusalem. Here is the basis of my hope.

I have a birth certificate. The Lord God has given me a new nature (2 Corinthians 5:17). There is in me a new man, created of God in righteousness and true holiness. I have a visa. I have a right to enter into heaven itself by the blood of Christ, because I am washed in his blood and robed in his righteousness (Colossians 1:12). God says, 'It shall be perfect to be accepted', and in Christ I am perfect! And I have a clear record. The Lord Jesus Christ has purged my sins with his own precious blood. God will never charge me with any sin (Romans 4:8). When I stand before God and he searches the books for iniquity and sin under my name, he will find none (Jeremiah 50:20).

Do you want to be clean? Come, with God given faith and bathe your soul in God's Laver, Christ Jesus.

Chapter 105

Do You Have The Anointing?

'Moreover the LORD spake unto Moses, saying, Take thou also unto thee principal spices, of pure myrrh five hundred shekels, and of sweet cinnamon half so much, even two hundred and fifty shekels, and of sweet calamus two hundred and fifty shekels, And of cassia five hundred shekels, after the shekel of the sanctuary, and of oil olive an hin: And thou shalt make it an oil of holy ointment, an ointment compound after the art of the apothecary: it shall be an holy anointing oil. And thou shalt anoint the tabernacle of the congregation therewith, and the ark of the testimony, And the table and all his vessels, and the candlestick and his vessels, and the altar of incense, And the altar of burnt offering with all his vessels, and the laver and his foot. And thou shalt sanctify them, that they may be most holy: whatsoever toucheth them shall be holy. And thou shalt anoint Aaron and his sons, and consecrate them, that they may minister unto me in the priest's office. And thou shalt speak unto the children of Israel, saying, This shall be an holy anointing oil unto me throughout your generations. Upon man's flesh shall it not be poured, neither shall ye make any other like it, after the composition of it: it is holy, and it shall be holy unto you. Whosoever compoundeth any like it, or whosoever putteth any of it upon a stranger, shall even be cut off from his people. And the LORD said unto Moses, Take unto thee sweet spices, stacte, and onycha, and galbanum; these sweet spices with pure frankincense: of each shall there be a like weight: And thou shalt make it a perfume, a confection after the art of the apothecary, tempered together, pure and holy: And thou shalt beat some of it very small, and put of it before the testimony in the tabernacle of the congregation, where I will meet with thee: it shall be unto you most holy. And as for the perfume which thou shalt make, ye shall not make to yourselves according to the composition thereof: it shall be unto thee holy for the LORD. Whosoever shall make like unto that, to smell thereto, shall even be cut off from his people.' (Exodus 30:22-38)

There is much talk in today's religious world about the Holy Spirit, the gifts of the Spirit, and the anointing of the Spirit. When some confused charismatic comes up to you and asks, 'Do you have the anointing?' do you feel a little bit dirty, a little lacking? Does that question make you uncomfortable? That's the reason the question is asked. It is intended to make you uncomfortable so you will begin to seek the anointing.

Yes, the Bible does speak about an anointing. There is an anointing without which we are dirty, without which we are lacking, without which we should be very uncomfortable. Do you have the anointing? If you do not have it you should feel dirty, lacking, and uncomfortable. Exodus 30:22-38 shows us the anointing without which we are in our consciences dirty and lacking before God.

Two Essentials

Two things essential to the worship of God in the tabernacle were holy oil and holy perfume. These two things were as essential as the blood of the paschal lamb and the ark of the covenant; and that represented by the holy oil and the holy perfume is just as necessary to the saving of our souls as the obedience and death of our Lord Jesus Christ.

The sanctifying work of God the Holy Spirit in us in regeneration, making us new creatures in Christ, making us partakers of the divine nature, forming Christ in us, is just as necessary to the everlasting salvation of our souls as the work of Christ for us in his obedience unto death as our Substitute. The righteousness of God imparted to us in the new birth is just as necessary and blessed as the righteousness of God imputed to us in free justification.

The tabernacle, the sanctuary of the Lord, would have been utterly unacceptable without the holy anointing oil and fragrant holy incense described in this passage. Without the holy oil and the holy incense, the blood of the paschal lamb would have been meaningless.

The Holy Oil

In verses 22-33 the Lord God commands Moses to make a special holy oil, 'an oil of holy ointment', by which everything connected with the worship of God, including Aaron and his sons, had to be anointed. This oil is specifically distinguished as 'holy anointing oil' (v. 31), because its chief purpose was to sanctify the tabernacle and its furnishings and Aaron and his sons and set them apart for the service of God.

God the Spirit is constantly spoken of as 'Holy', 'the Comforter', who is the 'Holy Ghost'. The Spirit is not more holy than the Father or the Son, but his great mission is to make chosen, redeemed sinners holy by making us new creatures in Christ. Thus, by the work of the Holy Spirit, we are consecrated to God, being created new 'in righteousness and true holiness' (Ephesians 4:24). The Lord God who commands, 'Be ye holy, for I am holy', is himself the One who makes chosen sinners holy. It is this work of God the Holy Spirit that is portrayed and typified in this 'holy anointing oil'.

Four spices had to be added to a hin of olive oil to make the 'holy ointment', myrrh, cinnamon, sweet calamus, and casia. Olive oil is used in Scripture as a type of God the Holy Spirit (Acts 10:38). The spices gave fragrance to the oil, and the oil was the element by which their aroma was borne through the air. So, the sweet graces manifested by Christ upon the earth were all according to the Spirit (Isaiah 11:1-5; 61:1-3), things wrought in him continually as our Mediator in the power of the blessed Spirit of God, because he was always full of the Spirit and always led by the Spirit (Luke 4:1; John 16:13, 14).

Whatever does not glorify Christ; a sermon, a prayer, a song, a good deed, a gift, is not of the Holy Spirit. No matter how good it looks or sounds, if it does not glorify Christ, the Holy Spirit has no hand in it. Whatever truly exalts our Lord Jesus and calls attention to him is of the Holy Spirit. The aroma of the anointing oil was the spices, diffused by the olive oil. He shall glorify me, our Saviour said, for he is a sweet-smelling savour to the Father. Let us look at those four spices.

Myrrh is the gum or sap of a tree obtained by incisions made in the tree. Pure Myrrh was sweet to the smell but bitter to the taste. In fact, the word comes from a word that means 'bitterness'.

Myrrh speaks beautifully of our Lord Jesus Christ (Psalm 45:8; Song of Solomon 1:13; 3:6; 5:2-5, 13). The sweet smell of myrrh speaks of love, immense, eternal, infinite love, poured out in a bitter but fragrant

391

death for us! The bitterness of the myrrh tells of the reality of the sufferings which our Lord endured. It was not physical pain, not even death, which gave intensity to his sufferings. What was it then? He who is holy, harmless, undefiled, and separate from sin, who knew no sin and did no sin, was made sin for us! When the Lord Jesus was made sin for us, he drank all the bitter dregs of the bitter cup of God's bitter wrath against sin. Now, from him comes the sweet smell of sin put away!

Sweet cinnamon was likely the same spice ladies today use to make cinnamon toast or cinnamon rolls. It is used four times in Scripture. The word 'cinnamon' comes from a word which means 'to erect or build'.

It is Christ who builds his church. He is our mighty Zerubbabel. He will finish the work. That is sweet cinnamon to all who know him. Cinnamon is attributed to the Church by the Lord Jesus as the gift of his grace (Song of Solomon 4:12-14). He attributes to us all he is and all that he has done.

In Proverbs 7:17 and Revelation 18:13, Babylon, the harlot church of freewill and works religion, pretends she has the cinnamon sinners need. With an insincere love she entices fools to her bed.

Sweet Calamus comes from sweet cane, which usually grows in miry soil. The fragrance is obtained by crushing the plant.

Our Lord Jesus came into all the mire of this world and grew erect and fragrant for God. He came to the mire of earth for a special work. Wicked men took him, bound and bruised him, but his fragrance fills heaven and earth through that bruising (Isaiah 53:5). Wherever he finds a 'bruised reed' he lifts it from the mire (John 8:11). That is his sweet-smelling purpose.

Cassia comes from a root word meaning 'to stoop or bow down', as in worship. What was foreshadowed here was our Lord's, submission to and worship of God as the perfect man, (Luke 4:16). What an example for us!

The only other mention of 'cassia' is in Ezekiel 27:19. What we learn there is that this was one of the articles in which Tyre, the great merchant nation of the world, traded (Ezekiel 27:2). Like Egypt, Tyre stands for the world. This tells us that even the world will traffic in the excellencies of Christ in order to further its own ends. In the next chapter of Ezekiel (28:12-19), Satan is presented as the 'King of Tyre'. The archenemy of God is always seeking to rob Christ of that adoration and worship which belongs to him alone.

When God the Holy Spirit comes in the saving operations of his grace, he reveals the Lord Jesus in the glory of his person and work, spoken of here as myrrh, cinnamon, calamus, and cassia, as a sweet-smelling savour, a sacrifice accepted and well pleasing to God. And he causes believing sinners to know that in Christ we are a sweet-smelling savour (2 Corinthians 2:15).

Jehovah's Claim

'This shall be an holy anointing oil unto me' (v. 31). The oil upon the tabernacle, upon all its furnishings, and upon Aaron and his sons, was God's claim of them. The oil was Jehovah's claim of all as his own! It was the Lord's seal. Everything it touched it sanctified. It was the voice of God asserting his ownership, approval, and acceptance. That is what the Holy Spirit is to the regenerate soul. When God pours out his Spirit upon the blood bought sinner, he claims the sinner for himself, and tells the sinner that he belongs to God (Galatians 4:4-6; Romans 8:16).

For God's Priests Alone

This holy anointing oil was put upon no one except Aaron and his sons, God's chosen priests (v. 30). Until they had the anointing, they were neither qualified nor worthy to minister in the priest's office. It was the anointing that consecrated them for the work. Even so, no sinner may approach or worship God until he is sanctified by the Spirit, until Christ is created in him. Then the sinner is worthy and serves God in the priest's office as a part of that royal priesthood who worship him.

This holy oil was for Aaron and his sons. The Lord God forbids any others to have it upon them (vv. 32, 33). It could not be poured upon any except those who wore the pure white mitre of the righteous priest. Yet, every chosen, redeemed priest is given the anointing; and it is by the anointing we are made to know we are God's (1 John 2:20-27).

Imitations Deadly

No imitations of the holy anointing were to be tolerated. 'Whosoever compoundeth any like it shall be cut off'' (v. 33). Any who dared presume to imitate God's holy anointing were to be put to death. What multitudes there are who today try to imitate the work of God's Holy Spirit in regeneration! All the churches and religious movements of the world try to put the anointing upon proud man. But man's nature is a barren soil; and the fruits of the Spirit will never spring from that desert land. A miracle must be performed. The sweet spices of Christ's person must be brought by the olive oil, the blessed, omnipotent Holy Spirit (John 3:6, 7). It is his own sovereign work of mercy (John 3:8).

No strange fire could be used at God's altar (Leviticus 10:1, 2). The fire had to come from the golden altar of incense. So, no imitation of this holy anointing oil was to be made. How this word condemns the imitations of divine worship, the Spirit's operations, and the fragrance of Christ in present day religion. Satan is a master imitator. It is frightening to think of the strange compositions of religion on every hand. We must be careful (1 John 4:1-3). Christ came and did all he came to do. If the spirit you listen to does not glorify Christ, the crucified and risen Christ, the interceding Christ, as the all-sufficient, effectual Saviour of his people, it is imitation oil, and a fake anointing.

Holy Perfume

In verses 34-38 the Lord commanded Moses to make holy perfume with which the anointed priests were to enter into the Holy of holies with the blood of the paschal lamb. This perfume was used in the censer they carried into that holy place before the Lord. It was a perfume made by mixing equal parts of three sweet spices: stacte, onycha, and galbanum. No one knows what these three spices were. But they were to be mixed with frankincense, tempered together, and beaten very small. Then, they were put in the fire from off the altar and carried with the blood of the paschal lamb to the mercy seat, 'where' the holy Lord God says, 'I will meet with thee'.

In Christ three things are tempered together: God, man, and merit, Christ's atonement and righteousness. These three things mixed with the whiteness of God's holiness, justice, and truth form the incense of our Saviour's intercession for us, the sweet perfume by which we draw near to God. It is a composition to which nothing can be added. Any attempts to add anything to this composition will end in being everlastingly cut off from God and his people (vv. 37, 38).

This is the holy anointing and the holy perfume by which we must come to and worship God. The anointing is Christ in you, the new birth! The perfume is Christ's for you, his work, his satisfaction! Do you have the anointing? I would not go to bed without it. If I were you, I would not give rest to my eyes without Christ.

Chapter 106

The Purpose Of The Sabbath

'And the LORD spake unto Moses, saying, See, I have called by name Bezaleel the son of Uri, the son of Hur, of the tribe of Judah: And I have filled him with the spirit of God, in wisdom, and in understanding, and in knowledge, and in all manner of workmanship, to devise cunning works, to work in gold, and in silver, and in brass, and in cutting of stones, to set them, and in carving of timber, to work in all manner of workmanship. And I, behold, I have given with him Aholiab, the son of Ahisamach, of the tribe of Dan: and in the hearts of all that are wise hearted I have put wisdom, that they may make all that I have commanded thee; The tabernacle of the congregation, and the ark of the testimony, and the mercy seat that is thereupon, and all the furniture of the tabernacle, and the table and his furniture, and the pure candlestick with all his furniture, and the altar of incense, and the altar of burnt offering with all his furniture, and the laver and his foot, and the cloths of service, and the holy garments for Aaron the priest, and the garments of his sons, to minister in the priest's office, and the anointing oil, and sweet incense for the holy place: according to all that I have commanded thee shall they do. And the LORD spake unto Moses, saying, Speak thou also unto the children of Israel, saying, Verily my sabbaths ye shall keep: for it is a sign between me and you throughout your generations; that ye may know that I am the LORD that doth sanctify you. Ye shall keep the sabbath therefore; for it is holy unto you: every one that defileth it shall surely be put to death: for whosoever doeth any work therein, that soul shall be cut off from among his people. Six days may work be done; but in the seventh is the sabbath of rest, holy to the LORD: whosoever doeth any work in the sabbath day, he shall surely be put to death. Wherefore the children of Israel shall keep the sabbath, to observe the sabbath throughout their generations, for a perpetual covenant. It is a sign between me and the children of Israel forever: for in six days the LORD made heaven and earth, and on the seventh day he rested, and was refreshed. And he gave unto Moses, when he had made an end of communing with him upon mount Sinai, two tables of testimony, tables of stone, written with the finger of God.' (Exodus 31:1-18)

How often have you read one of the commandments of the Old Testament and asked yourself, 'Why did God require that service? What is the significance of that law? What does that ceremony teach?' Without question, every law, every ceremony, every sacrifice given in the Old Testament Scriptures was designed and commanded by God to teach us something about the gospel, to show us our need of a Saviour, to show us who Christ is, what he would do, and how God saves sinners by the obedience, righteousness, and blood of his darling Son.

As that is true with regard to all the laws God gave to Israel, it is also true with regard to the tabernacle, all the furnishings of the tabernacle, the priesthood, the priestly garments, and the ceremonies performed by those priests. But, when we get to Exodus 31, the Lord God mixes one of the commandments given back in chapter 20 with the erection, the furnishings, and the services of the tabernacle. He gives specific instructions about sabbath keeping and tells us why he was so insistent upon sabbath observance. Here we are taught by the Spirit of God why the sabbath days of the law were established.

Workmen Provided

When God has a work to be done, he never lacks workmen, workmen he has specifically equipped to do the work to which he calls them.

'And the LORD spake unto Moses, saying, See, I have called by name Bezaleel the son of Uri, the son of Hur, of the tribe of Judah: And I have filled him with the spirit of God, in wisdom, and in understanding, and in knowledge, and in all manner of workmanship, To devise cunning works, to work in gold, and in silver, and in brass, and in cutting of stones, to set them, and in carving of timber, to work in all manner of workmanship' (vv. 1-5).

Every appointment of providence and of grace is the appointment of God (Ephesians 4:11, 12; Proverbs 16:33). And everything involved in or connected with the worship of God is also by divine appointment. We do not worship God if we do not worship him in the manner he prescribes. There is no true baptism except believer's baptism, the immersion of one who trusts the Lord Jesus Christ as his Saviour. Infant baptism, the sprinkling or pouring of water, is but a mockery of God and his ordinance. The Lord's Supper is the blessed remembrance and showing forth of our Saviour in his death. It cannot be done but by the eating of unleavened bread and drinking wine. If we would worship God in his house, our songs must be songs of divine praise, our worship must be done in simplicity, and all must be done focusing upon the preaching of the gospel.

'Bezaleel' means 'Shadow of God'. He was chosen of God for the specific work of erecting the tabernacle and making all its furnishings. He was not identified as the man God had chosen until it was time for him to do the work God chose him to do. But the Lord God gave Bezaleel everything he needed to do the work for which he was raised up by God. He was filled with the Spirit of God. And God gave his servant wisdom, understanding, and knowledge in those matters for which he needed wisdom, understanding, and knowledge.

The other man named for the work was Aholiab (v. 6). 'Aholiab' means 'Tent'. Aholiab and Bezaleel were chosen to erect the tabernacle, a tent that would be the shadow of God.

'And I, behold, I have given with him Aholiab, the son of Ahisamach, of the tribe of Dan: and in the hearts of all that are wise hearted I have put wisdom, that they may make all that I have commanded thee; The tabernacle of the congregation, and the ark of the testimony, and the mercy seat that is thereupon, and all the furniture of the tabernacle, and the table and his furniture, and the pure candlestick with all his furniture, and the altar of incense, and the altar of burnt offering with all his furniture, and the laver and his foot, and the cloths of service, and the holy garments for Aaron the priest, and the garments of his sons, to minister in the priest's office, and the anointing oil, and sweet incense for the holy place: according to all that I have commanded thee shall they do' (vv. 6-11).

Robert Hawker observed, 'If Bezaleel and Aholiab be appointed to the curious construction of the tabernacle building, the Holy Ghost will make them fit for the employment. And when Jesus called his poor fishermen of Galilee to be fishers of men, how soon were they qualified for the arduous work.'

If the Lord God so meticulously qualified these two men for the adorning of the tabernacle, which was but a shadow of good things to come, you can be sure he will not call and send forth men into the work of the gospel ministry who lack what is needed for the work to which he has called them, 'the edifying of the body of Christ' (Ephesians 4:11-13; Jeremiah 3:15). He will set in his church preachers and pastors fitted for their task. He will fill those men he sends forth to preach the gospel with the Spirit of God. He will equip them with knowledge of his word and understanding in all things spiritual. He will make them apt to teach, gifted to preach the gospel.

Let my God send a man where he will and for whatever purpose he will, if he be with that man, that man will soon demonstrate how God's strength is made perfect in human weakness. As Paul put it, 'Our sufficiency is of God'.

But, surely Bezaleel and Aholiab are names that point us above mere men to the Lord Jesus himself. Was he not, when he came to dwell upon this earth, the Revealer of God in a tent of humanity? As such, he was and is the only qualified workman for the true tabernacle, which the Lord pitched and not man. The tabernacle of which he is the author and finisher. He is the foundation stone of the spiritual building. He has raised up an everlasting tabernacle of redemption in his blood and righteousness and finished the work the Father gave him to do.

Sabbath Sign
'And the LORD spake unto Moses, saying, Speak thou also unto the children of Israel, saying, Verily my sabbaths ye shall keep: for it is a sign between me and you throughout your generations; that ye may know that I am the LORD that doth sanctify you. Ye shall keep the sabbath therefore; for it is holy unto you: every one that defileth it shall surely be put to death: for whosoever doeth any work therein, that soul shall be cut off from among his people. Six days may work be done; but in the seventh is the sabbath of rest, holy to the LORD: whosoever doeth any work in the sabbath day, he shall surely be put to death. Wherefore the children of Israel shall keep the sabbath, to observe the sabbath throughout their generations, for a perpetual covenant. It is a

sign between me and the children of Israel forever: for in six days the LORD made heaven and earth, and on the seventh day he rested, and was refreshed' (vv. 12-17).

Though they were constructing the tabernacle, the children of Israel are here reminded they still must observe the sabbath. They would not be excused, even to build the tabernacle. If they broke the sabbath, even to do God's work, even to build God's tabernacle, they were to be put to death. The Lord God gives a specific reason for this. He says, 'It is a sign between me and you throughout your generations; that ye may know that I am the LORD that doth sanctify you' (v. 13). 'Wherefore the children of Israel shall keep the sabbath, to observe the sabbath throughout their generations, for a perpetual covenant. It is a sign between me and the children of Israel forever: for in six days the LORD made heaven and earth, and on the seventh day he rested, and was refreshed' (vv. 16, 17).

God gave the law of the sabbath to stand as a perpetual sign, between him and his people, that it is his work alone to sanctify and save his people. His name is Jehovah-m'kaddesh. 'The LORD that doth sanctify you.' What a great name for our God! Our sanctification is God's work. It is a threefold work of grace. We are sanctified by God the Father in election (Jude 1), by God the Son in redemption (Hebrews 10:10-14), and by God the Spirit in regeneration (2 Corinthians 5:17; 2 Peter 1:4). The triune God makes us clean, washes us, and hallows us. God alone makes sinners holy, sanctifying us unto himself as his peculiar people.

Law Given
After declaring the whole work of making sinners holy is his work, the Lord God gave Moses the two tables of stone containing his law in the commandments.

'And he gave unto Moses, when he had made an end of communing with him upon mount Sinai, two tables of testimony, tables of stone, written with the finger of God' (v. 18).

The Lord had promised to give these tables back in Exodus 24:12. These commandments were written in stone 'with the finger of God'; and none but God himself can write his law on the stony heart of man (2 Corinthians 3:3; Hebrews 8:10). When God writes his law on the hearts of chosen sinners, then they rest in Christ and are refreshed, as they keep that blessed sabbath of faith.

Blessed Sabbath Rest

Christ is our Sabbath. The Old Testament laws of the sabbath all pointed to Christ and the blessed rest of faith in him. Our Saviour says, 'Come unto me, all ye that labour and are heavy laden, and I will give you rest. Take my yoke upon you, and learn of me; for I am meek and lowly in heart: and ye shall find rest unto your souls. For my yoke is easy, and my burden is light' (Matthew 11:28-30).

Here is Christ's word to lost, ruined, guilty sinners. 'Come unto me, all ye that labour and are heavy laden, and I will give you rest.' There is no salvation to be had but by coming to Christ. There can never be any true, peaceful, satisfying rest for your soul except you come to Christ, trusting him alone as your Lord and Saviour. Trusting his blood as your only atonement and his obedience as your only righteousness. Only Christ can give you rest.

Here is the Master's word to all, both to the unbeliever and the believer. 'Take my yoke upon you, and learn of me; for I am meek and lowly in heart: and you shall find rest unto your souls.'

In all circumstances of life, we find rest unto our souls only as we voluntarily submit to the rule and dominion of the Son of God as our Lord and King. The only way to find rest is to willingly slip your neck under his yoke. When you do, and only when you do, you will find his yoke really is easy and his burden really is light. Take the Master's yoke upon you and find rest unto your souls. Bow to him as your only Lord, take upon you his yoke of grace (Luke 14:25-33), and he will give you rest. Bow to his yoke of providence (Psalm 31:1-15). You will find rest for your soul.

Read the Word of God and you will discover that sabbath keeping was required in the Old Testament law to portray the blessed rest of faith in Christ. It had no other purpose. The ordinance of sabbath observance was established by God in the wilderness at the same time that Manna was given from heaven (Exodus. 16:22-30). The manna portrayed God's provision of life in Christ, the Bread of Life. The sabbath portrayed God's provision of rest in Christ.

The children of Israel were commanded not to do any work on the sabbath. They were not even allowed to pick up manna on the seventh day of the week. In Exodus 20:8-11, we read God's law commandment, forbidding any man to work on Saturday, or even to have anyone under his authority work for him.

Those who would impose upon us the carnal ordinance of sabbath keeping in this gospel day of liberty, who would bring us back under the yoke of bondage to the law, compelling us to keep the sabbath day, compel us to do what they themselves cannot do.

There are many who teach sabbath keeping as a so-called 'rule of life', who would impose upon God's saints strict rules and regulations for sabbath day observance. But all their teaching and preaching in that regard is sheer hypocrisy. Not one of them observes the sabbath day. Their teaching regarding the sabbath is nothing but 'a fair show in the flesh' (Galatians 6:12, 13). Their pretended reverence for the law of God, when examined, reveals a total disregard for God's law. They sift through the commandments, pick out what they like, and ignore the rest.

Let me show you again what I mean. Permit me to repeat here what I have already written elsewhere that these things might be reinforced and remembered. There are four things required in God's law for the observance of the sabbath day. If the sabbath day is observed, it must be observed in such a way as to include all four of these things.

The sabbath day must be observed on Saturday, the seventh day of the week (Exodus 20:10). Sunday is not the sabbath day. It never has been. Sunday is the Lord's Day, the day of Christ's resurrection; but nowhere in the Bible are we commanded to observe the sabbath on Sunday. No work can be done on the sabbath (Exodus 20:10).

Any genuine observance of the sabbath day necessitates a return to the ceremonial law of the Old Testament, because the sabbath day cannot be observed without the offering of a double sin offering, a double meal offering, and a double drink offering; and those offerings must be made in the temple at Jerusalem (Numbers 28:9, 10).

Those who insist upon keeping the sabbath must also demand the execution of all sabbath breakers (Exodus 31:15). We do not and cannot observe a legal, literal sabbath day because Christ is our Sabbath, we rest in him! In the New Testament epistles, Romans to Revelation, the sabbath is only mentioned in two places. It is mentioned in the four gospels and in the book of Acts many times, but always in connection with the Jews and Jewish worship. But in those epistles which prescribe all ordinances of divine worship in this gospel age, it is mentioned in just two places (Colossians 2:16, 17; Hebrews 4:3-9).

'Let no man therefore judge you in meat, or in drink, or in respect of an holyday, or of the new moon, or of the sabbath days: Which are a shadow of things to come; but the body is of Christ (Colossians 2:16, 17).

Here the Apostle Paul, writing by divine inspiration, forbids the observance of a legal sabbath day on the basis of the fact that in Christ every believer is completely, totally, entirely, and forever freed from the law (Romans 7:4; 10:4).

'For we which have believed do enter into rest, as he said, As I have sworn in my wrath, if they shall enter into my rest: although the works were finished from the foundation of the world. For he spake in a certain place of the seventh day on this wise, And God did rest the seventh day from all his works ... There remaineth therefore a rest to the people of God (Hebrews 4:3-9).

The word 'rest' in these verses is the word normally translated 'sabbath'. Here we are told that all who believe on the Lord Jesus Christ keep the sabbath spiritually, truly keep the sabbath, by faith in him. How do we keep the sabbath by faith? Just like our God kept the first sabbath, by coming to Christ, and believing on the Son of God. In this way we cease from our works and rest and are refreshed! Now, I bid you come to Christ and keep the sabbath of faith.

'Come unto me, all ye that labour and are heavy laden, and I will give you rest. Take my yoke upon you, and learn of me; for I am meek and lowly in heart: and ye shall find rest unto your souls. For my yoke is easy, and my burden is light' (Matthew 11:28-30).

Chapter 107

Lessons From The Golden Calf

'And when the people saw that Moses delayed to come down out of the mount, the people gathered themselves together unto Aaron, and said unto him, Up, make us gods, which shall go before us; for as for this Moses, the man that brought us up out of the land of Egypt, we wot not what is become of him ... And all the people brake off the golden earrings which were in their ears, and brought them unto Aaron ... After he had made it a molten calf: and they said, These be thy gods, O Israel, which brought thee up out of the land of Egypt. And when Aaron saw it, he built an altar before it; and Aaron made proclamation, and said, To morrow is a feast to the LORD. And they rose up early on the morrow, and offered burnt offerings, and brought peace offerings; and the people sat down to eat and to drink, and rose up to play ... And it came to pass on the morrow, that Moses said unto the people, Ye have sinned a great sin: and now I will go up unto the LORD; peradventure I shall make an atonement for your sin ... And the LORD plagued the people, because they made the calf, which Aaron made.'
(Exodus 32:1-35)

'The heart is deceitful above all things and desperately wicked.' How we prove those words day by day! How deceitful, how fickle is the heart of man! 'Who can know it?'

When Moses read the book of God's law to the children of Israel on Mount Sinai, in Exodus 24:7, the congregation spoke immediately, with unanimous voice, saying, 'All that the LORD hath said, will we do, and be obedient'. Less than six weeks later, while Moses was in the mount receiving the heavenly pattern of God's salvation and grace in Christ as portrayed and typified in the tabernacle, we find those very same men and women dancing around a golden calf, calling their creation their god and calling their naked revelry in idolatry the worship of Jehovah! What would God the Holy Ghost have us learn from the record of Israel's idolatry in worshipping the golden calf their hands had made?

We know this sad, sad portion of Israel's history came to pass according to the will of our God, that Israel might stand before us as a beacon, an example, lest we should follow them in the pursuit of our own heart's lusts. We know this because the Holy Spirit specifically points to this event and warns us not to follow their example (1 Corinthians 10).

'Now these things were our examples, to the intent we should not lust after evil things, as they also lusted. Neither be ye idolaters, as were some of them; as it is written, The people sat down to eat and drink, and rose up to play ... Now all these things happened unto them for ensamples: and they are written for our admonition, upon whom the ends of the world are come. Wherefore let him that thinketh he standeth take heed lest he fall' (1 Corinthians 10:6, 7, 11, 12).

Idolatry

The first thing we are taught here is that we are all superstitious idolaters at heart. The Egyptians had among their many gods the image of an ox and worshipped it. It must have been a very impressive image of strength, because the Jews remembered it, made a replica of it as an image of Jehovah, and worshipped it!

'And when the people saw that Moses delayed to come down out of the mount, the people gathered themselves together unto Aaron, and said unto him, Up, make us gods, which shall go before us; for as for this Moses, the man that brought us up out of the land of Egypt, we wot not what is become of him. And Aaron said unto them, Break off the golden earrings, which are in the ears of your wives, of your sons, and of your daughters, and bring them unto me' (Exodus 32:1, 2).

Aaron was a good speaker and orator, but he was not a leader. He lacked backbone and was apparently one whose heart craved approval. It is obvious the children of Israel knew they could manipulate Aaron.

They knew he would obey their whim. They did not ask for his counsel. They simply said, 'Get up and make us some gods'. And Aaron did. They spared no expense and Aaron willingly complied with their desire. 'The fear of man bringeth a snare: but whoso putteth his trust in the LORD shall be safe' (Proverbs 29:25).

'And all the people brake off the golden earrings which were in their ears, and brought them unto Aaron. And he received them at their hand, and fashioned it with a graving tool, after he had made it a molten calf: and they said, These be thy gods, O Israel, which brought thee up out of the land of Egypt' (Exodus 32:3, 4).

'They made a calf in Horeb, and worshipped the molten image. Thus they changed their glory into the similitude of an ox that eateth grass. They forgat God their saviour, which had done great things in Egypt' (Psalm 106:19-21).

'And when Aaron saw it, he built an altar before it; and Aaron made proclamation, and said, Tomorrow is a feast to the LORD. And they rose up early on the morrow, and offered burnt offerings, and brought peace offerings; and the people sat down to eat and to drink, and rose up to play' (Exodus 32:5, 6).

Robert Hawker observed, 'At the very moment the Lord, in the mount, was ordaining Aaron with peculiar honours to the priesthood, Aaron was aiding the Israelites to idolatry. Well might the Apostle say, the law maketh men high priests which have infirmity'. But, blessed be our God for his great grace! We have a Priest without infirmity (Hebrews 7:26-28).

Adding insult to insult and blasphemy to blasphemy, Aaron and the children of Israel called their sin the worship of Jehovah. The Spirit of God describes their religious ceremony with these words, 'They sat down to eat and to drink, and rose up to play'. Lascivious foolishness always accompanies idolatry. Idolatry is filth and always leads to the practise of filthy acts. 'Wherefore, my dearly beloved, flee from idolatry' (1 Corinthians 10:14). Every form of religious imagery is idolatry. Every addition to the worship of God is idolatry. Every mixture of false religion with the worship of God is idolatry. Every effort of man to mix the work of his own hands with the glory of God is idolatry.

What was it these people did that cost the lives of three thousand of them? What was their crime? They kept their feast unto the Lord. They offered burnt offerings and peace offerings. They used the strongest of images to represent Jehovah's might and power. They spared no expense. They ascribed their deliverance from Egypt to Jehovah their golden calf! What did they do that was so terrible? They worshipped the work of their own hands and called it the worship of God. They worshipped themselves, and called it worshipping Jehovah!

So it is with the idolatry of our age and every age. God save us from the religious idolatry running deep in every depraved heart; legalism, self-righteousness, will worship, works religion! There is no worship of God except the worship of Jesus Christ the Lord as our Saviour. If you would worship God, you must trust his Son. Christ alone is our Wisdom in the knowledge of God, our Righteousness for acceptance with God, our Sanctification and holiness before God, and our Redemption to bring us to God (1 Corinthians 1:30, 31; Philippians 3:1-3).

Moses' Intercession
Israel's sin was horrible and inexcusable. Their idolatry cannot be justified or lessened by any consideration, yet in verses 7-14 we see that Israel was spared, because Israel had a mighty intercessor with God. So, the second lesson to be learned from this chapter is that the wrath of God we deserve has been turned away by one God has ordained, one God has raised up for us, one God himself accepts as our Representative and Mediator, the Lord Jesus Christ.

'And the LORD said unto Moses, Go, get thee down; for thy people, which thou broughtest out of the land of Egypt, have corrupted themselves: They have turned aside quickly out of the way which I commanded them: they have made them a molten calf, and have worshipped it, and have sacrificed thereunto, and said, These be thy gods, O Israel, which have brought thee up out of the land of Egypt. And the LORD said unto Moses, I have seen this people, and, behold, it is a stiffnecked people: Now therefore let me alone, that my wrath may wax hot against them, and that I may consume them: and I will make of thee a great nation' (Exodus 32:7-10).

These Jews fully deserved God's wrath. They were more corrupt and wicked than the Egyptians God destroyed at the Red Sea. They were a people like you and me, far more deserving of God's wrath than many who have gone to hell before us. They corrupted themselves (v. 7). They turned aside quickly out of the way (v. 8). They made a molten calf (v.8). They worshipped the calf they made (v. 8). They called their hand-made god, Jehovah our Saviour (v. 8). They were a stiff-necked people (v. 9).

The Lord God said to Moses, 'Get out of my way, and I will kill them all and raise up from your loins a great nation.' But Moses interceded for the children of Israel as no mortal man ever interceded for other men. He said, 'Lord destroy me and spare them! Take me in their stead.' 'And Moses besought the LORD his God, and said, LORD, why doth thy wrath wax hot against thy people, which thou hast brought forth out of the land of Egypt with great power, and with a mighty hand? Wherefore should the Egyptians speak, and say, For mischief did he bring them out, to slay them in the mountains, and to consume them from the face of the earth? Turn from thy fierce wrath, and repent of this evil against thy people. Remember Abraham, Isaac, and Israel, thy servants, to whom thou swarest by thine own self, and saidst unto them, I will multiply your seed as the stars of heaven, and all this land that I have spoken of will I give unto your seed, and they shall inherit it forever. And the LORD repented of the evil which he thought to do unto his people' (Exodus 32:11-14).

Surely, it is the Holy Spirit's intent that we should lose sight of Moses in this place in order to behold him whom Moses typified, our Lord Jesus Christ, our mighty Intercessor. 'He saw that there was no man, and wondered that there was no intercessor: therefore his arm brought salvation unto him; and his righteousness, it sustained him' (Isaiah 59:16).

Notice the arguments Moses urged before the throne of God, giving him reasons why these sinful people should be spared. He said to God, 'These are thy people. You redeemed them, thy people, which thou hast brought forth out of the land of Egypt. Your name is at stake here. Your honour is pinned to the salvation of these people. Remember your covenant.'

'And the LORD repented of the evil which he thought to do unto his people' (v. 14; Psalm 106:8, 23, 45). How we ought to thank God for our all-glorious Christ who, like Moses, stands in the breach for us!

Satisfaction Demanded

In verses 15-19 we see in vivid, clear symbolism that God's broken law demands satisfaction.

'And Moses turned, and went down from the mount, and the two tables of the testimony were in his hand: the tables were written on both their sides; on the one side and on the other were they written. And the tables were the work of God, and the writing was the writing of God, graven upon the tables. And when Joshua heard the noise of the people as they shouted, he said unto Moses, There is a noise of war in the camp. And he said, It is not the voice of them that shout for mastery, neither is it the voice of them that cry for being overcome: but the noise of them that sing do I hear. And it came to pass, as soon as he came nigh unto the camp, that he saw the calf, and the dancing: and Moses' anger waxed hot, and he cast the tables out of his hands, and brake them beneath the mount' (Exodus 32:15-19).

When Moses came down from the Mount and saw the children of Israel dancing naked around their golden calf, he threw the tables of the law down on the ground, the tablets written by the finger of God, the work of God and the writing of God, and broke them; but he was never reproved for doing so. Symbolically, this action displays God's demands and God's work. His broken law demands satisfaction. But God alone can repair the law we have broken.

Justify God
In verses 20-26 we learn a fourth lesson. There is no reconciliation to God in our hearts until we justify God against ourselves.

'And he took the calf which they had made, and burnt it in the fire, and ground it to powder, and strawed it upon the water, and made the children of Israel drink of it. And Moses said unto Aaron, What did this people unto thee, that thou hast brought so great a sin upon them? And Aaron said, Let not the anger of my lord wax hot: thou knowest the people, that they are set on mischief. For they said unto me, Make us gods, which shall go before us: for as for this Moses, the man that brought us up out of the land of Egypt, we wot not what is become of him. And I said unto them, Whosoever hath any gold, let them break it off. So they gave it me: then I cast it into the fire, and there came out this calf. And when Moses saw that the people were naked; (for Aaron had made them naked unto their shame among their enemies:) Then Moses stood in the gate of the camp, and said, Who is on the LORD'S side? Let him come unto me. And all the sons of Levi gathered themselves together unto him' (Exodus 32:20-26).

Israel had to drink their golden calf. They had to take their corruption and sin to themselves. That is exactly what the Lord God requires of us (Psalm 51:1-5). If we confess our sins the Lord God is faithful and just to forgive us of our sins and cleanse us from all sin by the precious blood of Christ (1 John 1:7-10).

Repentance, faith, and the confession of sin do not accomplish our forgiveness. The judicial ground of our forgiveness is the shed blood of Christ alone. But until a man confesses his sin, he cannot receive the forgiveness accomplished at Calvary. Our hearts must be reconciled to God, and that reconciliation is begun in confession. Our confession must be made in humble sincerity towards God, with faith in Christ's atoning sacrifice. You cannot mention every offence, but you dare not hide one. Confess that you are vile by nature, wicked in practice, and evil in heart. Lie down as low as you can at the footstool of mercy. 'He that covereth his sins shall not prosper: but whoso confesseth and forsaketh them shall have mercy.'

God's forgiveness of such sinners as we are is both faithful and just. God has promised to forgive repenting, believing sinners for Christ's sake. And he is faithful to his word. But he can only forgive us in a way consistent with his justice. In holy justice God slew his Son as our Substitute. With that one sacrifice, justice is fully satisfied. And now, upon the ground of the finished work of Christ, the justice of God pleads as strongly as his mercy for our forgiveness. Our forgiveness is complete. If we confess our sins, trusting the blood of Christ alone to cleanse us from all unrighteousness, God will never impute iniquity to us (Romans 4:8). Blessed forgiveness!

Satisfaction Made

In verses 27-35, we learn the children of Israel were spared, because satisfaction was made by legal atonement. 'And he said unto them, Thus saith the LORD God of Israel, Put every man his sword by his side, and go in and out from gate to gate throughout the camp, and slay every man his brother, and every man his companion, and every man his neighbour. And the children of Levi did according to the word of Moses: and there fell of the people that day about three thousand men. For Moses had said, Consecrate yourselves today to the LORD, even every man upon his son, and upon his brother; that he may bestow upon you a blessing this day. And it came to pass on the morrow, that Moses said unto the people, Ye have sinned a great sin: and now I will go up unto the LORD; peradventure I shall make an atonement for your sin. And Moses returned unto the LORD, and said, Oh, this people have sinned a great sin, and have made them gods of gold. Yet now, if thou wilt forgive their sin ; and if not, blot me, I pray thee, out of thy book which thou hast written. And the LORD said unto Moses, Whosoever hath sinned against me, him will I blot out of my book. Therefore now go, lead the people unto the place of which I have spoken unto thee: behold, mine Angel shall go before thee: nevertheless in the day when I visit I will visit their sin upon them. And the LORD plagued the people, because they made the calf, which Aaron made' (Exodus 32:27-35).

None were spared except those for whom intercession was made; and all were spared for whom intercession was made (Deuteronomy 9:17-21). A great multitude was slain that the severity as well as the goodness of God be demonstrated. But all who were spared were spared by atonement; justice satisfying atonement made by a substitute (vv. 30-34). How sweet are the waters of forgiveness, flowing from a satisfied God! As we are reminded of and acknowledge our sin, we are refreshed and revived by God's great forgiveness.

Moses made symbolic, typical atonement; but real satisfaction, real atonement could only be made by one great Substitute, our Lord Jesus Christ, who fulfilled these very words when he was made sin for us (Proverbs 17:15; 2 Corinthians 5:20, 21; Galatians 3:13, 14). The Lord God declares, 'The soul that sinneth, it shall die'. He said to Moses, 'Whosoever hath sinned against me, him will I blot out of my book'. And in Christ, in union with our blessed Saviour, all God's elect suffered and died. Our great Saviour, God incarnate, has by the sacrifice of himself forever satisfied God's offended justice for us. In Christ, through Christ, by his blood atonement, the Holy Lord God is 'a just God and a Saviour'.

Chapter 108

Who Is On The Lord's Side?

'And when Moses saw that the people were naked; (for Aaron had made them naked unto their shame among their enemies:) Then Moses stood in the gate of the camp, and said, Who is on the LORD'S side? Let him come unto me. And all the sons of Levi gathered themselves together unto him. And he said unto them, Thus saith the LORD God of Israel, Put every man his sword by his side, and go in and out from gate to gate throughout the camp, and slay every man his brother, and every man his companion, and every man his neighbour. And the children of Levi did according to the word of Moses: and there fell of the people that day about three thousand men. For Moses had said, Consecrate yourselves today to the LORD, even every man upon his son, and upon his brother; that he may bestow upon you a blessing this day.'
(Exodus 32:25-29)

I call you who love Christ and love the truth of Christ, you whose hearts rejoice in the gospel of God's free, sovereign, saving grace, to a reaffirmation of your commitment and allegiance to Christ. I call you also who have, thus far, heard the gospel of the grace of God in vain. As the Spirit of God puts it, you have, thus far, received the grace of God in vain (2 Corinthians 6:1). You refuse to believe God. You trample under your feet the blood of the Son of God. You despise his grace. You resist his Spirit. And you rebel against his rule. You may even profess faith in Christ nominally; but you are yet an unbeliever. Your profession of faith is a sham, a mockery of Christ. Your heart's allegiance is not to Christ, but to yourself and to the world. You I call, even as you read these lines, to faith in Christ.

I set before you life and death, Christ and the world. Yes, I press you to make a decision. Like Elijah, I say to you, 'How long halt ye between two opinions? If the Lord be God, follow him' (1 Kings 18:21). Like Joshua, I say to you, 'Choose you this day whom ye will serve' (Joshua 24:15). That is precisely what Moses did in the text which heads this page. That is precisely what the Spirit of God says to all to whom this word of grace comes. 'Consecrate yourselves today to the LORD.'

While Moses was in the Mount receiving the law of God for Israel, Israel rebelled against the Lord. They did not openly deny God. In fact, they pretended to be worshipping the Lord. Dancing naked, like a bunch of barbarians around their golden calf, we read in verse 5 that they pretended to keep the feast of Jehovah! They persuaded Aaron to make them gods which they could see, and feel, and touch. So, Aaron made them a golden calf. You know the story. When Moses came down from the mount and saw their idolatry, he was furious. He smashed their 'god' to pieces, burned it, scattered it upon the waters, and made the children of Israel drink it. He rebuked Aaron sharply. And the children of Israel, fearing God and fearing his prophet, went to their tents.

But there were some, about three thousand, stout-hearted rebels, who brazenly defied Moses and the God he represented. Moses, knowing the rebellion had to be crushed and the rebels punished, issued a summons. He called for a decision. 'Moses stood in the gate of the camp, and said, Who is on the Lord's side? Let him come unto me'. He raised a standard, the name of God the Lord. He drew a line in the sand and called those who would follow the Lord to cross the line. A decision had to be made, a life and death decision. It had to be made right then. 'And all the sons of Levi gathered themselves together unto him.'

There is a dreadful conflict going on today, a warfare between Christ and Satan, light and darkness, truth and error, Zion and Babylon. And you must decide between the two. Regarding this conflict, neutrality is not possible. You must and will decide either to follow Christ or to pursue the world. May God be pleased to reveal Christ in you and give you a heart to follow him.

I want you to know that if you follow Christ, you must be prepared for spiritual warfare all the days of your life. So, while I seek recruits for Christ, I tell you plainly what the cost will be. Before you make your decision, I urge you to count the cost. I do not ask you to enlist blindly in the King's army. He will have only willing, loyal-hearted volunteers.

The Engagement

First, let me describe the engagement to which the Book of God calls us. It is warfare. I am seeking recruits for war. But before you volunteer, you have a right to know what is the warfare and who is the enemy you are about to engage. I call you to take sides with the Lord Jesus Christ against all his enemies. I call you to choose the path of faith and oppose all unbelief. Scepticism is the way of the world. Unbelief is the way of the flesh. Faith is the way of life. If you would live in Christ, you must believe God (Hebrews 11:6). To believe God is to rely upon him. It is to trust the revelation of God concerning his Son the Lord Jesus (1 John 5:10). Faith in Christ is reliance upon the promise of God in Christ (Romans 8:32). It is trusting the word of God in the face of trial, temptation, opposition, and heresy (2 Timothy 3:16; Hebrews 11:1-3).

I call you to choose the gospel of God's free and sovereign grace in Christ and reject all the religious superstitions of the world. If we would follow Christ, we must turn our backs upon the world, the religion of the world, and those who will not follow Christ (Galatians 1:6-8; 1 Corinthians 16:22). The religion of Christ is the gospel of pure, free, sovereign, unconditional grace (Ephesians 1:3-14; 2:8, 9). The religion of this world is any deviation from or addition to grace alone (Galatians 5:2-4). You cannot follow Christ unless you turn your back upon antichrist and come out of the great whore (2 Corinthians 6:16-7:1).

I am calling for utter surrender to King Jesus. Let us give our allegiance to Christ alone and deny ourselves (Luke 14:25-33). To do this we must give ourselves in unreserved surrender to him, setting our heart against our own fleshy desires, the world's allurements and charms, the devil's temptations. This is the engagement I set before you. It is a lifelong warfare, a bitter conflict in hostile, enemy territory, from which there is no reprieve and no truce as long as we live in this world.

The Eligibility

Second, you must be eligible to enlist in Christ's army. If we would follow Christ, we have to meet certain requirements. If you do not meet these three requirements, you can never be 'on the Lord's side'.

We must have forgiveness. We are sinners, justly condemned by the law of the Lord, our sins must be forgiven before we can serve the Lord. These sons of Levi were as guilty of idolatry as the rest of the people. They could not be accepted of God until their sins were forgiven.

Therefore, Moses interceded with God for their forgiveness (v. 32). Like those Levites, we are guilty, justly condemned sinners; but there is forgiveness with God; free, full, immutable, everlasting forgiveness of all sin through the Lord Jesus Christ (Psalm 130:4; 1 John 1:9).

We must have atonement. The only basis upon which the Lord God can or will forgive sin is satisfaction by blood atonement. God cannot forgive sin without atonement. There can be no atonement without satisfaction, and there can be no satisfaction without blood. 'Without shedding of blood is no remission' (Hebrews 9:22).

These Jews could never have been accepted without atonement. 'Moses said unto the people, Ye have sinned a great sin: and now I will go up unto the Lord; peradventure I shall make atonement for your sin' (v. 30). In a word, you and I are not eligible for grace except by blood atonement. We cannot obtain mercy except we come to God through faith in the blood of Christ (Hebrews 7:25). Our hope is in the merit of Christ's blood as the God-man, our Mediator. We must trust that blood, crying 'God be merciful to me a sinner'.

We must have consecration. Eligibility for service in the kingdom of Christ is decided consecration (v. 29). Faith in Christ is nothing less than deliberate, voluntary consecration of heart to Christ as Master.

These Levites were required to openly declare their allegiance to the Lord, and so are we. When we identify with God's truth, God's church, and God's messenger, we identify with Christ. The opposite is also true. When a person identifies with Christ's enemies, a false gospel, and a false prophet, he identifies with antichrist. What does this consecration to Christ involve? Read what Moses wrote by divine inspiration and you will see what it involved for these Levites. They had to be willing to be aligned with the minority, one tribe against eleven. That is the case with God's people in the world. They are always in the minority.

They had to be prepared for stern conflict. Moses said, 'Put every man his sword by his side' (v. 27). Their love for Christ meant hatred of their own kinsmen. They had to choose between Christ and family. And they chose Christ (v. 28). They had to obey the Lord. Their heart allegiance demanded they do the will of God, regardless of cost. And 'the children of Levi did according to the word of Moses' (v. 28).

Eligibility for the kingdom of God requires these three things; forgiveness, atonement, consecration.

The Encouragements

Third, God gives us some great encouragements. The Book of God calls us to the kind of commitment that possessed Jephthah's soul, the kind of commitment that these Levites exemplified, the kind of commitment that holds back nothing.

When Ignatius was martyred for his faith in Christ, he met death with utter commitment to the Lord Jesus, saying, 'Now I begin to be a Christian'. That is the commitment I want to give my Redeemer. That is the commitment to which I call all who read these lines. I make no promises of a happy, peaceful, easy life in this world. Allegiance to Christ is costly. It is a constant aggravation to the flesh. The way of faith is, more often than not, a path of isolation, trouble, temptation, and trial. I have tried to show you the cost and the conflict of faith in Christ.

Now, let me encourage you to pay the price. The cause I hold before you is the cause of Christ in this world. It is the cause of his glory and his truth. It is a cause with a sure foundation and certain end. Like David, let us go to meet God's enemies armed with the whole armour of God. 'Is there not a cause?' Our cause is the cause of Christ and Christ himself is with us (Matthew 28:18-20). The angels of God hold guard over us (2 Kings 6:17; Hebrews 1:14). We have no cause for fear. A great cloud of witnesses in heaven has led the way and marked it for us (Hebrews 12:1). Your own conscience bears witness. 'This is the way!' I call you to enlist in an army at war, but an army whose victory is sure, whose reward is eternal glory (Revelation 19:1-14). I set before you a strait gate. Will you enter? I call you to walk the narrow way.

The Enlistment

Fourth, I press on you the claims of Christ and call you to enlist. 'Who is on the Lord's side? Let him come unto me.' Have you decided to join ranks with the Son of God? Have you, in your heart, done so? If you have, then put on the colours of the King's army by confessing Christ in believer's baptism. Come out publicly for the Son of God! All who take sides with Christ against hell and antichrist, who take his cause to be their cause are like these Levites who came to Moses. Read what Moses tells us about them in Deuteronomy 33.

'And of Levi he said, Let thy Thummim and thy Urim be with thy holy one, whom thou didst prove at Massah, and with whom thou didst strive at the waters of Meribah; Who said unto his father and to his mother, I have not seen him; neither did he acknowledge his brethren, nor knew his own children: for they have observed thy word, and kept thy covenant. They shall teach Jacob thy judgments, and Israel thy law: they shall put incense before thee, and whole burnt sacrifice upon thine altar. Bless, LORD, his substance, and accept the work of his hands: smite through the loins of them that rise against him, and of them that hate him, that they rise not again' (Deuteronomy 33:8-11).

These Levites who came to Moses, who publicly demonstrated their allegiance to the Lord were all divinely chosen men; accepted, priestly men, greatly blessed men, eternally blessed and daily blessed! And these blessed, chosen, believing men were proved of God faithful men!

I call for you and call upon myself, let us now commit and consecrate ourselves this day unto the Lord, let us commit and consecrate ourselves this day to the Lord Jesus Christ our Saviour as decided, loyal soldiers in the cause of Christ (Romans 12:1, 2). Put on the whole armour of God (Ephesians 6:13-18). Make your first concern a matter of civil war. Wage war against your own self. Make no provision for the flesh. Engage the enemy at home. Go to war against your own hearts' lusts! Make it your business to oppose every proud, hissing serpent of hell, who dares raise his head in opposition to Christ and his gospel, who dares oppose the glory of our God and Saviour. Our Master's cause, his glory, his truth, and the souls of men are at stake. We must engage the enemy!

Martin Luther said, 'If I profess with the loudest voice and clearest exposition every portion of the truth of God except precisely that point which the world and the devil are at that moment attacking, then I am not confessing Christ, however boldly I may be professing him! Where the battle rages, there the loyalty of the soldier is proved; and to be steady on all the battle front besides is merely flight and disgrace if he flinches at that point.'

The gates of hell will fall before us. God will again send the Spirit of life upon his church. Moses' prayer for Levi is my prayer for you who take sides with Christ and carry his banner of light through the darkness of this world, assailing the gates of hell with the battering ram of free grace.

'Bless, LORD, his substance, and accept the work of his hands: smite through the loins of them that rise against him, and of them that hate him, that they rise not again' (Deuteronomy 33:11).

Chapter 109

Let Us Go To The Tabernacle

'And the LORD said unto Moses, Depart, and go up hence, thou and the people which thou hast brought up out of the land of Egypt, unto the land which I sware unto Abraham, to Isaac, and to Jacob, saying, Unto thy seed will I give it: And I will send an angel before thee; and I will drive out the Canaanite, the Amorite, and the Hittite, and the Perizzite, the Hivite, and the Jebusite: Unto a land flowing with milk and honey: for I will not go up in the midst of thee; for thou art a stiffnecked people: lest I consume thee in the way. And when the people heard these evil tidings, they mourned: and no man did put on him his ornaments. For the LORD had said unto Moses, Say unto the children of Israel, Ye are a stiffnecked people: I will come up into the midst of thee in a moment, and consume thee: therefore now put off thy ornaments from thee, that I may know what to do unto thee. And the children of Israel stripped themselves of their ornaments by the mount Horeb. And Moses took the tabernacle, and pitched it without the camp, afar off from the camp, and called it the tabernacle of the congregation. And it came to pass, that everyone which sought the LORD went out unto the tabernacle of the congregation, which was without the camp. And it came to pass, when Moses went out unto the tabernacle, that all the people rose up, and stood every man at his tent door, and looked after Moses, until he was gone into the tabernacle. And it came to pass, as Moses entered into the tabernacle, the cloudy pillar descended, and stood at the door of the tabernacle, and the LORD talked with Moses.

And all the people saw the cloudy pillar stand at the tabernacle door: and all the people rose up and worshipped, every man in his tent door. And the LORD spake unto Moses face to face, as a man speaketh unto his friend. And he turned again into the camp: but his servant Joshua, the son of Nun, a young man, departed not out of the tabernacle.' (Exodus 33:1-11)

When Moses came down from the mount, after receiving the law, he saw the children of Israel dancing naked around the calf Aaron had made. He knew the enormity of their sin. Immediately, he destroyed the golden calf. He ground it to powder, scattered it upon the water, and made the children of Israel drink it. 'Then Moses stood in the gate of the camp, and said, Who is on the Lord's side? Let him come unto me.' Before the day was over, the sons of Levi had killed three thousand of those idolaters who refused to repent.

Then Moses made his great, intercessory prayer for Israel, seeking God's forgiveness for them. The Lord God was merciful. He did not destroy the nation; but he said, 'I will not go up in the midst of thee; for thou art a stiffnecked people'. Broken, humbled, fearing the loss of God's presence, Moses and the children of Israel sought the Lord (vv. 4-7).

There is no physical tabernacle, temple, or holy place of worship on earth today. We do not want one! We worship God in the Spirit, if we worship him at all. We have no need for carnal ceremonies and fleshy rituals. But as we read about the tabernacle, we are taught much about the worship of God. Actually, the tabernacle was not finished and set up until we get to Exodus 40. The Lord God showed Moses how the tabernacle was to be made while he was in the Mount Sinai (Exodus 25–31). Then, after Israel's terrible act of idolatry, before the tabernacle could be completed and set up with all its ordinances of worship, Moses pitched a tent and called it 'the Tabernacle of the congregation' (v. 7). This temporary tabernacle was pitched afar off, outside the camp of Israel. Later, the actual tabernacle would be set up in the middle of the camp.

Moses' tabernacle here was a temporary representation of the tabernacle he was about to erect for the worship of God. Moses called this temporary structure 'the Tabernacle of the congregation', the same name that was given to the subsequent structure. It is the later tabernacle, the one Moses built exactly according to the pattern God showed him in the Mount Sinai, which has our attention in this chapter.

The outer court of that structure was approximately 75 feet by 150 feet and contained the brazen altar and the laver. The holy place was approximately 15 feet by 45 feet. It contained the table of shewbread, the golden candlestick, and the altar of incense. The holy of holies, the most holy place, was separated from the holy place by a thick veil. In the most holy place stood the ark of the covenant with the mercy seat.

The tabernacle was the sanctuary of God's presence, the place where God met with his people in the manifestation of his grace and glory (Exodus 25:8, 22; 29:42, 43). In accordance with his promise, when the tabernacle was finished, 'a cloud covered the tent of the congregation, and the glory of the LORD filled the tabernacle' (Exodus 40:34).

What does all of this mean to us? The tabernacle and its furnishings were destroyed long ago. Why should we be interested in it? Well, because, everything concerning the tabernacle was highly symbolical and spiritually instructive. For example, as well as being called the tabernacle of the congregation, it is also called 'the tabernacle of witness in the wilderness' and 'the tabernacle of the testimony', showing that it bore witness to God's presence and testified of God's dealings with his people.

The tabernacle is certainly a symbol of the church, which is 'an habitation of God through the Spirit' (Exodus 25:8; Ephesians 2:19-22). Without question, the tabernacle represents the believer, who is the 'temple of the Holy Ghost' (1 Corinthians 6:19; 2 Corinthians 6:16). And the tabernacle on earth was a pattern and representation of 'things in the heavens' (Hebrews 9:23, 24). But, first and foremost, the tabernacle was a beautiful, instructive picture of Christ, teaching us how sinful man can approach the holy Lord God and worship him.

All the 'ordinances of divine service', all the rites and ceremonies, and 'the worldly sanctuary' itself, the tabernacle were pictures of Christ. You will never understand the laws regarding the tabernacle and its many services, until you understand that these things are pictures of Christ and of our redemption by him, which is the revelation of the glory of God. The tabernacle was a simple tent of earthly material on the outside; but on the inside it was glorious. Everything inside the tabernacle was overlaid with pure gold. That is Christ, the meek and lowly man and the great and glorious God!

A Sacrificing Priest

As we approach the tabernacle, the first thing we see, standing by the gate and the brazen altar is a sacrificing high priest. This sacrificing priest represents Christ, our great High Priest (Hebrews 5:1-5) taken from among men, a man without blemish (Leviticus 21:17, 18), merciful and compassionate, chosen and ordained of God.

All the garments of the priest speak of Christ. His mitre with its golden plate, 'Holiness to the LORD', typified the holiness and perfection of Christ's nature. His white linen garments portrayed Christ's righteousness and the garments of salvation he has given to his elect. The priest's girdle signified Christ our Strength. His breastplate, with the names of twelve tribes of Israel engraved upon it, shows Christ as our Representative before God, with our names engraved upon his heart. His ephod, the apron that held the breastplate, with the twelve stones bearing the names of the twelve tribes of Israel, shows us that Christ bears all God's elect upon his shoulders in all his priestly functions. The work of our redemption is his work alone.

But a priest without a sacrifice is as useless as a bucket without a bottom. Every priest ordained of God was a sacrificing priest. Without a blood sacrifice, no man can come to God. All the sacrifices offered in the tabernacle by the high priest were typical of Christ our Sacrifice. Strong beasts, males of the first year, tame beasts led, not forced, to the slaughter, beasts without blemish, innocent victims, all were used to portray the Lamb of God, our all-glorious Christ.

Brazen Altar

The next thing we see as we approach the tabernacle is the brazen altar (Exodus 27:1-8). This altar and the burnt sacrifices offered upon it represented Christ our Altar (Hebrews 13:10). Dying upon the cross, our Lord Jesus was a burnt offering to God. The fire of God's wrath fell upon him there. All the excrement and filthy inward parts of the slain beasts were burned on this altar, so all our sins were laid on Christ, when he was made sin for us, and were purged away, being consumed by the fire of God's wrath.

Laver of Brass

Third, standing between the brazen altar and the holy place is the laver of brass (Exodus 30:18-25). Every priest, before entering the holy place to do any service for the Lord in the sanctuary, had to wash his hands and feet. This represents our sanctification and regeneration by God the Holy Spirit, creating us new creatures in Christ, creating in us that holiness without which no one shall ever see the Lord (Revelation 1:5; Titus 3:5; Hebrews 12:14).

Before we can serve God, we must personally wash and bathe in the laver of Christ's blood.

This washing involves personal faith in Christ. You must personally appropriate to yourself the merits of Christ's finished work. All who wash in this laver are holy before God! As the priests washed in this laver daily, so you and I must bathe daily in the Word of God, applying the blood of Christ to ourselves, asking the Saviour to wash us again, that we may be cleansed from the defilements of sin (John 13:2-10).

The Holy Place
Now, go with the priest into the holy place. In Moses' day none but the priests could go into that sanctuary. All who trust Christ are priests (1 Peter 2:9). So let us lift up the outer veil and go in. What do you see in the holy place? Three things.

On the south side, on your left, you see the golden candlestick with its seven lamps burning (Exodus 25:31).

This golden candlestick represents Christ the Light of the world. There were seven lamps in the candlestick. Seven, being the number of perfection, shows that Christ is the perfect revelation of God. The only light in the holy place was the candlestick and the only light any man has into the things of God is the light Christ gives by his Spirit (1 Corinthians 2:14, 15). These seven golden candlesticks also represent the churches of Christ holding forth the light of life in this dark world (Revelation 1:20).

On the north side of the sanctuary, on your right, is the table of shewbread (Exodus 25:23-30).

This is Christ the Bread of Life. There were twelve loaves on the table, bread provided for all the tribes of Israel. As God's manna was given to Israel alone, so his grace in Christ is given only to his chosen people. The bread was always on the table, representing Christ the Bread of Life being always available to our hungry souls.

Sitting in the back, against the veil, is the altar of incense (Exodus 30:1-10).

This represents Christ our Intercessor (John 17; Hebrews 7:25; 1 John 2:1, 2). Our prayers, sacrifices and services come to God and find acceptance with him through the sweet incense of Christ our Intercessor and Mediator (1 Peter 2:5; Hebrews 13:15; Revelation 8:3, 4). The incense burned perpetually on this altar because Christ's intercessions for us, as our Mediator in heaven, are perpetual.

The Veil

Fifth, standing between the holy place and the most holy place is the veil (Exodus 26:31). God the Holy Spirit tells us this heavy, thick veil was typical of Christ's humanity (Hebrews 10:20). This veil was the only way of access to God. Before man could enter in and have access to God, and be accepted of him, this veil had to come down. Christ had to die before any sinner could ever come to God. When the Lord Jesus Christ died upon the cursed tree at Calvary, the veil was rent in two, from top to bottom. The rent veil means righteousness is established, justice is satisfied, sin is gone, the law is fulfilled, reconciliation is made. There is no cause of separation between God and his elect, no reason for separation between God and those sinners redeemed by Christ's precious blood!

Come to God. The way is open. Coming to God by faith in Christ, you may come with full assurance of acceptance!

'Now where remission of these is, there is no more offering for sin. Having therefore, brethren, boldness to enter into the holiest by the blood of Jesus, by a new and living way, which he hath consecrated for us, through the veil, that is to say, his flesh; and having an high priest over the house of God; let us draw near with a true heart in full assurance of faith, having our hearts sprinkled from an evil conscience, and our bodies washed with pure water' (Hebrews 10:18-22).

The Ark Of The Covenant

Sixth, entering into the holy of holies, we see one glorious, magnificent piece of furniture, the ark of the covenant (Exodus 25:10-22).

'Then verily the first covenant had also ordinances of divine service, and a worldly sanctuary. For there was a tabernacle made; the first, wherein was the candlestick, and the table, and the shewbread; which is called the sanctuary. And after the second veil, the tabernacle which is called the Holiest of all; which had the golden censer, and the ark of the covenant overlaid round about with gold, wherein was the golden pot that had manna, and Aaron's rod that budded, and the tables of the covenant; and over it the cherubims of glory shadowing the mercyseat; of which we cannot now speak particularly' (Hebrews 9:1-5).

The ark was a beautiful type of Christ. It was made of shittim wood, overlaid with gold, representing both the humanity and the deity of our Saviour. The ark was the symbol of God's holiness, power, and glory. It was carried about from place to place by staves upon the shoulders of the priests. Even so, Christ is carried through the world upon the shoulders of chosen men by the preaching of the gospel. There are three things in the ark.

A golden pot. The golden pot that had manna was a large golden pot containing an omer of manna, the bread of heaven. This represented God's provision of life and grace for sinners in Christ (Exodus 16:33, 34).

Aaron's rod that budded was also here. This rod represents God's power, the gospel of Christ. Christ was smitten by Moses' rod, the law. The water of life flows out to sinners by Aaron's rod, the gospel. The gospel of Christ is the power of God unto salvation (Romans 1:16, 17). No wonder Dagon (1 Samuel 5) fell before the ark!

The two tables of the law are here. This represents God's purpose. The law was written upon tables of stone, representing both the hardness of our hearts and the inflexibility of God's justice. The law represents our curse and condemnation by reason of sin. The law was always kept in the ark, under the mercy seat, under the blood (Exodus 25:16, 21). That represents perfect redemption by Christ. And that is the purpose of God (Romans 8:28-31).

The Mercy Seat

Sitting on top of the ark, completely covering it, is the mercy seat (Exodus 25:17, 21, 22). The Word 'mercy seat' means 'a propitiatory covering'. That is what Christ is to us (1 John 2:2; Romans 3:24-26).

The mercy seat represented redemption by the blood of Christ, mercy flowing to sinners by the blood of Christ (Hebrews 9:12). The mercy seat was the symbol of God's presence. With the blood upon the mercy seat that covered the tables of the broken law, we see the glory of God in the pardon of sin by the sacrifice of Christ (Leviticus 9:23, 24). We see the glory of God in redemption (Psalm 85:9-11). God meets sinners upon the mercy seat (Exodus 25:22), only at the mercy seat, only in Christ.

We have made a reprise and taken a very brief tour of the tabernacle in this study because I want more for you than simply to understand the typical meaning of those Mosaic ordinances. I want you to come to Christ. Christ is the Priest you need. Christ is the Altar upon which you must do business with God. Christ is the Sacrifice by which you must come to God. Christ is the Laver in which you must wash. Christ is the Light in which you must walk. Christ is the Bread you must eat. Christ is the Mercy-Seat of propitiation upon which God will meet you!

Chapter 110

'Show Me Thy Glory'

'And Moses said unto the LORD, See, thou sayest unto me, Bring up this people: and thou hast not let me know whom thou wilt send with me. Yet thou hast said, I know thee by name, and thou hast also found grace in my sight. Now therefore, I pray thee, if I have found grace in thy sight, shew me now thy way, that I may know thee, that I may find grace in thy sight: and consider that this nation is thy people. And he said, My presence shall go with thee, and I will give thee rest. And he said unto him, If thy presence go not with me, carry us not up hence. For wherein shall it be known here that I and thy people have found grace in thy sight? is it not in that thou goest with us? so shall we be separated, I and thy people, from all the people that are upon the face of the earth. And the LORD said unto Moses, I will do this thing also that thou hast spoken: for thou hast found grace in my sight, and I know thee by name. And he said, I beseech thee, shew me thy glory. And he said, I will make all my goodness pass before thee, and I will proclaim the name of the LORD before thee; and will be gracious to whom I will be gracious, and will shew mercy on whom I will shew mercy. And he said, Thou canst not see my face: for there shall no man see me, and live. And the LORD said, Behold, there is a place by me, and thou shalt stand upon a rock: And it shall come to pass, while my glory passeth by, that I will put thee in a clift of the rock, and will cover thee with my hand while I pass by: And I will take away mine hand, and thou shalt see my back parts: but my face shall not be seen.'
(Exodus 33:12-23)

This portion of Holy Scripture contains one of the boldest prayers a man ever uttered. At first glance, it might appear that no mere man upon the earth could ever ask such a favour from God. This is a mighty request, a very great request. Moses said, in verse 18, 'I beseech thee, shew me thy glory'.

Moses could not have asked for more. This is, perhaps, the greatest request of faith to be found in all the Bible. Here, Moses stands out as a giant among giants. Abraham showed great faith when he went out into the plain to offer up intercession for such a guilty city as Sodom. It was a great faith that enabled Jacob to lay hold of the Angel of the Lord, refusing to release his hold until he had received the blessing he desired. Elijah was strong in faith when he was able to rend the heavens and bring rain from the skies that had been as brass before. But it seems to me, if you put all these requests together, they would pale in comparison with this prayer of Moses. It is the greatest request a man could ever make to God, 'I beseech thee, shew me thy glory'.

The revelation of the glory of God is the greatest blessing any man can ask, and the greatest blessing God can give to any man upon this earth.

After making his request, when he had put his desire into words, Moses' bones must have trembled, his blood must have chilled in his veins, his hair must have stood on end. Jacob was a man of great faith, but, when the Lord God revealed himself to him, Jacob was astonished that he had survived the revelation. 'Jacob called the name of that place Peniel: for I have seen God face to face, and my life is preserved' (Genesis 32:30). When Manoah saw the Angel of the Lord, the pre-incarnate Christ, he was struck with fear. 'Manoah said unto his wife, we shall surely die, because we have seen God (Judges 13:22). Isaiah's response to the vision he had of God's glory was 'Woe is me! For I am undone; (I am cut off) because I am a man of unclean lips, and I dwell in the midst of a people of unclean lips: for mine eyes have seen the King, the LORD of hosts' (Isaiah 6:5). The Apostle John was a truly noble man, an example we would be wise to follow. Not only did he lay his head upon the Saviour's breast physically, he walked in heart to heart communion with the Son of God. Yet, when he saw the exalted, glorified God-man, he said, 'I fell at his feet as dead' (Revelation 1:17).

Moses himself was astonished that God would even speak to him, much less that he should show him his glory. He said to the children of

Israel, 'Behold, the LORD our God hath shewed us his glory and his greatness, and we have heard his voice out of the midst of the fire: we have seen this day that God doth talk with man and he liveth ... For who is there of all flesh, that hath heard the voice of the living God speaking out of the midst of the fire, as we have, and lived?' (Deuteronomy 5:24, 26). Surely, Moses himself was astonished that he could ask such a favour as this. 'I beseech thee, shew me thy glory.'

Moses' Inspiration
But how did Moses come to make such a request? What was it that God used to put this prayer in his heart? What inspired this man to pray, 'I beseech thee, show me thy glory'?

Moses had been in Sinai's mount in communion with God for forty days (Exodus 24:18). For forty blessed days he dwelt in the presence of his God. Jehovah had spoken to him as a man speaks with his own friend. Such nearness to God gave the meekest man on earth the boldness of faith to ask the greatest blessing any man could ever enjoy upon the earth.

Moses' prayer was the culmination of God's gracious dealings with him and of his faithful reliance upon his God. Before Moses said, 'I beseech thee, show me thy glory', he had sought and received several other tokens of God's gracious favour. The Lord God revealed his good will to Moses, his purpose of grace in Christ, in the burning bush (Exodus 3). He revealed his great and glorious name, JEHOVAH, to his servant on Horeb's holy ground. Moses had seen God's wonders in the land of Ham. He saw Pharaoh and the armies of Egypt destroyed in the Red Sea.

Look back to chapter thirty-two. The Lord was angry with the children of Israel. They had made a golden calf and bowed down before it. The Lord said to Moses, 'Let me alone, that my wrath may wax hot against them, and that I may consume them: and I will make of thee a great nation' (v. 10). But Moses loved the children of Israel and sought God's glory. He was more concerned for God's people and God's glory than he was for himself. So, he put God in remembrance of his covenant with Abraham, and of his deliverance of the Israelites out of Egypt. He argued that if the nation were slain, God's name would be mocked and blasphemed by the Egyptians. Then, he prayed, 'Yet now, if thou wilt forgive their sin; and if not, blot me I pray thee, out of thy book which thou hast written' (v. 32). Like Jacob of old, Moses prevailed with God. By God sparing the guilty nation, he received a fresh testimony of God's grace.

Thy Way

This great prayer, 'I beseech thee, show me thy glory', was preceded by three other great prayers. Let us look at them.

'And Moses said unto the LORD, See, thou sayest unto me, Bring up this people: and thou hast not let me know whom thou wilt send with me. Yet thou hast said, I know thee by name, and thou hast also found grace in my sight' (Exodus 33:12).

In verse 1 the Lord told Moses to bring the children of Israel on to the Land of Canaan. In verse 3, the Lord told Moses he would not go in the midst of the stiff-necked people. Christ, the Angel of the Lord, would continue to go before them and behind them; but he said he would no longer walk in their midst. Moses knew he could not perform the task before him without God's help and presence. Watch him plead his case before the Lord. Watch him put God in remembrance (Isaiah 43:26).

'Thou hast said, I know thee by name.' You have declared that you love me, that you have chosen me, that you have redeemed me, that you approve of me, that you have ordained and predestined me, that you accept me. Then Moses said to the Lord God, you said to me, 'Thou has also found grace in my sight'. You are the object of my favour and good will.

'Now therefore, I pray thee, if I have found grace in thy sight, show me now thy way, that I may know thee, that I may find grace in thy sight: and consider that this nation is thy people' (Exodus 33:13).

Read the word 'if' as 'since'. Moses was not expressing doubt concerning God's grace nor of the fact that he was the object of God's grace. Rather, he is pleading his cause, offering a reason for his prayer. 'Since I have found grace in thy sight, show me now thy way.'

The Lord God had commanded his servant to guide his people. But Moses knew and confessed his weakness and ignorance and sought the guidance of God to walk in his way. He knew God's way was not the way man would choose. He knew God's way might be a rough and dark way. But he knew God's way to be the best and wisest way. Only as Israel walked in God's way would the name of God be glorified. So, he prayed, 'Shew me now thy way'. Thy Way through this wilderness! Thy Way among all these enemies! Thy Way to Canaan! Thy Way of providence! Thy Way of grace! Thy Way of salvation! Blessed is the poor, needy soul in this dark wilderness of earth and time who asks the Lord God, 'Show me now thy way'.

'Jesus saith unto him, I am the way, the truth, and the life: no man cometh unto the Father, but by me' (John 14:6).

'Lead me, O LORD, in thy righteousness because of mine enemies; make thy way straight before my face' (Psalm 5:8).

'Teach me thy way, O LORD, and lead me in a plain path, because of mine enemies' (Psalm 27:11).

'Our heart is not turned back, neither have our steps declined from thy way' (Psalm 44:18).

'Teach me thy way, O LORD; I will walk in thy truth: unite my heart to fear thy name' (Psalm 86:11).

'Turn away mine eyes from beholding vanity; and quicken thou me in thy way' (Psalm 119:37).

Look at the reasons Moses urges before the Lord, the reasons he desired to know God's way. 'That I may know him' (Philippians 3:10). 'That I may find grace in thy sight.' The Lord God, the God of all grace before whom Moses bowed was and is our Saviour, who declares, 'My grace is sufficient for thee'.

Thy People

Next, God's servant prays, 'Consider that this nation is thy people'. He put the Lord in remembrance of his elect people, his covenant people, whom he had chosen for his own heritage (Deuteronomy 9:26; Joel 2:17). 'Jacob is the lot of his inheritance' (Deuteronomy 32:9). 'Jacob (is) his people and Israel his inheritance' (Psalm 78:71). They are a sinful people; but they are your people. You chose them. They are a stiff-necked people; but they are your people. You redeemed them. They are a straying people; but they are your people. You called them. They are a weak people; but they are your people. You keep them. They are a fallen people; but they are your people. You gave them your name. They are a fickle people; but they are your people. You took them into covenant union with yourself. They are just people, just men and women, just flesh and blood; but they are your people. Your honour is wrapped up in them.

429

Thy Presence

In verse 14 the Lord God makes a great promise of great grace. 'And he said, My presence shall go with thee, and I will give thee rest.' God's presence is the Lord Jesus Christ, the Angel of his presence. 'In all their affliction he was afflicted, and the angel of his presence saved them: in his love and in his pity he redeemed them; and he bare them, and carried them all the days of old' (Isaiah 63:9).

The rest promised here speaks specifically of Canaan, the land of rest. Canaan typified God's salvation in Christ. The promise is the blessed sabbath rest of grace and salvation in Christ (Hebrews 4:9, 10; Matthew 11:28-30).

As soon as Moses heard God's promise, he said, I have got to have that, and laid hold of the promise, urging God's promise as the basis of his prayer. 'And he said unto him, If thy presence go not with me, carry us not up hence' (v. 15). Without his presence, without Christ, all else is worthless and insignificant. Even the land of Canaan, the promised land of rest and plenty, is nothing in comparison with God's presence, nothing in comparison with our Saviour.

It does not much matter what we have or where we are, if we do not enjoy the presence of God. But if God is with us, the greatest hardships in the wilderness are easy; and we pass through our difficulties with peace, if not pleasure. It is as though Moses had said, 'Lord, if you go with me, I can do all that you require. But, if you will not go with me, then all will come to nothing.'

Moses goes on to use even stronger pleas, with which to urge his request before the throne of grace. Like a child on his father's lap, he argues his case for the thing he wants. Like a poor, needy soul before one who is able to supply his need, Moses offers reasons for God to give him his abiding presence.

'For wherein shall it be known here that I and thy people have found grace in thy sight? Is it not in that thou goest with us? So shall we be separated, I and thy people, from all the people that are upon the face of the earth' (Exodus 33:16).

The Lord's presence with us is the manifestation and evidence of his grace toward us, upon us, and in us. His presence with us and in us is our sanctification, the thing that separates us and distinguishes us from 'all the people that are upon the face of the earth'. The word 'separated' might be better translated 'marvellously separated', and truly we are marvellously separated from all people by our God, by his purpose, by his purchase, by his providence, by his power!

In verse 17 we read the Lord's answer to Moses' prayer. 'And the LORD said unto Moses, I will do this thing also that thou hast spoken: for thou hast found grace in my sight, and I know thee by name.'

Thy Glory

Now, I want us to look at this great request to see God's glory and see God's gracious response to it. May it please God the Holy Spirit to show us something of God's greatness and his glory. 'And he said, I beseech thee, show me thy glory' (v. 18).

'And he said, I will make all my goodness pass before thee, and I will proclaim the name of the LORD before thee; and will be gracious to whom I will be gracious, and will show mercy on whom I will show mercy. And he said, Thou canst not see my face: for there shall no man see me, and live' (Exodus 33:19, 20).

In this present state we see through a glass darkly. We see nothing perfectly. We certainly do not and cannot see God's glorious face, his magnificent being fully.

'And the LORD said, Behold, there is a place by me, and thou shalt stand upon a rock: And it shall come to pass, while my glory passeth by, that I will put thee in a clift of the rock, and will cover thee with my hand while I pass by. And I will take away mine hand, and thou shalt see my back parts: but my face shall not be seen' (Exodus 33:21-23).

When the Lord God passed by Moses, the one who passed by him was Christ, the pre-incarnate Saviour, in human form. God's 'back parts' refer to our Saviour's humanity, specifically to his suffering and death in human flesh. It was his back parts, his humanity, his heel, that was bruised in our redemption. It was his back parts, his heel, his humanity, that crushed the serpent's head (Genesis 3:15).

It is only in the cleft of the Rock that you can behold the glory of God. In Western North Carolina there is a mountain called Grandfather Mountain. As you drive along the highway, you can look at that mountain from many different places and wonder where it got such a name. But, if you drive on until you get to the north side of it, you can look up from its base and see, clearly and distinctly, the image of a man with a flowing beard. And so it is with you. Come under the shadow of the cross. Come there as a penitent sinner. Look there upon that visage more marred than any man. Realize that the Sufferer hangs as the guiltless Substitute, dying for your sins. Look, and you will see in him the glory of God's goodness. His beauty will ravish your soul. But the only place to behold that glory is in the cleft of the Rock. Until you see God's glorious goodness in Christ, any sight of him will terrify you.

Isaac Watts wrote,

> Till God in human flesh I see,
> My thoughts no comfort find;
> The holy, just, and sacred Three,
> Are terrors to my mind!

Would you see the glory of God? Look to Christ. In the crucified Lamb of God, God shows his glory (2 Corinthians 4:3-6; 5:17-21).

Chapter 111

The Glory Revealed

'And he said, I beseech thee, shew me thy glory. And he said, I will make all my goodness pass before thee, and I will proclaim the name of the LORD before thee; and will be gracious to whom I will be gracious, and will shew mercy on whom I will shew mercy. And he said, Thou canst not see my face: for there shall no man see me, and live. And the LORD said, Behold, there is a place by me, and thou shalt stand upon a rock: And it shall come to pass, while my glory passeth by, that I will put thee in a clift of the rock, and will cover thee with my hand while I pass by: And I will take away mine hand, and thou shalt see my back parts: but my face shall not be seen. And the LORD said unto Moses, Hew thee two tables of stone like unto the first: and I will write upon these tables the words that were in the first tables, which thou brakest. And be ready in the morning, and come up in the morning unto mount Sinai, and present thyself there to me in the top of the mount. And no man shall come up with thee, neither let any man be seen throughout all the mount; neither let the flocks nor herds feed before that mount. And he hewed two tables of stone like unto the first; and Moses rose up early in the morning, and went up unto mount Sinai, as the LORD had commanded him, and took in his hand the two tables of stone. And the LORD descended in the cloud, and stood with him there, and proclaimed the name of the LORD. And the LORD passed by before him, and proclaimed, The LORD, The LORD God, merciful and gracious, longsuffering, and abundant in goodness and truth,

Keeping mercy for thousands, forgiving iniquity and transgression and sin, and that will by no means clear the guilty; visiting the iniquity of the fathers upon the children, and upon the children's children, unto the third and to the fourth generation. And Moses made haste, and bowed his head toward the earth, and worshipped. And he said, If now I have found grace in thy sight, O Lord, let my Lord, I pray thee, go among us; for it is a stiffnecked people; and pardon our iniquity and our sin, and take us for thine inheritance.'
(Exodus 33:18-34:9)

Moses prayed, 'I beseech thee, show me thy glory'. The revelation of the glory of God is the greatest blessing any man can ask, and the greatest blessing God can give to any man upon this earth, for the revelation of the glory of God is salvation. God had revealed his glory to Moses before. At the burning bush, God our Saviour revealed himself to Moses and there revealed 'the good will of him that dwelt in the bush' (Exodus 3:1-10; Deuteronomy 33:16). The triune Jehovah revealed his Christ and his salvation to Moses at the bush. And, as all who have experienced his grace will testify, once the Lord reveals his glory, his salvation of sinners by the sacrifice of his dear Son, the Lord Jesus Christ, he continues to reveal him more and more, and we continue to experience his salvation day by day, beholding his glory in the face of our crucified Redeemer (2 Corinthians 3:18). Moses saw the glory of God revealed in the manna he rained from heaven, in the water gushing from the smitten rock, in the top of Sinai's fiery mount, and in 'the pattern of the tabernacle, and the pattern of all the instruments thereof' (Exodus 25:9, 40). The pattern after which the tabernacle was made is Christ. The whole tabernacle, with its furnishings, its priesthood, the priestly garments, the priestly work, the sacrifices, everything was typical of God's salvation of sinners by the doing and dying of the Lord Jesus Christ. When the tabernacle furnishings were all completed, it was by divine design something that could be erected by one man in a single day, as we see in Exodus 40. Typically, it represented the fulfilment of God's promise by his servant Zechariah. 'I will remove the iniquity of that land in one day' (Zechariah 3:9). The complete salvation of his people was accomplished by the Lord Jesus in a single day when he who knew no sin was made sin for us, and died for our sins upon the cursed tree (2 Corinthians 5:20, 21; Galatians 3:13, 14).

God's Revelation

What did God reveal to Moses? Moses prayed, 'I beseech thee, shew me thy glory'. And God said, 'I will make all my goodness to pass before thee, and I will proclaim the name of the LORD before thee; and will be gracious to whom I will be gracious, and will shew mercy on whom I will shew mercy.'

Moses knew that 'God is a Spirit'. He knew that the mind of man can never conceive an adequate idea of the incomprehensible Jehovah. Moses had a great view of God. He knew that God is infinite, eternal, and incomprehensible. Yet, it seems Moses entertained the idea that the invisible God might be and would be seen.

The eyes of flesh are designed to show us only those things that are physical and material. They cannot reveal that which is spiritual. As long we are upon this earth, we cannot see God with the eyes of clay.

Yet, there is nothing that God's children desire more than the sight of God our Saviour in all his glory. This was that hope which gave David confidence toward God. 'Thou wilt shew me the path of life: in thy presence is fulness of joy: at thy right hand there are pleasures forever more ... As for me, I will behold thy face in righteousness; I shall be satisfied when I awake with thy likeness' (Psalm 16:11; 17:15).

This desire to behold God's glory is one sure result of sweet fellowship and communion with our God. Moses had spent forty days in the presence of God. We read, 'The LORD spake unto Moses face to face, as a man speaketh unto his friend' (v. 11). And what was the result? Moses said, 'Show me thy glory'. That is always the result of close communion with God. The more we know of him, the more we desire to know. The closer God draws to us, the more we are constrained to cry, 'LORD, lift thou up the light of thy countenance upon us' (Psalm 4:6).

The great purpose of the death of our Lord Jesus Christ to redeem his people was that we might behold the glory of God in him. Our Lord prayed, 'Father, I will that they also, whom thou hast given me, be with me where I am; that they may behold my glory' (John 17:24). And you can be sure of this, if we are redeemed by the blood of Christ, we shall behold the glory of God! Job said, 'I know that my Redeemer liveth, and that he shall stand at the latter day upon the earth; and though after my skin worms destroy this body, yet in my flesh shall I see God: whom I shall see for myself, and mine eyes shall behold, and not another;

though my reins be consumed in me' (Job 19:25-27). Turn to the end of the Book and read what is written of that Eternal City. 'And I saw no temple therein, for the Lord God Almighty and the Lamb are the temple of it. And the city had no need of the sun, neither of the moon, to shine in it; for the glory of God did lighten it, and the Lamb is the light thereof' (Revelation 21:22, 23).

Goodness

Now, turn from Moses prayer and consider God's response. Observe the gracious revelation that God made to his friend. Moses asked to see God's glory. As the Lord passed by, proclaiming his name, he covered Moses with his hand. When he removed his hand, Moses saw God's 'back parts', the crucified Christ. In the vision of Christ crucified, he understood the name, and the attributes that he heard while hidden in the cleft of the rock.

What attribute shall the man of God first see? Will he show him his holiness? Will he show him his wrath? Will he show him his justice? Will he show him his power? Will he bring his sins to remembrance, and show him his omniscience? No. I hear a still small voice saying, 'I will make all my goodness to pass before thee'.

Oh, sons of men, the essence of God is his glory, and the glory of God is his goodness! When we read chapter thirty-four, we see that God revealed his mercy, grace, longsuffering, truth, faithfulness, and justice. But the essence of them all is his goodness. The brightest gem in the crown of God is his goodness. God's greatest glory is that he is good.

My soul longs to make known to the sons of men that God, the infinite, holy, triune Jehovah, is the sum and substance of all good. 'There is none good but one, that is, God' (Matthew 19:17).

God alone can make men happy. He is the Father of mercy, the Fountain of goodness. He is the Source of all joy. 'Happy is that people, whose God is the LORD' (Psalm 144:15). The splendour of God's goodness is such that no mortal can begin to tell it all. There is nothing but goodness in God, and nothing but goodness comes from God.

There is no evil, iniquity, or unrighteousness in God's Person, his ways, or his works. 'God is light, and in him is no darkness at all' (1 John 1:5). Whatever God does is good, simply because he does it. He may ordain wickedness for a season, but he overrules it for good. He will eternally punish the wicked, but that punishment will prove at last to be good. When all is done and time is no more, the saints in heaven will sing God's praise even in the execution of his wrath (Revelation 18:20; 19:1-6); and the damned themselves will say, 'Amen', to his judgment (Isaiah 45:23-25; Philippians 2:9-11).

God is immutably and eternally good. The goodness of men is like the morning dew. It soon fades away. But the goodness of God is invariably the same. It continues forever. The entire universe shares in the goodness of God. The whole creation proclaims to us that God is good. 'The Word of the LORD is right: and all his works are done in truth. He loveth righteousness and judgment: the earth is full of the goodness of the LORD' (Psalm 33:4, 5). This world was created by the goodness of God. From his goodness he clothes the fields with green grass and feeds the cattle on a thousand hills. The sparrows come and peck their seed from the hands of the Almighty.

Even the wicked upon this earth enjoy the goodness of God. 'The LORD is good to all, and his tender mercies are over all his works' (Psalm 145:9). Out of his abundant goodness, God sends both sunshine and rain upon the just and the unjust.

Our great God rules this world in the goodness of his providence, simply because he is good. We are of yesterday and know nothing. Man is but a flower of the field, withering away. Yesterday he was an infant. Today he is an old man. Tomorrow he is gone. But God is the eternal good that rules them all.

Yet, if you would truly behold the goodness of God, you must see it revealed in the sovereign goodness of the triune Jehovah to his covenant people. O my soul, go back to old eternity and see your name in God's book of predestinating, unchanging grace! Behold the goodness of God the blessed Father. He chose you for himself. He loved you. He laid up all good things for you in Christ. He gave his only begotten Son for you.

Behold the goodness of God the eternal Son, your Redeemer. He became your Surety and Representative. He undertook all things for your good. He stooped to assume your nature. He lived before God as your Representative to work out righteousness for you. He died as your Substitute to purchase your soul from divine justice. He is the Fountain of all goodness to your soul. He ever lives to speak a good word in the presence of God for you.

Behold the goodness of God the Holy Ghost. All the gifts of divine grace are tokens of his goodness to you. He gives you faith and repentance, the hope of eternal life, and the gift of eternal life. He preserves and keeps you. He revives and refreshes you. He comforts and instructs you. Here is the great glory of God, the Father, the Son, and the Holy Ghost. He is 'keeping mercy for thousands, forgiving iniquity, transgression, and sin' (34:7).

Sovereignty

Alongside Jehovah's goodness, Moses saw his glorious sovereignty. The Lord God said, 'I will make all my goodness pass before thee'. But there is something more. He said, 'I will be gracious to whom I will be gracious, and will shew mercy on whom I will shew mercy'. This is another divine attribute. This speaks of God's great and glorious sovereignty. Moses not only saw that God is good, but also that he is sovereignly good.

God's goodness without his sovereignty does not completely set forth his nature. If you only see one attribute of God, you only see part of his glorious being. God is good, and he is sovereign. He does as he pleases. And, though he is good to all, he is not obliged to do good to any. He declares, 'I will be gracious to whom I will be gracious, and will shew mercy on whom I will shew mercy'.

God is an absolute sovereign. He has the right to do whatever he will. He can make man, or not make man. He can create man in his own image, or he can create a brute beast. He had the right to require of Adam anything he liked. When Adam broke his law, he had the right to destroy all the race or to save whomsoever he pleased. We are in the hands of God, like clay in the hands of the potter. We are creatures in the hands of the Creator. God has the right, if he pleases, to save anyone or to crush all into the deepest hell.

The glorious gospel doctrine of God's sovereignty crushes the pride of man. And men by nature do not like that, because man likes to think that he is something. But is it not right for a man to do as he will with his own? Surely, then, we cannot deny this right to God! If he chooses to let men go on in the error of their way, that is his right. But, if he chooses graciously to intervene, as indeed he has, and say, 'Come unto me, all ye that labour and are heavy laden, and I will give you rest', that is his right.

This blessed attribute of God ought to cheer the hearts of God's children, even as it did the heart of our Redeemer. 'I thank thee, O

Father, Lord of heaven and earth, because thou hast hid these things from the wise and prudent, and hast revealed them unto babes. Even so, Father, for so it seemed good in thy sight' (Matthew 11:25, 26).

We all deserve God's wrath. We have no claim to his mercy. But he is sovereignly good, so let us plead with him, and sue for mercy on the grounds of his goodness in Christ. And, maybe, maybe he will show us mercy. Edmund Jones wrote,

> Perhaps he will admit my plea,
> Perhaps will hear my prayer;
> But if I perish, I will pray,
> And perish only there.
>
> I can but perish if I go,
> I am resolved to try,
> For if I stay away, I know,
> I must forever die.
>
> But if I die with mercy sought,
> When I the King have tried,
> This were to die (delightful thought!)
> As sinner never died.

Matthew Henry rightly observed, 'It is never said, "I will be angry with whom I will be angry", for his wrath is always just and holy; but "I will show mercy on whom I will show mercy", for his grace is always free. He never damns by prerogative, but by prerogative he saves.'

Put these two things together, goodness and sovereignty, and we begin to see God's glory. God is not gracious alone. He is sovereignly gracious. And he is not sovereign alone. He is graciously sovereign.

God's Hiding

What did God conceal from Moses? 'He said, Thou canst not see my face; for there shall no man see me and live' (v. 20). This was a gracious concealment. There was as much mercy in what God hid from Moses as there is in what he revealed. And there is as much mercy in what God hides from us as there is in what he reveals. When God hides a thing from us, there is as much mercy in his hiding as there is in his revelation.

'The secret things belong to the LORD, but the things that are revealed to us and to our children.' There are some things God does not intend for us to know. And that man is a fool who tries to pry into them. Let us be earnest students. But let us study only what God has revealed. God said to Moses, 'Thou canst not see my face'.

This statement makes it abundantly clear that no man can see God's face as a sinner and live. Any man who stands before the face of God, clothed in the filthy rags of his own righteousness, must perish.

No man, even as a saint, can see God's face and live. There are such limitations to this physical body, that it could not endure the sight of God's absolute glory. Even when we stand glorified in heaven, we shall behold the glory of God in the person of the God-man.

All that we can ever behold of God upon this earth is that which Moses saw, his 'back parts'. Those words, 'my back parts', I think refer to his regal train, the train that Isaiah speaks of when he saw the Lord Jesus Christ in his exaltation and glory, having accomplished eternal redemption for us (Isaiah 6:1-6). Jehovah's 'back parts', his royal, majestic train is the Lord Jesus Christ. It is the incarnate, obedient, crucified, risen Son, our Saviour, by whom Satan's head is crushed, God's elect are saved, all that was ruined by Adam is restored, and all that was made wrong is made right!

I have not yet fully seen him, neither do I fully understand his being. He is incomprehensible! 'Who only hath immortality, dwelling in the light which no man can approach unto; whom no man hath seen, nor can see: to whom be honour and power everlasting. Amen!' (1 Timothy 6:16). But, blessed be his name forever, God has revealed his dear Son in me and I know him. 'I know whom I have believed, and am persuaded that he is able to keep that which I have committed unto him.' Oh, may he give the same revelation of his glory to all who read these lines!

Method of Revelation
How did God reveal his glory to Moses? 'And the LORD said, Behold, there is a place by me, and thou shalt stand upon a rock; and it shall come to pass, while my glory passeth by, that I will put thee in a clift of the rock, and will cover thee with my hand while I pass by; and I will take away mine hand, and thou shalt see my back parts: but my face shall not be seen' (vv. 21-23). There is much here that is yet hidden to

me. I will not speculate about them. But some things are obvious. These obvious things are of tremendous importance; instructive and glorious. Before any sinful man can behold the perfections of the infinitely glorious, righteous, and holy Lord God, he must be put into a place of security and peace. Moses had to be put into a clift or cleft of the rock before he could see God. That Rock was Christ. He is the Rock, the Rock of Israel, the Rock of Ages, the Rock of Refuge, Salvation, and Strength. Blessed be his name forever, our God has provided sinners a place of shelter in the cleft of the Rock, Christ Jesus!

> Rock of Ages, cleft for me,
> Grace has hid me safe in Thee!
> Let the water and the blood
> From Thy wounded side which flowed,
> Be of sin the double cure,
> Cleanse me from its guilt and power.

Look at the beautiful picture we have here of the believer's absolute security in Christ. 'Thou shalt stand upon a Rock.' We stand before God today, and for all eternity, upon this blessed Foundation, and we shall not be confounded.

> Jesus, Thy blood and righteousness,
> My beauty are, my glorious dress;
> Midst flaming worlds in these arrayed,
> With joy shall I lift up my head.

The Lord God said, 'I will put thee in a cleft of the rock', because no sinner can put himself into Christ. We were chosen in him, redeemed in him, accepted in him. We were 'created in Christ Jesus' (Ephesians 2:10; 1 Corinthians 1:30, 31; Colossians 2:9, 10). Then, God said, 'I will cover thee with my hand'. Not only is the believer in Christ, he is protected by the Father's hand. 'My Father, which gave them me, is greater than all; and no man shall pluck them out of my Father's hand' (John 10:29). 'He that dwelleth in the secret place of the Most High shall abide under the shadow of the Almighty' (Psalm 91:1).

Here is the great superiority of the gospel over the law. The law had only a shadow of good things to come, and not the very image of those things. But look at the fulness of the gospel, 'God, who commanded light to shine out of darkness, hath shined in our hearts, to give the light of the knowledge of the glory of God in the face of Jesus Christ' (2 Corinthians 4:6).

The Glory Revealed

What is the glory of God revealed in Christ?

'And the LORD descended in the cloud, and stood with him there, and proclaimed the name of the LORD. And the LORD passed by before him, and proclaimed, The LORD, The LORD God, merciful and gracious, longsuffering, and abundant in goodness and truth, keeping mercy for thousands, forgiving iniquity and transgression and sin, and that will by no means clear the guilty; visiting the iniquity of the fathers upon the children, and upon the children's children, unto the third and to the fourth generation' (Exodus 34:5-7).

The Lord God showed Moses his absolute sovereignty, his boundless mercy and grace, his indescribable long-suffering and goodness. He showed Moses the full, complete, free forgiveness of sin by, in, and with the Lord Jesus Christ, our crucified Saviour; forgiveness that shows how he can be and is, both 'a just God and a Saviour' (Isaiah 45:21), in strict, unbending truth and justice.

'And Moses made haste, and bowed his head toward the earth, and worshipped. And he said, If now I have found grace in thy sight, O Lord, let my Lord, I pray thee, go among us; for it is a stiffnecked people; and pardon our iniquity and our sin, and take us for thine inheritance' (Exodus 34:8, 9).

When Moses saw God's great glory in Christ Jesus, when he saw the fulness of God in the crucified Redeemer, when he saw the glory of God in the face of Jesus Christ, he hurriedly bowed his face to the ground and worshipped God with yet three more earnest prayers. 'I pray thee go among us, for it is a stiff-necked people'. 'Pardon our iniquity and our sin'. 'Take us for thine inheritance!'

Blessed, forever blessed are those sinners who do the same! That is what it is to see and experience the glory of the Lord. That is what it is to see and experience God's salvation in Christ. Soon you shall die. You will stand before the throne of infinite majesty, holiness, and glory. And what will become of you then? 'It is a fearful thing to fall into the hands of the living God.' God is so glorious, so pure, so full of light that it is written, 'God is a consuming fire'. Flee to Christ! Find shelter in the cleft of the Rock!

Now, understand this and rejoice. 'The whole earth is full of his glory' (Isaiah 6:3). What does that mean? God the Holy Ghost explains it to us in the eighth chapter of Romans.

'And we know that all things work together for good to them that love God, to them who are the called according to his purpose. For whom he did foreknow, he also did predestinate to be conformed to the image of his Son, that he might be the firstborn among many brethren. Moreover whom he did predestinate, them he also called: and whom he called, them he also justified: and whom he justified, them he also glorified. What shall we then say to these things? If God be for us, who can be against us?' (Romans 8:28-31).

Moses saw only the back parts of the living God; but upon the Mount of Transfiguration, he saw Christ's 'face shine as the sun'. And it shall be so, even with us. Now we see his glory. Now we see him who is invisible. We see his face, but only through a glass darkly. But, O blessed be God, we shall soon see him face to face! 'In my flesh shall I see God.' We shall see him, without sin. We shall see him, personally. We shall see him, as he is. We shall see him. And when we see him, we shall be like him. This is the glorious hope of every blood-bought child of God. Carrie Ellis Breck wrote,

> Face to face with Christ my Saviour,
> Face to face, what will it be;
> When with rapture I behold Him,
> Jesus Christ, who died for me?
>
> Only faintly now I see Him,
> With a darkling vail between;
> But a blessed day is coming,
> When His glory shall be seen.
>
> What rejoicing in his presence,
> When are banished grief and pain;
> When the crooked ways are straitened,
> And the dark things shall be plain.

Face to face, O blissful moment,
Face to face, to see and know;
Face to face with my Redeemer,
Jesus Christ who loves me so.

Face to face, I shall behold Him,
Far beyond the starry sky;
Face to face in all His glory,
I shall see Him by and by.

We shall see him face to face, and we shall live! God hasten the day, for Jesus' sake.

Chapter 112

'The LORD Whose Name Is Jealous'

'And he said, Behold, I make a covenant: before all thy people I will do marvels, such as have not been done in all the earth, nor in any nation: and all the people among which thou art shall see the work of the LORD: for it is a terrible thing that I will do with thee. Observe thou that which I command thee this day: behold, I drive out before thee the Amorite, and the Canaanite, and the Hittite, and the Perizzite, and the Hivite, and the Jebusite. Take heed to thyself, lest thou make a covenant with the inhabitants of the land whither thou goest, lest it be for a snare in the midst of thee: But ye shall destroy their altars, break their images, and cut down their groves: For thou shalt worship no other god: for the LORD, whose name is Jealous, is a jealous God: Lest thou make a covenant with the inhabitants of the land, and they go a whoring after their gods, and do sacrifice unto their gods, and one call thee, and thou eat of his sacrifice; And thou take of their daughters unto thy sons, and their daughters go a whoring after their gods, and make thy sons go a whoring after their gods. Thou shalt make thee no molten gods. The feast of unleavened bread shalt thou keep. Seven days thou shalt eat unleavened bread, as I commanded thee, in the time of the month Abib: for in the month Abib thou camest out from Egypt. All that openeth the matrix is mine; and every firstling among thy cattle, whether ox or sheep, that is male. But the firstling of an ass thou shalt redeem with a lamb: and if thou redeem him not, then shalt thou break his neck. All the firstborn of thy sons thou shalt redeem. And none shall appear before me empty. Six days thou shalt work, but on the seventh day thou shalt rest: in earing time and in harvest thou shalt rest. And thou shalt

observe the feast of weeks, of the firstfruits of wheat harvest, and the feast of ingathering at the year's end. Thrice in the year shall all your men children appear before the Lord GOD, the God of Israel. For I will cast out the nations before thee, and enlarge thy borders: neither shall any man desire thy land, when thou shalt go up to appear before the LORD thy God thrice in the year. Thou shalt not offer the blood of my sacrifice with leaven; neither shall the sacrifice of the feast of the passover be left unto the morning. The first of the firstfruits of thy land thou shalt bring unto the house of the LORD thy God. Thou shalt not seethe a kid in his mother's milk. And the LORD said unto Moses, Write thou these words: for after the tenor of these words I have made a covenant with thee and with Israel. And he was there with the LORD forty days and forty nights; he did neither eat bread, nor drink water. And he wrote upon the tables the words of the covenant, the ten commandments.'
(Exodus 34:10-28)

The Lord God reveals himself by many names in the Old Testament. He is 'Elohim', The One Worshipped (Genesis 1:1); 'El', The Mighty God (Genesis 12:7, 8); 'Eliom', The Most High God (Genesis 14:18-22); 'El-Shaddai', God All-sufficient (Genesis 17:1); 'The LORD of Sabaoth'; 'The LORD of Hosts'; The Absolute Sovereign of the Universe (1 Samuel 1:9-11); 'Adonai', The Cause, The Support (Genesis 15:2); and 'Ejeh', I AM, the Immutable Jehovah (Exodus 3:13, 14; Malachi 3:6). In Exodus 34:14 God the Holy Ghost gives us another of our God's great names, a name by which our blessed God and Saviour often identifies himself and distinguishes himself from the imaginary gods of man's making. Here we read that he who is our God is 'the LORD whose name is Jealous'. In the portion of Scripture before us (Exodus 34:10-28) the Lord God gives us explicit instructions about worshipping him in spirit and in truth, inspiring us by his great jealousy to adhere to him alone as God our Saviour.

A Covenant Admired
In verses 10, 11, the Lord God calls for us to admire his great covenant and all the works he performs on our behalf, by which he fulfils it.

'And he said, Behold.' That word, 'Behold', tells us to pause for a while and look at this. Do not read this hurriedly, but slowly, with thoughtfulness and deliberation. Admire and wonder at this. 'I make a covenant.' The covenant was made before the world began; but every time it is revealed, it is as though it were just made. 'Before all thy people I will do marvels, such as have not been done in all the earth, nor in any nation.' The inspired psalmist taught us to sing about God's covenant grace in Psalm 72:14-19.

'And all the people among which thou art shall see the work of the LORD.' When God gets done, everybody in heaven, earth, and hell will see his wonders toward us and upon us (Ephesians 2:7). 'For it is a terrible thing that I will do with thee.' The word 'terrible' means that which startles and frightens because it is unexpected, wondrous, and unexplainable!

In verse 11 we read, 'Observe thou that which I command thee this day'. That which God commands God performs. We see this in the next line of the verse. 'Behold, I drive out before thee the Amorite, and the Canaanite, and the Hittite, and the Perizzite, and the Hivite, and the Jebusite.' The Lord our God, our mighty Saviour, he and he alone has taken away all our sins. He and he alone will destroy all our enemies!

A Jealous God
In verses 12-17, the Lord God uses his jealousy to inspire our hearts' devotion to him. He does this by forbidding us to mingle with idolatry in any way. 'Take heed to thyself, lest thou make a covenant with the inhabitants of the land whither thou goest, lest it be for a snare in the midst of thee' (v. 12). Clearly, he does not forbid, as religion does, association with wicked people. That is both impossible and evil. He is here talking about mixing with the heathen in the exercise of religion.

'But ye shall destroy their altars, break their images, and cut down their groves: For thou shalt worship no other god' (vv. 13, 14). It is our responsibility, not by law or by sword, not by physical force, but by the preaching of the gospel, to destroy every refuge of lies men build, to destroy their altars, smash their gods, and demolish their religion.

Here's the motivation God gives for this devotion to him. 'For the LORD, whose name is Jealous, is a jealous God.' 'Thus saith the LORD of hosts; I was jealous for Zion with great jealousy, and I was jealous for her with great fury' (Zechariah 8:2). The word translated 'jealous' is the same as the word translated 'zealous'. Jealousy is zealousness. Where there is no jealousy, no burning zeal, there is no love. I do not love a person if I do not zealously do my utmost for that person. So it is with our God and Saviour, who 'is a consuming fire'. He declares that he is jealous for his church, 'with great fury', against those who would pull her away from him. Yet, he declares to the object of his love, for whom he is jealous, 'Fury is not in me' (Isaiah 27:4).

Solomon wrote, 'Jealousy is the rage of a man' (Proverbs 6:34), the rage of a man against any and all who would steal the heart of the wife he loves. The inspired apostle used that term when he wrote to the Corinthian believers expressing his concern for their souls in 2 Corinthians 11:2, 3.

'For I am jealous over you with godly jealousy: for I have espoused you to one husband, that I may present you as a chaste virgin to Christ. But I fear, lest by any means, as the serpent beguiled Eve through his subtlety, so your minds should be corrupted from the simplicity that is in Christ.'

As at first our Saviour loved us simply because he loved us (Deuteronomy 7:7, 8), he will bestow upon his chosen all good things simply because he loves us with an everlasting love. 'The zeal' (that is the tender love and free grace, the burning jealousy) 'of the LORD of hosts will perform this' (Isaiah 9:7). For his word's sake, that is to say 'for Christ's sake', and according to his own heart, the Lord God has done and will yet do great things for the salvation of his people (2 Samuel 7:21).

Jealousy causes a man to be watchful and quick sighted. Even the slightest glance of one who desires his wife's heart enrages the loving, jealous husband. So it is with our loving Saviour, who is jealous for our hearts. The slightest indignity done to his beloved spouse, his Hephzibah, seeking to take her heart from him, will be met with his utmost fury. If Ammon but claps his hands at God's Israel, if he stomps his feet, or if he merely rejoices in his heart, when Christ's bride is hurt, he will suffer for his daring insolence (Ezekiel 25:6, 7; Joel 2:18).

Jealousy is merciless, violent, and cruel as the grave, burning as fire in a man's heart (Song of Solomon 8:6). The word translated 'jealous' in Exodus 34 is elsewhere translated 'fiery thunderbolts' (Psalm 78:48) and 'burning heat' (Deuteronomy 32:24). Jealousy puts a man into a feverish fit of outrage and makes him burn for revenge. While those things are all evil in fallen man, they are gloriously just and righteous in our blessed Husband, the Lord Jesus. He will spit in the face of any

Miriam who dares but to mutter against his Moses (Numbers 12:14). What will he not do to those who would steal the heart of his bride?

Jealousy is implacable. It cannot be reconciled (Proverbs 6:34, 35). Balak was willing to give anything to have his way with Israel. Haman would pay ten thousand talents of silver to have the Jews destroyed. Ahasuerus was willing to comply with Haman. Esther said, 'We are sold, I and my people, to be destroyed, to be slain and to perish' (Esther 3:9; 7:4). But God was jealous for Israel and had Haman hanged upon his own gallows.

'For thus saith the LORD of hosts; After the glory hath he sent me unto the nations which spoiled you: for he that toucheth you toucheth the apple of his eye' (Zechariah 2:8). Our mighty Phineas, the Lord Jesus, will gird his sword upon his thigh and execute the great fury of his wrath upon any who dare oppose his beloved. He will smite his enemies in the hinder parts and put them to a perpetual shame and reproach forever (Psalm 78:66).

In Exodus 34:15-17, the Lord God, our Jealous Husband, who 'hateth putting away' (Malachi 2:16), shows us that his concern is as much for us as it is for himself. He will not share his glory with another; and his glory and the everlasting salvation of our souls cannot be separated. Therefore, he calls us here, as he does throughout Holy Scripture, to flee from every form of treachery, to flee the enticing arms of the great whore Babylon, which is freewill, works religion, and the wine of her fornications, with which the whole world is intoxicated (2 Corinthians 6:14-7:1; Revelation 18:4).

'Lest thou make a covenant with the inhabitants of the land, and they go a whoring after their gods, and do sacrifice unto their gods, and one call thee, and thou eat of his sacrifice; And thou take of their daughters unto thy sons, and their daughters go a whoring after their gods, and make thy sons go a whoring after their gods. Thou shalt make thee no molten gods' (Exodus 34:15-17).

'Be ye not unequally yoked together with unbelievers: for what fellowship hath righteousness with unrighteousness? and what communion hath light with darkness? And what concord hath Christ with Belial? or what part hath he that believeth with an infidel? And what agreement hath the temple of God with idols? for ye are the temple of the living God; as God hath said, I will dwell in them, and walk in them; and I will be their God, and they shall be my people. Wherefore come out from among them, and be ye separate, saith the Lord, and touch not the unclean thing; and I will receive you, and will be a Father unto you, and ye shall be my sons and daughters, saith the Lord Almighty. Having therefore these promises, dearly beloved, let us cleanse ourselves from all filthiness of the flesh and spirit, perfecting holiness in the fear of God' (2 Corinthians 6:14-7:1).

'And I heard another voice from heaven, saying, Come out of her, my people, that ye be not partakers of her sins, and that ye receive not of her plagues' (Revelation 18:4).

A Singular Worship
In verses 18-26, the Lord our Saviour, whose name is Jealous, demands we worship him alone. He will not share his glory with another; he will not share his wife with another. In Malachi 2, the Lord demands that we relentlessly beware of the treachery of false prophets who, following the example of Balaam, would share his bride with the gods of the world by profaning his holiness, making the blood and righteousness of Christ a meaningless sacrifice (Hebrews 10:29) and by feigned, pretentious, hypocritical worship (Malachi 2:13; Philippians 3:3)

God required his people to keep three distinct feasts, 'holy convocations', every year. Each of these feasts were typical of our Lord Jesus Christ and God's great salvation in and by him. Only two are specifically mentioned here. These two feasts represent the great works of our God in redemption, grace, and salvation. These two feasts specifically represent and typify our experience of grace by the gift of God creating life and faith in us.

Israel's first great feast, as given here, was the feast of unleavened bread (v. 18). The feast of unleavened bread was really a continuation of the feast of passover, which portrayed Christ our Passover who was sacrificed for us. On the passover night the children of Israel ate the lamb with their coats on their backs, their shoes on their feet, and their staffs in their hand, ready to go out of Egypt. The passover sacrifice was the cause. The feast of unleavened bread represents the effects of redemption. The sacrifice of the paschal lamb, speaking of Christ and his shed blood, is the effectual cause of pardon. The sweet fellowship of faith, represented in the feast of unleavened bread, is the effect, the sure and certain result of Christ's death as our Substitute. The feast of unleavened bread pictured faith in Christ (John 6:53-56).

Be sure you do not fail to see the connection of the feast of unleavened bread with the feast of passover. The feast of unleavened bread began the next day after the passover was ended. So, too, the gift of life and faith in Christ follows the accomplishments of Christ at Calvary. All who were redeemed by blood shall be made to live and feed upon Christ at God's appointed time (Galatians 3:13, 14).

As one great family, the children of Israel kept this feast as a 'holy convocation'. The people were all joined together, united in one holy body of redeemed souls, remembering what God had done for them. They were all bought with the same blood, saved by the same power, going to the same homeland, and they all ate the same bread. So it is with all God's elect. We are one people, one church, one body, the one bride of Christ, constantly under the care and protection of him who is 'the LORD whose name is Jealous' (Ephesians 3:18, 19; 4:1-7).

In verses 19 and 20, we see that in all our worship, our God and Saviour demands and deserves singleness of heart, and utter devotion.

'All that openeth the matrix is mine; and every firstling among thy cattle, whether ox or sheep, that is male. But the firstling of an ass thou shalt redeem with a lamb: and if thou redeem him not, then shalt thou break his neck. All the firstborn of thy sons thou shalt redeem. And none shall appear before me empty' (Exodus 34:19, 20).

Unclean sinners, saved by the grace of God, washed in the blood of Christ, and made clean before God by him, rejoice in the fact that our Lord includes the unclean ass among the things that might be redeemed to him with the blood of a lamb (Exodus 13:13).

In verse 22, the Lord commands Israel to observe the feast of weeks. 'And thou shalt observe the feast of weeks, of the firstfruits of wheat harvest, and the feast of ingathering at the year's end.' The feast of weeks was held fifty days (seven weeks and a day, a sabbath) after the feast of firstfruits. It is commonly called 'Pentecost', because it was held on the fiftieth day. This is the harvest or ingathering feast. This great harvest feast speaks of the ingathering of God's elect by Christ.

The risen Christ gave us a foretaste of the ingathering of his elect in Acts 2. When the Day of Pentecost was fully come, he poured out his Spirit upon all flesh and 3000 souls were gathered into the fold of his grace. Just as the harvest followed the firstfruits, so the salvation of God's elect follows the resurrection of Christ. All the redeemed shall be gathered unto God (Isaiah 43:5; John 10:15, 16; Romans 11:26).

The Holy Spirit tells us this feast also speaks of Christ's glorious resurrection and of our resurrection with him, in him, and by him. That shall be the glorious consummation of our salvation by Christ, our God and Saviour, 'the LORD whose name is Jealous' (Romans 11:16; 1 Corinthians 15:23; James 1:18; Revelation 14:4).

'For if the firstfruit be holy, the lump is also holy: and if the root be holy, so are the branches' (Romans 11:16). 'But every man in his own order: Christ the firstfruits; afterward they that are Christ's at his coming' (Romans 11:16). 'Of his own will begat he us with the word of truth, that we should be a kind of firstfruits of his creatures' (James 1:18). 'These are they which were not defiled with women; for they are virgins. These are they which follow the Lamb whithersoever he goeth. These were redeemed from among men, being the firstfruits unto God and to the Lamb' (Revelation 14:4).

Encouraging us still to worship and obey him, the Lord promises us he will not allow us to suffer loss by whole-hearted devotion to him.

'Thrice in the year shall all your men children appear before the Lord GOD, the God of Israel. For I will cast out the nations before thee, and enlarge thy borders: neither shall any man desire thy land, when thou shalt go up to appear before the LORD thy God thrice in the year' (Exodus 34:23, 24).

Now, read the special, distinct instructions given by our God, whose name is Jealous (vv. 25, 26). 'Thou shalt not offer the blood of my sacrifice with leaven.' Nothing is to be mixed with the sacrifice of our blessed Saviour. 'Neither shall the sacrifice of the feast of the passover be left unto the morning.' Nothing is to be rejected, despised, and refused.

'The first of the firstfruits of thy land thou shalt bring unto the house of the LORD thy God.' Bring God the first and the best, only the first and the best. 'Thou shalt not seethe a kid in his mother's milk.' There is to be no mixture of human invention, idolatry, superstition, custom, or tradition!

A Blessed Command
Look at verse 21. Here the Lord God gives us a blessed command. His sweet and blessed command is 'Rest'. 'Six days thou shalt work, but on the seventh day thou shalt rest: in earing time and in harvest thou shalt rest.'

It is obvious that the sabbath occupied a very prominent and independent place in Old Testament worship. In fact, each of Israel's feasts was specifically associated with sabbath observance. Whenever Moses gives instruction about keeping the feasts, he gives specific instruction from God about keeping the sabbath. It is as if the Lord is saying, 'These feasts I give are typical of my great salvation which shall give you everlasting rest in me and will give me everlasting rest in you.'

The sabbath was to be kept every week. It was a constant reminder to Israel of that sweet rest which Adam lost in the Garden and of that blessed rest that could and would be recovered only in and by Christ. The sabbath was entirely and only intended to typify salvation in Christ, the blessed rest of life, and faith, and reconciliation to God in him.

'No work' whatsoever was to be done on the sabbath, because salvation is altogether a matter of grace, a work of grace alone, enjoyed by faith in Christ, without our works of any kind. No other Old Testament ordinance had such a strict injunction put on it, except the Day of Atonement.

Do you see the significance of that? The rest of faith is the same as the rest of complete, perfect atonement, and the rest of complete, perfect reconciliation to God. This is what was typified in the beginning, when the Lord God rested from all his works on the seventh day.

Is it so with your soul? Do you have such rest in Christ with God as if you had never sinned? Do you have no more conscience of sin? This is the rest Christ has won for all who trust him. Oh, come now to the Lord Jesus Christ and rest! Cease from all work and labour and rest in him. He says to sinners everywhere,

'Come unto me, all ye that labour and are heavy laden, and I will give you rest. Take my yoke upon you, and learn of me; for I am meek and lowly in heart: and ye shall find rest unto your souls. For my yoke is easy, and my burden is light' (Matthew 11:28-30).

We read of this rest of faith, our gospel sabbath, in Hebrews 4. 'For we which have believed do enter into rest, as he said, As I have sworn in my wrath, if they shall enter into my rest: although the works were finished from the foundation of the world' (Hebrews 4:3). 'Again, he limiteth a certain day, saying in David, Today, after so long a time; as it is said, Today if ye will hear his voice, harden not your hearts' (Hebrews 4:7). The rest of faith is good. Heaven will be glorious! 'There remaineth therefore a rest to the people of God' (Hebrews 4:9).

A Foreshadowed Saviour

This blessed sabbath rest can be had only through the dying of that blessed Saviour, our all-glorious Lord Jesus Christ, foreshadowed by Moses in verses 27 and 28.

'And the LORD said unto Moses, Write thou these words: for after the tenor of these words I have made a covenant with thee and with Israel. And he was there with the LORD forty days and forty nights; he did neither eat bread, nor drink water. And he wrote upon the tables the words of the covenant, the ten commandments.'

As Moses, who gave the law, fasted forty days and forty nights, so our blessed Saviour, who fulfilled the law, satisfied the law, and ended the law, fasted forty days and forty nights when he commenced his public ministry as our Saviour (Matthew 4:2). Moses, who gave the law, could never give the children of Israel rest. But the Lord Jesus Christ, who alone is the end of the law, does! Erdmann Neumeister wrote,

> Come, and He will give you rest;
> Trust Him, for His Word is plain;
> He will take the sinfulest;
> Christ receiveth sinful men.
>
> Now my heart condemns me not,
> Pure before the law I stand;
> He who cleansed me from all spot,
> Satisfied its last demand.
>
> Christ receiveth sinful men,
> Even me with all my sin;
> Purged from every spot and stain,
> Heaven with Him I enter in.

I am sure of it, because he, who is God my Saviour, is 'the LORD whose name is Jealous'.

Chapter 113

The Veil On Moses' Face Removed

'And it came to pass, when Moses came down from mount Sinai with the two tables of testimony in Moses' hand, when he came down from the mount, that Moses wist not that the skin of his face shone while he talked with him. And when Aaron and all the children of Israel saw Moses, behold, the skin of his face shone; and they were afraid to come nigh him. And Moses called unto them; and Aaron and all the rulers of the congregation returned unto him: and Moses talked with them. And afterward all the children of Israel came nigh: and he gave them in commandment all that the LORD had spoken with him in mount Sinai. And till Moses had done speaking with them, he put a vail on his face. But when Moses went in before the LORD to speak with him, he took the vail off, until he came out. And he came out, and spake unto the children of Israel that which he was commanded. And the children of Israel saw the face of Moses, that the skin of Moses' face shone: and Moses put the vail upon his face again, until he went in to speak with him.'
(Exodus 34:29-35)

In this portion of Holy Scripture, God the Holy Spirit has recorded for our learning and consolation the shining and veiling of Moses' face. The things we read here are recorded in the Book of God 'for our learning, that we through patience and comfort of the scriptures might have hope' (Romans 15:4).

The Law
'And it came to pass, when Moses came down from mount Sinai with the two tables of testimony in Moses' hand, when he came down from the mount, that Moses wist not that the skin of his face shone while he talked with him' (Exodus 34:29).

The tables of the law Moses carried in his hands were written by the finger of God upon tables of stone. These tables of the law, the Ten Commandments, were laid up in the ark of the covenant under the mercy seat. The picture here given is highly symbolical.

These tables of stone, upon which the Lord God wrote out the law a second time, represented the fact that the law broken by man could only be repaired by God. The law could and would be fulfilled only by one who is himself God. The law would be fulfilled when Christ our Passover died for our sins and with his own blood entered into the holy place, having obtained eternal redemption for us. As God wrote the law upon these tables of stone, so the Spirit of the living God alone can and does write his law upon the fleshy tables of our hearts in the new birth (2 Corinthians 3:3).

Moses' Shining Face
But what is the meaning of the shining of Moses' face? Some have suggested that Moses' face shined brilliantly because he had been in intimate communion with the triune God. Others suggest Moses' shining face was prophetic of his appearance with the Lord Jesus upon the Mount of Transfiguration and prophetic of the glory of God's saints in the resurrection.

While those things may be so, I am certain there is more to the picture before us. The shining of Moses' face is directly connected with the revelation God gave him of his glory in the accomplishment of salvation by Christ in the death he accomplished as our Substitute at Calvary. In Christ's face the glory of God shines forth to chosen, redeemed sinners (2 Corinthians 4:3-6). The shining of Moses' face indicated the enlightenment of his own heart and of ours in the new birth, the light of the knowledge of the glory of God in the face of Jesus Christ shining in our hearts.

'And when Aaron and all the children of Israel saw Moses, behold, the skin of his face shone; and they were afraid to come nigh him. And Moses called unto them; and Aaron and all the rulers of the congregation returned unto him: and Moses talked with them' (Exodus 34:30, 31).

Enlightened souls always frighten those who are yet in darkness. As it is written, 'The world knoweth us not, because it knew him not' (1 John 3:1). Having veiled his face because of their fear, Moses spoke to Aaron and the children of Israel about the things the Lord God showed him in Mount Sinai, those things typified and foreshadowed by the law, the tabernacle, the sacrifices, the holy days, and the priesthood of Jesus Christ and him crucified.

'And afterward all the children of Israel came nigh: and he gave them in commandment all that the LORD had spoken with him in mount Sinai. And till Moses had done speaking with them, he put a veil on his face. But when Moses went in before the LORD to speak with him, he took the veil off, until he came out. And he came out, and spake unto the children of Israel that which he was commanded. And the children of Israel saw the face of Moses, that the skin of Moses' face shone: and Moses put the veil upon his face again, until he went in to speak with him' (Exodus 34:32-35).

The Veil

The veiling of Moses' face is significant and instructive. Anything under a veil is hard to see. It indicated the obscurity of the law. The law reveals the righteousness and holiness of God but gives no hint of how it can be obtained, except by the pictures, types, and ceremonies of it. The law speaks of judgment and death but gives no hint of mercy and life. The law exposes sin but allows no forgiveness. The law demands obedience but gives no ability. The law terrifies but cannot comfort. The law threatens death to anyone who puts his hand to it, but offers no grace to the needy soul. Still, the shining of Moses' face and the veil upon his shining face are even more significant. Many believe Moses' face continued to shine as long as he lived on earth. Whether that was the case, I cannot say. But once the light of the knowledge of the glory of God in the face of Jesus Christ begins to shine in the heart of the heaven-born soul, it never ceases but shines more brightly.

The Veil Removed

Read verse 34 again. 'When Moses went in before the LORD to speak with him, he took the veil off, until he came out.' When Moses went in before the Lord, he took the veil off his face. Why? I would think he would wear the veil before the Lord, if he wore it anywhere. Why, then, are we told, 'When Moses went in before the LORD to speak with him, he took the veil off, until he came out'? You will find the answer in 2 Corinthians 3. The best commentary on Exodus 34 is the commentary given by God the Holy Ghost himself in 2 Corinthians 3. When Moses went in before the Lord, he took the veil off his face, because he was standing before him by whom all the law must and would be fulfilled.

'Ye are our epistle written in our hearts, known and read of all men: Forasmuch as ye are manifestly declared to be the epistle of Christ ministered by us, written not with ink, but with the Spirit of the living God; not in tables of stone, but in fleshy tables of the heart. And such trust have we through Christ to God-ward: Not that we are sufficient of ourselves to think anything as of ourselves; but our sufficiency is of God; who also hath made us able ministers of the new testament; not of the letter, but of the spirit: for the letter killeth, but the spirit giveth life. But if the ministration of death, written and engraven in stones, was glorious, so that the children of Israel could not stedfastly behold the face of Moses for the glory of his countenance; which glory was to be done away: How shall not the ministration of the Spirit be rather glorious? For if the ministration of condemnation be glory, much more doth the ministration of righteousness exceed in glory. For even that which was made glorious had no glory in this respect, by reason of the glory that excelleth. For if that which is done away was glorious, much more that which remaineth is glorious. Seeing then that we have such hope, we use great plainness of speech: And not as Moses, which put a veil over his face, that the children of Israel could not stedfastly look to the end of that which is abolished: But their minds were blinded: for until this day remaineth the same veil untaken away in the reading of the Old Testament; which veil is done away in Christ. But even unto this day, when Moses is read, the veil is upon their heart. Nevertheless, when it shall turn to the Lord, the veil shall be taken away. Now the Lord is that Spirit: and where the Spirit of the Lord is, there is liberty' (2 Corinthians 3:2-17).

Two Covenants
Here the Spirit of God draws a comparison between the two covenants. The first was given at Mount Sinai; the law, the covenant of works. The

second from Mount Zion; the gospel, the covenant of grace. The law he calls the 'ministration of death', and of 'condemnation'. The gospel is called 'the ministration of life'. The law is fleshy and carnal. The gospel is spirit and righteousness. The law brings bondage. The gospel brings liberty. The law was glorious in the ministration of death and condemnation. The ministration of the gospel is much more glorious in the gift of life. The glory of the law was transient. The glory of the gospel is permanent. 'Much more doth the ministration of righteousness exceed in glory.' In fact, by comparison, when compared to the gospel, the law has no glory at all, 'by reason of the glory that excelleth'.

Done Away
Three times in this chapter the Spirit of God tells us the glory of the law, the law itself, was 'done away', done away by the coming, accomplishments, and revelation of Christ. And the very same word translated 'done away' in 2 Corinthians 3:7, 11, 14, is translated in verse 13 as 'abolished'. It is strong language. The Spirit of God uses the unveiling of Moses' face as a picture of the fact that the dispensation, economy, and service of the law is over in this gospel age! The law was our schoolmaster unto Christ. But since Christ has come, we are no longer under a schoolmaster (Galatians 3:15-29; 5:1-4).

The reason the law was given was to point us to Christ, who alone obeyed its requirements and satisfied its justice as the sinner's Substitute. It serves no other purpose. I defy anyone to find a solitary text of Scripture in the New Testament that uses the law to motivate, inspire, regulate, or even guide the believer. Believers are motivated by love, inspired by gratitude, regulated by grace, and guided by the Holy Spirit. The whole Word of God, the complete revelation of his will, is our law.

We are not ruled by the law but by grace. We are not motivated by the law, but 'the love of Christ constraineth us'. Condemnation by the law holds no fear for us. We have no covenant with the law. We keep no ceremonies of the law. We suffer no curse from the law. We owe no debt to the law (Romans 8:33, 34). When Satan raises Moses up to condemn us, the Lord Jesus stands by his redeemed and silences the devil's accusations in our hearts, assuring the believing sinner of his righteousness in, by, and with him (Jude 9; Zechariah 3:1-5; 1 John 2:1, 2).

We are not under the law, but under grace! 'Where the Spirit of the Lord is there is liberty' (2 Corinthians 3:17). The Scriptures declare this with unmistakable clarity (Romans 6:14, 15; 7:4; 8:1-4; 10:4). Truly, as Robert Hawker wrote, 'It is very blessed to read Moses in Christ; and to see that Christ "is the end of the law for righteousness to everyone that believeth".'

Taken Away

The veil that is spread upon God's Israel, the veil that is spread over God's elect scattered among all nations, is taken away when Christ is revealed in the hearts of chosen sinners by the mighty, saving operations of God the Holy Spirit. Until they are each taught of God by the revelation of Christ in their hearts, 'even unto this day, when Moses is read, the veil' of spiritual ignorance, blindness, and death, the veil of self-righteousness, idolatry, and religious superstition 'is upon their heart. Nevertheless when it', God's Israel, the elect, redeemed sinner, being born of God, taught of God, and granted repentance toward God, 'shall turn to the Lord, the veil shall be taken away' (2 Corinthians 3:15, 16). The veil is taken away by the revelation of the glory of God in the face of the Lord Jesus Christ, our all-glorious Saviour (2 Corinthians 4:1-7; 2 Timothy 1:9, 10; Isaiah 12:1-6; 29:15).

Yes, there is a veil upon the hearts of all by nature, a veil that only God the Holy Ghost can take away. In 2 Corinthians 3:18 we are reminded of the fact that as long as we are in this body of flesh, you and I can see but little of the glory of our dear God and Saviour, the Lord Jesus. But, blessed be his name forever, when we drop this veil of flesh, we shall see all things clearly! 'But we all, with open face beholding as in a glass the glory of the Lord, are changed into the same image from glory to glory, even as by the Spirit of the Lord' (2 Corinthians 3:18).

Soon that will change! 'As for me, I will behold thy face in righteousness: I shall be satisfied, when I awake, with thy likeness' (Psalm 17:15). Soon, we shall behold him face to face – forever!

Chapter 114

The High Honour God Puts Upon His People

'And Moses gathered all the congregation of the children of Israel together, and said unto them, These are the words which the LORD hath commanded, that ye should do them. Six days shall work be done, but on the seventh day there shall be to you an holy day, a sabbath of rest to the LORD: whosoever doeth work therein shall be put to death. Ye shall kindle no fire throughout your habitations upon the sabbath day. And Moses spake unto all the congregation of the children of Israel, saying, This is the thing which the LORD commanded, saying, Take ye from among you an offering unto the LORD: whosoever is of a willing heart, let him bring it, an offering of the LORD; gold, and silver, and brass, And blue, and purple, and scarlet, and fine linen, and goats' hair, And rams' skins dyed red, and badgers' skins, and shittim wood, And oil for the light, and spices for anointing oil, and for the sweet incense, And onyx stones, and stones to be set for the ephod, and for the breastplate. And every wise hearted among you shall come, and make all that the LORD hath commanded; The tabernacle, his tent, and his covering, his taches, and his boards, his bars, his pillars, and his sockets, The ark, and the staves thereof, with the mercy seat, and the vail of the covering, The table, and his staves, and all his vessels, and the shewbread, The candlestick also for the light, and his furniture, and his lamps, with the oil for the light, And the incense altar, and his staves, and the anointing oil, and the sweet incense, and the hanging for the door at the entering in of the tabernacle, The altar of burnt offering, with his brasen grate, his staves, and all his vessels, the laver and his foot, The hangings of the court, his pillars, and their sockets, and the hanging for the door of the court, The pins of the tabernacle, and the pins of the

court, and their cords, The cloths of service, to do service in the holy place, the holy garments for Aaron the priest, and the garments of his sons, to minister in the priest's office. And all the congregation of the children of Israel departed from the presence of Moses. And they came, every one whose heart stirred him up, and every one whom his spirit made willing, and they brought the LORD'S offering to the work of the tabernacle of the congregation, and for all his service, and for the holy garments. And they came, both men and women, as many as were willing hearted, and brought bracelets, and earrings, and rings, and tablets, all jewels of gold: and every man that offered offered an offering of gold unto the LORD. And every man, with whom was found blue, and purple, and scarlet, and fine linen, and goats' hair, and red skins of rams, and badgers' skins, brought them. Every one that did offer an offering of silver and brass brought the LORD'S offering: and every man, with whom was found shittim wood for any work of the service, brought it. And all the women that were wise hearted did spin with their hands, and brought that which they had spun, both of blue, and of purple, and of scarlet, and of fine linen. And all the women whose heart stirred them up in wisdom spun goats' hair. And the rulers brought onyx stones, and stones to be set, for the ephod, and for the breastplate; And spice, and oil for the light, and for the anointing oil, and for the sweet incense. The children of Israel brought a willing offering unto the LORD, every man and woman, whose heart made them willing to bring for all manner of work, which the LORD had commanded to be made by the hand of Moses. And Moses said unto the children of Israel, See, the LORD hath called by name Bezaleel the son of Uri, the son of Hur, of the tribe of Judah; And he hath filled him with the spirit of God, in wisdom, in understanding, and in knowledge, and in all manner of workmanship; And to devise curious works, to work in gold, and in silver, and in brass, And in the cutting of stones, to set them, and in carving of wood, to make any manner of cunning work. And he hath put in his heart that he may teach, both he, and Aholiab, the son of Ahisamach, of the tribe of Dan. Them hath he filled with wisdom of heart, to work all manner of work, of the engraver, and of the cunning workman, and of the embroiderer, in blue, and in purple, in scarlet, and in fine linen, and of the weaver, even of them that do any work, and of those that devise cunning work.'
(Exodus 35:1-35)

Everybody wants to be a part of something big. Everyone wants to be a part of something great, important, and significant. Here, in Exodus 35, we are told about some people who are a part of something truly great, men and women used of God to make for him a tabernacle of worship. What a great privilege and honour it is for God to allow such people as we are (fallen, depraved, fickle, unstable, sinful men and women) to perform his work in this world!

The highest honour we can give to the triune God, to the Lord Jehovah, our God and Saviour, is faith in him. Our faith in him is his gift to us; and our faith in Christ is our gift to him. Believing him, we honour him. And the Lord God has declared, 'Them that honour me I will honour' (1 Samuel 2:30). In this portion of Holy Scripture, we are given many pictures of the way God honours those who honour him by faith in Christ.

Because, at first glance, chapters 35-39 seem to be nothing more than a recapitulation of chapters 25-31, most of the commentaries have very little to say about these final chapters of Exodus, treating them almost as though they were redundant. That is a great pity. Nothing written in the Book of God is redundant, merely repetitive or unnecessary. At the very least, all repetitions given in Scripture are needful repetitions. None are redundant. When a man sharpens his pocket knife, is it redundant to go over the whetstone many times? No. The more strokes the better. And we are specifically told to teach the things of God with repetition (Deuteronomy 6:7; Philippians 3:1).

Exodus 25-31 is a description of the tabernacle as it was given directly to Moses by the Lord God himself. Chapters 35-39 record what was actually made according to the pattern shown to Moses. Typically, that fact alone is very significant because that which was accomplished by God in his purpose of grace in sovereign predestination shall be performed by the sovereign power of God in time.

Blessed Rest

Exodus 35 is all about serving God. In the previous chapters we are told about the pattern God gave Moses in the Mount. Here the work is actually begun; and it is begun with another declaration of God's command that the children of Israel must keep the sabbath.

'And Moses gathered all the congregation of the children of Israel together, and said unto them, These are the words which the LORD hath commanded, that ye should do them. Six days shall work be done, but on the seventh day there shall be to you an holy day, a sabbath of rest to the LORD: whosoever doeth work therein shall be put to death. Ye shall kindle no fire throughout your habitations upon the sabbath day' (vv. 1-3).

In this chapter, we see the children of Israel serving God with willing hearts. Here are God's chosen people making sacrifices with joy and labouring with gladness; but the chapter begins with a commandment to keep the sabbath day holy. So, the first thing evident in the chapter is that service begins with rest. We cannot do anything for God until we stop trying to do something to appease God. We cannot serve the Lord until we rest in Christ, our blessed Sabbath Rest. We cannot bring anything to God until we find rest in Christ.

Remember, the tabernacle was designed of God and given by God to portray and typify our Lord Jesus Christ and the full accomplishment of salvation by him and in him. So, before the work of erecting the tabernacle began, the Lord God gave this commandment again. 'Six days shall work be done, but on the seventh day there shall be to you an holy day, a sabbath of rest to the LORD: whosoever doeth work therein shall be put to death.' Before we are fit to serve the holy Lord God, we must rest in Christ. Before we can bring anything to him, we must receive grace from him. This is the seventh and last mention of the sabbath in the book of Exodus, the book of redemption and deliverance. It was Solomon, 'a man of rest' (1 Chronicles 22), who alone could build a house to Jehovah's name. Both the sabbath days of the Old Testament and Solomon, the man of rest, typified our Lord Jesus Christ, our blessed Sabbath, in whom and by whom we rest.

But in Exodus 35:3, an additional feature is added to the observance of the sabbath. Even the lighting of a fire on the sabbath day is here prohibited! The Lord never mentioned that before. Why is it added here? There may be other reasons for this additional requirement; but I am sure this is intended to show us at least these two things.

Faith in Christ is a complete cessation of works, a total dependence upon the Son of God for our entire salvation. Faith in Christ is the means by which God the Holy Spirit purges our consciences of guilt and imputes righteousness to the believing sinner, as he did to Abraham.

Having faith in the Son of God, trusting Christ alone as our Saviour, resting in him, every believer calls the sabbath a delight.

'If thou turn away thy foot from the sabbath, from doing thy pleasure on my holy day; and call the sabbath a delight, the holy of the LORD, honourable; and shalt honour him, not doing thine own ways, nor finding thine own pleasure, nor speaking thine own words: Then shalt thou delight thyself in the LORD; and I will cause thee to ride upon the high places of the earth, and feed thee with the heritage of Jacob thy father: for the mouth of the LORD hath spoken it' (Isaiah 58:13, 14).

Honour Bestowed
Next, in verses 4-19, we see the Lord God bestowing a great honour upon the children of Israel. He so highly honoured them that he allowed every man and woman in the nation of Israel to have a hand in making the tabernacle. Without question, God did not need Israel's assistance. Everything the children of Israel brought to him he had given them. Yet, the Lord condescended to use the people he brought out of Egypt to establish his place of worship and all the things connected with his worship while they were in the wilderness.

Great as that privilege was, high as that honour was, it pales into insignificance, when compared to the great, high honour and extraordinary privilege the Lord God has placed upon believing sinners in this world. God Almighty has chosen us as his witnesses and his servants in this world. What a high honour God has put upon his church! We are his witnesses.

'Ye are my witnesses, saith the LORD, and my servant whom I have chosen: that ye may know and believe me, and understand that I am he: before me there was no God formed, neither shall there be after me. I, even I, am the LORD; and beside me there is no saviour. I have declared, and have saved, and I have showed, when there was no strange god among you: therefore ye are my witnesses, saith the LORD, that I am God' (Isaiah 43:10-12).

'Fear ye not, neither be afraid: have not I told thee from that time, and have declared it? ye are even my witnesses. Is there a God beside me? yea, there is no God; I know not any' (Isaiah 44:8).

'Then said Jesus to them again, Peace be unto you: as my Father hath sent me, even so send I you' (John 20:21).

'Ye shall receive power, after that the Holy Ghost is come upon you: and ye shall be witnesses unto me both in Jerusalem, and in all Judaea, and in Samaria, and unto the uttermost part of the earth' (Acts 1:8).

'Therefore if any man be in Christ, he is a new creature: old things are passed away; behold, all things are become new. And all things are of God, who hath reconciled us to himself by Jesus Christ, and hath given to us the ministry of reconciliation; To wit, that God was in Christ, reconciling the world unto himself, not imputing their trespasses unto them; and hath committed unto us the word of reconciliation. Now then we are ambassadors for Christ, as though God did beseech you by us: we pray you in Christ's stead, be ye reconciled to God. For he hath made him to be sin for us, who knew no sin; that we might be made the righteousness of God in him' (2 Corinthians 5:17-21).

'We then, as workers together with him, beseech you also that ye receive not the grace of God in vain' (2 Corinthians 6:1).

The People and Their Gifts
Now, look in verses 20-29 at the people God uses to serve him and the gifts they bring to him, by which he is honoured. Let us apply the passage as personally as possible. Behold the people God uses to build his kingdom in this world, the people God uses to spread the gospel to the four corners of the earth, the people God uses to call out his elect in every generation.

'For ye see your calling, brethren, how that not many wise men after the flesh, not many mighty, not many noble, are called: But God hath chosen the foolish things of the world to confound the wise; and God hath chosen the weak things of the world to confound the things which are mighty; and base things of the world, and things which are despised, hath God chosen, yea, and things which are not, to bring to nought things that are: That no flesh should glory in his presence. But of him are ye in Christ Jesus, who of God is made unto us wisdom, and righteousness, and sanctification, and redemption: That, according as it is written, he that glorieth, let him glory in the Lord' (1 Corinthians 1:26-31).

'But we have this treasure in earthen vessels, that the excellency of the power may be of God, and not of us' (2 Corinthians 4:7).

Who are the people God uses to honour himself? Who were those people he used to make the tabernacle? They were a chosen, covenant people. 'All the congregation of the children of Israel' (v. 20). The offerings they brought were 'the Lord's offering' (v. 21), that which the Lord had given them, that which really was the Lord's, that which they acknowledged to be the Lord's. Men and women, rich and poor, the rulers and the labourers worked and brought their gifts to the Lord, each serving with what God gave them, and in the capacity God appointed.

The offerings were the offerings of willing hearts. That is the only service, the only offering, God will ever accept. Only what rises from and is performed by a willing heart. 'If there be first a willing mind, it is accepted according to that a man hath, and not according to that he hath not' (2 Corinthians 8:12).

'And the LORD spake unto Moses, saying, Speak unto the children of Israel, that they bring me an offering: of every man that giveth it willingly with his heart ye shall take my offering' (Exodus 25:1, 2).

The materials out of which the tabernacle was made were to be provided by the voluntary offerings of devoted hearts. 'And they came, everyone whose heart stirred him up, and everyone whom his spirit made willing … And they came, both men and women, as many as were willing hearted, and brought bracelets, and earrings, and rings, and tablets, all jewels of gold: and every man offered an offering of gold unto the Lord' (vv. 21, 22). Spontaneously, freely, joyfully they availed themselves of their great honour and high privilege (Exodus 35:22-28).

Everything offered to God must proceed from hearts made willing by his Spirit. It must be spontaneous and free, not the result of persuasion or of external pressure, but from the heart. It must be given, not taken, constrained by love, not by law, motivated by gratitude, not by fear, inspired by reverence, not by reward.

Nothing is more certain to ruin any missionary work, ministry, or church than the employment of carnal, fleshy, worldly schemes to raise money: tithing, pledges, deputation, bake sales, begging, etc.. Nothing more dishonours God and his people than the many ways churches, preachers, and religious organizations try to get their money!

Moses simply told the people that the Lord God Almighty, who brought them out of Egypt and destroyed all their enemies, God their Saviour and Redeemer, was willing to receive a gift from them. He did not tell them what to bring or how much to bring. He simply said, God is willing to receive your gifts. Each brought what he had in his possession (blue, silver, gold, shittim wood). Each brought only as much as he wanted to bring, no more and no less than his own heart dictated. And there was more than sufficient, 'much more than enough', to finish the work (Exodus 36:5-7).

If the God of Glory calls us to do a work, the God of Glory will supply everything needed to do the work. God's servants do not beg; and God's people are not mercenaries. We serve our God and do whatever it is the Lord God allows us to do for his glory, because we want to do it. 'The love of Christ constraineth us.'

Bezaleel and Aholiab
In verses 30-35, Moses introduces Bezaleel and Aholiab to us. Without question, these two men typify our blessed Saviour, the Lord Jesus Christ, who builds his church. But let me briefly show you that these two men also represent those men who are called and gifted of God to lead his people in building his house. Bezaleel and Aholiab clearly represent faithful pastors, gospel preachers, appointed of God as overseers in his house.

'And Moses said unto the children of Israel, See, the LORD hath called by name Bezaleel the son of Uri, the son of Hur, of the tribe of Judah; And he hath filled him with the Spirit of God, in wisdom, in understanding, and in knowledge, and in all manner of workmanship; And to devise curious works, to work in gold, and in silver, and in brass, and in the cutting of stones, to set them, and in carving of wood, to make any manner of cunning work. And he hath put in his heart that he may teach, both he, and Aholiab, the son of Ahisamach, of the tribe of Dan. Them hath he filled with wisdom of heart, to work all manner of work, of the engraver, and of the cunning workman, and of the embroiderer, in blue, and in purple, in scarlet, and in fine linen, and of the weaver, even of them that do any work, and of those that devise cunning work' (Exodus 35:30-35).

Like all those men called of God to the work of preaching the gospel, Bezaleel and Aholiab were divinely called (v. 30). They were filled with the Spirit of God (v. 31). They were gifted of God with wisdom, understanding, and knowledge to perform the work to which they were called (v. 31); and they were 'cunning (skilful) workman' (v. 35).

Little did Bezaleel or Aholiab know that while they were making bricks in Egypt, under the lash of cruel taskmasters, the God of Glory was preparing them to be skilled artisans by whose hands he would erect the tabernacle in the wilderness for the glory of his name and the everlasting good of his people!

Chapter 115

Brass Nails And Linen Cords

'The pins of the tabernacle, and the pins of the court, and their cords.' (Exodus 35:18)

While preaching in Australia more than 30 years ago, I ran into a man, a preacher, who, for some strange reason, objected to the fact that the whole Book of God is the revelation of the Lord Jesus Christ and him crucified (1 Corinthians 2:2; Luke 24:27, 45-47). Thankfully, I don't remember the man's name. I only spoke to him briefly. But he mockingly asked me a question I could not answer at the time, a question I had never really considered. He said, with a smirk on his face, 'If the whole Bible speaks of Christ, what was the purpose of the tent pins in the tabernacle'. I was not embarrassed that I did not know the answer to his question. As I said, I had never really thought about the pins (nails) that were used to hold the tabernacle in place. But I said to myself then, 'Perhaps, someday, the Lord will show me the meaning of those nails.'

Well, that day has come. I am confident the Lord taught me, at least in part, the spiritual significance of those brass nails and linen cords that were used to erect and hold together the tabernacle. Here, listed among all the things God required Moses to make for the tabernacle are, 'The pins of the tabernacle, and the pins of the court, and their cords'.

The tabernacle was secured in its place by these brass pins (nails) and linen cords. The nails were driven into the ground and the cords were stretched over the outer covering of badgers' skins, tying everything securely in place, much like we use nails and cords to secure a tent to the ground today. We are told these pins (nails) were made of brass (Exodus 27:19; 38:20). Though we are not specifically told the cords were linen, the only materials that could have been used to make these cords were blue, purple, scarlet, and fine linen (Exodus 35:5-19).

The word 'pin' is the same word that is translated 'nail' in the Book of Judges (4:21, 22; 5:26). You will remember that Heber's wife, Jael, drove a tent pin, an iron nail, through Sisera's temples, firmly attaching his head to the ground. In Isaiah 33:20 and 54:2, the same word is translated 'stake'. I point this out simply so you will not think of these tabernacle pins as small things. They were large, brass stakes, driven deep into the ground.

Security
The first thing suggested by these brass nails is security. They were used to securely attach and fasten the tabernacle and its court to the earth. So securely was it fastened that we never read that it was even slightly disturbed by all the strong winds it must have endured during all the years of Israel's sojourn through the wilderness. Many of the things inside the tabernacle such as the Shewbread, the candlestick, the censer, might have been easily swept away by high wind or a flood of water. But that never happened.

Like everything else connected with the tabernacle, those brass nails were typical of our Lord Jesus Christ. They were made of brass, a material that could not be corrupted though the nails were driven deep into the ground. They withstood all the elements of the earth. Clearly, they typified our blessed Saviour. We are given clear indication of this in Isaiah 22, where our Lord Jesus is described as 'a nail in a sure place'.

'And it shall come to pass in that day, that I will call my servant Eliakim the son of Hilkiah: And I will clothe him with thy robe, and strengthen him with thy girdle, and I will commit thy government into his hand: and he shall be a father to the inhabitants of Jerusalem, and to the house of Judah. And the key of the house of David will I lay upon his shoulder; so he shall open, and none shall shut; and he shall shut, and none shall open. And I will fasten him as a nail in a sure place; and he shall be for a glorious throne to his father's house. And they shall hang upon him all the glory of his father's house, the offspring and the issue, all vessels of small quantity, from the vessels of cups, even to all the vessels of flagons' (Isaiah 22:20-24).

We know this passage is talking about our Saviour, because he applies it to himself in Revelation 3:7. He alone has the key of David, and he alone opens and no man can shut, and shuts, so no man can open.

Stedfast Purpose

When we read about these brass nails that held the tabernacle in place, we should remember the stedfast purpose and resolve of our Lord Jesus. He faithfully and relentlessly pursued the path marked out for him by the counsels of God from everlasting, even though that path ended in a storm of divine judgment and billows of infinite wrath. Neither the fierce attacks of the tempter, nor the anticipation of the death he had to die, turned him aside from the settled purpose of his heart. He cried, 'Lo, I come to do thy will, O God', and never turned to the right hand nor to the left. And though he experienced the deep feelings expressed in Psalm 55, he was never once inclined to forsake his purpose for coming into this world, his purpose to save us from our sins.

'My heart is sore pained within me: and the terrors of death are fallen upon me. Fearfulness and trembling are come upon me, and horror hath overwhelmed me. And I said, Oh that I had wings like a dove! For then would I fly away, and be at rest. Lo, then would I wander far off, and remain in the wilderness. Selah. I would hasten my escape from the windy storm and tempest' (Psalm 55:4-8).

Jehovah's faithful Servant, our dear Saviour, refused to turn back from his mission. He refused to give up his work. He says,

'The Lord GOD hath opened mine ear, and I was not rebellious, neither turned away back. I gave my back to the smiters, and my cheeks to them that plucked off the hair: I hid not my face from shame and spitting. For the Lord GOD will help me; therefore shall I not be confounded: therefore have I set my face like a flint, and I know that I shall not be ashamed' (Isaiah 50:5-7).

What faith and faithfulness he exemplified all the days of his life! He knew how to cast his burden upon Jehovah, upon God who shall never suffer the righteous to be moved. His heart was fixed, and God was his exceeding joy.

Behold the God-man, your Saviour, fully God and fully man, fully man and fully God. Weak, yet immovably firm, himself the Mighty

God, yet dependent for everything on God his Father. He set his face stedfastly toward Jerusalem in order to suffer there, and cried in deep distress, 'O my Father if it be possible let this cup pass from me! Nevertheless not as I will, but as thou wilt'. Oh, the wondrous power of that weakness! Oh, the marvellous victory of that death! Oh, the eternal stability of our unchangeable Christ! He was laid low in the depths of the grave, yet he was and is life itself and alive for evermore!

The desert afforded a shifting foundation for a tabernacle of glory, but the solid sockets and nails of brass, driven deeply into the ground, made all secure. So, it is our Lord Jesus Christ, the nail in a sure place, who secures all things for us. It is he and he alone who is our security.

'Out of him came forth the corner, out of him the nail, out of him the battle bow, out of him every oppressor together' (Zechariah 10:4).

Here are three references to the Lord Jesus. He is the Corner, the Nail, and the Battle Bow. He is the Chief Cornerstone and Headstone of the corner. He is the Battle Bow by whom we conquer and prevail over every foe. And he is the Nail that firmly secures all the eternal counsels of love, mercy, grace, and blessing of the triune God and connects them with this earth. That means, that notwithstanding the desolation and ruin of such a wilderness as this world is, the purpose of God stands sure! No matter how barren this wilderness is, in Christ, with this Nail of Brass fixed in a sure place, covenant mercies constantly flow down in unceasing rivers of grace from our God in heaven.

Eliakim and Christ

Look at Eliakim, the man who typified our Saviour as 'a nail in a sure place'. God called Judah to repentance during the reign of Hezekiah. But the nation had no regard for God, his Word, or his prophet, because the leaders of the nation under Hezekiah were self-serving, godless men. The treasurer over the house of Israel, Shebna, was singled out by God for his sin. Shebna was as a nail in a sure place. But God pulled him down and set up Eliakim in his place. Go back to page 470 and 471 and again read Isaiah 22:20-24.

This man, Eliakim, who was exalted in the place of Shebna, is set before us as a type and picture of our Lord Jesus Christ. When Shebna was removed, there was room for Eliakim. And Eliakim was fastened by God as a nail in a sure place. His name (Eliakim) means 'my God shall establish or raise up'. Like Eliakim, our Lord Jesus Christ has been set up and fastened by God as 'a nail in a sure place'. Upon him the triune God hangs his glory. Upon him we confidently hang the weight of our immortal souls. Eliakim, was a type of Christ. Remember, his name means 'my God will raise up'. As he was raised up to be the ruler over the Lord's house in the days of Hezekiah, so the Lord Jesus was raised up and exalted to be Head over all things for his church (John 17:1-4; Ephesians 1:21-23; Philippians 2:8-11). Compare Isaiah 22:22 with Revelation 3:7.

'And the key of the house of David will I lay upon his shoulder; so he shall open, and none shall shut; and he shall shut, and none shall open' (Isaiah 22:22). 'And to the angel of the church in Philadelphia write; These things saith he that is holy, he that is true, he that hath the key of David, he that openeth, and no man shutteth; and shutteth, and no man openeth' (Revelation 3:7). The House of David is the church and kingdom of God. Christ is the Ruler, King, and Sovereign of his kingdom. Christ is the only Way, the only Door of access into his kingdom. When he opens, none can shut. When he shuts, none can open. Christ's throne is glorious in his Father's house.

An Overthrow

In his exaltation, Eliakim was a type of Christ. But there is more, much more. Before Eliakim could be set up, Shebna had to be removed, cut off, and destroyed (Isaiah 22:17-21, 25). Shebna, who seemed to be fastened like a nail in a sure place had to be pulled out and discarded, so Eliakim could be put in his place. Even so, in the experience of grace, in order for Christ to be established in the heart there must be an overthrow of someone else. The strong man must be bound, and the devils of self-righteousness must be cast out to make room for Christ in a man's soul (Matthew 12:28, 29). When Christ comes into a heart, when he sets up his throne in the City of Mansoul a battle takes place. Every rival must be cast out. King Jesus will not share his throne.

All personal worth, merit, and righteousness must be pulled out, cast down, and torn to shreds. All men by nature have some kind of self-righteousness. There is no man so vile, but he still wraps himself in his rags of self-righteousness and comforts himself with the belief that his moral, spiritual, or religious goodness will stand him in good stead with God. Like Adam's fig-leaf apron, your righteousness must be torn to shreds, every stitch unravelled! You cannot put on the robe of Christ's righteousness until you have taken off your own (Philippians 3:1-10). Christ will never go shares in the business of salvation. As he was alone in his suffering, he will be alone in his saving. All self-confidence must be cast down. Some seem to have the idea that we are to trust Christ for the past but look to ourselves for the future. Our only hope for the future is Christ. If I am kept, Christ is the one who keeps me (John 10:27-30). If I am lost, trusting him, Christ is the one who loses me!

Having cast away all self-righteousness and self-confidence, we must continue to do so as long as we live in this world. Though in theory we recognize the evil of self-righteousness and despise it, it is always the darling idol of our sinful flesh. With both hands, we must pull it out, cast it down, and trample it under foot. We must look to Christ alone as our Saviour. Christ is my Saviour, not my faith. Christ is my Saviour, not my repentance. Christ is my Saviour, not my knowledge. Christ is my Saviour, not my feelings. Christ is my Saviour, not my faithfulness.

As Eliakim was in the house of Hezekiah, so Christ in the palace of heaven is as 'a nail in a sure place'. The picture here given is of a large, strong nail, fastened as a bracket, or an anchor in a wall, or a post, upon which you might with confidence hang anything. Christ is as a nail fastened by God himself. It is the Lord God who said, 'I will fasten him as a nail'. He did it in eternity, at Calvary, and in his ascension. He does it in the hearts of chosen, redeemed sinners with the gift of faith.

Here is a nail upon which you may hang the weight of your immortal soul. Christ is the Mighty God! He is the Mighty Redeemer! He is the Mighty Saviour! He is the Mighty Advocate! The gospel proclaims redemption by Christ (1 Corinthians 15:3) and promises salvation to all who believe. Trust Christ alone and I tell you, as God is true, you shall never come into judgment. Our Lord Jesus Christ is as a nail fastened in a sure place. All the vessels of the Father's house hang upon this one nail, Christ alone. He is the Nail that secures the whole tabernacle of God. Eliakim was the glory of his father's house. The Lord Jesus Christ is all the glory of his Father's house (Isaiah 22:23, 24).

A Nail Proved

As those brass nails which held the tabernacle withstood every element of the earth, every storm, and the stress of every test, so our Lord Jesus Christ declares, 'Thou hast proved mine heart; thou hast visited me in the night; thou hast tried me' (Psalm 17:3). He was tempted in the wilderness, pressed hard in Gethsemane, and proved at Calvary. Like those brass nails, our blessed Saviour was tempted, tested, and proved in all points, like as we are, yet without sin.

The Amen

Here then we have the Lord Jesus spoken of as a Nail, a Nail fastened in a sure place. It seems remarkable to me that the word translated 'sure' is the same as the Hebrew word commonly translated 'amen'. The Lord Jesus is the Nail because he is the Amen, the holy and the true, the faithful and true witness, the beginning of the creation of God.

All 'the promises of God in him are yea, and in him amen'. They hang securely, utterly dependent on him like vessels of every capacity, filled with the wine of joy and blessing. On him hangs all the glory of his Father's house, the offspring and the issue. The nail driven down into earth in death, now raised up on high is all the strength of God's house and God's building. As the tabernacle was firmly fixed by its nails of brass, so our souls, all the house of God, and all God's blessings of salvation are firmly fixed by Christ, the Nail in a sure place!

'Look upon Zion, the city of our solemnities: thine eyes shall see Jerusalem a quiet habitation, a tabernacle that shall not be taken down; not one of the stakes thereof shall ever be removed, neither shall any of the cords thereof be broken' (Isaiah 33:20).

Linen Cords

If you read every passage in the Old Testament that speaks of tabernacle nails, you will see the nails of brass and linen cords were inseparable. Wherever there was a nail, there was a cord and vice versa.

The cords were fastened to the nails and stretched across the coverings. The cords were attached to the nails, holding everything tightly to the earth and holding the whole house of God tightly together, making it secure and complete. These cords set forth the drawing and holding power of our Lord Jesus Christ in his mighty love for his own. He calls them 'bands of love' (Hosea 11:4). This is beautifully pictured in 2 Corinthians 5:14. The word 'constraineth' signifies to 'hold together'. If our union with Christ depended on our love for him, then the winds of circumstance would blow us apart. It is his unchanging love for the church that holds it together.

The cords of love by which he draws us to himself are the powerful cords of love revealed in our crucified Saviour (John 12:32, 33). Someone suggested that the nails of brass speak of our Saviour's great and glorious person, and the cords speak of his work; and the two can never be separated. Another suggested that the nails refer to his accomplishments for us, and the cords refer to the Spirit's work binding all together in the sweet revelation of his grace.

The cords tied to the nails bound together as one all the parts of the tabernacle and secured everything! And so it is today. The crucified Christ, the Nail in the sure place, secures all the blessings of grace and salvation for all the house of God, for all God's elect. God the Holy Spirit, applying the work of Christ to chosen, redeemed sinners, secures all grace to our hearts, as the earnest of our Salvation. And in Christ all who are born of the Spirit are one.

The first time some smart alec asks you, 'What was the purpose of the tent pins and cords?' You have the answer. They typified our Lord Jesus Christ, who by his accomplishments and by his Spirit secures the everlasting salvation of God's elect and holds everything together. Because he is our mighty Nail in a sure place and because the Linen Cords of his everlasting love hold us together, all is well. God's tabernacle cannot be moved. Not by wind of adversity! Not by attack of heresy! Not by flood of iniquity!

'Look upon Zion, the city of our solemnities: thine eyes shall see Jerusalem a quiet habitation, a tabernacle that shall not be taken down; not one of the stakes thereof shall ever be removed, neither shall any of the cords thereof be broken' (Isaiah 33:20).

Chapter 116

Bezaleel And Aholiab

'And Moses said unto the children of Israel, See, the LORD hath called by name Bezaleel the son of Uri, the son of Hur, of the tribe of Judah; And he hath filled him with the spirit of God, in wisdom, in understanding, and in knowledge, and in all manner of workmanship; And to devise curious works, to work in gold, and in silver, and in brass, And in the cutting of stones, to set them, and in carving of wood, to make any manner of cunning work. And he hath put in his heart that he may teach, both he, and Aholiab, the son of Ahisamach, of the tribe of Dan. Them hath he filled with wisdom of heart, to work all manner of work, of the engraver, and of the cunning workman, and of the embroiderer, in blue, and in purple, in scarlet, and in fine linen, and of the weaver, even of them that do any work, and of those that devise cunning work.'
(Exodus 35:30-35)

Here are two men who were chosen and ordained of God to serve him in an extraordinary way, two men whose names are known only to a few, but two men who are held before us in Holy Scripture as eminent types of our Lord Jesus Christ: Bezaleel and Aholiab.

I remind you again that the tabernacle was typical of our Lord Jesus Christ and the salvation that is ours in him. It typified both the person of our blessed Saviour and the work he performed. Therefore, when the Lord God gave commandment for it to be erected, every detail was arranged by divine purpose, revealed to a mediator (Moses), and provided for by the hand of God. And the whole work was executed precisely according to the revealed will of God in his Word. Nothing was left to chance. No vote was taken. No mortal was consulted. No man was allowed to add anything or take anything away. Everything was exactly as God himself said it must be. And everything was done exactly as God himself said it must be done. No exceptions!

Though skilled in all the wisdom of the Egyptians, Moses was not left to draw the plans for Jehovah's dwelling-place. Rather, he was required to make all things after the pattern shown to him in the mount. Not even Moses was allowed to add anything or subtract anything. The pattern had been fully set before him, perfectly and clearly. There was no question about what was to be done or who was to do it. The Lord God even specified who would do the work, right down to who would carry the nails that were driven into the ground (Numbers 4:29-33).

So it is in all things relating to the salvation of our souls. It is God's work alone. 'Salvation is of the Lord.' It is a work planned and ordained from eternity (Romans 8:28-30; Ephesians 1:3-6). It is carried out according to God's predestinating purpose. Nothing is left to chance! Nothing is contributed by man! The man who brings the Word of God to the chosen sinner, the time it comes, the place and the circumstances, all are according to the immutable, eternal, unalterable, irresistible will and purpose of God.

Here, in Exodus 35:30-35, the Lord God names two specific men who were to be the primary artisans by whom all things were to be accomplished: Bezaleel from the tribe of Judah and Aholiab from the tribe of Dan. God chose them. God equipped them. God identified them. The tabernacle is now to be built and the Lord told Moses who must do the work. But, long before this, when God gave Moses the pattern of the tabernacle, he identified these two men in exactly the same words (Exodus 31:1-5).

Typical of Christ

Bezaleel and Aholiab are set before us here as very instructive pictures of our blessed Saviour. They were typical of the Lord Jesus Christ. None but Christ was capable of building a house for God and every detail given about these two men clearly establishes that fact. May the Spirit of God grant us eyes to see. In fact, the first thing Moses says about this revelation from God is, 'See'. Ponder this awhile!

Bezaleel

As is often the case in Holy Scripture, the names given to these two men and their ancestors are highly significant. The first man named here is Bezaleel. His name means 'in the shadow of God' or 'the protection of God'. Bezaleel was the son of Uri, which means 'light'. He was the grandson of Hur, which means 'free'. He was from the tribe of Judah, which means 'praise'. Our Lord Jesus Christ is that one who is the Shadow of God and Protection of God for his people (Psalm 17:8; 57:1; 63:7). Blessed are they who take refuge under the shadow of his wings!

Bezaleel was the son of Uri, 'Light'. And the Lord Jesus is 'the Light of the Lord' (Isaiah 2:5). The Urim of the high priest's breastplate is the same word in the plural number. As Bezaleel was the son of light, so Christ is the Son of God who is Light, in whom is no darkness at all. He who is the 'Son of Light' is the Son of God, our Saviour (1 John 1:5). He is 'the brightness of his glory, and the express image of his person' (Hebrews 1:3). He is 'the Light of the world' (John 9:5). He is 'the Sun of Righteousness' who arises upon the souls of men with healing in his wings (Malachi 4:2).

Bezaleel was the son of Uri, the son of 'Hur', which means 'free' or 'at liberty'. Christ is our Salvation. He is the Refuge for our poor souls, the Shadow and Protection of God. Christ is our Light, 'the Light of the Lord', in whom we walk. He is our Liberty, the One who sets us free from sin, free from the curse, free from the law, free from guilt, free from religious tradition, free from death, and free from the fear of death.

We are told that Bezaleel was 'of the tribe of Judah'. Judah was Benjamin's surety, portraying Christ our Surety (Genesis 43:9). Our Lord Jesus is called 'the Lion of the tribe of Judah'. Judah was the royal tribe of Israel from whom Christ our King descended (Genesis 49:10). Judah was the tribe God ordered to take the lead when Israel journeyed, just as Christ always goes before and leads the way for his Israel. The name Judah means 'praise' and our precious Christ shall have all the praise of his house (Revelation 5:11-14).

Divinely Equipped

We are told that Bezaleel was divinely equipped for the work he was to do (vv. 31-35). As Bezaleel was equipped, miraculously and divinely, to build the tabernacle, so our Lord Jesus was miraculously and divinely equipped to be our Redeemer and Saviour.

'And there shall come forth a rod out of the stem of Jesse, and a Branch shall grow out of his roots: And the Spirit of the LORD shall rest upon him, the spirit of wisdom and understanding, the spirit of counsel and might, the spirit of knowledge and of the fear of the LORD; and shall make him of quick understanding in the fear of the LORD: and he shall not judge after the sight of his eyes, neither reprove after the hearing of his ears: But with righteousness shall he judge the poor, and reprove with equity for the meek of the earth: and he shall smite the earth with the rod of his mouth, and with the breath of his lips shall he slay the wicked. And righteousness shall be the girdle of his loins, and faithfulness the girdle of his reins' (Isaiah 11:1-5).

Bezaleel was equipped 'to work in gold'. Gold was used throughout the tabernacle to represent God. Only one filled with 'the Spirit of God, in wisdom and understanding and in knowledge' was able to 'work in gold'. And only One who is God is fit to work in divine things. Our Saviour said, 'I have glorified thee on the earth: I have finished the work which thou gavest me to do.' 'I have manifested thy name.' 'I have given unto them the words which thou gavest.' 'I have kept them in thy name.' 'It is finished.'

Bezaleel, this divinely chosen builder of the tabernacle, was enabled to work 'in silver'. Silver speaks of atonement and redemption. Who was qualified to 'work in silver'? None but Christ! The work of redemption was a work more astonishing and wondrous than the work of creation. It was a work beyond the power of those who are redeemed (Psalm 49:7, 8). The redemption of the soul is 'precious', so precious that nothing but the 'the precious blood of Christ, as of a lamb without blemish and without spot' (1 Peter 1:19) could wash away our sins.

He was skilled to work 'in brass'. Brass is the symbol of divine judgment. No mere creature is capable of enduring the weight of God's judgment upon the sins of his people. Therefore, our God laid help upon One that is mighty. He exalted One chosen out of the people (Psalm 89:19). This is unspeakably solemn! Let us ever think and speak of these things in reverence. None but Christ could have been made sin for us, borne the wrath of God for our sins, and thereby redeem us from the curse of the law (Lamentations 1:12-14; 2 Corinthians 5:21; Galatians 3:13). As Moses lifted up the serpent of brass (John 3:14-16), Christ was crucified for us. The 'work in brass' was completed when he cried, 'It is finished', bowed his head, and breathed out his life (John 19:30).

'And in cutting of stones.' The reference is to the jewels which were to adorn the shoulders and breastplate of Israel's high priest, as he appeared before God on their behalf. On these jewels were engraved the names of all the twelve tribes. Thus, those gems spoke of the people of God, presented before him in all the merits and excellency of that great and blessed High Priest of God's Israel, the Lord Jesus Christ.

'And in carving of timber.' It is the Lord Jesus who, by his Spirit, felled the tree which he sets as a beam in his holy temple and on which he carves his own image with 'cunning work'. The trees, by his grace, he makes to be boards, standing upright in his tabernacle, boards of shittim wood, overlaid with pure gold, standing in fixed sockets of silver, made from the atonement money paid by our Substitute.

Aholiab

'Aholiab, the son of Ahisamach, of the tribe of Dan' (v. 34), portrays our Saviour too. It takes more than one man to foreshadow the God-man. Adam, Abel, Noah, Abraham, Joseph, Moses, Aaron, David, and Solomon are all types of Christ, each one pointing to some distinct aspect of his person, offices, or work. Here in Exodus 35, Bezaleel and Aholiab together typify our Saviour.

Aholiab means 'the tent of the father'. When I learned the meaning of Aholiab's name, John 1:14 immediately came to mind. 'And the Word was made flesh, and dwelt among us, (and we beheld his glory, the glory as of the only begotten of the Father,) full of grace and truth.'

Just as Jehovah took up his abode in the tabernacle in the wilderness, so he found a dwelling place on earth when God the Son became one of us. 'God was in Christ, reconciling the world unto himself' (2 Corinthians 5:19). He is 'God manifest in the flesh' (1 Timothy 3:16). So perfect and complete is that manifestation that he could say, 'He that hath seen me hath seen the Father' (John 14:9).

Aholiab was the son of Ahisamach. Ahisamach means 'brother of support'. And the Lord Jesus Christ is our Brother, our Brother born for adversity, and our Brother of Support (Hebrews 2:17, 18; 4:14-16).

Aholiab was of the tribe of Dan. As Judah took the lead when Israel was on the march, so Dan brought up the rear. Thus, in these two men all Israel was represented. So, all God's elect are in Christ and one with Christ. The Lord Jesus, both in his person and in the glorious work he accomplished, represented all God's Israel. The tabernacle of God is a place for worship and praise, because therein is revealed God's great act of judgment upon sin in the sacrifice of his dear Son, the Lamb of God. As Dan brought up the rear, so our Lord Jesus is both the Leader and the Rear Guard of his people (Isaiah 52:12; 58:8). He goes before; and he brings up the rear. That means all is well!

Both Bezaleel and Aholiab were 'filled with the Spirit of God, in wisdom, in understanding, and in knowledge, and in all manner of workmanship ... Them hath he filled with wisdom of heart, to work all manner of work, of the engraver, and of the cunning workman, and of the embroiderer, in blue, and in purple, in scarlet, and in fine linen, and of the weaver, even of them that do any work, and of those that devise cunning work.' And we are God's 'workmanship' (Ephesians 2:10), God's masterpieces created in Christ Jesus! It is in his heart to teach us (v. 34), to reveal the things of God, to reveal God to us. He knows how to work in us both to will and to do of his good pleasure. He will perform his work until his house is complete.

Thank God for our Lord Jesus Christ, our Bezaleel, the Shadow of God under whose wings we hide, the Light, the One who makes us free. He shall have our praise!

Blessed be our Lord Jesus, our Aholiab, in whom dwells all the fulness of the Godhead bodily, our Brother of Support who both goes before and comes behind to gather all his chosen into heavenly glory!

Chapter 117

Doing Things God's Way

'Then wrought Bezaleel and Aholiab, and every wise hearted man, in whom the LORD put wisdom and understanding to know how to work all manner of work for the service of the sanctuary, according to all that the LORD had commanded. And Moses called Bezaleel and Aholiab, and every wise hearted man, in whose heart the LORD had put wisdom, even every one whose heart stirred him up to come unto the work to do it: And they received of Moses all the offering, which the children of Israel had brought for the work of the service of the sanctuary, to make it withal. And they brought yet unto him free offerings every morning … According to all that the LORD commanded Moses, so the children of Israel made all the work. And Moses did look upon all the work, and, behold, they had done it as the LORD had commanded, even so had they done it: and Moses blessed them.'
(Exodus 36:1-39:43)

If we would worship and serve the Lord our God, the true and living God, we must worship and serve him in the way he prescribes. We either do things God's way, or all we call worship and service to the Lord is but will-worship and a vain show of religion.

In these four chapters, God the Holy Spirit tells us how the tabernacle was actually constructed by the children of Israel under the direction of Bezaleel and Aholiab. We have seen in the earlier chapters of Exodus what the Lord revealed to Moses in the mount and how Moses conveyed God's revelation to his people. There is no need to go over all the types again; but these chapters are not redundant repetitions.

These chapters were not written to fill up space, but as all the Book of God, 'were written for our learning, that we through patience and comfort of the Scriptures might have hope' (Romans 15:4).

The tabernacle in the wilderness portrays and typifies the person and work of Christ. It shows the redemption and salvation of God's elect by Christ's obedience unto death, by His righteousness and satisfaction, and the whole Church of God, built by Christ and upon Christ, as one habitation of God through the Spirit.

The boards of shittim wood overlaid with gold could not be set in their place except in the divinely prescribed order. Those boards represented sinners saved by grace, surrounding the mercy seat, around the throne of God. The boards all stood upright, fixed upon sockets of silver made from the atonement money given in the numbering of Israel, the atonement 'wherein ye stand'. Each board had two sockets: righteousness and satisfaction. The boards were all coupled together. They were held in place by the bars surrounding them, which appear to represent the attributes and promises of God. They were all shot through with the middle bar, which no one could see but the one who put it through them. That middle bar, I believe, represents 'Christ in you, the hope of glory'.

Generosity

What a picture of devotion and generosity we have before us! These men and women and their rulers, all the children of Israel, are here held up to us as examples of consecration to God in performing the work of the sanctuary. No effort was needed to move the hearts of the people to give. No appeals were made. No impressive arguments were given. Nothing was promised. Nothing was threatened.

Rather, their 'hearts stirred them up'. The streams of voluntary devotion flowed from within. 'Rulers', 'men', 'women' all felt it to be their sweet privilege to give to the Lord, not with a narrow heart or mean hand, but after such a princely fashion that Bezaleel and Aholiab told Moses that they had enough and too much.

Implicit Obedience

Not only did the children of Israel give with open hearts and hands, their obedience was implicit. They did exactly as the Lord commanded Moses (Exodus 39:42, 43), 'according to all that the Lord commanded

484

Moses, so the children of Israel made all the work. And Moses did look upon all the work, and, behold, they had done it as the Lord had commanded, even so had they done it: and Moses blessed them.'

The Lord God had given minute, detailed instructions concerning the entire work of the tabernacle. Every pin, socket, loop, buckle was to be made exactly as God said. There was no room for man's vote, reason, or common sense. Jehovah did not give a general outline and leave it for the children of Israel, or even Bezaleel, to fill in the details. He left no place for any man to enter an opinion, let alone a regulation. None! 'See, saith he, that thou make all things according to the pattern showed to thee in the mount' (Exodus 25:40; 26:30; Hebrews 8:5).

This left no room for human device. Had man been allowed to make a single pin, that pin would have been wrongly made and out of place in the tabernacle of God. We see what man's 'graving tool' produces in Exodus 32. It has no place in the worship and service of God! The people did as they were told, no more, no less. The Spirit constrained them to do exactly as instructed that we might have in their obedience an example to follow. There are many things in the history of Israel we must earnestly seek to avoid: their impatient murmurings, their legal vows, and their idolatry. But what is before us here in their giving and obedience is exemplary. Blessed are they who follow the example.

The tabernacle was, in all respects, according to the divine pattern, therefore it could be filled with the divine glory. We are prone to regard the Word of God as insufficient for the most minute details connected with his worship and service. This is a great mistake, it has proved the source of much evil and great error in the professing church. The Word of God is and must be our only rule of faith and practice. It is sufficient for everything in doctrine and service. It is our only rule of faith and practice in the worship and service of our God (2 Timothy 3:16, 17).

The Givers
Look at the givers. Those who brought the gifts were all the congregation of the children of Israel: men, women, and rulers, young and old, rich and poor, the well-known and the unknown. They were God's chosen, covenant people, his redeemed, a people to whom the Lord God revealed himself in saving grace. They were a people willingly obedient to the Lord.

The Users

Bezaleel and Aholiab were the men appointed by God to use the things the children of Israel brought for the service of God. These two men, typical of the Lord Jesus, also represent God's servants; pastors and gospel preachers, appointed by the Lord to be overseers in his house.

They were filled with the Spirit of God (Exodus 35:31). They were specifically gifted of God with wisdom and understanding to perform the work. God put it in their heart to do the work (Exodus 35:34). The Lord made it obvious to all Israel that they were the men he had chosen for the work. They were truly the servants of God. They wanted nothing but to serve him as he had ordained. And when they had all they needed to do the work, they refused to take any more!

The Gifts

There is much to be learned from the gifts themselves, the gifts the children of Israel brought, the gifts God received and used for his glory.

The gifts varied greatly: gold and oil, silver and spices, precious stones and wood, brass and goats' hair, wool and linen, dyes for blue and purple and scarlet, and onyx stones. The gifts all came from people with willing hearts, happy to give; from people who knew that what they brought to the Lord was not theirs, but his (Exodus 35:5, 21).

The Word of God supplies an abundance of instruction about the matter of giving. All of 1 Corinthians 9, and 2 Corinthians 8 and 9, are taken up with this subject. But there are no commands given to the people of God anywhere in the New Testament about how much we are to give, when we are to give, or where we are to give. Tithing and all systems like it are totally foreign to the New Testament. Giving, like all other acts of worship, is an act of faith and grace. It must be free and voluntary, or it is unacceptable. However, there are some plain, simple guidelines laid down in the Scriptures for us to follow. Here are ten things revealed in the New Testament about giving: our giving should be planned (2 Corinthians 9:7), free, voluntary, and unconstrained (2 Corinthians 9:7). Our giving must be motivated by love and gratitude towards Christ (2 Corinthians 8:7-9; 9:7) and arise from a willing heart (2 Corinthians 8:12; 9:7). Believers give to the work of the gospel according to personal ability (1 Corinthians 9:7; 16:2). Every believer should give a portion of his goods for the cause of Christ (1 Corinthians 9:7; 16:2). Our gifts for the gospel should be liberal and sacrificial

(Mark 12:41-44; 2 Corinthians 9:5-7). We are to give as unto the Lord (Matthew 6:1-5). This kind of giving is well pleasing to God (2 Corinthians 9:5-7; Philippians 4:18; Hebrews 13:16). If we are willing to give, God will supply us with the ability to give (Luke 6:38; 2 Corinthians 9:7, 10; Philippians 4:19).

The Result
Because the children of Israel were stirred up in their hearts by the Spirit of God, stirred up by the knowledge of what was to be represented in the tabernacle, the priesthood, the sacrifice, and the services of the sanctuary, they devoted themselves to do the work, giving whatever and all that was needed. 'The stuff they had was sufficient for the work' (36:7). And, 'Thus was all the work of the tabernacle of the tent of the congregation finished: and the children of Israel did according to all that the LORD commanded Moses, so did they' (Exodus 39:32).

'Then a cloud covered the tent of the congregation, and the glory of the LORD filled the tabernacle. And Moses was not able to enter into the tent of the congregation, because the cloud abode thereon, and the glory of the LORD filled the tabernacle' (Exodus 40:34, 35).

Chapter 118

Blessed Repetition

'And Bezaleel made the ark of shittim wood: two cubits and a half was the length of it, and a cubit and a half the breadth of it, and a cubit and a half the height of it: And he overlaid it with pure gold within and without, and made a crown of gold to it round about … And he made the holy anointing oil, and the pure incense of sweet spices, according to the work of the apothecary.'
(Exodus 37:1-29)

Everything written in Exodus 37 is written in almost the very same words in Exodus 25 and 30. In Exodus 25 and 30, the Lord God told Moses exactly how to make the ark with its mercy seat, the table of shewbread with its vessels, the golden candlestick with its bowls and snuff dishes, the golden altar of incense, and the holy anointing oil. Here we are told that Bezaleel made those things exactly as God had declared they must be made. We might wonder, why are these things recorded again in almost the very same words? Would it not have been just as useful for Moses to have written, 'Bezaleel made everything as the Lord commanded Moses'?

Of course, we dare not make such a presumption. If something is repeated in the Book of God, there is a reason for the repetition. May God the Holy Spirit who inspired Moses to make this repetition show us the blessedness of such inspired repetitions in the Book of God.

The Ark of the Covenant

In Exodus 37:1-5, Moses tells us Bezaleel made the ark of the covenant just as the Lord commanded it must be made in Exodus 25:10.

'And Bezaleel made the ark of shittim wood: two cubits and a half was the length of it, and a cubit and a half the breadth of it, and a cubit and a half the height of it: And he overlaid it with pure gold within and without, and made a crown of gold to it round about. And he cast for it four rings of gold, to be set by the four corners of it; even two rings upon the one side of it, and two rings upon the other side of it. And he made staves of shittim wood, and overlaid them with gold. And he put the staves into the rings by the sides of the ark, to bear the ark.'

Nothing in Holy Writ can be said to be unneedful or superfluous. And if, as it is written, our God does not forget our work of faith and labour of love, surely, we can never think too often, remember too dearly, or speak too frequently of his great acts of mercy, operations of grace, and works of love for our souls (Philippians 3:1).

Originally, these things were written to the children of Israel, to whom these sacred treasures were entrusted. Yet, none of the Israelites ever saw the interior furnishings of the tabernacle, except the priests. What a blessing it was then to be often reminded in the Book of God of those blessed types of the Saviour in whom they, like us, hoped and trusted. As often as they read, they were reminded and called to remember what God had done for them and what he would do for them.

In the New Testament, we frequently read the same things repeated. Many of the events in our Lord's earthly life and ministry, many of his works, the details of his agony at Gethsemane, Gabbatha, and Golgotha, and his resurrection and glory, are recorded two, three, and four times by the gospel writers. Who would have them written less often?

The Mercy Seat

In verse 6-9, we are told Bezaleel constructed the mercy seat with its cherubim exactly as the Lord commanded Moses.

'And he made the mercy seat of pure gold: two cubits and a half was the length thereof, and one cubit and a half the breadth thereof. And he made two cherubims of gold, beaten out of one piece made he them, on the two ends of the mercy seat; one cherub on the end on this side, and another cherub on the other end on that side: out of the mercy seat made he the cherubims on the two ends thereof. And the cherubims spread out their wings on high, and covered with their wings over the mercy seat, with their faces one to another; even to the mercy seatward were the faces of the cherubims.'

We cannot keep our blessed Lord Jesus in view sufficiently. It is he of whom both the ark, and mercy seat speak. Christ is the mercy seat, our propitiation (1 John 2:1; Romans 3:24-26). The spiritual riches and beauties of the gospel tabernacle are by these things recommended to our frequent consideration. Walk much around this Zion. 'Mark ye well her bulwarks, consider her palaces' (Psalm 48:13). 'Salvation will God appoint for walls and bulwarks' (Isaiah 26:1). The more we see the glories of Christ and the gospel of his grace, the more we will admire and love him. The everlasting covenant should be read often.

Table of Shewbread

'And he made the table of shittim wood: two cubits was the length thereof, and a cubit the breadth thereof, and a cubit and a half the height thereof: And he overlaid it with pure gold, and made thereunto a crown of gold round about. Also he made thereunto a border of an handbreadth round about; and made a crown of gold for the border thereof round about. And he cast for it four rings of gold, and put the rings upon the four corners that were in the four feet thereof. Over against the border were the rings, the places for the staves to bear the table. And he made the staves of shittim wood, and overlaid them with gold, to bear the table. And he made the vessels which were upon the table, his dishes, and his spoons, and his bowls, and his covers to cover withal, of pure gold' (Exodus 37:10-16).

This golden table on which the shewbread was perpetually kept was intended to portray the Lord Jesus who is the everlasting bread of life to his people. As the shewbread was always to be spread upon the table, the Lord Jesus is always in the presence of God for us.

But we must never fail to see the vast superiority of the gospel over the law. The shewbread was always upon the table indeed, but it was only to be looked upon, not eaten, except by the priests. But our blessed Saviour not only calls us to look on him and receive him, but he who is the Bread of Life bids hungry souls to eat the bread (Proverbs 9:5).

In our Father's house there is always bread enough and to spare. Come and eat! 'Come and dine, the Master calleth, Come and dine!' In the house of God bread is always on the table, and that Bread is Christ.

491

The Golden Candlestick

In Exodus 37:17-24, we are told Bezaleel made the golden candlestick.

'And he made the candlestick of pure gold: of beaten work made he the candlestick; his shaft, and his branch, his bowls, his knops, and his flowers, were of the same: And six branches going out of the sides thereof; three branches of the candlestick out of the one side thereof, and three branches of the candlestick out of the other side thereof: Three bowls made after the fashion of almonds in one branch, a knop and a flower; and three bowls made like almonds in another branch, a knop and a flower: so throughout the six branches going out of the candlestick. And in the candlestick were four bowls made like almonds, his knops, and his flowers: And a knop under two branches of the same, and a knop under two branches of the same, and a knop under two branches of the same, according to the six branches going out of it. Their knops and their branches were of the same: all of it was one beaten work of pure gold. And he made his seven lamps, and his snuffers, and his snuffdishes, of pure gold. Of a talent of pure gold made he it, and all the vessels thereof.'

The golden candlestick, or lamp stand, is used throughout Scripture to portray and typify both Christ the Light of the world and his gospel churches (Revelation 1-3), through whom the light shines in this dark world. The candlestick points us to Christ who shines into the hearts of chosen sinners by God the Holy Spirit and his Sacred Word.

'Thy word is a lamp unto my feet, and a light unto my path' (Psalm 119:105). 'The mystery of the seven stars which thou sawest in my right hand, and the seven golden candlesticks. The seven stars are the angels of the seven churches: and the seven candlesticks which thou sawest are the seven churches' (Revelation 1:20).

The branches of the candlestick were meant to show that this Light which shines in our hearts by the Holy Spirit and by the Word of his grace is Christ the Light. Everything our souls have in the sweet experience of God's saving grace is ours in, with, and by Christ Jesus (Zechariah 4:2, 3; 2 Corinthians 4:6).

A candlestick is a very faint, dim, light. Similarly, the light we have in this world is but as the light of a candle compared to the full day-light of glory in the Lord Jesus which is reserved for the upper world (1 Corinthians 13:12). Imagine that! We just now see a little, but what glory awaits us!

Altar of Incense

Next, we read about the altar of incense. It, too, was made exactly as the Lord commanded Moses (Exodus 30:1).

'And he made the incense altar of shittim wood: the length of it was a cubit, and the breadth of it a cubit; it was foursquare; and two cubits was the height of it; the horns thereof were of the same. And he overlaid it with pure gold, both the top of it, and the sides thereof round about, and the horns of it: also he made unto it a crown of gold round about. And he made two rings of gold for it under the crown thereof, by the two corners of it, upon the two sides thereof, to be places for the staves to bear it withal. And he made the staves of shittim wood, and overlaid them with gold' (Exodus 37:25-28).

The Lord Jesus Christ is both our Altar of Sacrifice, by whom we draw near to God, and our Altar of Incense, in and by whom we have perpetual acceptance with God.

'This is the covenant that I will make with them after those days, saith the Lord, I will put my laws into their hearts, and in their minds will I write them; And their sins and iniquities will I remember no more. Now where remission of these is, there is no more offering for sin. Having therefore, brethren, boldness to enter into the holiest by the blood of Jesus, by a new and living way, which he hath consecrated for us, through the veil, that is to say, his flesh; and having an high priest over the house of God; let us draw near with a true heart in full assurance of faith, having our hearts sprinkled from an evil conscience, and our bodies washed with pure water' (Hebrews 10:16-22).

'We have an altar, whereof they have no right to eat which serve the tabernacle' (Hebrews 13:10). 'By him therefore let us offer the sacrifice of praise to God continually, that is, the fruit of our lips giving thanks to his name' (Hebrews 13:15).

'And another angel came and stood at the altar, having a golden censer; and there was given unto him much incense, that he should offer it with the prayers of all saints upon the golden altar which was before the throne' (Revelation 8:3).

The Holy Anointing Oil

The last thing mentioned in Exodus 37 is the holy anointing oil and pure incense of sweet spices. In Exodus 37:29, we are told these things were mixed together just as the Lord directed Moses in Exodus 30:22-25.

'And he made the holy anointing oil, and the pure incense of sweet spices, according to the work of the apothecary.'

This holy oil represented God the Holy Spirit and the gifts and graces of the Spirit bestowed upon us by the merit and efficacy of Christ's shed blood.

'Christ hath redeemed us from the curse of the law, being made a curse for us: for it is written, Cursed is every one that hangeth on a tree: That the blessing of Abraham might come on the Gentiles through Jesus Christ; that we might receive the promise of the Spirit through faith' (Galatians 3:13, 14).

May God the Holy Spirit teach us to read his Word with care and thoughtfulness, earnestly praying that he will cause us to see our blessed Saviour in every picture and hear his voice in every line. Pause as you read and remember as you go how very precious Christ Jesus ought to be to us. He who was shadowed forth by the Holy Spirit in these rich pictures makes the types themselves precious. May God the Spirit ever give us grace when we pass by the picture to pause and remember the Saviour. Christ is my Ark of salvation, my Mercyseat of propitiation, my Living Bread, my everlasting Light, my Altar of Sacrifice, my Incense of Acceptance, and my Holy Anointing. He makes his priest fit to draw near to God!

Thank you, our God, for every repeated reminder of Christ Jesus our Lord. Blessed repetitions are good for our souls.

Chapter 119

Entering The Lord's Courts

'And he made the altar of burnt offering of shittim wood: five cubits was the length thereof, and five cubits the breadth thereof; it was foursquare; and three cubits the height thereof ... And he made the laver of brass, and the foot of it of brass, of the lookingglasses of the women assembling, which assembled at the door of the tabernacle of the congregation. And he made the court: on the south side southward the hangings of the court were of fine twined linen, an hundred cubits ... This is the sum of the tabernacle, even of the tabernacle of testimony, as it was counted, according to the commandment of Moses, for the service of the Levites, by the hand of Ithamar, son to Aaron the priest.' (Exodus 38:1-31)

Do you hope to dwell in the courts of the Lord's house forever? Is it your joy to sing with David, 'Surely goodness and mercy shall follow me all the days of my life: and I shall dwell in the house of the Lord for ever'? Salvation, as is presented in Holy Scripture, is about entering the courts of the Lord, worshipping God in sweet communion, both while you live in this world and forever in the world to come (Psalm 65:4; 96:8, 9; 100:1-5).

Throughout the Scriptures faith is portrayed as a matter of coming to Christ. To believe on the Son of God is to come to him. To come to him is to believe on him. We come to him by following after him, as disciples follow after their Master. Our all-glorious Christ says, 'Whosoever will come after me, let him deny himself' (Mark 8:34). To worship God is to come to Christ.

Coming to Christ is the result of a deliberate, purposeful choice. It is an act of the will. Our Master says, 'whosoever will'. Let us never alter his Word. I know faith is a gift of God. I know none will ever come to Christ, none will ever worship God, unless God the Holy Ghost graciously and effectually causes them to come and worship. Yet, it is certain that any who come to him, do so because they want him and choose him. God does not save sinners by knocking them on the head and dragging them to Christ. He saves sinners by causing them to want Christ more than life itself.

Faith in Christ is not a matter of conscription, it is a voluntary act. Soldiers in Christ's army are volunteers, not drafted and forced to serve. It is written, 'Thy people shall be willing in the day of thy power' (Psalm 110:3). 'Blessed is the man whom thou choosest, and causest to approach unto thee, that he may dwell in thy courts' (Psalm 65:4).

Coming to Christ is an act of the heart, a spiritual not a carnal thing. No one has ever come to Christ by walking a church aisle, kneeling at an altar, saying a prayer someone taught him to repeat, or signing a decision card. If you would come to Christ, you must come to him in your heart. Faith is a heart work (Romans 10:8-10). True faith is wilful, deliberate confidence of heart in the power and grace of the Lord Jesus Christ. It is trusting the merits of his blood and righteousness as my acceptance before God. Faith in Christ involves the willing surrender of my heart to him as my Lord. It is the bowing and submission of my heart to him as my Lord (Luke 14:25-33).

Coming to Christ is a continual thing. Our Saviour does not speak of coming to him as a one-time thing, as a single act, but as a constant, continual, lifelong thing. If I worship God, I do not worship him one day in seven. I worship him with my life. If I do not worship the Lord Jesus with my life, I do not worship at all. Faith in Christ is not an event in life, but a way of life. 'If so be ye have tasted that the Lord is gracious. To whom coming, as unto a living stone, disallowed indeed of men, but chosen of God, and precious' (1 Peter 2:3, 4).

Not only are sinners bidden to come to Christ, we are commanded to come (1 John 3:23). The warrant of faith is not my feeling, my emotion, my meeting certain prescribed conditions, but God's Word. If the Son of God says for me to come to him, then I may come to him!

Any sinner in all the world who will come to Christ may come to Christ. Our Master uses that blessed word of universal application and uses it frequently, 'Whosoever'. I am so thankful he said, 'Whosoever will', rather than, 'if Don Fortner will'. Had he said that, I would have concluded he must have meant some other Don Fortner. But I cannot doubt that 'whosoever' includes me (Matthew 11:28-30; John 3:36; Revelation 22:17).

Salvation is coming to Christ, worshipping God in Spirit and in truth. It is dwelling in the courts of our God. 'A day in thy courts is better than a thousand. I had rather be a doorkeeper in the house of my God, than to dwell in the tents of wickedness' (Psalm 84:10). 'Those that be planted in the house of the LORD shall flourish in the courts of our God' (Psalm 92:13). How can I enter into the courts of the Lord? What is required? By what means can a poor, vile sinner enter and dwell in the courts of the Lord? Exodus 38 shows us. The tabernacle in the wilderness was made up of three sections, three courts: the outer court representing the church and people of God on earth, the inner court, the holy place, representing heaven, the place of divine worship, and the holy of holies representing the very throne of God.

The only gate by which we can enter these courts of our God, the only door of access to God is the Lord Jesus Christ, our Mediator, who is represented by all the curtains hanging between the courts. Here in Exodus 38, we see in vivid type and picture how sinners like you and me may enter into and dwell in the courts of our God. Here are five things essential to the worship of God, five things that are always involved in and essential to the everlasting salvation of God's elect.

Atonement

The very first thing required if we would come to God, if we would enter his courts and be saved, is blood atonement. We must come to God by an altar of sacrifice he has made, with the sacrifice he has given.

'And he made the altar of burnt offering of shittim wood: five cubits was the length thereof, and five cubits the breadth thereof; it was foursquare; and three cubits the height thereof. And he made the horns thereof on the four corners of it; the horns thereof were of the same: and he overlaid it with brass. And he made all the vessels of the altar, the pots, and the shovels, and the basons, and the fleshhooks, and the firepans: all the vessels thereof made he of brass. And he made for the altar a brasen grate of network under the compass thereof beneath unto the midst of it. And he cast four rings for the four ends of the grate of brass, to be places for the staves. And he made the staves of shittim wood, and overlaid them with brass. And he put the staves into the rings on the sides of the altar, to bear it withal; he made the altar hollow with boards' (Exodus 38:1-7).

Clearly this altar is a picture of our Lord Jesus Christ. He is our altar. But we must never separate the altar from the sacrifice. Christ is both our altar and our sacrifice (Hebrews 13:7-13; Psalm 118:1, 14-29).

The horns of the altar upon which the sacrifice must be bound spoke of the strength and efficacy of the sacrifice. There were four of them, pointing to the four corners of the earth. From thence the ransomed of the Lord must be fetched. The sacrifice was bound to the altar by the hand of God as a matter of justice, grace, mercy and truth. When the holy Lamb of God was made sin for us, made a curse for us, the justice and truth of God as well as the grace and mercy of God was obtained for God's elect (2 Corinthians 5:17-21; Galatians 3:13).

Do you recall where the word 'sin' is first used in the Bible? What is the context in which we find the word sin for the first time? What is the first thing that is specifically called sin in the Book of God? Read Genesis 4 and you will see the first thing named sin in Holy Scripture is the attempt of proud man to do away with God's sacrifice (Genesis 4:7). Everything about salvation begins with and hinges upon God's sacrifice for sin. Yet, that which men most despise and most viciously trample under their feet (Hebrews 10:29) is the precious blood of Christ.

Cleansing

The first thing is atonement. We cannot come to God, be accepted of God, worship God, enter the courts of his house without blood atonement by the sacrifice of God's darling Son, the Lord Jesus Christ. The second thing required is the cleansing depicted in the laver of brass.

'And he made the laver of brass, and the foot of it of brass, of the lookingglasses of the women assembling, which assembled at the door of the tabernacle of the congregation' (Exodus 38:8).

This laver of brass and the ceremonial cleansing performed at the laver typified the gospel of Christ as it is applied to the hearts of chosen sinners by God the Holy Spirit, purging our consciences from the dead works of dead men in dead religion to serve the living God.

'For we ourselves also were sometimes foolish, disobedient, deceived, serving divers lusts and pleasures, living in malice and envy, hateful, and hating one another. But after that the kindness and love of God our Saviour toward man appeared, not by works of righteousness which we have done, but according to his mercy he saved us, by the washing of regeneration, and renewing of the Holy Ghost; which he shed on us abundantly through Jesus Christ our Saviour; that being justified by his grace, we should be made heirs according to the hope of eternal life' (Titus 3:3-7).

The laver was made from the brass 'lookingglasses of the women assembling'. Why is that stated? I know the word 'lookingglasses' refers to mirrors. James compares the gospel to a mirror in which we behold ourselves (James 1:23). In that same context, James speaks of the gospel not only as a mirror in which to behold ourselves, but also as a looking glass through which to 'behold the perfect law of liberty' (James 1:25). Perhaps, the Holy Spirit used the phrase looking glass because the gospel is the looking glass in which and by which we behold our Lord Jesus, looking to him for life everlasting (Isaiah 45:22; Zechariah 12:10; John 1:29; Hebrews 11:3; 1 John 3:3).

Communion
When the sinner comes to God trusting Christ, when we come to God through faith in his blood, beholding Christ in the gospel, we enter into his courts and dwell with him in sweet communion. We walk with God in sweet fellowship and intimate communion. That is the third picture set before us in the courts of the Lord's house.

'And he made the court: on the south side southward the hangings of the court were of fine twined linen, an hundred cubits: Their pillars were twenty, and their brasen sockets twenty; the hooks of the pillars and their fillets were of silver. And for the north side the hangings were an hundred cubits, their pillars were twenty, and their sockets of brass twenty; the hooks of the pillars and their fillets of silver. And for the west side were hangings of fifty cubits, their pillars ten, and their sockets ten; the hooks of the pillars and their fillets of silver. And for the east side eastward fifty cubits. The hangings of the one side of the gate were fifteen cubits; their pillars three, and their sockets three. And for the other side of the court gate, on this hand and that hand, were hangings of fifteen cubits; their pillars three, and their sockets three. All the hangings of the court round about were of fine twined linen. And the sockets for the pillars were of brass; the hooks of the pillars and their fillets of silver; and the overlaying of their chapiters of silver; and all the pillars of the court were filleted with silver. And the hanging for the gate of the court was needlework, of blue, and purple, and scarlet, and fine twined linen: and twenty cubits was the length, and the height in the breadth was five cubits, answerable to the hangings of the court' (Exodus 38:9-18).

Everything in the courts of the Lord's house is in perfect symmetry. Everything had reference to and pointed to our blessed Saviour. It was in perfect harmony. Oh, what wonderful, wonderful grace the grace of God is! In Christ, by Christ, and with Christ, saved sinners walk with God in sweet fellowship and perfect intimate communion!

Security

The fourth thing essential to this matter of worship, and without which we cannot worship, is security; the complete security of our souls in Christ. That security is pictured in the pillars, pins, posts and nails that held everything together, securing all the pieces of the tabernacle.

'And their pillars were four, and their sockets of brass four; their hooks of silver, and the overlaying of their chapiters and their fillets of silver. And all the pins of the tabernacle, and of the court round about, were of brass' (Exodus 38:19, 20).

The word 'pin' is the same word that is translated 'nail' in the book of Judges (4:21, 22; 5:26). You will remember that Heber's wife, Jael, drove a tent pin, an iron nail, through Sisera's temples, firmly attaching his head to the ground. You will remember in Isaiah 33:20 and 54:2, the same word is translated 'stake'. Do not think of these tabernacle pins as small things. They were large brass stakes driven deep into the ground and used to attach and fasten the tabernacle and its court to the earth. So securely was it fastened that we never read it was even slightly disturbed by all the strong winds it must have endured during all the years of Israel's sojourn through the wilderness.

These brass nails were typical of our Lord Jesus Christ. The nails were made of brass, a material that could not be corrupted though the nails were driven deep into the ground. They withstood all the elements of the earth. Clearly, they typified our blessed Saviour, who is described by Isaiah as one fastened as a nail in a sure place (Isaiah 22:20-24). He is the security of our souls.

Sacrifice
There is another thing always involved in the worship of our God and
Saviour, and that is sacrifice. I mean personal sacrifice. We cannot
come to God without Christ our Sacrifice, trusting his blood and
righteousness. Nor can we come to God, or trust Christ without the
surrender and sacrifice of ourselves to him in the totality of our being.

'This is the sum of the tabernacle, even of the tabernacle of
testimony, as it was counted, according to the commandment of Moses,
for the service of the Levites, by the hand of Ithamar, son to Aaron the
priest. And Bezaleel the son of Uri, the son of Hur, of the tribe of Judah,
made all that the LORD commanded Moses. And with him was
Aholiab, son of Ahisamach, of the tribe of Dan, an engraver, and a
cunning workman, and an embroiderer in blue, and in purple, and in
scarlet, and fine linen. All the gold that was occupied for the work in
all the work of the holy place, even the gold of the offering, was twenty
and nine talents, and seven hundred and thirty shekels, after the shekel
of the sanctuary. And the silver of them that were numbered of the
congregation was an hundred talents, and a thousand seven hundred and
threescore and fifteen shekels, after the shekel of the sanctuary: A bekah
for every man, that is, half a shekel, after the shekel of the sanctuary,
for every one that went to be numbered, from twenty years old and
upward, for six hundred thousand and three thousand and five hundred
and fifty men. And of the hundred talents of silver were cast the sockets
of the sanctuary, and the sockets of the vail; an hundred sockets of the
hundred talents, a talent for a socket. And of the thousand seven
hundred seventy and five shekels he made hooks for the pillars, and
overlaid their chapiters, and filleted them. And the brass of the offering
was seventy talents, and two thousand and four hundred shekels. And
therewith he made the sockets to the door of the tabernacle of the
congregation, and the brasen altar, and the brasen grate for it, and all
the vessels of the altar, and the sockets of the court round about, and the
sockets of the court gate, and all the pins of the tabernacle, and all the
pins of the court round about' (Exodus 38:21-31).

The total cost in sheer value of materials used in the construction of
the tabernacle was immense. If you go back to chapter 35 and read
about the gifts the children of Israel brought to the Lord with willing
hearts, you will see there was not a stingy person among them. They all
seemed to speak as David did many years later when he sought a place

to build the house of God, 'I will not offer to God that which doth cost me nothing'.

O Holy Spirit, so let us worship our God in the beauty of holiness, in the beauty of our Saviour's holiness, which you alone can convey to mortals upon the earth.

Read these last verses of Exodus 38 again. You will see how everything connected with the worship of God in the tabernacle was built upon, arose from, was held together, and kept secure for the glory of God by atonement. That is, the atonement money paid in the numbering of Israel as it is set before us in Exodus 30:11-16.

'And the LORD spake unto Moses, saying, when thou takest the sum of the children of Israel after their number, then shall they give every man a ransom for his soul unto the LORD, when thou numberest them; that there be no plague among them, when thou numberest them. This they shall give, every one that passeth among them that are numbered, half a shekel after the shekel of the sanctuary: (a shekel is twenty gerahs:) an half shekel shall be the offering of the LORD. Every one that passeth among them that are numbered, from twenty years old and above, shall give an offering unto the LORD. The rich shall not give more, and the poor shall not give less than half a shekel, when they give an offering unto the LORD, to make an atonement for your souls. And thou shalt take the atonement money of the children of Israel, and shalt appoint it for the service of the tabernacle of the congregation; that it may be a memorial unto the children of Israel before the LORD, to make an atonement for your souls.'

This numbering of the children of Israel and the atonement money they paid, so no plague come upon them, was typical of our ransom by Christ. None but Israelites were ransomed. A specific, numbered people were ransomed. The ransom price was the same for all. And all those who were ransomed were preserved from any plague (Proverbs 12:21; Psalm 91:10). How I thank God for atonement; the specific, effectual atonement of God's elect by the precious blood of Christ, which forever secures the everlasting salvation of every sinner for whom he died upon the cursed tree. He has obtained for us eternal salvation, and an eternal dwelling in the courts of our God!

Chapter 120

Clothes Of Service

'And of the blue, and purple, and scarlet, they made cloths of service, to do service in the holy place, and made the holy garments for Aaron; as the LORD commanded Moses ... Thus was all the work of the tabernacle of the tent of the congregation finished: and the children of Israel did according to all that the LORD commanded Moses, so did they ... And Moses did look upon all the work, and, behold, they had done it as the LORD had commanded, even so had they done it: and Moses blessed them.'
(Exodus 39:1-43)

As the Mosaic record of the tabernacle's construction ended, Moses was inspired of God to give us a description of 'the holy garments' that were made for Aaron, those garments Aaron was required to wear whenever he went into the tabernacle doing service before the Lord God as Israel's high priest. They are called 'clothes of service'.

Two Sets of Garments
These 'clothes of service' were very significant and highly symbolical. They are listed three times by Moses (Exodus 28, Exodus 39, and Leviticus 8). Aaron was not allowed to appear before the Lord God as Israel's priest to do service in the holy place without these 'holy garments', without these 'clothes of service'. They were vital to his priestly work. We are specifically told that they were garments of consecration (Exodus 28:3), 'for glory and for beauty' (Exodus 28:40).

These garments were made specifically for Aaron to show forth the glory and beauty of his work as Israel's high priest. But they show more than that. These garments were made for and put upon Aaron to show forth the glory and beauty of our Lord Jesus Christ, our great High Priest, of whom Aaron was but a type and picture.

Actually, Aaron had two sets of priestly garments: this glorious apparel, which he wore before Israel and before the Lord in his common, daily functions in the tabernacle, and those holy linen garments mentioned in verse 28, and more fully described in Leviticus 16:4, which he wore only once a year on the Day of Atonement. On that great Day of Atonement, when he went with the blood of the paschal lamb before the Lord God into the holy of holies, Aaron was robed only in spotless white, portraying the infinitely meritorious obedience and personal righteousness and holiness of the Lord Jesus Christ.

The garments described here in Exodus 39 were ordained of God to show Aaron's glory and beauty to the people he represented and served as a priest. These garments are described in detail so we might see the glory and beauty of our Lord Jesus Christ as our great High Priest.

Aaron wore seven specific, highly symbolic garments: an ephod, a girdle, a breastplate, a robe, a coat, a mitre, and a holy crown. Let us look at each briefly. May the Holy Spirit give us eyes to behold our great High Priest, our Saviour, the Lord Jesus Christ. If ever you see him as he is here set forth, you will believe him.

The Ephod

First, Moses put the ephod on Aaron's shoulders. 'And he made the ephod of gold, blue, and purple, and scarlet, and fine twined linen. And they did beat the gold into thin plates, and cut it into wires, to work it in the blue, and in the purple, and in the scarlet, and in the fine linen, with cunning work. They made shoulder pieces for it, to couple it together: by the two edges was it coupled together' (Exodus 39:2-4).

The ephod was the outer apron that hung over Aaron's robe. It was made of two parts, covering both his back and his chest. The two pieces of it were joined together at the shoulders by golden clasps. Those golden clasps were the setting for the onyx stones. Like Aaron's robe, the ephod was made of gold, blue, purple, scarlet, and fine twined linen. The breastplate with the names of twelve tribes of Israel and the Urim and Thummim, the Lights and Perfections, were worn on the ephod.

Try to get the picture in your mind's eye. Here is Aaron, wearing his gorgeous, costly robe. Strapped over his shoulders, held by gold clasps, is this equally gorgeous, costly apron. Upon his heart and shoulders hangs the breastplate with the names of God's chosen people engraved in precious stones. In the ephod or the breastplate are those mysterious emblems of light and perfection called the Urim and Thummim.

What does it all mean? I can but scratch the surface; yet it certainly means the Lord Jesus Christ constantly has his people upon his heart and carries us on his shoulders. He guides us according to the light and perfection of his purpose and grace. We are the sparkling jewels of his glory and beauty (Malachi 3:17). Because our all glorious, omnipotent, ever gracious Christ carries us upon his shoulders, in his heart, and in his hands, we are beyond the reach of any enemy and totally safe.

The Girdle
Second, Moses was commanded of God to gird Aaron with a girdle. This was not just the ordinary girdle worn by the other priests, Aaron's sons. This was 'the curious girdle of his ephod'. 'And the curious girdle of his ephod, that was upon it, was of the same, according to the work thereof; of gold, blue, and purple, and scarlet, and fine twined linen; as the LORD commanded Moses' (Exodus 39:5).

We are told in verse 29 that this girdle was made of 'needlework'. The 'girdle' itself speaks of our Saviour's readiness to serve the needs of his people for the glory of God (Psalm 40; Hebrews 10). It is written, 'Righteousness shall be the girdle of his loins, and faithfulness the girdle of his reins' (Isaiah 11:5). 'Blessed are those servants, whom the Lord, when he cometh, shall find watching: verily I say unto you, that he shall gird himself, and make them sit down to meat, and will come forth and serve them' (Luke 12:37).

While he was in this world, our Lord Jesus 'took a towel, and girded himself ... and began to wash the disciples' feet' (John 13:5). Today he stands in the midst of his churches, 'girt about the paps with a golden girdle' (Revelation 1:13), ready to serve his people on earth.

The Lord God commanded Moses to make the girdle just as he did the ephod. 'It shall be of the same, according to the work thereof' (Exodus 28:8). The girdle of the high priest was of the same materials and the same splendorous colours as the ephod itself, indicating in picture that our Saviour's present priestly work in heaven, as well as

505

the work he performed on earth, is according to the perfection of his character as the God-man, our Mediator. Though glorified, Christ is Jehovah's Righteous Servant still. He has gone into heaven to appear in the presence of God for us (Hebrews 9:24), having 'obtained eternal redemption for us' (Hebrews 9:12), and there 'he ever liveth to make intercession for' us (Hebrews 7:25; 1 John 2:1, 2).

The Breastplate

Now Moses put the breastplate on Aaron. 'And he made the breastplate of cunning work, like the work of the ephod; of gold, blue, and purple, and scarlet, and fine twined linen. It was foursquare; they made the breastplate double: a span was the length thereof, and a span the breadth thereof, being doubled. And they set in it four rows of stones: the first row was a sardius, a topaz, and a carbuncle: this was the first row. And the second row, an emerald, a sapphire, and a diamond. And the third row, a ligure, an agate, and an amethyst. And the fourth row, a beryl, an onyx, and a jasper: they were inclosed in ouches of gold in their inclosings. And the stones were according to the names of the children of Israel, twelve, according to their names, like the engravings of a signet, every one with his name, according to the twelve tribes. And they made upon the breastplate chains at the ends, of wreathen work of pure gold. And they made two ouches of gold, and two gold rings; and put the two rings in the two ends of the breastplate. And they put the two wreathen chains of gold in the two rings on the ends of the breastplate. And the two ends of the two wreathen chains they fastened in the two ouches, and put them on the shoulderpieces of the ephod, before it. And they made two rings of gold, and put them on the two ends of the breastplate, upon the border of it, which was on the side of the ephod inward. And they made two other golden rings, and put them on the two sides of the ephod underneath, toward the forepart of it, over against the other coupling thereof, above the curious girdle of the ephod. And they did bind the breastplate by his rings unto the rings of the ephod with a lace of blue, that it might be above the curious girdle of the ephod, and that the breastplate might not be loosed from the ephod; as the LORD commanded Moses' (Exodus 39:8-21).

Exodus 28:30 gives this description of Aaron's priestly breastplate. 'And thou shalt put in the breastplate of judgment the Urim and the Thummim; and they shall be upon Aaron's heart, when he goeth in

506

before the LORD: and Aaron shall bear the judgment of the children of Israel upon his heart before the LORD continually.'

Not only does this breastplate upon Aaron's chest portray our Saviour's constant love and care for us, it speaks of our constant, perfect, acceptance with God in him. The names of God's elect are known to our great High Priest. They are engraved on his heart not to be erased. 'I know them … I give unto them eternal life; and they shall never perish!' For them he makes continual intercession (John 17).

Can you see your Priest yonder in heaven, with your name upon his heart? Not only are you, my brother, my sister, beyond the reach of any enemy. In Christ, we are beyond the influence of any foe or evil!

What a consolation this is to this poor sinner! The Lord God Almighty always sees me, and only sees me, in his Son as a sparkling jewel, shining in him gloriously! In his eyes, I shine with all the brilliance of Christ himself! Is he precious? We are precious in him. Is he accepted? We are accepted in him. Does he live? We live in him.

In heaven's glory, before the dazzling purity of the white light of God's holiness, things are seen as they really are. That, my tempted, tried, tempest tossed, heavy hearted, sinning, weeping brother and sister, ought to comfort our hearts. We are jewels in Christ, with Christ, upon his heart, in his heart, in heaven. The more brilliantly the light shines upon a diamond, the more it sparkles with radiant beauty. He has set us as a seal upon his heart (Song of Solomon 8:6). What grace! What joy! What peace! What a cause for devotion and consecration to God our Saviour! We are partakers of his beauty and his glory!

Did you notice the Lord God made special arrangements to attach the breastplate to the ephod in such a way that it could not be loosed from the ephod, hanging on the broad shoulders of his priest? This breastplate of judgment speaks loudly and beautifully of our everlasting salvation and absolute security in Christ Jesus (Romans 8:32-39).

The Robe
The fourth garment Aaron wore was a robe. Moses clothed Aaron with the priestly robe as God commanded. This was the robe of the ephod the outer apron, worn under the ephod, and had a hem of golden bells and pomegranates. 'And he made the robe of the ephod of woven work, all of blue. And there was an hole in the midst of the robe, as the hole of an habergeon, with a band round about the hole, that it should not

rend. And they made upon the hems of the robe pomegranates of blue, and purple, and scarlet, and twined linen. And they made bells of pure gold, and put the bells between the pomegranates upon the hem of the robe, round about between the pomegranates; A bell and a pomegranate, a bell and a pomegranate, round about the hem of the robe to minister in; as the LORD commanded Moses' (Exodus 39:22-26).

This was a robe that was blue in colour, but was woven of gold, blue, purple, and scarlet, and was made of fine linen. Gold symbolized our Saviour's divinity. Blue is the colour of heaven above. Purple is the colour of royalty. Scarlet represents blood. Fine linen portrays purity. This robe represented the righteousness of Christ. It is that with which Christ himself is clothed, and with which we are clothed in him. It is a robe covering the whole man from head to foot.

This was a robe prepared according to the law of God. In the parable of The Prodigal Son, our Lord Jesus portrays it as 'the best robe' (Luke 15:22), the robe of Christ's perfect righteousness, which the Lord God puts upon every sinner who comes to him by faith in Christ, because his righteousness is our righteousness (Jeremiah 23:6; 33:16). Yes, we are made the very righteousness of God in him (2 Corinthians 5:21).

The golden bells portray the perfection and sweetness of Christ's intercession for us. As Aaron moved about inside the holy place of the tabernacle, the ringing bells told the people, 'All is well. Aaron is alive. God accepts your priest.' They speak of our living, exalted High Priest and the sweet savour of his intercession in heaven for us.

The pomegranates speak of the fruitfulness of Christ's priesthood. Cut a pomegranate, you will find it full of seeds in a red fluid. If you look at Exodus 28:35, you will see that Aaron was required to wear these bells and pomegranates on the hem of his robe 'that he die not'. 'And thou shalt make the robe of the ephod all of blue. And there shall be an hole in the top of it, in the midst thereof: it shall have a binding of woven work round about the hole of it, as it were the hole of an habergeon, that it be not rent. And beneath upon the hem of it thou shalt make pomegranates of blue, and of purple, and of scarlet, round about the hem thereof; and bells of gold between them round about: A golden bell and a pomegranate, a golden bell and a pomegranate, upon the hem of the robe round about. And it shall be upon Aaron to minister: and his sound shall be heard when he goeth in unto the holy place before the LORD, and when he cometh out, that he die not' (Exodus 28:31-35).

No man can come before God, none can approach the holy Lord God without the robe of God's Priest, arrayed in the clothes of service God requires, the holy garments God provides in his Son. And all who come to God by Christ Jesus, walking before him in the joy of faith, have the bells and pomegranates of perfect acceptance ringing about them.

The Coat

Fifth, Moses was commanded to put a coat upon Aaron. This was not a coat as we think of it, but an inner garment. It is described in Exodus 28:4 and 39, and in Exodus 39:27 as an embroidered 'coat of fine linen' of woven work. This special embroidered coat of fine linen, along with the linen breeches or trousers, were Aaron's undergarments. They were not commonly seen by the people. I rather doubt Moses put these on Aaron in public, but rather gave them to him publicly and Aaron put them on in private. But they were here held before all the congregation, because their typical significance was important.

Fine linen is for purity and righteousness (Revelation 19:8). Christ's purity and righteousness is sufficient for all his saints. 'Righteousness' in Revelation 19:8 is really in the plural righteousnesses. Many imagine it refers to righteous works the saints of God perform on the earth. You and I know better. We have no ability to perform righteousness. But we do have a righteousness that exceeds the righteousness of the scribes and Pharisees. We have the righteousness of God imputed to us in justification and imparted to us in sanctification and regeneration.

The undergarments speak of the righteousness of Christ. All his other perfections were displayed in the outer garments of the priest. This embroidered linen coat was a seamless garment, like that worn by our Redeemer (John 19:23). It was worn next to Aaron's body as he served as priest. I see three things here. First, to come to and be accepted of God, we must have a complete clothing of righteousness. Second, God's supply of Christ is our righteousness. Third, by linen breeches the priest's nakedness was covered. The blood and righteousness of Christ covers our nakedness as we walk before our God (Exodus 28:42).

The Mitre

Sixth, Moses was commanded of God to put the mitre of fine linen upon Aaron's head (Exodus 39:28). The mitre, or turban, was made of fine white linen. It was both a symbol of honour and humility. It was worn

509

by kings and by servants. When Zechariah saw the vision of Joshua the high priest standing before the Lord (Zechariah 3:1-5), the first thing the Lord commanded, after he put away his filthy garments, was this mitre. He 'set a fair mitre upon his head, and clothed him with garments'. God has given his own Son to be for us the helmet of salvation. This mitre, made of white linen, like Aaron's robe, portrays that perfect righteousness which is ours in Christ (Revelation 19:8).

The Crown

Moses put the holy crown on Aaron's head. 'And they made the plate of the holy crown of pure gold, and wrote upon it a writing, like to the engravings of a signet, HOLINESS TO THE LORD. And they tied unto it a lace of blue, to fasten it on high upon the mitre; as the LORD commanded Moses. Thus was all the work of the tabernacle of the tent of the congregation finished: and the children of Israel did according to all that the LORD commanded Moses, so did they' (Exodus 39:30-32).

Moses, representing the law of God, put the crown upon Aaron's head. When the Lord Jesus finished the work of redemption portrayed in the tabernacle, the very law and justice of God crowned him, our great High Priest, Lord and King forever. Let this comfort our souls. This golden plate, the holy crown, emblazoned on Aaron's forehead pictured the perfect holiness of our Lord Jesus Christ.

It is this holiness that enabled our Lord Jesus to bear our iniquities. He not only put away our sins, he has washed away forever the iniquity of our 'holy things' (Exodus 28:38), our best deeds of righteousness, faith, and worship. The Lord Jesus wears this crown, emblazoned before the holy Lord God, 'HOLINESS TO THE LORD', that we may be forever and ever 'accepted before the Lord'.

What rest there is here for our weary hearts! Amid all our failings, in spite of all our sin, though we may be often harassed by hell with doubts and fears, though our hearts be cold as ice, and hard as steel, our acceptance with God is as unvarying, perfect, and sure as Christ's own (Ecclesiastes 9:7, 8). All the 'clothes of service', these priestly garments represent Christ's glory and beauty. Do you see how beautiful, how glorious a Saviour the Lord Jesus is? His glory and beauty are ours (Ezekiel 16:8-14). Believe him, trust him as God your Saviour, and his glory and beauty are yours! 'He shall beautify the meek with salvation' (Psalm 149:4; Isaiah 61:1-3).

Chapter 121

God's Tabernacle: God's Salvation

'And the LORD spake unto Moses, saying, On the first day of the first month shalt thou set up the tabernacle of the tent of the congregation … And it came to pass in the first month in the second year, on the first day of the month, that the tabernacle was reared up. And Moses reared up the tabernacle, and fastened his sockets, and set up the boards thereof, and put in the bars thereof, and reared up his pillars. And he spread abroad the tent over the tabernacle, and put the covering of the tent above upon it; as the LORD commanded Moses … Then a cloud covered the tent of the congregation, and the glory of the LORD filled the tabernacle … For the cloud of the LORD was upon the tabernacle by day, and fire was on it by night, in the sight of all the house of Israel, throughout all their journeys.'
(Exodus 40:1-38)

One year after the Lord God brought the children of Israel out of the land of Egypt, one year after he set his captive people free from the bondage, affliction, and tyranny of Pharaoh and the Egyptians, one year after the children of Israel crossed over the Red Sea and sang Jehovah's praise in the fresh, sweet experience of divine deliverance, the Lord God commanded Moses to set up the tabernacle and to set in order the things to be set in order. And on the first day of the first month of Israel's first new year, 'Moses finished the work. Then a cloud covered the tent of the congregation, and the glory of the LORD filled the tabernacle'.

I remind you once more that the tabernacle and everything connected with it was typical of our Lord Jesus Christ and of God's salvation in and by him. Everything we read here refers to things spiritual. In the book of Hebrews, the Spirit of God tells us all these things were the 'shadow of heavenly things' (8:5), 'patterns of things in the heavens' (9:23), and 'figures of the true' (9:24). Those blind to spiritual things see neither beauty nor meaning in this wonderful arrangement; but the tabernacle was God's own picture to his people of 'good things to come' (Hebrews 9:11; 10:1). When we read about it, we ought to always pray, 'Open thou mine eyes, that I may behold wondrous things out of thy law' (Psalm 119:18), for the law of God relating to the tabernacle is full of truly wondrous things.

Its Purpose
The very purpose for the tabernacle was wondrous. It was to be a sanctuary for God, that the holy Lord God might dwell among men (Exodus 25:8). The triune Jehovah so loved his people, the people of his choice whom he had redeemed and delivered out of the hands of Pharaoh, that he desired a place for himself among them, that his presence might abide with them.

That tabernacle typified the incarnate Christ, our blessed Saviour, the Lord Jesus. Immanuel in, with, and by whom God dwells with us and we with him, both now and forever (Hebrews 9:11). Consider that! The Almighty desires to dwell with us; and in Christ he does! 'Ye are the temple of God.' O, Spirit of God, make my heart truly a sanctuary for my God!

Its Priests
In verses 12-16 we read about Aaron and his sons, God's priests. Here five things were done for Aaron the high priest and for his sons, who were made priests with him. Without these five things, they could not minister before God, they could not serve in the tabernacle, they could not function in the priest's office. These five things were done for Christ and are done for all he makes priests unto God. The priest was chosen by God. The priest was washed with holy water and made clean. The priest was clothed with holy garments. The priest was anointed with holy oil. The priest was sanctified.

Its Time

There seems to be something very singular about the time God appointed for the tabernacle to be raised. We are told in verse 17, 'In the first month in the second year, on the first day of the month, that the tabernacle was reared up'. The house of God was to be set up on Israel's 'New Year's Day'. The erection of the tabernacle symbolized a new beginning, a new beginning and more. It symbolized a new beginning with God (2 Corinthians 5:17).

Its Structure

The tabernacle was a very simple structure. Yet, the very structure was wondrous. Everything had to be made and set in order according to the pattern shown to Moses on the mount. In the worship of God everything must be done according to his order.

The sockets which formed the foundation (v. 18) were made of solid silver. That silver came from the 'atonement money' (Exodus 38:25-27). So those golden boards all around the tabernacle, representing as they do God's elect standing before him, stood upon that which represented redemption by blood atonement, redemption by the precious blood of the Lord Jesus Christ.

Those boards, built upon the sockets of ransom money, were 'fitly joined together' and strengthened by the 'bars thereof'; encircling arms of omnipotent power and grace. This represents our standing in Christ and our union one with another within the everlasting arms of divine strength and faithfulness. The bars encircling the boards speak of us in Christ. The middle bar, shot through the boards, speaks of Christ in us. 'Christ in you, the hope of glory.'

Its Contents

All the contents of the tabernacle spoke of things truly wondrous. The tabernacle was divided into three parts: 'the holiest of all', 'the holy place', and 'the court'. In the 'holiest of all', Moses was commanded to place the ark of the covenant, which contained the tables of the broken law, broken by us and repaired, fulfilled and satisfied by Christ. The lid covering the ark was called 'the mercy seat'. There God promised to meet with his people.

'And he took and put the testimony into the ark, and set the staves on the ark, and put the mercy seat above upon the ark: And he brought the ark into the tabernacle, and set up the vail of the covering, and covered the ark of the testimony; as the LORD commanded Moses' (Exodus 40:20, 21).

'And there I will meet with thee, and I will commune with thee from above the mercy seat, from between the two cherubims which are upon the ark of the testimony, of all things which I will give thee in commandment unto the children of Israel' (Exodus 25:22).

Christ is our mercy seat. He is our propitiation. God meets, accepts, approves of, smiles upon, and delights in sinners in Christ (Romans 3:24-26; 1 John 2:1, 2).

In the 'holy place', Moses set the table of shewbread (v. 22) and set the bread in order upon the table. That table and its bread spoke of the believer's fellowship with God in Christ, the Bread of Life. The candlestick, with its branches and lights (vv. 24, 25), pointed to Christ, the Light of the world, and his churches and people, by whom the light is held forth in this world. The golden altar (vv. 26, 27) with its sweet incense, speaks of our acceptance with God in Christ. It speaks also of the acceptance of our works and worship through the sweet incense of Christ's perfection. We offer up prayers and praises, sacrifices and services 'acceptable to God by Jesus Christ' (1 Peter 2:5).

Outside the door of the holy place stood the 'altar of burnt offering' (v. 29). This was the place of sacrifice, declaring that there can be no approach to God, but by blood. God will not allow fallen, sinful, corrupt man to come to him without atonement. The altar points to the cross of Christ. Between the altar of sacrifice and the door of communion, Moses set the laver (v. 30) with its water for cleansing, teaching the need for cleansing by the Holy Spirit. There must be substitution and sanctification if the sinner is to walk in fellowship with God.

Its Glory
The tabernacle had a wondrous glory about it. In verse 34, we read, 'The glory of the LORD filled the tabernacle'.

'Then a cloud covered the tent of the congregation, and the glory of the LORD filled the tabernacle. And Moses was not able to enter into the tent of the congregation, because the cloud abode thereon, and the glory of the LORD filled the tabernacle. And when the cloud was taken up from over the tabernacle, the children of Israel went onward in all their journeys' (Exodus 40:34-36).

The glory of the tabernacle was the manifest presence of God. This cloud of glory is the same pillar of cloud that appeared to Israel and led them out of Egypt and across the Red Sea. But now it appeared in a different form, not so much as a pillar as a great covering, an umbrella over the camp of Israel, with its shaft dropping down on the tabernacle and filling it. This cloud filled the tabernacle with a glory, a brightness, a glorious stream of light. The glory of the Lord that filled the tabernacle was representative of Christ, the Light of Life, the brightness of the Father's glory and the express image of his person, the Shechinah, the Divine Majesty embodied in humanity (Colossians 2:9).

As the completed tabernacle typified the whole of God's salvation in Christ, the glory of the Lord that filled the tabernacle, the Shechinah into which Moses could not enter, was symbolic of the revelation of the glory of God shining forth in the face of Jesus Christ, our Saviour (2 Corinthians 4:6). When Christ appears in the dazzling glory of his accomplished redemption, Moses cannot enter the house with him. The law fulfilled must stand aside.

The Pillar of Cloud

The pillar of cloud was a type of the incarnate Son of God. God was in the pillar; and God was in Christ (2 Corinthians 5:19). In both we see the union of weakness and power. It was as weak as a cloud and as strong as a pillar. 'Great is the mystery of godliness. God was manifest in the flesh.' To those outside, the pillar may seem only a column of smoke, but to those who through the atoning blood had witnessed the glory within, it was the visible presence of the eternal God. To some, Christ is 'without form or comeliness', but we rejoice to confess that he is 'the Christ, the Son of the Living God' (Matthew 16:16).

God in the pillar may also be a foreshadowing of Christ in the Scriptures. Our Saviour declares, 'They are they which testify of me' (John 5:39). There is a living, divine personality abiding and breathing through this holy pillar. 'His name is called The Word of God' (Revelation 19:13). Let us bow before the Sacred Volume and with obedient hearts follow this Pillar of Light.

This pillar of cloud was to the children of Israel the presence of a personal God. The cloudy pillar was the visible evidence of the invisible God. 'God is in the midst of her; she shall not be moved' (Psalm 46:5). Jesus Christ is to us what the pillar was to Israel, the visible revelation of the invisible God (Hebrews 1:3). He says, 'I and my Father are one' (John 10:30). The glory was hidden until the veil was rent, the veil of his flesh. Then the glory shined forth in his resurrection and ascension, and in the coming of the Holy Ghost sent down from heaven.

The pillar of cloud was an abiding testimony of fellowship and communion with the living God. 'These words the Lord spake unto all your assembly in the mount out of the midst of the fire, of the cloud, and of the thick darkness, with a great voice' (Deuteronomy 5:22). He was a sojourner with them. Wonderful condescension this! 'Lo, I am with you alway' (Matthew 28:20). Out of the pillar of his Word, God still speaks to his people. The Holy Spirit guides us by the Word of Light and Christ the 'Urim and Thummim' within. He takes the things of Christ and shows them to us. Our fellowship is with the Father, with the Son, and with the Holy Ghost.

The pillar was also the guarantee of abundant supply. While abiding with the pillar, all their needs were met. Here the manna fell daily from Heaven. The waters, also, from the smitten rock followed the guiding pillar. 'They drank of that spiritual Rock that followed them: and that Rock was Christ' (1 Corinthians 10:4). All the promises of God are yea and amen in him.

The presence of the pillar also meant unfailing divine protection. At the Red Sea the pillar came between the Israelites and the Egyptians (Exodus 14), delivering Israel and destroying the Egyptians. It was light to Israel and darkness to Egypt. 'The LORD looked ... through the pillar, ... and troubled the host of the Egyptians' (Exodus 14:24). The Lord God looked through Christ and saved us. He still looks through him to protect and keep us. He will one day look through him in judgment upon the ungodly. 'He will judge the world in righteousness by that man whom he hath ordained' (Acts 17:31). And in that day, the Lord will look through him and declare us 'holy and unblameable and unreproveable in his sight' (Colossians 1:22).

The pillar was a shelter to Israel. A parasol overshadowing the whole camp, yet with its shaft resting in the midst, upon the mercy seat. They could truly sing, 'the LORD is thy shade upon thy right hand' (Psalm 121:5). The presence of Christ with the believer has a wonderful shading and comforting effect when the hot, fierce rays of adversity are falling upon us. 'In the day of adversity consider' (Ecclesiastes 7:14), consider that the Lord keeps you. The Lord is your shade. He shelters from sin and wrath by his blood, and from sadness and sorrow by his comforting Spirit. Abide under his shadow, and you will have great delight.

The pillar was their source of light. It was a pillar of cloud by day and a pillar of fire by night. They had no light of their own. Apart from the cloud, they had no light to lighten their darkness. Christ is the Light of the world. 'He that followeth me', he says, 'shall not walk in darkness, but shall have the light of life'.

The pillar was their guide, too (vv. 36-38). When it moved, they moved. When it rested, they rested, whether for a day, or a month, or a year. To go without the pillar was to go without God. That meant without light, shelter, protection, or provision; and without a promise. This guide was infallible, because it was God in the pillar who guided.

Its Gate
The court of the tabernacle was a hundred and fifty feet long, seventy-five feet broad, and was enclosed by a wall, or hangings of 'fine twined linen', seven and a half feet high. But there was only one way of access to God in the tabernacle. It had just one gate.

The tabernacle was erected by one man, Moses. And our salvation was accomplished by one man, the Lord Jesus Christ. The whole tabernacle was erected by one man in one day. And our salvation was accomplished by God our Saviour in one day (Zechariah 3:9).

The tabernacle had just one gate, one door of entrance. At the east end there was the gate through which the worshippers entered and approached the altar of burnt offering. Thank God, there is a gate! What a dark world this would have been had there been no way of entrance into the knowledge of and into fellowship with God! 'Behold, I have set before thee an open door' (Revelation 3:8).

Yet there was but one gate. Christ alone is the Gate, the Door by which poor, needy sinners enter into God's salvation. The Gate said, 'I am the Way' (John 14:6). The wall of curtains said, 'There is none other name under heaven given among men, whereby ye must be saved' (Acts 4:12). These hangings were suspended from 'rods of silver' made from 'redemption money', hanging on atonement!

How suggestive. They seem to occupy the place and do the work of the evangelist. They were made of 'fine linen', representing the righteousness of saints. They depended entirely upon the price of ransom, rods of silver, for their support (Exodus 30:12-16). They bore a united testimony that the only way to God was by the altar of sacrifice, the cross of our Lord Jesus Christ.

This was a wide gate. 'Whosoever will, let him come.' The gate of atonement is as wide as the breadth of our sin (1 John 2:2). The way of substitution is as broad as our need, as broad as the very righteousness, justice, and truth of God.

The tabernacle gate was a strongly supported gate. It hung on four pillars. The gospel of our Lord Jesus Christ is supported by four infallible pillars: the mercy of God and the truth of God, the grace of God and the justice of God.

The gate was of the same material as the veil. 'Fine-twined linen, blue, purple, and scarlet.' Christ is the Way. Christ opened the way. Christ puts us in the way. Christ guides us in the way. Christ keeps us in the way. And Christ is at the end of the way!

This gate was the way into life. Immediately in front of the gate stood the altar of sacrifice. It was impossible to enter the tabernacle without seeing and coming through God's provision for the guilty sinner. God's sacrifice, Christ Jesus! There is no way to God, no salvation, no acceptance with God, but by the cross of our Lord Jesus Christ!

> I must needs go home by the way of the cross,
> There's no other way but this.
> I shall ne'er get sight of the gates of light,
> If the way of the cross I miss!
> The way of the cross leads home!
> It is sweet to know as I onward go,
> The way of the cross leads home!

Index Of Bible Verses

527

Galatians continued

3:23	54
3:24	169, 195
3:27	89
4:4-6	393
4:6	144
4:22	149
4:22-29	149
5:1	81
5:1-4	237, 238, 459
5:2-4	413
5:17	148, 150, 152, 227
5:22, 23	244
6:12, 13	134, 401
6:14	275
6:16	241, 378

Ephesians

1:3	218, 283, 306
1:3-6	102, 270, 278, 350, 379, 478
1:3-14	108, 211, 413
1:3-2:10	222
1:5	109
1:5, 6	222
1:6	200, 304
1:7	222, 252, 306
1:10	291
1:11	15, 109, 269
1:12-14	88
1:13, 14	21
1:20, 21	373
1:21-23	473
2:1-9	166
2:1-10	26
2:4-7	210
2:7	109, 211, 447
2:8	80
2:8, 9	81, 220, 413
2:10	441, 482
2:11-13	228
2:13	252
2:19-22	290, 298, 419
2:21, 22	291
3:8	161, 164

3:15	291
3:17-19	203
3:18, 19	235, 451
4:1-7	235, 261, 300, 451
4:3-5	291
4:4-6	106
4:11	397
4:11-13	398
4:16	291
4:24	391
4:28	195
4:32-5:1	228
5:2	323
5:14	347
5:25	201
5:25-27	204, 205
5:30	334
6:2	194
6:13-18	416

Philippians

1:6	61
2:5	206
2:5-8	128
2:6-8	200
2:8-11	473
2:9-11	437
2:15	260
3:1	463, 490
3:1, 3	99
3:1-3	238, 406
3:1-10	474
3:3	21, 88, 107, 331, 351, 450
3:7-15	83
3:10	429
3:21	156
4:4-6	99
4:13	163
4:18	487
4:19	487

Colossians

1	307
1:10	111

1:12	348, 388
1:12-29	305
1:19, 20	269
1:22	516
1:27	149, 266, 306
2:3	346
2:9	349, 515
2:9, 10	212, 265, 268, 306, 441
2:10-12	88
2:11	21
2:12	81
2:13-15	101
2:16, 17	401, 402
3	287
3:1-3	117
3:4	292

1 Thessalonians

4:6	195
4:13-18	48
5:16-18	119

2 Thessalonians

2:13	365
2:13, 14	309

1 Timothy

2:5	91, 106, 218, 268, 332, 337
2:8	153
2:14	204
3:5	331
3:15	331
3:16	313, 481
4:8	308
5:23	121
6:15, 16	110
6:16	106, 440

2 Timothy

1:9	220
1:9, 10	220, 307, 379, 460
1:12	44
2:19	287

1 Peter continued

3:18-22	93
3:21	92
4:1,2	17, 50
4:12	44
5:4	308
5:6-11	61

2 Peter

1:4	149, 152, 333, 364, 387, 399
1:19	259
3:9-14	49

1 John

1:1-3	317
1:5	436, 479
1:7	385
1:7-9	245
1:7-10	409
1:8-10	355
1:9	143, 414
2:1	491
2:1, 2	198, 303, 317, 357, 370, 422, 459, 506, 514
2:2	423, 518
2:19, 20	365
2:20, 27	365
2:20-27	260, 393
2:25	308
2:27	340
3:1	214, 226, 457
3:1, 2	306
3:1-10	227
3:3	419
3:5	203
3:9	149
3:16	143, 214
3:23	197, 496
3:23, 24	266
4:1-3	394
4:9, 10	214, 275
4:12	266
5:7	108, 200
5:10	413

Jude

1	357, 365, 399
4	213
9	459
24, 25	205, 259

Revelation

1:5	421
1:5, 6	206
1:6	320, 336
1:8	349
1:10-20	256
1:13	341, 363, 505
1:17	426
1:20	257, 259, 421, 492
2:28	259
3	275
3:1	260
3:7	471, 473
3:8	517
3:12	331
4	259, 274
4:1, 2	316
4:5	259
4:6-11	275
4:7	184
4:8	101, 128
4:11	53, 110
5:5	374
5:6	374
5:9-14	19
5:10	320, 336
5:11-14	479
7:4	282, 380
7:9-12	19
7:9-14	381
7:14, 15	253, 294
8:3	154, 376, 493
8:3, 4	372, 422
11:15	103
11:19	273
12:1-17	181
12:9-11	101
12:11	154
12:12	60, 101

12:13-16	61
12:16	102
13:8	251, 294, 303
14:1-3	282
14:4	452
15:3, 4	97
15:5	265
18:4	449, 450
18:3	392
18:20	437
19:1-6	57, 437
19:1-14	415
19:8	331, 340, 509, 510
19:11	101
19:13	515
20:6	336
21:1-7	236
21:3	267
21:5-7	237
21:6	18
21:22, 23	436
21:23	348
21:24	18
22:2	119, 122
22:15	195
22:16	259
22:17	497

531